American
Constitutional
Essays, Cases, and Comparative Notes # Law

American Constitutional Law

Essays, Cases, and Comparative Notes

Law
Volume 1

Donald P. Kommers
University of Notre Dame

John E. Finn
Wesleyan University

West/Wadsworth
I(T)P®   An International Thomson Publishing Company

Belmont, CA • Albany, NY • Bonn • Boston • Cincinnati • Detroit • Johannesburg • London • Madrid
Melbourne • Mexico City • New York • Paris • Singapore • Tokyo • Toronto • Washington

Political Science Editor: Clark Baxter
Senior Developmental Editor: Sharon Adams Poore
Editorial Assistant: Amy Guastello
Print Buyer: Barbara Britton
Production: Tobi Giannone, Michael Bass & Associates
Composition: G & S Typesetters, Inc.
Marketing Manager: Jay Hu
Cover Design: Harry Voigt
Cover Photograph: S. Barrow/SuperStock
Printer: R. R. Donnelley & Sons

Printed in the United States of America
1   2   3   4   5   6   7   8   9   10

ISBN 0-534-53937-8

For more information, contact Wadsworth Publishing Company, 10 Davis Drive, Belmont, CA
94002, or electronically at http://www.thomson.com/wadsworth.html

International Thomson Publishing Europe
Berkshire House 168-173
High Holborn
London, WC1V 7AA, England

International Thomson Editores
Campos Eliseos 385, Piso 7
Col. Polanco
11560 México D.F. México

Thomas Nelson Australia
102 Dodds Street
South Melbourne 3205
Victoria, Australia

International Thomson Publishing Asia
221 Henderson Road
#05-10 Henderson Building
Singapore 0315

Nelson Canada
1120 Birchmount Road
Scarborough, Ontario
Canada M1K 5G4

International Thomson Publishing Japan
Hirakawacho Kyowa Building, 3F
2-2-1 Hirakawacho
Chiyoda-ku, Tokyo 102, Japan

International Thomson Publishing GmbH
Königswinterer Strasse 418
53227 Bonn, Germany

International Thomson Publishing Southern
   Africa
Building 18, Constantia Park
240 Old Pretoria Road
Halfway House, 1685 South Africa

 This book is printed on acid-free recycled paper.

For Nancy and Linda

There is no remedy for love
but to love more.
—THOREAU

Contents in Brief

Contents

Preface

This book is borne of the conviction that the study of constitutional law is an integral part of—and should draw upon—a liberal arts education. In light of this, we have tried to produce a unique casebook, one that will encourage students to think critically about the American constitutional order and to engage the great questions of political life that the Constitution and constitutional interpretation address. Among these issues are questions that concern the meaning of the good life, of justice, and of power.

We have written the introductory essays, edited the cases, and prepared notes and queries in ways that highlight three basic themes, or perspectives. Each theme is designed to facilitate critical thinking and draws upon knowledge and skills central to the liberal arts. Our first theme, the interpretive perspective, stresses the nature and process of constitutional interpretation. It asks students to consider how judges and other interpreters find meaning in the wonderfully elastic language of the Constitution. Our second theme, the normative perspective, invites students to consider how constitutional argument, both at the founding and in our time, has concentrated on a few basic conflicts, including the conflict over the proper limits of state and federal authority, the conflict between democracy and constitutionalism, and the meaning of and conflict between the values of liberty and community. Our third theme, the comparative perspective, represents our belief that the study of American constitutional law should be informed by the great variety and richness of comparative materials. A comparative perspective can enrich the study of American constitutional law in several ways, not least by encouraging students to consider what, if anything, is unique in American constitutional life and what we share with other constitutional democracies. Some readers may find the inclusion of comparative materials novel. We prefer to think of comparative analysis as a longstanding part of constitutional argument in the United States, one that reaches at least as far back as the *Federalist Papers*.

In most other respects, the organization of these materials should seem familiar. The casebook is divided into three parts, one focusing on the Court and the Constitution, one on governmental structures and powers, and one on civil liberties and basic freedoms. We hope that teachers accustomed to the canon will find much that is familiar, as well as recognize why and where our themes have led us to depart from the normal course.

It took several years to produce this book. Along the way we received the wise counsel and, no less important, the encouragement of numerous colleagues and teachers of constitutional law. Colleagues who read and commented on parts of the manuscript include Kenneth Betsalel (University of North Carolina, Asheville), Gary Jacobsohn (Williams College), Michael Tolley (Northeastern University), Stephen Shaw (Nazareth College), Nancy Schwartz (Wesleyan University), and Theodore Vestal (Oklahoma State University). We also thank our anonymous reviewers among whom, we discovered later, are David G. Barnum (De Paul University), Lauren Bowen (John Carroll University), Jerry L. Simich (University of Nevada, Las Vegas), Robert C. Bradley (Illinois State University), Jennifer A. Segal (University of Kentucky), Shannon Smithey (University of Pittsburgh), and James G. Dickson (Stephen F. Austin State University). In heeding their comments and suggestions, we have produced a better book. For their help on selected aspects of the book, we are grateful to Cathleen Kaveny (Notre Dame Law School) and Johan DeWaal (Stellenbosch University, South Africa). We also want to thank Paul Mullen, of the University of Pittsburgh, for preparing the Instructor's Manual and for his comments on the text. Finally, we are happy to acknowledge the great benefit we received from discussions about this and other projects from Sotirios A. Barber (University of Notre Dame) and Walter F. Murphy (Princeton University).

We are also grateful to the members of Professor Kommers' 1989, 1991, and 1993 National Endowment for the Humanities Summer Seminars for College Teachers on the topic "American Constitutionalism in Comparative Perspective." These thirty-six college teachers, most of whom teach American constitutional law, helped to convince us to stay the course and bring this book to completion. We also thank the students in Professor Finn's courses on comparative constitutional interpretation and civil liberties, who suffered through earlier versions of the manuscript.

This book would not have been possible without the hard work of our many talented research assistants. Especially deserving of our thanks are Deb Baker, Melissa Brown, Brian Burchett, Michael E. Chaplin, Frank Colluci, Christopher Kukla, Bradley Lewis, Peter Meilander, Shane Tucker, John Wilcox, and Brian Wong. We also thank our tireless secretaries, Janet Demicco and Debbie Sumption, law librarians Dwight King and Patti Ogden, and two great computer wizards, Pat Curley (Public Affairs Center Data Lab, Wesleyan) and Jeff Morgan (Office of Computer Technology, Notre Dame). For institutional support we are grateful to Deans Patricia Leonard and David Link of the Notre Dame Law School; Richard Boyd, Vice President of Academic Affairs, Wesleyan; and Jochen Frowein and Helmut Steinberger of the Max Planck Institute of Comparative and International Public Law in Heidelberg, Germany.

We are also grateful for the hard work of so many people in formatting and designing the book. We want especially to thank Tobi Giannone, of Michael Bass & Associates, and Hal Humphrey, of Wadsworth. A word of appreciation is due to Robert Jucha, of West Publishing, who signed on to this project way back when and to Clark Baxter, of Wadsworth, who pleaded, prodded, and even cajoled when necessary. We thank them both for their patience and for their confidence in our work.

Finally, and most importantly, we thank our families for their patience.

Donald P. Kommers
Heidelberg, Germany

John E. Finn
Maple Juice Cove, Maine

American Constitutional Law

Essays, Cases, and Comparative Notes

Introduction

*I*t takes a measure of audacity to produce yet another course book in American constitutional law. We have done so, however, in an effort to relate the cases presented here to important developments in American constitutional theory and comparative constitutional law. Our years of teaching constitutional law have persuaded us that the topic should serve not simply as professional preparation but, because of the questions it raises about the nature of our polity and the political morality of our Constitution, as an integral part of a student's liberal education. Seen from this perspective, a constitutional law course can be—and is—no less than an extended commentary on the meaning of America. We have tried to produce a casebook appropriate for such a commentary—one that goes beyond the facts and rulings of particular cases to engage the great issues of constitutional interpretation and one that avoids the insularity of an exclusively domestic focus.

We think it is most helpful to consider constitutional theory and Supreme Court opinions as embracing two interrelated concerns, one dealing with the forms and methods of judicial review and the other with the political theory of the Constitution as a whole. The first highlights the process of constitutional interpretation and directs attention to how judges decide cases and when they should declare legislation valid or invalid. The second concern, which emphasizes the political theory of the Constitution, emphasizes efforts to reinterpret American liberalism and revive an older tradition of civic republicanism. Both concerns, the interpretive and the normative, promise to make the study of American constitutional cases more inviting, challenging, and relevant to the creation of a stable political order in the United States.

Furthermore, we think the time has finally arrived to view American constitutional law in a comparative light. The globalization of constitutional law is a reality today, owing in part to the growth of international human rights law and to the rich and voluminous jurisprudence of foreign constitutional courts created after the Second World War, not to mention the transnational European Court of Human Rights.[1] Moreover, in interpreting their respective

---

[1] David Weissbrodt, *Globalization of Constitutional Law and Civil Rights,* 43 Journal of Legal Education 261–70 (1993). For an account of the rise and spread of judicial review around the globe see Mauro Cap-

constitutions, foreign constitutional courts have been consulting each other's case law, including American cases, with increasing frequency. In a fascinating development, the new constitution of South Africa (1996) even contains an interpretive provision expressly advising the courts, in protecting basic rights, that it "must consider international law" and "may consider foreign law."[2] The United States Supreme Court, by contrast, like the general study of American constitutional law, remains relatively isolated from these foreign developments. Indeed, constitutional law is one of the few areas of contemporary law and political science that remains resistant to the comparative approach. We may doubt, however, whether Americans can any longer ignore the ideas and practices of other nations with liberal constitutions similar to their own and designed for the governance of modern, secular, and pluralistic societies. So we have introduced carefully selected materials from countries and jurisdictions whose constitutional law parallels that of the United States.

Yet this book remains emphatically a text on *American* constitutional law. We have, therefore, introduced comparative elements in three limited ways: by including boxes featuring extracts from foreign cases, carefully spliced into the text so as to focus on points of special interest; by reserving the concluding section of each introductory essay to discuss some recent foreign developments; and by raising comparative issues in the notes and queries following each case. Our goal, then, is to combine these three perspectives—interpretive, normative, and comparative—in a single integrated text. The book is thus aimed at students who may welcome an approach to constitutional law that draws upon the learning they have acquired in a liberal arts curriculum. We hope to challenge and encourage these students to reflect upon constitutional law in the light of both new thinking currently taking place in American constitutional law and of comparative developments.

In reading the cases reproduced here, students will find that the interpretive, normative, and comparative perspectives interact and overlap. *How* judges interpret the Constitution often depends on their underlying vision of the kind of society or political democracy the Constitution was designed to promote, but this vision has itself unfolded within a world where ideas, values, and attitudes—constitutional and political as well as social and philosophical—easily migrate across national borders. For purposes of further clarifying the goals and concerns of this casebook, however, we shall keep the three perspectives analytically distinct in the following remarks.

The Interpretive Perspective

In recent years, Americans have watched and participated in a fierce national debate over the source and scope of judicial power. The debate has been ongoing since before *Marbury v. Madison*,[3] but in recent decades, due to the robust "activism" of the Warren and Burger Courts and the so-called "counter-revolution" staged by the

---

pelletti, *Judicial Review in the Contemporary World* (Indianapolis: The Bobbs-Merrill Company, Inc., 1971). For a more updated study see his *The Judicial Process in Comparative Perspective* (Oxford: Oxford University Press, 1989) and A. R. Brewer-Carias, *Judicial Review in Comparative Law* (Cambridge: Cambridge University Press, 1989). See also Andrzej Rapaczynski, "Bibliographical Essay: The Influence of U.S. Constitutionalism Abroad" in Louis Henkin and Albert J. Rosenthal, eds., *Constitutionalism and Rights* (New York: Columbia University Press, 1990), 405–62.

[2]South African Constitution, 1996. Sec 39(1)b and c.

[3]5 U.S. (1 Cranch) 137 (1803).

Rehnquist Court, it has reached a level of intensity unmatched in the history of American constitutional discourse, and it shows no signs of abating.[4] At the center of this debate are two basic questions: *Who* shall be responsible for interpreting the Constitution and *how* shall it be interpreted? But there is a prior question. Before any interpretation can take place, we must know *what* we are interpreting. What, in short, is the Constitution? Is it the seven thousand-word document that emerged from the Philadelphia Convention? Or does the Constitution include other foundational documents, such as the Declaration of Independence and President Lincoln's First Inaugural Address (see Appendixes A and C), or other principles, precepts, practices, rights, or theories that are not explicit in the written text? One aim of the course is to read the opinions of the Supreme Court with these queries in mind. Another is to draw attention to the sources of information, interpretive techniques, and styles of argument the Court uses to decide cases. Certain approaches to constitutional interpretation (e.g., historical, textual, structural, doctrinal, ethical, and prudential) compete for supremacy on and off the Supreme Court and, as the Senate hearings on the Robert Bork and Clarence Thomas nominations showed, many Americans are themselves caught up in the argument.

Although in dealing with these interpretive issues we are mainly concerned with the approaches and techniques used by the Court in construing the Constitution, institutional issues also loom large. When and under what circumstances should the judiciary, rather than the legislature or other political actors, decide a particular question of constitutional law? It is, of course, no secret that legislative and executive officials—even the police officer on the beat—also interpret the Constitution. If senators and representatives, all sworn to uphold the Constitution, have vigorously and conscientiously debated the constitutionality of a legislative bill before enacting it, should the Supreme Court then reject their judgment and declare the law unconstitutional? What deference, if any, do judicial decision makers owe to legislators and executive officials who have made independent assessments of the constitutionality of their actions? These and related issues are presented mainly in the notes and queries to each case.

The Normative Perspective

This casebook seeks to frame the debate over what the Constitution means within the broader context of political theory. Here, too, constitutional argument in our time is largely a revived and sophisticated version of a much older debate reaching back to the "founding" disputes between Federalists and anti-Federalists. This debate has traditionally focused on three central normative tensions: (1) the conflict over the limits of federal and state power; (2) the conflict between democracy (rule by political majorities) and constitutionalism (limits on majoritarian democracy); and (3) the meaning of and conflict between liberty and community. The playing out of these overlapping tensions forms the basis of the doctrinal history of American constitutional law.

These normative issues are important because they go to the heart of the kind of nation Americans aspire to be and the Supreme Court's role in defining that people. Should the Supreme Court, for example, seek to promote individualism and personal liberty, striking down laws that impinge on individual autonomy or entrepre-

---

[4] A poignant example of the depth and sharpness of the debate is Sotirios A. Barber, *The Constitution of Judicial Power* (Baltimore: Johns Hopkins University Press, 1993).

neurialism? Or should the Court use its moral authority to protect the rights of groups and reinforce a sense of community based on widely-shared and deeply-held visions of the good life? Through substantial introductory essays, in the notes and queries, and by the manner in which we have edited cases, we have sought to encourage students to focus on central issues of liberty, equality, community, individualism, and personhood.

The Comparative Perspective

By introducing comparative materials into the standard course in American constitutional law, this casebook serves not only as a springboard for fresh reflection on the American Constitution, but it also anticipates an important trend in teaching constitutional law. Foreign constitutional texts and judicial opinions, along with international human rights law, are inviting targets of study, particularly if they are chosen to illuminate aspects of domestic constitutionalism. The outsider's perspective may furnish students with insights into their own society that would otherwise have remained invisible. In the same vein, Richard Stewart writes: "[A] glimpse into the households of our neighbors serves the better to illuminate our own, as when by pressing hard against the pane we see not only the objects on the other side but our own features reflected in the glass."[5] Carefully selected comparative references can help students better appreciate the work of our Supreme Court and enhance their understanding of the American Constitution.

A comparative perspective enriches the study of constitutional law in several ways. First, by looking at foreign models of constitutional governance or other traditions of freedom, students may begin to discern what is purely historical and contingent in the American experience and what is more universal and permanent. Second, Americans may take a great deal of pride in knowing something about the extent to which their constitutional ideals and practices are embedded in the provisions and features of other liberal democracies. Third, they may also find great value in the distinctive aspects of foreign constitutions and the sharp contrasts to American law found in foreign constitutional doctrine. For example, the idea of an "objective order of values" or an "unconstitutional constitutional amendment" or "the unity of the constitution" or the distinction between negative and positive rights, all found in German constitutional theory, may hold fascinating implications for Americans seeking new ways of understanding their own Constitution.

For purposes of illustration, we might briefly compare *Bowers v. Hardwick*,[6] the American homosexual sodomy case, with *Dudgeon v. United Kingdom*,[7] a similar case decided by the European Court of Human Rights. In *Dudgeon*, the European Court ruled that Northern Ireland's law prohibiting homosexual conduct between consenting adults constituted an interference with the respect for private life guaranteed by Article 8(1) of the European Convention on Human Rights. Five years later, in 1986, the U.S. Supreme Court, in a five to four vote, came to the opposite conclusion. It sustained the constitutionality of a Georgia statute criminalizing homosexual sod-

---

[5] *Courts and Free Markets: Perspectives from the United States and Europe* (Oxford: Clarendon Press, 1982), viii.

[6] 478 U.S. 186 (1986).

[7] 4 *European Human Rights Reports* (hereinafter E. H. R. R.) 149 (1981).

omy even when engaged in by consenting adults.[8] That the two cases produced opposite results invites reflection in its own right, but the distinctive analytical approaches of the two tribunals are equally compelling. Justice White's majority opinion held that the Fourteenth Amendment's concept of due process liberty does not confer a fundamental right on homosexuals to engage in acts of consensual sodomy. Justice Blackmun, writing for the minority, held that Georgia's law violated the fundamental right to privacy implicit in the due process liberty clause of the Fourteenth Amendment. The two opinions are marked by an irreconcilable polarity. Under the majority's holding that there is no fundamental right to engage in homosexual conduct, the state won easily; had the minority prevailed, declaring that such conduct is included in the fundamental right to privacy, the individual would have won just as easily.

In sharp contrast to both of these opinions, the European Court's holding engages in a nuanced and sensitive balancing of the valid interests of both state and individual. The Court recognized the state's interest in regulating sexual morality but also the individual's interest in protecting the most intimate aspects of one's private life. After examining the policies of other European nations and finding that in Northern Ireland itself there appeared to be no "pressing need" to criminalize homosexual conduct, the Court concluded that the "detrimental effects [of the legislation] on the life of a person of homosexual orientation" outweighs "the state's justification . . . for retaining the law in force."[9] There was some faint suggestion in the opinion, however, that in other circumstances and with different facts, the decision could have conceivably gone the other way.

We need not decide here which of the three opinions is right. Suffice to say that *Bowers* is rich for the interpretive, normative, and comparative issues it raises. First, *Bowers* prompts questions about the interpretive approaches used by the Court in construing the Constitution—its reliance on history, text, precedent, structure, natural law, social utility, and consensus, among other possibilities—along with the institutional question of when federal judicial power should be used to overturn majoritarian policies. Second, it revolves around the crucial normative tensions we mentioned earlier, raising important questions: What theory of liberty should inform the general meaning of the Constitution? How shall individual rights be reconciled (if they should be reconciled) with the desire to enforce the community's prevailing conception of social morality? What visions of society and human personality emerge from the case? Finally, students may be driven to wonder about the relative wisdom of the European Court's analytical approach, as opposed to the approaches of the majority and minority opinions in *Bowers*. They may also wonder why the Supreme Court failed to cite the European Court's opinion. Was it a conscious omission, and if so, why? At any rate, the opinions of the Supreme Court may well appear differently when seen through the lens of a foreign constitutional tribunal.

We wish to reemphasize, however, that our insertion of comparative materials is extremely selective and largely for the purpose of illustrating issues and problems of American constitutional law. Thus we draw these materials mainly from the decisions of foreign constitutional courts in countries which face social and political problems similar to those of the United States in the last half of the twentieth century, which

---

[8] Georgia's criminal code also punished heterosexual sodomy. For present purposes, however, it is sufficient to focus on the statute's punishment of homosexual conduct.

[9] *Ibid.*, at 167.

share constitutional language similar to the words and phrases of the U.S. Constitution, and whose supreme judicial tribunals play roles analogous to that of the United States Supreme Court—primarily (but not only) Germany, Canada, Japan, South Africa, Ireland, and the Council of Europe. All of these nations have produced bodies of constitutional law comparable in complexity and learning to the jurisprudence of our Supreme Court and their opinions are accessible to students unfamiliar with the complex judicial structures, legal systems, and doctrinal writings of the foreign jurisdictions. In a book such as this we can only open the door a tiny crack to ways in which other constitutional democracies have dealt with the issues discussed in this introduction. Nevertheless, we believe that the comparative perspective, for the reasons given earlier, can offer guidance to Americans engaged in reexamining the goals and content of their own Constitution, and perhaps this book will encourage interested students to explore that perspective further.

Apart from the comparative materials, the organization of this book is fairly conventional, covering the usual topics and leading cases found in the standard course on American constitutional law. We hope, therefore, that teachers of American constitutional law accustomed to presenting the standard course materials may find this book simultaneously useful and challenging.

The casebook is divided into three parts: Part 1 includes two introductory chapters. Chapter 1 focuses on the organization, procedures, powers, and personnel of the United States Supreme Court. Chapter 2 introduces students to the structure and principles of the United States Constitution, describes various approaches to judicial review, and discusses competing theories of the Constitution. These chapters also compare the process of constitutional interpretation and the institution of judicial review in the United States with their variants in other advanced constitutional democracies, a discussion intended to help students think comparatively about the larger issues of liberty and community underlying particular constitutional cases and controversies in the United States.

Part 2 covers five chapters dealing with governmental structures and relationships. These chapters include edited cases and materials dealing respectively with the expansion of judicial power (chapter 3), divided and separated powers (chapter 4), federalism (chapter 5), the powers of Congress (chapter 6), and foreign and military affairs (chapter 7). Finally, Part 3 includes seven additional chapters on civil rights and basic freedoms. They deal respectively with the Bill of Rights and the Fourteenth Amendment (chapter 8); liberty and property (chapter 9); liberty, life, and personhood (chapter 10); freedom of expression (chapter 11); freedom of religion (chapter 12); race, slavery, and the equal protection clause (chapter 13); and fundamental rights, gender discrimination, and other discriminatory classifications (chapter 14). Each of the case law chapters is preceded by an original essay that calls attention to interpretive and normative issues raised by the edited cases and readings. In addition, each essay describes parallel developments in selected nonAmerican jurisdictions for the purpose of raising questions about American constitutional values and their transmission to other cultures.

We have also included several useful appendixes. Appendixes A, B, and C reproduce the texts of the Declaration of Independence, the U.S. Constitution, and President Lincoln's First Inaugural Address, respectively. Appendix D offers tips on how to study constitutional law and an example of how to summarize or brief a constitutional case. Appendix E features a glossary of technical legal terms. Finally, Appendix F presents a chronological chart of the justices. An additional appendix that would have included selected provisions from foreign constitutions, particularly in the area of basic rights and liberties, had to be deleted for reasons of space. A sampling of these provisions, however, appear in comparative notes featured throughout this book.

We the People

Article. I.

Section. 1. All legislative Powers herein granted shall be vested in a Congress of the United States, which shall consist of a Senate and House of Representatives.

Section. 2. The House of Representatives shall be composed of Members chosen every second Year by the People of the several States, and the Electors in each State shall have the Qualifications requisite for Electors of the most numerous Branch of the State Legislature.

No Person shall be a Representative who shall not have attained to the Age of twenty five Years, and been seven Years a Citizen of the United States, and who shall not, when elected, be an Inhabitant of that State in which he shall be chosen.

Representatives and direct Taxes shall be apportioned among the several States which may be included within this Union, according to their respective Numbers, which shall be determined by adding to the whole Number of free Persons, including those bound to Service for a Term of Years, and excluding Indians not taxed, three fifths of all other Persons. The actual Enumeration shall be made within three Years after the first Meeting of the Congress of the United States, and within every subsequent Term of ten Years, in such Manner as they shall by Law direct. The Number of Representatives shall not exceed one for every thirty Thousand, but each State shall have at Least one Representative; and until such enumeration shall be made, the State of New Hampshire shall be entitled to chuse three, Massachusetts eight, Rhode-Island and Providence Plantations one, Connecticut five, New-York six, New Jersey four, Pennsylvania eight, Delaware one, Maryland six, Virginia ten, North Carolina five, South Carolina five, and Georgia three.

When vacancies happen in the Representation from any State, the Executive Authority thereof shall issue Writs of Election to fill such Vacancies.

The House of Representatives shall chuse their Speaker and other Officers; and shall have the sole Power of Impeachment.

Section. 3. The Senate of the United States shall be composed of two Senators from each State, chosen by the Legislature thereof, for six Years; and each Senator shall have one Vote.

Immediately after they shall be assembled in Consequence of the first Election, they shall be divided as equally as may be into three Classes. The Seats of the Senators of the first Class shall be vacated at the Expiration of the second Year, of the second Class at the Expiration of the fourth Year, and of the third Class at the Expiration of the sixth Year, so that one third may be chosen every second Year; and if Vacancies happen by Resignation, or otherwise, during the Recess of the Legislature of any State, the Executive thereof may make temporary Appointments until the next Meeting of the Legislature, which shall then fill such Vacancies.

No Person shall be a Senator who shall not have attained to the Age of thirty Years, and been nine Years a Citizen of the United States, and who shall not, when elected, be an Inhabitant of that State for which he shall be chosen.

The Vice President of the United States shall be President of the Senate, but shall have no Vote, unless they be equally divided.

The Senate shall chuse their other Officers, and also a President pro tempore, in the Absence of the Vice President, or when he shall exercise the Office of President of the United States.

The Senate shall have the sole Power to try all Impeachments. When sitting for that Purpose, they shall be on Oath or Affirmation. When the President of the United States is tried, the Chief Justice shall preside: And no Person shall be convicted without the Concurrence of two thirds of the Members present.

Judgment in Cases of Impeachment shall not extend further than to removal from Office, and disqualification to hold and enjoy any Office of honor, Trust or Profit under the United States: but the Party convicted shall nevertheless be liable and subject to Indictment, Trial, Judgment and Punishment, according to Law.

Section. 4. The Times, Places and Manner of holding Elections for Senators and Representatives, shall be prescribed in each State by the Legislature thereof; but the Congress may at any time by Law make or alter such Regulations, except as to the Places of chusing Senators.

The Congress shall assemble at least once in every Year, and such Meeting shall be on the first Monday in December, unless they shall by Law appoint a different Day.

Section. 5. Each House shall be the Judge of the Elections, Returns and Qualifications of its own Members, and a Majority of each shall constitute a Quorum to do Business; but a smaller Number may adjourn

Part One

Institutional
and Interpretive
Foundations

he first part of this book (chapters 1 and 2) provides students with background on the Supreme Court and the Court's role in the American system of government as well as an overview of the process of constitutional interpretation. It locates the Court within our "dual" system of state and federal courts and focuses on its organization, composition, and decision-making procedures. Among the Court's important decisional procedures is its discretionary authority to decide only those cases it chooses to decide, a prerogative that accounts for its heavy emphasis on *constitutional* adjudication. Prior to 1950, barely five percent of the Court's dispositions with full opinions dealt with constitutional issues, whereas today such issues form the principal question in some sixty percent of cases decided with full opinions. Indeed, over the years, the Supreme Court has evolved, for all practical purposes, into a constitutional tribunal not unlike the specialized constitutional courts created in Western Europe after the Second World War.

Part 1 also offers advice on how to read Supreme Court opinions. Reading constitutional cases is not like reading P. G. Wodehouse or S. J. Perelman. Judicial opinions require close reading. They are manifestations of legal reasoning, which is not a simple thing. Felix Frankfurter once remarked that judicial opinions often "convey accents and nuances which the ear misses on a single reading, and [they] reveal meanings in silences." Unveiling these nuances and "listening" to these silences is one of the exciting intellectual challenges in reading constitutional cases.

The purpose of this volume, however, is not merely to introduce students to the policies, principles, and rulings of the Supreme Court in constitutional cases. An equally important inquiry is *how* the Court reaches its decisions. Accordingly, chapter 2 introduces students to various methods and sources of constitutional advocacy. As we will see, constitutional arguments may be drawn from a variety of valid sources. Constitutional interpretation itself involves the various ways by which judges, and others, seek to determine what the Constitution means. Familiarity with these methods is important because a constitutional doctrine or policy enunciated by the Court may well depend on the particular judicial method or approach to interpretation. It is also important to understand that the various methods of interpretation play an important role in assisting the Court to reconcile the tension between democracy and constitutionalism. Finally, chapter 2 compares American interpretive approaches with those used by foreign constitutional tribunals.

Chapter 1

The Supreme Court

I n *Federalist* 78, Hamilton concluded that "the judiciary is beyond comparison the weakest of the three branches. . . ." Whether Hamilton's conclusion is an accurate description of the Court's place in our constitutional life is a question we shall consider throughout this book. In 1787, Hamilton's observation was surely accurate. Today, appointment to the Court is a prize, the culmination of a career in law. President Washington, though, had to plead with friends and twist arms to find competent individuals to serve on the Court. The first chief justice, John Jay, left the Court after only five years, finding a more prestigious and powerful position as governor of New York. Another justice resigned his commission in favor of a seat on the South Carolina Supreme Court.

When the Court first convened on 1 February 1790, it met in the Royal Exchange Building in New York City. Thereafter and until 1939, it met in a spare room in the basement of the capitol building. Today, the Court holds office in an impressive palace of white marble on the corner of First and A Streets in Washington, D.C. Inside, the justices and their clerks are surrounded by polished wood and gleaming brass. The Court has its own library, printing press, cafeteria, museum, gift shop, and even a basketball court.

The splendor of the Court's residence mirrors the prominence of the Court as an institution. The Court presides over a vast bureaucracy that includes more than one hundred lower courts staffed by over seven hundred judges. It controls a budget in excess of two million dollars. More importantly, the Court is at the center of public debate and policymaking in such areas as abortion, affirmative action, sexuality, gun control and state's rights, and privacy. Just this past Term, the Court decided a case involving physician-assisted suicide, as well as other cases that go to the very heart of the separation of powers, federalism, and the Bill of Rights. As Alexis de Tocqueville wrote, "there is hardly a political question in the United States which does not sooner or later turn into a judicial one."[1]

It was not always so. Under the Articles of Confederation there was no Supreme Court—indeed, no federal judiciary at all. In contrast, Article 3 of

---

[1] J. P. Mayer, ed., *Democracy in America* (Garden City, N.Y.: Doubleday, 1969), 270.

the Constitution provides that "there shall be a Supreme Court and such inferior courts" as Congress may desire. To ensure the independence of the federal judiciary, it also gives judges lifetime tenure and protects against a reduction of their salaries. In broad language Article 3 also defines what kind of cases the Court can hear.

On the other hand, the text tells us nothing about who the justices should be or how many there should be. Moreover, Article 3 provides no information about how the Court works, about how the Court decides which cases to hear, or how the justices should decide the cases. Thus, the federal court system is a product of an evolution that has been profoundly influenced by other features of the constitutional order, such as federalism, the separation of powers, and the tension between individual liberty and popular rule. And as we shall see in chapter 3, the development of the federal courts has been advanced by Congress, which has expanded the jurisdiction of the federal courts and given the Supreme Court greater control over its own jurisdiction.

Article 3's vagueness is due, in part, to conflict at the Philadelphia Convention about whether a national judiciary was a necessary concomitant of national power. Some delegates, such as Alexander Hamilton, argued in favor of a national judiciary because "the majesty of the national authority must be manifested through the medium of the courts of justice."[2] Some of the other delegates thought a national judiciary would be a terrible threat to the sovereignty of the individual states, each of which possessed its own judiciary.

The Justices: Politics of Appointment

The appointment of a Supreme Court justice is one of the notable events of American political life. As specified in Article 2, justices are nominated by the president and must be confirmed by a majority of the Senate. If confirmed, a justice serves for life on "good behavior" and can be removed only through impeachment by the House of Representatives and conviction by the Senate.[3] On average, there is a vacancy on the Court every two years. Franklin Roosevelt made no appointments in his first term but had nine opportunities between 1937 and 1943. President Carter made no appointments to the Court, President Reagan made three, and President Bush two. As of late 1997 President Clinton has made two appointments.

Presidents typically seek out Supreme Court nominees whose judicial philosophy and record are similar to the president's own political views. As often as not, however, Supreme Court justices go their own way, surprising and disappointing presidential expectations. President Eisenhower, for example, appointed both Chief Justice Earl Warren and Justice William J. Brennan. Their "liberal" inclinations on the Court disappointed Eisenhower, who later called them "the biggest damned-fool mistakes" of his presidency.[4]

The nomination process has always been political and, in recent years, is often controversial, as the nominations of Robert Bork in 1987 and Clarence Thomas in 1991 vividly demonstrate. In addition to the president and the Senate, important players in the confirmation process include the American Bar Association, which on its own initiative has chosen to evaluate nominees based on judicial experience and temperament. A wide array of interest groups and political associations are also involved, such

---

[2] Clinton Rossiter, ed., *The Federalist Papers* (#16) (New York: New American Library, Mentor Books, 1961).

[3] Only one Supreme Court justice—Samuel Chase—has been impeached. Charges were brought in 1805 by leaders of the Jeffersonian Party in Congress. The Senate did not convict him. For an account, see Bernard Schwartz, *A History of the Supreme Court* (N.Y.: Oxford University Press, 1993), 57–58.

[4] For a more detailed discussion, see Phillip Cooper and Howard Ball, *The United States Supreme Court: From the Inside Out* (Upper Saddle River, N.J.: Prentice-Hall, 1996), 31–74.

as the American Civil Liberties Union, the National Association for the Advancement of Colored People, and the National Organization for Women. At times, sitting members of the Court have also tried to influence the process. The presence of so many actors testifies to the significance of the nomination process: It is one of the most important ways the community has of influencing the Court and enforcing a measure of political accountability.

Most of the individuals appointed to the Court have had long and distinguished careers in the law and an exemplary record of public service. Many have been members of Congress, some have aspired to the presidency, and, since 1975, all have been judges on lower courts. The overwhelming majority have been Protestant, white, and males of economic means. A great number have graduated from the country's most prestigious law schools, and several justices began their careers as clerks to Supreme Court justices after graduating from law school. There is, however, no constitutional requirement that a justice have a law degree or be a lawyer.

Notwithstanding this similarity of background, presidents have usually considered diversity an important factor in the Court's composition. For many years the Court had a "Jewish" seat, and geographical and ideological diversity have also influenced the makeup of the Court. President Johnson appointed Thurgood Marshall as the first African American on the Court in 1967, and in 1980 President Reagan appointed Sandra Day O'Connor as the first woman on the Court.

Most nominees are confirmed without great difficulty. Between 1900 and 1967 the Senate rejected only one nominee. Since 1967, however, the Senate has rejected six nominees. On what basis may the Senate reject an appointment? There is much disagreement about how the confirmation process should work.[5] Should the Senate assess the moral character of a nominee? The nation struggled with this question during the Senate's hearings on Clarence Thomas. Should it inquire into the political or jurisprudential views of nominees? Much of the controversy surrounding Robert Bork's nomination involved these issues.

Some senators and scholars argue vehemently that the Senate's role should be limited to determining whether the nominee is "competent." They argue that the Senate is a threat to judicial independence when it inquires into a nominee's substantive views.[6] Others have called for an aggressive review of a candidate's constitutional philosophy, claiming that the Senate has an obligation to the people to assess the candidate's views on matters of public importance.[7] Both positions rest upon a particular understanding about the relationship between constitutionalism and democracy. That tension haunts nearly every area of American constitutional law and is one of the central themes of this book.

The Federal Court System

What kinds of cases may the Court hear? Article 3 gives us little guidance. It provides that "the judicial Power shall extend to all Cases, in Law and Equity, arising under this Constitution, the Laws of the United States, and Treaties. . . ." The phrase presents two immediate difficulties: First, the article refers to "judicial power" but does not say what

---

[5] See Susan Low Bloch and Thomas G. Krattenmaker, *Supreme Court Politics: The Institution and Its Procedures* (St. Paul, Minn.: West Publishing Company, 1994), chapter 2.

[6] Robert F. Nagel, *Advice, Consent, and Influence,* 84 Northwestern University Law Review 858 (1990).

[7] Stephen Carter, *The Confirmation Mess,* 101 Harv. L. Rev. 1185 (1988); Nina Totenberg, *The Confirmation Process and the Public: To Know or Not To Know,* 101 Harvard Law Review 1213 (1988); see also Lawrence Tribe, *God Save This Honorable Court: How the Choice of Supreme Court Justices Shapes Our History* (New York: Random House, 1985).

the power is or what it includes. Second, the Court's "power" to hear cases depends upon whether it has "jurisdiction" over the particular case. As we shall see, the Court has "original" jurisdiction in a group of cases set forth explicitly in Section 2, including those affecting ambassadors and other public ministers, disputes in which the United States is a party, disputes between two or more states, and disputes between a state and citizens of another state. In all other cases the Court has "appellate" jurisdiction, with such exceptions and regulations as Congress shall make.

The great majority of the cases the Court hears come to the Court under its appellate jurisdiction, or on appeal from a federal or state court. The Constitution does not itself create lower federal courts, instead entrusting their creation and organization to Congress. Congress first created a system of lower federal courts in the Judiciary Act of 1789. Just below the Supreme Court were three circuit courts, each serving a group of states. Thirteen district courts served at the lowest level. Although there have been substantial changes in the particular arrangements of these courts, the tripartite structure of the federal court system has remained in place ever since.

The Supreme Court is at the apogee of the system. Since 1869 the Court has had nine justices, but nine is not a constitutional command. President Washington's Court had just six justices. There have been many efforts to change the number, often as a result of straightforward political maneuvering by presidents and Congresses. President Adams tried to reduce the number to five, President Lincoln expanded the number to ten, and Franklin Roosevelt's "court-packing" plan, if it had succeeded, might have increased the number to fifteen. Sometimes sitting members of the Court have joined the fray as well. Justice Field, for example, proposed that the Court should have twenty-one Justices.[8]

In the current arrangement, the United States Courts of Appeals sit directly below the Supreme Court. These courts are organized by territory (except for the District of Columbia Court, which hears cases from federal administrative agencies and the District of Columbia). Each court, or "circuit," covers at least three states. The First Circuit, for example, hears cases from Maine, New Hampshire, Massachusetts, and Rhode Island. The circuit courts hear appeals from the United States District Courts and from federal agencies. Usually a three judge panel hears cases and decides them by majority vote. On rare occasions, when an issue is especially difficult or contentious, the entire roster of judges on a circuit court may choose to hear a case *en banc*.

The United States District Courts are the entry level to the federal court system. The district courts are trial courts: One judge hears criminal and civil cases, sometimes with a jury. There are ninety-four district courts with at least one in every state. The District of Columbia also has a district court, and there is a court for each of the U.S. territories of Guam, Puerto Rico, the Virgin Islands, and the Northern Mariana Islands. In addition, Congress has created a wide variety of specialized courts, including military courts, tax courts, and customs courts. Many of these courts were created by Congress under Article 1 and not under Article 3 of the Constitution. The provenance of the court is important, for unlike Article 3 courts, judges on Article 1 courts are not guaranteed lifetime tenure.

Jurisdiction: The Power to Hear Cases and Controversies

No court may hear a case unless the court has "jurisdiction" over it. The Supreme Court has two kinds of jurisdiction—original and appellate. In cases of original jurisdiction, the Supreme Court hears a case "on first impression." In other words, the

---

[8] Howard J. Graham, *Everyman's Constitution* (Madison: Historical Society of Wisconsin, 1968), 136ff.

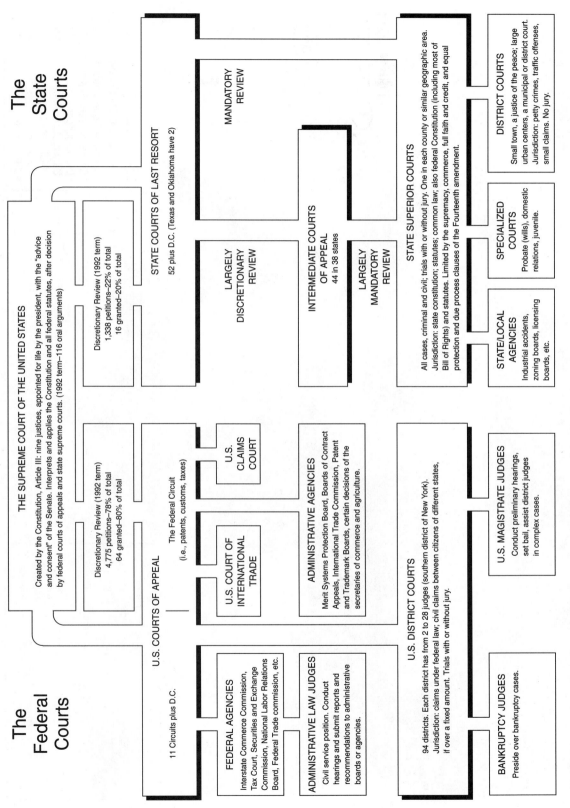

FIGURE 1.1 *Federal and state court organization and jurisdiction.*

Source: Frank M. Coffin, *On Appeal* (New York: W.W. Norton, 1994), 48–49.

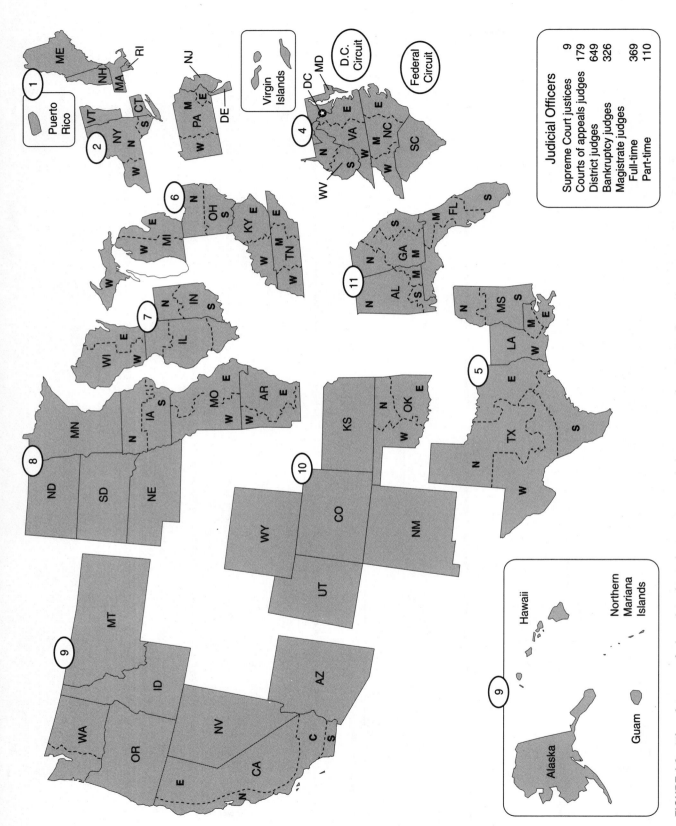

Judicial Officers	
Supreme Court justices	9
Courts of appeals judges	179
District judges	649
Bankruptcy judges	326
Magistrate judges	
Full-time	369
Part-time	110

FIGURE 1.2 *The thirteen federal judicial circuits and the ninety-four U.S. district courts.*

Source: *Understanding the Federal Courts*, 2d Ed. (Washington, D.C.: Administrative Office of the Courts, 1994), 8.

litigants bypass state courts and the lower federal courts and go straight to the Supreme Court. Partly because of the Eleventh Amendment, congressional legislation, and the Court's own rules (which provide that original jurisdiction may be held "concurrently" with lower federal courts), such cases are extremely rare.

The Court's workload is therefore largely a function of its appellate jurisdiction. Although the Court is a passive, reactive institution and may not formally initiate cases, it does have great control over how many and what kinds of cases it will hear. In a typical year the Court receives approximately 4,900 petitions, or requests, by litigants to hear their appeals. The Court usually decides to hear between 120 to 150 petitions yearly.[9] In these cases, the Court will accept briefs from the parties, schedule oral arguments, and issue an opinion.

There are three kinds of appellate jurisdiction. Every case the Court hears under appellate jurisdiction follows one of these paths:

1. Certification. A United States Court of Appeals can "certify" to the Supreme Court that a particular case poses exceptional difficulties. When it certifies a case, the lower court asks the Supreme Court to provide instruction about how some matter of law should be settled.

2. Appeal. For much of its history, the Supreme Court was required to hear cases on appeal that raised certain kinds of questions about federal law. In practice, though, the Court routinely dismissed such cases, explaining that they did not present a "substantial federal question." In 1988, Congress passed legislation that sanctioned the practice, thus transforming the Court's "mandatory" jurisdiction in such cases into "discretionary" jurisdiction.

3. Certiorari. In most cases, a party appealing a decision files a "writ of certiorari" with the Supreme Court. A "cert" petition is a formal request by a party that the Court hear a case. The decision to accept or deny the writ is entirely within the Court's discretion.

Writs of certiorari are the primary means of access to the Court. The Court will grant the writ if four justices agree that a case warrants the Court's attention. The Rules of the Supreme Court indicate under what circumstances it will be likely to grant the writ. Important considerations include a conflict among the courts of appeals on a question of law; a conflict between a circuit court and a state supreme court; when a state court has decided a federal question in a way that conflicts with another state court or a U.S. Court of Appeals; and when a state or federal court has decided a question of federal law that the Supreme Court has not yet settled or has settled differently. In each of these instances, the Court's position at the top of the judicial hierarchy allows it to settle conflicts among lower courts and to ensure some measure of uniformity in the interpretation and application of the law.

These rules indicate when the Supreme Court has jurisdiction over a case. Whether the Court will choose to hear a case, though, is not only a function of jurisdiction. As we shall see in chapter 3, the Court has developed a number of additional devices it uses to decide whether to hear a case. Among these "prudential" considerations are the doctrines of standing, ripeness, mootness, and the political questions doctrine. Each represents a policy choice by the Court to limit its jurisdiction to avoid certain kinds of cases and issues, usually for reasons that go to the limited role of the Court in the larger political order.

---

[9]This number held more or less constant for the last fifty years. There is some indication, however, that the number of cases the Court accepts for review has steadily decreased under the leadership of Chief Justice Rehnquist. See, e.g., Bloch and Krattenmaker, *supra* note 5 at 334.

Congressional Control Over Appellate Jurisdiction

Article 3, Section 2 of the Constitution provides that the Court shall have appellate jurisdiction "with such Exceptions, and under such Regulations as the Congress shall make." Section 2 is one of the primary means we have of assuring that the federal courts are accountable to the community. The principle of accountability, however, exists in some tension with the principle of judicial independence.

As we discuss in chapter 3, Congress has exercised its power to control the Court's appellate jurisdiction on several occasions. In each case the tension between democratic accountability and judicial independence has colored the specific facts and interpretive controversies involved.

Among the interpretive issues raised by Section 2 are questions about the definition and scope of the words "Exceptions" and "Regulations." May Congress remove the Court's entire appellate jurisdiction, or would this exceed the meaning of "exception"? Are there other limits to congressional power under Section 2? If so, what are they and what is their source?

Deciding to Decide: Decision-Making Procedures

As mentioned, every year the Court receives approximately 4,900 requests for writs of certiorari. Because the Court has almost complete discretion in deciding which cases to hear, the procedures and criteria it uses to winnow the multitude to the worthy 120 to 150 cases are extremely important. The Court's rules give litigants some basic guidelines about what kinds of cases the Court is likely to entertain.

The first cut in the case load is made by law clerks. Clerks are typically law school graduates with distinguished academic records. Each justice has several clerks. The clerks review every petition and prepare summaries for their justices. Some justices have asked their clerks to combine their efforts—called the cert pool—to help offset the sheer number of petitions flooding the Court every year. The clerks review the petitions in light of Rule 17 of the Court's Rules of Procedure and following any additional instructions they receive from their individual justices. The memos the clerks prepare are then circulated to the justices who have chosen to participate in the cert pool.

The chief justice then prepares a "discuss list": a list of petitions the various justices have indicated they believe merit the Court's consideration. If a petition is not on the chief justice's list, or added to the list by another justice, it is dismissed. Nearly three-quarters of the petitions are rejected at this stage.[10]

The justices discuss the surviving petitions in conferences soon after the Court's Term begins, always on the first Monday in October. They continue to discuss petitions throughout the Term, which usually ends in late June or early July. The justices have adopted a "Rule of Four" to decide which cases on the discuss list they will hear. If at least four justices do not agree to hear the case, the petition will be dismissed.

Why do some petitions pique the interest of four justices and others not? Aside from Rule 10, there are no written guidelines. As a general matter, the factors include:

1. the importance of the issue or issues the case raises;
2. the clarity of the issues involved;
3. whether the lower court has developed a clear and complete record of the case; and
4. the potential impact of the case on the Court's own credibility and prestige.

---

[10] Cooper and Ball, *supra* note 4, at 112–13.

In an address to the American Bar Association, Chief Justice Vinson underscored the importance of these factors:

> *The debates in the Constitutional Convention make clear that the purpose of the establishment of one supreme national tribunal was, in the words of John Rutledge of South Carolina, "to secure the national rights and uniformity of judgments." The function of the Supreme Court is, therefore, to resolve conflicts of opinion on federal questions that have arisen among lower courts, to pass upon questions of wide import under the Constitution, laws, and treaties of the United States, and to exercise supervisory power over lower federal courts. If we took every case in which an interesting legal question is raised . . . we could not fulfill the constitutional and statutory responsibilities placed upon the Court. To remain effective, the Supreme Court must continue to decide only those cases which present questions whose resolution will have immediate importance far beyond the particular facts and parties involved.[11]*

In addition, each justice will bring to the conference individual interests and concerns. One justice might be especially interested in petitions that raise issues of federalism. Another might be on the lookout for cases that raise free exercise of religion issues. And, of course, justices will assess cases based on the likelihood that they can get four other justices to agree with their resolution of the issue.[12]

Finally, the kinds of petitions the Court accepts will be influenced by the kinds of issues—political, economic, moral, and social—that preoccupy society at the time. From the founding to the Civil War, for example, the Court's agenda was dominated by questions concerning the distribution of political power between the national government and the states. The post–Civil War period and the early twentieth century brought to the Court issues about the growth of monopoly and industrialization. In the past several decades the rapid rise of the administrative welfare state has led the Court to concentrate on issues surrounding the individual's relationship to the state. We may be on the cusp of yet another change: In recent years the Court has increasingly considered cases that go to the heart of concentrated power, both political and economic. These questions present themselves in renewed debates about the limits of federal power vis-à-vis the states, as well as in cases that address the limits of the state action doctrine. Similarly, rapid technological change has led the Court to consider new and intractable issues about the nature of the individual and his or her relationship to the state and community.

Once the Court accepts a case and puts it on the "docket," it informs the parties and schedules a deadline for them to file legal briefs. A brief is a formal legal document in which an attorney tries to persuade the Court that the relevant case law and other legal materials support his or her client's arguments. Many briefs include a great variety of nonlegal materials—such as medical information or social science—to support or to challenge the statute or policy at issue. Sometimes called "Brandeis

---

[11] Fred Vinson, speech to the American Bar Association, 7 Sept. 1949, reprinted in 69 S. Ct. vi (1949).

[12] H. W. Perry, Jr. *Deciding to Decide: Agenda Setting in the United States Supreme Court* (Cambridge: Harvard University Press, 1991); Doris Marie Provine, *Case Selection in the United States Supreme Court* (Chicago: University of Chicago Press, 1980); Walter F. Murphy, *Elements of Judicial Strategy* (Chicago: University of Chicago Press, 1964).

[13] Before he became Justice Brandeis, attorney Louis Brandeis used these kinds of materials to help persuade the Court to uphold an Oregon law that regulated the number of hours women could work. The case was *Muller v. Oregon*, 208 U.S. 412 (1908). Brandeis' tactic met with outraged disapproval in some camps. See Clement E. Vose, *The National Consumer's League and the Brandeis Brief,* 1 Midwest Journal of Political Science 267 (1957).

briefs,"[13] these briefs illustrate how constitutional interpretation is not simply an academic or legal exercise, but it also concerns and is shaped by conceptions of what constitutes good and wise public policy. In addition to the briefs of counsel, the Court will often receive *amicus curiae* briefs, or briefs filed by "friends of the Court." These briefs are prepared by various interest groups and other organizations that have an interest or expertise in a particular area, such as the American Civil Liberties Union, National Association for the Advancement of Colored People, the National Organization for Women, and Citizens for Decency Through Law. The briefs often support the arguments taken by one of the parties to the case, but they sometimes raise issues or present arguments the litigants have not addressed.

More dramatic than legal briefs, but not necessarily as important to the process of decision making, is oral argument. In a routine case, each party is entitled to one-half hour; in exceptional cases the Court may schedule more time, but no longer do the arguments run for days, as they sometimes used to in the previous century. Argument in *Gibbons v. Ogden* (1824), for example, lasted five days. Opinions vary about the importance of the arguments. Some justices, such as Justice Harlan, hold that a good argument may make the difference between winning and losing.[14] Others, such as former Chief Justice Burger, complain that the consistently poor quality of arguments makes them considerably less useful than the briefs. The Court hears oral argument from ten to twelve o'clock on Monday, Tuesday, and Wednesday mornings.

What are oral arguments like? It depends on the case, the justices, and the lawyers. The Rules of the Court state clearly that the Court "looks with disfavor on any oral argument that is read from a prepared text."[15] The justices frequently pepper the lawyers—and sometimes each other—with questions. As Chief Justice Rehnquist has written, oral argument is not a "brief with gestures," but instead a conversation with "nine flesh and blood men and women."[16]

Coming to Decision: Voting on Cases and Writing Opinions

The Court meets to discuss and decide cases on Wednesdays and Fridays. The meetings take place without clerks or staff. Some justices keep private records, but there is no formal or public record of the meetings, no collective record about who said what to whom or how each justice voted.

After all of the justices have shaken hands, the chief justice states his views on the case under discussion and indicates how he intends to vote. Then each of the other justices, in descending order of seniority, gives his or her view and intended vote. The dynamics of this discussion are a matter of conjecture. The papers of some justices, such as William O. Douglas, suggest the discussions can be heated and intense.[17] On the other hand, Chief Justice Rehnquist has said there is more presentation than persuasion in the current Court's conferences,[18] a matter of ongoing concern for some justices, including Justice Scalia.[19] Similarly, Justice Powell observed that "for the most

---

[14] As quoted in Anthony Lewis, *Gideon's Trumpet* (New York: Vintage Books, 1966), 162, n. 23.

[15] *Rule 10,* 28 U.S.C. Rules of the Supreme Court of the United States (1993).

[16] "Oral Advocacy: A Disappearing Art," Brainerd Currie Lecture, Mercer University School of Law, 20 October 1983, msp. 4.

[17] For a general review, see Cooper and Ball, *supra* note 4 at 224–44.

[18] As quoted in David M. O'Brien, *Storm Center: The Supreme Court in American Politics.* 3d ed. (New York: Norton, 1993), 294. See also William H. Rehnquist, *The Supreme Court: How It Was, How It Is* (New York: Willam Morrow and Company, Inc.), 287–303.

[19] See Stuart Taylor, Jr., "Ruing Fixed Opinions." *New York Times*, 22 February 1988 at A–16.

part, perhaps as much as 90 percent of our total time, we function as nine small, independent law firms."[20] No doubt the personality of the justices, and the leadership style of the chief justice, play an important role in determining how the conferences work.

After the tentative vote the justices must decide who will write the opinion. If the chief justice is in the majority, the opinion is his to assign. If the chief justice is in the minority, the power to assign falls to the senior associate justice in the majority. The assignment decision is frequently influenced by political and strategic factors. The chief justice, for example, may assign the majority opinion to a justice whose own vote was tentative, hoping that in the process of drafting an opinion the justice may become more certain of his or her convictions.[21]

Each justice has a unique way of writing an opinion. Some rely heavily on their clerks, entrusting first drafts to them and only lightly editing thereafter. Others insist upon writing themselves and limit their clerks to research or editorial assistance. The drafting stage is often crucial to the final outcome of a case. The justices circulate opinions to each other and solicit remarks, especially if they are worried about keeping a majority or are seeking to persuade a justice who may be uncertain. In short, the drafting stage is often a continuation of the conference discussions. Voting alignments often change as opinions are circulated; dissenting and concurring opinions come and go in the process of deliberation and compromise, a process that usually lasts several months.[22]

The Court makes its decisions public on "Opinion Days." The decisions are announced to reporters and attorneys in the courtroom. The Justices usually limit themselves to announcing the result in the case, but in unusual or controversial cases they may read aloud all or part of their opinions. In *Brown v. Board of Education* (1954), for example, Chief Justice Warren read the opinion in its entirety to a full and silent room. The public information office of the Court provides summaries of the decisions to reporters.

The Impact of Decisions

What happens after the Court reaches a decision? Hamilton observed in *Federalist* 78 that the Court has neither the power of purse nor sword: The Court's opinions do not enforce themselves, and the Court itself has very little power to force other actors to comply with its rulings. In the narrowest sense, the impact of a judicial decision extends first and primarily to the parties to the case. The Court's decision thus creates a legal obligation *inter partes*, or between the parties to the case. In the great majority of cases, however, a decision has important ramifications for the polity at large. When the Court decided *Roe v. Wade* (1973), for example, its decision voided the particular

---

[20]Lewis F. Powell, Jr., *What the Justices are Saying . . . ,* 62 American Bar Association Journal 1454 (1976).

[21]For a more elaborate discussion, see Walter F. Murphy, *Elements of Judicial Strategy* (Chicago: University of Chicago Press, 1964), 84–5. In *Roe v. Wade* (1973), the private papers of some of the justices indicate that there was some confusion about how Justice Blackmun had voted at the conference, and likewise some doubt about whether there was a majority to strike or uphold the statute. Chief Justice Burger, who had voted to sustain the law, assigned the opinion to Blackmun. Douglas, thinking Blackmun had voted with Burger, objected because Burger was in the minority. Later, Justices Douglas and Brennan decided to wait to see Blackmun's draft before pressing the issue any further. In the end, Justice Blackmun wrote the majority opinion striking the Texas abortion law. See Bernard Schwartz, *The Ascent of Pragmatism: The Burger Court in Action* (New York: Addison-Wesley Publishing Company, 1990), 297–307.

[22]See David M. O'Brien, *Storm Center: The Supreme Court in American Politics.* 3d ed. (New York: W. W. Norton & Company, Inc., 1993), 304–06.

Texas antiabortion law that gave rise to the case. But more broadly, it put into question the antiabortion laws of every state in the Union. When the Court decides a matter of law in ways that go beyond the particular parties to the case, it purports to create a rule of legal obligation that is *erga omnes*, or one that applies to all similarly situated parties.

Whether and when a Supreme Court decision is *erga omnes* or *inter partes* is often a matter of some conflict. Unpopular decisions are likely to provoke congressional or presidential responses that seek to overturn or limit the ruling. The forms of these responses can vary from outright disobedience, as was often the case following *Brown v. Board of Education* (1954), to feigned blindness following *INS v. Chadha* (1983), to constitutional and statutory efforts to reverse specific rulings as happened following the Court's controversial ruling in *Texas v. Johnson* (1989), the flag-burning case. In some instances, the Court's decisions have provoked claims by other institutional actors that they possess a coordinate and coequal right to interpret the Constitution for themselves. As we shall see in chapter 3, President Jefferson responded to the Court's opinion in *Marbury v. Madison* (1803) by insisting that "The Constitution intended that the three great branches of the government should be co-ordinate, & independent of each other. As to acts, therefore, which are to be done by either, it has given no controul to another branch."[23] Likewise, President Lincoln concluded in his first Inaugural Address (Appendix C) that

> *At the same time, the candid citizen must confess that if the whole policy of the government, upon vital questions, affecting the whole people, is to be irrevocably fixed by decisions of the Supreme Court, the instant they are made, in ordinary litigation between parties, in personal actions, the people will have ceased to be their own rulers, having, to that extent practically resigned their government into the hands of that eminent tribunal.*

As we note in chapter 2, questions about the impact and enforcement of judicial opinions inevitably raise questions of power and accountability in interpretation, questions that go to the very heart of the constitutional order.

Understanding Judicial Opinions

For most students, judicial opinions are an unusual and sometimes frustrating object of study. Filled with jargon, complicated arguments, and references to obscure legal materials, judicial opinions *are* somewhat puzzling. Most, however, follow a standard format. Learning to recognize the various parts of an opinion will make the process of reading and understanding cases easier.

Every case includes:

• A Title. The title usually includes the names of the parties to a case. Hence, *Bowers v. Hardwick*, 478 U.S. 186 (1986), tells us that Bowers and Hardwick are the primary parties in the case. The first party—here it is Bowers—is the party that lost in the lower court. He or she is called the "appellant" or the "petitioner." The second party—usually the one seeking to have the lower court decision upheld—is the "appellee" or "respondent."

• A Citation. Every title is followed by a string of numbers, or a citation. In the *Bowers* case, the citation is 478 U.S. 186 (1986). The decisions of the Supreme Court (and of all federal courts) are kept in "reporters," or collections, that are organized

---

[23] Jefferson's letter to the prosecutor in the Burr treason case, 2 June 1807.

chronologically. The volume number is "478." The initials "U.S." tell us that the reporter is the official reporter—or collection—of Supreme Court cases. (There are also unofficial reporters prepared by private companies. The initials "L. Ed" and "S. C." refer to these other reporters.) The number "186" indicates the page number where the case begins. The last number, "1986" in our example, tells us the year when the case was decided.

• Facts of the Case. Usually, although not always, the Court will begin its opinion by stating the facts of the case. Often the facts are in dispute or subject to interpretation, so concurring and dissenting opinions may also include an account of the facts.

• Questions Presented. Every case raises at least one and usually several constitutional questions. It is important to determine what those questions are. The Court will often list them near the beginning of its opinion. As with the facts, the precise nature of the questions involved—or how they are framed—is often a matter of dispute among the justices.

• The Majority Opinion. Most cases are decided by a majority of the justices. One justice, speaking for the majority, writes the Opinion of the Court. (If no opinion commands a majority, it will be a "plurality" opinion.) The majority opinion announces the holding, or the result, of the case and sets forth the reasons for the decision.

• Concurring Opinions. Sometimes one or more justices will agree with the majority's result but not entirely with its reasoning. In such cases the justice will write a "concurring opinion." Justices who joined the majority opinion may write to add something or to clarify a point in the majority opinion.

• Dissenting Opinions. A justice who disagrees with the result in the case may simply note the disagreement, or he or she may choose to write a "dissenting opinion." Unlike the majority opinion, a dissent does not have the force of law. Nevertheless, it may have a considerable impact on the law, perhaps by highlighting flaws in the majority opinion or by making a forceful argument that will influence the thinking of a future Court.

As you read the opinions, you will find it helpful to assess them in light of the three themes—interpretive, normative, and comparative—we identified in the text introduction. Every opinion, for example, adopts one or more methods of constitutional interpretation. Similarly, in every opinion the justices wrestle—sometimes explicitly—with the political theory and ideals that inform the Constitution and give it meaning.

Constitutional Courts in Comparative Perspective

Although its antecedents are ancient, the practice of judicial review is essentially an American invention. The Supreme Court's power to review legislation for its constitutionality, whether a consequence of decision or evolution, has struck many observers as the very essence of constitutional democracy. Consequently, the Court has served as a model, both of attraction and repulsion, for many other countries. In *Democracy in America*, Alexis de Tocqueville praised the institution, but in the nineteenth century few Europeans shared his enthusiasm for a strong judicial body equipped with the power of constitutional review. In France and many other civil law jurisdictions the process of democratization resulted in a profound distrust of judicial power and judges, who were often associated with reactionary or aristocratic elements of society. The introduction of judicial review was easier in Latin and South America, although the transplant did not often take.

In the twentieth century, especially following World War II and later the collapse of the Iron Curtain, judicial review and constitutional courts have become common around the world. Constitutional democracy and the structures associated with it have blossomed in the latter half of this century, so much so that some scholars have argued that the expansion of judicial review is one of the distinguishing features of contemporary political life.[24]

The popularity of constitutionalism has contributed to the spread of judicial review and constitutional courts. More than one hundred countries have constitutions that provide for judicial review, at least on paper. Constitutional courts exercise the power of judicial review in Canada, Germany, Spain, Italy, Austria, Israel, India, Australia, Venezuela, Japan, Ireland, South Africa, Eritrea, Uruguay, Brazil, Colombia, and in many other countries. In the former Eastern bloc countries of Europe, there are new constitutional courts in the Czech Republic, Hungary, Poland, Ukraine, and elsewhere. Indeed, the idea has proven so persuasive that in Europe there are two supranational tribunals with the power of constitutional review. The European Court of Justice, established in 1952, enforces the Treaty of the European Economic Community. The European Court of Human Rights, established in 1953, enforces the European Convention on Human Rights and Fundamental Freedoms. The Court of Human Rights consists of judges, one from each member-state, elected by the Council of Europe to renewable nine-year terms. As we shall see in later chapters, the Convention includes a number of far-reaching guarantees for the protection of civil liberties, including guarantees of the freedom of expression (Article 10), the right to a fair trial (Article 6), and respect for private and family life (Article 8).

Why have constitutional courts become so popular? The appeal is partly practical. Many countries have come to see judicial review as a mechanism for protecting democracy and human rights. The appeal is also political: In an era when appeals to many other forms of political legitimacy, such as communism and organic statism, have lost much of their attraction, the forms of constitutional democracy have become common currency.

Broadly speaking, we can identify two systems of judicial review—or two different kinds of constitutional courts—one based on the American experience, the other based on the European model.[25] The models differ in the structure, methods, and effects of judicial review.[26] Even within the two species, though, there is wide room for variation. Different constitutions provide for different judicial structures and kinds of organizations, for different procedures, and for different methods of appointing and removing justices.

Generalized or Specialized Jurisdiction

The American Supreme Court is a court of general jurisdiction. It may hear a wide range of cases, many of which raise no constitutional issue at all. Its jurisdiction extends to all areas of public law, including administrative law, federal statutory law, and admiralty. It may also hear private law cases, such as torts or contracts, that raise no questions of public import.

In contrast, many constitutional courts in other constitutional democracies have

---

[24] C. Neal Tate and Torbjörn Vallinder, "The Globalization of Judicial Power: The Judicialization of Politics," in Tate and Vallinder, *The Global Expansion of Judicial Power* (New York: New York University Press, 1995), 5.

[25] See generally Mauro Cappelletti, *The Judicial Process in Comparative Perspective* (Oxford: Clarendon Press, 1989); A. R. Brewer-Carias, *Judicial Review in Comparative Law* (Cambridge: Cambridge University Press, 1989); Louis Favoreu, "American and European Models of Constitutional Justice," in D. S. Clark, ed., *Essays in Honor of J. H. Merryman* (Berlin: Duncker & Humblot, 1990).

[26] Louis Favoreu, *supra* note 21, at 111–15.

only special, or limited jurisdiction. These courts, such as the Federal Constitutional Court of Germany and the Italian Constitutional Court, hear only cases that raise constitutional issues. They do not hear private law cases unless those cases raise an issue of constitutional interpretation. Their limited jurisdiction means that these courts do not have the appellate jurisdiction that makes up such a prominent part of the United States Supreme Court's jurisdiction. Similarly, they do not sit at the top of an elaborate judicial hierarchy, as does the American Court. Instead, they exist alongside or outside of the hierarchy of ordinary courts.

Centralized and Decentralized Systems of Constitutional Review

In the European model (sometimes called the Austrian model), only specialized constitutional courts have the power to resolve constitutional controversies. These courts usually do not share the power of review with lower courts. Hence the power of review is centralized or concentrated in a single court. The most prominent example of a centralized system with a court of specialized jurisdiction is the Federal Republic of Germany. Created in 1951, the Federal Constitutional Court has served as a model for similar courts in Hungary, Russia, Poland, and the Czech Republic.

Even within systems of centralized review there are significant differences. The German Court may hear constitutional controversies brought by various branches and officers of the state and national governments, as well as disputes submitted by individual citizens. The Italian Court, in contrast, can hear cases only if they are brought by one of the branches of government or if they are certified by a judge on a lower court. The Italian model is the more common in Europe, though there are provisions for individual complaints in Austria, Belgium, Hungary, and in Spain, the latter through an elaborate procedure called an "amparo." The amparo allows individuals and "defenders of the people" to file a complaint against an administrative or judicial act (but not directly against a statute), but the Constitutional Court itself must determine whether the cause raises a constitutional question.

The American model is characterized by decentralized, or diffuse, review. The Supreme Court shares its power to hear constitutional cases with other federal and state courts. Moreover, constitutional review takes place only in the context of a concrete case. Implicit in the two models are different understandings about the demands of federalism and how the relationship between the center and periphery should be moderated by judicial structures. As we saw, this issue was a source of great conflict at the Philadelphia Convention in 1789. It remains one of the great sources of conflict in contemporary constitutional regimes. As we discuss in chapter 3, differences in the structure and form of constitutional courts and systems of constitutional review also reflect various understandings about which governmental actors bear primary responsibility for safeguarding and protecting the Constitution.

The Effects of Judicial Review

In every case that comes before a court, the court's decision is binding on the parties to the case. The decision, in other words, binds *inter partes*. If a decision binds all other actors, even those not party to the suit, we say that the decision binds *erga omnes*. As mentioned earlier, in the United States, there is always room for question about whether any particular decision is *inter partes* or *erga omnes*. In some other constitutions, the text plainly indicates whether a decision binds the parties alone. The decisions of the Federal Constitutional Court of the German Republic bind *erga omnes*, as do the decisions of the Austrian Supreme Court and the Italian Constitutional Court. The Canadian Charter provides that most decisions of their Supreme

Court may in certain cases be overridden by the national legislature and sometimes by provincial legislatures. As the Canadian case makes clear, behind the technical issues of *inter partes* and *erga omnes* are fundamental political questions about how to weigh the balance between judicial protection of individual liberty and respect for popular rule and democratic ideals.

Differences in Judicial Opinions

In the United States, judicial opinions are often long, elaborately reasoned, and argued in unique and highly stylized ways. Judges and justices frequently write for themselves, either in concurring opinions or dissents, and they do not hesitate to criticize other opinions, sometimes very harshly. In other countries, though, it is not unusual to find very short opinions that simply announce a conclusion or provide only sparse accounts of the reasoning the justices used to reach their conclusion. Similarly, there are courts where the use of separate opinions is rare and discouraged. As we shall see in chapter 2, the interpretive styles of courts vary widely as well.

Methods of Judicial Appointment and Terms of Office

One of the most striking differences among constitutional courts are the methods used for appointing and removing justices. In general, judicial appointments, especially in parliamentary systems, are an elaborate affair, entrusted in large measure to legislative bodies. The Italian Constitutional Court, for example, has fifteen judges, five nominated by the president, five by Parliament, and five by the highest state courts. The term of appointment is for nine years, with no reappointment allowed. The German Court has sixteen judges, divided into two distinct chambers. The lower house of the German legislature appoints one-half of the justices, and the upper house appoints the other half. Terms are for twelve years, with no reappointment. In Austria the fourteen members of the Court are appointed by the president acting upon the recommendation of the National and Federal Councils. There are similar processes in Belgium, Spain, and Portugal.

Perhaps the most notable contrast between the foregoing systems and the United States is that the justices on these other courts do not hold lifetime appointments. In the United States, lifetime appointments are generally thought to be a critical means of ensuring judicial independence. Most other constitutional democracies have devised alternate means of ensuring judicial independence, such as immunities from prosecution, salary guarantees, autonomy over budgets and internal administration, as well as prohibitions against intervention by government ministries. No less important, limited appointments reflect a judgment that judicial independence must be weighed against the equally compelling demands of democratic and popular accountability.[27]

Although the ideas of judicial review and constitutional courts find their source in the American Supreme Court, other countries have not slavishly duplicated American practice. For the most part, the European model of specialized judicial review has been the more persuasive. In part, the aversion to the American model has stemmed from different understandings about the meaning of separation of powers and equality under law, as well as differences occasioned by the predominance of parliamentarianism rather than presidential regimes.

The prestige and influence of constitutional courts varies. Some of them, such as

---

[27] See Cappelletti, *supra* note 21 at 83–6.

the German and the Canadian Courts, have attained considerable influence and are important, persuasive voices in their countries. Other courts, especially in Latin America and the newly democratic states of Eastern Europe, are still embryonic.

All of them, however, wrestle with the same kinds of issues and questions that dominate American constitutional interpretation. The great similarity of issues and problems that dominate constitutional politics in all countries are a testimony to what is universal in human life. But if the themes are much the same, the approaches to resolving these questions vary widely in constitutional democracies. As we shall see throughout this book, an appreciation of what we share with and how we differ from others can be a powerful tool for understanding constitutional interpretation in the United States.

Selected Bibliography

Abraham, Henry J. *Justices and Presidents: A Political History of Appointments to the Supreme Court*. 3d ed. New York: Oxford University Press, 1992.

Barnum, David G. *The Supreme Court and American Democracy*. New York: St. Martin's Press, 1992.

Baum, Lawrence. *The Supreme Court*. 4th ed. Washington, D.C.: CQ Press, 1992.

Bloch, Susan Low and Thomas G. Krattenmaker. *Supreme Court Politics: The Institution and Its Procedures*. St. Paul, Minn.: West Publishing Company, 1994.

Brewer-Carias, A. R. *Judicial Review in Comparative Law*. Cambridge: Cambridge University Press, 1989.

Cappelletti, Mauro. *The Judicial Process in Comparative Perspective*. Oxford: Oxford University Press, 1989.

Coffin, Frank M. *On Appeal: Courts, Lawyers, and Judging*. New York: W. W. Norton and Co., 1994.

Cooper, Phillip and Howard Ball. *The United States Supreme Court: From the Inside Out*. Upper Saddle River, N.J.: Prentice Hall, 1996.

Dinnage, James D. and John F. Murphy. *The Constitutional Law of the European Union*. Cincinnati, Ohio: Anderson Publishing Co., 1996.

Hall, Kermit, ed. *The Oxford Companion to the Supreme Court of the United States*. New York: Oxford University Press, 1992.

Jacob, Herbert et al. *Courts, Law, and Politics in Comparative Perspective*. New Haven: Yale University Press, 1996.

Kavass, Igor I., ed. *Supranational and Constitutional Courts in Europe: Functions and Sources*. Buffalo, N.Y.: William S. Hein & Co., Inc. 1992.

McCloskey, Robert. *The American Supreme Court*. Chicago: University of Chicago Press, 1960.

Meador, Daniel J. *American Courts*. St. Paul, Minn.: West Publishing Co., 1991.

Murphy, Walter. *Elements of Judicial Strategy*. Chicago: University of Chicago Press, 1964.

Perry, H. W., Jr. *Deciding to Decide: Agenda Setting in the United States Supreme Court*. Cambridge: Harvard University Press, 1991.

Provine, Doris Marie. *Case Selection in the United States Supreme Court*. Chicago: University of Chicago Press, 1980.

Rehnquist, William H. *The Supreme Court: How It Was, How It Is*. New York: William Morrow & Co., 1987.

Schwartz, Bernard. *A History of the Supreme Court*. New York: Oxford University Press, 1993.

Tate, C. Neal and Torbjorn Vallinder. *The Global Expansion of Judicial Power*. New York: New York University Press, 1995.

Tribe, Lawrence. *God Save This Honorable Court: How the Choice of Supreme Court Justices Shapes Our History*. New York: Random House, 1985.

Van Geel, T. R. *Understanding Supreme Court Opinions*. New York: Longman, 1991.

Chapter 2

The Constitution and Its Interpretation

The Constitution

Thomas Reed Powell once advised his first-year students in the Harvard Law School not to read the Constitution because it would only confuse them. We would prefer to ignore his legendary advice and advise students to read the document before they plunge into the "why and what" of interpretation. In doing so, they should not overlook the importance of the preamble, for it lays out the broad purposes of the Constitution among which is the creation of "a more perfect union" that would secure the "Blessings of Liberty" and the achievement of "justice." Nor should we overlook the significance of its opening line, "We the People of the United States," words that prompt us to ask who the Framers meant by the "people"? We know they excluded some people, such as slaves. But did they exclude others? An equally important consideration is why we are the "We" of the preamble. Because we tacitly consent to be bound by the Constitution? Because we are citizens or voters? Because we as a people are committed to a given political ideology? Or because we share certain values and want to foster preferred ways of life? Each of these possibilities implicates the manner in which the Constitution might be interpreted.

Related questions may be asked about the content and scope of the Constitution as a whole. Is it more than the original document ratified in 1789, along with its twenty-seven amendments? Or does it also include extratextual practices and traditions that define Americans as a people or their political system as exceptional? Does the Constitution include values, beliefs, or written sources apart from the documentary text? The Constitution, for example, was drafted in the long shadow of the Declaration of Independence, an American revolutionary confession of faith that certain self-evident truths must be respected by any government established on these shores. Should the Constitution accordingly be interpreted in the light of its values? If so, what indeed are its "truths," what does it mean to say that Americans "hold" these truths, and why do Americans regard them as "self-evident"? Whatever meaning is extracted from its terms, the Declaration is arguably an integral part of the American constitutional tradition and thus worthy of study and analysis in its own right.[1] (See Appendix A for the text of the Declaration.)

---

[1] Similarly, as Edward Corwin reminds us, principles of higher law or natural justice were commonly accepted by the founders, and many of these principles worked their way into the Supreme Court's interpre-

On the other hand, not everything in the written text is regarded today as part of our "living" Constitution. The development of the two party system, for example, has reduced the electoral college—part of the written Constitution—to a virtual nullity. Other constitutional provisions, too, like muscles that have atrophied from disuse, have lost their vitality. A prominent example is the provision of the Fourteenth Amendment that requires Congress to reduce a state's congressional delegation proportionate to the number of citizens denied the right to vote in federal elections. To the extent that such provisions are ignored or unenforced, they could not be said to have been a normative part of the Constitution.[2]

For present purposes, however, we confine our attention to the documentary text. First, we might observe that the Framers wrote the Constitution for ordinary people and thus refrained from using arcane language or the irritating "legalese" often found in statutory law, legal contracts and, alas, even in the decisions of the Supreme Court. Unlike many American state and nearly all foreign constitutions, they also shunned the minutiae of excessive detail. They produced a document distinguished not only for its graceful style but also for its judicious use of language broad and flexible enough to withstand the changes of time and circumstance. John Marshall captured the genius of the Framers' accomplishment when he remarked in *McCulloch v. Maryland* (1819) that "we must never forget, that it is a *constitution* we are expounding"—that is, one marked by "its great outlines" and "important objects" unburdened by "the prolixity of a legal code [that] would probably never be understood by the public."[3]

The original document is composed of seven articles, most of them comparatively short. The first three establish the branches of the national government, specifying their structures and powers; the remaining articles lay down, respectively, the duties the states owe each other, procedures for amending the Constitution, the rule affirming the supremacy of the Constitution and laws of the United States, and the method by which the Constitution is to be ratified. These structures and procedures embody the main principles of American constitutionalism: They include federalism, separation of powers, checks and balances, the rule of law, government by consent, and republican government. (Judicial review, which is also a fundamental principle of American constitutionalism, emerged from *Marbury v. Madison* (1803) and its progeny [see chapter 3].) In addition, the Constitution identifies three sources of power, namely, the national government, the individual states, and the people. The national government is one of enumerated or limited powers while the Tenth Amendment reserves all other powers "to the States respectively, or to the people." Under the Ninth Amendment, the people alone reserve to themselves certain rights that remain unspecified in the documentary text.

---

tation of the original Constitution. See Edward S. Corwin, *The Higher Law Background of American Constitutional Law*, 42 Harvard Law Review 149–85; 365–409, (1928). In 1898 Justice Henry Brown struck a familiar note when he wrote that "the object of the first eight amendments to the Constitution was to incorporate into the fundamental law of the land certain principles of natural justice." See *Brown v. Walker*, 161 U.S. 591 (1896). In the same vein, Supreme Court justices have often appealed to the moral and ethical values of society in resolving difficult constitutional issues.

[2] More recently, constitutional scholars have even debated whether the Twenty-Seventh Amendment, ratified in 1992, belongs in the Constitution. The provision requires a congressional election to intervene between the passage of a law raising the salaries of senators and representatives and the law's going into effect. Proposed in 1789, it was ratified 203 years later after some thirty states had approved the measure between 1979 and 1992. Because the proposed amendment—initially introduced by James Madison—lay dormant for nearly two hundred years, some scholars urged that it had "died" and therefore could not legitimately be part of the Constitution unless proposed by a new Congress and submitted once again for ratification by the states. See Sanford Levinson, *Authorizing the Constitutional Text: Or the (So-Called) Twenty-Seventh Amendment*, 10 Constitutional Commentary 101 (1994).

[3] 17 U.S. (4 Wheat.) 316, 407 (1819).

As for specified rights, the first eight amendments to the Constitution include a list of personal freedoms that the state may not infringe, including numerous procedural guarantees in criminal investigations and prosecutions. The main body of the Constitution also enhances liberty by prohibiting bills of attainder, *ex post facto* laws, and laws impairing the obligation of contracts, not to mention its ban on suspending the privilege of habeas corpus unless "the public Safety may require it." Finally, ten of the seventeen amendments added to the Constitution since the incorporation of the Bill of Rights (i.e., Amendments I through X) have served either to expand the right to vote—resulting in universal adult suffrage—or to enhance the general principle of popular representation in government.

The expansion of popular government through the amendatory process has transformed the American polity from what was originally a limited representative republic into a modern political democracy. Democracy, however, remains conceptually in tension with the idea of constitutionalism. If the essence of democracy is universal suffrage combined with majority rule, then the people through their representatives are entitled to write their policy preferences into law. As Lincoln succinctly put forth in his elegant Gettysburg Address, ours is a "government of, by, and for the people." Chief Justice John Marshall, on the other hand, regarded the Constitution as a superior legal norm that limits what the people may legislate. Lincoln's democracy and Marshall's constitutionalism may embrace each other in certain contexts, but they collide in many cases that come before the Supreme Court. (The tension between the two ideals, as noted in our general introduction, is a major theme of this coursebook.)

The Why and What of Constitutional Interpretation

In *Texas v. Johnson* (1989), the controversial flag-burning case, Justice Anthony Kennedy wrote,

> *The hard fact is that sometimes we must make decisions we do not like. We make them because they are right, right in the sense that the law and the Constitution, as we see them, compel the result. And so great is our commitment to the process that, except in rare cases, we do not pause to express our distaste for the result, perhaps for fear of undermining a valued principle that dictates the decision.*

Justice Felix Frankfurter made a similar point when he spoke of the "awful task of judging." In the United States, unlike in some other constitutional democracies, the justices of the Supreme Court have many duties other than interpreting the Constitution, for the Court sits at the top of a hierarchy of federal and state courts. Its business as an appellate court includes responsibility for making final decisions in a wide variety of cases that ordinarily have nothing to do with the Constitution.

It is in constitutional cases, however, where the awful task of judging weighs most heavily. The burden is great, in part because the responsibility is profound and far reaching. Every year the Court must decide cases that raise issues of fundamental importance to us all. But the burden is great, too, because the justices must often tease what Justice Kennedy called "right answers" from materials as enigmatic as a Jackson Pollock painting. The search for right answers would be far easier, and of less consequence, if the Constitution simply and clearly laid them out. It is easy to overstate its indeterminacy. A nominee for the presidency must be thirty-five or older, candidates for the Senate thirty years, and for the House twenty-five; presidential elections are held at prescribed times; and all states, large and small, are equally represented in the United States Senate.

The specificity of these provisions contrasts sharply with other parts of the text. What do the Fifth and Fourteenth Amendments mean by "due process of law"? What does "equal protection" of the law mean? When is a search and seizure "unreasonable"? What makes a punishment "cruel and unusual" or a bail "excessive"? When the Court is asked to apply these vague guarantees to specific cases, it is engaged in an act of interpretation—that is, an effort to discern what these expansive phrases require or prohibit in ordinary life. In this sense, constitutional interpretation is the process we use to give concrete expression to the ideals and values contained in the Constitution.

One of the difficulties in this definition of interpretation is that it tells us nothing about "the process" itself. The definition suggests, if it does not say, that constitutional interpretation is a routine, mechanical matter. Some justices have seemed to agree. In a well-known opinion, Justice Owen Roberts described constitutional interpretation this way:

> When an act of Congress is appropriately challenged in the court as not conforming to the constitutional mandate, the judicial branch . . . has only one duty; to lay the article of the Constitution which is invoked beside the statute which is challenged and to decide whether the latter squares with the former. All the court does, or can do, is to announce its considered judgment upon the question. The only power it has, if such it may be called, is the power of judgment.[4]

One would never guess from Roberts's description that constitutional interpretation involves an element of doubt and indecision. Sometimes the "article invoked" seems to conflict with some other part of the constitutional text. Sometimes the Constitution is so hopelessly and wonderfully vague that it appears to say nothing at all—or perhaps worse, too much. In difficult cases constitutional interpretation demands insight, creativity and, not least, political acumen. And if, as Justice Kennedy claimed, constitutional interpretation is really about finding "right answers," and not simply as stating one's preferences, then it demands also that we have some understanding of the polity the Constitution seeks to invent. It requires, in other words, an appreciation of the ends it seeks to achieve and the means it adopts to achieve those ends. Constitutional interpretation, in this larger sense, is an ongoing act of self-definition.

For reasons we shall briefly explore, interpretation is a practical necessity. We should not forget, however, that the practice rests on an important, indeed critical, assumption. When we say interpretation is necessary, we mean first that it must occur because the constitutional text gives us less than complete guidance. In such cases, we might choose simply to disregard the Constitution. When we interpret, however, we accept that the Constitution should guide our collective behavior. The act of interpretation is an act of fidelity, a decision to become citizens of the constitutional order and to order our collective affairs according to its ideals and terms.

Constitutional interpretation is thus simultaneously a choice and a necessity: a choice because we may choose not to bother; a necessity because, having chosen to be governed by the Constitution, it is not always obvious how it is to govern us. The causes of the Constitution's vagueness are not difficult to find. First, as James Madison noted in *Federalist* 37, "When the Almighty himself condescends to address mankind in their own language, his meaning, luminous as it must be, is rendered dim and doubtful by the cloudy medium through which it is communicated." Language is an imprecise and imperfect means of communication. Words have many meanings, and sometimes their meaning changes over time.

Ambiguity in the constitutional document is not simply an unavoidable consequence of imperfect communication. A second cause of imprecision is a deliberate

---

[4] *United States v. Butler*, 297 U.S. 1 (1936).

choice by the Founders to use elastic words and phrases. Conflict among the delegates about many important issues was resolved by finding language sufficiently pliant to let all parties think they might win the issue at some later point. The most litigated of these elastic phrases are contained in the Fourteenth Amendment. They include the guarantee of "equal protection" and the command that forbids the states from "depriv[ing] any person of life, liberty, or property, without due process of law." Just what "life," "liberty," and "due process" mean has bedeviled the Court for decades, and the Court's attempts to specify what these terms do mean are among its most controversial decisions.

A third, and related, cause of imprecision rests in the nature of constitution making itself. Although the Founders did not claim that the new constitution would exist "in perpetuity," as had the Framers of the Articles of Confederation, the Founders were acutely aware that they were constructing a political order that would endure through time. Many of the Constitution's most important provisions, in the words of Ronald Dworkin, refer to general "concepts" and not to specific "conceptions."[5] The Eighth Amendment's prohibition of "cruel and unusual punishments," for example, represents a choice by the Founders to enshrine a general concept of fairness. They might have chosen instead to simply list those punishments they thought were cruel and unusual, or to give us specific conceptions about what fairness means in particular cases. Instead, each generation must find for itself what the concept means.

Another cause of vagueness is similarly related to the nature of the constitutional enterprise. Constitutional democracies are committed to a number of values. The preamble tells us, as noted earlier, that the Constitution promises "Blessings and Liberty" in the context of a more perfect union capable of promoting the general welfare. These goals, or ends, are not always compatible with each other. At times the general welfare is in tension with liberty. It was inevitable that a Constitution committed to these ideals would find it necessary to adopt the vague language of compromise. In addition, the Founders could not have foreseen every contingency and problem, so the text they gave us is incomplete and imperfect.

For reasons both unavoidable and desirable, then, the Constitution requires interpretation if it is to be realized. The reasons that give rise to the need for interpretation—human imperfection, the need for compromise, and a multiplicity of ideals—also make the process of interpretation difficult and complex. The complexity is heightened when we see that in the United States, especially, questions about constitutional interpretation often overlap with contentious questions about the nature and limits of judicial power in a constitutional democracy. These questions are so closely related that many students of the Constitution treat them as though they were just one question. One definition of constitutional interpretation, for example, holds that it "is concerned with the justification, standards, and methods by which a court exercises the power of judicial review."[6] There is much to commend in this definition, not least that it combines constitutional interpretation with judicial power.

We would stress, however, that constitutional interpretation is not necessarily the same thing as judicial review. When the Court exercises the power of judicial review, it does indeed interpret the Constitution, but interpretation is not an exclusively judicial responsibility. It is a task performed also—and often—by legislators, administrative officials, police officers, constitutional scholars, journalists, and even citizens who write letters to the editor.

---

[5] See Ronald Dworkin, *Taking the Constitution Seriously* (Cambridge: Harvard University Press, 1977), 134–36.

[6] Craig R. Ducat and Harold W. Chase, *Constitutional Interpretation*, 5th ed. (St. Paul, Minn.: West Publishing Co., 1992), 82.

Matters are complicated, too, because constitutional interpretation takes place within a larger political environment, one that includes a great number of institutional, cultural, and social factors, any one of which can influence an interpreter. Moreover, interpretation is itself a political act—that is, an exercise of political power. The Court is intricately caught up in the basics of politics, and it frequently decides who gets what, when, and how much.[7] As we saw in chapter 1, there are a variety of constitutional provisions relating to the Court that acknowledge its status as a political actor.

In a larger sense, the activity of interpretation—as opposed to its results—is also fundamentally political because it represents a collective, deliberative choice to exercise power through reason. A written opinion, like a written constitution, represents an effort to engage and to persuade. The effort to persuade tells us something, too, about the requirements of "good" or "correct" interpretation. A good interpretation must ground itself in the Constitution or trace it to the Constitution. Some interpretive methods are surely out of bounds. An interpretation that says simply "give me that" is not an interpretation. The opinion must be expanded to include a rational basis for what is said: For example, "Give me that, it belongs to me" or "It's part of my inheritance." Constitutional jurisprudence, like the legal enterprise generally, begins when "discourse is expanded to include a rational basis for what is said."[8]

Sources and Methods of Interpretation

It is well worth asking what we are looking for when examining various methods of interpretation. We have seen why interpretation is necessary, but we have to ask whether we can distinguish between right and wrong, or better and worse, methods of interpretation. What criteria of interpretation shall be used and where do these methods come from? Surprisingly, these questions receive less attention than they deserve. To begin with, we would hope that interpretation seriously considers the fact that we have a written Constitution. Second, we would hope that a judicial opinion interpreting the Constitution is one that the public can understand. Citizens have a right to know what their judges are saying about the Constitution's meaning and why.[9] Finally, we would hope that in interpreting the Constitution, judges recognize the limits of their power and find some way to curtail their discretion.

To limit its role in deciding constitutional cases, the Supreme Court often follows guidelines known as the *Ashwander* rules. (They are discussed in greater detail in chapter 3.) These rules are really self-imposed canons of restraint. Out of respect for the principle of separated powers, they exhort the Supreme Court to presume the constitutionality of legislative acts, to reach constitutional issues last not first, and never to anticipate a constitutional question in advance of the necessity of deciding it. The rules reflect the seriousness of any judicial decision that interprets the Constitution since there is no way to get around a constitutional decision unless—short of noncompliance—the Constitution is amended or the Supreme Court changes its mind. Relatedly, by observing these rules, the Court pays proper respect for the results of the democratic political process.

Beyond these general guidelines, however, scholars and justices have developed a number of mechanisms or methods of interpretation to discern the Constitution's meaning. Taking a written constitution seriously means that interpretation must al-

---

[7] Harold Lasswell, *Politics: Who Gets What, When, How* (New York: McGraw Hill, 1936).

[8] Robert E. Rodes, Jr., *The Legal Enterprise* (Port Washington, N.Y.: Kennikat Press, 1976), 22.

[9] See Joseph Goldstein, *The Intelligible Constitution: The Supreme Court's Obligation to Maintain the Constitution as Something We the People Can Understand* (Oxford: Oxford University Press, 1992) and Lawrence M. Solan, *The Language of Judges* (Chicago: University of Chicago Press, 1993).

ways begin with the constitutional text. But it must also account for omissions, contradictions, and imperfections in the text. The following methods are most frequently used in constitutional argument, both on and off the Court. We shall encounter them as we read the cases. Justices rarely, if ever, commit themselves to just one of these methods. Instead, they typically take a pragmatic approach, using one here and one there, or using several methods together, as circumstances warrant.

Textualism

Textualism is based on the unremarkable claim that constitutional interpretation must begin with the written word. At times, the words of the Constitution are sufficiently plain, and they provide an answer without recourse to any other source of meaning. Sometimes called the "plain words" approach, advocates of textualism claim that we should read the words of the Constitution for their ordinary meaning and apply them accordingly. Justice Joseph Story wrote in his celebrated *Commentaries on the Constitution*, "It is obvious that there can be no security to the people in any constitution of government if they are not to judge of it by the fair meaning of the words of the text."[10] Story's insistence on "plain" meaning was grounded in what Philip Bobbitt has called an "ongoing social contract, whose terms are given their contemporary meanings continually reaffirmed by the refusal of the People to amend the instrument."[11] It was grounded also—as are all theories of interpretation—in a specific conception of judicial power. As Bobbitt notes, "Story believed that this obligation to apply contemporary meanings constrained judges; one cannot appeal to superior learning to establish the meaning of a common phrase."[12]

The textual approach, however, is also profoundly limited. First, and most troublesome, the words of the text are anything but clear in a great many places. Indeed, it is this lack of clarity that necessitates interpretation in the first place. Or words may take on several meanings. In such cases, which meaning should govern? Worse, there are some provisions, such as the Ninth Amendment, that by their very terms seem to call for a method of interpretation that reaches beyond the text. The text of the Ninth Amendment, for example—once referred to by Judge Bork as an "ink blot"[13]—seems to counsel interpreters to reach beyond the text. In addition, the commonsense meaning of constitutional provisions sometimes fail to catch or appreciate the way that the concepts behind those words have changed or have grown more complex with time. To put it bluntly, the commonsense meanings of words are often limited or simplistic. Finally, the textual method of constitutional interpretation fails to account for the many cases where constitutional words or phrases conflict with one another.

Original History

Some judges and scholars have argued that the aim of constitutional interpretation is to discover what the Founders "intended" the provision at hand to mean. Once discovered, intent governs the case. For many people, there is an intuitive appeal to the search for intent. When we seek the meaning of any text we often begin by asking,

---

[10] *Commentaries on the Constitution of the United States*, vol. I (New York: De Capo Press, 1970), s. 407, 390, n. 1.

[11] Philip Bobbitt, *Constitutional Fate* (New York: Oxford University Press, 1982), 26.

[12] Ibid.

[13] See Walter F. Murphy, *et al.*, *American Constitutional Interpretation*, 2d ed. (Westbury, N.Y.: The Foundation Press, 1995), 385.

"What did the author mean?" And like textualism, appeals to intent promise to limit judicial power by putting constraints on what judges may do. Bobbitt writes that this strict intentionalist approach "draws legitimacy from the social contract negotiated from an original position."[14] If, therefore, the Constitution is in fact the supreme law of the land, it must be interpreted in terms of the original will that informs its content. This use of history is usually coupled with an argument rooted in democratic theory. Robert Bork, for example, asserts that out of respect for our political democracy judges must "accept any value choice the legislature makes unless it runs clearly contrary to a choice made in framing the Constitution."[15]

Despite these obvious attractions, appeals to the Founders' intent as a method of interpretation are subject to a great many reservations. As a practical matter, we have very little evidence about what the Founders actually intended. No official record of the Philadelphia Convention exists. Several delegates did take notes, but often they are incomplete, subject to bias, and some may even be forged.[16] And what are we to do when, as is sometimes the case, the fifty-five delegates disagreed with each other or sought compromise? Whose intent governs and why? A similar but even more basic problem points to a fascinating question: Just who, exactly, counts as a Founder? All fifty-five delegates? Some did not participate in any meaningful sense; Hamilton even quit the proceedings at one point. And why not consult the intentions of the state ratifying conventions? After all, without those conventions, the Constitution would have no binding force.

One way around some of these problems is to focus less on the Founders' intent and instead to search for the "original meaning" of the Constitution's words as they were used at the time of their drafting. Aids to interpretation would include dictionaries and etymological sources used in 1789. Like original intent, this approach—favored, for example, by Justice Scalia—has much to be said for it. The approach requires judges to appeal to authoritative sources of meaning outside their personal preferences and thus to "objectify" the process of constitutional interpretation. To some extent, however, all of the difficulties that accompany the search for intent apply, albeit sometimes with less urgency, to originalism. But the move from intent to "original meaning" highlights another difficulty that attends both variations. Why should the Constitution's meaning be a function of what its authors, however broadly defined, intended it to mean? Even if intent could be objectively determined, would Americans living on the threshold of the year 2000 want to be governed by prevailing attitudes and definitions of the eighteenth century or, as some would have it, by the "dead hand of the past"?

Still there may be good reasons to put forth some effort to determine what the Founders intended when they wrote the Constitution. The Founders are an obvious source of great wisdom and insight into the nature and purposes of the constitutional order they created. Many of our problems—concerning the relationship between individual liberty and the common good, or the relationship between executive and legislative power—were their problems. And the basic tools we use both to formulate and to resolve many of those problems are tools they created and bequeathed to us. Consequently, it would be a great mistake not to seek their guidance. But it is important to recognize a distinction between seeking guidance and being bound, by definition, to follow their intentions.

---

[14] *Ibid.*, 26.

[15] See *Neutral Principles and Some First Amendment Problems*, 47 Indiana Law Journal 10–11 (1971).

[16] See James H. Hutson, *The Creation of the Constitution: The Integrity of the Documentary Record*, 65 Texas Law Review 1 (1986).

Doctrinalism

Much of contemporary constitutional law consists of "doctrines," or verbal formulas, that the Court uses to decide specific cases. When the Court is examining state legislation that touches a "fundamental right," for example, it applies the "compelling state interest" doctrine. This doctrine provides simply that the state must have a "compelling" interest to regulate a fundamental right—for example, the right to privacy. But how do we know which rights are fundamental? The Court applies another doctrine—or test: Is such a right one that is "implicit in the concept of ordered liberty"? (See *Palko v. Connecticut*, discussed in chapter 8.) Doctrinal tests appear in nearly every area of constitutional law, some of which consist of three or four parts.[17] The increasing importance of these doctrines is what prompted Thomas Reed Powell to tell his Harvard students not to read the constitutional text, for it would only confuse their understanding of the case law.

In its purest form, doctrinalism is both a way of deciding cases and a way of organizing constitutional law. Doctrinalism attempts to superimpose a coherent analytical framework for an entire area of the law, such as equal protection, or no establishment of religion, and to use that overarching order to decide particular cases. The source of these doctrines is an eclectic mix of cases (precedents), logical reasoning, and judicial creativity. Its proponents insist that the use of doctrines helps to minimize judicial mischief by constraining discretion. Moreover, they allow for the orderly progression and evolution of the law by striking a middle course between respect for the past and the need for change.

Critics of the approach often begin by noting that it is a simple matter to manipulate doctrine to achieve a desired result. Similarly, many of the doctrines are themselves so vague and ambiguous that, instead of providing interpretive guidance, they exacerbate the need for it. For example, what possibly would qualify—or not qualify—as a "compelling state interest" in equal protection analysis? Perhaps the most fundamental objection to doctrinalism, however, is that it may not take the Constitution seriously at all. This may happen when doctrines and formulas dominate judicial reasoning, which is the meaning of the quote by T. R. Powell. What may be worse is that these doctrines, formulas, or multipart tests often communicate a false sense of certainty, as if to suggest that a right answer will mechanically follow their invocation.[18]

Doctrinalism thus runs the risk of substituting verbal tests and formulas for the Constitution. As Justice Black noted, this kind of substitution may result in an expansion of the text's meaning—an expansion Black objected to as simply judicial lawmaking—but it might also result in the contraction of meaning: "One of the most effective ways of diluting or expanding a constitutionally guaranteed right is to substitute for the crucial word or words or a constitutional guarantee another word or words more or less flexible or more or less restricted in meaning."[19] Another objection to doctrinalism recalls Justice Story's view that the interpretation of constitutional language must center on the ordinary meaning of the words. Implicit in Story's approach was his insistence that the Constitution is ultimately a public document whose mean-

---

[17] The following three-part test, for example, has often been used to determine whether a law violates the First Amendment's Establishment Clause: "First, the statute must have a secular legislative purpose; second, its principal or primary effect must be one that neither advances nor inhibits religion; finally, the statute must not foster 'an excessive government entanglement with religion.'" See *Lemon v. Kurtzman*, 403 U.S. 602 (1971).

[18] Robert F. Nagel, *Constitutional Cultures: The Mentality and Consequences of Judicial Review* (Berkeley: University of California Press, 1989), 121–56.

[19] *Griswold v. Connecticut*, 381 U.S. 479, 486 (1965).

ing must be accessible to any citizen. Complex and changing verbal formulas tend to make the meaning of the Constitution less public and more remote, for few citizens will have the time or the resources to wade through a swampland of doctrine.

Precedent

Closely related to doctrinalism is a method of interpretation called *stare decisis*. *Stare decisis*—to stand by what has already been decided—is basically a doctrine built on the importance of precedent. A precedent is simply a case that has already been decided. *Stare decisis*, then, refers to a method of interpretation that decides current cases by looking at how similar cases were decided in the past. Neither doctrinalism nor precedent are unique to constitutional interpretation. Rather, they are the characteristic methods of legal reasoning in the common law tradition. The great attraction of precedent as a method of interpretation is its promise of consistency and predictability through time. These are critically important values in any system of law. Indeed, one may well wonder whether the rule of law can exist without them.[20] Like doctrinalism, an appeal to precedent offers stability while leaving room for evolution and change. And like doctrinalism, it constrains judicial discretion.

Unfortunately, appeals to precedent are also subject to a great number of criticisms, some of which will seem familiar. Any good lawyer knows that there is almost always a precedent "out there" to support either side of an issue. To the extent this is true, precedents do little to guide decision making. Similarly, it is not always clear just for what principle a precedent stands. The precedents themselves demand interpretation. Most critically, and like doctrinalism, precedent as a method of interpretation is subject to the criticism that it does not have much to do with the Constitution. Respect for the Constitution must also mean, as Justice Frankfurter argued, that "the ultimate touchstone of constitutionality is the Constitution itself and not what we have said about it."[21] For this reason, some justices have argued that *stare decisis* should carry less weight in constitutional interpretation. Unlike the common law, which has no touchstone but instead develops and evolves in response to felt necessities, constitutional interpretation must revolve around a set of knowable and defined purposes, values, and rules. Especially in constitutional interpretation, therefore, it is more important to get the case "right" than to follow a wrongly decided precedent for the purpose of maintaining consistency.

Prudentialism

Prudentialism is often identified with the work of Alexander Bickel who celebrated various "passive virtues" which Bobbitt calls "mediating devices by which the Court can introduce political realities into its decisional process."[22] In appreciation of the judiciary's limited powers under the Constitution and the caution demanded by the so-called counter-majoritarian difficulty—i.e., the problem of reconciling judicial review with democracy—Bickel advised the Court to creatively exploit jurisdictional doctrines such as ripeness, standing, and mootness, together with the judicial application of the political question doctrine. (See chapter 3 for a discussion of these doctrines.) Each of these rules is a subcategory of the basic concept of justiciability, one designed to ensure, as Chief Justice Earl Warren wrote in *Flast v. Cohen* (1968), that

---

[20] See Lon Fuller, *The Morality of Law* (New Haven: Yale University Press, 1969).

[21] *Graves v. New York*, 306 U.S. 466, 491 (1939).

[22] See Bobbitt, *supra* note 11, at 65.

"the business of the federal courts [is limited] to questions presented in an adversary context" and "to assure that the federal courts will not intrude into areas committed to other branches of government."[23]

Bickel felt that a politically unaccountable judiciary has a limited amount of moral and political capital to spend, and if its voice were to be heeded and respected by the American people, judges should reserve their power to declare legislation unconstitutional only to vindicate the most important values at the foundation of our political system. Justices Frankfurter and Brandeis were among the most prominent of those who advocated prudentialism, though nearly every justice has used it at some point. Bickel argued that "The accomplished fact, affairs and interests that have formed around it, and perhaps popular acceptance of it—these are elements . . . that may *properly* enter into a decision to abstain from rendering constitutional judgment or to allow room and time for accommodation to such a judgment; and they may also enter into the shaping of the judgment, the applicable principle itself"[24] (emphasis added). The key word here is "properly." Prudentialists insist that it is appropriate that judges should account for prudential considerations in coming to a decision.

If this is its strength, the importance of such considerations is also the weakness of prudentialism. Prudential arguments seem less of an interpretive enterprise than strategies for avoiding a decision in politically sensitive cases or for balancing interests in particularly complicated ones. Thus, its harshest critics suggest that prudentialism is simply consequentialism dressed in finery. Both, they argue, do violence to the Constitution because they permit the push and pull of politics—not principle, and not the Constitution proper—to determine judicial decision making. The Constitution, or at least its text, these critics complain, becomes subordinate to "extraconstitutional" considerations. Moreover, the "weight" attached to these considerations and their relative importance must also be a matter of judgment, a judgment, again, to which the Constitution does not speak.

Structuralism

One of the principles of the American constitutional order is the separation of powers or, as Richard Neustadt put it more appropriately, the existence of separate institutions sharing power. The constitutional document does not contain the phrase "separation of powers," but the very structure of the text—and the larger political order it constitutes—gives life to the principle. As a method of interpretation, structuralism believes that the meaning of individual constitutional provisions can only be discerned by a thorough examination of the entire Constitution. Thus "[s]tructural arguments are inferences from the existence of constitutional structures and the relationships which the Constitution ordains among these structures."[25]

In its narrowest sense, this means we should not focus on the meaning of specific, isolated clauses, but rather on the location of the clause and its interaction with the whole text. In a somewhat broader sense, structuralism seeks unity and coherence not only in the text, but in the larger political order the text signifies. Advocates of this more expansive understanding of structuralism stress the way the constitutional document and the larger political order interact. Judicial review, for example, has been justified on structural grounds because the Supreme Court has the power to hear cases

---

[23] 392 U.S. 83 (1968).

[24] Alexander M. Bickel, *The Least Dangerous Branch,* 2nd ed. (New Haven: Yale University Press, 1986), 116.

[25] Bobbitt, *supra* note 11, at 74.

and controversies arising under a constitutional provision that makes the Constitution the supreme law of the land.

One of structuralism's strengths is its attention to the Constitution. Unlike doctrinalism or appeals to precedent, its proponents claim, structuralism concentrates on the meaning of the Constitution and not on what has been said about it. On the other hand, structuralism does little to lessen the discretion of its practitioners. It is all well and good to see a provision as part of a whole, but just how it fits into the whole, and indeed just what the whole means, are themselves open questions, ones that cannot be answered without interpretation. The problems multiply if structuralism moves beyond the text to the political order—that is, any effort to "read" a theory into that order must itself require a bold act of interpretation. Vincent Blasi has offered a similar objection, claiming that agreement about the existence and importance of constitutional structures, or about the desirability of structural understandings of the Constitution, does not tell us very much about what these structures demand in particular cases.[26]

All of these criticisms share a common bond. Structuralism, its critics argue, fails one of the most basic requirements of "good" constitutional interpretation. It does not limit discretion and thus does not adequately cope with the problem of judicial power. A second objection suggests that structural arguments may work well in cases that involve structural issues and relationships, such as federalism and separation of powers, but are less useful in cases that involve constitutional liberties. Presumably, structuralism would hold that rights derive from a structural relationship between citizens and the state. On this view, citizenship is the foundation of liberties—and arguably, not a very firm foundation, if, as Professor Bickel argued, citizenship may be regulated and perhaps even taken away by the state.

Philosophical and Aspirational Argument

Our political system incorporates elements of both democratic and constitutional theory. The fundamental principles that inform our polity—including principles of self-government, of respect for liberty, and the need for limited but energetic government—have their source and much of their meaning in philosophical assumptions about human nature, what constitutes the good life, and the relationship of law to politics. More particularly, constitutional commitments to republican government, to freedom of speech, or to religious freedom, themselves rest upon larger philosophical commitments and understandings about the relationship of the individual to the community, and between state and society.

It should be no surprise then that many justices interpret the Constitution in light of these philosophical understandings, or through the lenses of democratic and constitutional theory. One might well wonder, in fact, whether any kind of constitutional interpretation is really possible without making reference—either knowingly or unknowingly—to such things. One of the advantages of philosophical approaches to constitutional interpretation is their ability to engage fundamental questions and assumptions about constitutional democracy and to do so in ways that address the Constitution seriously as a political text.

On the other hand, critics charge that judges are not and should not be philosophers because judges lack the kind of expertise required to deal with sophisticated questions of moral or political philosophy. Similarly, they argue that equating or reducing constitutional interpretation to a question of philosophy is to make the Constitution even more remote and less accessible to ordinary citizens.

---

[26] See Vincent Blasi, *Creativity and Legitimacy in Constitutional Law*, 80 Yale Law Journal 176 (1970).

A related method of interpretation is sometimes called the "aspirational" approach. This method of interpretation, sometimes promoted by Justice Brennan, argues that the Constitution is a vision of a state of affairs we hope to achieve, or to which we aspire. Individual provisions must be read in light of those aspirations and interpreted in ways that help us to realize those aspirations.[27] Some justices are uncomfortable with such interpretation. Justices Rehnquist and Scalia, for example, have argued that judicial appeals to "aspirations" are simply ways for judges to "short-circuit" majoritarian government. There is a point to such criticisms. It is also true, however, that no justice could possibly be free of relying upon "aspirations" as a tool in decision making. The criticism of "aspirational" jurisprudence as undemocratic, for example, itself depends upon the assertion that the Constitution aspires predominantly toward democratic values.

The great difficulty, then, is that it is not always clear just what these aspirations are or whose aspirations we should incorporate into the Constitution. The abortion controversy provides an example of the difficulty. Is it the aspiration toward liberty construed as freedom of choice that we should defend, or is it the aspiration toward the protection of all human life, born and unborn, that we should protect? Since aspirations compete for ascendancy in our society, it is unclear—or, it cannot be clear without an act of interpretation—how we are to choose between or rank-order aspirations when they push in different directions. Similarly, agreement in the abstract about the nature and definition of our collective aspirations does not go very far in telling us what those aspirations mean or require in specific cases. In this respect, then, aspirational and philosophical approaches to constitutional interpretation do little to constrain judicial power and interpretive creativity.

Griswold v. Connecticut: *A Case Study in Interpretation*

We have already seen that no one method of interpretation commands universal assent. Judges rarely commit to one method to the exclusion of others, and sometimes they seem unaware or profess to be uninterested in which methods they use. In part this is because the methods often overlap or complement each other. For an illustration we can look at a single case and make an effort to discern what methods the various justices used to interpret the Constitution. *Griswold v. Connecticut* (1963), the well known birth control case, provides us with an excellent opportunity to see how the methods work.[28] *Griswold* concerned the constitutionality of a state statute that imposed a penalty on the use of any drug or instrument for the purpose of preventing conception. Even before reaching the merits of the case, the Court was confronted with a complex issue of justiciability: Did the physician bringing the case on behalf of his patient have the necessary standing to invoke the power of the federal judiciary under the "case and controversy" requirement of Article 3? A narrow application of standing, as the rigorous prudentialist might advise, would probably have resulted in the dismissal of *Griswold*.[29] The fact that standing was granted is just one measure of the flexibility with which prudential considerations are applied in particular situations.

On the merits, most students tend to see *Griswold* as a simple case, and they usually cheer when they hear its result. In examining the case, however, we find that it

---

[27] For a cogent defense of the aspirational approach, see Sotirios A. Barber, *On What the Constitution Means* (Baltimore: The Johns Hopkins University Press, 1984).

[28] 381 U.S. 479.

[29] The Supreme Court had earlier declined to decide the constitutionality of Connecticut's birth control statute on the ground that the law was not being enforced and thus posed no harm to persons seeking contraceptive information or purchasing contraceptive devices. See *Poe v. Ullman*, 367 U.S. 497 (1961).

contains six opinions, two of which are dissenting, and it incorporates at least six interpretive approaches. In addition, the seven justices in the majority could not agree on the constitutional basis for the right they voted to uphold. No fewer than six constitutional amendments were invoked in support of *Griswold's* holding that a person's liberty interest in marital privacy is fundamental and thus protected by the Constitution.

To begin with, Justice Douglas, author of the main opinion, declined to rely on the due process clause of the Fourteenth Amendment, which prohibits states from depriving persons within their jurisdiction of life, liberty, or property without due process of law. He was well aware of the criticism triggered by the Court's use of the due process clause to strike down protective labor laws in an earlier period on the basis of a general theory of economic liberty. To deflect the charge that the Court would not similarly function as a "super-legislature," Douglas relied heavily on both textual and doctrinal analysis. He recapitulated the relevant case law under the First, Third, Fourth, and Fifth Amendments that protects aspects of personal privacy. Then, arguing from the text itself he noted: "The foregoing cases suggest that specific guarantees in the Bill of Rights have penumbras, formed by emanations from those guarantees that give them life and substance." At the end of his opinion, however, Douglas felt the urge to utter what is essentially an aspiration or ethical argument well beyond the words of the Constitution itself:

> *We deal with a right of privacy older than the Bill of Rights—older than our political parties, older than our school system. Marriage is a coming together for better or for worse, hopefully enduring, and intimate to the degree of being sacred. It is an association that promotes a way of life, not causes; a harmony in living, not political faiths; a bilateral loyalty, not commercial or social projects. Yet it is an association for as noble a purpose as any involved in our prior decisions.*[30]

Douglas's ode to the wonder and majesty of marriage anticipates the arguments about to be made by Justices Goldberg, Harlan, and White.

Justice Goldberg, who joined Douglas's opinion and judgment, went on to emphasize that the concept of liberty in the Fourteenth Amendment includes not only those personal rights confined to the specific terms of the Bill of Rights, but also those found to be "so rooted in the tradition and conscience of our people as to be ranked as fundamental." Marital privacy, he concluded, drawing now on doctrine and precedent, partakes of this fundamentality. What is new about Goldberg's argument, however, is his appeal to the "language and history of the Ninth Amendment which exist alongside those fundamental rights specifically mentioned in the first eight constitutional amendments." Goldberg's appeal to the original history of the long-neglected Ninth Amendment—later in the opinion he would draw on the words of James Madison who proposed the amendment—was designed to show that the term "liberty" was not confined to the specified rights mentioned in the Bill of Rights. In an interesting twist, Goldberg was also responding to Black, who accused him of turning "somersaults" with the Constitution. Goldberg, however, was also trying to reason from the text—in this instance the text of the Ninth Amendment. He appealed to the text to validate what was essentially a structural reading of the Constitution as a whole; in short, the Ninth Amendment tells us how to read other parts of the Constitution. He was thus able to conclude, on the basis of the text, that the term "liberty" in the Fourteenth Amendment included the unwritten right to marital privacy.

---

[30] 381 U.S. 479, 486.

Justice Harlan, on the other hand, vigorously rejected the textualism of Douglas's opinion as well as the literalism advanced in the dissenting opinions of Justices Black and Stewart. Harlan, like Frankfurter before him, was a strong proponent of the view that the due process clause of the Fourteenth Amendment "is not dependent on the provisions of the Bill of Rights or any of their radiations"—referring of course to Douglas's "penumbras"—but "stands on its own bottom." Justice White joined Harlan in resting squarely on the due process clause. For White and Harlan the due process clause provided adequate standards to keep "most judges from roaming at large in the constitutional field." What the due process clause requires in determining its meaning, wrote Harlan, is a "continual insistence on open respect for the teachings of history, solid recognition of the basic values that underlie our society, and [in coming close to invoking a structural argument] wise appreciation of the great roles that the doctrines of federalism and separation of powers have played in establishing and preserving American freedoms."[31]

Justice Black, dissenting, would have none of this. The Harlan-Goldberg-White approach was, in his view, judicial subjectivism at its worst and a blatant usurpation of the rightful power of legislatures to make law. A confirmed textualist—and the Court's leading advocate of the *total* incorporation (see chapter 8) of *all* the specified guarantees of the Bill of Rights into the due process clause of the Fourteenth Amendment (validated for him, incidentally, by original history)—as well as one of the Court's most ardent civil libertarians, he nevertheless objected to any open-ended approach that would give judges a license to declare laws unconstitutional because they believe that the laws are unwise, unnecessary, dangerous, or offensive to the justices' notions of "natural justice." "I like my privacy as well as the next one," wrote Black, "but I am nevertheless compelled to admit that government has a right to invade it unless prohibited by some specific constitutional provision."

Justice Stewart was equally blunt—and succinct: "I think this [statute against the use of contraceptives] is an uncommonly silly law. . . . But we are not asked in this case to say whether we think this law is unwise, or even asinine. We are asked to hold that it violates the United States Constitution. And that I cannot do."[32] Needless to say, neither Stewart nor Black could find a right of married persons to use contraceptives—or even the more general right of marital privacy—in the Constitution.

The *Griswold* case underscores the different perspectives and attitudes that the justices bring to the process of constitutional interpretation. The justices also draw upon a variety of sources in interpreting the Constitution. In the order of their legitimacy, the text, history, and structure of the Constitution, along with precedent or *stare decisis*, have gained the widest acceptance among judges and scholars. Yet, as *Griswold* demonstrates, judges often reach different results even though they apply the same judicial methodology. When this happens, students must decide for themselves who among the justices has reasoned most convincingly from the source or method employed to the conclusion that he or she has reached.

Comparative Perspectives

The late twentieth century is an age of judicial review. What was generally regarded as a unique feature of the American Constitution prior to the Second World War is now a major feature of numerous constitutions around the world. The proliferation of constitutional courts in Western Europe, Latin America, Asia, and, lately, in the former

[31] *Ibid.*, 501.

[32] *Ibid.*, 527.

communist countries of Eastern Europe, is one of the most fascinating constitutional developments of our time. In truth, we live in an era of spreading democracy but one that places elective governments under the rule of written constitutions and under the guidance of courts empowered to nullify governmental actions contrary to the Constitution. In the light of twentieth-century dictatorships, judicial review has also been seen as a potent weapon against the enemies of democracy.

The particular institutional form that judicial review takes often depends on the culture and tradition of a country's legal tradition. Germany's Federal Constitutional Court provides the model that most European countries (east and west) and, most recently, the Republic of South Africa, have adopted. As noted in chapter 1, these countries have established constitutional courts separate from and independent of the regular judiciary. In addition, only these courts are empowered to declare laws unconstitutional. Many of them, like Germany's Constitutional Court and unlike the U.S. Supreme Court, are authorized to decide constitutional disputes on the basis of what is called "abstract judicial review" (*abstrakte Normenkontrolle*), that is, outside the framework of adverse litigation or what is technically regarded as a "case or controversy" in the American sense. In Germany, for example, the federal or a state government or one-third of the members of the national parliament may request the Constitutional Court to review the validity of an enacted law even before it enters into force or becomes the object of a conventional lawsuit.

In the comparative section of each introductory essay in chapters 3 through 14, we discuss many of the doctrinal differences between American and foreign constitutional law, so there is no need to anticipate those steps. We limit ourselves now to some general observations about the interpretive orientation of foreign constitutional courts that contrast most sharply with American approaches. We must caution ourselves, however, not to exaggerate these differences because principles of rationality and proportionality seem to constitute the core of judicial review wherever it is practiced, despite wide variations in the vigor with which the powers of judicial review are exercised.

Again it may be helpful to use Germany as an example of a contrasting—although not wholly different—approach to constitutional interpretation. One significant difference is the lesser role that prudentialism appears to play in German constitutional law, probably because the counter-majoritarian difficulty, which so preoccupies American constitutional lawyers and judges, is not a major issue in German constitutional theory. One of the characteristics of the Basic Law is the normativity of all its provisions. Every provision is a legally binding norm requiring full and unambiguous implementation. In short, the Constitution may be said to represent the basic norm that governs and legitimates the entire legal order. It controls public law directly but it also influences, indirectly, the interpretation of private law. When serious doubts arise over the validity of a law or practice having the force of law, the Constitutional Court's function, in a case properly before it, is to resolve these doubts in the interest of constitutional clarity and the rule of law. This approach, which envisions the Constitutional Court as *the* guardian of the Basic Law, has little in common with the political question doctrine or the maxim that the courts reach constitutional questions last not first.

In interpreting the Basic Law, the German Court employs four classic modes of interpretation drawn from the history and practice of statutory construction. These four modes of analysis are textual, contextual or systematic, historical, and teleological. Textual and contextual analysis focus on *what is said* in the constitution, the former dwelling on the ordinary meaning of a word or its legal usage, the latter on the grammatical context or structure of a provision. Historical analysis attempts to determine *what was willed* by the Framers at the time of the constitution's adoption. Teleological analysis, finally, examines the purpose—or *what was intended*—behind the various provisions of the Basic Law or the document as a whole. Like American judges, German constitutionalists have established no fixed order in which to apply these methods. Original history, however, is less important in determining the meaning of the Constitution than the other three methods. History is often used to support, and not to determine, constitutional meaning and carries far less weight than in the United States. German and European constitutionalists generally focus more heavily on the broad purposes of constitutional words and phrases than on their historical background.

In contrast to the tendency in American constitutional analysis to focus on isolated phrases and passages of the Constitution, German constitutional theorists and practitioners place a heavy emphasis on the Basic Law as a unified structure of principles and values. In fact, the Constitutional Court has declared that "no single provision may be taken out of its context and interpreted by itself, [for] every constitutional provision must always be interpreted so as to render it compatible with the fundamental principles of the Constitution." In other instances, the Court has alluded to the Basic Law as "logical-teleological unity."[33] This accent on the Basic Law's unity has resulted in several supplementary interpretive standards, among the most important of which are the principles of practical concordance (*praktische Konkordanz*), integration, and optimization.

When two or more constitutional values are in conflict, practical concordance requires the Court to harmonize these values rather than realizing one at the expense of the other. Integration instructs the Court to honor, to the extent possible, the constitutional values represented by the various parties before it and thereby to promote social and political cohesion. Optimization, finally, requires the Court to "actualize," to the extent possible, each and every value in the constitution, including those institutional values flowing from the structure of federalism and separation of powers. In all these ways, the Court seeks to legitimate the constitution in all of its parts, reinforcing its legitimacy in the conscience of the people. One by-product of this extraordinary emphasis on the unity of the Basic Law is the doctrine of an unconstitutional constitutional amendment. On several occasions, the Federal Constitutional Court has announced its readiness to strike down any constitutional amendment that would erode the Basic Law's core principles.

The optimizing and harmonizing strategies of the Federal Constitutional Court make the balancing of obligations and rights a prominent feature of German constitutional analysis. In freedom of speech cases, for example, there is less of an effort in Germany to engage in "definitional" balancing; that is, to define a particular action or expression as an unprotected value rather than including it within the ambit of those actions or behaviors requiring independent constitutional assessment. The reverse side of definitional balancing is the "preferred freedoms" approach which has often led the Supreme Court, as in Justice Black's textualism, to renounce any balancing at all. Also noteworthy in this connection, and absent in the U.S. Constitution, are the reservation clauses that limit almost all basic rights provisions of modern constitutions. Canada's Charter of Rights and Freedoms actually contains a general reservation clause almost identical to the many reservation clauses appended to particular provisions of the European Convention on Human Rights. It reads: "The *Canadian Charter of Rights and Freedoms* guarantees the rights and freedoms set out in it subject only to such reasonable limits prescribed by law as can be demonstrably justified in a free and democratic society."

---

[33] *Church Construction Tax Case*, 19 *Entscheidungen des Bundesverfassungsgerichts* (hereinafter cited as BVerfGE) 206, 220 (1965).

TABLE 2.1   *Teleological or Purposive Analysis*
("What is Intended")

Variations	Schools of Jurisprudence
politics	critical legal studies
procedural fairness	democracy and representation
substantive justice	natural law and moral theory
inclusion, nonsubordination	feminism, race theory
order, stability	conservatism
ordered liberty	communitarianism
choice maximization	individualism
interest satisfaction	utilitarianism
wealth maximization	economic theory of law
expediency, practicality	pragmatism

Source: Winfried Brugger, *Legal Interpretation, Schools of Jurisprudence, and Anthropology: Some Remarks from a German Point of View*, XLII American Journal of Comparative Law (1994): 403.

In applying interpretive provisions such as this, as noted earlier, constitutional courts almost everywhere apply the principles of rationality and proportionality. The case law of constitutional courts such as the Supreme Courts of Canada, the United States, India, and Ireland as well as the European Court of Human Rights and the Constitutional Courts of Germany, Italy, and Spain may apply the principles in dramatically different ways and with different results. But the fact that all of these courts invoke some variation on these principles suggests that something universal is at work here and that some degree of objectivity and determinacy informs the process of constitutional interpretation. There also seems to be a widespread tendency of constitutional courts around the world to rely to a lesser or greater extent on unwritten textual values that reflect a particular country's history and culture. This observation recalls Justice Holmes's comment that constitutional cases "must be considered in the light of our whole experience and not merely in that of what was said a hundred years ago."[34]

In turning back to Germany we might also note that the teleological approach has much in common with the variations on purpose analysis that one finds in American constitutional theory. Table 2.1 is from a chart devised by Winfried Brugger in his seminal article comparing German and American methods of constitutional interpretation. The variations on the teleological approach have been ingeniously paired with their corresponding schools of jurisprudence, several of which hold a prominent place in the literature of American and foreign constitutional theory.

How you interpret the Constitution may very well depend on what you think is its overall purpose, or theory. Various schools of jurisprudence compete for ascendancy in constitutional interpretation, and each of the schools listed in table 2.1 has its advocates. The critical legal studies movement, of whom the constitutional scholar, Mark Tushnet, is a well-known representative, sees constitutional law as "politics" carried on by other means, just as doctrine and precedent are to be manipulated and exploited for correct political purposes. The view of the Constitution as a set of procedures for the conduct of politics is best illustrated in the United States by John Ely's book, *Democracy and Distrust*,[35] an attempt to build an American theory of judicial review around the democratic and representational underpinnings of the Constitution.

---

[34]*Missouri v. Holland*, 252 U.S. 416, 433 (1920).

[35]See John H. Ely, *Democracy and Distrust* (Cambridge: Harvard University Press, 1980).

Public choice theory and wealth maximization, on the other hand, have become dominant themes in the constitutional views of American scholars such as U.S. Court of Appeals Judge Richard Posner. But in Western and Eastern Europe, ordered liberty and communitarianism interpreted as solidarity informs the approach to constitutional decision making. Finally, it is no surprise that choice maximization and its corresponding emphasis on personal autonomy and individualism is the background theory that informs a number of abortion decisions in the United States and abroad. Like the particular approaches to constitutional interpretation discussed earlier, these theories are often used in combination and rarely, if ever, does any one theory predominate in constitutional interpretation, a reality that applies to foreign jurisdictions as much as to the United States.

Selected Bibliography

American References

Abraham, Henry. *The Judicial Process*. 6th ed. Oxford: Oxford University Press, 1993.

Ackerman, Bruce A. *Beyond Carolene Products*, Harvard Law Review 98 (1985): 713.

Antieau, Chester James. *Constitutional Construction*. New York: Oceana Publications, 1982.

Barber, Sotirios A. *On What the Constitution Means*. Baltimore: Johns Hopkins University Press, 1984.

Bickel, Alexander. *The Least Dangerous Branch*. 2d ed. New Haven: Yale University Press, 1986.

Black, Charles L., Jr. *The People and the Court*. Westport, Conn.: Greenwood Press, 1960.

Bobbitt, Philip. *Constitutional Fate*. New York: Oxford University Press, 1982.

———. *Constitutional Interpretation*. New York: Oxford University Press, 1991.

Cardozo, Benjamin N. *The Nature of the Judicial Process*. New Haven: Yale University Press, 1921.

Corwin, Edward S. *The Higher Law Background of American Constitutional Law*, Harvard Law Review 42 (1928): 149.

Ducat, Craig R. *Modes of Constitutional Interpretation*. St. Paul, Minn.: West Publishing Co., 1978.

Dworkin, Ronald. *A Matter of Principle*. Cambridge: Harvard University Press, 1985.

Ely, John H. *Democracy and Distrust*. Cambridge: Harvard University Press, 1980.

Gerhardt, Michael J. and Thomas D. Rowe, Jr., eds. *Constitutional Theory*. Charlottesville, Va.: The Michie Company, 1993.

Harris, William III. *The Interpretable Constitution*. Baltimore: Johns Hopkins University Press, 1993.

Jacobsohn, Gary. *The Supreme Court and the Decline of Constitutional Aspiration*. Princeton, N.J.: Princeton University Press, 1986.

Jacobsohn, Gary. *Apple of Gold: Constitutionalism in Israel and the United States*. Princeton, N.J.: Princeton University Press, 1993.

Kaplin, William A. *The Concepts and Methods of Constitutional Law*. Durham, N.C.: Carolina Academic Press, 1992.

Monaghan, Henry P. *Our Perfect Constitution*, New York University Law Review 56 (1981): 353.

Nagel, Robert F. *Constitutional Cultures*. Berkeley: University of California Press, 1989.

———. *Judicial Power and American Character*. New York: Oxford University Press, 1994.

Perry, Michael J. *The Constitution in the Courts*. New Haven: Yale University Press, 1980.

Powell, H. Jefferson. *The Moral Tradition of American Constitutionalism: A Theological Interpretation*. Durham, N.C.: Duke University Press, 1993.

Rakove, Jack N. *Original Meanings: Politics and Ideas in the Making of the Constitution*. New York: Alfred A. Knopf, 1996.

Scalia, Antonin. *A Matter of Interpretation: Federal Courts and the Law*. Princeton, N.J.: Princeton University Press, 1997.

Thayer, James B. *The Origin and Scope of the American Doctrine of Constitutional Law*, Harvard Law Review 7 (1883): 129.

Tribe, Laurence. *Constitutional Choices*. Cambridge: Harvard University Press, 1985.

——— and Michael C. Dorf. *On Reading the Constitution*. Cambridge: Harvard University Press, 1991.

Tushnet, Mark V. *Red, White, and Blue: A Critical Analysis of Constitutional Law*. Cambridge: Harvard University Press, 1988.

Wechsler, Herbert. *Toward Neutral Principles of Constitutional Law*, Harvard Law Review 73 (1959): 1.

Comparative References

Alexy, Robert. *A Theory of Legal Argumentation*. Oxford: Clarendon Press, 1989.

Beatty, David M., ed. *Human Rights and Judicial Review: A Comparative Perspective*. Dordrecht: Martinus Nijhoff Publishers, 1994.

———. *Constitutional Law In Theory and Practice*. Toronto: University of Toronto Press, 1995.

Beer, Laurence and Hiroshi Itoh, *Japanese Constitutional Law: 1956–1990*. Seattle: University of Washington Press, 1996.

Beaudoin, Gerald A. and Errol Mendes. *The Canadian Char-*

ter of *Rights and Freedoms*. 3d ed. Toronto: Carswell, 1996.

Bryden, Philip *et al. Protecting Rights and Freedoms: Essays on the Charters Placed in Canada's Political, Legal, and Intellectual Life*. Toronto: University of Toronto Press, 1994.

Friedrich, Carl J. *Constitutional Government and Democracy*. rev. ed. Boston: Ginn and Company, 1950.

Herget, James E. *Contemporary German Legal Philosophy*. Philadelphia: University of Pennsylvania Press, 1996.

Hogan, Gerard and Gerry Whyte. *The Irish Constitution*. Dublin: Butterworths, 1994.

Janis, Mark et al. *European Human Rights Law*. Oxford: Clarendon Press, 1995.

Kommers, Donald P. *The Constitutional Jurisprudence of the Federal Republic of Germany*. 2d ed. Durham: Duke University Press, 1997.

Kommers, Donald P. *The Value of Comparative Constitutional Law*, John Marshall Journal of Practice and Procedure, 9 (1976).

McKenna, Marian C., ed. *The Canadian and American Constitutions in Comparative Perspective*. Calgary: University of Calgary Press, 1993.

Murphy, Walter F. and Joseph Tanenhaus. *Comparative Constitutional Law: Cases and Commentaries*. New York: St. Martin's Press, 1977.

Singh, Mahendra P., ed. *Comparative Constitutional Law*. Lucknow, India: Eastern Book Co., 1989.

Starck, Christian, ed. *Studies in German Constitutionalism*. Baden-Baden: Nomos Verlagsgesellschaft, 1995.

van Wyk, Dawid *et al. Rights and Constitutionalism: The New South African Constitution*. Oxford: Clarendon Press, 1996.

We the People of the United States, in Order to form a more perfect Union, establish Justice, insure domestic Tranquility, provide for the common defence, promote the general Welfare, and secure the Blessings of Liberty to ourselves and our Posterity, do ordain and establish this Constitution for the United States of America.

Article. I.

Section. 1. All legislative Powers herein granted shall be vested in a Congress of the United States, which shall consist of a Senate and House of Representatives.

Section. 2. The House of Representatives shall be composed of Members chosen every second Year by the People of the several States, and the Electors in each State shall have the Qualifications requisite for Electors of the most numerous Branch of the State Legislature.

No Person shall be a Representative who shall not have attained to the Age of twenty five Years, and been seven Years a Citizen of the United States, and who shall not, when elected, be an Inhabitant of that State in which he shall be chosen.

Representatives and direct Taxes shall be apportioned among the several States which may be included within this Union, according to their respective Numbers, which shall be determined by adding to the whole Number of free Persons, including those bound to Service for a Term of Years, and excluding Indians not taxed, three fifths of all other Persons. The actual Enumeration shall be made within three Years after the first Meeting of the Congress of the United States, and within every subsequent Term of ten Years, in such Manner as they shall by Law direct. The Number of Representatives shall not exceed one for every thirty Thousand, but each State shall have at Least one Representative; and until such enumeration shall be made, the State of New Hampshire shall be entitled to chuse three, Massachusetts eight, Rhode Island and Providence Plantations one, Connecticut five, New York six, New Jersey four, Pennsylvania eight, Delaware one, Maryland six, Virginia ten, North Carolina five, South Carolina five, and Georgia three.

When vacancies happen in the Representation from any State, the Executive Authority thereof shall issue Writs of Election to fill such Vacancies.

The House of Representatives shall chuse their Speaker and other Officers; and shall have the sole Power of Impeachment.

Section. 3. The Senate of the United States shall be composed of two Senators from each State, chosen by the Legislature thereof, for six Years; and each Senator shall have one Vote.

Immediately after they shall be assembled in Consequence of the first Election, they shall be divided as equally as may be into three Classes. The Seats of the Senators of the first Class shall be vacated at the Expiration of the second Year, of the second Class at the Expiration of the fourth Year, and of the third Class at the Expiration of the sixth Year, so that one third may be chosen every second Year; and if Vacancies happen by Resignation, or otherwise, during the Recess of the Legislature of any State, the Executive thereof may make temporary Appointments until the next Meeting of the Legislature, which shall then fill such Vacancies.

No Person shall be a Senator who shall not have attained to the Age of thirty Years, and been nine Years a Citizen of the United States, and who shall not, when elected, be an Inhabitant of that State for which he shall be chosen.

The Vice President of the United States shall be President of the Senate, but shall have no Vote, unless they be equally divided.

The Senate shall chuse their other Officers, and also a President pro tempore, in the Absence of the Vice President, or when he shall exercise the Office of President of the United States.

The Senate shall have the sole Power to try all Impeachments. When sitting for that Purpose, they shall be on Oath or Affirmation. When the President of the United States is tried, the Chief Justice shall preside: And no Person shall be convicted without the Concurrence of two thirds of the Members present.

Judgment in Cases of Impeachment shall not extend further than to removal from Office, and disqualification to hold and enjoy any Office of honor, Trust or Profit under the United States: but the Party convicted shall nevertheless be liable and subject to Indictment, Trial, Judgment and Punishment, according to Law.

Section. 4. The Times, Places and Manner of holding Elections for Senators and Representatives, shall be prescribed in each State by the Legislature thereof; but the Congress may at any time by Law make or alter such Regulations, except as to the Places of chusing Senators.

The Congress shall assemble at least once in every Year, and such Meeting shall be on the first Monday in December, unless they shall by Law appoint a different Day.

Section. 5. Each House shall be the Judge of the Elections, Returns and Qualifications of its own Members, and a Majority of each shall constitute a Quorum to do Business; but a smaller Number may adjourn from day to day, and may be authorized to compel the Attendance of absent Members, in such Manner, and under such Penalties as each House may provide.

Part Two

Intergovernmental Powers and Relationships

The United States Constitution is a blueprint for the conduct of politics. By dividing power between federal and state governments and by placing legislative, executive, and judicial power in separate departments at the national level, the Founders hoped to combine representative democracy with limited rulership. The Founders reinforced the "limited rulership" side of the ledger by importing a system of checks and balances into the structure of separated powers. They knew that this bundle of institutional structures and relationships would complicate the process of governing, but they placed a higher value on restraint and reflection than on speed and efficiency, all for the purpose of preventing the abuse of power by keeping rulers within the bounds of their constituted authority. Conflict and tension would mark interbranch and intergovernmental relations, but the Founders hoped—and expected—that these stresses and strains would engender creativity and forbearance rather than rigidity and deadlock.

Part two highlights some of the most notable federalism and separation of powers conflicts in American history. Such conflicts, however, have not been the staple of ordinary politics; if they were, the machinery of American government would cease to operate. No democratic polity could withstand a steady diet of foundational collisions over the proper lines of its constituted authority. The cases featured here represent the occasions on which one branch or level of government has allegedly invaded the rightful domain of another branch or level. Occasionally, too, as the cases show, creative innovations in the art of governance overstep defined competencies, as do certain well meaning collaborative efforts between and within governments. When this happens, and adjudication ensues, the Supreme Court often serves as the guardian of the spheres of authority framed by the Constitution.

The following five chapters contain important illustrations of the Court's guardianship. Chapter 3 includes cases that show how the Court has sought to confine and expand the power of judicial review, and we pay particular attention to cases in which the Court has emphasized both the finality of its rulings and the importance of its moral voice in American constitutional politics. Chapter 4 consists of cases that define the complex relations between the three branches of the national government. Chapter 5 features classic conflicts in the field of federal-state relations; the cases underscore alternative visions of the American polity while showing the extent to which arguments over state sovereignty echo those sounded originally in the *Federalist Papers* and in debates over the Constitution's ratification. Chapter 6 shifts to the powers of Congress, sketching the checkered history of the Court's perspective on the permissible range of national power and its clash with state claims to reserved powers under the Tenth Amendment. Chapter 7, which deals with foreign and military affairs, allows us to revisit issues of federalism and separation of powers in this most difficult and sensitive area of national and international politics.

Part two, like parts one and three, includes comparative constitutional perspectives. We are reminded here that the American Founders were themselves students of comparative constitutionalism. They looked to the experiences of Sparta, Athens, Rome, and Carthage for guidance in crafting a new constitution for the United States. But their constitution was originally crafted for a preindustrial society. Modern democratic constitutions—i.e., those framed after World War II and after the collapse of communism in Eastern Europe—and their interpretation may have lessons for Americans, both negative and positive.

Most of these modern constitutions embrace mixed structures of presidential and parliamentary governments—favoring weak presidents elected by parliament or strong presidents chosen in direct popular elections. Contrasting sharply with the American system of separated powers, these constitutions feature dual executives [president and cabinet], occasionally one-house legislatures, and often popularly unaccountable institutions such as central banks and specialized constitutional courts. They seek to achieve a system of checks and balances through devices such as central financial controls, popular initiatives, the creation of ombudsmen, abstract judicial review, presidential or legislative calls for referenda, parliamentary override of constitutional court decisions, and limits on the power to dissolve parliament.[1]

It is doubtful whether Americans would be prepared to transplant any of these practices or institutions into their constitutional system. Americans critical of the deadlock and inefficiency that often characterize policy making at the national level have often envied what appears to be the more responsible and democratic procedures of some parliamentary governments.[2] Before transporting to these shores any version of parliamentary democracy, however, a new set of American constitution-makers would have to be convinced that the American presidential form is less resilient, less focused, and less democratic over the long haul than parliamentary systems, whatever the variety. Such proof does not seem to be available. And, as Robert Dahl has noted, a nation's underlying political culture is likely to be equally determinative of how politics operates as any set of constitutional structures.[3]

Were Americans given the chance to hold a new constitutional convention, they would in all probability give some thought to perfecting their democracy. A modern-day Madison, drawing on comparative knowledge, might find that the present tripartite division of power is as outmoded as it is [or sometimes seems] democratically unaccountable. Given the complexity of modern government, he or she might wish to replace the existing document with one that recognizes the critical role of administrative agencies, but which includes the two-house legislative veto—struck down

[1] See Rett R. Ludwikowski, *Constitution-Making in the Region of Former Soviet Dominance* (Durham and London: Duke University Press, 1996).

[2] See, for example, Daniel Lazare, *The Frozen Republic: How the Constitution is Paralyzing our Democracy* (New York: Harcourt Brace & Co., 1996).

[3] Robert A. Dahl, "Thinking About Democratic Constitutions: Conclusions from Democratic Experience" in Ian Shapiro and Russell Hardin, eds., *Political Order: Nomos XXXIII* (New York: New York University Press, 1966), 175–202.

by the Supreme Court in *INS v. Chadha* (1983) and installs, like Germany's Basic Law, a strong version of the doctrine of nondelegation. He or she might also be inclined to follow the lead of most modern constitutions by specifying in greater detail the powers and duties of state and local governments. In addition, our modern Madison might seek to resolve the perennial dispute between the president and Congress over their respective powers in the field of military affairs, perhaps by constitutionalizing some version of the War Powers Resolution. Finally, in the interest of democratizing major foreign policy decisions and again heeding foreign constitutional developments, he or she might shift the Senate's treaty-making power to the House of Representatives and eliminate the two-thirds vote requirement for the ratification of treaties.

Failing these reforms, the new Madison would surely abandon the electoral college as an aberration among modern constitutional democracies. In a further effort to reinforce the representative character of American government, and in view of the legal changes that have taken place in Europe, Canada, South Africa, and elsewhere, he or she might also consider experimenting with compulsory voting, limiting the terms of Supreme Court justices, recognizing political parties and regulating their finances, and adopting a variation of Germany's system of modified proportional representation, an electoral system that has so impressed the world's constitution-makers that even the British are thinking of adopting it.[4]

There is one other structural change—one that goes to the heart of America's national identity—that our contemporary Madison might consider if indeed he or she would wish to be guided by constitutional developments abroad. That is a tax system more in conformity with democratic communal values and one that insures a better and more equitable distribution of tax revenues between levels of government. This would entail a major redefinition of the taxing and spending power of the national government; in short, a fiscal system that announces who we Americans are and what we would like to be.[5] The time may thus be ripe, as many European constitution-makers have long recognized, to democratize, and perhaps to decentralize, the power to tax and spend.

As you read the cases and materials in part two, you may wish to consider whether there is anything that Americans or the Supreme Court can learn from foreign constitutional developments pertaining to constitutional structures and relationships.

---

[4] William Rees-Mogg, "See Democracy Die in a Hail of Ballots," *The Times* (London), 27 July 1997.

[5] See generally Edward J. McCaffery, *The Political Liberal Case Against the Estate Tax*, 23 Philosophy and Public Affairs 281 (1994).

Chapter 3

The Judicial Power

The Constitution and Judicial Review

arbury v. Madison[1] (1803, reprinted later in the chapter) is the cornerstone of American constitutional law. In this seminal case, the first time the Supreme Court nullified a provision of federal law, Chief Justice John Marshall laid down the doctrine that judges are authorized to nullify and void any law that in their view violates the Constitution. The case was equally resourceful because Marshall enunciated the doctrine of judicial review in the absence of any constitutional provision clearly authorizing its adoption. As noted in chapter 2, the Constitution says nothing about whether the judicial power of the United States extends to the voidance of laws incompatible with the Constitution. For Marshall, however, judicial review could be inferred from the Constitution's general principles.

Marshall's chain of reasoning in *Marbury* was deceptively simple: He declared that under the Constitution "it is emphatically the province and duty of the judicial department to say what the law is." In so declaring, Marshall called attention to the significance and purpose of a written constitution. "All those who have framed written constitutions," he wrote, "contemplate them as forming the fundamental and paramount law of the nation, and consequently, the theory of every such government must be, that an act of the legislature, repugnant to the Constitution, is void." It follows, therefore, that a constitution is "a law of superior obligation, unchangeable by ordinary means." From this premise, Marshall inferred the power of the judiciary to nullify a law contrary to the Constitution, a power fortified in his view by the supremacy clause, the judicial oath to defend the Constitution, and the extension of federal judicial power to all cases and controversies arising under the Constitution.[2]

Marshall's decision was a strong rebuke to Thomas Jefferson, and the ensuing clash of personalities focused attention on the conflict between judicial review and political democracy. Indeed, the congressional cancellation of the

---

[1] 5 U.S. (1 Cranch) 137 (1803).

[2] In proclaiming the power of judicial review, Marshall was not writing on a clean slate. Colonial judges were known to have voided laws deemed contrary to their state constitutions and in an earlier case, *Hylton v. U.S.* (3 Dall.) 171 (1796), the Supreme Court implied that it could refuse to enforce unconstitutional laws or practices. Alexander Hamilton also advocated judicial review in *Federalist* 78.

Supreme Court's 1801–02 term, recommended by Jefferson, was a warning shot across Marshall's bow. Jefferson was telling him to stay out of presidential affairs and to let the president run the executive branch as he sees fit. The president reacted bitterly to Marshall's opinion. He described it as nothing more than "an *obiter* dissertation of the Chief Justice,"[3] and he went on to recommend the impeachment of federal judges who would dare to disallow acts of the coordinate and equal branches of the federal government.

Marshall's decision met with another sharp rejoinder in Judge Gibson's dissenting opinion in *Eakin v. Raub*,[4] an otherwise unremarkable case decided by Pennsylvania's Supreme Court. Like many of his contemporaries, Judge Gibson assumed that in the event of a collision between the Constitution and ordinary law, the latter would have to give way to the former; unlike Marshall, however, he denied that any such "collision [could] be resolved *before the Judiciary*." Gibson's view—one that in time would be shared by Presidents Jackson, Lincoln, and Franklin Roosevelt—was that no one department or branch of the national government may conclusively interpret the Constitution for another. The system of checks and balances overlaying the American structure of separated powers, Gibson maintained, would be sufficient to negate any exercise of unconstitutional power. He added that public opinion would serve as the only effective guard against legislative usurpation. In short, argued Gibson, "it rests with the people, in whom full and absolute sovereign power resides, to correct abuses in legislation."[5]

Whether the Framers wanted federal judges to hold laws and other governmental acts unconstitutional remains disputed. Judicial review, as such, was not discussed at the Constitutional Convention, although in the debate over a council of revision some delegates assumed that courts would have the final power of interpretation. Yet as Hamilton remarked in *Federalist* 81, the "doctrine [of judicial review] is not deducible from any circumstance peculiar to the plan of the convention."[6] Even so, suspicious commentators examined the judiciary article and feared what they saw. Robert Yates, writing as Brutus in a preratification debate, charged that the powers vested in the judiciary would enable the federal courts "to mould the government into almost any shape they please."[7] To allay this fear, Hamilton avowed that the judiciary would always be the national government's "least dangerous" branch. Although conceding that the courts would have the "right . . . to pronounce legislative acts void, because contrary to the Constitution," he sought to disarm his critics by claiming that they would "have neither Force nor Will, but merely judgment."[8]

Hamilton's response to Brutus glossed over the substantial political power the Constitution conferred on the judiciary. He also ignored the problem of interpretive in-

---

[3] Quoted in Gerald Gunther, *Constitutional Law*, 12th ed. (Mineola, N.Y.: The Foundation Press, 1991), 12.

[4] 12 Sergeant & Rawle 330 (1825).

[5] Judge Gibson failed to emphasize what may be Marshall's most audacious claim, namely that the Constitution is paramount law. Paramountcy, however, seems not to be the main problem. Rather it is Marshall's uncritical claim that the Constitution should be understood essentially, if not only, as a *legal* instrument. In the understanding of many other nations, constitutions are not law as such, but rather frameworks for the conduct of government, guidelines for political action, or counsels of aspiration that elected officials and units of government are *morally* obligated to pursue.

[6] Hamilton did say, however, that judicial review is "deducible . . . from the general theory of a limited Constitution." See *Federalist* 81, edited by Benjamin Fletcher Wright (New York: Barnes & Noble, Inc., 1996), 506.

[7] Brutus, No. 11 (31 January 1788) in Michael Kammen, ed., *The Origins of the American Constitution: A Documentary History* (New York: Penguin Books, 1986), 337.

[8] *Federalist* 78, *supra* note 6, at 490.

determinacy, as would Marshall in *Marbury v. Madison* (1803). Robert Yates was also aware of the perils of interpretation, predicting that by a certain "latitude of interpretation," the Supreme Court would begin to dominate the legislature and render the states subservient to the national government.[9]

The judicial controversy over how to interpret the Constitution—indeed, over what it actually includes—was already in full swing in *Calder v. Bull* (1798)—where Justices Chase and Iredell clashed over the standard of review to be applied in assessing the validity of a state statute.[10] Whereas Iredell argued that the Court must confine itself to the written text of the Constitution, Chase invoked principles of natural justice, claiming that "the purposes for which men enter into society will determine the nature and terms of the social compact." The debate is far from over. Because of the issues of interpretation discussed in chapter 2, the debate continues today in even more heightened form. As *Planned Parenthood of Southeast Pennsylvania v. Casey* (1992, reprinted later in the chapter) shows, the debate reflects the deep tension between the right of the community to embed its values in law and the authority of the Supreme Court to void such laws in the interest of the higher values of the Constitution.

The Early Struggle for Judicial Supremacy

In 1787, no one could have predicted how the Constitution would transform the system of government it created. As John Marshall noted in *McCulloch v. Maryland*, the Constitution was not a mere legal code; only its "great outlines" and "important objects" were set down in writing; the rest would be left to interpretation. What would be interpreted, however, was likely to be more than the words laid down in the documentary text. Robert McCloskey observed that "the Constitution was potentially the convergence point for all the ideas about fundamental law that had been current in America since the colonization period."[11] These ideas included the principles of popular sovereignty and government by consent; unwritten principles of liberty and freedom embedded in the idea of "higher" law; and common law doctrines relating to property, contract, and criminal procedure. Which of these written and unwritten principles and doctrines would be "constitutionalized" and how they would be balanced or ranked in the process of interpretation could never be known in advance. Equally uncertain was who or what branch of government would have the final word in the interpretation of the Constitution.

Whether *Marbury v. Madison* attempted to resolve the question of which branch would have the final say depends on how broadly or narrowly the case is construed. A narrow reading could be understood as saying that the Supreme Court has the final word with respect to the meaning of Article 3. *Marbury* struck down Section 13 of the Judiciary Act of 1789 because it was thought to vest the Supreme Court with original jurisdiction that Article 3 forbade. In short, consistent with the view that each department of government should be able to interpret for itself the powers granted to it, the Supreme Court would take charge of its *own* house. The broad reading, by contrast, sees the Supreme Court as the final arbiter of all the Constitution's provisions.

Dred Scott v. Sandford (1857, reprinted later in the chapter) appeared to vindicate a broad reading.[12] In striking down the Missouri Compromise—an act of Congress

---

[9] Brutus, No. 15 (20 March 1788), *Ibid.*, 358 and Brutus, No. 11 (31 January 1788), *Ibid.*, 335.

[10] 3 Dall. 386 (1798).

[11] *The American Supreme Court*, rev. ed. (Chicago: University of Chicago Press, 1994), 5.

[12] 60 U.S. (19 Howard) 393 (1857). *Dred Scott* lives in infamy because it held that African Americans could not be regarded as "citizens" within the meaning of the Constitution.

banning slavery in the Louisiana Territory—it may be said that the Supreme Court took the power of judicial review to a new level. Now, instead of reviewing a statute pertaining to the exercise of its own power under Article 3, the court invalidated a statute enacted pursuant to a grant of authority vested in Congress. Here the Court was telling Congress [and by implication the president] what it may or may not do under its constitutional powers. Judicial review had begun to transform itself into a principle of judicial supremacy. For its part, *Dred Scott*—the second instance in which the Court struck down an act of Congress—prompted President Lincoln to remark in his first inaugural address that "the policy of the government, upon vital questions, affecting the whole people," could not properly "be irrevocably fixed by the decisions of the Supreme Court" (see Appendix C). *Dred Scott* was eventually reversed by the Fourteenth Amendment.

Long before *Dred Scott*, however, the Supreme Court had held that its power also extended to reviewing the constitutionality of state laws. In *Fletcher v. Peck*,[13] decided seven years after *Marbury*, Chief Justice John Marshall relied on the Constitution's contract clause to invalidate a Georgia statute that nullified a corrupt land grant sale and the property rights derived from it. In so doing, he employed judicial review as an instrument of national unity. But *Fletcher* was not the first demonstration of judicial nationalism. Already in *Chisholm v. Georgia*, decided in 1793, the Supreme Court delivered a devastating blow to state sovereignty when it decided a state could be sued in federal court without the state's consent.[14] Under the Constitution, the people of the United States, not the states, were now sovereign, wrote Justice James Wilson, and it is they who ordained in Article 3 that the states would be "amendable to the jurisdiction of the supreme court." The decision created a firestorm of protest, with Georgia going so far as to impose the death penalty on anyone who would enforce the Court's ruling within the state. Instead, and in record time, the states administered a death blow to *Chisholm* by ratifying the Eleventh Amendment.[15] The Eleventh Amendment reaffirmed the principle of sovereign immunity that kept states from being sued in federal courts, but it also constituted an implicit acceptance of the proposition that only a constitutional amendment could override the Supreme Court's authoritative interpretation of a constitutional provision.

A brief discussion of *Martin v. Hunter's Lessee* (1816) and *Cohens v. Virginia* (1821, reprinted later in the chapter) will help to round out this Section on the early struggle for judicial supremacy. *Martin* sustained the constitutionality of Section 25 of the Judiciary Act of 1789 over Virginia's vehement objection that the act could not validly extend the Supreme Court's appellate jurisdiction to *state* judicial decisions arising under federal law. Under the terms of the Constitution, wrote Justice Story, it is the nature of the case, not the identity of the court, that determines the reach of the Supreme Court's appellate jurisdiction. Story's opinion is historically important for its unambiguous affirmation of national judicial supremacy in the interpretation of the Constitution. Similarly, *Cohens v. Virginia* (1821) held that the Supreme Court's jurisdiction extended to an appeal from a defendant convicted in a state court for a state criminal offense over his objection that the state law conflicted with a federal law.

---

[13] 6 Cranch 87 (1810).

[14] 2 Dall. (2 U.S.) 419 (1793). Article 3, Section 2, of the Constitution extends the judicial power of the United States, *inter alia*, "to controversies between a State and Citizens of another State." The Supreme Court read this language literally in allowing a South Carolina merchant to sue Georgia for its failure to pay for the supplies he sold the state in 1777.

[15] "The judicial power of the United States shall not be construed to extend to any suit in law or equity, commenced or prosecuted against one of the United States by Citizens of another State, or by Citizens or Subjects of any Foreign States." Adopted in 1798.

Relying heavily on Story's opinion in *Martin*, John Marshall ruled that the Eleventh Amendment did not bar the Supreme Court from hearing the case to resolve a question of federal law—here whether the state law did in fact conflict with a federal statute on the same subject—even though the appeal was brought against the state after the case had been fully adjudicated in the state's judicial system.

The reference to the Eleventh Amendment prompts us to fast-forward the clock of history to 1996, when the Supreme Court declared, in *Seminole Tribe of Florida v. Florida*,[16] that the amendment prevents Congress from authorizing suits by Native American tribes against the states to enforce legislation enacted pursuant to the Indian Commerce Clause. The decision caught Congress off guard and appeared to reverse, in the opinion of the dissenting justices, the prevailing historical view, which originated with Justice James Iredell's dissenting opinion in *Chisholm v. Georgia*. In his opinion, the Eleventh Amendment does not bar Congress from creating a private federal cause of action against a state for the violation of a *federal* right. [*Seminole Tribe* will be taken up again in chapter 6 on congressional power, but it is noted here because it revisits two issues central to this and other chapters in this book; that is, the relationship of the Supreme Court to a coequal branch of the federal government and the position of the states in the federal union.] *Seminole Tribe* is cited not for the rightness or wrongness of its result but to underscore the perennial nature of the debate that began with *Chisholm* in 1793.

Expansion of Judicial Power

The struggle for judicial supremacy has been an ongoing battle, and the Supreme Court has not always emerged victorious. We have seen that *Marbury v. Madison* was at best grudgingly accepted at the time of its deliverance. In addition, a Supreme Court decision interpreting the Constitution could be overturned by a constitutional amendment; *Chisholm v. Georgia* suffered this fate in 1798. Occasionally, however, in order to diminish the possibility of political retaliation, the Supreme Court reverses itself, as it did in 1937 with *NLRB v. Jones & Laughlin Steel Corporation*.[17] Finally, as we shall see in the next subsection, the Supreme Court has developed a number of doctrinal strategies for limiting its power of judicial review.

The concept of judicial independence might have assumed a variety of forms. First, as in *Marbury*, the Supreme Court might have limited itself, out of respect for the principle of separated powers, to holding acts unconstitutional only when necessary to defend itself against encroachments by the other branches. Second, the Court might have invalidated actions of the other branches, but the enforcement of its rulings would depend on the latters' concurrence. Third, the Court might have claimed for itself the right to invalidate the actions of the elected branches but only in cases where it is obvious that a violation has occurred. Finally, the Court might have claimed the power to nullify acts of the other branches but confined the enforcement of its rulings to the parties before the Court.[18] It is unclear which of these variations on judicial review would have been most acceptable to the Framers, but each would have safeguarded the Court's independence.

As the cases featured in this subsection show, however, judicial power has risen to new levels of prestige and influence in the last half of the twentieth century. Three

---

[16] 134 L. Ed. 2d 252 (1996).

[17] 301 U.S. 1 (1937). Reprinted in chapter 6.

[18] For an extended discussion of these variations, see Stephen M. Griffin, *American Constitutionalism* (Princeton: Princeton University Press, 1996), 90–9.

sets of constitutional cases illustrate the extent to which the Supreme Court affects the life and law of modern America. Each set represents an unprecedented exertion of judicial power. The first deals with school desegregation. *Brown v. Board of Education* (1954) and its progeny, which struck down state-enforced segregation of the races in the nation's public schools, ushered in a new era of judicial review. In so doing, *Brown* triggered no less than a cultural revolution in America. Although *Marbury* and *Dred Scott* produced political explosions, they were nonetheless limited in their practical effects. The desegregation cases, by contrast, required the abandonment of existing social practices. They effectively called for the transformation of society. *Brown* and its progeny declared that schools segregated by law must be dismantled and replaced with integrated schools where white and African American children would be required to attend school together. Even Americans convinced of *Brown*'s legal, political, and moral correctness would concede that the Supreme Court had lifted judicial power to a new peak.

The Supreme Court remained steadfast and unwavering in its adherence to *Brown* even in the face of massive Southern resistance. Perhaps the most flagrant defiance of *Brown* was the refusal of the governor and legislators of Arkansas to enforce a federal court order to integrate Little Rock's public schools. *Cooper v. Aaron* (1958, reprinted later in the chapter) arose out of the state's refusal to enforce *Brown*, and the Supreme Court used the occasion to make what many acknowledge to be one of the most vigorous assertions of federal judicial power in American history. In a decision signed by all nine justices, the Supreme Court reminded Americans that its interpretation of the Constitution is binding not only on courts of law but also on all state legislative and executive officials. *Cooper* is significant for its unambiguous claim to "judicial exclusivity in constitutional interpretation."[19]

With its decision in *Baker v. Carr* (1962, reprinted later in the chapter), the Supreme Court engaged in what Justice Frankfurter in dissent described as "a massive repudiation of the experience of our whole past." By entering the "political thicket" of legislative apportionment the Court was, he wrote, "asserting destructively novel judicial power." The decision triggered no less than a political revolution in America. *Baker* declared, for the first time, and in contrast to decisions of the Court in prior cases, that the Constitution provides a judicial remedy for malapportioned state legislative districts. In subsequent cases, the Court not only extended *Baker*'s reach to congressional and local legislative districts, but it also laid down the rule that all legislative districts must be as equal in population as circumstances would permit. Clear, also, was the Court's resolve to determine whether any such circumstances warranted deviation from the rule of equal population. And so the Court installed the principle of one person–one vote as the only legitimate basis of legislative representation in America.

Roe v. Wade (1973) launched the Court on still another constitutional adventure. [Its detractors would call it a misadventure.] *Roe* established a woman's constitutional right to procure an abortion. The right to have an abortion, declared the Court, is a "fundamental liberty" protected against state invasion by the due process liberty clauses of the Fifth and Fourteeth Amendments. By effectively nullifying the anti-abortion statutes of nearly all the states, *Roe* inflamed passions that resisted compromise. It caused divisions between "pro-life" and "pro-choice" forces in political campaigns and became a burning issue in assessing the credentials of Supreme Court nominees. *Brown* and *Baker* also ignited passions and invited resistance to the Court's

---

[19] See Geoffrey Stone *et al.*, *Constitutional Law*, 3d ed. (Boston: Little Brown and Company, 1996), 53.

decrees, but a generation later they were seen by most Americans as landmarks in the development of their constitutional democracy. The same cannot be said of *Roe*, and the controversy over its correctness and legitimacy shows no signs of abating.

The debate over *Roe* has raged as bitterly in the Supreme Court itself as in the public at large. In dissenting, Justice Bryon White saw the Court's vindication of the abortion liberty as "an exercise of raw judicial power." [20] From his point of view, *Baker* and *Brown* were at least rooted in logic founded respectively on the importance of the franchise to American democratic theory and on the antidiscrimination value of the equal protection clause. The right of privacy that produced the abortion liberty, however, seemed far less anchored in the Constitution's language or structure. Sixteen years later, in *Webster v. Reproductive Health Services*,[21] *Roe* narrowly escaped being overruled. The split decision prompted Justice Blackmun to end his concurring opinion on this inauspicious note: "For today," he wrote, "the women of this nation still retain the liberty to control their destinies. But the signs are evident and very ominous, and a chill wind blows." [22] The chill wind was expected to turn icy in the 1992 case of *Planned Parenthood of Southeastern Pennsylvania v. Casey* (reprinted later in the chapter). Some commentators predicted that the Court would use *Casey* to overrule *Roe*. As it turned out, *Casey* reaffirmed what the joint opinion described as *Roe*'s "essential holding," although it did collapse much of *Roe*'s original reasoning.

The focus here is not on the substantive merits of *Casey* but on the Court's understanding of its judicial role. First, *Casey* appeared to anchor the right to an abortion in a definition of liberty broader than any previous judicial pronouncement. "At the heart of liberty," said the Court, "is the right to define one's own concept of existence, of meaning, of the universe, and of the mystery of human life." [23] The language was new, the assertion untestable, and the implications boundless. Equally boundless was the Court's certitude: "Liberty finds no refuge in a jurisprudence of doubt," [24] proclaimed the first sentence of the joint opinion. Thus, the "core" of the abortion liberty had to be protected, although the joint opinion went on to declare that states could pass legislation to protect the fetus so long as the states did not impose an "undue burden" on the right of a woman to procure an abortion.

But then the joint opinion appeared to shift the analysis from a focus on the substantive right to the abortion liberty—one that no political majority can validly interfere with—to an argument rooted in majoritarian political theory. The opinion focused now on the importance of social expectations as well as the Court's own institutional integrity. The justices felt obligated to adhere to precedent, because for two decades "people have organized intimate relationships and made choices that define their views of themselves and their places in society, in reliance on the availability of abortion in the event that contraception should fail." The joint opinion then proceeded to remind Americans of *their* responsibility to heed the voice of the Supreme Court when it decides cases "grounded truly in principle." [25] It pointed out that *Roe* is one of those "rare" cases—*Brown* being the other example—that "has a dimension that the resolution of the normal case does not carry. It is the dimension present whenever the Court's interpretation of the Constitution calls the contending sides of a national

---

[20] *Doe v. Bolton*, 410 U.S. 113 at 222 (1973).

[21] 492 U.S. 490 (1989).

[22] *Ibid.*, at 560.

[23] 505 U.S. 833, 851.

[24] *Ibid.*, at 844.

[25] *Ibid.*, at 856.

controversy to end their national divisions by accepting a common mandate rooted in the Constitution."[26] This is the closest the Court has ever come to instructing Americans generally to honor its judgments, even to the point of asking them to accept the Court's vision of who they are as a people. Heretofore, as in *Cooper v. Aaron*, the Court's judgments were said to be binding on "every state legislator and executive and judicial officer [who] is solemnly committed by oath taken pursuant to Art. VI, cl. 3, 'to support this Constitution.'"[27] Now the Court was asking Americans to share its view of the meaning of life and liberty.

As we have seen, the Court in *Casey* preoccupied itself with the legitimacy of its authority, a problem the Court faces whenever it is called upon to deal with new issues on the frontiers of life and law. Examples of newer issues reaching the courts are state limits on assisted suicide, same-sex marriages, and the use of narcotic drugs. Here again the question poses itself: At what point is it proper for the courts to overturn a decision or policy of the elected representatives of the people? Should the Court take it upon itself "to confront some aspect of the general culture and to transform it by force of the superior virtue of the Constitution?"[28] What exactly is the process by which the judiciary discovers unenumerated fundamental rights? This process is by no means clear in the face of varying judicial strategies used to justify such rights. It is likely to become more problematic as the judiciary begins to decide cases in areas of national controversy that might be deemed to implicate, as in *Casey*, "one's own concept of existence, of meaning, of the universe, and of the mystery of human life."[29]

Self-Imposed Limits on Judicial Power

Despite the expansion of judicial authority in recent decades, the Supreme Court has created a number of doctrines that restrict access to the federal judiciary. These "justiciability" doctrines, as they are called, are counsels of judicial self-restraint. The Court feels compelled to place limits on itself because the traditional self-understood role of the judiciary is to interpret the law, not to make it. While the line between interpreting and making law is fuzzy, as we pointed out in chapter 2, our legal culture sees courts as independent and impartial agents of justice. Trying to handle an overabundance of cases, deciding when it need not decide, or taking on too many politically charged cases at the same time could, as Alexander Bickel has reminded us, undermine the Supreme Court's moral authority in America. Self-discipline, Bickel argues, not only helps to preserve the Court's institutional integrity—and independence; it is also a gesture of respect for the capacity of people to govern themselves through their legislative and executive institutions.

Perhaps the most important of the Court's justiciability doctrines is the "case and controversy" requirement. Article 3 of the Constitution extends the "judicial power of the United States" to "cases and controversies." The Supreme Court underscored the importance of this language in 1793 when President George Washington asked the Supreme Court for advice on whether the Franco-American Treaty of 1778 conflicted with the recent Proclamation of Neutrality. In a letter to the president dated 8 August 1793, the Court, then led by Chief Justice John Jay, noted that it was powerless under the Constitution to tender such advice. The "precedent" stuck. To this day, the federal

---

[26] *Ibid.*, at 867.

[27] *Cooper v. Aaron*, 358 U.S. 1, 18 (1958).

[28] Robert F. Nagel, *Judicial Power and the American Character* (Oxford: Oxford University Press, 1994), 72.

[29] *Planned Parenthood v. Casey*, 505 U.S. 833, 851 (1992).

courts refuse to give advisory opinions since their jurisdiction extends only to *real* cases and controversies arising under federal law or the Constitution.

As *Ex Parte McCardle* (1869, reprinted later in the chapter) underscores, Article 3 contains another serious limit on the exercise of federal judicial power. Section 2 of Article 3 subjects the Supreme Court's appellate jurisdiction to "such Exceptions . . . as the Congress shall make." *McCardle* sustained this constitutional power of Congress by declining to decide a case brought under a provision of a habeas corpus statute that Congress had repealed, even though McCardle's case had reached the Supreme Court on appeal prior to the congressional action. Congress's power to withdraw this jurisdiction constitutes a powerful legislative check on the Supreme Court. But the exercise of the "exceptions" power may also be seen as a threat to the Court's independence. Most congressional efforts to limit the Court's appellate jurisdiction are responses to politically controversial cases. Many of the cases discussed in this essay, including *Cohens v. Virginia*, *Baker v. Carr*, *Brown v. Board of Education*, and *Roe v. Wade*, triggered legislation to repeal provisions of the judicial code under which they arose. *McCardle*, however, represents one of the few instances in which Congress succeeded in limiting the Court's jurisdiction.[30]

We have noted that the Supreme Court decides only "controversies" within the meaning of Article 3. The Court usually invokes the doctrines of standing, mootness, and ripeness to determine whether a real controversy exists. Standing focuses on the capacity of the plaintiff or litigant to sue in a federal court. The party who invokes this power must be able to show that he or she has suffered an injury in fact—an injury that is concrete, particularized, actual and imminent, and one that results from unlawful governmental action. The Supreme Court's standing jurisprudence, as pointed out in the concluding section of this introductory essay, contrasts sharply with norms of judicial review in some other advanced democracies. The following summary of this jurisprudence may sharpen the student's appreciation of the contrast.

Standing issues are commonly adjudicated in the Supreme Court. *Frothingham v. Mellon* (1923), in which the Court determined that an individual taxpayer did not have standing to challenge the constitutionality of a federal spending program, is a seminal case. "The party who invokes the power [of judicial review]," declared the *Frothingham* Court, "must be able to show not only that the statute is invalid but that he has sustained or is immediately in danger of sustaining some direct injury as the result of its enforcement, and not merely that he suffers in some indefinite way in common with people generally."[31] The Warren Court, however, relaxed the requirements for standing, especially for claims based on the express provisions of the Bill of Rights. For example, in *Flast v. Cohen* (1968) the Court decided that taxpayers had standing to sue in challenging aid to religious schools. Chief Justice Warren's majority opinion concluded that "the *Frothingham* barrier should be lowered when a taxpayer attacks a federal statute on the ground that it violates the Establishment and Free Exercise Clause of the First Amendment."[32] But later the Burger Court would tighten requirements for standing and do so in such a way as to make some provisions of the

---

[30] The potential limits of congressional power, if any, have been the source of much speculation. See, e.g., Gerald Gunther, *Congressional Power to Curtail Federal Court Jurisdiction*, 36 Stan. L. Rev. 895 (1984); Michael J. Perry, *The Constitution, the Courts, and Human Rights* (New Haven: Yale University Press, 1982), 129–145; Lawrence G. Sager, *Constitutional Limitations on Congress' Authority to Regulate the Appellate Jurisdiction of the Federal Courts*, 95 Harv. L. Rev. 17 (1981); Henry M. Hart, *The Power of Congress to Limit the Jurisdiction of the Federal Courts*, 66 Harv. L. Rev. 1362 (1953).

[31] 262 U.S. 444, 488.

[32] 392 U.S. 83, 85.

Constitution unenforceable. Despite the constitutional provision requiring the publication "from time to time" of all receipts and expenditures of public money, the Burger Court ruled in 1974 that a taxpayer did not have standing to challenge the statute that prohibits the budget of the Central Intelligence Agency from being made public.[33]

Allen v. Wright is a more recent example of the Court's application of the standing doctrine. Parents of African American public school children sued the Internal Revenue Service for its failure to deny tax-exempt status, as required by law, to racially discriminatory private schools. In dismissing the case for lack of standing, the Court said that the denial of equality to the African American public school children did not result from the IRS's failure to act. As for the omission itself, the Court recalled a common refrain in its justiciability jurisprudence: there is no standing to challenge a violation of law *per se* absent an "actual present or immediately threatened injury resulting from unlawful governmental action."[34] Invoking the separation of powers principle, the Court rejected any approach to judicial review that would turn the federal judiciary into "continuing monitors of the wisdom and soundness of Executive action." Such oversight, said the Court, is the function of Congress and the executive branch. The Rehnquist Court reinforced this view of separation of powers in the recent case of *Lujan v. Defenders of Wildlife* (1992, reprinted later in the chapter).

Mootness and ripeness are similarly concerned with the principle of separated powers. A case becomes moot when the litigated complaint loses its adversarial character; that is, when the facts constituting the dispute are no longer "live" and the parties no longer have anything at stake. One such case is *DeFunis v. Odegaard*.[35] An unsuccessful white law school applicant sued the University of Washington for its preferential treatment of certain minorities. The applicant was later admitted to the law school under a court order while the case made its way to the United States Supreme Court. But by the time the case reached the Supreme Court, the applicant was about to finish law school with the University's blessing. This being so, the case was dismissed for being moot: there was no longer a dispute between the applicant and the University, and to render a decision in the absence of an adversarial relationship, the Supreme Court noted, would be an advisory opinion.[36]

Finally, the requirement of ripeness is also designed to enhance the adversarial character of constitutional litigation. Before the Supreme Court will decide a "case" or "controversy," all questions of fact and law must be fully developed. The facts must be hard and the issues clear; if they are not, or if there is a possibility that adjudication would not end the dispute, the Supreme Court may regard the case as unripe for review. Justice Powell's concurring opinion in *Goldwater v. Carter* (reprinted in chapter 7) illustrates one use of the doctrine of ripeness. In *Carter*, the Court dismissed a suit initiated by several United States senators against the president for his unilateral termination of an international treaty without the advice and consent of the Senate.[37] Unlike the plurality opinion—which ruled that the issue before the Court was a "political question" inappropriate for judicial resolution—Powell preferred to dismiss the complaint "as not ripe for review" because of his conviction that the conflict had yet

---

[33] *United States v. Richardson*, 418 U.S. 166.

[34] *Allen v. Wright*, 468 U.S. 737 (1984).

[35] 416 U.S. 312 (1974).

[36] *Roe v. Wade* represents a major exception to the doctrine of mootness. A pregnant woman who initiates a complaint against a restrictive abortion law is unlikely to be pregnant by the time the courts get around to her case. The birth of the child or a miscarriage would render the case moot, thus evading judicial review. The pregnancy, however, may be repeated. In this situation—where the condition is "capable of repetition yet evading review"—the doctrine of mootness will not usually apply.

[37] 444 U.S. 996 (1979).

to reach the stage of a final impasse between Congress and the president. As Powell's disagreement with the *Carter* plurality shows, the doctrine of ripeness, like those of standing and mootness, is anything but a rigid formula. In the hands of the Supreme Court it has been flexibly and variously applied for both prudential and constitutional reasons.

The Political Question Doctrine

The "political question" doctrine is even tougher to define. One commentator describes it as "the most amorphous aspect of justiciability."[38] He notes further that the doctrine is driven mainly by "underlying policy concerns," the most important of which, as we would expect, is "to avoid an improper interference with the political judgments of the other branches of the federal government."[39] *Luther v. Borden* (1849, reprinted later in the chapter) is the classic example of a nonjusticiable political question. Writing for the Court, Chief Justice Taney held that the guarantee clause of Article 4, Section 4 of the Constitution was *judicially* unenforceable because it vested Congress alone with the authority to decide whether a state has a republican form of government.

A century later, the guarantee clause would be invoked once again in legislative apportionment controversies.[40] Some litigants argued that apportionment cases were political because the guarantee clause left to Congress the decision whether malapportioned legislative districts violated the concept of "republican" government. In *Baker v. Carr* (1962), the Court rejected this argument, holding that challenges to such districts were reviewable under the equal protection standards of the Fourteenth Amendment. In its labored discussion of the guarantee clause, however, the Court found it necessary to define the contours and limits of the political question doctrine. Writing for the *Baker* majority, Justice Brennan enumerated the situations which would involve a political question:

> *Prominent on the surface of any case held to involve a political question is found a textually demonstrable constitutional commitment of the issue to a coordinate political department; or a lack of judicially discoverable and manageable standards for resolving it; or the impossibility of deciding without an initial policy determination of a kind clearly for nonjudicial discretion; or the impossibility of a court's undertaking independent resolution without expressing lack of the respect due coordinate branches of government; or an unquestioning adherence to a political decision already made; or the potentiality of embarrassment from multifarious pronouncements by various departments on one question.*[41]

In applying the political question doctrine to specific cases, the Supreme Court does not always make clear whether it is doing so for prudential or constitutional reasons (see discussion of prudentialism in chapter 2). In *Carter v. Goldwater*, the political question doctrine appeared to have been applied for prudential reasons; that

---

[38] Kenneth F. Ripple, *Constitutional Litigation* (Charlottesville, Va.: The Michie Company, 1984), 96.

[39] *Ibid.*

[40] In 1946, the Supreme Court dismissed a constitutional challenge against Illinois' malapportioned congressional districts, partially on the ground that the question was political and thus beyond judicial resolution. *Colegrove v. Green* 328 U.S. 549 (1946). In 1964 the Court reversed, now holding that congressional apportionments are subject to judicial review under the equal protection clause. See *Wesberry v. Sanders*, 376 U.S. 1 (1964).

[41] *Baker v. Carr*, 369 U.S. 186, 217 (1962).

is, the Court declined to interfere with a foreign policy decision of the president as a matter of propriety given the sensitive issue of international politics involved. On the other hand, in *Nixon v. United States* (1993, reprinted later in the chapter), the Court applied the doctrine because, in its view, the *Constitution* stipulated that the impeachment of a federal judge is the *sole* prerogative of the Senate. But as the various opinions show, the justices were far from unanimous over whether the impeachment of Judge Nixon was a nonjusticiable political question.[42]

Yet there is some hint in the concurring opinion of Justice White that prudential reasoning may have dictated the result in *Nixon*. Whether prudential rather than constitutional reasons are offered for applying the political question doctrine is largely a matter of judgment. In short, the Court may decline to decide a case if it is politically too "hot" to handle or if the justices feel that the exercise of jurisdiction would manifest lack of regard for the competence or judgment of the legislature. As with most of the "passive virtues" that serve as guides to the legitimacy of judicial review, the doctrine of political questions seems to be the American way of reconciling the principles of constitutionalism and democracy.

Finally, the Court has more or less adhered to various maxims of judicial restraint set forth by Justice Brandeis in his often cited concurring opinion in *Ashwander v. Tennessee Valley Authority* (1936).[43] Known as the "Ashwander rules," these maxims or "considerations of propriety," as Brandeis called them, may be summarized as follows:

1. The Court will not anticipate a question of constitutional law in advance of the necessity of deciding it, nor will the Court formulate a rule of constitutional law broader than is required by the precise facts to which it is to be applied.

2. The Court will not decide a constitutional question properly presented by the record if some other ground upon which the case may be disposed of is also present.

3. If a statute is challenged on constitutional grounds, the Court will first ascertain whether a construction of the statute is fairly possible by which the constitutional question may be avoided.[44]

In brief, the Court reaches constitutional questions last not first. To the extent that these rules continue to be observed, they also suggest that a constitutional decision is a serious matter, for such a decision can be overruled only by the Court itself or by a constitutional amendment—which is far more difficult to achieve. Americans tend to see these rules and other norms of constitutional adjudication discussed in this section as logical and natural ingredients of any viable regime of judicial review. The next section shows that they are uniquely American.

Judicial Review in Comparative Perspective

In his classic treatise on American democracy, Alexis de Tocqueville observed that "the representative system of government has been adopted in several states of Europe, but we are not aware that any nation of the globe has hitherto organized a

---

[42] *Goldwater v. Carter*, cited previously, provides another illustration of these differing perspectives. The Court's plurality (consisting of Chief Justice Burger and Justices Rehnquist, Stewart, and Stevens) regarded President Carter's decision to abrogate the defense treaty with Taiwan as nonjusticiable "because it involves the authority of the President in the conduct of our country's foreign relations." Justice Powell, as indicated above, thought the issue was justiciable but preferred to decline review because the complaint was not ripe for review. Justice Brennan, the only member of the Court to decide the case on its merits, ruled that the decision to abrogate the treaty "rests upon the President's well-established authority to recognize, and withdraw recognition from, foreign governments."

[43] 297 U.S. 288.

[44] *Ibid.*, 346–8.

judicial power on the principle now adopted by the Americans."[45] He was, of course, speaking of judicial review. If Tocqueville were to observe the world today, he would be astonished to note that judicial review has emerged as a principle of governance in many if not most of the world's advanced constitutional democracies. This is mainly a post Second World War development, to no small degree the product of American influence, and primarily in response to the excesses of prewar popular democracies.[46] Judicial review in the United States, as we have seen, was—and remains—largely a product of judicial interpretation. What is new about the emergence of judicial review in Europe, Asia, and Canada—and, most recently, in the former communist countries of Eastern Europe—is not merely the broad scale on which it has been adopted, but the conscious decision of constitution makers to place the guardianship of fundamental law in judicial hands.[47]

What accounts for this astonishing institutional development? One possible explanation—besides the historical memory of popular democracies succumbing to totalitarian appeals—is the more recent growth of big government and its increasing tendency to colonize areas of life and society previously consigned to the private sphere. Judicial review cannot slow the growth of government, but it can check the exercise of public power at crucial points, particularly when individual rights are implicated. Indeed, judicial review has expanded in some countries with the adoption of a constitutionally entrenched bill of rights, a most prominent illustration of which is Canada's Charter of Rights and Freedoms, adopted in 1982. Both developments—the growth of big government and the adoption of entrenched bills of rights—go hand-in-hand with the challenge that modern constitutionalism has mounted against the principle of parliamentary supremacy. Yet, as in the United States, the exercise of judicial review in other countries has also created severe tensions between the principles of constitutionalism and democracy.

The United States might be most gainfully compared in this short treatment of foreign constitutionalism to the judicial review administrations of Canada and selected European jurisdictions. Among the countries of Europe which have adopted judicial review on a scale equal to and in some instances exceeding that of the United States are Germany, France, Italy, and Spain. As we saw in chapter 1, each of these countries has housed judicial review in specialized courts of constitutional review created apart from and independent of the ordinary judicial establishment. Unlike the United States Supreme Court, these constitutional courts are not courts of general appellate jurisdiction. In common law systems such as the United States and Canada, any court may decide a constitutional issue in the normal course of litigation. In civil law systems, constitutional courts have no general appellate jurisdiction; their competence is confined to determining whether laws or other state acts having the force of law conform to the Constitution. Finally, the most prominent example of a transnational constitutional tribunal is the European Court of Human Rights, which is entrusted with the enforcement of the European Convention on Human Rights in the member-states of the Council of Europe.

---

[45] Alexis de Tocqueville, *Democracy in America* (London: Oxford University Press, 1952), 79.

[46] See Louis Henkin and Albert J. Rosenthal, *Constitutionalism and Rights: The Influence of the United States Constitution Abroad* (New York: Columbia University Press, 1990).

[47] See generally A.R. Brewer-Carias, *Judicial Review in Comparative Law* (Cambridge: Cambridge University Press, 1989); Lawrence W. Beer, *Constitutionalism in Asia: Asian Views of the American Influence*, Occasional Papers in Contemporary Asian Studies (Baltimore: School of Law, University of Maryland, 1988); Symposium on *Comparative Constitutionalism: Theoretical Perspectives on the Role of Constitutions in the Interplay Between Identity and Diversity*, 14 Cardozo Law Review 497–956 (January 1993); and Herman Schwartz, *The New East European Constitutional Courts*, 13 Michigan Journal of International Law 741 (1992).

Of the constitutional tribunals just mentioned, Germany's Federal Constitutional Court, created in 1951, is the oldest. The German Court is also one of the world's most powerful constitutional tribunals, rivaled in prestige and influence only by the United States Supreme Court. In fact, Germany's Constitutional Court has inspired the creation of most European constitutional tribunals, including the new constitutional courts of Hungary, Russia, Bulgaria, Lithuania, Poland, and the Czech Republic. Of course, there are significant differences in the powers conferred on these tribunals. Italy, for example, confines the competence of its constitutional court to hearing constitutional disputes between branches and levels of government. The Italian Court may also hear issues of constitutionality certified to it by judges of ordinary courts. On the other hand, France's Constitutional Council exercises what is known as "preventive" judicial review; that is, it can only examine the constitutionality of pending legislative bills and only on the request of the president, prime minister, president of one of the parliamentary assemblies, or a prescribed number of parliamentary representatives—the opposite of the U.S. rule against advisory opinions. In addition, the council is empowered to review the constitutionality of parliamentary and presidential elections as well as referenda.

Germany's Federal Constitutional Court combines all the foregoing jurisdiction along with many other competences, including the power to declare political parties unconstitutional and to hear the complaints of ordinary citizens whose constitutional rights have been infringed by any law or act of government. Even more powerful is the Hungarian Constitutional Court, recently described as "the most activist court in the former Soviet world."[48] Pursuant to the so-called "popular action"—a complaint or petition that can be brought by any citizen or public official against any law that he or she deems unconstitutional—the Court decides cases mainly on abstract judicial review. On the average, the Court strikes down about one law per week and, in addition, has often ruled that parliament acts "unconstitutionally by omission" if it fails to enact a law that the Constitution requires.[49] Contrary to the canons of restraint [discussed earlier] observed by the U.S. Court, the Hungarian Court will declare a law unconstitutional if it *can be* construed as unconstitutional. The German Court, by contrast, nearly always sustains a statute if it *can be* interpreted to conform to the Constitution.

The American system of judicial review thus differs in many respects from the continental systems. We have already noted that judicial review in the United States is a power exercised by all courts but subject to "case" and "controversy" requirements, the political question doctrine, and certain prudential guidelines for avoiding a ruling on constitutional grounds—all passive virtues that would seem to be vices in Hungary. Germany's Federal Constitutional Court also finds the passive virtues unacceptable. Its approach to constitutional review has been described as follows:

> *The preservation of the constitutional state in* all *of its particulars is . . . the function of the Federal Constitutional Court. . . . [T]he Court's role is to* decide *constitutional issues, not to avoid them or to resolve them as a matter of last resort. When serious doubts arise over the validity of a law or practice having the force of law, the Court's function is to resolve the doubt in the interest of constitutional clarity and certainty. Gaps in the Constitution cry out for closure, for which reason all issues arising under the Basic Law's provisions relating to the maintenance of peace and security appear to be justiciable. Vague constitutional terms such as "human dignity," "de-*

---

[48] See remarks of Kim Scheppele in Symposium: *Constitutional "Refolution" in the Ex-Communist World: The Rule of Law*, 12 American University Journal of International Law and Policy 95 (1997).

[49] *Ibid.*, 96.

mocracy," and "social state" have also been found to possess a sharp set of teeth capable of killing legislation and even to compel certain forms of state action if public officials are to avoid its bite. In the United States, by contrast, major constitutional provisions like the republican form of government clause . . . and the clause on the ratification of amendments to the Constitution have been relegated to the limbo of nonjusticiability.[50]

In brief, a specialized constitutional court is conceptualized as the *supreme* guardian of the constitution, its main function being to review laws of doubtful constitutionality and to annul them if they are unconstitutional. A proceeding known as abstract judicial review is, as already noted, one common method of examining such laws. In Germany, for example, upon the request of a state government or one-third of the members of the national parliament, a duty enacted and promulgated law—even before it enters into force—may be reviewed by the constitutional court. In this way, the losers in a legislative battle are able to turn a political dispute almost immediately into a constitutional controversy.

What this means in the German context is that all provisions of the Constitution are enforceable. In the United States, by contrast, some constitutional provisions are unenforceable because they give rise to "political" questions or because the plaintiff in a case lacks standing to challenge an unconstitutional action. *Constitutional* review in Europe is thus different from *judicial* review in the United States. Yet we are also seeing some kind of convergence taking place between judicial power in Europe and in the United States. First, in recent years the Supreme Court has been given total control over its own docket, allowing it to take only those cases it wishes to decide. With such discretion, the Court has been able to concentrate on constitutional issues and thus to transform itself into a virtual European-style constitutional court. Second, the political question doctrine has been narrowed in recent years, so that much of what was previously nonjusticiable is now open to adjudication.

Relatedly, we have seen that the doctrine of standing is as open or closed as the Supreme Court wants it to be. In addition, academic legal critics have weighed in with their own criticism of the standing cases discussed earlier. One of these critics has remarked: "When a genuine disagreement about the meaning of the Constitution erupts that affects the lives of a significant segment of the population, the Court's duty is to construe the Constitution, whether or not the disagreement can be choreographed as a classic *Marbury* dispute."[51] With regard to environmental matters, Congress appears to have had a similar model of judicial review in mind; it has often defined new injuries—e.g., interfering with recreational activities such as whale watching and outdoor hiking—and articulated chains of causation that give rise to a case or controversy where none existed before. *Lujan v. Defenders of Wildlife*, for example, involved a citizen-suit authorized by Congress for the protection of endangered species. Although the citizen-suit in *Lujan* failed, there were strong dissenting opinions to the contrary.

On the other hand, if the barriers to standing and the political question doctrine were to be dropped altogether, the Supreme Court's power might increase dramatically. This would raise significant questions about the relationship between constitutionalism and democracy. The tension between these contrasting principles seems more easily accommodated under the Canadian and German constitutions. Section 33

---

[50] See Donald P. Kommers, *German Constitutionalism: A Prolegomenon*, 40 Emory Law Journal 848–9 (1991).

[51] See "Justiciability, Remedies, and the Burger Court" in Herman Schwartz, ed., *The Burger Years: Rights and Wrongs in the Supreme Court 1969–1986* (New York: Viking Penguin Inc., 1987), 16.

of Canada's Charter of Rights and Liberties contains an override provision, allowing the Parliament to declare that one of its enactments "shall operate notwithstanding" a judicial decision to the contrary. In Germany, the Federal Constitutional Court often declares a statute "incompatible" with the Constitution but declines to nullify it, a procedure which keeps the statute on the law books but allows the legislature to take a second look at it while proceeding to correct the constitutional deficiency. In addition, the German Court is unbound by the doctrine of *stare decisis* and, finally, the German Basic Law is much easier to amend than the Constitution of the United States.

Selected Bibliography

Ackerman, Bruce. *We the People*. Cambridge: Harvard University Press, 1991.

Agresto, John. *The Supreme Court and Constitutional Democracy*. Ithaca, N.Y.: Cornell University Press, 1984.

Barber, Sotirios A. *On What the Constitution Means*. Baltimore: Johns Hopkins University Press, 1984.

Beaty, David M., ed. *Human Rights and Judicial Review: A Comparative Perspective*. Dordrecht, Boston and London: Martinus Nijhoff Publishers, 1994.

Bickel, Alexander M. *The Least Dangerous Branch: The Supreme Court at the Bar of Politics*. New York: Bobbs-Merrill, 1962.

Brewer-Carias, A.R. *Judicial Review in Comparative Law*. Cambridge: Cambridge University Press, 1989.

Burgess, Susan R. *Contest for Constitutional Authority: The Abortion and War Powers Debate*. Lawrence, Kan.: University of Kansas Press, 1992.

Caenegem, R.C. van *An Historical Introduction to Western Constitutional Law*. Cambridge: Cambridge University Press, 1995.

Cappelletti, Mauro. *The Judicial Process in Comparative Perspective*. Oxford: Clarendon Press, 1989.

Choper, Jesse H. *Judicial Review and the National Political Process*. Chicago: University of Chicago Press, 1980.

Clinton, Robert Lowry. *Marbury v. Madison and Judicial Review*. Lawrence, Kan.: University Press of Kansas, 1989.

Dworkin, Ronald. *Taking Rights Seriously*. Cambridge: Harvard University Press, 1977.

Ely, John Hart. *Democracy and Distrust: A Theory of Judicial Review*. Cambridge: Harvard University Press, 1980.

Fisher, Louis. *Constitutional Dialogues: Interpretation as Political Process*. Princeton, N.J.: Princeton University Press, 1988.

Franck, Matthew J. *Against the Imperial Judiciary*. Lawrence, Kan.: University Press of Kansas, 1996.

Gant, Scott. *Judicial Supremacy and Nonjudicial Interpretation of the Constitution*, 24 Hastings Constitutional Law Quarterly 359 (1997).

Greenberg, Douglas *et al.*, eds. *Constitutionalism and Democracy: Transitions in the Contemporary World*. New York: Oxford University Press, 1993.

Harris, William F. *The Interpretable Constitution*. Baltimore: Johns Hopkins University Press, 1993.

Jacobsohn, Gary L. *The Supreme Court and the Decline of Constitutional Aspiration*. Totowa, N.J.: Rowman & Littlefield, 1986.

Kavas, Igor I. *Supranational and Constitutional Courts in Europe: Functions and Sources*. Buffalo, N.Y.: William S. Hein & Co., 1992.

King, Preston and Andrea Bosco, eds. *A Constitution For Europe*. London: Lothian Foundation Press, 1991.

Mandel, Michael. *The Charter of Rights and the Legalization of Politics in Canada*. Toronto: Thompson Educational Publishing, Inc., 1994.

McDowell, Gary L. *Curbing the Courts: The Constitution and the Limits of Judicial Power*. Baton Rouge: Louisiana State University Press, 1988.

McKenna, Marian C., ed. *The Canadian and American Constitutions in Comparative Perspective*. Calgary: University of Calgary Press, 1993.

Melone, Albert P. and George Mace. *Judicial Review and American Democracy*. Ames, Iowa: Iowa State University Press, 1988.

Murphy, Walter F. *Who Shall Interpret: The Quest for the Ultimate Constitutional Interpreter*, 48 Review of Politics 401 (1986).

Nagel, Robert F. *Constitutional Cultures: The Mentality and Consequences of Judicial Review*. Berkeley: University of California Press, 1989.

Perry, Michael J. *The Constitution, Courts, and Human Rights*. New Haven, Conn.: Yale University Press, 1982.

Powell, Jefferson H. *The Moral Tradition of American Constitutionalism*. Durham, N.C.: Duke University Press, 1993.

Sartori, Giovanni. *Comparative Constitutional Engineering*. New York: New York University Press, 1994.

Seidman, Louis Michael and Mark V. Tushnet. *Remnants of Belief*. Oxford: Oxford University Press, 1996.

Shapiro, Martin. *Courts: A Comparative and Political Analysis*. Chicago: University of Chicago Press, 1981.

Smith, Rogers M. *Liberalism and American Constitutional Law*. Cambridge: Harvard University Press, 1985.

Stone, Alec. *The Birth of Judicial Politics in France: The Constitutional Council in Comparative Perspective*. Oxford: Oxford University Press, 1992.

Sunstein, Cass R. *The Partial Constitution*. Cambridge: Harvard University Press, 1993.

Marbury v. Madison
5 U.S. 137, 1 Cranch 137, 2 L. Ed. 60 (1803)

Near the end of his term of office President Adams nominated William Marbury to the office of justice of the peace in the District of Columbia. The nomination was affirmed by the Senate, the commission was signed by the president, and the seal of the United States was affixed by the secretary of state. When Adams's term of office expired, Marbury applied to James Madison, secretary of state under Jefferson, for the delivery of his commission. Jefferson maintained that the commission was not valid until delivered and ordered Madison to withhold it, whereupon Marbury applied to the Supreme Court for a writ of *mandamus*. The Court ordered Madison to show cause why the writ should not be issued. The case proceeded after a showing of no cause. Opinion of the Court: *Marshall*, Chase, Patterson, Washington. Not participating: Cushing, Moore.

**Mr. Chief Justice MARSHALL delivered
the opinion of the Court.**

In the order in which the court has viewed this subject, the following questions have been considered and decided.

1st. Has the applicant a right to the commission he demands? . . .

It is . . . decidedly the opinion of the court, that when a commission has been signed by the President, the appointment is made; and that the commission is complete when the seal of the United States has been affixed to it by the Secretary of State. . . .

Mr. Marbury, then, since the commission was signed by the President. and sealed by the Secretary of State, was appointed. . . .

To withhold his commission, therefore, is an act deemed by the court not warranted by law, but violative of a vested legal right.

This brings us to the second inquiry; which is

2d. If he has a right, and that right has been violated, do the laws of his country afford him a remedy?

The very essence of civil liberty certainly consists in the right of every individual to claim the protection of the laws, whenever he receives an injury. One of the first duties of government is to afford that protection. . . .

3d. If they do afford him a remedy, is it a mandamus issuing from this court? . . .

It is then the opinion of the court,

1. That by signing the commission of Mr. Marbury, the president of the United States appointed him a justice of peace for the county of Washington in the district of Columbia; and that the seal of the United States, affixed thereto by the secretary of state, is conclusive testimony of the verity of the signature, and of the completion of the appointment; and that the appointment conferred on him a legal right to the office for the space of five years.
2. That, having this legal title to the office, he has a consequent right to the commission; a refusal to deliver which is a plain violation of that right, for which the laws of his country afford him a remedy.

It remains to be inquired whether

3. He is entitled to the remedy for which he applies. This depends on,
   1. The nature of the writ applied for; and,
   2. The power of this court

. . . The intimate political relation subsisting between the President . . . and the heads of departments, necessarily renders any legal investigation of these acts of one of those high officers peculiarly irksome, as well as delicate; and excites some hesitation with respect to the propriety of entering into such investigation. . . .

It is scarcely necessary for the court to disclaim all pretension to such jurisdiction. An extravagance, so absurd and excessive, could not have been entertained for a moment. The province of the court is, solely, to decide on the rights of individuals, not to inquire how the executive, or executive officers, perform duties in which they have a discretion. Questions in their nature political, or which are, by the constitution and laws, submitted to the executive, can never be made in this court. . . .

This, then, is a plain case of a *mandamus*, either to deliver the commission, or a copy of it from the record; and it only remains to be inquired,

Whether it can issue from this court.

The act to establish the judicial courts of the United States authorizes the supreme court "to issue writs of *mandamus*, in cases warranted by the principles and usages of law, to any courts appointed, or persons holding office, under the authority of the United States."

The secretary of state, being a person, holding an office under the authority of the United States, is precisely within the letter of the description; and if this court is not authorized to issue a writ of *mandamus* to such an officer, it must be because the law is unconstitutional, and therefore absolutely incapable of conferring the authority, and assigning the duties which its words purport to confer and assign.

The constitution vests the whole judicial power of the United States in one supreme court, and such inferior courts as congress shall, from time to time, ordain and establish. This power is expressly extended to all cases arising under the laws of the United States; and consequently, in some form, may be exercised over the present case; because the right claimed is given by a law of the United States.

In the distribution of this power it is declared that "the supreme court shall have original jurisdiction in all cases affecting ambassadors, other public ministers and consuls, and those in which a state shall be a party. In all other cases, the supreme court shall have appellate jurisdiction."

It has been insisted at the bar, that as the original grant of jurisdiction to the supreme and inferior courts is general, and the clause, assigning original jurisdiction to the supreme court, contains no negative or restrictive words; the power remains to the legislature to assign original jurisdiction to that court in other cases than those specified in the article which has been recited; provided those cases belong to the judicial power of the United States.

If it had been intended to leave it in the discretion of the legislature to apportion the judicial power between the supreme and inferior courts according to the will of that body, it would certainly have been useless to have proceeded further than to have defined the judicial power, and the tribunals in which it should be vested. The subsequent part of the section is mere surplusage, is entirely without meaning, if such is to be the construction. If congress remains at liberty to give this court appellate jurisdiction, where the constitution has declared their jurisdiction shall be original; and original jurisdiction where the constitution has declared it shall be appellate; the distribution of jurisdiction made in the constitution, is form without substance.

Affirmative words are often, in their operation, negative of other objects than those affirmed; and in this case, a negative or exclusive sense must be given to them or they have no operation at all.

It cannot be presumed that any clause in the constitution is intended to be without effect; and therefore, such a construction is inadmissible, unless the words require it.

When an instrument organizing fundamentally a judicial system, divides it into one supreme, and so many inferior courts as the legislature may ordain and establish; then enumerates its powers, and proceeds so far to distribute them, as to define the jurisdiction of the supreme court by declaring the cases in which it shall take original jurisdiction, and that in others it shall take appellate jurisdiction, the plain import of the words seems to be, that in one class of cases its jurisdiction is original, and not appellate; in the other it is appellate, and not original. If any other construction would render the clause inoperative, that is an additional reason for rejecting such other construction, and for adhering to the obvious meaning.

To enable this court then to issue a *mandamus*, it must be shown to be an exercise of appellate jurisdiction, or to be necessary to enable them to exercise appellate jurisdiction.

It has been stated at the bar that the appellate jurisdiction may be exercised in a variety of forms, and that if it be the will of the legislature that a *mandamus* should be used for that purpose, that will must be obeyed. This is true; yet the jurisdiction must be appellate, not original. It is the essential criterion of appellate jurisdiction, that it revises and corrects the proceedings in a cause already instituted, and does not create that case. Although, therefore, a *mandamus* may be directed to courts, yet to issue such a writ to an officer for the delivery of a paper is in effect the same as to sustain an original action for that paper, and therefore seems not to belong to appellate, but to original jurisdiction. Neither is it necessary in such a case as this, to enable the court to exercise its appellate jurisdiction.

The authority, therefore, given to the supreme court, by the act establishing the judicial courts of the United States, to issue writs of *mandamus* to public officers, appears not to be warranted by the constitution; and it becomes necessary to inquire whether a jurisdiction, so conferred, can be exercised.

The question, whether an act, repugnant to the constitution, can become the law of the land, is a question deeply interesting to the United States; but, happily, not of an intricacy proportioned to its interest. It seems only necessary to recognise certain principles, supposed to have been long and well established, to decide it.

That the people have an original right to establish, for their future government, such principles as, in their opinion, shall most conduce to their own happiness, is the basis on which the whole American fabric has been erected. The exercise of this original right is a very great exertion; nor can it nor ought it to be frequently repeated. The principles, therefore, so established are deemed fundamental. And as the authority, from which they proceed, is supreme, and can seldom act, they are designed to be permanent. This original and supreme will organizes the government, and assigns to different departments their respective powers. It may either stop here; or establish certain limits not to be transcended by those departments.

The government of the United States is of the latter description. The powers of the legislature are defined and limited; and that those limits may not be mistaken or forgotten, the constitution is written. To what purpose are powers limited, and to what purpose is that limitation committed to writing; if these limits may at any time, be passed

Comparative Note 3.1

A. Article 93, German Basic Law (1949)

(1) The Federal Constitutional Court shall decide:

1. in cases of differences of opinion or doubts on the formal and material compatibility of federal law or Land law with this Basic Law . . . at the request of the Federal Government, of a Land government or of one third of the Bundestag members.

4a. on complaints of unconstitutionality, which may be entered by any person who claims that one of his basic rights or one of his rights . . . has been violated by public authority.

B. Canadian Charter of Rights and Freedoms (1982)

Sec. 24 (1). Anyone whose rights or freedoms, as guaranteed by this Charter, have been infringed or denied may apply to a court of competent jurisdiction to obtain such remedy as the court considers appropriate and just in the circumstances.

Sec. 33 (1). Parliament or the legislature of a province may expressly declare in an Act of Parliament or of the legislature, as the case may be, that the Act or a provision thereof shall operate notwithstanding a provision included in section 2 or sections 7 to 15 of this Charter.

Sec. 52. The Constitution of Canada is the supreme law of Canada, and any law that is inconsistent with the provisions of the Constitution is, to the extent of the inconsistency, of no force or effect.

C. South African Constitution (1996)

Art. 39 (1). When interpreting the Bill of Rights, a court, tribunal or forum (a) must promote the values that underlie an open and democratic society based on human dignity, equality, and freedom; (b) must consider international law; and (c) may consider foreign law.

---

by those intended to be restrained? The distinction, between a government with limited and unlimited powers is abolished, if those limits do not confine the persons on whom they are imposed, and if acts prohibited and acts allowed are of equal obligation. It is a proposition too plain to be contested, that the constitution controls any legislative act repugnant to it; or, that the legislature may alter the constitution by an ordinary act.

Between these alternatives there is no middle ground. The constitution is either a superior, paramount law, unchangeable by ordinary means, or it is on a level with ordinary legislative acts, and like other acts, is alterable when the legislature shall please to alter it.

If the former part of the alternative be true, then a legislative act contrary to the constitution is not law: if the latter part be true, then written constitutions are absurd attempts, on the part of the people, to limit a power in its own nature illimitable.

Certainly all those who have framed written constitutions contemplate them as forming the fundamental and paramount law of the nation, and consequently the theory of every such government must be, that an act of the legislature repugnant to the constitution is void.

This theory is essentially attached to a written constitution, and is consequently to be considered by this court as one of the fundamental principles of our society. It is not therefore to be lost sight of in the further consideration of this subject.

If an act of the legislature, repugnant to the constitution, is void, does it, notwithstanding its invalidity, bind the courts and oblige them to give it effect? Or, in other words, though it be not law, does it constitute a rule as operative as if it was a law? This would be to overthrow in fact what was established in theory; and would seem, at first view, an absurdity too gross to be insisted on. It shall, however, receive a more attentive consideration.

It is emphatically the province and duty of the judicial department to say what the law is. Those who apply the rule to particular cases, must of necessity expound and interpret that rule. If two laws conflict with each other, the courts must decide on the operation of each.

So if a law be in opposition to the constitution; if both the law and the constitution apply to a particular case, so that the court must either decide that case conformably to the law, disregarding the constitution; or conformably to the constitution, disregarding the law; the court must determine which of these conflicting rules governs the case. This is of the very essence of judicial duty.

If then the courts are to regard the constitution, and the constitution is superior to any ordinary act of the legislature, the constitution, and not such ordinary act, must govern the case to which they both apply.

Those, then, who controvert the principle that the constitution is to be considered, in court, as a paramount law, are reduced to the necessity of maintaining that courts must close their eyes on the constitution, and see only the law.

This doctrine would subvert the very foundation of all written constitutions. It would declare that an act, which, according to the principles and theory of our government, is entirely void, is yet, in practice, completely obligatory. It would declare, that if the legislature shall do what is expressly forbidden, such act, notwithstanding the express prohibition, is in reality effectual. It would be giving to the legislature a practical and real omnipotence with the same breath which professes to restrict their powers within narrow limits. It is prescribing limits, and declaring that those limits may be passed at pleasure.

That it thus reduces to nothing what we have deemed the greatest improvement on political institutions, a written constitution, would of itself be sufficient, in America, where written constitutions have been viewed with so much reverence, for rejecting the construction. But the peculiar expressions of the constitution of the United States furnish additional arguments in favour of its rejection.

The judicial power of the United States is extended to all cases arising under the constitution.

Could it be the intention of those who gave this power, to say that, in using it, the constitution should not be looked into? That a case arising under the constitution should be decided without examining the instrument under which it arises?

This is too extravagant to be maintained.

In some cases then, the constitution must be looked into by the judges. And if they can open it at all, what part of it are they forbidden to read, or to obey?

Why otherwise does it direct the judges to take an oath to support it? This oath certainly applies, in an especial manner, to their conduct in their official character. How immoral to impose it on them, if they were to be used as the instruments, and the knowing instruments, for violating what they swear to support!

Why does a judge swear to discharge his duties agreeably to the constitution of the United States, if that constitution forms no rule for his government? If it is closed upon him and cannot be inspected by him?

If such be the real state of things, this is worse than solemn mockery. To prescribe, or to take this oath, becomes equally a crime.

It is also not entirely unworthy of observation, that in declaring what shall be the supreme law of the land, the constitution itself is first mentioned; and not the laws of the United States generally, but those only which shall be made in pursuance of the constitution, have that rank.

Thus, the particular phraseology of the constitution of the United States confirms and strengthens the principle, supposed to be essential to all written constitutions, that a law repugnant to the constitution is void, and that courts, as well as other departments, are bound by that instrument.

The rule must be discharged.

Notes/Queries/Readings

1. Why was section 13 of the Judiciary Act of 1789 found unconstitutional? Where does Marshall find the power of the judiciary to declare the actions of a coordinate branch of the federal government unconstitutional? How does he differentiate the issue in this case from a political question, or one submitted to the executive, that courts cannot rule upon? What interpretive method or methods does Marshall employ in reaching his conclusion in *Marbury*?

2. The Court concluded that "The constitution is either a superior, paramount law, unchangeable by ordinary means, or it is on a level with ordinary legislative acts, and like other acts, is alterable when the legislature shall please to alter it." Is it true that there is "no middle ground" between these two alternatives? How does Marshall's insistence that the Constitution must be superior to ordinary legislation justify the practice of judicial review?

3. Marshall wrote that the question "whether an act repugnant to the Constitution, can become the law of the land, is a question deeply interesting to the United States, but, happily, not of an intricacy proportioned to its interests." Do you agree? Consider the response by Alexander M. Bickel: "Marshall's confidence . . . is understandable, since he had already begged the question-in-chief, which was not whether an act repugnant to the Constitution could stand, but who should be empowered to decide that the act is repugnant." See *The Least Dangerous Branch: The Supreme Court at the Bar of Politics* (Indianapolis: Bobbs-Merrill Educational Publishing, 1962), 3.

4. How would our system of government differ if the Supreme Court could not declare actions of Congress or the executive unconstitutional? Could individual freedom and limited government be sustained under such a system? Or do you agree with the idea expressed by Justice Oliver Wendell Holmes at the beginning of this century: "I do not think the United States would come to an end if we lost our power to declare an Act of Congress void"? Is there any support in the text or structure of the Constitution for Holmes's view?

5. Does Marshall's opinion establish the judiciary as an equal branch of the federal government, or does it ultimately establish a groundwork for a system of judicial supremacy over all other branches of government?

6. Marshall's argument for judicial review was not accepted by all. In *Eakin v. Raub*, an 1825 case before the Pennsylvania Supreme Court, Justice John Gibson argued that the judiciary should not have the power to rule that acts of coordinate branches of government are unconstitutional. His opinion directly attacked Marshall's reasoning in *Marbury*. It stated, in part: "The constitution is said to be a law of superior obligation; and consequently, that if it were to come into collision with an act of the legislature, the latter would have to give way; that is conceded. But it is a fallacy, to suppose, that they can come into collision before the judiciary. . . . It is by no means clear, that to declare a law void, which has been enacted according to the forms prescribed in the constitution, is not a usurpation of legislative power. . . . It is the business of the judiciary to interpret the laws, not scan the authority of the law-giver; . . . I am of the opinion that it rests with the people, in whom full and absolute sovereign power resides, to correct abuses in legislation, by instructing their representatives to repeal the obnoxious act, [for] it is a postulate in the theory of our government, and the very basis of the super-structure, that the people are wise, virtuous, and competent to manage their own affairs: and if they are not so, in fact, still, every question of this sort must be determined according to the principles of the constitution, as it came from the hands of its framers, and the existence of a defect which was not foreseen, would not justify those who administer the government, in applying a corrective in practice, which can be provided only by a convention. . . ."

7. In what way does Gibson's conception of the people's will differ from Marshall's? Is one of these views more democratic than the other? Is one of them more consistent with constitutional government?

8. As indicated in Comparative Note 3.1, the Canadian Constitution empowers the Supreme Court to strike down legislative acts, but it includes an "override" clause [Sec. 33 [1]] that establishes parliament's supremacy. Assuming that the legislature—state or federal—would invoke the override clause sparingly, do you think it is a good way of resolving the tension between constitutionalism and democracy? Or is Canada's override the very antithesis of constitutionalism?

9. Comparative Note 3.1 also includes the text of Article 39 of South Africa's Constitution. Would you favor adding a similar provision to the U.S. Constitution?

10. For additional reading on *Marbury* and other opinions of Chief Justice Marshall, see Robert F. Faulkner, *The Jurisprudence of John Marshall* [Westport, Conn.: Greenwood Press, 1968]. For a general biography of Marshall, see Albert J. Beveridge, *The Life of John Marshall*, 4 Vols. [New York: Houghton Mifflin, 1916].

Cohens v. Virginia

19 U.S. 264, 6 Wheat. 264, 5 L. Ed. 257 (1821)

In 1802 Congress passed a law authorizing the District of Columbia to conduct lotteries for the purpose of raising money for improvements in the city of Washington. Accordingly, the city passed an ordinance permitting the lottery. The state of Virginia, however, had a law prohibiting the sale of lottery tickets. The Cohens were arrested in Norfolk, Virginia, for selling Washington lottery tickets. The local court found them guilty and imposed a fine of $100. The Cohens claimed that they were protected under the act of Congress. A principal question in this case was whether the Supreme Court's appellate jurisdiction extends to a case commenced and adjudicated in a state court. Opinion of the Court: *Marshall*, Duvall, Johnson, Livingston, Story, Todd. Not participating: Washington.

Mr. Chief Justice MARSHALL delivered the opinion of the Court.

1st. The first question to be considered is, whether the jurisdiction of this Court is excluded by the character of the parties, one of them being a State, and the other a citizen of that State?

[Recall from our discussion in the introductory essay to this chapter that the Eleventh Amendment, adopted in response to *Chisholm v. Georgia*, excluded from the judicial power of the United States "any suit . . . commenced or prosecuted against one of the United States by Citizens of another State." Virginia maintained the Eleventh Amendment prevents the U.S. Supreme Court from hearing the Cohens' appeal. Section 25 of the Judiciary Act of 1789, however, extended the Supreme Court's appellate jurisdiction to any final judgment of a state court which upholds a state law against a claim based on a federal statute or treaty.]

The second section of the third article of the constitution defines the extent of the judicial power of the United States. Jurisdiction is given to the Courts of the Union in two classes of cases. In the first, their jurisdiction depends on the character of the cause, whoever may be the parties. This class comprehends "all cases in law and equity arising under this constitution, the laws of the United States, and treaties made, or which shall be made, under their authority." This clause extends the jurisdiction of the Court to all the cases described, without making in its terms any exception whatever, and without any regard to the condition of the party. If there be any exception, it is to be implied against the express words of the article.

In the second class, the jurisdiction depends entirely the character of the parties. In this are comprehended "controversies between two or more States, between a State and citizens of another State, and between a State foreign States, citizens or subjects." If these be the par, it is entirely unimportant what may be the subject oftroversy. Be it what it may, these parties have a constitutional right to come into the Courts of the Union.

The jurisdiction of the Court, then, being extended by the letter of the constitution to all cases arising under it, or under the laws of the United States, it follows that those who would withdraw any case of this description from that jurisdiction, must sustain the exemption they claim on the spirit and true meaning of the constitution, which spirit and true meaning must be so apparent as to overrule the words which its framers have employed.

The counsel for the defendant have undertaken to do this; and have laid down the general proposition, that a sovereign independent State is not suable, except by its own consent.

This general proposition will not be controverted. But its consent is not requisite in each particular case. It may be given in a general law. And if a State has surrendered any portion of its sovereignty, the question whether a liability to suit be a part of this portion, depends on the instrument by which the surrender is made. If, upon a just construction of that instrument, it shall appear that the State has submitted to be sued, then it has parted with this sovereign right of judging in every case on the justice of its own pretensions, and has entrusted that power to a tribunal in whose impartiality it confides.

The American States, as well as the American people, have believed a close and firm Union to be essential to their liberty and to their happiness. They have been taught by experience, that this Union cannot exist without a government for the whole; and they have been taught by the same experience that this government would be a mere shadow, that must disappoint all their hopes, unless invested with large portions of that sovereignty which belongs to independent States. Under the influence of this opinion, and thus instructed by experience, the American people, in the conventions of their respective States, adopted the present constitution.

If it could be doubted, whether from its nature, it were not supreme in all cases where it is empowered to act, that doubt would be removed by the declaration, that "this constitution, and the laws of the United States, which shall be made in pursuance thereof, and all treaties made, or which shall be made, under the authority of the United States, shall be the supreme law of the land; and the judges in every State shall be bound thereby; any thing in the constitution or laws of any State to the contrary notwithstanding."

This is the authoritative language of the American people; and, if gentlemen please, of the American States. It marks, with lines too strong to be mistaken, the characteristic distinction between the government of the Union, and those of the States. The general government, though limited as to its objects, is supreme with respect to those objects. This principle is a part of the constitution; and if there be any who deny its necessity, none can deny its authority.

To this supreme government ample powers are confided; and if it were possible to doubt the great purposes for which they were so confided, the people of the United States have declared, that they are given "in order to form a more perfect union, establish justice, ensure domestic tranquillity, provide for the common defence, promote the general welfare, and secure the blessings of liberty to themselves and their posterity."

With the ample powers confided to this supreme government, for these interesting purposes, are connected many express and important limitations on the sovereignty of the States, which are made for the same purposes. The powers of the Union, on the great subjects of war, peace, and commerce, and on many others, are in themselves limitations of the sovereignty of the States; but in addition to these, the sovereignty of the States is surrendered in many instances where the surrender can only operate to the benefit of the people, and where, perhaps, no other power is conferred on Congress than a conservative power to maintain the principles established in the constitution. The maintenance of these principles in their purity, is certainly among the great duties of the government. One of the instruments by which this duty may be peaceably performed, is the judicial department. It is authorized to decide all cases of every description, arising under the constitution or laws of the United States. From this general grant of jurisdiction, no exception is made of those cases in which a State may be a party. When we consider the situation of the government of the Union and of a State, in relation to each other; the nature of our constitution; the subordination of the State governments to that constitution; the great purpose for which jurisdiction over all cases arising under the constitution and laws of the United States, is confided to the judicial department; are we at liberty to insert in this general grant, an exception of those cases in which a State may be a party? Will the spirit of the constitution justify this attempt to control its words? We think it will not. We think a case arising under the constitution or laws of the United States, is cognizable in the Courts of the Union, whoever may be the parties to that case.

. . . The constitution gave to every person having a claim upon a State, a right to submit his case to the Court of the nation. However unimportant his claim might be, however little the community might be interested in its decision, the framers of our constitution thought it necessary for the purposes of justice, to provide a tribunal as superior to influence as possible, in which that claim might be decided. Can it be imagined, that the same persons considered a case involving the constitution of our country and the majesty of the laws, questions in which every American citizen must be deeply interested, as withdrawn from this tribunal, because a State is a party?

The mischievous consequences of the construction contended for on the part of Virginia, are also entitled to great consideration. It would prostrate, it has been said, the government and its laws at the feet of every State in the Union. And would not this be its effect? What power of the government could be executed by its own means, in any State disposed to resist its execution by a course of legislation? The laws must be executed by individuals acting within the several States. If these individuals may be exposed to penalties, and if the Courts of the Union cannot correct the judgments by which these penalties may be enforced, the course of the government may be, at any time, arrested by the will of one of its members. Each member will possess a veto on the will of the whole.

The answer which has been given to this argument, does not deny its truth, but insists that confidence is reposed, and may be safely reposed, in the State institutions; and that, if they shall ever become so insane or so wicked as to seek the destruction of the government, they may accomplish their object by refusing to perform the functions assigned to them.

But a constitution is framed for ages to come, and is designed to approach immortality as nearly as human institutions can approach it. Its course cannot always be tranquil. It is exposed to storms and tempests, and its framers must be unwise statesmen indeed, if they have not provided it, as far as its nature will permit, with the means of self-preservation from the perils it may be destined to encounter. No government ought to be so defective in its organization, as not to contain within itself the means of securing the execution of its own laws against other dangers than those which occur every day. Courts of justice are the means most usually employed; and it is reasonable to expect that a government should repose on its own Courts, rather than on others. There is certainly nothing in the circumstances under which our constitution was formed; nothing in the history of the times, which would justify the opinion that the confidence reposed in the States was so

implicit as to leave in them and their tribunals the power of resisting or defeating, in the form of law, the legitimate measures of the Union.

It has been also urged, as an additional objection to the jurisdiction of the Court, that cases between a State and one of its own citizens, do not come within the general scope of the constitution; and were obviously never intended to be made cognizable in the federal Courts.

This is very true, so far as jurisdiction depends on the character of the parties; and the argument would have great force if urged to prove that this Court could not establish the demand of a citizen upon his State, but is not entitled to the same force when urged to prove that this Court cannot inquire whether the constitution or laws of the United States protect a citizen from a prosecution instituted against him by a State. If jurisdiction depended entirely on the character of the parties, and was not given where the parties have not an original right to come into Court, that part of the 2d section of the 3d article, which extends the judicial power to all cases arising under the constitution and laws of the United States, would be mere surplusage. It is to give jurisdiction where the character of the parties would not give it, that this very important part of the clause was inserted. It may be true, that the partiality of the State tribunals, in ordinary controversies between a State and its citizens, was not apprehended, and therefore the judicial power of the Union was not extended to such cases; but this was not the sole nor the greatest object for which this department was created. A more important, a much more interesting object, was the preservation of the constitution and laws of the United States, so far as they can be preserved by judicial authority; and therefore the jurisdiction of the Courts of the Union was expressly extended to all cases arising under that constitution and those laws. If the constitution or laws may be violated by proceedings instituted by a State against its own citizens, and if that violation may be such as essentially to affect the constitution and the laws, such as to arrest the progress of government in its constitutional course, why should these cases be excepted from that provision which expressly extends the judicial power of the Union to all cases arising under the constitution and laws?

After bestowing on this subject the most attentive consideration, the Court can perceive no reason founded on the character of the parties for introducing an exception which the constitution has not made; and we think that the judicial power, as originally given, extends to all cases arising under the constitution or a law of the United States, whoever may be the parties.

It is most true that this Court will not take jurisdiction if it should not: but it is equally true, that it must take jurisdiction if it should. The judiciary cannot, as the legislature may, avoid a measure because it approaches the confines of the constitution. We cannot pass it by because it is doubtful. With whatever doubts, with whatever difficulties, a case may be attended, we must decide it, if it be brought before us. We have no more right to decline the exercise of jurisdiction which is given, than to usurp that which is not given. The one or the other would be treason to the constitution. Questions may occur which we would gladly avoid; but we cannot avoid them. All we can do is, to exercise our best judgment, and conscientiously to perform our duty. In doing this, on the present occasion, we find this tribunal invested with appellate jurisdiction in all cases arising under the constitution and laws of the United States. We find no exception to this grant, and we cannot insert one.

2d. The second objection to the jurisdiction of the Court is, that its appellate power cannot be exercised, in any case, over the judgment of a State Court.

This objection is sustained chiefly by arguments drawn from the supposed total separation of the judiciary of a State from that of the Union, and their entire independence of each other. The argument considers the federal judiciary as completely foreign to that of a State; and as being no more connected with it in any respect whatever, than the Court of a foreign State. If this hypothesis be just, the argument founded on it is equally so; but if the hypothesis be not supported by the constitution, the argument fails with it.

This hypothesis is not founded on any words in the constitution, which might seem to countenance it, but on the unreasonableness of giving a contrary construction to words which seem to require it; and on the incompatibility of the application of the appellate jurisdiction to the judgments of State Courts, with that constitutional relation which subsists between the government of the Union and the governments of those States which compose it.

Let this unreasonableness, this total incompatibility, be examined.

That the United States form, for many, and for most important purposes, a single nation, has not yet been denied. In war, we are one people. In making peace, we are one people. In all commercial regulations, we are one and the same people. In many other respects, the American people are one; and the government which is alone capable of controlling and managing their interests in all these respects, is the government of the Union. It is their government, and in that character they have no other. America has chosen to be, in many respects, and to many purposes, a nation; and for all these purposes, her government is complete; to all these objects, it is competent. The people have declared, that in the exercise of all powers given for these objects, it is supreme. It can, then, in effecting these objects, legitimately control all individuals or governments within the American territory. The constitution and laws of a State, so far as they are repugnant to the constitution and laws of the United States, are absolutely void. These States are constituent parts of the United States. They are members of one great empire—for some purposes sovereign, for some purposes subordinate.

In a government so constituted, is it unreasonable that the judicial power should be competent to give efficacy to the constitutional laws of the legislature? That department can decide on the validity of the constitution or law of a State, if it be repugnant to the constitution or to a law of

---

Comparative Note 3.2

It is clear that the meaning of "unreasonable" cannot be determined by recourse to a dictionary, nor for that matter, by reference to the rules of statutory construction. The task of expounding a Constitution is crucially different from that of construing a statute. A statute defines present rights and obligations. It is easily enacted and as easily repealed. A Constitution, by contrast, is drafted with an eye to the future. Its function is to provide a continuing framework for the legitimate exercise of governmental power and, when joined by a Bill or a Charter of Rights, for the unremitting protection of individual rights and liberties. Once enacted, its provisions cannot easily be repealed or amended. It must, therefore, be capable of growth and development over time to meet new social, political and historical realities often unimagined by its framers. The Judiciary is the guardian of the Constitution and must, in interpreting its provisions, bear these considerations in mind. Professor Paul Freund expressed this idea aptly when he admonished the American courts "not to read the provisions of the Constitution like a last will and testament lest it become one."

SOURCE: *Hunter v. Southam*. In the Supreme Court of Canada [1984] 2 S.C.R. 145.

the United States. Is it unreasonable that it should also be empowered to decide on the judgment of a State tribunal enforcing such unconstitutional law? Is it so very unreasonable as to furnish a justification for controlling the words of the constitution?

We think it is not. We think that in a government acknowledgedly supreme, with respect to objects of vital interest to the nation, there is nothing inconsistent with sound reason, nothing incompatible with the nature of government, in making all its departments supreme, so far as respects those objects, and so far as is necessary to their attainment. The exercise of the appellate power over those judgments of the State tribunals which may contravene the constitution or laws of the United States, is, we believe, essential to the attainment of those objects.

The propriety of entrusting the construction of the constitution, and laws made in pursuance thereof, to the judiciary of the Union, has not, we believe, as yet, been drawn into question. It seems to be a corollary from this political axiom, that the federal Courts should either possess exclusive jurisdiction in such cases, or a power to revise the judgment rendered in them, by the State tribunals. If the federal and State Courts have concurrent jurisdiction in all cases arising under the constitution, laws, and treaties of the United States; and if a case of this description brought in a State Court cannot be removed before judgment, nor revised after judgment, then the construction of the constitution, laws, and treaties of the United States, is not confided particularly to their judicial department, but is confided equally to that department and to the State Courts, however they may be constituted. "Thirteen independent Courts," says a very celebrated statesman (and we have now more than twenty such Courts), "of final jurisdiction over the same causes, arising upon the same laws, is a hydra in government, from which nothing but contradiction and confusion can proceed."

Dismissing the unpleasant suggestion, that any motives which may not be fairly avowed, or which ought not to exist, can ever influence a State or its Courts, the necessity of uniformity, as well as correctness in expounding the constitution and laws of the United States, would itself suggest the propriety of vesting in some single tribunal the power of deciding, in the last resort, all cases in which they are involved.

We are not restrained, then, by the political relations between the general and State governments, from construing the words of the constitution, defining the judicial power, in their true sense. We are not bound to construe them more restrictively than they naturally import.

They give to the Supreme Court appellate jurisdiction in all cases arising under the constitution, laws, and treaties of the United States. The words are broad enough to comprehend all cases of this description, in whatever Court they may be decided. In expounding them, we may be permitted to take into view those considerations to which Courts have always allowed great weight in the exposition of laws. . . .

. . . Let the nature and objects of our Union be considered; let the great fundamental principles, on which the fabric stands, be examined; and we think the result must be, that there is nothing so extravagantly absurd in giving to the Court of the nation the power of revising the decisions of local tribunals on questions which affect the nation, as to require that words which import this power should be restricted by a forced construction. . . .

Motion denied.

Notes/Queries/Readings

1. On what grounds does Chief Justice Marshall justify federal judicial review of actions taken by state courts?

2. What vision of federalism is articulated in this decision, and how does it follow from Marshall's understanding of the Constitution and of the nation as a whole? What conception of the American Union—and the ratification of the Constitution—does Marshall advance in this opinion? How does he argue that "we are all one people"? Is the argument consistent with the account he presented in *Marbury*?

3. How does Marshall envision the Constitution? Does he consider the Constitution as the means to a just government or as an end in itself? Does his argument lose some of its force in the fact that this case occurred more than thirty years after the ratification of the Constitution, and that most people living at the time could not have been said to have given their consent to it?

4. How convincing is his argument? How does it derive from—or differ from—the reasoning justifying judicial review in *Marbury*? How does the result in this case expand the power and reach of the judiciary?

5. How does the state of Virginia understand the limits of national power and the federal courts? What would be the consequence upon our system of government if Virginia's argument about state supremacy had been adopted?

6. In *Cohens*, Marshall rules that the Constitution required that state court rulings be subject to review by federal courts. Does it follow from his reasoning that state governments should be subject to the same limits as the federal government? For example, should actions of state governments conform to the Bill of Rights, just as actions of the federal government must? To see how Marshall decided this question, see *Barron v. Baltimore* (chapter 8).

Dred Scott v. Sandford

60 U.S. 393, 19 How. 393, 15 L. Ed. 691 (1857)

Dred Scott, a slave, belonged to Dr. Emerson, a U.S. Army surgeon stationed in Missouri. In 1834 Emerson was transferred to Rock Island, Illinois, a state that forbade slavery, yet he took Scott with him. Later, Emerson was transferred to Fort Snelling in what is now Minnesota, a free territory under the Missouri Compromise of 1820, and he again took Scott with him. Emerson and Scott returned to Missouri in 1838. In 1846, Dred Scott sued for his freedom in a Missouri state court because he was brought into and had resided in a free territory. Scott won the initial case, but the Missouri Supreme Court reversed the judgment. Unsatisfied, abolitionists arranged a fictitious sale of Scott to John Sandford, a resident of New York and a relative of Emerson, so that the Federal Circuit Court could assert jurisdiction because of diversity of state citizenship. The Circuit Court ruled against Scott, and the decision was appealed to the Supreme Court on a writ of error. Opinion of the Court: *Taney*, Campbell, Catron, Grier, Nelson, Wayne. Concurring opinions: *Campbell, Catron, Grier, Nelson, Wayne*. Dissenting opinions: *Curtis, McLean*.

Mr. Chief Justice TANEY delivered the opinion of the Court.

The question is simply this: Can a negro, whose ancestors were imported into this country, and sold as slaves, become a member of the political community formed and brought into existence by the Constitution of the United States, and as such become entitled to all the rights, and privileges, and immunities, guaranteed by that instrument to the citizen? One of which rights is the privilege of suing in a court of the United States in the cases specified in the Constitution.

It will be observed, that the plea applies to that class of persons only whose ancestors were negroes of the African race, and imported into this country, and sold and held as slaves. The only matter in issue before the court, therefore, is, whether the descendants of such slaves, when they shall be emancipated, or who are born of parents who had become free before their birth, are citizens of a State, in the sense in which the word citizen is used in the Constitution of the United States. And this being the only matter in dispute on the pleadings, the court must be understood as speaking in this opinion of that class only, that is, of those persons who are the descendants of Africans who were imported into this country, and sold as slaves. . . .

The words "people of the United States" and "citizens" are synonymous terms, and mean the same thing. They both describe the political body who, according to our republican institutions, form the sovereignty, and who hold the power and conduct the Government through their representatives. They are what we familiarly call the "sovereign people," and every citizen is one of this people, and a constituent member of this sovereignty. The question before us is, whether the class of persons described in the plea in abatement compose a portion of this people, and are constituent members of this sovereignty? We think they are not, and that they are not included, and were not intended to be included, under the word "citizens" in the Constitution, and can therefore claim none of the rights and privileges which that instrument provides for and secures to citizens of the United States. On the contrary, they were at that time considered as a subordinate and inferior class of beings, who had been subjugated by the dominant race, and, whether emancipated or not, yet remained subject to their authority, and had no rights or privileges but such as those who held the power and the Government might choose to grant them.

It is not the province of the court to decide upon the justice or injustice, the policy or impolicy, of these laws. The decision of that question belonged to the political or law-making power; to those who formed the sovereignty and framed the Constitution. The duty of the court is, to interpret the instrument they have framed, with the best lights we can obtain on the subject, and to administer it as we find it, according to its true intent and meaning when it was adopted.

In discussing this question, we must not confound the rights of citizenship which a State may confer within its own limits, and the rights of citizenship as a member of the Union. It does not by any means follow, because he has all the rights and privileges of a citizen of a State, that he must be a citizen of the United States. He may have all of the rights and privileges of the citizen of a State, and yet not be entitled to the rights and privileges of a citizen in any other State. For, previous to the adoption of the Constitution of the United States, every State had the undoubted right to confer on whomsoever it pleased the character of citizen, and to endow him with all its rights. But this character of course was confined to the boundaries of the State, and gave him no rights or privileges in other States beyond those secured to him by the laws of nations and the comity of States. Nor have the several States surrendered the power of conferring these rights and privileges by adopting the Constitution of the United States. Each State may still confer them upon an alien, or any one it thinks proper, or upon any class or description of persons; yet he would not be a citizen in the sense in which that word is used in the Constitution of the United States, nor entitled to sue as such in one of its courts, nor to the privileges and immunities of a citizen in the other States. The rights which he would acquire would be restricted to the State which gave them. The Constitution has conferred on Congress the right to establish an uniform rule of naturalization, and this right is evidently exclusive, and has always been held by this court to be so. Consequently, no State, since the adoption of the Constitution, can by naturalizing an alien invest him with the rights and privileges secured to a citizen of a State under the Federal Government, although, so far as the State alone was concerned, he would undoubtedly be entitled to the rights of a citizen, and clothed with all the rights and immunities which the Constitution and laws of the State attached to that character.

It is very clear, therefore, that no State can, by any act or law of its own, passed since the adoption of the Constitution, introduce a new member into the political community created by the Constitution of the United States. It cannot make him a member of this community by making him a member of its own. And for the same reason it cannot introduce any person, or description of persons, who were not intended to be embraced in this new political family, which the Constitution brought into existence, but were intended to be excluded from it.

The question then arises, whether the provisions of the Constitution, in relation to the personal rights and privileges to which the citizen of a State should be entitled, embraced the negro African race, at that time in this country, or who might afterwards be imported, who had then or should afterwards be made free in any State; and to put it in the power of a single State to make him a citizen of the United States, and endow him with the full rights of citizenship in every other State without their consent? Does the Constitution of the United States act upon him whenever he shall be made free under the laws of a State, and raised there to the rank of a citizen, and immediately clothe him with all the privileges of a citizen in every other State, and in its own courts?

The court thinks the affirmative of these propositions cannot be maintained. And if it cannot, the plaintiff could not be a citizen of the State of Missouri, within the meaning of the Constitution of the United States, and, consequently, was not entitled to sue in its courts.

It is true, every person, and every class and description of persons, who were at the time of the adoption of the Constitution recognised as citizens in the several States, became also citizens of this new political body; but none other; it was formed by them, and for them and their posterity, but for no one else. And the personal rights and privileges guaranteed to citizens of this new sovereignty were intended to embrace those only who were then members of the several State communities, or who should afterwards by birthright or otherwise become members, according to the provisions of the Constitution and the principles on which it was founded. It was the union of those who were at that time members of distinct and separate political communities into one political family, whose power, for certain specified purposes, was to extend over the whole territory of the United States. And it gave to each citizen rights and privileges outside of his State which he did not before possess, and placed him in every other State upon a perfect equality with its own citizens as to rights of person and rights of property; it made him a citizen of the United States.

It becomes necessary, therefore, to determine who were citizens of the several States when the Constitution was adopted.

The legislation of the States therefore shows, in a manner not to be mistaken, the inferior and subject condition

---

Comparative Note 3.3

An individual constitutional provision cannot be considered as an isolated clause and interpreted alone. A constitution has an inner unity, and the meaning of any one part is linked to that of other provisions. Taken as a unit, a constitution reflects certain overarching principles and fundamental decisions to which individual provisions are subordinate. . . . [It is therefore the case] that a constitutional provision itself may be null and void [even though] it is part of the constitution itself.

There are constitutional principles that are so fundamental. . . . that they even bind the framers of the constitution, and other constitutional provisions that do not rank as high may be null and void because they contravene these principles. From this rule of interpretation it follows that any constitutional provision must be interpreted in such a way that it is compatible with those elementary principles and with the basic values of the framers of the constitution.

SOURCE: *The Southwest State Case* (1951), Federal Constitutional Court, in Donald P. Kommers, *The Constitutional Jurisprudence of the Federal Republic of Germany*, 2d ed. (Durham, N.C.: Duke University Press, 1997), 63. (Hereinafter *Constitutional Jurisprudence.*)

of that race at the time the Constitution was adopted, and long afterwards, throughout the thirteen States by which that instrument was framed; and it is hardly consistent with the respect due to these States, to suppose that they regarded at that time, as fellow-citizens and members of the sovereignty, a class of beings whom they had thus stigmatized; whom, as we are bound, out of respect to the State sovereignties, to assume they had deemed it just and necessary thus to stigmatize, and upon whom they had impressed such deep and enduring marks of inferiority and degradation; or, that when they met in convention to form the Constitution, they looked upon them as a portion of their constituents, or designed to include them in the provisions so carefully inserted for the security and protection of the liberties and rights of their citizens. It cannot be supposed that they intended to secure to them rights, and privileges, and rank, in the new political body throughout the Union, which every one of them denied within the limits of its own dominion. More especially, it cannot be believed that the large slaveholding States regarded them as included in the word citizens, or would have consented to a Constitution which might compel them to receive them in that character from another State. For if they were so received, and entitled to the privileges and immunities of citizens, it would exempt them from the operation of the special laws and from the police regulations which they considered to be necessary for their own safety. It would give to persons of the negro race, who were recognised as citizens in any one State of the Union, the right to enter every other State whenever they pleased, singly or in companies, without pass or passport, and without obstruction, to sojourn there as long as they pleased, to go where they pleased at every hour of the day or night without molestation, unless they committed some violation of law for which a white man would be punished; and it would give them the full liberty of speech in public and in private upon all subjects upon which its own citizens might speak; to hold public meetings upon political affairs, and to keep and carry arms wherever they went. And all of this would be done in the face of the subject race of the same color, both free and slaves, and inevitably producing discontent and insubordination among them, and endangering the peace and safety of the State. . . .

Undoubtedly, a person may be a citizen, that is, a member of the community who form the sovereignty, although he exercises no share of the political power, and is incapacitated from holding particular offices. Women and minors, who form a part of the political family, cannot vote; and when a property qualification is required to vote or hold a particular office, those who have not the necessary qualification cannot vote or hold the office, yet they are citizens.

So, too, a person may be entitled to vote by the law of the State, who is not a citizen even of the State itself. And in some of the States of the Union foreigners not naturalized are allowed to vote. And the State may give the right to free negroes and mulattoes, but that does not make them citizens of the State, and still less of the United States. And the provision in the Constitution giving privileges and immunities in other States, does not apply to them.

Neither does it apply to a person who, being the citizen of a State, migrates to another State. For then he becomes subject to the laws of the State in which he lives, and he is no longer a citizen of the State from which he removed. And the State in which he resides may then, unquestionably, determine his status or condition, and place him among the class of persons who are not recognised as citizens, but belong to an inferior and subject race; and may deny him the privileges and immunities enjoyed by its citizens.

No one, we presume, supposes that any change in public opinion or feeling, in relation to this unfortunate race, in the civilized nations of Europe or in this country, should induce the court to give to the words of the Constitution a more liberal construction in their favor than they were intended to bear when the instrument was framed and adopted. Such an argument would be altogether inadmissible in any tribunal called on to interpret it. If any of its provisions are deemed unjust, there is a mode prescribed in the instrument itself by which it may be amended; but while it remains unaltered, it must be construed now as it was understood at the time of its adoption. It is not only the same in words, but the same in meaning, and delegates the same powers to the Government, and reserves and secures the same rights and privileges to the citizen; and as long as it continues to exist in its present form, it speaks not only in the same words, but with the same meaning and intent with which it spoke when it came from the hands of its framers, and was voted on and adopted by the people of the United States. Any other rule of construction would abrogate the judicial character of this court, and make it the mere reflex of the popular opinion or passion of the day. This court was not created by the Constitution for such purposes. Higher and graver trusts have been confided to it, and it must not falter in the path of duty.

What the construction was at that time, we think can hardly admit of doubt. We have the language of the Declaration of Independence and of the Articles of Confederation, in addition to the plain words of the Constitution itself; we have the legislation of the different States, before, about the time, and since, the Constitution was adopted; we have the legislation of Congress, from the time of its adoption to a recent period; and we have the constant and uniform action of the Executive Department, all concurring together, and leading to the same result. And if anything in relation to the construction of the Constitution can be regarded as settled, it is that which we now give to the word "citizen" and the word "people."

And upon a full and careful consideration of the subject, the court is of opinion, that . . . Dred Scott was not a citizen of Missouri within the meaning of the Constitution of the United States, and not entitled as such to sue in its courts; and, consequently, that the Circuit Court had no jurisdiction of the case . . .

We proceed, therefore, to inquire whether the facts relied on by the plaintiff entitled him to his freedom.

In considering this part of the controversy, two questions arise: 1. Was he, together with his family, free in Missouri by reason of the stay in the territory of the United States . . . ? And 2. If they were not, is Scott himself free by reason of his removal to Rock Island, in the State of Illinois . . . ?

We proceed to examine the first question.

The act of Congress, upon which the plaintiff relies, declares that slavery and involuntary servitude, except as a punishment for crime, shall be forever prohibited in all that part of the territory ceded by France, under the name of Louisiana, which lies north of thirty-six degrees thirty minutes north latitude, and not included within the limits of Missouri. And the difficulty which meets us at the threshold of this part of the inquiry is, whether Congress was authorized to pass this law under any of the powers granted to it by the Constitution; for if the authority is not given by that instrument, it is the duty of this court to declare it void and inoperative, and incapable of conferring freedom upon any one who is held as a slave under the laws of any one of the States.

The counsel for the plaintiff has laid much stress upon that article in the Constitution which confers on Congress the power "to dispose of and make all needful rules and regulations respecting the territory or other property belonging to the United States"; but, in the judgment of the court, that provision has no bearing on the present controversy, and the power there given, whatever it may be, is confined, and was intended to be confined, to the territory which at that time belonged to, or was claimed by, the United States, and was within their boundaries as settled by the treaty with Great Britain, and can have no influence upon a territory afterwards acquired from a foreign Government. It was a special provision for a known and particular territory, and to meet a present emergency, and nothing more. . . .

This brings us to examine by what provision of the Constitution the present Federal Government, under its delegated and restricted powers, is authorized to acquire territory outside of the original limits of the United States, and what powers it may exercise therein over the person or property of a citizen of the United States, while it remains a Territory, and until it shall be admitted as one of the States of the Union.

There is certainly no power given by the Constitution to the Federal Government to establish or maintain colonies bordering on the United States or at a distance, to be ruled and governed at its own pleasure; nor to enlarge its territorial limits in any way, except by the admission of new States. That power is plainly given; and if a new State is admitted, it needs no further legislation by Congress, because the Constitution itself defines the relative rights and powers, and duties of the State, and the citizens of the State, and the Federal Government. But no power is given to acquire a Territory to be held and governed permanently in that character.

. . . [T]he government and the citizen both enter [the territory] under the authority of the Consitution, with their respective rights defined and marked out; and the Federal Government can exercise no power over his person or property, beyond what that instrument confers, nor lawfully deny any right which it has reserved.

Upon these considerations, it is the opinion of the court that the act of Congress which prohibited a citizen from holding and owning property of this kind in the territory of the United States north of the line therein mentioned, is not warranted by the Constitution, and is therefore void; and that neither Dred Scott himself, nor any of his family, were made free by being carried into this territory; even if they had been carried there by the owner, with the intention of becoming a permanent resident.

But there is another point in the case which depends on State power and State law. And it is contended, on the part of the plaintiff, that he is made free by being taken to Rock Island, in the State of Illinois, independently of his residence in the territory of the United States; and being so made free, he was not again reduced to a state of slavery by being brought back to Missouri.

Our notice of this part of the case will be very brief; for the principle on which it depends was decided in this court, upon much consideration, in the case of *Strader et al. v. Graham* [1880]. In that case, the slaves had been taken from Kentucky to Ohio, with the consent of the owner, and afterwards brought back to Kentucky. And this court held that their status or condition, as free or slave, depended upon the laws of Kentucky, when they were brought back into that State, and not of Ohio; and that this court had no jurisdiction to revise the judgment of a State court upon its own laws. This was the point directly before the court, and the decision that this court had not jurisdiction turned upon it, as will be seen by the report of the case.

So in this case. As Scott was a slave when taken into the State of Illinois by his owner, and was there held as such, and brought back in that character, his status, as free or slave, depended on the laws of Missouri, and not of Illinois.

Upon the whole, therefore, it is the judgment of this court, that it appears by the record before us that the plaintiff is not a citizen of Missouri, in the sense in which that word is used in the Constitution; and that the Circuit Court of the United States, for that reason, had no jurisdiction in the case, and could give no judgment in it. Its judgment for the defendant must, consequently, be reversed, and a mandate issued, directing the suit to be dismissed for want of jurisdiction.

Mr. Justice CURTIS dissenting.

I dissent from the opinion pronounced by the Chief Justice, and from the judgment which the majority of the court think it proper to render in this case.

To determine whether any free persons, descended from Africans held in slavery, were citizens of the United States under the Confederation, and consequently at the time of the adoption of the Constitution of the United States, it is only necessary to know whether any such persons were citizens of either of the States under the Confederation, at the time of the adoption of the Constitution.

Of this there can be no doubt. At the time of the ratification of the Articles of Confederation, all free native-born inhabitants of the States of New Hampshire, Massachusetts, New York, New Jersey, and North Carolina, though descended from African slaves, were not only citizens of those States, but such of them as had the other necessary qualifications possessed the franchise of electors, on equal terms with other citizens.

The fourth of the fundamental articles of the Confederation was as follows: "The free inhabitants of each of these States, paupers, vagabonds, and fugitives from justice, excepted, shall be entitled to all the privileges and immunities of free citizens in the several States."

The fact that free persons of color were citizens of some of the several States, and the consequence, that this fourth article of the Confederation would have the effect to confer on such persons the privileges and immunities of general citizenship, were not only known to those who framed and adopted those articles, but the evidence is decisive, that the fourth article was intended to have that effect, and that more restricted language, which would have excluded such persons, was deliberately and purposely rejected.

On the 25th of June, 1778, the Articles of Confederation being under consideration by the Congress, the delegates from South Carolina moved to amend this fourth article, by inserting after the word "free," and before the word "in-habitants," the word "white," so that the privileges and immunities of general citizenship would be secured only to white persons. Two States voted for the amendment, eight States against it, and the vote of one State was divided.

Did the Constitution of the United States deprive them or their descendants of citizenship?

That Constitution was ordained and established by the people of the United States, through the action, in each State, of those persons who were qualified by its laws to act thereon, in behalf of themselves and all other citizens of that State. In some of the States, as we have seen, colored persons were among those qualified by law to act on this subject. These colored persons were not only included in the body of "the people of the United States," by whom the Constitution was ordained and established, but in at least five of the States they had the power to act, and doubtless did act, by their suffrages, upon the question of its adoption. It would be strange, if we were to find in that instrument anything which deprived of their citizenship any part of the people of the United States who were among those by whom it was established.

I can find nothing in the Constitution which, *proprio vigore*, deprives of their citizenship any class of persons who were citizens of the United States at the time of its adoption, or who should be native-born citizens of any State after its adoption; nor any power enabling Congress to disfranchise persons born on the soil of any State, and entitled to citizenship of such State by its Constitution and laws. And my opinion is, that, under the Constitution of the United States, every free person born on the soil of a State, who is a citizen of that State by force of its Constitution or laws, is also a citizen of the United States.

I dissent, therefore, from that part of the opinion of the majority of the court, in which it is held that a person of African descent cannot be a citizen of the United States; and I regret I must go further, and dissent both from what I deem their assumption of authority to examine the constitutionality of the act of Congress commonly called the Missouri compromise act, and the grounds and conclusions announced in their opinion.

Having first decided that they were bound to consider the sufficiency of the plea to the jurisdiction of the Circuit Court, and having decided that this plea showed that the Circuit Court had not jurisdiction, and consequently that this is a case to which the judicial power of the United States does not extend, they have gone on to examine the merits of the case as they appeared on the trial before the court and jury, on the issues joined on the pleas in bar, and so have reached the question of the power of Congress to pass the act of 1820. On so grave a subject as this, I feel obliged to say that, in my opinion, such an exertion of judicial power transcends the limits of the authority of the court, as described by its repeated decisions, and, as I understand, acknowledged in this opinion of the majority of the court.

Notes/Queries/Readings

1. Why does Chief Justice Taney say that African Americans have no standing to sue in federal court? What methods of interpretation does he use to arrive at his conclusion?

2. According to Taney, why is the Missouri Compromise of 1820 unconstitutional? What view of congressional power does he take?

3. What theory of federalism does Taney articulate? How does he distinguish between state and federal citizenship? Why did he have to do so? Is his resulting definition overly cramped considering the social and political changes between the time of the Founding and the hearing of this case?

4. Does *Dred Scott* expand the power of judicial review beyond the limits of *Marbury*, as the introductory essay suggests? Chief Justice Taney wrote that the Constitution "must be construed now as it was understood at the time of its adoption." A different rule, he argued, "would abrogate the judicial character of this court, and make it the mere reflex of the popular opinion or passion of the day." Does Taney's preferred method of constitutional interpretation therefore rest upon a particular understanding of ju-

dicial power? Is that conception of judicial power consistent with the Court's approach in *Marbury*?

5. *Dred Scott* is generally regarded as the Court's most disastrous decision. Does this suggest practical limits to the Court's power to resolve divisive political and moral issues? Do any of the opinions in *Dred Scott* avoid the perils of judicial subjectivity?

6. Suppose we knew, absolutely and positively, what the Founding Fathers actually intended to include within the meaning of a given constitutional provision. Should justices today be bound by that belief? Why or why not? If not, how would they get around Chief Justice Taney's objection that "any other rule of construction would abrogate the judicial character of this court"? Does constitutional language supply any guidance to answering this question?

7. If the Supreme Court had taken the German approach to constitutional interpretation described in Comparative Note 3.3, would—or could—the result in *Dred Scott* have been different?

8. Much has been written about this case. Among the best treatments are Paul Finkelman, *Dred Scott versus Sandford: A Brief History with Documents* (Boston: Bedford Books, 1997); Don E. Fehrenbacher, *The Dred Scott Case* (New York: Oxford University Press, 1978); Christopher L. Eisbruger, Dred *Again: Originalism's Forgotten Past*, 10 Constitutional Commentary 37 (1993); and Stanley Kutler, *The Dred Scott Decision: Law or Politics* (Boston: Houghton-Mifflin, 1967).

Brown v. Board of Education of Topeka
347 U.S. 483, 74 S. Ct. 686, 98 L. Ed. 873 (1954)

The facts of the case are set forth in the following extracts. Other parts of this unanimous opinion are included in chapter 13 at page 753. Opinion of the Court: *Warren*, Black, Burton, Clark, Douglas, Frankfurter, Jackson, Minton, Reed.

**Mr. Chief Justice WARREN delivered
the opinion of the Court.**

These cases come to us from the States of Kansas, South Carolina, Virginia, and Delaware. They are premised on different facts and different local conditions, but a common legal question justifies their consideration together in this consolidated opinion.

In each of the cases, minors of the Negro race, through their legal representatives, seek the aid of the courts in obtaining admission to the public schools of their community

on a nonsegregated basis. In each instance, they have been denied admission to schools attended by white children under laws requiring or permitting segregation according to race. This segregation was alleged to deprive the plaintiffs of the equal protection of the laws under the Fourteenth Amendment. In each of the cases other than the Delaware case, a three-judge federal district court denied relief to the plaintiffs on the so-called "separate but equal" doctrine announced by this Court in *Plessy v. Ferguson* (1896). Under that doctrine, equality of treatment is accorded when the races are provided substantially equal facilities, even though these facilities be separate. In the Delaware case, the Supreme Court of Delaware adhered to that doctrine, but ordered that the plaintiffs be admitted to the white schools because of their superiority to the Negro schools.

The plaintiffs contend that segregated public schools are not "equal" and cannot be made "equal," and that hence they are deprived of the equal protection of the laws. Because of the obvious importance of the question presented, the Court took jurisdiction. Argument was heard in the 1952

Term, and reargument was heard this Term on certain questions propounded by the Court.

Reargument was largely devoted to the circumstances surrounding the adoption of the Fourteenth Amendment in 1868. It covered exhaustively consideration of the Amendment in Congress, ratification by the states, then existing practices in racial segregation, and the views of proponents and opponents of the Amendment. This discussion and our own investigation convince us that, although these sources cast some light, it is not enough to resolve the problem with which we are faced. At best, they are inconclusive. The most avid proponents of the post-War Amendments undoubtedly intended them to remove all legal distinctions among "all persons born or naturalized in the United States." Their opponents, just as certainly, were antagonistic to both the letter and the spirit of the Amendments and wished them to have the most limited effect. What others in Congress and the state legislatures had in mind cannot be determined with any degree of certainty.

An additional reason for the inconclusive nature of the Amendment's history, with respect to segregated schools, is the status of public education at that time. In the South, the movement toward free common schools, supported by general taxation, had not yet taken hold. Education of white children was largely in the hands of private groups. Education of Negroes was almost nonexistent, and practically all of the race were illiterate. In fact, any education of Negroes was forbidden by law in some states. Today, in contrast, many Negroes have achieved outstanding success in the arts and sciences as well as in the business and professional world. It is true that public school education at the time of the Amendment had advanced further in the North, but the effect of the Amendment on Northern States was generally ignored in the congressional debates. Even in the North, the conditions of public education did not approximate those existing today. The curriculum was usually rudimentary; ungraded schools were common in rural areas; the school term was but three months a year in many states; and compulsory school attendance was virtually unknown. As a consequence, it is not surprising that there should be so little in the history of the Fourteenth Amendment relating to its intended effect on public education.

In the first cases in this Court construing the Fourteenth Amendment, decided shortly after its adoption, the Court interpreted it as proscribing all state-imposed discriminations against the Negro race. The doctrine of "separate but equal" did not make its appearance in this court until 1896 in the case of *Plessy v. Ferguson*, involving not education but transportation. American courts have since labored with the doctrine for over half a century. In this Court, there have been six cases involving the "separate but equal" doctrine in the field of public education. In *Cumming v. Board of Education of Richmond County* (1899) and *Gong Lum v. Rice* (1927) the validity of the doctrine itself was not challenged. In more recent cases, all on the graduate school level, inequality was found in that specific benefits enjoyed by white students were denied to Negro students of the same educational qualifications. In none of these cases was it necessary to re-examine the doctrine to grant relief to the Negro plaintiff. And in *Sweatt v. Painter* (1950), the Court expressly reserved decision on the question whether *Plessy v. Ferguson* should be held inapplicable to public education.

In the instant cases, that question is directly presented. Here, unlike *Sweatt v. Painter*, there are findings below that the Negro and white schools involved have been equalized, or are being equalized, with respect to buildings, curricula, qualifications and salaries of teachers, and other "tangible" factors. Our decision, therefore, cannot turn on merely a comparison of these tangible factors in the Negro and white schools involved in each of the cases. We must look instead to the effect of segregation itself on public education.

In approaching this problem, we cannot turn the clock back to 1868 when the Amendment was adopted, or even to 1896 when *Plessy v. Ferguson* was written. We must consider public education in the light of its full development and its present place in American life throughout the Nation. Only in this way can it be determined if segregation in public schools deprives these plaintiffs of the equal protection of the laws.

Today, education is perhaps the most important function of state and local governments. Compulsory school attendance laws and the great expenditures for education both demonstrate our recognition of the importance of education to our democratic society. It is required in the performance of our most basic public responsibilities, even service in the armed forces. It is the very foundation of good citizenship. Today it is a principal instrument in awakening the child to cultural values, in preparing him for later professional training, and in helping him to adjust normally to his environment. In these days, it is doubtful that any child may reasonably be expected to succeed in life if he is denied the opportunity of an education. Such an opportunity, where the state has undertaken to provide it, is a right which must be made available to all on equal terms.

We come then to the question presented: Does segregation of children in public schools solely on the basis of race, even though the physical facilities and other "tangible" factors may be equal, deprive the children of the minority group of equal educational opportunities? We believe that it does. In *Sweatt v. Painter*. . . in finding that a segregated law school for Negroes could not provide them equal educational opportunities, this Court relied in large part on "those qualities which are incapable of objective measurement but which make for greatness in a law school." In *McLaurin v. Oklahoma State Regents*. . . the Court, in requiring that a Negro admitted to a white graduate school be treated like all other students, again resorted to intangible considerations: ". . . his ability to study, to engage in discussions and exchange views with other students, and, in general, to learn his profession."

Such considerations apply with added force to children in grade and high schools. To separate them from others of similar age and qualifications solely because of their race generates a feeling of inferiority as to their status in the community that may affect their hearts and minds in a way unlikely ever to be undone. The effect of this separation on their educational opportunities was well stated by a finding in the Kansas case by a court which nevertheless felt compelled to rule against the Negro plaintiffs:

Segregation of white and colored children in public schools has a detrimental effect upon the colored children. The impact is greater when it has the sanction of the law; for the policy of separating the races is usually interpreted as denoting the inferiority of the negro group. A sense of inferiority affects the motivation of a child to learn. Segregation with the sanction of law, therefore, has a tendency to [retard] the educational and mental development of Negro children and to deprive them of some of the benefits they would receive in a racial[ly] integrated school system.

Whatever may have been the extent of psychological knowledge at the time of *Plessy v. Ferguson*, this finding is amply supported by modern authority.* Any language in *Plessy v. Ferguson* contrary to this finding is rejected.

We conclude that in the field of public education the doctrine of "separate but equal" has no place. Separate educational facilities are inherently unequal. Therefore, we hold that the plaintiffs and others similarly situated for whom the actions have been brought are, by reason of the segregation complained of, deprived of the equal protection of the laws guaranteed by the Fourteenth Amendment. This disposition makes unnecessary any discussion whether

such segregation also violates the Due Process Clause of the Fourteenth Amendment.

It is so ordered.

Cases ordered restored to docket for further argument on question of appropriate decrees.

Notes/Queries/Readings

1. To what extent does the Court's opinion rely on original intent? Does the reasoning expose problems with theories that claim to rely on original intent?

2. What other interpretive strategies does the Court employ? How does the Court defend overturning the precedent of *Plessy v. Ferguson*? Is the social science evidence cited in the footnote persuasive? Should the Court take such data into account? Suppose scientific studies had not shown that African American children displayed evidence of a feeling of inferiority. Would *Brown* then have to be decided differently, and would *Plessy* have to be reaffirmed? What other evidence and argument does the Court use to support its opinion? Ultimately, how important is social science data to the Court's conclusion? Consider this question in the light of Justice Barak's remarks in Comparative Note 3.7.

3. Consider Justice Barak's remarks once again. Do you see any problems with his approach to constitutional interpretation? What are these fundamental values that a democracy seeks to attain? How is a statute to be assessed in terms of these values?

4. There is a large body of commentary on the Court's opinion in this case. For influential reactions to the decision and to the methods of constitutional interpretation used in *Brown*, see Herbert Wechsler, *Toward Neutral Principles of Constitutional Law*, 73 Harvard Law Review 1 (1959) and Alexander Bickel, *The Original Understanding and the Segregation Decision*, 69 Harvard Law Review 1 (1955). For the history of *Brown* and an equally detailed account of the dynamics of decision making in the case see Richard Kluger, *Simple Justice: The History of* Brown v. Board of Education *and Black America's Struggle for Equality* (New York: Knopf, 1976).

5. In *Bolling v. Sharpe*, 347 U.S. 497 1954, a companion case to *Brown*, the Supreme Court reviewed the validity of segregation in the public schools of the District of Columbia. The legal problem was whether the due process clause of the Fifth Amendment, which is applicable to the District of Columbia, contains an equal protection guarantee. Again speaking through Chief Justice Warren, a unanimous Court held that while the concepts of equal protection and due process are not "always interchangeable phrases," segregated educational facilities are "so unjustifiable as to be violative of due process." Is this disingenu-

---

*K. B. Clark, Effect of Prejudice and Discrimination on Personality Development (Midcentury White House Conference on Children and Youth, 1950); Witmer and Kotinsky, Personality in the Making (1952), ch VI; Deutscher and Chein, The Psychological Effects of Enforced Segregation: A Survey of Social Science Opinion, 26 J Psychol 259 (1948); Chein, What are the Psychological Effects of Segregation Under Conditions of Equal Facilities?, 3 Int J Opinion and Attitude Res. 229 (1949); Brameld, Educational Costs, in Discrimination and National Welfare (MacIver, ed, 1949), 44–48; Frazier, The Negro in the United States (1949), 674–681. And see generally Myrdal, An American Dilemma (1944).

ous manipulation of constitutional language or a justifiable construction of the Fifth Amendment's due process clause? Would there have been another valid approach to constitutional interpretation in *Bolling*? In deciding *Bolling*, the Court announced that "[c]lassifications based solely upon race must be scrutinized with particular care, since they are contrary to our traditions and hence constitutionally suspect." The application of this standard of review to related cases on racial discrimination is treated in chapter 13.

Cooper v. Aaron
358 U.S. 1, 78 S. Ct. 1401, 3 L. Ed 2d 5 (1958)

The governor and legislature of Arkansas actively resisted the implementation of a Little Rock School Board plan, approved by the Federal District Court for the Eastern District of Arkansas, to begin desegregating Little Rock's public school system in the fall of 1957. Claiming that *Brown v. Board of Education* was itself unconstitutional, the governor dispatched units of Arkansas's National Guard to place Central High School "off-limits" to African American students. (In September 1957 President Eisenhower stationed federal troops at the high school to protect these students.) In early 1958 the school board, fearing more turmoil and an outbreak of violence, petitioned the district court for a postponement of its desegregation plan. The Court granted the relief requested. The U.S. Court of Appeals reversed. Opinion of the Court: *Warren, Black, Frankfurter, Douglas, Burton, Clark, Harlan, Brennan, Whittaker.* Concurring opinion: *Frankfurter.*

The Chief Justice, Mr. Justice BLACK, Mr. Justice FRANKFURTER, Mr. Justice DAVIS, Mr. Justice BURTON, Mr. Justice CLARK, Mr. Justice HARLAN, Mr. Justice BRENNAN and Mr. Justice WHITTAKER delivered the opinion of the Court.

As this case reaches us it raises questions of the highest importance to the maintenance of our federal system of government. It necessarily involves a claim by the Governor and Legislature of a State that there is no duty on state officials to obey federal court orders resting on this Court's considered interpretation of the United States Constitution. Specifically it involves actions by the Governor and Legislature of Arkansas upon the premise that they are not bound by our holding in *Brown v. Board of Education* [1954]. We are urged to uphold a suspension of the Little Rock School Board's plan to do away with segregated public schools in Little Rock until state laws and efforts to upset and nullify our holding in *Brown v. Board of Education* have been further challenged and tested in the courts. We reject these contentions.

The controlling legal principles are plain. The command of the Fourteenth Amendment is that no "State" shall deny to any person within its jurisdiction the equal protection of the laws. "A State acts by its legislative, its executive, or its judicial authorities. It can act in no other way. The constitutional provision, therefore, must mean that no agency of the State, or of the officers or agents by whom its powers are exerted, shall deny to any person within its jurisdiction the equal protection of the laws. Whoever, by virtue of public position under a State government, denies or takes away the equal protection of the laws, violates the constitutional inhibition; and as he acts in the name [of] and for the State, and is clothed with the State's power, his act is that of the State. This must be so, or the constitutional prohibition has no meaning." Thus the prohibitions of the Fourteenth Amendment extend to all action of the State denying equal protection of the laws; whatever the agency of the State taking the action, or whatever the guise in which it is taken. In short, the constitutional rights of children not to be discriminated against in school admission on grounds of race or color declared by this Court in the *Brown* case can neither be nullified openly and directly by state legislators or state executive or judicial officers, nor nullified indirectly by them through evasive schemes for segregation whether attempted "ingeniously or ingenuously."

What has been said, in the light of the facts developed, is enough to dispose of the case. However, we should answer the premise of the actions of the Governor and Legislature that they are not bound by our holding in the *Brown* case. It is necessary only to recall some basic constitutional propositions which are settled doctrine.

Article VI of the Constitution makes the Constitution the "supreme Law of the Land." In 1803, Chief Justice Marshall, speaking for a unanimous Court, referring to the Constitution as "the fundamental and paramount law of the nation," declared in the notable case of *Marbury v. Madison* [1803] that "It is emphatically the province and duty of the judicial department to say what the law is." This decision declared the basic principle that the federal judiciary is supreme in the exposition of the law of the Constitution, and that principle has ever since been respected by this Court and the Country as a permanent and indispensable feature of our constitutional system. It follows that the interpretation of the Fourteenth Amendment enunciated by this Court in the *Brown* case is the supreme law of the land, and Art. VI of the Constitution makes it of binding effect on the States "any Thing in the Constitution or Laws of any State to the Contrary notwithstanding." Every state legislator and executive and judicial officer is solemnly committed

Comparative Note 3.4

A state, it is said, is sovereign and it is not for the courts to pass upon the policy or wisdom of legislative will. As a broad statement of principle that is undoubtedly correct, but the general principle must yield to the requisites of the constitution in a federal state. By it the bounds of sovereignty are defined and supremacy circumscribed. The court will not question the wisdom of enactments which, by the terms of the Canadian Constitution, are within the competence of the legislatures, *but it is the high duty of the court to insure that the legislatures do not transgress the limits of their constitutional mandate and engage in the illegal exercise of power.*

SOURCE: *Amax Potash Ltd. v. Saskatchewan.* In the Supreme Court of Canada [1977] 2 S.C.R. 576.

by oath taken pursuant to Art. VI, cl. 3 "to support this Constitution." Chief Justice Taney, speaking for a unanimous Court in 1859, said that this requirement reflected the framers' "anxiety to preserve it [the Constitution] in full force, in all its powers, and to guard against resistance to or evasion of its authority, on the part of a State. . . ."

No state legislator or executive or judicial officer can war against the Constitution without violating his undertaking to support it. Chief Justice Marshall spoke for a unanimous Court in saying that: "If the legislatures of the several states may, at will, annul the judgments of the courts of the United States, and destroy the rights acquired under those judgments, the constitution itself becomes a solemn mockery. . . ." A Governor who asserts a power to nullify a federal court order is similarly restrained. If he had such power, said Chief Justice Hughes, in 1932, also for a unanimous Court, "it is manifest that the fiat of a state Governor, and not the Constitution of the United States, would be the supreme law of the land; that the restrictions of the Federal Constitution upon the exercise of state power would be but impotent phrases. . . ."

It is, of course, quite true that the responsibility for public education is primarily the concern of the States, but it is equally true that such responsibilities, like all other state activity, must be exercised consistently with federal constitutional requirements as they apply to state action. The Constitution created a government dedicated to equal justice under law. The Fourteenth Amendment embodied and emphasized that ideal. State support of segregated schools through any arrangement, management, funds, or property cannot be squared with the Amendment's command that no State shall deny to any person within its jurisdiction the equal protection of the laws. The right of a student not to be segregated on racial grounds in schools so maintained is indeed so fundamental and pervasive that it is embraced in the concept of due process of law. . . . The basic decision in *Brown* was unanimously reached by this Court only after the case had been briefed and twice argued and the issues had been given the most serious consideration. Since the first *Brown* opinion three new Justices have come to the Court. They are at one with the Justices still on the Court who participated in that basic decision as to its correctness, and that decision is now unanimously reaffirmed. The principles announced in that decision and the obedience of the States to them, according to the command of the Constitution, are indispensable for the protection of the freedoms guaranteed by our fundamental charter for all of us. Our constitutional ideal of equal justice under law is thus made a living truth.

Concurring opinion of Mr. Justice FRANKFURTER.

. . . When defiance of law judicially pronounced was last sought to be justified before this Court, views were expressed which are now especially relevant:

The historic phrase "a government of laws and not of men" epitomizes the distinguishing character of our society. [Such a government] was the rejection in positive terms of rule by fiat, whether by the fiat of governmental or private power. . . . The conception of a government by laws dominated the thoughts of those who founded this Nation and designed its Constitution, although they knew as well as the belittlers of the conception that laws have to be made, interpreted and enforced by men. To that end, they set apart a body of men, who were to be the depositories of law, who by their disciplined training and character and by withdrawal from the usual temptations of private interest may reasonably be expected to be "as free, impartial, and independent as the lot of humanity will admit." So strongly were the framers of the Constitution bent on securing a reign of law that they endowed the judicial office with extraordinary safeguards and prestige. No one, no matter how exalted his public office or how righteous his private motive, can be judge in his own case. That is what courts are for. *United States v. United Mine Workers* [1947].

The duty to abstain from resistance to "the supreme Law of the Land," as declared by the organ of our Government for ascertaining it, does not require immediate approval of it nor does it deny the right of dissent. Criticism need not be stilled. Active obstruction or defiance is barred. Our kind of society cannot endure if the controlling authority of the Law as derived from the Constitution is not to be the tribunal specially charged with the duty of ascertaining and declaring what is "the supreme Law of the Land." Particularly is this so where the declaration of what is "the supreme Law" commands on an underlying moral issue is not the dubious pronouncement of a gravely divided Court but is the unanimous conclusion of a long-matured deliberative process. The Constitution is not the formulation of the merely personal views of the members of this Court, nor can its authority be reduced to the claim that state officials are its controlling interpreters. Local customs, however hardened by time, are not decreed in heaven. . . .

That the responsibility of those who exercise power in a democratic government is not to reflect inflamed public feeling but to help form its understanding, is especially true when they are confronted with a problem like a racially discriminatory public school system. . . .

Notes/Queries/Readings

1. Does *Cooper* elevate the power of judicial review to a new plateau in American political life? Or is it simply a forthright reaffirmation of *Marbury v. Madison*? Did *Marbury* declare the "basic principle that the federal judiciary is supreme in the exposition of the law of the Constitution," as Chief Justice Warren asserted in this case?

2. What room is left for dissent or criticism of the Court's reasoning in *Brown* or *Cooper*? Is it proper for the Court to equate its opinions with the text of the Constitution? Are certain opinions more important than others? How might this be determined?

3. In his concurrence, Justice Frankfurter notes that the role of the Court is not to "reflect public feeling but to help form its understanding." He notes that on the grave moral issue of integration, the decision in *Brown* was unanimous and that all subsequent Supreme Court justices had concurred with its ruling.

4. How does Frankfurter support his proposition that the Court has a better understanding of the Constitution and should be a body to form public understanding? Should unanimity or consensus among Supreme Court justices be considered proof of the rightness of a constitutional interpretation? Can one oppose a particular decision of the Supreme Court as being "at war with the Constitution"? If so, then what makes the decision in *Brown* different from those that can be opposed?

5. Is judicial exclusivity over constitutional interpretation necessary for the operation of a stable constitutional system? What problems might it raise?

6. The U.S. Supreme Court, like the Canadian Supreme Court, would sharply distinguish between questioning the wisdom of legislation and transgressing the limits of the constitution (see Comparative Note 3.4). Is there any objective way of making this distinction? Would the approach of the German Constitutional Court in Comparative Note 3.3 help us to identify an objective constitutional morality in terms of which the distinction could be appropriately made? Is Frankfurter's appeal to the gravity of the moral issue of any help here?

7. For additional reading on *Cooper*, see Daniel Farber, *The Supreme Court and the Rule of Law: Cooper v. Aaron Revisited*, 1983 University of Illinois Law Review 387.

Planned Parenthood of Southeastern Pennsylvania v. Casey

505 U.S. 833, 114 S. Ct. 909, 127 L. Ed. 2d 352 (1992)

This case, unlike *Cooper v. Aaron*, was decided by a deeply fractured Court. Four of the *Casey* justices sought to overrule *Roe v. Wade* (1973), the case which upheld a woman's right to procure an abortion. The joint opinion, however, part of which is reprinted below, upheld the "essential core" of the abortion liberty. The facts of the case are set forth in chapter 10 at page 477. Opinion of the Court: *O'Connor*, Kennedy, Souter. Concurring and dissenting opinions: *Stevens*, *Blackmun*. Dissenting opinion: *Scalia*, Rehnquist, White, Thomas.

Justice O'CONNOR, Justice KENNEDY, and Justice SOUTER announced the judgment of the Court . . . in which Justice STEVENS joins. . .

Liberty finds no refuge in a jurisprudence of doubt. Yet 19 years after our holding that the Constitution protects a woman's right to terminate her pregnancy in its early stages, *Roe v. Wade* [1973], that definition of liberty is still questioned. Joining the respondents as *amicus curiae*, the United States, as it has done in five other cases in the last decade, again asks us to overrule *Roe*.

After considering the fundamental constitutional questions resolved by *Roe*, principles of institutional integrity, and the rule of *stare decisis*, we are led to conclude this: the essential holding of *Roe v. Wade* should be retained and once again reaffirmed.

It must be stated at the outset and with clarity that *Roe*'s essential holding, the holding we reaffirm, has three parts. First is a recognition of the right of the woman to choose to have an abortion before viability and to obtain it without undue interference from the State. Before viability, the State's interests are not strong enough to support a prohibition of abortion or the imposition of a substantial obstacle to the woman's effective right to elect the procedure. Second is a confirmation of the State's power to restrict abortions after fetal viability, if the law contains exceptions for pregnancies which endanger a woman's life or health. And third is the principle that the State has legitimate interests from the outset of the pregnancy in protecting the health of the woman and the life of the fetus that may become a child. These principles do not contradict one another; and we adhere to each.

Men and women of good conscience can disagree, and we suppose some always shall disagree, about the profound moral and spiritual implications of terminating a pregnancy, even in its earliest stage. Some of us as individuals find abortion offensive to our most basic principles of morality, but that cannot control our decision. Our obligation is to define the liberty of all, not to mandate our own moral code. The underlying constitutional issue is whether the State can resolve these philosophic questions in such a definitive way that a woman lacks all choice in the matter, except perhaps in those rare circumstances in which the pregnancy is itself a danger to her own life or health, or is the result of rape or incest.

It is conventional constitutional doctrine that where reasonable people disagree the government can adopt one position or the other. That theorem, however, assumes a state of affairs in which the choice does not intrude upon a protected liberty. Thus, while some people might disagree about whether or not the flag should be saluted, or disagree about the proposition that it may not be defiled, we have ruled that a State may not compel or enforce one view or the other.

. . . [O]ur cases recognize "the right of the individual, married or single, to be free from unwarranted governmental intrusion into matters so fundamentally affecting a person as the decision whether to bear or beget a child." Our precedents "have respected the private realm of family life which the state cannot enter." These matters, involving the most intimate and personal choices a person may make in a lifetime, choices central to personal dignity and autonomy, are central to the liberty protected by the Fourteenth Amendment. At the heart of liberty is the right to define one's own concept of existence, of meaning, of the universe, and of the mystery of human life. Beliefs about these matters could not define the attributes of personhood were they formed under compulsion of the State.

To eliminate the [respondents'] issue of reliance [upon the law already in place] that easily, however, one would need to limit cognizable reliance to specific instances of sexual activity. But to do this would be simply to refuse to face the fact that for two decades of economic and social developments, people have organized intimate relationships and made choices that define their views of themselves and their places in society, in reliance on the availability of abortion in the event that contraception should fail. The ability of women to participate equally in the economic and social life of the Nation has been facilitated by their ability to control their reproductive lives. The Constitution serves human values, and while the effect of reliance on *Roe* cannot be exactly measured, neither can the certain cost of overruling *Roe* for people who have ordered their thinking and living around that case be dismissed.

The root of American governmental power is revealed most clearly in the instance of the power conferred by the Constitution upon the Judiciary of the United States and specifically upon this Court. As Americans of each succeeding generation are rightly told, the Court cannot buy support for its decisions by spending money and, except to a minor degree, it cannot independently coerce obedience to its decrees. The Court's power lies, rather, in its legitimacy, a product of substance and perception that shows itself in the people's acceptance of the Judiciary as fit to determine what the Nation's law means and to declare what it demands.

The underlying substance of this legitimacy is of course the warrant for the Court's decisions in the Constitution and the lesser sources of legal principle on which the Court draws. That substance is expressed in the Court's opinions, and our contemporary understanding is such that a decision without principled justification would be no judicial act at all. But even when justification is furnished by apposite legal principle, something more is required. Because not every conscientious claim of principled justification will be accepted as such, the justification claimed must be beyond dispute. The Court must take care to speak and act in ways that allow people to accept its decisions on the terms the Court claims for them, as grounded truly in principle, not as compromises with social and political pressures having, as such, no bearing on the principled choices that the Court is obliged to make. Thus, the Court's legitimacy depends on making legally principled decisions under circumstances in which their principled character is sufficiently plausible to be accepted by the Nation.

The need for principled action to be perceived as such is implicated to some degree whenever this, or any other appellate court, overrules a prior case. This is not to say, of course, that this Court cannot give a perfectly satisfactory explanation in most cases. People understand that some of the Constitution's language is hard to fathom and that the Court's Justices are sometimes able to perceive significant facts or to understand principles of law that eluded their predecessors and that justify departures from existing decisions. However upsetting it may be to those most directly affected when one judicially derived rule replaces another, the country can accept some correction of error without necessarily questioning the legitimacy of the Court.

In two circumstances, however, the Court would almost certainly fail to receive the benefit of the doubt in overruling prior cases. There is, first, a point beyond which frequent overruling would overtax the country's belief in the Court's good faith. Despite the variety of reasons that may inform and justify a decision to overrule, we cannot forget that such a decision is usually perceived [and perceived correctly] as, at the least, a statement that a prior decision was wrong. There is a limit to the amount of error that can plausibly be imputed to prior courts. If that limit should be exceeded, disturbance of prior rulings would be taken as evidence that justifiable reexamination of principle had given way to drives for particular results in the short term. The legitimacy of the Court would fade with the frequency of its vacillation.

That first circumstance can be described as hypothetical; the second is to the point here and now. Where, in the performance of its judicial duties, the Court decides a controversy reflected in *Roe* and those rare, comparable cases, its decision has a dimension that the resolution of the normal case does not carry. It is the dimension present whenever the Court's interpretation of the Constitution calls the contending sides of a national controversy to end their national division by accepting a common mandate rooted in the Constitution.

The Court is not asked to do this very often, having thus addressed the Nation only twice in our lifetime, in the decisions of *Brown* and *Roe*. But when the Court does act in this way, its decision requires an equally rare precedential force to counter the inevitable efforts to overturn it and to thwart its implementation. Some of those efforts may be mere unprincipled emotional reactions; others may proceed from principles worthy of profound respect. But whatever the premises of opposition may be, only the most convincing justification under accepted standards of precedent could suffice to demonstrate that a later decision overruling the first was anything but a surrender to political pressure, and an unjustified repudiation of the principle on which the Court staked its authority in the first instance. So to overrule under fire in the absence of the most compelling reason to reexamine a watershed decision would subvert the Court's legitimacy beyond any serious question.

The country's loss of confidence in the Judiciary would be underscored by an equally certain and equally reasonable condemnation for another failing in overruling unnecessarily and under pressure. Some cost will be paid by anyone who approves or implements a constitutional decision where it is unpopular, or who refuses to work to undermine the decision or to force its reversal. The price may be criticism or ostracism, or it may be violence. An extra price will be paid by those who themselves disapprove of the decision's results when viewed outside of constitutional terms, but who nevertheless struggle to accept it, because they respect the rule of law. To all those who will be so tested by following, the Court implicitly undertakes to remain steadfast, lest in the end a price be paid for nothing. The promise of constancy, once given, binds its maker for as long as the power to stand by the decision survives and the understanding of the issue has not changed so fundamentally as to render the commitment obsolete. From the obligation of this promise this Court cannot and should not assume any exemption when duty requires it to decide a case in conformance with the Constitution. A willing breach of it would be nothing less than a breach of faith, and no Court that broke its faith with the people could sensibly expect credit for principle in the decision by which it did that.

. . . Like the character of an individual, the legitimacy of the Court must be earned over time. So, indeed, must be the character of a Nation of people who aspire to live according to the rule of law. Their belief in themselves as such a people is not readily separable from their understanding of the Court invested with the authority to decide their constitutional cases and speak before all others for their constitutional ideals. If the Court's legitimacy should be undermined, then, so would the country be in its very ability to see itself through its constitutional ideals. The Court's concern with legitimacy is not for the sake of the Court but for the sake of the Nation to which it is responsible.

The Court's duty in the present case is clear. In 1973, it confronted the already-divisive issue of governmental power to limit personal choice to undergo abortion, for which it provided a new resolution based on the due process guaranteed by the Fourteenth Amendment. Whether or not a new social consensus is developing on that issue, its divisiveness is no less today than in 1973, and pressure to overrule the decision, like pressure to retain it, has grown only more intense. A decision to overrule *Roe*'s essential holding under the existing circumstances would address error, if error there was, at the cost of both profound and unnecessary damage to the Court's legitimacy, and to the Nation's commitment to the rule of law. It is therefore imperative to adhere to the essence of *Roe*'s original decision, and we do so today.

Notes/Queries/Readings

1. The seminal case of *Roe v. Wade* has been characterized by no less than Justice Bryon White as a "raw exercise of judicial power." If *Roe* is considered an example of judicial activism, then must continued judicial activism be necessary to maintain stability in the law? Might activism in some cases be less disruptive of the nation's social and political life than judicial restraint?

2. Consider the plurality's discussion of the problems of morality inherent in determining whether the abortion liberty is constitutionally anchored. How does the plurality arrive at the distinction between "the liberty of all" and "one's own moral code"?

3. The opinion also states that the government cannot resolve important and divisive philosophic questions such as when life begins, and thus such questions ought to be left to the individual. Doesn't the Court's opinion in *Casey* amount to taking sides? If it does, why should the Court be the body that makes these determinations, rather than legislative majorities at the state level?

4. How does the plurality distinguish betwen normal cases and cases involving "intensely divisive controvers[ies]" such as *Roe*?

5. Is this opinion as truly grounded in principle as the plurality claims? Does it, in reality, rest only on public opinion, public expectations, and the importance of the institutional prestige of the judiciary? To what extent should the Court rely on such nonjudicial factors? Can they be ignored? What role should public opinion and public expec-

tations have on judicial decision making? Is this influence consistent with the idea of an independent judiciary? With the ideal of a democratic society?

6. Does the Court ultimately state that once it has resolved such a divisive question, it should not be raised again? On what grounds could one then criticize or overturn *Casey*?

7. How does the plurality's discussion echo that of *Cooper v. Aaron*? Are the two cases analogous? Should certain Supreme Court decisions have a privileged protection against being overruled? Why or why not? If so, to which other opinions besides *Roe* and *Brown* should the Court extend this protection? Does the Constitution provide any guidance for arriving at this determination? Is this decision necessarily subjective?

8. Should the Court consider itself as the final arbiter of not only legal but moral decisions, as it appears to do in this case? Can the Court adequately infer this role from the judiciary's duty to "say what the law is"? Is the Court capable of this? Does it shirk its constitutional responsibilities if it does not attempt to resolve these controversies?

9. *Casey* has generated a great deal of commentary, some of it directly concerned with the issue of judicial legitimacy and public support for Supreme Court decisions. See, for example, William Mishler and Reginald Sheehan, *The Supreme Court as a Countermajoritarian Institution? The Impact of Public Opinion on Supreme Court Decisions*, 87 American Political Science Review 87 (1993) and the response by Helmut Norpoth and Jeffrey Segal, *Popular Influence on Supreme Court Decisions*, 88 *ibid.* 711 (1994).

Ex Parte McCardle

74 U.S. 506, 7 Wall. 506, 19 L. Ed. 264 (1868)

In the aftermath of the Civil War, the Radical Republican Congress passed a series of acts imposing programs of reconstruction on the former states of the rebellion. McCardle, a Mississippi newspaper editor and a fierce opponent of reconstruction, was held in custody by military authorities for publishing "incendiary and libelous" articles against the enforcement of the reconstruction acts. While awaiting trial, he petitioned a U.S. Circuit Court for a writ of habeas corpus and being denied the writ, he appealed to the Supreme Court. The Supreme Court's announcement that it would take the case alarmed the Radical Republicans. Fearing the fate of the reconstruction program in the hands of the Supreme Court, Congress enacted a statute taking away from the Court its power to hear appeals in habeas corpus cases. The law was passed after the Court

had heard arguments in the case, but before it had handed down a decision. Opinion of the Court: *CHASE*, Clifford, Davis, Field, Grier, Miller, Nelson, Swayne.

**Mr. Chief Justice CHASE delivered
the opinion of the Court.**

The first question necessarily is that of jurisdiction; for, if the act of March, 1868, takes away the jurisdiction defined by the act of February, 1867, it is useless, if not improper, to enter into any discussion of other questions.

It is quite true, as was argued by the counsel for the petitioner, that the appellate jurisdiction of this court is not derived from acts of Congress. It is, strictly speaking, conferred by the Constitution. But it is conferred "with such exceptions and under such regulations as Congress shall make."

It is unnecessary to consider whether, if Congress had made no exceptions and no regulations, this court might not have exercised general appellate jurisdiction under rules prescribed by itself. For among the earliest acts of the first Congress, at its first session, was the act of September 24th, 1789, to establish the judicial courts of the United States. That act provided for the organization of this court, and prescribed regulations for the exercise of its jurisdiction.

The source of that jurisdiction, and the limitations of it by the Constitution and by statute, have been on several occasions subjects of consideration here. In the case of *Durousseau v. The United States* [1810], particularly, the whole matter was carefully examined, and the court held, that while "the appellate powers of this court are not given by the judicial act, but are given by the Constitution," they are, nevertheless, "limited and regulated by that act, and by such other acts as have been passed on the subject." The court said, further, that the judicial act was an exercise of the power given by the Constitution to Congress "of making exceptions to the appellate jurisdiction of the Supreme Court. They have described affirmatively," said the court, "its jurisdiction, and this affirmative description has been understood to imply a negation of the exercise of such appellate power as is not comprehended within it."

The principle that the affirmation of appellate jurisdiction implies the negation of all such jurisdiction not affirmed having been thus established, it was an almost necessary consequence that acts of Congress, providing for the exercise of jurisdiction, should come to be spoken of as acts granting jurisdiction, and not as acts making exceptions to the constitutional grant of it.

The exception to appellate jurisdiction in the case before us, however, is not an inference from the affirmation of other appellate jurisdiction. It is made in terms. The provision of the act of 1867, affirming the appellate jurisdiction of this court in cases of habeas corpus is expressly repealed. It is hardly possible to imagine a plainer instance of positive exception.

We are not at liberty to inquire into the motives of the legislature. We can only examine into its power under the Constitution; and the power to make exceptions to the appellate jurisdiction of this court is given by express words.

What, then, is the effect of the repealing act upon the case before us? We cannot doubt as to this. Without jurisdiction the court cannot proceed at all in any cause. Jurisdiction is power to declare the law, and when it ceases to exist, the only function remaining to the court is that of announcing the fact and dismissing the cause. And this is not less clear upon authority than upon principle.

Several cases were cited by the counsel for the petitioner in support of the position that jurisdiction of this case is not affected by the repealing act. But none of them, in our judgment, afford any support to it. They are all cases of the exercise of judicial power by the legislature, or of legislative interference with courts in the exercising of continuing jurisdiction.

On the other hand, the general rule, supported by the best elementary writers, is, that "when an act of the legislature is repealed, it must be considered, except as to transactions past and closed, as if it never existed." . . .

It is quite clear, therefore, that this court cannot proceed to pronounce judgment in this case, for it has no longer jurisdiction of the appeal; and judicial duty is not less fitly performed by declining ungranted jurisdiction than in exercising firmly that which the Constitution and the laws confer.

The appeal of the petitioner in this case must be dismissed for want of jurisdiction.

Notes/Queries/Readings

1. Why does the Court ignore the merits of McCardle's case? Might this case fall under the Constitution's prohibition of *ex post facto* laws or bills of attainder?

2. What theory of judicial power is advanced in this opinion? How does it compare to that laid down in *Marbury* and *Dred Scott*?

3. The Court notes that "we are not at liberty to inquire into the motives of the legislature. We can only examine into its power under the Constitution." If the Court is to uphold constitutionalism and individual rights, should it not inquire into these motives? What might be the dangers of courts inquiring into legislative motives? How can it discover these motives if they are not obvious?

4. Are there limits on Congress's power to limit or regulate the appellate jurisdiction of the Supreme Court? Suppose Congress passed a law forbidding the Supreme Court from deciding cases on appeal dealing with abortion or freedom of speech. Could you make the case that, in this instance, Congress has exceeded its power under the Constitution?

5. For readings on *McCardle*, see Charles Fairman, *Reconstruction and Reunion 1864–1888* (New York: Macmillan, 1971), I, ch. 10 and William Van Alstyne, *A Critical Guide to* Ex Parte McCardle, 15 Arizona Law Review 229 (1973).

Lujan v. Defenders of Wildlife

505 U.S. 555, 112 S. Ct. 2130, 119 L. Ed. 351 (1992)

Under Section 7 of the Endangered Species Act of 1973 federal agencies are required to insure, in consultation with the secretary of interior, that their activities will not threaten or adversely affect an endangered species or its habitat. The secretary promulgated a rule extending the coverage of Section 7 to projects in the United States and on the high seas but not in foreign lands. The respondent and several wildlife organizations challenged the legality of the rule's limited geographic scope and petitioned for a declaratory judgment to that effect. The Federal District Court granted the secretary's motion to dismiss for lack of standing. The Court of Appeals for the Eighth Circuit reversed. Opinion of the Court: *Scalia*, Rehnquist, White, Kennedy, Souter. Concurring in part: *Kennedy*, Souter, *Stevens*. Dissenting opinions: *Blackmun*, O'Connor.

Justice SCALIA delivered the opinion of the Court with respect to Parts I, II, III-A, and IV, and an opinion with respect to Part III-B, in which the Chief Justice, Justice WHITE, and Justice THOMAS join.

[In this multifaceted opinion, six justices held that the wild-life groups involved could not validly assert standing on the basis of an "ecosystem nexus" theory, an "animal nexus" approach, or a "vocational nexus" approach. The concurring justices, who agreed with the judgment, nevertheless noted that in different circumstances the nexus theory might support a claim to standing. The dissenting opinion, which is omitted in the following extracts, claimed that environmental plaintiffs who allege an ecosystem nexus or a vocational or professional injury should not be required to show physical proximity to the alleged wrong.]

II

While the Constitution of the United States divides all power conferred upon the Federal Government into "legislative Powers," Art. I, s 1, "the executive Power," Art. II, s 1, and "[t]he judicial Power," Art. III, s 1, it does not attempt to define those terms. To be sure, it limits the jurisdiction of federal courts to "Cases" and "Controversies," but an executive inquiry can bear the name "case" (the *Hoffa* case) and a legislative dispute can bear the name "controversy" (the Smoot-Hawley controversy). Obviously, then, the Constitution's central mechanism of separation of powers depends largely upon common understanding of what activities are appropriate to legislatures, to executives, and to courts. In *The Federalist* No. 48, Madison expressed the view that "it is not infrequently a question of real nicety in legislative bodies whether the operation of a particular measure will, or will not, extend beyond the legislative sphere," whereas "the executive power [is] restrained within a narrower compass and . . . more simple in its nature," and "the judiciary [is] described by landmarks still less uncertain." . . . One of those landmarks, setting apart the "Cases" and "Controversies" that are of the justiciable sort referred to in Article III—"serving to identify those disputes which are appropriately resolved through the judicial process," . . . —is the doctrine of standing. Though some of its elements express merely prudential considerations that are part of judicial self-government, the core component of standing is an essential and unchanging part of the case-or-controversy requirement of Article III. . . .

Over the years, our cases have established that the irreducible constitutional minimum of standing contains three elements. First, the plaintiff must have suffered an "injury in fact"—an invasion of a legally protected interest which is (a) concrete and particularized, . . . and (b) "actual or imminent, not 'conjectural' or 'hypothetical,' " . . . Second, there must be a causal connection between the injury and the conduct complained of—the injury has to be "fairly . . . trace[able] to the challenged action of the defendant, and not . . . the result [of] the independent action of some third party not before the court." . . . Third, it must be "likely," as opposed to merely "speculative," that the injury will be "redressed by a favorable decision."

. . . The party invoking federal jurisdiction bears the burden of establishing these elements. . . . Since they are not mere pleading requirements but rather an indispensable part of the plaintiff's case, each element must be supported in the same way as any other matter on which the plaintiff bears the burden of proof, i. e., with the manner and degree of evidence required at the successive stages of the litigation. . . .

When the suit is one challenging the legality of government action or inaction, the nature and extent of facts that must be averred (at the summary judgment stage) or proved (at the trial stage) in order to establish standing depends considerably upon whether the plaintiff is himself an object of the action (or forgone action) at issue. If he is, there is ordinarily little question that the action or inaction has caused him injury, and that a judgment preventing or requiring the action will redress it. When, however, as in this case, a plaintiff's asserted injury arises from the government's allegedly unlawful regulation [or lack of regulation] of someone else, much more is needed. In that circumstance, causation and redressability ordinarily hinge on the response of the regulated (or regulable) third party to the government action or inaction—and perhaps on the response of others as well. The existence of one or more of the essential elements of standing "depends on the unfettered choices made by independent actors not before the courts and whose exercise of broad and legitimate discretion the courts cannot presume either to control or to predict," . . . and it becomes the burden of the plaintiff to adduce facts showing that those choices have been or will be made in such manner as to produce causation and permit redressability of injury. . . . Thus, when the plaintiff is not himself the object of the government action or inaction he challenges, standing is not precluded, but it is ordinarily "substantially more difficult" to establish. . . .

III

We think the Court of Appeals failed to apply the foregoing principles in denying the Secretary's motion for summary judgment. Respondents had not made the requisite demonstration of [at least] injury and redressability.

A

Respondents' claim to injury is that the lack of consultation with respect to certain funded activities abroad "increas[es] the rate of extinction of endangered and threatened species." Of course, the desire to use or observe an animal species, even for purely esthetic purposes, is undeniably a cognizable interest for purpose of standing. . . . "But the 'injury in fact' test requires more than an injury to a cognizable interest. It requires that the party seeking review be himself among the injured." . . . To survive the Secretary's summary judgment motion, respondents had to submit affidavits or other evidence showing, through specific facts, not only that listed species were in fact being threatened by funded activities abroad, but also that one or more of respondents' members would thereby be "directly" affected apart from their "'special interest' in the subject." . . .

With respect to this aspect of the case, the Court of Appeals focused on the affidavits of two Defenders' members—Joyce Kelly and Amy Skilbred. Ms. Kelly stated that she traveled to Egypt in 1986 and "observed the traditional habitat of the endangered nile crocodile there and intend[s] to do so again, and hope[s] to observe the crocodile directly," and that she "will suffer harm in fact as the result of [the] American . . . role . . . in overseeing the rehabilitation of the Aswan High Dam on the Nile . . . and [in] developing . . . Egypt's . . . Master Water Plan." Ms. Skilbred averred that she traveled to Sri Lanka in 1981 and "observed the habitat" of "endangered species such as the Asian elephant and the leopard" . . .

We shall assume for the sake of argument that these affidavits contain facts showing that certain agency-funded projects threaten listed species—though that is questionable. They plainly contain no facts, however, showing how damage to the species will produce "imminent" injury to Mses. Kelly and Skilbred. That the women "had visited" the areas of the projects before the projects commenced proves nothing. As we have said in a related context, "Past exposure to illegal conduct does not in itself show a present case or controversy regarding injunctive relief . . . if unaccompanied by any continuing, present adverse effects." . . . And the affiants' profession of an "intent" to return to the places they had visited before—where they will presumably, this time, be deprived of the opportunity to observe animals of the endangered species—is simply not enough. Such "some day" intentions—without any description of concrete plans, or indeed even any specification of when the some day will be—do not support a finding of the "actual or imminent" injury that our cases require. . . .

Besides relying upon the Kelly and Skilbred affidavits,

Comparative Note 3.5

I recognize that any attempt to place standing in a federal taxpayer suit on the likely tax burden or debt resulting from an illegal expenditure, by analogy to one of the reasons given for allowing municipal taxpayer's suits, is as unreal as it is in the municipal taxpayer cases. Certainly, a federal taxpayer's interest may be no less than that of a municipal taxpayer in that respect. It is not the alleged waste of public funds alone that will support standing but rather the right of the citizenry to constitutional behaviour by Parliament where the issue in such behavior is justiciable as a legal question.

In my opinion, standing of a federal taxpayer seeking to challenge the constitutionality of federal legisla-

tion is a matter particularly appropriate for the exercise of judicial discretion, relating as it does to the effectiveness of process. . . . [T]he court may decide, as it did in the *Smith* case, that a member of the public . . . is too remotely affected to be accorded standing.

On the other hand, where all members of the public are affected alike, as in the present case, and there is a justiciable issue respecting the validity of legislation, the court must be able to say that as between allowing a taxpayer's action and denying any standing at all when the Attorney General refuses to act, it may choose to hear the case on the merits.

SOURCE: *Thorson v. The Attorney General of Canada.* In the Supreme Court of Canada [1975] 1 S.C.R. 138.

respondents propose a series of novel standing theories. The first, inelegantly styled "ecosystem nexus," proposes that any person who uses any part of a "contiguous ecosystem" adversely affected by a funded activity has standing even if the activity is located a great distance away. This approach, as the Court of Appeals correctly observed, is inconsistent with our opinion in *National Wildlife Federation*, which held that a plaintiff claiming injury from environmental damage must use the area affected by the challenged activity and not an area roughly "in the vicinity" of it. . . .

It makes no difference that the general-purpose section of the ESA states that the Act was intended in part "to provide a means whereby the ecosystems upon which endangered species and threatened species depend may be conserved," . . . To say that the Act protects ecosystems is not to say that the Act creates (if it were possible) rights of action in persons who have not been injured in fact, that is, persons who use portions of an ecosystem not perceptibly affected by the unlawful action in question.

Respondents' other theories are called, alas, the "animal nexus" approach, whereby anyone who has an interest in studying or seeing the endangered animals anywhere on the globe has standing; and the "vocational nexus" approach, under which anyone with a professional interest in such animals can sue. Under these theories, anyone who goes to see Asian elephants in the Bronx Zoo, and anyone who is a keeper of Asian elephants in the Bronx Zoo, has standing to sue because the Director of the Agency for International Development (AID) did not consult with the Secretary regarding the AID-funded project in Sri Lanka. This is beyond all reason. Standing is not "an ingenious academic exercise in the conceivable," but as we have said requires, at the summary judgment stage, a factual showing of perceptible harm. It is clear that the person who observes or works with a particular animal threatened by a federal decision is facing perceptible harm, since the very subject of his interest will no longer exist. It is even plausible—though it goes to the outermost limit of plausibility—to think that a person who observes or works with animals of a particular species in the very area of the world where that species is threatened by a federal decision is facing such harm, since some animals that might have been the subject of his interest will no longer exist. It goes beyond the limit, however, and into pure speculation and fantasy, to say that anyone who observes or works with an endangered species, anywhere in the world, is appreciably harmed by a single project affecting some portion of that species with which he has no more specific connection. . . .

B

Besides failing to show injury, respondents failed to demonstrate redressability. Instead of attacking the separate de-

cisions to fund particular projects allegedly causing them harm, respondents chose to challenge a more generalized level of Government action (rules regarding consultation), the invalidation of which would affect all overseas projects. This programmatic approach has obvious practical advantages, but also obvious difficulties insofar as proof of causation or redressability is concerned. As we have said in another context, "suits challenging, not specifically identifiable Government violations of law, but the particular programs agencies establish to carry out their legal obligations . . . [are], even when premised on allegations of several instances of violations of law, . . . rarely if ever appropriate for federal-court adjudication." . . .

The most obvious problem in the present case is redressability. Since the agencies funding the projects were not parties to the case, the District Court could accord relief only against the Secretary: He could be ordered to revise his regulation to require consultation for foreign projects. But this would not remedy respondents' alleged injury unless the funding agencies were bound by the Secretary's regulation, which is very much an open question. Whereas in other contexts the ESA is quite explicit as to the Secretary's controlling authority, . . . with respect to consultation the initiative, and hence arguably the initial responsibility for determining statutory necessity, lies with the agencies, . . .

The short of the matter is that redress of the only injury in fact respondents complain of requires action (termination of funding until consultation) by the individual funding agencies; and any relief the District Court could have provided in this suit against the Secretary was not likely to produce that action. . . .

We have consistently held that a plaintiff raising only a generally available grievance about government—claiming only harm to his and every citizen's interest in proper application of the Constitution and laws, and seeking relief that no more directly and tangibly benefits him than it does the public at large—does not state an Article III case or controversy. . . .

Whether the courts were to act on their own, or at the invitation of Congress, in ignoring the concrete injury requirement described in our cases, they would be discarding a principle fundamental to the separate and distinct constitutional role of the Third Branch—one of the essential elements that identifies those "Cases" and "Controversies" that are the business of the courts rather than of the political branches. "The province of the court," as Chief Justice Marshall said in *Marbury v. Madison* [1803] "is, solely, to decide on the rights of individuals." Vindicating the public interest (including the public interest in Government observance of the Constitution and laws) is the function of Congress and the Chief Executive. The question presented here is whether the public interest in proper administration of the laws (specifically, in agencies' observance of a particular, statutorily prescribed procedure) can be converted into an individual right by a statute that denominates it as such, and that permits all citizens (or, for that matter, a subclass of citizens who suffer no distinctive concrete harm) to sue. If the concrete injury requirement has the separation-of-powers significance we have always said, the answer must be obvious: To permit Congress to convert the undifferentiated public interest in executive officers' compliance with the law into an "individual right" vindicable in the courts is to permit Congress to transfer from the President to the courts the Chief Executive's most important constitutional duty, to "take Care that the Laws be faithfully executed," Art. II, s 3. It would enable the courts, with the permission of Congress, "to assume a position of authority over the governmental acts of another and co-equal department," . . . and to become "virtually continuing monitors of the wisdom and soundness of Executive action." . . . We have always rejected that vision of our role . . .

We hold that respondents lack standing to bring this action and that the Court of Appeals erred in denying the summary judgment motion filed by the United States. The opinion of the Court of Appeals is hereby reversed, and the cause is remanded for proceedings consistent with this opinion.

It is so ordered.

Mr. Justice KENNEDY, with whom Justice SOUTER joins, concurring in part and concurring in the judgment. . . .

As Government programs and policies become more complex and far reaching, we must be sensitive to the articulation of new rights of action that do not have clear analogs in our common-law tradition. Modern litigation has progressed far from the paradigm of Marbury suing Madison to get his commission, *Marbury v. Madison*, or Ogden seeking an injunction to halt Gibbons' steamboat operations. . . . In my view, Congress has the power to define injuries and articulate chains of causation that will give rise to a case or controversy where none existed before, and I do not read the Court's opinion to suggest a contrary view. . . . In exercising this power, however, Congress must at the very least identify the injury it seeks to vindicate and relate the injury to the class of persons entitled to bring suit. The citizen-suit provision of the Endangered Species Act does not meet these minimal requirements, because while the statute purports to confer a right on "any person . . . to enjoin . . . the United States and any other governmental instrumentality or agency . . . who is alleged to be in violation of any provision of this chapter," it does not of its own force establish that there is an injury in "any person" by virtue of any "violation."

The Court's holding that there is an outer limit to the power of Congress to confer rights of action is a direct and necessary consequence of the case and controversy limitations found in Article III. I agree that it would exceed those limitations if, at the behest of Congress and in the absence of any showing of concrete injury, we were to entertain citizen suits to vindicate the public's nonconcrete interest in the proper administration of the laws. While it does not matter how many persons have been injured by the challenged action, the party bringing suit must show that the action injures him in a concrete and personal way. This requirement is not just an empty formality. It preserves the vitality of the adversarial process by assuring both that the parties before the court have an actual, as opposed to professed, stake in the outcome, and that "the legal questions presented . . . will be resolved, not in the rarified atmosphere of a debating society, but in a concrete factual context conducive to a realistic appreciation of the consequences of judicial action." . . .

In addition, the requirement of concrete injury confines the Judicial Branch to its proper, limited role in the constitutional framework of Government.

An independent judiciary is held to account through its open proceedings and its reasoned judgments. In this process it is essential for the public to know what persons or groups are invoking the judicial power, the reasons that they have brought suit, and whether their claims are vindicated or denied. The concrete injury requirement helps assure that there can be an answer to these questions; and, as the Court's opinion is careful to show, that is part of the constitutional design. . . .

Notes/Queries/Readings

1. Can standing in a particular case be determined by the text of the Constitution? Or are such considerations necessarily prudential judgments? Are they necessarily subjective?

2. The rule of standing, like other so-called rules of justiciability, derives from the *Marbury v. Madison* model of judicial decision making; namely, that courts decide constitutional issues as a by-product of a real dispute between adverse litigants. For a major criticism of this approach, see Burt Neuborne, "Justiciability, Remedies, and the Burger Court" in Herman Schwartz, ed., *The Burger Court* (New York: Viking, 1987), 3–20. Neuborne praises the Warren Court for "stretch[ing] the [*Marbury*] model to its outermost limits (as in *Baker*) or to jettison it entirely . . . in order to make sure that the Supreme Court fulfilled its role as enforcer of the Constitution." The Burger Court, however, "declined to [follow this trend when certain] challengers could not be characterized as *Marbury*-style plaintiffs with particularized grievances caused by the unlawful activity,

and could not articulate an individualized injury-in-fact." *Ibid.*, 7.

3. For other decisions in which important constitutional questions remained undecided because the plaintiffs failed to meet the standing rule, see *Laird v. Tatum*, 408 U.S. 1 (1972); *Schlesinger v. Reservists Committee to Stop the War*, 418 U.S. 208 (1974); and *Allen v. Wright*, 468 U.S. 737 (1984). See also *Frothingham v. Mellon*, 262 U.S. 447 (1923), in which the Supreme Court ruled that a taxpayer could not enjoin the execution of a federal appropriation act, on the ground that it is invalid and will result in taxation for illegal purposes. Frothingham's suit was dismissed for lack of standing. "[T]he relation of a taxpayer of the United States to the federal Government," declared the Court, "is shared with millions of others; is comparatively minute and indeterminable; and the effect upon future taxation [is] so remote . . . that no basis is afforded for an appeal to the preventive powers of a court of equity." In addition, "If one taxpayer may champion and litigate such a cause, then every other taxpayer may do the same, not only in respect of the statute here under review but also in respect of every other appropriation . . . whose validity may be questioned." For a Canadian perspective on taxpayer suits see Comparative Note 3.5.

4. How is it possible for the Supreme Court to serve as the guardian of the Constitution in light of the standing rule or of the "political question" doctrine discussed in the upcoming cases *Luther v. Borden*, *Baker v. Carr*, and *Nixon v. United States*? In other constitutional democracies, such as Germany and Italy, constitutional courts do serve as *the* guardian of the Constitution, for they are empowered to declare the meaning of all constitutional provisions when asked to do so and entirely outside the technical context of a "case" or "controversy" as understood in the United States.

The Supreme Court recently acknowledged the difference between the exercise of judicial review in the United States and other countries. In *Raines v. Byrd*, 138 L. Ed. 2d

849 (1997), in which the Court cited *Lujan*, Chief Justice Rehnquist remarked: "There would be nothing irrational about a system which granted standing in [certain] cases; some European constitutional courts operate under one or another variant of such a regime. But it is obviously not the regime that has obtained under our Constitution to date. Our regime contemplates a more restricted role for Article III courts, well expressed by Justice Powell in his concurring opinion in *United States v. Richardson* (1947):

> The irreplaceable value of the power articulated by Mr. Chief Justice Marshall [in *Marbury v. Madison* (1803)] lies in the protection it has afforded the constitutional rights and liberties of individual citizens and minority groups against oppressive or discriminatory government action. It is this role, not some amorphous general supervision of the operations of government, that has maintained public esteem for the federal courts and has permitted the peaceful coexistence of the countermajoritarian implications of judicial review and the democratic principles upon which our Federal Government in the final analysis rests.

But what if the "operations of government" to which Justice Powell refers—in *Raines* it was the president's line item veto—violate the Constitution? Should these operations be permitted to continue simply because the litigants do not have standing to sue? In Germany, as Chief Justice Rehnquist recognizes, the Federal Constitutional Court is empowered to rule on the constitutionality of a law, immediately after its passage, on a petition of one-third of parliament's membership if there is a disagreement or even doubts about the statute's validity. Moreover, the Court's rulings in such abstract judicial review cases is absolutely binding on all state officials and branches of government. Would "public esteem for the federal courts" drop significantly, as Justice Powell suggests, if the United States were to adopt the German system of constitutional review?

Luther v. Borden
48 U.S. 1, 7 Howard 1, 12 L. Ed. 581 (1849)

This case grew out of Thomas W. Dorr's rebellion against the government of Rhode Island, whose constitution was almost identical to the colonial charter that Charles II had granted in 1663. The constitution strictly limited the right to vote and had no provision for amendment. In 1841 Dorr and his supporters held mass meetings throughout the state, convened a constitutional convention, and drafted a new constitution that established universal manhood suffrage. Dorr was then elected governor under the new con-

stitution. When he sought to put the new constitution into force, the state's charter government declared martial law, crushed the "insurrection," and jailed many of its supporters, including Luther, one of Dorr's followers. The charter government appealed to President Tyler for help, but no federal troops had to be sent. Dorr was later tried and convicted of treason, although he was eventually pardoned. In 1842 the charter government gave way to popular sentiment and a new democratic constitution entered into force.

During the rebellion, Borden and other state agents had arrested Luther after breaking into his home. Luther sued Borden for illegal entry on the grounds that the charter government was illegal and had been replaced by the new constitution. Luther had moved to Massachusetts which allowed him to bring a diversity suit against Borden, a resident of Rhode Island. The Court was called upon to decide which of the two claimants was the legal government of Rhode Island. Opinion of the Court: *Taney*, Grier, McLean, Nelson, Wayne. Dissenting Opinion: *Woodbury*, Catron, Daniel. Not participating: McKinley.

**Mr. Chief Justice TANEY delivered
the opinion of the Court.**

The fourth section of the fourth article of the Constitution of the United States provides that the United States shall guarantee to every State in the Union a republican form of government, and shall protect each of them against invasion; and on the application of the legislature or of the executive (when the legislature cannot be convened) against domestic violence.

Under this article of the Constitution it rests with Congress to decide what government is the established one in a State. For as the United States guarantee to each State a republican government, Congress must necessarily decide what government is established in the State before it can determine whether it is republican or not. And when the senators and representatives of a State are admitted into the councils of the Union, the authority of the government under which they are appointed, as well as its republican character, is recognized by the proper constitutional authority. And its decision is binding on every other department of the government, and could not be questioned in a judicial tribunal. It is true that the contest in this case did not last long enough to bring the matter to this issue; and as no senators or representatives were elected under the authority of the government of which Mr. Dorr was the head, Congress was not called upon to decide the controversy. Yet the right to decide is placed there, and not in the courts.

So, too, as relates to the clause in the above-mentioned article of the Constitution, providing for cases of domestic violence. It rested with Congress, too, to determine upon the means proper to be adopted to fulfill this guarantee. They might, if they had deemed it most advisable to do so, have placed it in the power of a court to decide when the contingency had happened which required the federal government to interfere. But Congress thought otherwise, and no doubt wisely; and by the act of February 28, 1795, provided, that, "in case of an insurrection in any State against the government thereof, it shall be lawful for the President of the United States, on application of the legislature of such State or of the executive [when the legislature cannot be convened], to call forth such number of the militia of any other State or States, as may be applied for, as he may judge sufficient to suppress such insurrection."

By this act, the power of deciding whether the exigency had arisen upon which the government of the United States is bound to interfere, is given to the President. He is to act upon the application of the legislature or of the executive, and consequently he must determine what body of men constitute the legislature, and who is the governor, before he can act. The fact that both parties claim the right to the government cannot alter the case, for both cannot be entitled to it. If there is an armed conflict, like the one of which we are speaking, it is a case of domestic violence, and one of the parties must be in insurrection against the lawful government. And the President must, of necessity, decide which is the government, and which party is unlawfully arrayed against it, before he can perform the duty imposed upon him by the act of Congress.

After the President has acted and called out the militia, is a Circuit Court of the United States authorized to inquire whether his decision was right? Could the court, while the parties were actually contending in arms for the possession of the government, call witnesses before it and inquire which party represented a majority of the people? If

---

Comparative Note 3.6

. . . s. 24 (1) of the Charter, also part of the Constitution, makes it clear that the adjudication of that question is the responsibility of a "court of competent jurisdiction." While the court is entitled to grant such remedy as it "considers appropriate and just in the circumstances," I do not think it is open to it to relinquish its jurisdiction, either on the basis that the issue is inherently non-justiciable or that it raises a so-called "political question."

If we are to look at the Constitution for the answer to the question whether it is appropriate for the courts to "second guess" the executive on matters of defense, we would conclude that it is not appropriate. However, if what we are being asked to do is to decide whether any particular act of the executive violates the rights of citizens, then it is not only appropriate that we answer the question; it is our obligation to do so.

SOURCE: *Operation Dismantle v. R.* In the Supreme Court of Canada [1985] 1 S.C.R. 441.

it could, then it would become the duty of the court (provided it came to the conclusion that the President had decided incorrectly) to discharge those who were arrested or detained by the troops in the service of the United States or the government which the President was endeavouring to maintain. If the judicial power extends so far, the guarantee contained in the Constitution of the United States is a guarantee of anarchy, and not of order. Yet if this right does not reside in the courts when the conflict is raging, if the judicial power is at that time bound to follow the decision of the political, it must be equally bound when the contest is over. It cannot, when peace is restored, punish as offences and crimes the acts which it before recognized, and was bound to recognize, as lawful.

It is true that in this case the militia were not called out by the President. But upon the application of the governor under the charter government, the President recognized him as the executive power of the State, and took measures to call out the militia to support his authority if it should be found necessary for the general government to interfere; and it is admitted in the argument, that it was the knowledge of this decision that put an end to the armed opposition to the charter government, and prevented any further efforts to establish by force the proposed constitution. The interference of the President, therefore, by announcing his determination, was as effectual as if the militia had been assembled under his orders. And it should be equally authoritative. For certainly no court of the United States, with a knowledge of this decision, would have been justified in recognizing the opposing party as the lawful government; or in treating as wrongdoers or insurgents the officers of the government which the President had recognized, and was prepared to support by an armed force. In the case of foreign nations, the government acknowledged by the President is always recognized in the courts of justice. And this principle has been applied by the act of Congress to the sovereign States of the Union.

It is said that this power in the President is dangerous to liberty, and may be abused. All power may be abused if placed in unworthy hands. But it would be difficult, we think, to point out any other hands in which this power would be more safe, and at the same time equally effectual. When citizens of the same State are in arms against each other, and the constituted authorities unable to execute the laws, the interposition of the United States must be prompt, or it is of little value. The ordinary course of proceedings in courts of justice would be utterly unfit for the crisis. And the elevated office of the President, chosen as he is by the people of the United States, and the high responsibility he could not fail to feel when acting in a case of so much moment, appear to furnish as strong safeguards against a wilful abuse of power as human prudence and foresight could well provide. At all events, it is conferred upon him by the Constitution and laws of the United States, and must therefore be respected and enforced in its judicial tribunals.

. . . Undoubtedly, if the President in exercising this power shall fall into error, or invade the rights of the people of the State, it would be in the power of Congress to apply the proper remedy. But the courts must administer the law as they find it.

Much of the argument on the part of the plaintiff turned upon political rights and political questions, upon which the court has been urged to express an opinion. We decline doing so. The high power has been conferred on this court of passing judgment upon the acts of the State sovereignties, and of the legislative and executive branches of the federal government, and of determining whether they are beyond the limits of power marked out for them respectively by the Constitution of the United States. This tribunal, therefore, should be the last to overstep the boundaries which limit its own jurisdiction. And while it should always be ready to meet any question confided to it by the Constitution, it is equally its duty not to pass beyond its appropriate sphere of action, and to take care not to involve itself in discussions which properly belong to other forums. No one, we believe, has ever doubted the proposition, that, according to the institutions of this country, the sovereignty in every State resides in the people of the State, and that they may alter and change their form of government at their own pleasure. But whether they have changed it or not by abolishing an old government, and establishing a new one in its place, is a question to be settled by the political power. And when that power has decided, the courts are bound to take notice of its decision, and to follow it.

The judgment of the Circuit Court must therefore be affirmed.

Notes/Queries/Readings

1. What reasoning does the Court use to vest in Congress—and not the judiciary—the determination of whether a state has a republican form of government?

2. Chief Justice Marshall noted in *Marbury* that "questions in their nature political, or which are, by the Constitution and laws, submitted to the Executive, can never be made by this court." How does the Court determine when a question is, in fact, political?

3. Should the judiciary have the final authority to resolve such essentially political questions? Do the political considerations cited by the Court in deferring to the other branches of government outweigh what Marshall considered the duty of the judiciary to say what the law is?

4. Can you imagine circumstances in which the application of the "political questions" doctrine would be an abdication of judicial responsibility or place at risk the principle of constitutionalism?

5. Do you find it troubling that the Court has determined that it will not or cannot enforce certain provisions of the Constitution? How can this judicial practice of refusing to intervene in political questions be reconciled with Marshall's statement that the judicial power of the United States is extended to all cases arising under the Constitution? Consider in this connection the remarks of Justice Claire L'Heureux-Dube of the Supreme Court of Canada in Comparative Note 3.6.

6. For additional reading, see William M. Wiecek, *The Guarantee Clause of the United States Constitution* (Ithaca, N.Y.: Cornell University Press, 1972) and Marvin E. Gettleman, *The Dorr Rebellion: A Case Study in American Radicalism* (New York: Random House, 1973).

Baker v. Carr

369 U.S. 186, 82 S. Ct. 691, 7 L. Ed. 2d 663 (1962)

This case arose out of a constitutional challenge to Tennessee's apportionment of its state legislative districts. The state had not reapportioned its districts since 1901, notwithstanding a provision in its constitution requiring reapportionment on the basis of population every ten years. Demographic changes over the ensuing decades had resulted in legislative districts that varied widely in population. Voters in Tennessee sued the state on the grounds that the system of representation caused by malapportionment was "utterly arbitrary" and a dilution of the strength of their votes in violation of the equal protection clause of the Constitution. Citing *Colegrove v. Green* (1946), a three-judge federal district court dismissed the suit, after which the case went to the Supreme Court on appeal. Opinion of the Court: *Brennan*, Black, Clark, Douglas, Stewart, Warren. Concurring Opinion: *Clark*, Douglas, Stewart. Dissenting Opinion: *Frankfurter*, Harlan. Not participating: Whittaker.

Mr. Justice BRENNAN delivered the opinion of the Court.

. . . [W]e hold today only (a) that the court possessed jurisdiction of the subject matter; (b) that a justiciable cause of action is stated upon which appellants would be entitled to appropriate relief; and (c) because appellees raise the issue before this Court, that the appellants have standing to challenge the Tennessee apportionment statutes. Beyond noting that we have no cause at this stage to doubt the District Court will be able to fashion relief if violations of constitutional rights are found, it is improper now to consider what remedy would be most appropriate if appellants prevail at the trial.

Jurisdiction of the Subject Matter

The District Court was uncertain whether our cases withholding federal judicial relief rested upon a lack of federal jurisdiction or upon the inappropriateness of the subject matter for judicial consideration—what we have designated "nonjusticiability." The distinction between the two grounds is significant. In the instance of nonjusticiability, consideration of the cause is not wholly and immediately foreclosed; rather, the Court's inquiry necessarily proceeds to the point of deciding whether the duty asserted can be judicially identified and its breach judicially determined, and whether protection for the right asserted can be judicially molded. In the instance of lack of jurisdiction the cause either does not "arise under" the Federal Constitution, laws or treaties (or fall within one of the other enumerated categories of Art. III, s 2), or is not a "case or controversy" within the meaning of that section; or the cause is not one described by any jurisdictional statute. Our conclusion that this cause presents no nonjusticiable "political question" settles the only possible doubt that it is a case or controversy. . . .

Standing

A federal court cannot "pronounce any statute, either of a state or of the United States, void, because irreconcilable with the constitution, except as it is called upon to adjudge the legal rights of litigants in actual controversies." Have the appellants alleged such a personal stake in the outcome of the controversy as to assure that concrete adverseness which sharpens the presentation of issues upon which the court so largely depends for illumination of difficult constitutional questions? This is the gist of the question of standing. It is, of course, a question of federal law.

We hold that the appellants do have standing to maintain this suit. Our decisions plainly support this conclusion. Many of the cases have assumed rather than articulated the premise in deciding the merits of similar claims. . . .

These appellants seek relief in order to protect or vindicate an interest of their own, and of those similarly situated. Their constitutional claim is, in substance, that the 1901 statute constitutes arbitrary and capricious state action, offensive to the Fourteenth Amendment in its irrational disregard of the standard of apportionment prescribed by the State's Constitution or of any standard, effecting a gross disproportion of representation to voting population. The injury which appellants assert is that this classification disfavors the voters in the counties in which they reside, placing them in a position of constitutionally unjustifiable inequality vis-a-vis voters in irrationally favored counties. A citizen's right to a vote free of arbitrary impairment by state action has been judicially recognized as a right secured by the Constitution, when such impairment resulted from dilution by a false tally, or by a refusal to count votes from arbitrarily selected precincts, . . . or by a stuffing of the ballot box.

It would not be necessary to decide whether appellants' allegations of impairment of their votes by the 1901 apportionment will, ultimately, entitle them to any relief, in order to hold that they have standing to seek it. If such impairment does produce a legally cognizable injury, they are among those who have sustained it. They are asserting "a plain, direct and adequate interest in maintaining the effectiveness of their votes," not merely a claim of the right possessed by every citizen "to require that the government be administered according to law . . ." They are entitled to a hearing and to the District Court's decision on their claims. "The very essence of civil liberty certainly consists in the right of every individual to claim the protection of the laws, whenever he receives an injury."

Justiciability

In holding that the subject matter of this suit was not justiciable, the District Court relied on *Colegrove v. Green* [1946]. The court stated: "From a review of these decisions there can be no doubt that the federal rule . . . is that the federal courts . . . will not intervene in cases of this type to compel legislative reapportionment." We understand the District Court to have read the cited cases as compelling the conclusion that since the appellants sought to have a legislative apportionment held unconstitutional, their suit presented a "political question" and was therefore nonjusticiable. We hold that this challenge to an apportionment presents no nonjusticiable "political question." The cited cases do not hold the contrary.

Of course the mere fact that the suit seeks protection of a political right does not mean it presents a political question. Such an objection "is little more than a play upon words." Rather, it is argued that apportionment cases, whatever the actual wording of the complaint, can involve no federal constitutional right except one resting on the guaranty of a republican form of government, and that complaints based on that clause have been held to present political questions which are nonjusticiable.

We hold that the claim pleaded here neither rests upon nor implicates the Guaranty Clause and that its justiciability is therefore not foreclosed by our decisions of cases involving that clause. . . . To show why we reject the argument based on the Guaranty Clause, we must examine the authorities under it. But because there appears to be some uncertainty as to why those cases did present political questions, and specifically as to whether this apportionment case is like those cases, we deem it necessary first to

consider the contours of the "political question" doctrine.

Our discussion . . . requires review of a number of political question cases, in order to expose the attributes of the doctrine—attributes which, in various settings, diverge, combine, appear, and disappear in seeming disorderliness. . . . That review reveals that in the Guaranty Clause cases and in the other "political question" cases, it is the relationship between the judiciary and the coordinate branches of the Federal Government, and not the federal judiciary's relationship to the States, which gives rise to the "political question." . . .

The nonjusticiability of a political question is primarily a function of the separation of powers. Much confusion results from the capacity of the "political question" label to obscure the need for case-by-case inquiry. Deciding whether a matter has in any measure been committed by the Constitution to another branch of government, or whether the action of that branch exceeds whatever authority has been committed, is itself a delicate exercise in constitutional interpretation, and is a responsibility of this Court as ultimate interpreter of the Constitution. To demonstrate this requires no less than to analyze representative cases and to infer from them the analytical threads that make up the political question doctrine. We shall then show that none of those threads catches this case.

. . . Prominent on the surface of any case held to involve a political question is found a textually demonstrable constitutional commitment of the issue to a coordinate political department; or a lack of judicially discoverable and manageable standards for resolving it; or the impossibility of deciding without an initial policy determination of a kind clearly for nonjudicial discretion; or the impossibility of a court's undertaking independent resolution without expressing lack of the respect due coordinate branches of government; or an unusual need for unquestioning adherence to a political decision already made; or the potentiality of embarrassment from multifarious pronouncements by various departments on one question.

Unless one of these formulations is inextricable from the case at bar, there should be no dismissal for nonjusticiability on the ground of a political question's presence. The doctrine of which we treat is one of "political questions," not one of "political cases." The courts cannot reject as "no law suit" a bona fide controversy as to whether some action denominated "political" exceeds constitutional authority. . . .

But it is argued that this case shares the characteristics of decisions that constitute a category not yet considered, cases concerning the Constitution's guaranty, in Art. IV, s 4, of a republican form of government. . . .

Just as the Court has consistently held that a challenge to state action based on the Guaranty Clause presents no justiciable question so has it held, and for the same reasons, that challenges to congressional action on the ground of inconsistency with that clause present no justiciable question. In *Georgia v. Stanton* [1867], the State sought by an original bill to enjoin execution of the Reconstruction Acts, claiming that it already possessed "A republican State, in every political, legal, constitutional, and juridical sense," and that enforcement of the new Acts "Instead of keeping the guaranty against a forcible overthrow of its government by foreign invaders or domestic insurgents . . . is destroying that very government by force." Congress had clearly refused to recognize the republican character of the government of the suing State. It seemed to the Court that the only constitutional claim that could be presented was under the Guaranty Clause, and Congress having determined that the effects of the recent hostilities required extraordinary measures to restore governments of a republican form, this Court refused to interfere with Congress' action at the behest of a claimant relying on that very guaranty. . . .

We come, finally, to the ultimate inquiry whether our precedents as to what constitutes a nonjusticiable "political question" bring the case before us under the umbrella of that doctrine. A natural beginning is to note whether any of the common characteristics which we have been able to identify and label descriptively are present. We find none: The question here is the consistency of state action with the Federal Constitution. We have no question decided, or to be decided, by a political branch of government coequal with this Court. Nor do we risk embarrassment of our government abroad, or grave disturbance at home if we take issue with Tennessee as to the constitutionality of her action here challenged. Nor need the appellants, in order to succeed in this action, ask the Court to enter upon policy determinations for which judicially manageable standards are lacking. Judicial standards under the Equal Protection Clause are well developed and familiar, and it has been open to courts since the enactment of the Fourteenth Amendment to determine, if on the particular facts they must, that a discrimination reflects no policy, but simply arbitrary and capricious action.

This case does, in one sense, involve the allocation of political power within a State, and the appellants might conceivably have added a claim under the Guaranty Clause. Of course, as we have seen, any reliance on that clause would be futile. But because any reliance on the Guaranty Clause could not have succeeded it does not follow that appellants may not be heard on the equal protection claim which in fact they tender. True, it must be clear that the Fourteenth Amendment claim is not so enmeshed with those political question elements which render Guaranty Clause claims nonjusticiable as actually to present a political question itself. But we have found that not to be the case here. . . .

We conclude that the complainant's allegations of a denial of equal protection present a justiciable constitutional cause of action upon which appellants are entitled to a trial and a decision. The right asserted is within the reach of judicial protection under the Fourteenth Amendment.

The judgment of the District Court is reversed and the cause is remanded for further proceedings consistent with this opinion. Reversed and remanded.

Mr. Justice FRANKFURTER, whom Mr. Justice HARLAN joins, dissenting.

The Court today reverses a uniform course of decision established by a dozen cases, including one by which the very claim now sustained was unanimously rejected only five years ago. The impressive body of rulings thus cast aside reflected the equally uniform course of our political history regarding the relationship between population and legislative representation—a wholly different matter from denial of the franchise to individuals because of race, color, religion or sex. Such a massive repudiation of the experience of our whole past in asserting destructively novel judicial power demands a detailed analysis of the role of this Court in our constitutional scheme. Disregard of inherent limits in the effective exercise of the Court's "judicial Power" not only presages the futility of judicial intervention in the essentially political conflict of forces by which the relation between population and representation has time out of mind been and now is determined. It may well impair the Court's position as the ultimate organ of "the supreme Law of the Land" in that vast range of legal problems, often strongly entangled in popular feeling, on which this Court must pronounce. The Court's authority—possessed of neither the purse nor the sword—ultimately rests on sustained public confidence in its moral sanction. Such feeling must be nourished by the Court's complete detachment, in fact and in appearance, from political entanglements and by abstention from injecting itself into the clash of political forces in political settlements.

A hypothetical claim resting on abstract assumptions is now for the first time made the basis for affording illusory relief for a particular evil even though it foreshadows deeper and more pervasive difficulties in consequence. The claim is hypothetical and the assumptions are abstract because the Court does not vouchsafe the lower courts—state and federal—guidelines for formulating specific, definite, wholly unprecedented remedies for the inevitable litigations that today's umbrageous disposition is bound to stimulate in connection with politically motivated reapportionments in so many States. In such a setting, to promulgate jurisdiction in the abstract is meaningless. It is as devoid of reality as "a brooding omnipresence in the sky," for it conveys no intimation what relief, if any, a District Court is capable of affording that would not invite legislatures to play ducks and drakes with the judiciary. For this Court to direct the District Court to enforce a claim to which the Court has over the years consistently found itself required to deny legal enforcement and at the same time to find it necessary to withhold any guidance to the lower court how to enforce this turnabout, new legal claim, manifests an odd—indeed an esoteric—conception of judicial propriety. One of the Court's supporting opinions, as elucidated by commentary, unwittingly affords a disheartening preview of the mathematical quagmire (apart from diverse judicially inappropriate and elusive determinants) into which this Court today catapults the lower courts of the country without so much as adumbrating the basis for a legal calculus as a means of extrication. Even assuming the indispensable intellectual disinterestedness on the part of judges in such matters, they do not have accepted legal standards or criteria or even reliable analogies to draw upon for making judicial judgments. To charge courts with the task of accommodating the incommensurable factors of policy that underlie these mathematical puzzles is to attribute, however flatteringly, omnicompetence to judges. . . .

We were soothingly told at the bar of this Court that we need not worry about the kind of remedy a court could effectively fashion once the abstract constitutional right to have courts pass on a state-wide system of electoral districting is recognized as a matter of judicial rhetoric, because legislatures would heed the Court's admonition. This is not only a euphoric hope. It implies a sorry confession of judicial impotence in place of a frank acknowledgment that there is not under our Constitution a judicial remedy for every political mischief, for every undesirable exercise of legislative power. The Framers carefully and with deliberate forethought refused so to enthrone the judiciary. In this situation, as in others of like nature, appeal for relief does not belong here. Appeal must be to an informed, civically militant electorate. In a democratic society like ours, relief must come through an aroused popular conscience that sears the conscience of the people's representatives. In any event there is nothing judicially more unseemly nor more self-defeating than for this Court to make *in terrorem* pronouncements, to indulge in merely empty rhetoric, sounding a word of promise to the ear, sure to be disappointing to the hope.

In sustaining appellants' claim, based on the Fourteenth Amendment, that the District Court may entertain this suit, this Court's uniform course of decision over the years is overruled or disregarded. Explicitly it begins with *Colegrove v. Green, supra*, decided in 1946, but its roots run deep in the Court's historic adjudicatory process.

Colegrove held that a federal court should not entertain an action for declaratory and injunctive relief to adjudicate the constitutionality, under the Equal Protection Clause and other federal constitutional and statutory provisions, of a state statute establishing the respective districts for the State's election of Representatives to the Congress. . . . [The

---

Comparative Note   3.7

. . . [O]ne must examine again the claim that determination of policy by the judge is incompatible with a democratic regime. As the argument goes, a democratic regime demands that policy be made by the people, through their elected representatives, not by the judges, who do not represent the nation and who are not accountable to it. It seems that this claim must now be seen in a different light. When a judge makes policy in the context of the fundamental values of the democracy, he does not act against the democracy but rather according to it. If democracy is a balance between majority rule and certain fundamental values, then the judge who makes policy on the basis of the fundamental values puts into effect those values that the democracy seeks to protect. A judge who adopts policy on the basis of the democracy's fundamental values makes the democracy faithful to itself. . . .

Of course, the assumption is that the judge acts lawfully within the frontiers of the zone of legitimacy. One also assumes that the legislature can at any time establish the balance that appeals to it. Yet as long as the legislature does not act and the judge operates within the limits of the zone of formal legitimacy, a determination of policy that is based on the fundamental values of the democratic regime should not be perceived as an undemocratic act. All the judge is doing is determining the borderline, as he sees it, between the power of the majority and its self-restraint. If the legislature, representing the majority, does not approve of this borderline, it has the authority to move it into the zone it believes is appropriate.

SOURCE: Aharon Barak, *Judicial Discretion.* Translated by Yadin Kaufmann (New Haven: Yale University Press, 1987), 196–197. Aharon Barak is a Justice of the Supreme Court of Israel.

two opinions written by the majority] demonstrate a predominant concern, first, with avoiding federal judicial involvement in matters traditionally left to legislative policy making; second, with respect to the difficulty—in view of the nature of the problems of apportionment and its history in this country—of drawing on or devising judicial standards for judgment, as opposed to legislative determinations, of the part which mere numerical equality among voters should play as a criterion for the allocation of political power; and, third, with problems of finding appropriate modes of relief—particularly, the problem of resolving the essentially political issue of the relative merits of at-large elections and elections held in districts of unequal population.

What, then, is this question of legislative apportionment? Appellants invoke the right to vote and to have their votes counted. But they are permitted to vote and their votes are counted. They go to the polls, they cast their ballots, they send their representatives to the state councils. Their complaint is simply that the representatives are not sufficiently numerous or powerful—in short, that Tennessee has adopted a basis of representation with which they are dissatisfied. Talk of "debasement" or "dilution" is circular talk. One cannot speak of "debasement" or "dilution" of the value of a vote until there is first defined a standard of reference as to what a vote should be worth. What is actually asked of the Court in this case is to choose among competing bases of representation—ultimately, really, among competing theories of political philosophy—in order to establish an appropriate frame of government for the State of Tennessee and thereby for all the States of the Union.

. . . What Tennessee illustrates is an old and still widespread method of representation—representation by local geographical division, only in part respective of population—in preference to others, others, forsooth, more appealing. Appellants contest this choice and seek to make this Court the arbiter of the disagreement. They would make the Equal Protection Clause the charter of adjudication, asserting that the equality which it guarantees comports, if not the assurance of equal weight to every voter's vote, at least the basic conception that representation ought to be proportionate to population, a standard by reference to which the reasonableness of apportionment plans may be judged.

To find such a political conception legally enforceable in the broad and unspecific guarantee of equal protection is to rewrite the Constitution. Certainly, "equal protection" is no more secure a foundation for judicial judgment of the permissibility of varying forms of representative government than is "Republican Form." Indeed since "equal protection of the laws" can only mean an equality of persons standing in the same relation to whatever governmental action is challenged, the determination whether treatment is equal presupposes a determination concerning the nature of the relationship. This, with respect to apportionment, means an inquiry into the theoretic base of representation in an acceptably republican state. For a court could not determine the equal-protection issue without in fact first determining the Republican-Form issue, simply because what is reasonable for equal-protection purposes will depend upon what frame of government, basically, is allowed. To divorce "equal protection" from "Republican Form" is to talk about half a question.

The notion that representation proportioned to the geographic spread of population is so universally accepted as a necessary element of equality between man and man that it must be taken to be the standard of a political equality preserved by the Fourteenth Amendment—that it is, in appellants' words "the basic principle of representative government"—is, to put it bluntly, not true. However desirable and however desired by some among the great political thinkers and framers of our government, it has never been generally practiced, today or in the past. It was not the English system, it was not the colonial system, it was not the system chosen for the national government by the Constitution, it was not the system exclusively or even predominantly practiced by the States at the time of adoption of the Fourteenth Amendment, it is not predominantly practiced by the States today. Unless judges, the judges of this Court, are to make their private views of political wisdom the measure of the Constitution—views which in all honesty cannot but give the appearance, if not reflect the reality, involvement with the business of partisan politics so inescapably a part of apportionment controversies—the Fourteenth Amendment, "itself a historical product," provides no guide for judicial oversight of the representation problem. . . .

Manifestly, the Equal Protection Clause supplies no clearer guide for judicial examination of apportionment methods than would the Guarantee Clause itself. Apportionment, by its character, is a subject of extraordinary complexity, involving—even after the fundamental theoretical issues concerning what is to be represented in a representative legislature have been fought out or compromised—considerations of geography, demography, electoral convenience, economic and social cohesions or divergencies among particular local groups, communications, the practical effects of political institutions like the lobby and the city machine, ancient traditions and ties of settled usage, respect for proven incumbents of long experience and senior status, mathematical mechanics, censuses compiling relevant data, and a host of others. Legislative responses throughout the country to the reapportionment demands of the 1960 Census have glaringly confirmed that these are not factors that lend themselves to evaluations of a nature that are the staple of judicial determinations or for which judges are equipped to adjudicate by legal training or experience or native wit. And this is the more so true because in every strand of this complicated, intricate web of values meet the contending forces of partisan politics. The practical significance of apportionment is that the next election results may differ because of it. Apportionment battles are overwhelmingly party or intra-party contests. It will add a virulent source of friction and tension in federal-state relations to embroil the federal judiciary in them.

Notes/Queries/Readings

1. What vision of political society animates the reasoning of the majority opinion? It might be suggested that in *Roe v. Wade* the Court envisions civil society as a collection of morally autonomous persons independent of any connection with or loyalty to other persons or groups. Does *Baker v. Carr* advance a similar view of political society? What conception of the citizen is inherent in the majority's reasoning?

2. To what ideal of representation does your answer to the previous query lead? In *Reynolds v. Sims* (1964), the Court declared that the Constitution requires state legislatures to be apportioned on the principle of "one person, one vote." Does the majority opinion allow states to take into account representation of particular communities or groups when apportioning their legislatures? Should states be allowed to do so?

3. In *Wesberry v. Sanders* (1964), the Supreme Court declared that the states must also apportion their congressional legislative districts on the basis of the one person, one vote rule. Can it be plausibly argued that a challenge to malapportioned congressional districts—as opposed to state legislative districts—poses a political question that the Supreme Court should not decide?

4. Does Justice Frankfurter offer a better theory of representation? Is the fact that representation solely on the basis of population "has never been generally practiced, today or in the past," necessarily fatal to the majority's argument that the Constitution mandates states to apportion their legislatures on the basis of one person, one vote?

5. In his dissent, Justice Frankfurter wrote that "What is actually asked of the Court in this case is to choose among competing bases of representation—ultimately, really, among competing theories of political philosophy. . . ." Do you agree? Is this a proper task for judges? Are there ways for judges to ground such choices in the Constitution?

6. *Baker* generated a wealth of commentary. Among the best efforts are Robert McCloskey, *Foreword: The Reapportionment Case*, 76 Harvard Law Review 54 [1962] and Phil C. Neal, Baker v. Carr: *Politics in Search of Law*, 1962 Supreme Court Review 252.

Nixon v. United States

506 U.S. 224, 113 S. Ct. 732, 122 L. Ed. 2d 1 (1993)

Walter Nixon, a federal district court judge, was convicted of making false statements before a federal grand jury and sentenced to prison. On 10 May 1989, the House of Representatives adopted three articles of impeachment for high crimes and misdemeanors. After the articles were presented to the Senate, the Senate appointed a committee of senators to "receive evidence and testimony" under its Rule XI. The committee held four days of hearings during which ten witnesses, including Nixon, testified. Nixon and the House impeachment managers submitted extensive final briefs to the full Senate and delivered arguments from the Senate floor during the oral argument in front of that body. The Senate voted by more than the constitutionally required two-thirds majority to convict Nixon on the first two articles, whereupon Nixon was removed from his office as United States District Judge. Nixon thereafter filed this suit arguing that the Senate Rule XI violates the constitutional grant of authority to the Senate to "try" all impeachments because it prohibits the whole Senate from taking part in the evidentiary hearings. The district court held that his claim was nonjusticiable. The court of appeals affirmed. Opinion of the Court: *Rehnquist*, Stevens, O'Connor, Scalia, Kennedy, Thomas. Concurring opinions: *Stevens*, Blackmun, *White*, *Souter*.

Mr. Chief Justice REHNQUIST delivered the opinion of the Court.

A controversy is nonjusticiable—i.e., involves a political question—where there is "a textually demonstrable constitutional commitment of the issue to a coordinate political department; or a lack of judicially discoverable and manageable standards for resolving it. . . ." But the courts must, in the first instance, interpret the text in question and determine whether and to what extent the issue is textually committed. As the discussion that follows makes clear, the concept of a textual commitment to a coordinate political department is not completely separate from the concept of a lack of judicially discoverable and manageable standards for resolving it; the lack of judicially manageable standards may strengthen the conclusion that there is a textually demonstrable commitment to a coordinate branch.

In this case, we must examine Art. I, s 3, cl. 6, to determine the scope of authority conferred upon the Senate by the Framers regarding impeachment. It provides: "The Senate shall have the sole Power to try all Impeachments. When sitting for that Purpose, they shall be on Oath or Affirmation. When the President of the United States is tried, the Chief Justice shall preside: And no Person shall be convicted without the Concurrence of two thirds of the Members present." The language and structure of this Clause are revealing. The first sentence is a grant of authority to the Senate, and the word "sole" indicates that this authority is reposed in the Senate and nowhere else. The next two sentences specify requirements to which the Senate proceedings shall conform: the Senate shall be on oath or affirmation, a two-thirds vote is required to convict, and when the President is tried the Chief Justice shall preside.

Petitioner argues that the word "try" in the first sentence imposes by implication an additional requirement on the Senate in that the proceedings must be in the nature of a judicial trial. From there petitioner goes on to argue that this limitation precludes the Senate from delegating to a select committee the task of hearing the testimony of witnesses, as was done pursuant to Senate Rule XI. . . .

There are several difficulties with this position which lead us ultimately to reject it. The word "try," both in 1787 and later, has considerably broader meanings than those to which petitioner would limit it. . . . Based on the variety of definitions, however, we cannot say that the Framers used the word "try" as an implied limitation on the method by which the Senate might proceed in trying impeachments. . . .

The conclusion that the use of the word "try" in the first sentence of the Impeachment Trial Clause lacks sufficient precision to afford any judicially manageable standard of review of the Senate's actions is fortified by the existence of the three very specific requirements that the Constitution does impose on the Senate when trying impeachments: the members must be under oath, a two-thirds vote is required to convict, and the Chief Justice presides when the President is tried. These limitations are quite precise, and their nature suggests that the Framers did not intend to impose additional limitations on the form of the Senate proceedings by the use of the word "try" in the first sentence.

Petitioner devotes only two pages in his brief to negating the significance of the word "sole" in the first sentence of Clause 6. As noted above, that sentence provides that "[t]he Senate shall have the sole Power to try all Impeachments." We think that the word "sole" is of considerable significance. Indeed, the word "sole" appears only one other time in the Constitution—with respect to the House of Representatives' "*sole* Power of Impeachment." Art. I, s 2,

cl. 5 (emphasis added). The common sense meaning of the word "sole" is that the Senate alone shall have authority to determine whether an individual should be acquitted or convicted. The dictionary definition bears this out. "Sole" is defined as "having no companion," "solitary," "being the only one," and "functioning . . . independently and without assistance or interference." If the courts may review the actions of the Senate in order to determine whether that body "tried" an impeached official, it is difficult to see how the Senate would be "functioning . . . independently and without assistance or interference."

Petitioner also contends that the word "sole" should not bear on the question of justiciability because Art. II, s 2, cl. 1, of the Constitution grants the President pardon authority "except in Cases of Impeachment." He argues that such a limitation on the President's pardon power would not have been necessary if the Framers thought that the Senate alone had authority to deal with such questions. But the granting of a pardon is in no sense an overturning of a judgment of conviction by some other tribunal; it is "[a]n executive action that mitigates or sets aside *punishment* for a crime." Authority in the Senate to determine procedures for trying an impeached official, unreviewable by the courts, is therefore not at all inconsistent with authority in the President to grant a pardon to the convicted official. . . .

Petitioner finally argues that even if significance be attributed to the word "sole" in the first sentence of the clause, the authority granted is to the Senate, and this means that "the Senate—not the courts, not a lay jury, not a Senate Committee—shall try impeachments." It would be possible to read the first sentence of the Clause this way, but it is not a natural reading. Petitioner's interpretation would bring into judicial purview not merely the sort of claim made by petitioner, but other similar claims based on the conclusion that the word "Senate" has imposed by implication limitations on procedures which the Senate might adopt. Such limitations would be inconsistent with the construction of the Clause as a whole, which, as we have noted, sets out three express limitations in separate sentences.

The history and contemporary understanding of the impeachment provisions support our reading of the constitutional language. The parties do not offer evidence of a single word in the history of the Constitutional Convention or in contemporary commentary that even alludes to the possibility of judicial review in the context of the impeachment powers. This silence is quite meaningful in light of the several explicit references to the availability of judicial review as a check on the Legislature's power with respect to bills of attainder, *ex post facto* laws, and statutes.

The Framers labored over the question of where the impeachment power should lie. Significantly, in at least two considered scenarios the power was placed with the Federal Judiciary. . . . Despite these proposals, the Convention ultimately decided that the Senate would have "the sole Power to Try all Impeachments." Art. I, s 3, cl. 6. According to Alexander Hamilton, the Senate was the "most fit depository of this important trust" because its members are representatives of the people. The Supreme Court was not the proper body because the Framers "doubted whether the members of that tribunal would, at all times, be endowed with so eminent a portion of fortitude as would be called for in the execution of so difficult a task" or whether the Court "would possess the degree of credit and authority" to carry out its judgment if it conflicted with the accusation brought by the Legislature—the people's representative. In addition, the Framers believed the Court was too small in number: "The awful discretion, which a court of impeachments must necessarily have, to doom to honor or to infamy the most confidential and the most distinguished characters of the community, forbids the commitment of the trust to a small number of persons."

There are two additional reasons why the Judiciary, and the Supreme Court in particular, were not chosen to have any role in impeachments. First, the Framers recognized that most likely there would be two sets of proceedings for individuals who commit impeachable offenses—the impeachment trial and a separate criminal trial. In fact, the Constitution explicitly provides for two separate proceedings. The Framers deliberately separated the two forums to avoid raising the specter of bias and to ensure independent judgments. . . . Certainly judicial review of the Senate's "trial" would introduce the same risk of bias as would participation in the trial itself.

Second, judicial review would be inconsistent with the Framers' insistence that our system be one of checks and balances. In our constitutional system, impeachment was designed to be the *only* check on the Judicial Branch by the Legislature. . . . Judicial involvement in impeachment proceedings, even if only for purposes of judicial review, is counter-intuitive because it would eviscerate the "important constitutional check" placed on the Judiciary by the Framers. Nixon's argument would place final reviewing authority with respect to impeachments in the hands of the same body that the impeachment process is meant to regulate.

Nevertheless, Nixon argues that judicial review is necessary in order to place a check on the Legislature. Nixon fears that if the Senate is given unreviewable authority to interpret the Impeachment Trial Clause, there is a grave risk that the Senate will usurp judicial power. The Framers anticipated this objection and created two constitutional safeguards to keep the Senate in check. The first safeguard is that the whole of the impeachment power is divided between the two legislative bodies, with the House given the right to accuse and the Senate given the right to judge. . . .

This split of authority "avoids the inconvenience of making the same persons both accusers and judges; and guards against the danger of persecution from the prevalency of a factious spirit in either of those branches." The second safeguard is the two-thirds supermajority vote requirement. Hamilton explained that "[a]s the concurrence of two-thirds of the senate will be requisite to a condemnation, the security to innocence, from this additional circumstance, will be as complete as itself can desire."

In addition to the textual commitment argument, we are persuaded that the lack of finality and the difficulty of fashioning relief counsel against justiciability. We agree with the Court of Appeals that opening the door of judicial review to the procedures used by the Senate in trying impeachments would "expose the political life of the country to months, or perhaps years, of chaos." This lack of finality would manifest itself most dramatically if the President were impeached. The legitimacy of any successor, and hence his effectiveness, would be impaired severely, not merely while the judicial process was running its course, but during any retrial that a differently constituted Senate might conduct if its first judgment of conviction were invalidated. Equally uncertain is the question of what relief a court may give other than simply setting aside the judgment of conviction. Could it order the reinstatement of a convicted federal judge, or order Congress to create an additional judgeship if the seat had been filled in the interim?

In the case before us, there is no separate provision of the Constitution which could be defeated by allowing the Senate final authority to determine the meaning of the word "try" in the Impeachment Trial Clause. We agree with Nixon that courts possess power to review either legislative or executive action that transgresses identifiable textual limits. As we have made clear, "whether the action of [either the Legislative or Executive Branch] exceeds whatever authority has been committed, is itself a delicate exercise in constitutional interpretation, and is a responsibility of this Court as ultimate interpreter of the Constitution." But we conclude, after exercising that delicate responsibility, that the word "try" in the Impeachment Clause does not provide an identifiable textual limit on the authority which is committed to the Senate.

For the foregoing reasons, the judgment of the Court of Appeals is
Affirmed.

Justice WHITE, with whom Justice BLACKMUN joins, concurring in the judgment.

Petitioner contends that the method by which the Senate convicted him on two articles of impeachment violates Art. I, s 3, cl. 6 of the Constitution, which mandates that the Senate "try" impeachments. The Court is of the view that the Constitution forbids us even to consider his contention. I find no such prohibition and would therefore reach the merits of the claim. I concur in the judgment because the Senate fulfilled its constitutional obligation to "try" petitioner.

The majority states that the question raised in this case meets two of the criteria for political questions set out in *Baker v. Carr* [1962]. It concludes first that there is "a textually demonstrable constitutional commitment of the issue to a coordinate political department." It also finds that the question cannot be resolved for "a lack of judicially discoverable and manageable standards."

Of course the issue in the political question doctrine is not whether the Constitutional text commits exclusive responsibility for a particular governmental function to one of the political branches. There are numerous instances of this sort of textual commitment, e.g., Art. I, s 8, and it is not thought that disputes implicating these provisions are nonjusticiable. Rather, the issue is whether the Constitution has given one of the political branches final responsibility for interpreting the scope and nature of such a power.

The majority finds a clear textual commitment in the Constitution's use of the word "sole" in the phrase "the Senate shall have the sole Power to try all impeachments." Art. I, s 3, cl. 6. . . .

. . . The significance of the Constitution's use of the term "sole" lies not in the infrequency with which the term appears, but in the fact that it appears exactly twice, in parallel provisions concerning impeachment. That the word "sole" is found only in the House and Senate Impeachment Clauses demonstrates that its purpose is to emphasize the distinct role of each in the impeachment process. As the majority notes, the Framers, following English practice, were very much concerned to separate the prosecutorial from the adjudicative aspects of impeachment. . . . Giving each House "sole" power with respect to its role in impeachments effected this division of labor. While the majority is thus right to interpret the term "sole" to indicate that the Senate ought to "functio[n] independently and without assistance or interference," . . . it wrongly identifies the judiciary, rather than the House, as the source of potential interference with which the Framers were concerned when they employed the term "sole."

The majority also claims support in the history and early interpretations of the Impeachment Clauses, noting the various arguments in support of the current system made at the Constitutional Convention and expressed powerfully by Hamilton in *The Federalist* Nos. 65 and 66. In light of these materials there can be little doubt that the Framers came to the view at the Convention that the trial of officials' public misdeeds should be conducted by representatives of the people; that the fledgling judiciary lacked the wherewithal to adjudicate political intrigues; that the judiciary ought not to try both impeachments and subsequent criminal cases emanating from them; and that the impeachment power must reside in the Legislative Branch to provide a check on the largely unaccountable judiciary.

The majority's review of the historical record thus explains why the power to try impeachments properly resides with the Senate. It does not explain, however, the sweeping statement that the judiciary was "not chosen to have any role in impeachments." Not a single word in the historical materials cited by the majority addresses judicial review of the Impeachment Trial Clause. And a glance at the arguments surrounding the Impeachment Clauses negates the majority's attempt to infer nonjusticiability from the Framers' arguments in support of the Senate's power to try impeachments.

The historical evidence reveals above all else that the Framers were deeply concerned about placing in any branch the "awful discretion, which a court of impeachments must necessarily have." . . . Viewed against this history, the discord between the majority's position and the basic principles of checks and balances underlying the Constitution's separation of powers is clear. In essence, the majority suggests that the Framers' conferred upon Congress a potential tool of legislative dominance yet at the same time rendered Congress' exercise of that power one of the very few areas of legislative authority immune from any judicial review. While the majority rejects petitioner's justiciability argument as espousing a view "inconsistent with the Framers' insistence that our system be one of checks and balances," it is the Court's finding of nonjusticiability that truly upsets the Framers' careful design. In a truly balanced system, impeachments tried by the Senate would serve as a means of controlling the largely unaccountable judiciary, even as judicial review would ensure that the Senate adhered to a minimal set of procedural standards in conducting impeachment trials.

The majority also contends that the term "try" does not present a judicially manageable standard. . . .

This argument comes in two variants. The first, which asserts that one simply cannot ascertain the sense of "try" which the Framers employed and hence cannot undertake judicial review, is clearly untenable. To begin with, one would intuitively expect that, in defining the power of a political body to conduct an inquiry into official wrongdoing, the Framers used "try" in its legal sense. That intuition is borne out by reflection on the alternatives. The third clause of Art. I, s 3 cannot seriously be read to mean that the Senate shall "attempt" or "experiment with" impeachments. It is equally implausible to say that the Senate is charged with "investigating" impeachments given that this description would substantially overlap with the House of Representatives' "sole" power to draw up articles of impeachment. Art. I, s 2, cl. 5. . . .

The other variant of the majority position focuses not on

which sense of "try" is employed in the Impeachment Trial Clause, but on whether the legal sense of that term creates a judicially manageable standard. The majority concludes that the term provides no "identifiable textual limit." Yet, as the Government itself conceded at oral argument, the term "try" is hardly so elusive as the majority would have it. Were the Senate, for example, to adopt the practice of automatically entering a judgment of conviction whenever articles of impeachment were delivered from the House, it is quite clear that the Senate will have failed to "try" impeachments. Indeed in this respect, "try" presents no greater, and perhaps fewer, interpretive difficulties than some other constitutional standards that have been found amenable to familiar techniques of judicial construction, including, for example, "Commerce . . . among the several States," Art. I, s 8, cl. 3, and "due process of law."

The majority's conclusion that "try" is incapable of meaningful judicial construction is not without irony. One might think that if any class of concepts would fall within the definitional abilities of the judiciary, it would be that class having to do with procedural justice. Examination of the remaining question—whether proceedings in accordance with Senate Rule XI are compatible with the Impeachment Trial Clause—confirms this intuition.

Petitioner bears the rather substantial burden of demonstrating that, simply by employing the word "try," the Constitution prohibits the Senate from relying on a fact-finding committee. It is clear that the Framers were familiar with English impeachment practice and with that of the States employing a variant of the English model at the time of the Constitutional Convention. Hence there is little doubt that the term "try" as used in Art. I, s 3, cl. 6 meant that the Senate should conduct its proceedings in a manner somewhat resembling a judicial proceeding. Indeed, it is safe to assume that Senate trials were to follow the practice in England and the States, which contemplated a formal hearing on the charges, at which the accused would be represented by counsel, evidence would be presented, and the accused would have the opportunity to be heard.

Petitioner argues, however, that because committees were not used in state impeachment trials prior to the Convention, the word "try" cannot be interpreted to permit their use. It is, however, a substantial leap to infer from the absence of a particular device of parliamentary procedure that its use has been forever barred by the Constitution. . . .

It is also noteworthy that the delegation of fact-finding by judicial and quasijudicial bodies was hardly unknown to the Framers. Jefferson, at least, was aware that the House of Lords sometimes delegated fact-finding in impeachment trials to committees and recommended use of the same to the Senate. The States also had on occasion employed legislative committees to investigate whether to draw up articles of impeachment. More generally, in colonial governments and state legislatures, contemnors appeared before committees to answer the charges against them. . . . Particularly in light of the Constitution's grant to each House of the power to "determine the Rules of its Proceedings," see Art. I, s 5, cl. 2, the existence of legislative and judicial delegation strongly suggests that the Impeachment Trial Clause was not designed to prevent employment of a fact-finding committee.

In short, textual and historical evidence reveals that the Impeachment Trial Clause was not meant to bind the hands of the Senate beyond establishing a set of minimal procedures. Without identifying the exact contours of these procedures, it is sufficient to say that the Senate's use of a fact-finding committee under Rule XI is entirely compatible with the Constitution's command that the Senate "try all impeachments." Petitioner's challenge to his conviction must therefore fail.

Justice SOUTER, concurring in the judgment.

I agree with the Court that this case presents a nonjusticiable political question. Because my analysis differs somewhat from the Court's, however, I concur in its judgment by this separate opinion. . . .

Whatever considerations feature most prominently in a particular case, the political question doctrine is "essentially a function of the separation of powers," existing to restrain courts "from inappropriate interference in the business of the other branches of Government," and deriving in large part from prudential concerns about the respect we owe the political departments. Not all interference is inappropriate or disrespectful, however, and application of the doctrine ultimately turns, as Learned Hand put it, on "how importunately the occasion demands an answer."

This occasion does not demand an answer. The Impeachment Trial Clause commits to the Senate "the sole Power to try all Impeachments," subject to three procedural requirements: the Senate shall be on oath or affirmation; the Chief Justice shall preside when the President is tried; and conviction shall be upon the concurrence of two-thirds of the Members present. U.S. Const., Art. I, s 3, cl. 6. It seems fair to conclude that the Clause contemplates that the Senate may determine, within broad boundaries, such subsidiary issues as the procedures for receipt and consideration of evidence necessary to satisfy its duty to "try" impeachments. Other significant considerations confirm a conclusion that this case presents a nonjusticiable political question: the "unusual need for unquestioning adherence to a political decision already made," as well as "the potentiality of embarrassment from multifarious pronouncements by various departments on one question." As the Court observes, . . . judicial review of an impeachment trial would under the best of circumstances entail significant disruption of government.

One can, nevertheless, envision different and unusual circumstances that might justify a more searching review of impeachment proceedings. If the Senate were to act in a manner seriously threatening the integrity of its results, convicting, say, upon a coin-toss, or upon a summary determination that an officer of the United States was simply "a bad guy," judicial interference might well be appropriate. In such circumstances, the Senate's action might be so far beyond the scope of its constitutional authority, and the consequent impact on the Republic so great, as to merit a judicial response despite the prudential concerns that would ordinarily counsel silence. "The political question doctrine, a tool for maintenance of governmental order, will not be so applied as to promote only disorder."

Notes/Queries/Readings

1. How does Chief Justice Rehnquist distinguish the issue in this case from the one in *Baker v. Carr* (1962)? What sorts of analysis does Rehnquist use to determine the definition of the word "try" as used in Article I? How does he answer Nixon's arguments for a limited definition of the term?

2. Why does Rehnquist refuse Nixon's argument for judicial review of judicial impeachment proceedings? What historical materials does he use to come to this conclusion? What does he see as the potential implications if judicial review of impeachments were allowed?

3. How do the concurring opinions of Justices White and Souter differ from Rehnquist's analysis? What larger judicial oversight of impeachment proceedings would they allow?

4. According to Justice White, the issue in *Nixon* is not whether the constitutional text commits a power exclusively to one of the political branches, but whether it has given that branch "final responsibility" for interpreting the scope of such a power. Do you agree?

5. Michael J. Gerhardt, *Rediscovering Nonjusticiability: Judicial Review of Impeachments after Nixon*, 44 Duke Law Journal 231 (1994); Jennifer L. Blum, *How Much Process is Due: The Senate Impeachment Process After* Nixon v. United States, 44 Catholic University Law Review.

Chapter 4

Separation of Powers

The principle of separation of powers traces its origin back to Aristotle. The celebrated political philosopher developed the idea that government should be composed of three organs, namely, the "deliberative" (i.e., legislative), the magisterial [i.e., executive], and the judicial.[1] The full implications of this distribution of public power, however, were not worked out until Locke and Montesquieu revisited the problem in the eighteenth century. Both philosophers made separation of powers cardinal features of their proposed systems of modern governance, and both had a major influence on the American Founders.[2] In justifying separation of powers, James Madison, following Locke, wrote in *Federalist* 47: "The accumulation of all powers, legislative, executive, and judiciary, in the same hands, whether of one, a few, or many, and whether hereditary, self-appointed, or elective, may justly be pronounced the very definition of tyranny."[3]

The View of the Framers

Madison remains America's preeminent theorist of separated powers. Therefore it is important to highlight the essentials of his thought as set forth in Numbers 47 to 51 of *The Federalist Papers*. Madison advocated a new political order based on a tripartite division of powers designed to avoid the twin evils of tyranny and anarchy. The plan of the Constitution, he argued, would achieve this result by channeling power into separate departments of government, each of which would possess a will of its own. "The fundamental principles of a free constitution are subverted," he said, "where the *whole* power

---

[1] *Politics*, Bk. 6, chap. XI, sec. 1.

[2] "Political liberty," Locke wrote, "is to be found only in moderate governments; even in these it is not always found. It is there only when there is no abuse of power. . . . To prevent this abuse, it is necessary from the very nature of things that power should be a check to power. . . . In every government there are three sorts of power: the legislative, the executive . . . and the judicial power. . . . When the legislative and executive powers are united in the same person, or in the same body of magistrates, there can be no liberty." *Treatise on Government*, Book II, chap. XII (1690). For Montesquieu's argument see *The Spirit of the Laws*, published in 1793. (The Legal Classics Library, 1984), vol. 1, Bk. 11, chap. 6.

[3] *The Federalist* (New York: Barnes & Noble, 1996), 336.

of one department is exercised by the same hands which possess the *whole* power of another department,"[4] an insight that he attributed to Montesquieu. Yet Madison was not writing on a clean slate; the constitutional experience of Massachusetts, for example, with its "watertight" separation between departments encouraged him to favor a system of shared powers at the federal level.

In defending the Constitution, Madison and the Framers held that government would be most effective in protecting both liberty and democracy by incorporating a series of checks and balances into the system of separated powers so long as each department retained its *essential* independence. The merit of the Convention's plan, Madison observed, lay in its judicious mixture of the three powers of government. "[U]nless these departments be so far connected and blended as to give each a constitutional control over the others, the degree of separation which the maxim requires, as essential to a free government, can never in practice be duly maintained."[5] Madison particularly feared the unfiltered power of public opinion and its potential sway over legislation. As it was, he remarked, "The legislative department is everywhere extending the sphere of its activity, and drawing all power into its impetuous vortex."[6] To stem the extension of this power, the Constitution vested the executive and judiciary with countervailing powers of resistance, just as they were equipped to resist the ambitions of each other. Finally, bicameralism within the legislative branch, with each House's representatives differing in their mode of selection and terms of office, would provide additional security against rash legislative action and the excesses of democracy.

Madison's theory of separated powers rooted itself in a particular vision of politics. Although he hoped that the governed and their rulers would be men and women of virtue, he expected self-interest and factional strife to dominate their behavior. He also thought that institutional power once established tends to aggrandize itself at the expense of rival centers of power. Madison deserves to be quoted in full:

> *But the great security against a gradual concentration of the several powers in the same department, consists in giving to those who administer each department the necessary constitutional means and personal motives to resist encroachments of the others. The provision for defense must in this, as in all other cases, be made commensurate to the danger of attack. Ambition must be made to counteract ambition. The interest of the man must be connected with the constitutional rights of the place. It may be a reflection on human nature, that such devices should be necessary to control the abuses of government. But what is government itself, but the greatest of all reflections on human nature? If men were angels, no government would be necessary. If angels were to govern men, neither external nor internal controls on government would be necessary. In framing a government which is to be administered by men over men, the great difficulty lies in this: you must first enable the government to control the governed; and in the next place oblige it to control itself. A dependence on the people is, no doubt, the primary control on the government; but experience has taught mankind the necessity of auxiliary precautions.*[7]

Madison—and the Founders generally—rooted these forms and structures in the soil of popular sovereignty. "We, the people of the United States," reads the first line of the Constitution's Preamble, "do ordain and establish this Constitution." In short,

---

[4] *Ibid.*, at 338.

[5] *Ibid.*, at 343.

[6] *Ibid.*, at 343.

[7] *Ibid.*, at 356.

the people rule, but they do so indirectly through separate legislative, executive, and judicial institutions. By putting distance between the people and their ruling institutions, Madison hoped that the Constitution's governmental design would create a republic of reason in the United States, one that would reflect the voice of enlightened public opinion rather than the passions of the moment or the self-interest of private groups.[8] Madison, however, believed that neither reason nor popular sovereignty would alone be sufficient to protect liberty or a commitment to the public good. Thus "deviations . . . from the principle [of separated powers] must be admitted" in the form of "auxiliary precautions," ones that allow the separate departments to retain their essential independence but simultaneously to blend them together in a relationship of creative tension.

Separation of Powers Today

Constitutions, however, rarely work as planned. Although the formal distribution of power among the branches still prevails today, the executive branch has become dominant, largely at the expense of Congress and the judiciary. Congress and the judiciary, however, have contributed to this growth, the former by its creation of a massive federal bureaucracy and the latter by its expansive interpretation of executive power. As for the Supreme Court, it too has evolved into a much more powerful institution than originally anticipated. Moreover, it is often overlooked that Congress itself is responsible for much of the authority wielded by the Supreme Court today. For one thing, Congress has expanded the jurisdiction of the federal courts over the years; for another, Congress has given the Supreme Court complete control over its docket, virtually allowing the Court to convert itself into a European-style constitutional tribunal. Congress has also customarily invited the judiciary to review laws of doubtful constitutionality, thus abdicating, in the minds of some commentators, its own authority to enforce the Constitution. In addition, Congress is responsible for allowing public interest groups, with their diverging agendas, to invoke the power of the federal judiciary in overseeing the execution of federal law.[9]

Facilitated by a broad construction of its enumerated powers, Congress's authority has also increased over the decades; yet the president often overshadows Congress in the face of his constant visibility and important role in advancing his own legislative program. A significant change in the nature of the presidency took place in the 1820s, when the Jacksonians overthrew the congressional caucus as a method of choosing party candidates for the presidency. President Jackson turned the presidency into an office representative of the people as a whole and claimed to base much of his power on that fact, as would other presidents after him. By the middle of the twentieth century, the president would preside over an awesome federal bureaucracy, which he has never fully been able to control. The president has had even less control over the work of independent regulatory commissions whose combination of legislative, adjudicatory, and executive functions fits uneasily, if at all, into Madison's original scheme of separation of powers.

Yet, as the executive branch has expanded into the affirmative state we have become, Congress found various ways to limit and obstruct the execution of federal law. The growth of the congressional committee system, the power of committee chairs,

---

[8] For a detailed modern application of Madison's theory of the reasoned republic, see Cass R. Sunstein, *The Partial Constitution* (Cambridge: Harvard University Press, 1993).

[9] *Lujan v. Defenders of Wildlife*, 505 U.S. 555 (1992) is a leading example, although the Court denied standing in this case. See also Steven G. Calabresi, *Some Normative Arguments for the Unitary Executive,* 48 Arkansas Law Review 48–50 (1995).

the explosive growth of congressional staffs, the development and use of the legislative veto, and the increasing tendency of the Senate to confirm cabinet secretaries subject to winning their agreement on how to construe statutes have all checked the executive branch in ways unmentioned in the constitutional text. Congress has adopted these "extra-constitutional" restraints largely in response to the growth of executive power. Still, some believe these measures have undermined the unity and energy in the executive that Hamilton thought were necessary for effective and accountable government.[10] On the other hand, changes in the office of the president and presidential claims to certain prerogative powers, particularly in the field of foreign affairs (see chapter 7), have led others to speak of an "imperial" presidency capable of lording it over Congress. Further complicating this picture is the growth and operation of the American party system. When Congress and the presidency are controlled by different political parties, as in recent decades, the existing system of nontextual checks and balances often serves to exacerbate the problem of democratic control and accountability in American politics.

In reading and assessing the cases reprinted in this chapter, students should bear in mind these contemporary realities of American government. The Supreme Court has rarely made Olympian pronouncements on the meaning of separation of powers; the actual administration of the separated powers and checks and balances systems is more the result of usage, practice, and politics than of constitutional adjudication. This does not mean that separation of powers has lost all of its vitality in American constitutionalism. Actually, it has experienced a jurisprudential revival in recent years, as several cases reprinted in this chapter show. The cases are important not only for what they tell us about the changing nature of the relations between the branches of the federal government, but also for the Supreme Court's limited role in defining that relationship.

Congressional Powers and Their Limits

Before proceeding to discuss cases involving interbranch relationships, we might pause to underscore a universally accepted principle: Neither the executive nor the legislature can fully define for itself the extent of its own power. As already suggested, the Supreme Court reserves the right to define the limits of each branch's power unless, of course, a legislative decision or an executive practice falls within the scope of the political question doctrine. Rarely, however, does the Court intrude itself into the internal processes of the other branches of government. A major exception to this generalization is *Powell v. McCormack* (1969, reprinted later in the chapter). *Powell*, like *Baker v. Carr* (1962), decided seven years earlier, appeared to place significant limits on the political question doctrine.

In 1967, the House of Representatives voted overwhelmingly to exclude one of its members from taking his seat, to which he had been duly elected, because of improprieties in his management of congressional funds in the previous session of Congress. The congressman sued to retain his seat, arguing that his exclusion violated the provision of the Constitution (Art. 1, sec. 2, cl. 3) that bases House eligibility on age, citizenship, and residence, all of which the member—Adam Clayton Powell—had satisfied. The speaker of the House, John McCormack, and other House leaders invoked in their defense the speech and debate clause (Art.1, Sec. 6) and the political question doctrine. The Court concluded that the speech and debate clause—the pro-

---

[10] For an account of this debate see Stephen M. Griffin, *American Constitutionalism* (Princeton, N.J.: Princeton University Press, 1996), esp. 59–87.

vision that bars senators and representatives from being questioned in any other place for any speech or debate in either House—required the removal of the speaker and other House members as defendants, but it allowed the continuance of the lawsuit against House employees charged with enforcing the exclusion order.

The argument that the case presented a nonjusticiable political question derives from Art. 1, Sec. 5. This provision makes each House the judge of its members' qualifications and empowers it to expel an already-seated member by a two-thirds vote. In affirming its authority to enforce the qualifications clause, the Court differentiated sharply between excluding and expelling a member. Members could be expelled from Congress for misconduct after being seated, but Congress could exclude them from being seated only if they failed to meet one of the three conditions laid down by the constitutional text. The Court ruled in favor of the excluded member after its long and detailed examination of the original intent behind the qualifications clause, including an historical analysis of preconvention precedents going back to early English precedents. (Years later, in *U.S. Terms Limits, Inc. v. Thornton* [1995, reprinted in chapter 5], the Court would draw heavily on *Powell*'s historical analysis to invalidate state-imposed congressional term limits.) Whether the *Powell* Court would have proclaimed an *expulsion* to have been a nonjusticiable political question remained unanswered.

In *Powell*, members of Congress successfully invoked the speech and debate clause to remove themselves as defendants. In *Gravel v. United States* [1972], however, the speech and debate clause failed as a defense against a prosecution for legislative-related activities. *Gravel* warrants notice because the Court extended the constitutional privilege to the aides and assistants of senators and representatives who served as their "alter egos" in the "day-to-day" work of Congress. If the independence of the legislature is to be protected against intimidation or threats from the executive, said the Court, the privilege must be extended to such aides and assistants. To this extent, the Court faced up to the realities of the modern legislative process, the complexities of which require the assistance of large congressional staffs. In a sharply divided opinion, the majority extended the privilege only to activities that are "an integral part of the deliberative and communicative processes by which Members participate in committee and House proceedings."[11] *Gravel* involved a senator who, after rising in the Senate to read from the Pentagon Papers [classified documents entitled "History of U.S. Decision-Making Process on Viet Nam Policy" stolen from the Department of State] instructed one of his aides to arrange for private publication of the documents with the Beacon Press. The speech and debate clause protected Senator Gravel against a grand jury investigation of a possible violation of federal law but did not protect, the Court ruled, his aide. Why? Because the aide's relations with the Beacon Press fell outside "the essential deliberations of the Senate." Justice Brennan, joined by Justices Douglas and Marshall, dissenting, found this view of the legislative process severely cramped. They would have extended the privilege of the speech and debate clause to a "legislator's duty to inform the public about matters affecting the administration of government."[12]

Here again, we find how different opinions rely on different visions of politics and the polity. The majority opinion in *Gravel* envisioned the legislative process as a rather insulated activity confined to committee hearings and debates on the floor of the House and Senate. There is merit in this view. It accords with the concept of legislators as independent decision makers capable of making rational decisions in the public

---

[11] *Gravel v. United States*, 408 U.S. 606, 625 (1972).

[12] *Ibid.*, at 649.

interest. It includes the view of Congress as a place of democratic representation where the people as a whole rule, in their collective sovereignty, and not as an assembly of party and group interests where policy results from "unholy" compromises inimical to the general welfare. The dissenting view, on the other hand, envisioned politics—i.e., legislative politics—as an open-ended process that does not end or begin with what occurs within the halls of Congress. The minority view embraces a more fluid concept of democracy, one that emphasizes the people's right to know and the importance of the media in communicating with the public. It sees the informing function of Congress as crucial to the legislative process as the enactment of laws.

Similarly, the majority and minority opinions in *Powell* represent different pictures not only of the principle of separated powers, but also of the nature of political representation. Apart from the view that Congress, as a coordinate branch of government, ought to have the right to establish and govern its own procedures, the minority opinion seems based on the conviction that democratic representation in the American polity requires men and women of integrity. The majority view, however, sees representation in a more pragmatic and, perhaps, realistic light, resting on the right of voters in any congressional district to elect who they want to represent them, regardless of whether he or she is a scoundrel.

Congressional Investigations

The Supreme Court has declared "that the power of inquiry—with process to enforce it—is an essential and appropriate auxiliary to the legislative function." [13] This power to ask questions is not written in the Constitution but has been inferred as a matter of practical construction and historical practice. Indeed, Congress's power to investigate is as broad as its competence to legislate. Accordingly, Congress may compel the appearance and testimony of any private individual who possesses information relevant to its lawmaking authority. In short, if Congress seeks information concerning a matter on which it is authorized to legislate, Congress may require an investigation into that matter. For "a legislative body cannot legislate wisely or effectively in the absence of information respecting the conditions which the legislation is intended to affect or change." [14]

But as *Watkins v. United States* (1957) underscores, the power to ask questions is limited. [15] Watkins, who was a labor organizer and Communist activist in the 1930s, was called before the House Un-American Activities Committee to testify about his activities and to identify persons who had previously been active in the Communist Party but who were no longer members. For refusing to answer questions about these persons, he was tried for contempt of Congress. The Court overruled his conviction because neither Congress nor the committee before which Watkins appeared had informed him of the purpose of the inquiry. The committee's purpose appeared to be one of exposure for the sake of exposure, placing the witness "in the glare of publicity" and "subject[ing him] to public stigma, scorn, and obloquy." "No inquiry is an end in itself," said the Court. "[I]t must be related to, and in furtherance of, a legitimate task of the Congress. Investigations conducted solely for personal aggrandizement of the investigators or to 'punish' those investigated are indefensible." Because the subject of the inquiry was not clearly identified, the witness was unable to determine whether the interrogation was pertinent to a legitimate legislative objective, thus ren-

---

[13] *McGrain v. Daugherty*, 273 U.S. 135 (1927).

[14] *Ibid.*, at 175.

[15] 354 U.S. 178.

dering him incapable of "determin[ing] whether he was within his rights in refusing to answer." [16] Accordingly, his conviction for contempt violated the due process clause of the Fifth Amendment.

As with *Powell* and *Gravel*, *Watkins* embraces alternative, and largely inarticulate, visions of how a constitutional democracy is supposed to work. Here, once again, the principle of democracy and constitutionalism appear to clash. A democratic Congress in touch with the people and empowered to investigate—and operating within a system of free speech that Justice Brennan has characterized as "uninhibited, robust, and wide-open," [17]—might be said to have the right to put witnesses "in the glare of publicity" if those persons have knowledge of individuals or facts of political interest to the American people. Constitutionalism, however, embraces the principle of human dignity and, apart from any procedural right that a person may have in the context of a congressional inquiry, that principle requires people to be treated with forbearance and respect.

Executive-Legislative Relations

The Principle of Nondelegation

The doctrine that Congress may not delegate its lawmaking power to any other department or body derives from the principle of separation of powers. "All legislative powers herein granted," declares the Constitution, "shall be vested in [the] Congress," just as Congress is empowered "to make all laws which shall be necessary and proper" for carrying these general powers into execution. But as Madison and the Founders knew from their insistence on checks and balances, the theory of separated powers would necessarily give way to the practical realities of public administration. If government were to function at all, Congress would have to confer rulemaking [i.e., legislative] authority on executive agencies lest the wheels of government grind to a halt, a self-evident proposition in the modern regulatory state.

Schechter v. United States (1935, reprinted later in the chapter), one of only two cases in which the Supreme Court has invalidated a legislative delegation of power, [18] arose out of the National Industrial Recovery Act [NIRA], the Roosevelt administration's main weapon in coping with the Great Depression of the 1930s. The NIRA authorized various industrial groups to adopt codes of fair trade which, if approved by the president, would constitute binding law. The president could, however, use his discretionary authority to modify the codes, any violation of which would be punishable by law. *Schechter* faulted Congress because it allowed the president to determine for himself the purpose and limits of the law. In effect, Congress said to the president: "Here is a serious problem; you resolve it." Accordingly, Congress had abdicated its authority by failing to establish an intelligible principle to guide the exercise of its delegated discretion. As Justice Cardozo said in his concurring opinion, the authority delegated here is "unconfined and vagrant;" it sets up "a roving commission to inquire into evils and upon discovery [to] correct them." *Schechter* teaches that Congress may authorize a governmental body to execute the law, but it must define for itself important choices of social policy and identify the boundaries within which the policy is to be carried out.

---

[16] *Ibid.*, at 215.

[17] See *Sullivan v. New York Times*, 376 U.S. 254 (1964).

[18] *Panama Refining Co. v. Ryan* (1935), decided four months before *Schechter*, was the one other case in which the Court invalidated a congressional delegation of authority. *Panama*, like *Schechter*, emerged from a presidential directive based on the National Industrial Recovery Act of 1933.

The nondelegation doctrine survives in theory, but in practice it has declined into virtual obsolescence in view of the Court's apparent reluctance, since the New Deal era, to review congressional delegations of authority. (We might add, however, that a version of the nondelegation doctrine lives on in the canon of construction that says we should interpret in ways that obviate constitutional objections.) Congress regularly entrusts to agency expertise the task of discerning the purpose and boundaries of law. According to some critics, the broad discretionary authority that federal law has conferred on executive agencies has eroded both the rule of law and our representative democracy, meriting in their opinion a revival of the delegation doctrine.[19] Justice Rehnquist joined the critics in *Industrial Union v. American Petroleum Institute* (1980), which involved a statute (Occupational Safety and Health Act [OSHA]) authorizing the Secretary of Labor to promulgate standards which are "reasonably necessary or appropriate to provide safe or healthful employment and places of employment." In this case the Court set aside certain rules limiting the exposure of employees to cancer-producing chemicals, but on the ground that the Secretary of Labor's finding was unsupported by appropriate evidence. In asking the Court to "reshoulder the burden of ensuring that Congress itself make the critical policy decisions," Rehnquist was alone in deciding the case on nondelegation grounds.[20]

With his appointment to the Supreme Court, Justice Antonin Scalia joined Rehnquist in seeking to revitalize the doctrine of "unconstitutional delegation." As a law professor, Scalia had faulted Congress for delegating "vague and standardless rulemaking authority" to administrative agencies.[21] He was equally critical of the "legislative veto," claiming, as the Supreme Court would hold several years later, that it invaded the authority of the president in violation of Article 2 of the Constitution (see the Legislative Veto Case [*INS v. Chadha*] later in the chapter). As his dissenting opinions in *Morrison v. Olson* (1988) and *Mistretta v. United States* (1989) show—both cases are also featured later in this chapter—Scalia's vision of the American state is one that draws a sharp legal distinction between the powers of the three branches.

The Steel Seizure Case

Under the Constitution's formal distribution of power among the three branches of the federal government, Congress *makes* law, the president *executes* it, and the judiciary *interprets* it. *Youngstown Sheet & Tube Company v. Sawyer* (1952, reprinted later in the chapter) represents a monumental struggle over the meaning of these powers. President Truman insisted that his seizure of the steel mills was necessary to avert a strike that would shut them down in the face of a United Nation's Resolution obligating the United States to send troops into armed combat in Korea. In justifying his action, Truman invoked "the aggregate of his powers" under Article 2; to wit, his general executive power, his authority as commander-in-chief, and his responsibility to "take care that the laws be faithfully executed." *Youngstown* ruled against the president because Congress denied him the authority to seize private property in the present circumstances. This denial, however, had no relevance for Justice Black, in whose view the president's action would have been unlawful even in the *absence* of an authorizing statute. Black's literalist approach to the interpretation of separation of powers amounted to a simple syllogism: Only Congress may provide for the taking of

---

[19] See, especially, Theodore Lowi, *The End of Liberalism*, 2d ed. (New York: Norton, 1979).

[20] 448 U.S. 607, at 687. In 1996, the Court once again refused to invoke the nondelegation doctrine in a constitutional challenge to a federal statute that directed the president to define the aggravating conditions that would warrant the death penalty in court martial cases. See *Loving v. United States*, 116 S. Ct. 1737 (1996).

[21] See Richard A. Brisbin, Jr., *Justice Antonin Scalia and the Conservative Revival* (Baltimore: Johns Hopkins University Press, 1997), 26–27.

property; here the president took property without congressional approval; *ergo*, the president acted unconstitutionally.

Justice Frankfurter, on the other hand, resisted the temptation to define what the president could or could not do in the absence of congressional authorizing legislation. After alluding to the history of presidential seizures of property, he remarked: "Deeply embedded traditional ways of conducting government cannot supplant the Constitution or legislation, but they give meaning to the words of a text. . . . In short, a systematic, unbroken, executive practice, long pursued to the knowledge of Congress and never before questioned, engaged in by Presidents who have also sworn to uphold the Constitution, making as it were such exercise part of the structure of our government, may be treated as a gloss on 'executive Power' vested in the President by Sec. 1 of Art. II." Yet Frankfurter concurred with the result in *Youngstown* because the action of the president did "not come to us sanctioned by long-continued [congressional] acquiescense."

Like Frankfurter, Justice Jackson declined to ascertain the exact meaning of the three powers of government. He wrote: "Just what our forefathers did envision by (separation of powers), or would have envisioned had they foreseen modern conditions, must be divined from materials almost as enigmatic as the dreams Joseph was called upon to interpret for Pharaoh."[22] His opinion is noted for its flexible analytical framework for determining whether the president has acted constitutionally when he undertakes an executive action. The president's power is "at its maximum," he wrote, when he "acts pursuant to an express or implied authorization of Congress." On the other hand, if the president "takes measures incompatible with the expressed or implied will of Congress, his power is at its lowest ebb," in which case his authority must be justified by reference to one of his own powers under Article 2. But there is also a "twilight zone" where the president acts in the absence of a grant or denial of authority and where the legitimacy of his actions "depends on the imperatives of events and contemporary imponderables rather than on abstract theories of law." For Jackson, these "events" and "imponderables" were not enough to warrant the president's seizure of the steel mills.

The different views advanced in *Youngstown* focus attention on the interpretive and normative themes of this book. Certainly, they illustrate the "awful task" of interpretation that the Supreme Court faces in difficult cases. Few persons correctly predicted *Youngstown*'s outcome. Chief Justice Vinson is even reported to have advised the president that the seizure of the steel mills would meet with the Court's approval.[23] In addition, the case places in sharp relief the tension between constitutionalism and democracy. In a time of emergency, a popularly elected leader might be expected to take whatever measures he deems constitutionally necessary to avert a crisis. Yet the Constitution controls the president just as it controls the other branches of government. Indeed President Truman paid tribute to the constitutionalism implicit in the Supreme Court's opinion by immediately bending to its will and ordering the return of the steel mills to their rightful owners.

Separation of Powers Reasserted

Bowsher v. Synar (1986, reprinted later in the chapter) featured an interesting variation on *Schechter*. *Bowsher* challenged a provision of the Gramm-Rudman-Hollings Act conferring broad authority on the comptroller general—an official subject to removal

---

[22] *Youngstown Sheet & Tube Co. v. Sawyer*, 343 U.S. 579, 634.

[23] See remarks of Richard Schifter in *Constitutional "Refolution" Symposium*, 12 American University Journal of International Law and Policy 131 (1997).

by a joint resolution of Congress—to establish spending cuts under the statute's anti-deficit provisions which the president would then be required to implement. The Court bypassed legitimate issues of delegation to decide the case on the basis of separation of powers. In as much as the comptroller general could be removed by Congress, said the Court, he was to be regarded as a congressional official and, as such, could not constitutionally perform a function—i.e., determining spending reductions under the statute—clearly within the scope of executive responsibility. Chief Justice Burger, writing for the majority, relied heavily on *Immigration and Naturalization Service v. Chadha* (1983, reprinted later in the chapter), noting that "to permit an officer controlled by Congress to execute the laws would be, in essence, to permit a legislative veto."

Chadha, a truly historic opinion, invalidated the so-called legislative veto, which was a device used by Congress to monitor the execution of federal law. Congressional legislation has frequently incorporated legislative veto provisions. Normally, an agency will be required to notify the House or Senate, or both, when it promulgates a rule or issues an order, with the result that the rule or order will not go into effect if the House or Senate—or both, depending on the terms of the statute—vetos it within a specified time. By reserving to itself the power to rescind a rule promulgated by an agency under one of its statutes, Congress has equipped itself with an effective check over the rulemaking powers of the federal bureaucracy. The use of the veto has a long history and, as Justice White noted in his dissent, its importance to Congress in our contemporary political system can hardly be overstated.

Yet by a seven to two vote, the Court held the legislative veto unconstitutional as violative of the presentment clauses and the principle of bicameralism. Because the legislative veto constitutes lawmaking in its own right, said the Court, the legislation in question must be presented to the president for his approval or veto. In addition, the one house veto offended the requirement that laws be passed by both houses of Congress. More broadly, the Court held that Congress had expanded its role to one of shared administration and by doing so had encroached on the executive's duty to execute the law. Justice White thought the Court had saddled Congress with a Hobson's choice: "either to refrain from delegating the necessary authority, leaving itself with a hopeless task of writing laws with the requisite specificity to cover endless special circumstances across the entire policy landscape, or in the alternative, to abdicate its lawmaking function to the executive branch and independent agencies."

Appointment and Removal Power

Article 2 (sec. 2, par. 2) empowers the president to nominate, by and with the advice and consent of the Senate, ambassadors, judges, and "all other officers of the United States, whose appointments are not herein otherwise provided for, and which shall be established by law: but the Congress may by law vest the appointment of such inferior officers, as they think proper, in the President alone, in the courts of law, or in the heads of departments." This provision says nothing about the extent of the president's power of removing his appointees. For example, may the Senate require the president to seek its consent prior to his removal of an officer whose appointment it approved? "No," the Supreme Court answered in *Myers v. United States*.[24] Drawing on the Convention debates, the Court declared that the Founders—citing Madison in particular—intended "to give the President the sole power of removal in his responsibility for the conduct of the executive branch." If he is to "take care that the laws be faithfully executed," he must have the power to remove officials when "he loses con-

---

[24] 272 U.S. 52 (1926).

fidence in the intelligence, ability, judgment or loyalty of any one of them [and] he must have the power to remove them without delay." The power of removal, declared the Court, is incident to the power of appointment, not to the power of advising and consenting to the appointment. With this decision, the Court underscored the importance of the unitary presidency, one that envisions the executive branch as a separate entity responsible to the president alone.

In *Humphrey's Executor v. United States*,[25] however, the Supreme Court limited the President's power to remove members of *independent* regulatory commissions. By doing so, the Court projected a less unified vision of the executive branch. In *Humphrey's Executor*, the Court faced one of the realities of modern government, namely, administrative agencies created by Congress to regulate various phases of the national economy. Vested with rulemaking and adjudicatory authority in highly specialized fields, these agencies are staffed with nonpartisan experts appointed for specified terms of office and insulated from political pressures. "Such a body," said the Court, "cannot in any proper sense be characterized as an arm or an eye of the executive. Its duties are performed without executive leave and, in the contemplation of the statute, must be free from executive control."[26] Accordingly, the Court confined the reach of *Myers*, holding that the president could remove a person from such an agency only for causes specified by statute.[27] He could not validly remove a member of an independent commission simply for reasons of policy.

Myers and *Humphrey's Executor* are rare examples of judicial interference in conflicts between the legislative and executive branches. The president and Congress have found various ways of conducting the business of government without regard to the bright lines that constitutional formalists of an earlier period had drawn between the three powers of government. Only in recent years, with decisions such as *Chadha* and *Bowsher*, has the Court returned to the formalist view of separation of powers expounded in *Myers*. This view advances "the goal of greater accountability of an energetic and efficient government to all the people it represents."[28] White's dissenting opinion in *Chadha*, on the other hand, envisions the three branches as interacting entities marked by balance and reciprocity. Justice White found nothing wrong with congressional arrangements or adaptations designed to regulate a huge modern bureaucracy in the interest of responsive and responsible government.

Executive-Judicial Relations

In *Morrison v. Olsen* (1988, reprinted later in the chapter) and *Mistretta v. United States* (1989), the pendulum swung back to a more functional—as opposed to a formalist—view of separation of powers. *Morrison* deals with still another relatively new phenomenon in American political life, namely, the creation of the office of an independent counsel. Congress has established the office to undertake investigations of high-ranking officials accused of committing serious crimes under federal law. The process of investigation and prosecution is clearly an executive function. Arguably, the president's command over this process is unconstitutionally limited when, as in *Morrison*, the right to appoint such counsel is vested in a special division of a court of appeals. *Morrison*, however, ruled that this arrangement did not violate the principle of separation of powers.

---

[25] 295 U.S. 602 (1935).

[26] *Ibid.*, at 603.

[27] See also *Wiener v. United States*, 357 U.S. 349 (1958).

[28] Martin S. Flaherty, *The Most Dangerous Branch*, 105 Yale Law Journal 1732 (1966).

Another critical issue in *Morrison* was whether the independent counsel constituted a superior or inferior officer of the United States. Were she a superior officer within the meaning of the appointments clause, she would have to be appointed by the president. Her tenure and duties were limited, however, and for this reason the Court regarded her as an inferior officer whose appointment, under the terms of the appointments clause, may be placed by Congress in the hands of the judiciary. Justice Scalia, the Court's most ardent textualist, dissented. In his view, the line between executive and judicial power must remain clear and distinct. The executive power conferred on the president, he wrote, means *"all* of the executive power," and this requires the executive's total control over criminal investigations and prosecutions. The Court, he wrote, "simply *announces*, with no analysis," this major "depart[ure] from the text of the Constitution."[29]

Justice Scalia wrote an equally passionate dissenting opinion in *Mistretta*. "I dissent from today's decision because I can find no place within our constitutional system for an agency created by Congress to exercise no governmental power other than the making of laws."[30] Congress had created an independent sentencing commission within the judiciary to develop guidelines that federal judges would be obligated to follow in handing down sentences for various categories of offenses and offenders. The commission's membership included at least three federal judges, each of whom would participate in what was admittedly a legislative task. The Court acknowledged that the placement of a rulemaking commission within the judicial branch and its composition approached the borderline of constitutionality. In the end, however, the Court found that the arrangement was a practical way of dealing with the problem of disparate sentencing practices in the federal judiciary and that the work of the commission compromise neither the independence nor the integrity of either the legislature or the judiciary.

United States v. Nixon (1974, reprinted later in the chapter), however, did implicate the independence of the judiciary. This well known decision, better known as the Watergate Tapes case, involved presidential assistants accused of conspiring to burglarize the headquarters of the Democratic Party during the presidential election campaign of 1972. The special prosecutor in charge of the investigation obtained a subpoena directing the president to produce as evidence certain tape recordings and notes of conversations held in the White House. In his defense, the president claimed executive privilege, a doctrine that refers to his discretion to withhold information of confidential communications for reasons of state. He claimed as well that the federal court lacked jurisdiction in the case "because the matter was an intrabranch dispute between a subordinate and superior officer of the Executive Branch and hence not subject to judicial resolution." The Supreme Court rejected both claims. As for executive privilege, the Court underscored its importance in protecting the confidentiality of presidential communications, and for the first time it anchored this right in the Constitution itself. But the Court rejected the president's claim that the privilege is absolute. On the facts of this case, the Court concluded that "the ends of criminal justice would be defeated if judgments were to be founded on a partial or speculative presentation of the facts. The very integrity of the judicial system and public confidence in the system depend on full disclosure of all the facts."

The claim of presidential immunity from suit was more successful in *Nixon v. Fitzgerald* (1982).[31] Fitzgerald was discharged from his government post allegedly for his

---

[29] *Ibid.*, at 711.

[30] 488 U.S. 361, at 413.

[31] 457 U.S. 731 (1982).

testimony on cost overruns that embarassed his superiors, whereupon he filed a civil damage suit against President Nixon. By a five to four vote, the Court held that the president was immune from such an action. "The President occupies a unique position in our constitutional scheme," declared the Court. Any "diversion of his energies by concern with private lawsuits would raise unique risks to the effective functioning of government." Suits for civil damages, said the Court, "could distract a President from his public duties, to the detriment not only of the President and his office but also to the Nation that the Presidency was designed to serve."

Fitzgerald, however, involved the actions of a sitting president. More recently, the question has arisen whether the president is entitled to temporary immunity from a civil lawsuit for a wrong committed prior to his election as president. A former Arkansas state employee brought a sexual harassment suit against President Clinton in 1996 for an event that allegedly occurred when he was governor. The president argued that as a sitting president he could not be required to submit as a defendant to a civil damage action directed at him personally. The argument from immunity, as suggested in *Fitzgerald*, proceeds from the view that the president is never off duty; to be required to defend himself in court would be a judicial interference with his capacity to carry out his constitutional responsibilities and thus violate the principle of separation of powers. On 9 January 1996, a U.S. Court of Appeals rejected this claim, holding that the president is not immune from suit for his unofficial acts.[32] In *Clinton v. Jones* (1997), the Supreme Court affirmed, holding that the doctrine of separation of powers does not require federal courts to stay all private actions against the president until he leaves office. The Court rejected the claim that this case would place unacceptable burdens on the president's performance of his official duties. The Court did, however, acknowledge the burdens of the presidency and noted that these "burdens are appropriate matters for the District Court to evaluate in its management of the case."[33]

Comparative Notes

In the interest of limiting the exercise of governmental power, all modern *constitutional* democracies include some variation on the principle of separation of powers. The independence and autonomy of the judiciary is a matter of fundamental importance. In most constitutional democracies, however, the structure of legislative-executive relations differs markedly from the American presidential system. Nearly all of the regimes with which we could compare the United States have adopted parliamentary systems in which the executive and legislative branches are intermingled. In such systems, the government or the executive consists of the prime minister and the members of his cabinet, all of whom normally hold seats in the national legislature. Any such commingling of legislative and executive officialdom would violate the American principle of separated powers. Parliamentary systems also tend to divide executive authority between the head of government (i.e., prime minister, chancellor, or premier) and a head of state (usually a president), although here variations abound both in the power conferred on heads of state and in the manner of their selection.

The parliamentary executive, finally, is typically responsible to the national legislature, and the government can be brought down by a parliamentary vote of no confidence. In the United States, by contrast, the president is independent of Congress. ("[E]ach department should have a will of its own," wrote Madison.) Moreover, the president and Congress often govern with different popular mandates, a condition

---

[32] *Jones v. Clinton*, 72 F.3d 1354 (8th Cir. 1996).

[33] *Clinton v. Jones*, 65 LW 4372, 4380 (1997).

that breeds conflict and occasionally deadlock between the branches. In the view of many foreign critics, Congress's separation from the executive tends to frustrate majority rule and weaken electoral accountability. As the Founders planned—out of their concern for liberty—American constitutionalism does indeed inhibit the smooth translation of majority opinion into public policy. Parliamentary constitutionalism, on the other hand, aspires to create legislatures more directly responsive to popular majorities and to produce governments responsible to the parliaments that elect them. The ideal of parliamentary government is to mobilize the electorate behind finding solutions to national problems and to ensure that all actions taken by the government proceed from the consent of the legislature.[34]

Because the United States differs from other systems of government, foreign constitutional provisions and constitutional case law on separation of powers may seem to have little relevance for Americans. But when so many Americans have begun to doubt the capacity of their national government to function properly, the comparative perspective may provide some basis for rethinking the relationship among the three branches. Short of amending the Constitution, the American system of presidential government will not change, and most Americans would probably not want it to change. Still, foreign constitutional practices may help Americans to reflect more critically on their structure of separation of powers, especially as defined by certain decisions of the Supreme Court. Since Germany's Basic Law is one of the most influential models of constitutional governance in the world today, the following discussion confines itself to the Basic Law and its interpretation.

The Basic Law lays down separation of powers as an unamendable principle of Germany's constitutional order, a status it shares with other unalterable features of the Constitution such as the rule of law, federalism, the social state, and the multi-party state. Article 20 (2) proclaims that "all public authority emanates from the people," but then declares that "it shall be exercised . . . by specific legislative, executive, and judicial bodies." Article 79 (3) establishes the separation of these branches in perpetuity by "[prohibiting] any amendment to this Basic Law affecting the . . . principles laid down in [this] Article." This well known "eternity clause," incidentally, is one source of the doctrine of an unconstitutional constitutional amendment, for the Federal Constitutional Court has on several occasions declared its readiness to strike down any amendment to the Basic Law that would erode the permanence of one of these principles (e.g., separation of powers). To this extent, separation of powers is more firmly anchored in Germany than in the United States.

As *the* guardian of the Basic Law, the Federal Constitutional Court plays a key role in overseeing the integrity of the three branches and maintaining the proper balance among them. In fact, the Basic Law confers on the Constitutional Court express authority to settle disputes among the highest institutions of the Federal Republic—i.e., the legislature (Bundestag), Council of State Governments (Bundesrat), chancellor, and president. Should these institutions disagree among themselves over their respective rights and obligations under the Basic Law, they may petition the Constitutional Court to resolve the conflict. As we shall see in the *Military Deployment* case, this jurisdiction also extends to units of these institutions—e.g., the parliamentary parties within the Bundestag—vested with rights of their own under the Constitution. Accordingly, the Basic Law itself endorses an active judicial role in monitoring Germany's system of separated powers. No prudential canons of self-restraint or precepts

---

[34] Harvey C. Mansfield, Jr., on the other hand, has written: "The end of the [U.S.] Constitution—for which its forms are designed—is to produce an equilibrium among the separated powers, not to move the whole government toward the solution of problems, in the direction of progress." See *The Soul of the Constitution* (Baltimore: Johns Hopkins University Press, 1991), 6.

such as the political question doctrine stand in the way of a judicial ruling when a dispute between branches of the government is properly before the Court.

Three well known cases illustrate the Federal Constitutional Court's central role in separation of powers disputes. In a case that recalls issues posed in *United States v. Nixon* (1974), the Court ruled that the Federal Finance and Economics Ministry was required to deliver certain corporate records to a parliamentary committee investigating illegal tax exemptions granted to a private corporation. The ministry refused to produce the documents on the ground that they contained trade and tax secrets whose confidentiality the tax code required. The Court recognized a "core sphere of executive autonomy" in which certain communications are immune to parliamentary oversight, but here the Court held that the cabinet is accountable to parliament. In the Court's unanimous view, it emphasized that parliament's right to inspect the records in this case is an essential aspect of the principle of separated powers.[35]

So that parliament may carry out its obligations to superintend the executive branch as well as to legislate, the Court has even handed down a ruling under the constitutional provision that guarantees adequate remuneration to all legislators. In the *Legislative Pay* case (1975) the Court held that in the interest of parliament's independence, a legislator's income "must be keyed to the significance of the office, the burden and responsibility connected with it, and the proper rank of the office within the constitutional structure."[36] The Court has been equally insistent on keeping the judiciary independent of the civil service. In the *Josef-Franziska* case (1959), the Court invalidated Baden-Württemberg's creation of special justice-of-the-peace courts staffed in part by local civil servants. Invoking the principle of judicial autonomy, the Court has even held that it is unconstitutional for a physician to be disciplined by a professional tribunal staffed in part by members of the medical association's chamber of deputies.

Two situations in particular may be of interest to Americans, namely, the delegation of legislative authority to administrative agencies and legislative-executive responsibility in the field of military affairs. As for the delegation of legislative power, Germany's Constitutional Court exercises more vigilance over this process than does the U.S. Supreme Court. American critics such as Theodore Lowi have viewed with dismay the post-*Schechter* decline in the vitality of the delegation doctrine (see note 19, *supra*). In Germany, by contrast, the doctrine prospers. One reason it prospers is due to the limits that the constitutional text itself imposes on the delegation of legislative authority. Article 80 (1) of the Basic Law authorizes national and state officials to issue regulations having the force of law, but specifies that "the content, purpose, and scope of any such authorization must be set forth in such laws." Statutes that confer general rulemaking power on an agency without specifying the scope and purpose of the power are likely to be viewed with distrust by the Federal Constitutional Court. As one commentator on the Basic Law notes, Article 80 represents a "conscious departure" from the practice during the Weimar Republic of conferring virtually unlimited discretion on executive officials to carry out the will of the lawmaker.[37]

Decisions of the Federal Constitutional Court reflect the high degree of rationality, predictability, and accountability required of administrative rulemaking in Germany. The Court has declared that a "statute must regulate the agency's activity and not confine itself to articulating general principles." In its view, as critics of agency government in the United States have charged, vague delegations of legislative authority

---

[35] See discussion of the *Flick* case in Donald P. Kommers, *The Constitutional Jurisprudence of the Federal Republic of Germany*, 2nd ed. (Durham, N.C.: Duke University Press, 1997), 122.

[36] *Ibid.*, 135.

[37] See Mahendra P. Singh, *German Administrative Law* (Berlin: Springer-Verlag, 1985), 21–22.

tend to encourage administrative agencies to substitute their policies for those of the legislature, risking violations of the principle of "legality" (i.e., rule of law) as well as separation of powers. On this ground, the German Court carefully reviews the validity of contested delegations of legislative power.

At the same time, the Federal Constitutional Court has not confronted parliament with the Hobson's choice that Justice White thought the majority opinion in *Chadha* imposed on Congress. In a well known case involving Germany's Atomic Energy Act—a statute dealing with the licensing of nuclear power plants—the question was whether parliament had adequately laid down guidelines for the safe development of nuclear power. To require parliament to specify rigid safety rules in this rapidly developing field, said the Court, "would impair rather than promote technical development and adequate safeguards (for the protection of the population.)" Parliament and government must be accorded a "[measure of discretion] in making pragmatic decisions within the confines of their authority." The Court sustained the validity of the statute because it specified "with sufficient precision requirements for the construction, operation, and modification of nuclear installations." But this was not the end of parliament's responsibility. Since the legislation affected the basic rights of individuals under the Constitution—here the right to life and physical integrity—parliament would be constitutionally responsible for monitoring developments in the field of nuclear technology to ensure that the authority it confers on an agency conforms to the broad safety requirements of the statute.

The German Court's approach in the nuclear energy case is one way of reconciling tensions between judicial review and majority rule. While recognizing the political character of legislative fact finding and the primacy of the legislature's competence in given subject areas, the case underscores the strong possibility of judicial intervention if, in the Court's judgment, newly accumulated facts seriously challenge the original legislative assessment. The degree of judicial scrutiny in such cases depends on the particularity with which parliament examines the factual basis of a regulatory plan of action. If this process is exacting, and if parliament indentifies the facts on the basis of which it enacts law, taking care to protect constitutional interests, the Court will not invalidate the regulatory scheme merely because the legislature did not accurately predict the results of its action. In this situation, however, the rule of law requires continuing parliamentary vigilance.

Finally, German constitutional law may have some relevance for the seemingly unresolvable conflict between president and Congress over their respective foreign and military powers. It may suffice to focus on Germany's recent *Military Deployment* case, for this decision contrasts sharply with the U.S. Supreme Court's reluctance to examine the validity of executive decisions to deploy military forces abroad. The German experience demonstrates that judicial review of military decisions taken by the executive, over the objection that such decisions have usurped the prerogatives of the legislature, need not lead to excessive judicial intervention in this sensitive field of international politics.

Germany's government had deployed its military force abroad in United Nations peacekeeping operations without explicit parliamentary approval. Ordinarily, the government (i.e., chancellor and cabinet) could count on the tacit support of a parliamentary majority. In one of the contested deployments, however—Germany's participation in the enforcement of the "no-fly zone" over Bosnia and Herzegovina—the government lacked even this tacit consent, for the operation failed to win the support not only of the opposition parties but also of the Free Democratic Party (FDP), the junior partner in coalition with the ruling Christian Democrats. In applying to the Federal Constitutional Court for a preliminary injunction against the action over Bosnia, the FDP took the unusual step of suing the government of which it was an indispensable part.

The dispute reduced itself to an argument over competing provisions of the Basic Law. Article 87a (2) declares that the armed forces, except for purposes of national defense, "may be employed only to the extent explicitly permitted by this Basic Law," whereas Article 24 (2) explicitly allows the Federal Republic to become a party to a system of collective security in the interest of international peace. The Court chose to interpret Article 87a (2) in the light of Article 24 (2) and thus sustained the validity of the military deployments. But the Court went on to hold that under the Basic Law, the chancellor and his cabinet would be required to seek parliament's explicit approval prior to any deployment of the armed services even under a valid international agreement. In so ruling, the Court vindicated parliament's right to participate in cabinet decisions to deploy military units outside the area covered by NATO.

The principle of democracy was crucial to the Court's reasoning. The government's actions were taken under treaties that constitutionally require parliamentary approval. Here, however, argued the petitioners, the military deployments were beyond the contemplation of the original treaties, thus requiring further parliamentary approval. Although the Court did not accept this view of the original treaties, its decision was clearly a response to its concern for the principle of democratic legitimacy in military matters. In Germany, then, the unamendable principle of separation of powers combines with the equally entrenched principle of popular sovereignty and executive responsibility to produce an accountable government supported by the consent of parliament.

Selected Bibliography

Arnold, Peri E. *Making the Managerial Presidency*. Princeton, N.J.: Princeton University Press, 1986.

Barber, Sotirios. *The Constitution and the Delegation of Congressional Power*. Chicago: University of Chicago Press, 1975.

Berger, Raoul. *Executive Privilege: A Constitutional Myth*. Cambridge: Harvard University Press, 1974.

Calabresi, Steven G. and Saikrishna B. Prakash. *The President's Power to Execute the Laws*, 104 Yale Law Journal 541–665 (1994).

Corwin, Edward S. *The President: Office and Powers*, 4th rev. ed. New York: New York University Press, 1957.

Craig, Barbara H. *Chadha: The Story of an Epic Constitutional Struggle*. Berkeley: University of California Press, 1990.

Fisher, Louis. *Constitutional Conflicts Between Congress and the President*. Princeton: Princeton University Press, 1985.

———. *Judicial Misjudgments About the Lawmaking Process: The Legislative Veto Case*. 45 Public Administration Review 705 (1985).

Flaherty, Martin S. *The Most Dangerous Branch*, 105 Yale Law Journal 1725–1839 (1996).

Hamilton, James. *The Power To Probe: A Study in Congressional Investigations*. New York: Random House, 1976.

Jones, Gordon S. and John A. Marini, eds. *The Imperial Congress: Crisis in the Separation of Powers*. New York: Pharos Books, 1988.

Labovitz, John R. *Presidential Impeachments*. New Haven: Yale University Press, 1978.

Murphy, Walter F. *Congress and the Court*. Chicago: University of Chicago Press, 1962.

Pierce, Richard. J. "*Morrison v. Olsen*, Separation of Powers, and the Structure of Government." In Gerhard Casper and Dennis J. Hutchinson, eds. *The Supreme Court Review 1988*. Chicago: University of Chicago Press, 1989.

Pyle, Christopher H. and Richard Pious. *The President, Congress, and the Constitution*. New York: The Free Press, 1984.

Ratnapala, Suri. *John Locke's Doctrine of Separation of Powers: A Reevaluation*. 38 American Journal of Jurisprudence 189–220 (1993).

Rohr, John. *To Run A Constitution: The Legitimacy of the Administrative State*. Lawrence: University Press of Kansas, 1986.

Shapiro, Martin. *Law and Politics in the Supreme Court*, chapter 2. New York: The Free Press, 1964.

Schlesinger, Arthur M. *The Imperial Presidency*. Boston: Houghton-Mifflin, 1973.

Stephens, Otis H. and Gregroy J. Rathjen. *The Supreme Court and the Allocation of Constitutional Power*. San Francisco: W. H. Freeman and Company, 1980.

Westin, Alan F. *The Anatomy of a Constitutional Law Case*. New York: Macmillan, 1958.

Schechter Poultry Corporation v. United States

295 U.S. 495, 55 S. Ct. 837, 79 L. Ed. 1570 (1935)

The National Industrial Recovery Act of 1933, a major New Deal measure designed to revive and develop the national economy, authorized various trades and industries to adopt codes of fair competition. The codes, which typically covered wages, hours of work, trade practices, and labor conditions, entered into force with the president's approval. Pursuant to the act, the president approved the "Live Poultry Code" for the New York metropolitan area, one purpose of which was to prevent sellers from requiring buyers to purchase "sick" chickens along with the healthy ones offered for sale. The Schechter Poultry Company was indicted and convicted in a federal district court for violating the code's provisions. Schechter challenged the conviction, contending that the code had been adopted pursuant to an unconstitutional delegation by Congress of legislative power and that it regulated local transactions outside of Congress's authority. The following extract deals with the issue of delegation. Opinion of the Court: *Hughes*, Van Devanter, McReynolds, Brandeis, Sutherland, Butler, Roberts. Concurring opinion: *Cardoza*, Stone.

Mr. Chief Justice HUGHES delivered the opinion of the Court.

. . . We recently had occasion to review the pertinent decisions and the general principles which govern the determination of this question. The Constitution provides that "All legislative powers herein granted shall be vested in a Congress of the United States, which shall consist of a Senate and House of Representatives." Article 1, s 1. And the Congress is authorized "To make all Laws which shall be necessary and proper for carrying into Execution" its general powers. Article 1, s 8, par. 18. The Congress is not permitted to abdicate or to transfer to others the essential legislative functions with which it is thus vested. We have repeatedly recognized the necessity of adapting legislation to complex conditions involving a host of details with which the national Legislature cannot deal directly. We pointed out in the *Panama Refining Company* case [1935] that the Constitution has never been regarded as denying to Congress the necessary resources of flexibility and practicality, which will enable it to perform its function in laying down policies and establishing standards, while leaving to selected instrumentalities the making of subordinate rules within prescribed limits and the determination of facts to which the policy as declared by the Legislature is to apply.

But we said that the constant recognition of the necessity and validity of such provisions, and the wide range of administrative authority which has been developed by means of them, cannot be allowed to obscure the limitations of the authority to delegate, if our constitutional system is to be maintained.

Accordingly, we look to the statute to see whether Congress has overstepped these limitations—whether Congress in authorizing "codes of fair competition" has itself established the standards of legal obligation, thus performing its essential legislative function, or, by the failure to enact such standards, has attempted to transfer that function to others.

The aspect in which the question is now presented is distinct from that which was before us in the case of the *Panama Company*. There, the subject of the statutory prohibition was defined. That subject was the transportation in interstate and foreign commerce of petroleum and petroleum products which are produced or withdrawn from storage in excess of the amount permitted by state authority. The question was with respect to the range of discretion given to the President in prohibiting that transportation. As to the "codes of fair competition," under section 3 of the Act, the question is more fundamental. It is whether there is any adequate definition of the subject to which the codes are to be addressed.

What is meant by "fair competition" as the term is used in the Act? Does it refer to a category established in the law, and is the authority to make codes limited accordingly? Or is it used as a convenient designation for whatever set of laws the formulators of a code for a particular trade or industry may propose and the President may approve (subject to certain restrictions), or the President may himself prescribe, as being wise and beneficent provisions for the government of the trade or industry in order to accomplish the broad purposes of rehabilitation, correction, and expansion which are stated in the first section of Title 1?

The Act does not define "fair competition." "Unfair competition," as known to the common law, is a limited concept. Primarily, and strictly, it relates to the palming off of one's goods as those of a rival trader. In recent years, its scope has been extended. It has been held to apply to misappropriation as well as misrepresentation, to the selling of another's goods as one's own—to misappropriation of what equitably belongs to a competitor. Unfairness in competition has been predicated of acts which lie outside the ordinary course of business and are tainted by fraud or coercion or conduct otherwise prohibited by law. But it is evident that in its widest range, "unfair competition," as it has been understood in the law, does not reach the objectives of the codes which are authorized by the National Industrial Recovery Act. The codes may, indeed, cover conduct which existing law condemns, but they are not limited to conduct of that sort. The government does not contend that the Act contemplates such a limitation. It would be opposed both to the declared purposes of the Act and to its administrative construction.

The Federal Trade Commission Act introduced the expression "unfair methods of competition," which were declared to be unlawful. That was an expression new in the law. . . .What are "unfair methods of competition" are thus to be determined in particular instances, upon evidence, in the light of particular competitive conditions and of what is found to be a specific and substantial public interest . . .

To make this possible, Congress set up a special procedure. A Commission, a quasi judicial body, was created. Provision was made for formal complaint, for notice and hearing, for appropriate findings of fact supported by adequate evidence, and for judicial review to give assurance that the action of the commission is taken within its statutory authority.

In providing for codes, the National Industrial Recovery Act dispenses with this administrative procedure and with any administrative procedure of an analogous character. But the difference between the code plan of the Recovery Act and the scheme of the Federal Trade Commission Act lies not only in procedure but in subject-matter. We cannot regard the "fair competition" of the codes as antithetical to the "unfair methods of competition" of the Federal Trade Commission Act. The "fair competition" of the codes has a much broader range and a new significance. The Recovery Act provides that it shall not be construed to impair the powers of the Federal Trade Commission, but, when a code is approved, its provisions are to be the "standards of fair competition" for the trade or industry concerned, and any violation of such standards in any transaction in or affecting interstate or foreign commerce is to be deemed "an unfair method of competition" within the meaning of the Federal Trade Commission Act.

For a statement of the authorized objectives and content of the "codes of fair competition," we are referred repeatedly to the "Declaration of Policy" in section 1 of Title 1 of the Recovery Act. Thus the approval of a code by the President is conditioned on his finding that it "will tend to effectuate the policy of this title." The President is authorized to impose such conditions "for the protection of consumers, competitors, employees, and others, and in furtherance of the public interest, and may provide such exceptions to and exemptions from the provisions of such code, as the President in his discretion deems necessary to effectuate the policy herein declared." The "policy herein declared" is manifestly set forth in section one. That declaration embraces a broad range of objectives. Among them we find

the elimination of "unfair competitive practices." But, even if this clause were to be taken to relate to practices which fall under the ban of existing law, either common law or statute, it is still only one of the authorized aims described in section one. It is there declared to be

> the policy of Congress—to remove obstructions to the free flow of interstate and foreign commerce which tend to diminish the amount thereof; and to provide for the general welfare by promoting the organization of industry for the purpose of cooperative action among trade groups, to induce and maintain united action of labor and management under adequate governmental sanctions and supervision, to eliminate unfair competitive practices, to promote the fullest possible utilization of the present productive capacity of industries, to avoid undue restriction of production (except as may be temporarily required), to increase the consumption of industrial and agricultural products by increasing purchasing power, to reduce and relieve unemployment, to improve standards of labor, and otherwise to rehabilitate industry and to conserve natural resources.

Under section 3, whatever "may tend to effectuate" these general purposes may be included in the "codes of fair competition." We think the conclusion is inescapable that the authority sought to be conferred by section 3 was not merely to deal with "unfair competitive practices" which offend against existing law, and could be the subject of judicial condemnation without further legislation, or to create administrative machinery for the application of established principles of law to particular instances of violation. Rather, the purpose is clearly disclosed to authorize prohibitions through codes of laws which would embrace what the formulators would propose, and what the President would approve, or prescribe, as wise and beneficent measures for the government of trades and industries in order to bring about rehabilitation, correction and development, according to the general declaration of policy in section 1. Codes of laws of this sort are styled "codes of fair competition."

The question, then, turns upon the authority which section 3 of the Recovery Act vests in the President to approve or prescribe. If the codes have standing as penal statutes, this must be due to the effect of the executive action. But Congress cannot delegate legislative power to the President to exercise an unfettered discretion to make whatever laws he thinks may be needed or advisable for the rehabilitation and expansion of trade or industry.

To summarize and conclude upon this point: Section 3 of the Recovery Act is without precedent. It supplies no standards for any trade, industry, or activity. It does not undertake to prescribe rules of conduct to be applied to par-

Comparative Note 4.1

The following considerations apply to the relationship between the legislature and the executive. In a free democratic and constitutional system, parliament has the constitutional task of enacting laws. Only parliament possesses the democratic legitimacy to make fundamental political decisions. To be sure, the Basic Law sanctions "delegated" legislation by the executive. However, the executive can legislate only within limits which the legislature prescribes. Parliament cannot neglect its responsibility as a legislative body by delegating part of its legislative authority to the executive without beforehand reflecting upon and determining the limitations of these delegated powers. If the legislature does not satisfy this requirement, then it will shift unfavorably the balance of powers presupposed by the Basic Law in the area of legislation. A total delegation of legislative power to the executive branch violates the principle of separation of powers.

. . .

To the extent that a statute delegates the authority to issue regulations to the exeuctive, the legislative intent must provide . . . a guide for the content of the regulation. The statute must give expression to the legislative intent. It must be clear whether or not the executive confined itself to the express limits [of the delegating statute] in issuing the regulation. If the content [of the regulation] goes beyond the legislative intent, then the issuer of the regulation has overstepped the boundaries of its delegated power. The regulation is then invalid because it has an insufficient legal basis.

SOURCE: *Judicial Qualifications Case* (1972), Federal Constitutional Court (Germany) in Kommers, *Constitutional Jurisprudence*, 2d ed., 147.

---

ticular states of fact determined by appropriate administrative procedure. Instead of prescribing rules of conduct, it authorizes the making of codes to prescribe them. For that legislative undertaking, section 3 sets up no standards, aside from the statement of the general aims of rehabilitation, correction, and expansion described in section 1. In view of the scope of that broad declaration and of the nature of the few restrictions that are imposed, the discretion of the President in approving or prescribing codes, and thus enacting laws for the government of trade and industry throughout the country, is virtually unfettered. We think that the code-making authority thus conferred is an unconstitutional delegation of legislative power.

Mr. Justice CARDOZO, concurring.

The delegated power of legislation which has found expression in this code is not canalized within banks that keep it from overflowing. It is unconfined and vagrant, if I may borrow my own words in an earlier opinion.

This court has held that delegation may be unlawful though the act to be performed is definite and single, if the necessity, time, and occasion of performance have been left in the end to the discretion of the delegate. I thought that ruling went too far. I pointed out in an opinion that there had been "no grant to the Executive of any roving commission to inquire into evils and then, upon discovering them, do anything he pleases." Choice, though within limits, has been given to him "as to the occasion, but none whatever as to the means." Here, in the case before us, is an attempted delegation not confined to acts identified or described by reference to a standard. Here in effect is a roving commission to inquire into evils and upon discovery correct them.

I have said that there is no standard, definite or even approximate, to which legislation must conform. Let me make my meaning more precise. If codes of fair competition are codes eliminating "unfair" methods of competition ascertained upon inquiry to prevail in one industry or another, there is no unlawful delegation of legislative functions when the President is directed to inquire into such practices and denounce them when discovered. For many years a like power has been committed to the Federal Trade Commission with the approval of this court in a long series of decisions. Delegation in such circumstances is born of the necessities of the occasion. The industries of the country are too many and diverse to make it possible for Congress, in respect of matters such as these, to legislate directly with adequate appreciation of varying conditions. Nor is the substance of the power changed because the President may act at the instance of trade or industrial associations having special knowledge of the facts. Their function is strictly advisory; it is the *imprimatur* of the President that begets the quality of law. When the task that is set before one is that of cleaning house, it is prudent as well as usual to take counsel of the dwellers.

But there is another conception of codes of fair competition, their significance and function, which leads to very different consequences, though it is one that is struggling now for recognition and acceptance. By this other conception a code is not to be restricted to the elimination of business practices that would be characterized by general acceptation as oppressive or unfair. It is to include whatever ordinances may be desirable or helpful for the well-being or prosperity of the industry affected. In that view, the function of its adoption is not merely negative, but positive; the planning of improvements as well as the extirpation of abuses. What is fair, as thus conceived, is not something to be contrasted with what is unfair or fraudulent or tricky. The extension becomes as wide as the field of industrial regulation. If that conception shall prevail, anything that Congress may do within the limits of the commerce clause for the betterment of business may be done by the President upon the recommendation of a trade association by calling it a code. This is delegation running riot. No such plenitude of power is susceptible of transfer. The statute, however, aims at nothing less, as one can learn both from its terms and from the administrative practice under it. Nothing less is aimed at by the code now submitted to our scrutiny.

Notes/Queries/Readings

1. *Schechter*, along with *Panama Refining Co. v. Ryan* (1935, holding unconstitutional the NIRA's delegation of authority to the president to prohibit the transportation of petroleum products in excess of an amount provided by law but containing no definition of the circumstances and condition in which the transportation is to be allowed or prohibited) represented the height of the Supreme Court's enforcement of the nondelegation doctrine. In the sixty-three years since these two cases, the Supreme Court has invalidated no federal law on the basis of the nondelegation doctrine despite broad delegations of authority by Congress to administrative agencies. For recent, although unsuccessful, efforts to revive the nondelegation doctrine see *Industrial Union Department v. American Petroleum Institute*, 448 U.S. 607 (1980) and *Loving v. United States*, 116 S. Ct. 1737 (1996).

2. Do you detect any difference between the delegation doctrine espoused in *Schechter* and the view set forth by Germany's Federal Constitutional Court in Comparative Note 4.1?

3. Chief Justice Hughes states that the "explicit terms" of the Tenth Amendment imply that "extraordinary conditions do not create or enlarge constitutional power." Do you agree with this statement? Does this statement square with actions taken by the executive office and the legislature in wartime or with the economic legislation enacted by Congress since the New Deal (see chapters 5 and 7)? If it is admitted that the government can extend its power during a declared war, does it follow that it can do so in times of civil and economic crises as well?

4. Why should the judiciary concern itself with how Congress delegates its rightful powers? Is there something wrong with such delegation from the standpoint of democratic accountability?

5. President Roosevelt responded to the Court's decision by asking: "Does this decision mean that the United States Government has no control over any national economic problem?" Roosevelt, of course, continued his efforts to rework the national economy. Among his efforts was a statute that would have established a regulatory framework for coal that was similar to the one the Court struck down in *Schechter*. In a letter to the congressional committee considering the legislation, Roosevelt wrote that "[I] hope your committee will not permit doubts as to unconstitutionality, however reasonable, to block the suggested legislation." Letter to Congressman Hill, 6 July 1935, 4 *The Public Papers and Addresses of Franklin D. Roosevelt* (1938), 297–98. Congress passed the legislation, the Bituminous Coal Conservation Act of 1935. The Court struck it down in the case of *Carter v. Carter Coal Co.*, 298 U. S. 238 (1936).

6. For additional reading on the nondelegation doctrine, see Sotirios A. Barber, *The Constitution and the Delegation of Congressional Power* (Chicago: University of Chicago Press, 1975) and Theodore W. Lowi, *The End of Liberalism*, 2d ed. (New York: Norton, 1979).

Youngstown Sheet & Tube v. Sawyer

343 U.S. 579, 72 S. Ct. 863, 96 L. Ed. 1153 (1952)

This case arose out of President Harry Truman's executive order directing the secretary of commerce to seize and operate the nation's steel mills. Other relevant facts are set forth in chapter 7 at page 290. The following extracts feature the respective views of Justices Black and Jackson.

Opinion of the Court: *Black*, Frankfurter, Burton, Jackson. Concurring opinions: *Frankfurter, Burton, Jackson, Clark, Douglas*. Dissenting opinion: *Vinson*, Reed, Minton.

Mr. Justice BLACK delivered the opinion of the Court.

We are asked to decide whether the President was acting within his constitutional power when he issued an order directing the Secretary of Commerce to take possession of and operate most of the Nation's steel mills. The mill owners argue that the President's order amounts to lawmaking, a legislative function which the Constitution has expressly confided to the Congress and not to the President. The Government's position is that the order was made on findings of the President that his action was necessary to avert a national catastrophe which would inevitably result from a stoppage of steel production, and that in meeting this grave emergency the President was acting within the aggregate of his constitutional powers as the Nation's Chief Executive and the Commander in Chief of the Armed Forces of the United States.

The President's power, if any, to issue the order must stem either from an act of Congress or from the Constitution itself. There is no statute that expressly authorizes the President to take possession of property as he did here. Nor is there any act of Congress to which our attention has been directed from which such a power can fairly be implied. Indeed, we do not understand the Government to rely on statutory authorization for this seizure.

Moreover, the use of the seizure technique to solve labor disputes in order to prevent work stoppages was not only unauthorized by any congressional enactment; prior to this controversy, Congress had refused to adopt that method of settling labor disputes. When the Taft-Hartley Act was under consideration in 1947, Congress rejected an amendment which would have authorized such governmental seizures in cases of emergency. Apparently it was thought that the technique of seizure, like that of compulsory arbitration, would interfere with the process of collective bargaining. . . .

It is clear that if the President had authority to issue the order he did, it must be found in some provision of the Constitution. And it is not claimed that express constitutional language grants this power to the President. The contention is that presidential power should be implied from the aggregate of his powers under the Constitution. Particular reliance is placed on provisions in Article II which say that "the executive Power shall be vested in a President . . . ," that "he shall take Care that the Laws be faithfully executed"; and that he "shall be Commander in Chief of the Army and Navy of the United States."

The order cannot properly be sustained as an exercise of the President's military power as Commander in Chief of the Armed Forces. The Government attempts to do so by citing a number of cases upholding broad powers in military commanders engaged in day-to-day fighting in a theater of war. Such cases need not concern us here. Even though "theater of war" be an expanding concept, we cannot with faithfulness to our constitutional system hold that the Commander in Chief of the Armed Forces has the ultimate power as such to take possession of private property in order to keep labor disputes from stopping production.

This is a job for the Nation's lawmakers, not for its military authorities.

Nor can the seizure order be sustained because of the several constitutional provisions that grant executive power to the President. In the framework of our Constitution, the President's power to see that the laws are faithfully executed refutes the idea that he is to be a lawmaker. The Constitution limits his functions in the lawmaking process to the recommending of laws he thinks wise and the vetoing of laws he thinks bad. And the Constitution is neither silent nor equivocal about who shall make laws which the President is to execute. . . .

The Founders of this Nation entrusted the law making power to the Congress alone in both good and bad times. It would do no good to recall the historical events, the fears of power and the hopes for freedom that lay behind their choice. Such a review would but confirm our holding that this seizure order cannot stand.

Affirmed

Mr. Justice FRANKFURTER, concurring.

. . . A constitutional democracy like ours is perhaps the most difficult of man's social arrangements to manage successfully. . . . The Founders of this nation were not imbued with the modern cynicism that the only thing that history teaches is that it teaches nothing. They acted on the conviction that the experience of man sheds a good deal of light on his nature. It sheds a good deal of light not merely on the need for effective power, if a society is to be at once cohesive and civilized, but also on the need for limitations on the power of governors over the governed.

To that end (the Founders) rested the structure of our central government on the system of checks and balances. For them the doctrine of separation of powers was not mere theory; it was a felt necessity. . . . The accretion of dangerous power does not come in a day. It does come, however slowly, from the generative force of unchecked disregard of the restrictions that fence in even the most disinterested assertion of authority.

The Framers, however, did not make the judiciary the overseer of our government. . . . Rigorous adherence to the narrow scope of the judicial function is especially demanded in controversies that arouse appeals to the Constitution. The attitude with which this Court must approach its duty when confronted with such issues is precisely the opposite of that normally manifested by the general public. So-called constitutional questions seem to exercise a mesmeric influence over the popular mind. This eagerness to settle—preferably forever—a specific problem on the basis of the broadest possible constitutional pronouncements may not unfairly be called one of our minor national traits. An English observer of our scene has acutely described it: "At the first sound of a new argument over the United States Constitution and its interpretation the hearts of Americans leap with a fearful joy. The blood stirs powerfully in their veins and a new lustre brightens their eyes. Like King Harry's men before Harfleur, they stand like greyhounds in the slips, straining upon the start."

The path of duty for this Court, it bears repetition, lies in the opposite direction. Due regard for the implications of the distribution of powers in our Constitution and for the nature of the judicial process as the ultimate authority in interpreting the Constitution, has . . . confined the Court within the narrow domain of appropriate adjudication. . . . A basic rule is the duty of the Court not to pass on a constitutional issue at all, however narrowly it may be confined, if the case may, as a matter of intellectual honesty, be decided without even considering delicate problems of power under the Constitution.

. . . Not the least characteristic of great statesmanship which the Framers manifested was the extent to which they did not attempt to bind the future. It is no less incumbent upon this Court to avoid putting fetters upon the future by needless pronouncements today.

. . . The issue before us can be met, and therefore should be, without attempting to define the President's powers comprehensively. . . . The judiciary may, as this case proves, have to intervene in determining where authority lies as between the democratic forces in our scheme of government. But in doing so we should be wary and humble. Such is the teaching of this Court's role in the history of the country.

It is in this mood and with this perspective that the issue before the Court must be approached. We must therefore put to one side consideration of what powers the President would have had if there had been no legislation whatever bearing on the authority asserted by the seizure, or if the seizure had been only for a short, explicitly temporary period, to be terminated automatically unless Congressional approval were given. . . .

To be sure, the content of the three authorities of government is not to be derived from an abstract analysis. The areas are partly interacting, not wholly disjointed. The Constitution is a framework for government. Therefore the way the framework has consistently operated fairly establishes that it has operated according to its true nature. Deeply embedded traditional ways of conducting government cannot supplant the Constitution or legislation, but they give meaning to the words of a text or supply them. It is an inadmissibly narrow conception of American constitutional law to confine it to the words of the Constitution and to disregard the gloss which life has written upon

them. In short, a systematic, unbroken, executive practice, long pursued to the knowledge of the Congress and never before questioned, engaged in by Presidents who have also sworn to uphold the Constitution, making as it were such exercise of power part of the structure of our government, may be treated as a gloss on the "executive Power" vested in the President by section 1 of Art. 2.

[Frankfurter went on to hold the seizure of the steel mills unconstitutional because the President had acted contrary to the specific procedures laid down by Congress to meet the emergency in this case.]

Mr. Justice JACKSON, concurring in the judgment and opinion of the Court.

A judge, like an executive adviser, may be surprised at the poverty of really useful and unambiguous authority applicable to concrete problems of executive power as they actually present themselves. Just what our forefathers did envision, or would have envisioned had they foreseen modern conditions, must be divined from materials almost as enigmatic as the dreams Joseph was called upon to interpret for Pharaoh. A century and a half of partisan debate and scholarly speculation yields no net result but only supplies more or less apt quotations from respected sources on each side of any question. They largely cancel each other. And court decisions are indecisive because of the judicial practice of dealing with the largest questions in the most narrow way.

The actual art of governing under our Constitution does not and cannot conform to judicial definitions of the power of any of its branches based on isolated clauses or even single Articles torn from context. While the Constitution diffuses power the better to secure liberty, it also contemplates that practice will integrate the dispersed powers into a workable government. It enjoins upon its branches separateness but interdependence, autonomy but reciprocity. Presidential powers are not fixed but fluctuate, depending upon their disjunction or conjunction with those of Congress. We may well begin by a somewhat over-simplified grouping of practical situations in which a President may doubt, or others may challenge, his powers. . . .

1. When the President acts pursuant to an express or implied authorization of Congress, his authority is at its maximum, for it includes all that he possesses in his own right plus all that Congress can delegate. In these circumstances, and in these only, may he be said (for what it may be worth), to personify the federal sovereignty. If his act is held unconstitutional under these circumstances, it usually means that the Federal Government as an undivided whole lacks power. A seizure executed by the President pursuant

to an Act of Congress would be supported by the strongest of presumptions and the widest latitude of judicial interpretation, and the burden or persuasion would rest heavily upon any who might attack it.

2. When the President acts in absence of either a congressional grant or denial of authority, he can only rely upon his own independent powers, but there is a zone of twilight in which he and Congress may have concurrent authority, or in which its distribution is uncertain. Therefore, congressional inertia, indifference or quiescence may sometimes, at least as a practical matter, enable, if not invite, measures on independent presidential responsibility. In this area, any actual test of power is likely to depend on the imperatives of events and contemporary imponderables rather than on abstract theories of law.

3. When the President takes measures incompatible with the expressed or implied will of Congress, his power is at its lowest ebb, for then he can rely only upon his own constitutional powers minus any constitutional powers of Congress over the matter. Courts can sustain exclusive presidential control in such a case only by disabling the Congress from acting upon the subject. Presidential claim to a power at once so conclusive and preclusive must be scrutinized with caution, for what is at stake is the equilibrium established by our constitutional system.

Into which of these classifications does this executive seizure of the steel industry fit? It is eliminated from the first by admission, for it is conceded that no congressional authorization exists for this seizure. That takes away also the support of the many precedents and declarations which were made in relation, and must be confined, to this category.

Can it then be defended under flexible tests available to the second category? It seems clearly eliminated from that class because Congress has not left seizure of private property an open field but has covered it by three statutory policies inconsistent with this seizure. In cases where the purpose is to supply needs of the Government itself, two courses are provided: one, seizure of a plant which fails to comply with obligatory orders placed by the Government, another, condemnation of facilities, including temporary use under the power of eminent domain. The third is applicable where it is the general economy of the country that is to be protected rather than exclusive governmental interests. None of these were invoked. In choosing a different and inconsistent way of his own, the President cannot claim that it is necessitated or invited by failure of Congress to legislate upon the occasions, grounds and methods for seizure of industrial properties.

This leaves the current seizure to be justified only by the severe tests under the third grouping, where it can be supported only by any remainder of executive power after subtraction of such powers as Congress may have over the subject. In short, we can sustain the President only by holding that seizure of such strike-bound industries is within his domain and beyond control by Congress. Thus, this Court's first review of such seizures occurs under circumstances which leave Presidential power most vulnerable to attack and in the least favorable of possible constitutional postures. . . .

The Solicitor General seeks the power of seizure in three clauses of the Executive Article, the first reading, "The executive Power shall be vested in a President of the United States of America." Lest I be thought to exaggerate, I quote the interpretation which his brief puts upon it: "In our view, this clause constitutes a grant of all the executive powers of which the Government is capable." If that be true, it is difficult to see why the forefathers bothered to add several specific items, including some trifling ones.

The example of such unlimited executive power that must have most impressed the forefathers was the prerogative exercised by George III, and the description of its evils in the Declaration of Independence leads me to doubt that they were creating their new Executive in his image. Continental European examples were no more appealing. And if we seek instruction from our own times, we can match it only from the executive powers in those governments we disparagingly describe as totalitarian. I cannot accept the view that this clause is a grant in bulk of all conceivable executive power but regard it as an allocation to the presidential office of the generic powers thereafter stated.

The clause on which the Government next relies is that "The President shall be Commander in Chief of the Army and Navy of the United States. . . ." These cryptic words have given rise to some of the most persistent controversies in our constitutional history. Of course, they imply something more than an empty title. But just what authority goes with the name has plagued presidential advisers who would not waive or narrow it by nonassertion yet cannot say where it begins or ends. It undoubtedly puts the Nation's armed forces under presidential command. Hence, this loose appellation is sometimes advanced as support for any presidential action, internal or external, involving use of force, the idea being that it vests power to do anything, anywhere, that can be done with an army or navy.

That seems to be the logic of an argument tendered at our bar—that the President having, on his own responsibility, sent American troops abroad derives from that act "affirmative power" to seize the means of producing a supply of steel for them. To quote, "Perhaps the most forceful illustrations of the scope of Presidential power in this connection is the fact that American troops in Korea, whose safety and effectiveness are so directly involved here, were sent to the field by an exercise of the President's constitutional powers." Thus, it is said he has invested himself with "war powers."

I cannot foresee all that it might entail if the Court should indorse this argument. Nothing in our Constitution is plainer than that declaration of a war is entrusted only to Congress. Of course, a state of war may in fact exist without a formal declaration. But no doctrine that the Court could promulgate would seem to me more sinister and alarming than that a President whose conduct of foreign affairs is so largely uncontrolled, and often even is unknown, can vastly enlarge his mastery over the internal affairs of the country by his own commitment of the Nation's armed forces to some foreign venture. I do not, however, find it necessary or appropriate to consider the legal status of the Korean enterprise to discountenance argument based on it.

We should not use this occasion to circumscribe, much less to contract, the lawful role of the President as Commander-in-Chief. I should indulge the widest latitude of interpretation to sustain his exclusive function to command the instruments of national force, at least when turned against the outside world for the security of our society. But, when it is turned inward, not because of rebellion but because of a lawful economic struggle between industry and labor, it should have no such indulgence. His command power is not such an absolute as might be implied from that office in a militaristic system but is subject to limitations consistent with a constitutional Republic whose law and policy-making branch is a representative Congress. . . .

In the practical working of our Government we already have evolved a technique within the framework of the Constitution by which normal executive powers may be considerably expanded to meet an emergency. Congress may and has granted extraordinary authorities which lie dormant in normal times but may be called into play by the Executive in war or upon proclamation of a national emergency. . . .

In view of the ease, expedition and safety with which Congress can grant and has granted large emergency powers, certainly ample to embrace this crisis, I am quite unimpressed with the argument that we should affirm possession of them without statute. Such power either has no beginning or it has no end. If it exists, it need submit to no legal restraint. I am not alarmed that it would plunge us straightway into dictatorship, but it is at least a step in that wrong direction.

But I have no illusion that any decision by this Court can keep power in the hands of Congress if it is not wise and timely in meeting its problems. A crisis that challenges the President equally, or perhaps primarily, challenges Congress. If not good law, there was worldly wisdom in the maxim attributed to Napoleon that "The tools belong to the man who can use them." We may say that power to legislate for emergencies belongs in the hands of Congress, but only Congress itself can prevent power from slipping through its fingers.

The essence of our free Government is "leave to live by no man's leave, underneath the law"—to be governed by those impersonal forces which we call law. Our Government is fashioned to fulfill this concept so far as humanly possible. The Executive, except for recommendation and veto, has no legislative power. The executive action we have here originates in the individual will of the President and represents an exercise of authority without law. No one, perhaps not even the President, knows the limits of the power he may seek to exert in this instance and the parties affected cannot learn the limit of their rights. We do not know today what powers over labor or property would be claimed to flow from Government possession if we should legalize it, what rights to compensation would be claimed or recognized, or on what contingency it would end. With all its defects, delays and inconveniences, men have discovered no technique for long preserving free government except that the Executive be under the law, and that the law be made by parliamentary deliberations.

Such institutions may be destined to pass away. But it is the duty of the Court to be last, not first, to give them up.

Notes/Queries/Readings

1. Who among the three justices, in your opinion, adopts the most intellectually compelling approach to constitutional interpretation in the *Steel Seizure* case? Who among them advances the most flexible conception of the relationship between the legislative and executive branches?

2. Do you find Justice Jackson's reasoning consistent with *Schechter*? With the idea of a limited government? What role should the long-accepted historical practices mentioned by Justice Frankfurter play in constitutional interpretation?

3. The case of *Dames & Moore v. Regan* illustrates a more recent and perhaps different conception of the president's power to act during times of congressional silence. An executive agreement was negotiated in 1981 to obtain the release of American hostages held by Iran. The agreement released Iranian assets that had been frozen in the United States and shifted all claims against Iran pending in American courts to a new Iran-United States claims tribunal for binding arbitration. The president defended the agreement on the basis of his inherent power as chief executive

under Article 2 of the Constitution. Justice Rehnquist, writing for the Court, upheld the government's claim, but rested his opinion on a less expansive conception of executive power. Rehnquist noted that the agreement with Iran could be justified either by specific congressional authorization or implied congressional approval. He emphasized that "the President does have some measure of power to enter into executive agreements without obtaining the advice and consent of the Senate."

Rehnquist cited the opinions of Justices Jackson and Frankfurter in *Youngstown Sheet & Tube*. He found Jackson's three-pronged approach "analytically useful," yet he observed that any particular instance does not fit exactly into one of the three categories but on a spectrum from express congressional authorization to express congressional proscription. This case is a narrow one, Rehnquist stated, because Congress had not "in some way resisted the exercise of Presidential authority." He relied instead on Frankfurter's analysis, stating that, "in light of the fact that Congress may be considered to have consented to the President's action in suspending claims, we can not say that the action exceeded the President's power."

4. In what situations should the president be able to act in opposition to the expressed provisions of congressional legislation? Can this be reconciled with the presidential oath to "faithfully execute the Office of the President of the United States"? Might acting contrary to the will of Congress be necessary for the president to "preserve, protect and defend the Constitution of the United States"?

5. Did the Court review President Truman's determination that the seizure of the steel mills was necessary for national security? Is this the type of political question that is beyond the capability of the judiciary to answer? Must it decide this question in order to decide the case? Does the view of the German Constitutional Court in Comparative

Note 4.1 provide any guidance in the judicial resolution of this case?

6. Do you agree with Justice Frankfurter that a "systematic, unbroken, executive practice, long pursued to the knowledge of the Congress and never before questioned, engaged in by Presidents who have also sworn to uphold the Constitution . . . may be treated as a gloss on the 'executive Power' vested in the President"?

7. In his concurring opinion, Justice Jackson wrote that "contemporary foreign experience may be inconclusive as to the wisdom of lodging emergency powers somewhere in the modern government. But it suggests that emergency powers are consistent with free government only when their control is lodged elsewhere than in the Executive who exercises them." Is this expression a simple restatement about the wisdom of separation of powers? Is the separation of powers fundamentally inconsistent with the doctrine of "inherent powers," as Jackson suggested? For a discussion of the role and limits of emergency powers in a constitutional democracy, see chapter 7. See also John E. Finn, *Constitutions in Crisis: Political Violence and the Rule of Law* (New York: Oxford University Press, 1991) and Clinton Rossiter, *Constitutional Dictatorship* (Princeton, N.J.: Princeton University Press, 1948).

8. There is considerable literature on *Youngstown*. See, for example, Macva Marcus, *Truman and the Steel Seizure Case: The Limits of Presidential Power* (New York: Columbia University Press, 1977); Grant McConnell, *The President Seizes the Steel Mills* (University of Alabama Case Study Program, 1960); Alan F. Westin, ed., *The Anatomy of a Constitutional Law Case* (New York: Macmillan, 1958); Edward S. Corwin, *The Steel Seizure Case: A Judicial Brick Without Straw*, 53 Columbia Law Review 53 (1953); and Paul G. Kauper, *The Steel Seizure Case*, 51 Michigan Law Review 141 (1952).

Powell v. McCormack
395 U.S. 486, 89 S. Ct. 1944, 23 L. Ed. 2d 491 (1969)

In November 1966, Adam Clayton Powell was duly elected from the 18th Congressional District of New York to serve in the House of Representatives for the 90th Congress. A special subcommittee of the 89th Congress, however, found that he had falsified his expense accounts and made illegal salary payments to his wife. After further investigation and debate, and in the face of Powell's refusal to testify about matters other than his eligibility to serve in Congress under the qualifications of Article 1, sec. 2 of the Constitu-

tion, the House voted 307 to 116 to exclude him from the 90th Congress and declared his seat vacant. Powell and thirteen voters from the 18th District sued the speaker (John McCormack), clerk, doorkeeper, and sergeant at arms for keeping him from taking his seat. The voters argued that they were being deprived of their representation in Congress and requested a declaratory judgment that Powell's exclusion was unconstitutional. The federal district court granted the defendants' motion to dismiss the complaint for lack of jurisdiction over the subject matter, and the court of appeals affirmed. Opinion of the Court: *Warren*, Black, Douglas, Harlan, Brennan, White, Fortas, Marshall. Concurring opinion: Douglas. Dissenting opinion: *Stewart*.

Mr. Chief Justice WARREN delivered the opinion of the Court.

Speech or Debate Clause

Respondents assert that the Speech or Debate Clause of the Constitution, Art. I, s 6, is an absolute bar to petitioners' action. . . .

The Speech or Debate Clause, adopted by the Constitutional Convention without debate or opposition, finds its roots in the conflict between Parliament and the Crown culminating in the Glorious Revolution of 1688 and the English Bill of Rights of 1689. Drawing upon this history, we concluded in *United States v. Johnson* [1966], that the purpose of this clause was "to prevent intimidation [of legislators] by the executive and accountability before a possibly hostile judiciary." Although the clause sprang from a fear of seditious libel actions instituted by the Crown to punish unfavorable speeches made in Parliament, we have held that it would be a "narrow view" to confine the protection of the Speech or Debate Clause to words spoken in debate. Committee reports, resolutions, and the act of voting are equally covered, as are "things generally done in a session of the House by one of its members in relation to the business before it." Furthermore, the clause not only provides a defense on the merits but also protects a legislator from the burden of defending himself.

Our cases make it clear that the legislative immunity created by the Speech or Debate Clause performs an important function in representative government. It insures that legislators are free to represent the interests of their constituents without fear that they will be later called to task in the courts for that representation. . . .

Legislative immunity does not, of course, bar all judicial review of legislative acts. That issue was settled by implication as early as 1803, [in] *Marbury v. Madison*, . . . and expressly in *Kilbourn v. Thompson* [1881], the first of this Court's cases interpreting the reach of the Speech or Debate Clause. . . . While holding that the Speech or Debate Clause barred Kilbourn's action for false imprisonment brought against several members of the House, the Court nevertheless reached the merits of Kilbourn's attack and decided that, since the House had no power to punish for contempt, Kilbourn's imprisonment pursuant to the resolution was unconstitutional. It therefore allowed Kilbourn to bring his false imprisonment action against Thompson, the House's Sergeant at Arms, who had executed the warrant for Kilbourn's arrest.

The Court first articulated in *Kilbourn* and followed in *Dombrowski v. Eastland* [1967], the doctrine that, although an action against a Congressman may be barred by the Speech or Debate Clause, legislative employees [such as the Sergeant at Arms] who participated in the unconstitutional activity are responsible for their acts. . . .

That House employees are acting pursuant to express order of the House does not bar judicial review of the constitutionality of the underlying legislative decision. Kilbourn decisively settles this question, since the Sergeant at Arms was held liable for false imprisonment even though he did nothing more than execute the House Resolution that Kilbourn be arrested and imprisoned. . . . [W]e thus dismissed the action against members of Congress but did not regard the Speech or Debate Clause as a bar to reviewing the merits of the challenged congressional action since congressional employees were also sued. Similarly, though this action may be dismissed against the Congressmen, petitioners are entitled to maintain their action against House employees and to judicial review of the propriety of the decision to exclude petitioner Powell. . . .

Exclusion or Expulsion

The resolution excluding petitioner Powell was adopted by a vote in excess of two-thirds of the 434 Members of Congress—307 to 116. Article I, s 5, grants the House authority to expel a member "with the Concurrence of two thirds." Respondents assert that the House may expel a member for any reason whatsoever and that, since a two-thirds vote was obtained, the procedure by which Powell was denied his seat in the 90th Congress should be regarded as an expulsion, not an exclusion. . . .

Although respondents repeatedly urge this Court not to speculate as to the reasons for Powell's exclusion, their attempt to equate exclusion with expulsion would require a similar speculation that the House would have voted to expel Powell had it been faced with that question. . . . The Speaker ruled that the House was voting to exclude Powell, and we will not speculate what the result might have been if Powell had been seated and expulsion proceedings subsequently instituted.

Nor is the distinction between exclusion and expulsion merely one of form. The misconduct for which Powell was charged occurred prior to the convening of the 90th Congress. On several occasions the House has debated whether a member can be expelled for actions taken during a prior Congress and the House's own manual of procedure applicable in the 90th Congress states that "both Houses have distrusted their power to punish in such cases." The House rules manual reflects positions taken by prior Congresses. For example, the report of the Select Committee appointed to consider the expulsion of John W. Langley states unequivocally that the House will not expel a member for misconduct committed during an earlier Congress. . . .

Comparative Note 4.2

[A Japanese Prefectural Assembly expelled one of its members for grossly insulting members of the opposition party. He was expelled despite his subsequent apology. This case arose out of an effort to quash a trial court's injunction against the legislator's expulsion. The Japanese Supreme Court sustained the validity of the injunction. What follows is a dissenting opinion.]

Inasmuch as the assembly of a local public entity is like each House of the Diet, a deliberative organ, its essential mission is to deliberate. Hence . . . it has an inherent power to establish such internal rules as may be necessary for discharging this duty. . . . It goes without saying that Art. 93 of the Constitution, which provides

that assemblies shall be established as the deliberative organs of local public entities, presumes the existence of the inherent power to make internal rules for internal discipline. The inherent power with respect to internal discipline is based on the principle that one can manage one's own house by one's self and means that the deliberative organ maintains the independence of its deliberative activities against outside interference. (There is no essential difference between Diet and assembly in this respect.) Since the imposition of discipline for these ends is part of the actual operation of the assembly, a disciplinary resolution is final. . . .

SOURCE: Dissenting opinion of Justice Kuriyama, *Aomori Assembly Case*, Grand Bench, 16 January 1953 in Walter F. Murphy and Joseph Tanenhaus, *Comparative Constitutional Law* (New York: St. Martin's Press, 1977), 130.

Finally, the proceedings which culminated in Powell's exclusion cast considerable doubt upon respondents' assumption that the two-thirds vote necessary to expel would have been mustered. These proceedings have been succinctly described by Congressman Eckhardt:

> The House voted 202 votes for the previous question leading toward the adoption of the (Select) Committee report. It voted 222 votes against the previous question, opening the floor for the Curtis Amendment which ultimately excluded Powell.
>
> Upon adoption of the Curtis Amendment, the vote again fell short of two-thirds, being 248 yeas to 176 nays. Only on the final vote, adopting the Resolution as amended, was more than a two-thirds vote obtained, the vote being 307 yeas to 116 nays. On this last vote, as a practical matter, members who would not have denied Powell a seat if they were given the choice to punish him had to cast an aye vote or else record themselves as opposed to the only punishment that was likely to come before the House. Had the matter come up through the processes of expulsion, it appears that the two-thirds vote would have failed, and then members would have been able to apply a lesser penalty.

We need express no opinion as to the accuracy of Congressman Eckhardt's prediction that expulsion proceedings would have produced a different result. However, the House's own views of the extent of its power to expel combined with the Congressman's analysis counsel that exclusion and expulsion are not fungible proceedings. The Speaker ruled that House Resolution No. 278 contemplated an exclusion proceeding. We must reject respond-

ents' suggestion that we overrule the Speaker and hold that, although the House manifested an intent to exclude Powell, its action should be tested by whatever standards may govern an expulsion.

Subject Matter Jurisdiction

Respondents first contend that this is not a case "arising under" the Constitution within the meaning of Art. III. They emphasize that Art. I, s 5, assigns to each House of Congress the power to judge the elections and qualifications of its own members and to punish its members for disorderly behavior. Respondents also note that under Art. I, s 3, the Senate has the "sole power" to try all impeachments. Respondents argue that these delegations (to "judge," to "punish," and to "try") to the Legislative Branch are explicit grants of "judicial power" to the Congress and constitute specific exceptions to the general mandate of Art. III that the "judicial power" shall be vested in the federal courts. Thus, respondents maintain, the "power conferred on the courts by article III does not authorize this Court to do anything more than declare its lack of jurisdiction to proceed."

We reject this contention. Article III, s 1, provides that the "judicial Power . . . shall be vested in one supreme Court, and in such inferior Courts as the Congress may . . . establish." Further, s 2 mandates that the "judicial Power shall extend to all Cases . . . arising under this Constitution. . . ." It has long been held that a suit "arises under" the Constitution if a petitioner's claim "will be sustained if the Constitution . . . [is] given one construction and will be defeated if [it is] given another." Thus, this case clearly is one "arising under" the Constitution as the Court has interpreted that phrase. Any bar to federal courts reviewing the judgments made by the House or Senate in excluding a member arises from the allocation of powers between the two branches of the Federal Government (a question of justiciability), and not from the petitioners' failure to state a claim based on federal law.

Justiciability

Having concluded that the Court of Appeals correctly ruled that the District Court had jurisdiction over the subject matter, we turn to the question whether the case is justiciable. Two determinations must be made in this regard. First, we must decide whether the claim presented and the relief sought are of the type which admit of judicial resolution. Second, we must determine whether the structure of the Federal Government renders the issue presented a "political question"—that is, a question which is not justiciable in federal court because of the separation of powers provided by the Constitution.

General Considerations

In deciding generally whether a claim is justiciable, a court must determine whether "the duty asserted can be judicially identified and its breach judicially determined, and whether protection for the right asserted can be judicially molded." Respondents do not seriously contend that the duty asserted and its alleged breach cannot be judicially determined. If petitioners are correct, the House had a duty to seat Powell once it determined he met the standing requirements set forth in the Constitution. It is undisputed that he met those requirements and that he was nevertheless excluded.

Respondents do maintain, however, that this case is not justiciable because, they assert, it is impossible for a federal court to "mold effective relief for resolving this case." Respondents emphasize that petitioners asked for coercive relief against the officers of the House, and, they contend, federal courts cannot issue mandamus or injunctions compelling officers or employees of the House to perform specific official acts. Respondents rely primarily on the Speech or Debate Clause to support this contention.

We need express no opinion about the appropriateness of coercive relief in this case, for petitioners sought a declaratory judgment, a form of relief the District Court could have issued. . . . We thus conclude that in terms of the general criteria of justiciability, this case is justiciable.

Political Question Doctrine
Textually Demonstrable Constitutional Commitment. . . .
Respondents' first contention is that this case presents a political question because under Art. I, s 5, there has been a "textually demonstrable constitutional commitment" to the House of the "adjudicatory power" to determine Pow-

ell's qualifications. Thus it is argued that the House, and the House alone, has power to determine who is qualified to be a member.

In order to determine whether there has been a textual commitment to a coordinate department of the Government, we must interpret the Constitution. In other words, we must first determine what power the Constitution confers upon the House through Art. I, s 5, before we can determine to what extent, if any, the exercise of that power is subject to judicial review. Respondents maintain that the House has broad power under s 5, and, they argue, the House may determine which are the qualifications necessary for membership. On the other hand, petitioners allege that the Constitution provides that an elected representative may be denied his seat only if the House finds he does not meet one of the standing qualifications expressly prescribed by the Constitution.

. . . [W]hether there is a "textually demonstrable constitutional commitment of the issue to a coordinate political department" of government and what is the scope of such commitment are questions we must resolve for the first time in this case. . . .

In order to determine the scope of any "textual commitment" under Art. I, s 5, we necessarily must determine the meaning of the phrase to "be the Judge of the Qualifications of its own Members." . . . When the Constitution and the debates over its adoption are . . . viewed in historical perspective, argue respondents, it becomes clear that the "qualifications" expressly set forth in the Constitution were not meant to limit the long-recognized legislative power to exclude or expel at will, but merely to establish "standing incapacities," which could be altered only by a constitutional amendment. Our examination of the relevant historical materials leads us to the conclusion that petitioners are correct and that the Constitution leaves the House without authority to exclude any person, duly elected by his constituents, who meets all the requirements for membership expressly prescribed in the Constitution.

Had the intent of the Framers emerged from these materials with less clarity, we would nevertheless have been compelled to resolve any ambiguity in favor of a narrow construction of the scope of Congress' power to exclude members-elect. A fundamental principle of our representative democracy is, in Hamilton's words, "that the people should choose whom they please to govern them." As Madison pointed out at the Convention, this principle is undermined as much by limiting whom the people can select as by limiting the franchise itself. In apparent agreement with this basic philosophy, the Convention adopted his suggestion limiting the power to expel. To allow essentially that same power to be exercised under the guise of judging qualifications, would be to ignore Madison's warning . . . against "vesting an improper & dangerous power in the Legislature." Moreover, it would effectively nullify the Convention's decision to require a two-thirds vote for expulsion. Unquestionably, Congress has an interest in preserving its institutional integrity, but in most cases that interest can be sufficiently safeguarded by the exercise of its power to punish its members for disorderly behavior and, in extreme cases, to expel a member with the concurrence of two-thirds. In short, both the intention of the Framers, to the extent it can be determined, and an examination of the basic principles of our democratic system persuade us that the Constitution does not vest in the Congress a discretionary power to deny membership by a majority vote.

For these reasons, we have concluded that Art. I, s 5, is at most a "textually demonstrable commitment" to Congress to judge only the qualifications expressly set forth in the Constitution. Therefore, the "textual commitment" formulation of the political question doctrine does not bar federal courts from adjudicating petitioners' claims.

Other Considerations.   Respondents' alternate contention is that the case presents a political question because judicial resolution of petitioners' claim would produce a "potentially embarrassing confrontation between coordinate branches" of the Federal Government. But, as our interpretation of Art. I, s 5, discloses, a determination of petitioner Powell's right to sit would require no more than an interpretation of the Constitution. Such a determination falls within the traditional role accorded courts to interpret the law, and does not involve a "lack of the respect due [a] coordinate [branch] of government," nor does it involve an "initial policy determination of a kind clearly for nonjudicial discretion." Our system of government requires that federal courts on occasion interpret the Constitution in a manner at variance with the construction given the document by another branch. The alleged conflict that such an adjudication may cause cannot justify the courts' avoiding their constitutional responsibility.

. . . [W]e conclude that petitioners' claim is not barred by the political question doctrine, and, having determined that the claim is otherwise generally justiciable, we hold that the case is justiciable.

Conclusion

. . . Therefore, we hold that, since Adam Clayton Powell, Jr., was duly elected by the voters of the 18th Congressional District of New York and was not ineligible to serve under any provision of the Constitution, the House was without power to exclude him from its membership.

Petitioners seek additional forms of equitable relief, including mandamus for the release of petitioner Powell's back pay. The propriety of such remedies, however, is

more appropriately considered in the first instance by the courts below. . . .

It is so ordered.

Mr. Justice DOUGLAS.

While I join the opinion of the Court, I add a few words. As the Court says, the important constitutional question is whether the Congress has the power to deviate from or alter the qualifications for membership as a Representative contained in Art. I, s 2, cl. 2, of the Constitution. Up to now the understanding has been quite clear to the effect that such authority does not exist. To be sure, Art. I, s 5, provides that: "Each House shall be the Judge of the Elections, Returns and Qualifications of its own Members. . . ." Contests may arise over whether an elected official meets the "qualifications" of the Constitution, in which event the House is the sole judge. But the House is not the sole judge when "qualifications" are added which are not specified in the Constitution.

At the root of all these cases, however, is the basic integrity of the electoral process. Today we proclaim the constitutional principle of "one man, one vote." When that principle is followed and the electors choose a person who is repulsive to the Establishment in Congress, by what constitutional authority can that group of electors be disenfranchised?

By Art. I, s 5, the House may "expel a Member" by a vote of two-thirds. And if this were an expulsion case I would think that no justiciable controversy would be presented, the vote of the House being two-thirds or more. But it is not an expulsion case. . . .

Notes/Queries/Readings

1. What constitutional provisions does the House claim to support its power to exclude *Powell*? How does the Court determine that none of these provisions justify the House's action? Is the Court's reading consistent with the words of the constitutional text? With the constitutional structure as a whole?

2. What is the difference between exclusion and expulsion in constitutional terms? Should that difference matter?

3. Is the opinion in this case consistent with the "hands-off" stance of the majority opinion concerning the Senate's power to try impeachments in *Nixon v. United States* (1993, reprinted in Chapter 3)?

4. Consider the argument advanced by Justice Kuriyama in Comparative Note 4.2. Might one plausibly have made such an argument within the text of the U.S. Constitution?

5. For an analysis of the Court's decision, see Terrance Sandalow, *Comments on* Powell v. McCormack, 17 University of California, at Los Angeles Law Review 164 (1969).

For treatments of Powell, a fascinating figure in American politics, see William Haygood, *King of the Cats: The Life and Times of Adam Clayton Powell, Jr.* (Boston: Houghton-Mifflin, 1993) and Charles V. Hamilton, *Adam Clayton Powell, Jr.: The Political Biography of an American Dilemma* (New York: Atheneum, 1991).

Immigration and Naturalization Service v. Chadha

462 U.S. 919, 103 S. Ct. 2764, 77 L. Ed. 2d 317 (1983)

Jagdish Rai Chadha, an East Indian born in Kenya and holding a British passport, was lawfully admitted to the United States in 1966 on a nonimmigrant student visa. His visa expired on 30 June 1972. In a subsequent deportation hearing, the Immigration and Naturalization Service (INS) allowed Chadha to apply for a suspension of his deportation. The attorney general suspended Chadha's deportation under a provision that authorizes him to do so if the lawfully admitted alien has lived in the United States for seven years, proves that he is of good moral character, and is a person whose deportation would cause "extreme hardship." The act, however, requires that such a suspension be reported to the Congress, and if either the House or the Senate vetos the suspension during the session at which a case is reported, the attorney general is obligated to deport the alien. A House subcommittee introduced a resolution opposing Chadha's continued residence in the United States, a veto that the House passed without debate or a recorded vote. Chadha then moved to terminate the proceedings against him on the ground that the legislative veto was unconstitutional. The Board of Immigration Appeals dismissed his appeal. The U.S. Court of Appeals held that the House had no constitutional authority to order the alien's deportation and the legislative veto provision violated the doctrine of separation of powers. Opinion of the Court: *Burger*, Brennan, Marshall, Blackmun, Stevens, O'Connor. Concurring opinion: *Powell*. Dissenting opinions: *White, Rehnquist*.

**Chief Justice BURGER delivered
the opinion of the Court.**

[Both Houses of Congress challenged the authority of the Supreme Court to resolve the issue raised in this case. They contended that the Court had no jurisdiction to hear Chadha's appeal, that he lacked standing to sue, that the case was not a genuine controversy, and that it presented a nonjusticiable political question. The Supreme Court rejected all of these contentions.]

We turn now to the question whether action of one House of Congress under s 244(c)(2) violates strictures of the Constitution. We begin, of course, with the presumption that the challenged statute is valid. Its wisdom is not the concern of the courts; if a challenged action does not violate the Constitution, it must be sustained. . . .

By the same token, the fact that a given law or procedure is efficient, convenient, and useful in facilitating functions of government, standing alone, will not save it if it is contrary to the Constitution. Convenience and efficiency are not the primary objectives—or the hallmarks—of democratic government and our inquiry is sharpened rather than blunted by the fact that Congressional veto provisions are appearing with increasing frequency in statutes which delegate authority to executive and independent agencies. . . .

"Since 1932, when the first veto provision was enacted into law, 295 congressional veto-type procedures have been inserted in 196 different statutes as follows: from 1932 to 1939, five statutes were affected; from 1940–49, nineteen statutes; between 1950–59, thirty-four statutes; and from 1960–69, forty-nine. From the year 1970 through 1975, at least one hundred sixty-three such provisions were included in eighty-nine laws." Abourezk, *The Congressional Veto: A Contemporary Response to Executive Encroachment on Legislative Prerogatives*, 52 Ind L Rev 323, 324 (1977). . . .

Explicit and unambiguous provisions of the Constitution prescribe and define the respective functions of the Congress and of the Executive in the legislative process. Since the precise terms of those familiar provisions are critical to the resolution of this case, we set them out verbatim. Art. I provides:

> All legislative Powers herein granted shall be vested in a Congress of the United States, which shall consist of a Senate *and* a House of Representatives." Art. I, s 1. [Emphasis added.]

> Every Bill which shall have passed the House of Representatives *and* the Senate, *shall*, before it becomes a Law, be presented to the President of the United States . . . Art. I, s 7, cl. 2. (Emphasis added.)

> *Every* Order, Resolution, or Vote to which the Concurrence of the Senate and House of Representatives may be necessary (except on a question of Adjournment) *shall be* presented to the President of the United States; and before the Same shall take Effect, *shall be* approved by him, or being disapproved by him, *shall be* repassed by two thirds of the Senate and House of Representa-

Comparative Note 4.3

[In this case, South Africa's new Constitutional Court ruled on the constitutional validity of a parliamentary act delegating subordinate regulatory authority to other bodies. The extracts are from the main opinion of Justice P. Chaskalson.]

. . . There is nothing in the Constitution which prohibits Parliament from delegating subordinate regulatory authority to other bodies. . . . In the United States, delegation of legislative power to the executive is dealt [with] under the doctrine of separation of powers. Congress as the body in which all federal lawmaking power has been vested must make legislative decisions in accordance with the "single, finely wrought and exhaustively considered, procedure" laid down by the United States Constitution, which requires laws to be passed bicamerally and then presented to the President for consideration of a possible veto. *INS v. Chadha*. . . . In Ireland. . . the courts have adopted a similar approach. . . . The influence of English law is referred to by Dixon J in his judgment in the Australian High Court. . . .

Seevai in his work on the Indian Constitution deals at length with the Indian jurisprudence on the power of Parliament to delegate legislative power to the executive. . . . In Canada . . . it seems to be accepted that Parliament has wide powers of delegation. . . .

This brief and somewhat limited survey of the law as it has developed in other countries is sufficient to show that where Parliament is established under a written constitution, the nature and extent of its power to delegate legislative powers to the executive depends ultimately on the language of the Constitution, construed in the light of the country's own history. . . . [But our] new Constitution establishes a fundamentally different order to that which previously existed. Parliament can no longer claim supreme power subject to limitations imposed by the Constitution; it is subject in all respects to the provisions of the Constitution and has only the powers vested in it by the Constitution expressly or by necessary implication.

SOURCE: *Executive Council of the Western Cape Legislature v. President of the Republic of South Africa and Others*, Constitutional Court Judgment of 22 September 1995, Butterworths Law Reports (October 1995), 1312–17.

---

tives, according to the Rules and Limitations prescribed in the Case of a Bill. Art. I, s 7, cl. 3. (Emphasis added.)

These provisions of Art. I are integral parts of the constitutional design for the separation of powers. We have recently noted that "[t]he principle of separation of powers was not simply an abstract generalization in the minds of the Framers: it was woven into the document that they drafted in Philadelphia in the summer of 1787." *Buckley v. Valeo* [1976]. Just as we relied on the textual provision of Art. II, s 2, cl. 2, to vindicate the principle of separation of powers in *Buckley*, we see the purposes underlying the Presentment Clauses, Art. I, s 7, cls. 2, 3 and the bicameral requirement of Art. I, s 1, and s 7, cl. 2, guide our resolution of the important question presented in these cases. The very structure of the articles delegating and separating powers under Arts. I, II, and III exemplifies the concept of separation of powers, and we now turn to Art. I.

The Presentment Clauses

The records of the Constitutional Convention reveal that the requirement that all legislation be presented to the President before becoming law was uniformly accepted by the Framers. Presentment to the President and the Presi-

dential veto were considered so imperative that the draftsmen took special pains to assure that these requirements could not be circumvented. . . .

The decision to provide the President with a limited and qualified power to nullify proposed legislation by veto was based on the profound conviction of the Framers that the powers conferred on Congress were the powers to be most carefully circumscribed. It is beyond doubt that lawmaking was a power to be shared by both Houses and the President. . . .

[To support this view, the Court draws heavily on Hamilton's discussion of the President's role in *The Federalist* No. 73. The Court also cites *The Federalist* No. 51 and Joseph Story's *Commentaries on the Constitution of the United States* (1858).]

Bicameralism

The bicameral requirement of Art. I, s 1, 7 was of scarcely less concern to the Framers than was the Presidential veto and indeed the two concepts are interdependent. By providing that no law could take effect without the concurrence of the prescribed majority of the Members of both

Houses, the Framers reemphasized their belief, already re-marked upon in connection with the Presentment Clauses, that legislation should not be enacted unless it has been carefully and fully considered by the Nation's elected officials. . . .

. . . The President's participation in the legislative pro-cess was to protect the Executive Branch from Congress and to protect the whole people from improvident laws. The division of the Congress into two distinctive bodies assures that the legislative power would be exercised only after opportunity for full study and debate in separate set-tings. The President's unilateral veto power, in turn, was limited by the power of two thirds of both Houses of Con-gress to overrule a veto thereby precluding final arbitrary action of one person. . . .

The Constitution sought to divide the delegated powers of the new Federal Government into three defined cate-gories, Legislative, Executive and Judicial, to assure, as nearly as possible, that each Branch of government would confine itself to its assigned responsibility. The hydraulic pressure inherent within each of the separate Branches to exceed the outer limits of its power, even to accomplish desirable objectives, must be resisted.

Although not "hermetically" sealed from one another, the powers delegated to the three Branches are function-ally identifiable. When any Branch acts, it is presumptively exercising the power the Constitution has delegated to it. When the Executive acts, it presumptively acts in an execu-tive or administrative capacity as defined in Art. II. And when, as here, one House of Congress purports to act, it is presumptively acting within its assigned sphere.

Beginning with this presumption, we must nevertheless establish that the challenged action under s 244(c)(2) is of the kind to which the requirements of Art. I, s 7, apply. Not every action taken by either House is subject to the bicameralism and presentment requirements of Art. I. Whether actions taken by either House are, in law and fact, an exercise of legislative power depends not on their form but upon "whether they contain matter which is properly to be regarded as legislative in its character and effect."

Examination of the action taken here by one House pur-suant to s 244(c)(2) reveals that it was essentially legislative in purpose and effect. In purporting to exercise power de-fined in Art. I, s 8, cl. 4 to "establish an uniform Rule of Naturalization," the House took action that had the pur-pose and effect of altering the legal rights, duties and rela-tions of persons, including the Attorney General, Executive Branch officials and Chadha, all outside the legislative branch. Section 244(c)(2) purports to authorize one House of Congress to require the Attorney General to deport an individual alien whose deportation otherwise would be canceled under s 244. The one-House veto operated in this case to overrule the Attorney General and mandate Chadha's deportation; absent the House action, Chadha would remain in the United States. Congress has *acted* and its action has altered Chadha's status.

Since it is clear that the action by the House under s 244(c)(2) was not within any of the express constitutional exceptions authorizing one House to act alone, and equally clear that it was an exercise of legislative power, that action was subject to the standards prescribed in Arti-cle I. The bicameral requirement, the Presentment Clauses, the President's veto, and Congress' power to override a veto were intended to erect enduring checks on each Branch and to protect the people from the improvident ex-ercise of power by mandating certain prescribed steps. To

---

Comparative Note 4.4

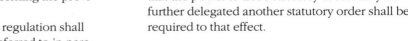

Article 92

1. Regulations shall be issued on the basis of spe-cific authorization contained in, and for the pur-pose of implementation of, statutes by the organs specified in the Constitution. The authorization shall specify the organ appropriate to issue a regulation and the scope of matters to be regu-lated as well as guidelines concerning the provi-sions of such act.

2. An organ authorized to issue a regulation shall not delegate its competence, referred to in para-graph 1 above, to another organ.

SOURCE: Constitution of the Republic of Poland (1997)

Article 80

1. The Federal Government, a Federal Minister or the Land governments may be empowered by law to issue statutory orders. The content, pur-pose and scope of that power shall be specified in the law. Statutory orders shall contain a refer-ence to their legal basis. Where the law provides that the power to issue statutory orders may be further delegated another statutory order shall be required to that effect.

SOURCE: Basic Law of the Federal Republic of Germany (1949)

preserve those checks, and maintain the separation of powers, the carefully defined limits on the power of each Branch must not be eroded. To accomplish what has been attempted by one House of Congress in this case requires action in conformity with the express prescription for legislative action: passage by a majority of both Houses and presentment to the President.

The choices we discern as having been made in the Constitutional Convention impose burdens on governmental processes that often seem clumsy, inefficient, even unworkable, but those hard choices were consciously made by men who had lived under a form of government that permitted arbitrary governmental acts to go unchecked. There is no support in the Constitution or decisions of this Court for the proposition that the cumbersomeness and delays often encountered in complying with explicit Constitutional standards may be avoided, either by the Congress or by the President. With all the obvious flaws of delay, untidiness, and potential for abuse, we have not yet found a better way to preserve freedom than by making the exercise of power subject to the crafted restraints spelled out in the Constitution. . . .

Affirmed.

Justice POWELL, concurring in the judgment.

The court's decision, based on the Presentment Clauses, Art. I, s 7, cls. 2 and 3, apparently will invalidate every use of the legislative veto. The breadth of this holding gives one pause. Congress has included the veto in literally hundreds of statutes, dating back to the 1930s. Congress clearly views this procedure as essential to controlling the delegation of power to administrative agencies. One reasonably may disagree with Congress' assessment of the veto's utility, but the respect due its judgment as a coordinate branch of Government cautions that our holding should be no more extensive than necessary to decide this case. In my view, the case may be decided on a narrower ground. When Congress finds that a particular person does not satisfy the statutory criteria for permanent residence in this country it has assumed a judicial function in violation of the principle of separation of powers. Accordingly, I concur only in the judgment.

Functionally, the doctrine [of separation of powers] may be violated in two ways. One branch may interfere impermissibly with the other's performance of its constitutionally assigned function. Alternatively, the doctrine may be violated when one branch assumes a function that more properly is entrusted to another. These cases present the later situation.

Justice WHITE, dissenting.

Today the Court not only invalidates s 244(c)(2) of the Immigration and Nationality Act, but also sounds the death knell for nearly 200 other statutory provisions in which Congress has reserved a "legislative veto." For this reason, the Court's decision is of surpassing importance. And it is for this reason that the Court would have been well-advised to decide the case, if possible, on the narrower grounds of separation of powers, leaving for full consideration the constitutionality of other congressional review statutes operating on such varied matters as war powers and agency rulemaking, some of which concern the independent regulatory agencies.

The prominence of the legislative veto mechanism in our contemporary political system and its importance to Congress can hardly be overstated. It has become a central means by which Congress secures the accountability of executive and independent agencies. Without the legislative veto, Congress is faced with a Hobson's choice: either to refrain from delegating the necessary authority, leaving itself with a hopeless task of writing laws with the requisite specificity to cover endless special circumstances across the entire policy landscape, or in the alternative, to abdicate its law-making function to the Executive Branch and independent agencies. To choose the former leaves major national problems unresolved; to opt for the latter risks unaccountable policymaking by those not elected to fill that role. Accordingly, over the past five decades, the legislative veto has been placed in nearly 200 statutes. The device is known in every field of governmental concern: reorganization, budgets, foreign affairs, war powers, and regulation of trade, safety, energy, the environment and the economy.

. . . The Court's holding today that all legislative-type action must be enacted through the lawmaking process ignores that legislative authority is routinely delegated to the Executive branch, to the independent regulatory agencies, and to private individuals and groups. . . .

This Court's decisions sanctioning such delegations make clear that Article I does not require all action with the effect of legislation to be passed as a law.

The wisdom and the constitutionality of these broad delegations are matters that still have not been put to rest. But for present purposes, these cases establish that by virtue of congressional delegation, legislative power can be exercised by independent agencies and Executive departments without the passage of new legislation. . . .

If Congress may delegate lawmaking power to independent and executive agencies, it is most difficult to understand Article I as forbidding Congress from also reserving a check on legislative power itself. Absent the veto, the agencies receiving delegations of legislative or quasi-legislative power may issue regulations having the force of law without bicameral approval and without the President's signature. It is thus not apparent why the reservation of a veto over the exercise of that legislative power must be subject to a more exacting test. In both cases, it is enough that the initial statutory authorizations comply with the Article I requirements.

The Court also takes no account of perhaps the most relevant consideration: However resolutions of disapproval under section 244(c)(2) are formally characterized, in reality, a departure from the status quo occurs only upon the concurrence of opinion among the House, Senate, and President. Reservations of legislative authority to be exercised by Congress should be upheld if the exercise of such reserved authority is consistent with the distribution of and limits upon legislative power that Article I provides.

Section 244(a)(1) authorizes the Attorney General, in his discretion, to suspend the deportation of certain aliens who are otherwise deportable and, upon Congress' approval, to adjust their status to that of aliens lawfully admitted for permanent residence. In order to be eligible for this relief, an alien must have been physically present in the United States for a continuous period of not less than seven years, must prove he is of good moral character, and must prove that he or his immediate family would suffer "extreme hardship" if he is deported. Judicial review of a denial of relief may be sought. Thus, the suspension proceeding "has two phases: a determination whether the statutory conditions have been met, which generally involves a question of law, and a determination whether relief shall be granted, which [ultimately] is confided to the sound discretion of the Attorney General [and his delegates]."

. . . Under s 244(c)(1) the Attorney General must report all such suspensions, with a detailed statement of facts and reasons, to the Congress. Either House may then act, in that session or the next, to block the suspension of deportation by passing a resolution of disapproval. s 244(c)(2). Upon Congressional approval of the suspension—by its silence—the alien's permanent status is adjusted to that of a lawful resident alien.

The history of the Immigration Act makes clear that s 244(c)(2) did not alter the division of actual authority between Congress and the Executive. At all times, whether through private bills, or through affirmative concurrent resolutions, or through the present one-House veto, a permanent change in a deportable alien's status could be accomplished only with the agreement of the Attorney General, the House, and the Senate.

Notes/Queries/Readings

1. Identify the interpretive approach used by Chief Justice Burger in this case. How does his approach differ from the reasoning of Justice White?

2. Why, according to Chief Justice Burger, is the legislative veto a legislative act and not oversight?

3. There is an old maxim that the Supreme Court should not lay down a rule of law broader than required by the facts of a case, in part out of respect for the principle of separation of powers. Does the *Chadha* majority ignore this maxim?

4. If Congress can constitutionally delegate powers under the Immigration and Naturalization Act, why shouldn't it be able to have the ultimate control of a veto upon the use of its delegated authority?

5. Justice Powell concurred with the result, but wrote separately to argue that the statute violated the separation of powers doctrine because its action was "clearly adjudicatory." The majority, however, had concluded that the congressional action was "legislative" in nature. Which of these two characterizations is correct? Does the dispute suggest that it is not always possible to clearly distinguish between the executive, legislative, and judicial powers?

6. Do you find Justice White's dissent convincing? Is Congress really faced with a "Hobson's choice" as a result of the Court's decision? Why should we not demand that Congress take more responsibility to draft statutes with clear and well-defined standards? Would it be more proper for Congress to check with the executive before rather than after executive action?

7. Powell concluded that the doctrine of separation of powers may "be violated in two ways." In the first, one branch may interfere with another's exercise of its constitutionally assigned duties. In the second, a branch may assume a function the Constitution assigns to another branch. Is this a useful way to approach separation of powers cases? Which of these alternatives is implicated in *Chadha*?

8. Recall our earlier discussion of the nondelegation doctrine. In light of that doctrine, does *Chadha* stand for the proposition that Congress may delegate its power to any branch but itself?

9. Comparative Note 4.3 is an example of the guidance that constitutional courts often seek from foreign jurisdictions. Should Chief Justice Burger have consulted the experience of other constitutional democracies in deciding *Chadha*? Would the Court be well-advised to do this as a regular practice?

10. For additional reading, see Barbara Hinkson Craig, *Chadha: The Story of an Epic Constitutional Struggle* (New York: Oxford University Press, 1988); Stephen Breyer, *The Legislative Veto after Chadha*, 72 Georgia Law Journal 785 (1984); Elliot H. Levitas and Stanley M. Brand, *The Son of Legislative Veto Lives On*, Georgetown Law Journal 801 (1984); and Louis Fisher, *Constitutional Conflicts Between Congress and the President*, 4th ed. (Lawrence: University Press of Kansas, 1997).

11. The president's line item veto is as controversial as Congress's legislative veto. In 1996, Congress passed the Line Item Veto Act, giving the president the authority to

cancel certain spending and tax benefit measures after he has signed such measures into law. Several members of Congress challenged the law as a violation of separation of powers in *Raines v. Byrd*, 138 L. Ed. 2d 849 (1997), but the Supreme Court avoided dealing with the merits of the case when it ruled that members of Congress lack standing to challenge the statute. (See query in *Lujan* at page 98.) The Court announced that only a party outside the federal government who has been directly harmed by the line item veto would be qualified to raise the constitutional question. In October 1997 the president used the line item veto to cancel a budget provision that allowed New York to keep its Medicaid financing scheme. "Without the provision," wrote the *New York Times*, "the state may have to pay back hundreds of millions of dollars to the Federal Government." Local hospitals have taken up the fight in the hope that the federal courts will now reach the constitutional merits of the line item veto.

In its editorial of 18 October 1997, the *Times* wrote:

The financial harm to New York is substantial, but the graver harm is the unconstitutional transfer of power from Congress to the President. The Constitution provides only a single procedure for making or changing Federal law. When a bill is approved by Congress, it is presented to the President, who may sign the whole bill into law, veto it or allow it to become without his signature. The line item veto, by allowing the President to cancel items from a budget bill after signing that budget into law, in effect gives the President power to change the law unilaterally, a result at odds with the fundamental doctrine of separation of powers.

Do you agree with the *New York Times*?

Bowsher v. Synar

478 U.S. 714, 106 S. Ct. 3181, 92 L. Ed. 2d 583 (1986)

The Balanced Budget and Emergency Deficit Control Act, better known as the Gramm-Rudman-Hollings Act, established deficit targets for federal spending for each of the fiscal years 1986 through 1991. The act authorized the comptroller general of the United States to recommend "across-the-board" spending cuts if the budget deficit were to exceed the maximum deficit amount by more than the specified sum in a given fiscal year. The president could then issue an order mandating the spending reduction specified by the comptroller general. This case arose when twelve members of Congress filed complaints challenging the act's constitutionality. A separate action was brought by the National Treasury Employees Union, which alleged that its members were injured by the act's automatic spending reduction provisions when they lost certain benefit increases as a result of a presidential order pursuant to the act. A three-judge federal district court ruled that the statute violated the principle of separation of powers. Opinion of the Court: *Burger*, Brennan, Powell, Rehnquist, O'Connor. Concurring opinions: *Stevens*, Marshall. Dissenting opinions: *White, Blackmun*.

Chief Justice BURGER delivered the opinion of the Court.

The question presented by these appeals is whether the assignment by Congress to the Comptroller General of the United States of certain functions under the Balanced Budget and Emergency Deficit Control Act of 1985 violates the doctrine of separation of powers.

We noted recently that "[t]he Constitution sought to divide the delegated powers of the new Federal Government into three defined categories, Legislative, Executive, and Judicial." The declared purpose of separating and dividing the powers of government, of course, was to "diffus[e] power the better to secure liberty." . . .

Even a cursory examination of the Constitution reveals the influence of Montesquieu's thesis that checks and balances were the foundation of a structure of government that would protect liberty. The Framers provided a vigorous Legislative Branch and a separate and wholly independent Executive Branch, with each branch responsible ultimately to the people. The Framers also provided for a Judicial Branch equally independent with "[t]he judicial Power . . . extend[ing] to all Cases, in Law and Equity, arising under this Constitution, and the Laws of the United States." Art. III, s 2.

Other, more subtle, examples of separated powers are evident as well. Unlike parliamentary systems such as that of Great Britain, no person who is an officer of the United States may serve as a Member of the Congress. Art. I, s 6. Moreover, unlike parliamentary systems, the President, under Article II, is responsible not to the Congress but to the people, subject only to impeachment proceedings which are exercised by the two Houses as representatives of the people. Art. II, s 4. And even in the impeachment of a President the presiding officer of the ultimate tribunal is not a member of the Legislative Branch, but the Chief Justice of the United States. Art. I, s 3.

That this system of division and separation of powers produces conflicts, confusion, and discordance at times is inherent, but it was deliberately so structured to assure full, vigorous, and open debate on the great issues affecting the people and to provide avenues for the operation of checks on the exercise of governmental power.

The Constitution does not contemplate an active role for Congress in the supervision of officers charged with the execution of the laws it enacts. The President appoints "Officers of the United States" with the "Advice and Consent of the Senate. . . ." Art. II, s 2. Once the appointment has been made and confirmed, however, the Constitution explicitly provides for removal of Officers of the United States by Congress only upon impeachment by the House of Representatives and conviction by the Senate. An impeachment by the House and trial by the Senate can rest only on "Treason, Bribery or other high Crimes and Misdemeanors." Article II, s 4. A direct congressional role in the removal of officers charged with the execution of the laws beyond this limited one is inconsistent with separation of powers.

. . . [W]e conclude that Congress cannot reserve for itself the power of removal of an officer charged with the execution of the laws except by impeachment. To permit the execution of the laws to be vested in an officer answerable only to Congress would, in practical terms, reserve in Congress control over the execution of the laws. . . . The structure of the Constitution does not permit Congress to execute the laws; it follows that Congress cannot grant to an officer under its control what it does not possess.

To permit an officer controlled by Congress to execute the laws would be, in essence, to permit a congressional veto. Congress could simply remove, or threaten to remove, an officer for executing the laws in any fashion found to be unsatisfactory to Congress. This kind of congressional control over the execution of the laws . . . is constitutionally impermissible.

Appellants urge that the Comptroller General performs his duties independently and is not subservient to Congress. We agree with the District Court that this contention does not bear close scrutiny.

The critical factor lies in the provisions of the statute defining the Comptroller General's office relating to removability. Although the Comptroller General is nominated by the President from a list of three individuals recommended by the Speaker of the House of Representatives and the President *pro tempore* of the Senate, and confirmed by the Senate, he is removable only at the initiative of Congress. He may be removed not only by impeachment but also by joint resolution of Congress "at any time" resting on any one of the following bases:

(i) permanent disability;

(ii) inefficiency;

(iii) neglect of duty;

(iv) malfeasance; or

(v) a felony or conduct involving moral turpitude.

This provision was included, as one Congressman explained in urging passage of the Act, because Congress "felt that [the Comptroller General] should be brought under the sole control of Congress, so that Congress at any moment when it found he was inefficient and was not carrying on the duties of his office as he should and as the Congress expected, could remove him without the long, tedious process of a trial by impeachment."

The removal provision was an important part of the legislative scheme, as a number of Congressmen recognized. . . .

. . . [T]he dissent's assessment of the statute fails to recognize the breadth of the grounds for removal. The statute permits removal for "inefficiency," "neglect of duty," or "malfeasance." These terms are very broad and, as interpreted by Congress, could sustain removal of a Comptroller General for any number of actual or perceived transgressions of the legislative will. . . .

This much said, we must also add that the dissent is simply in error to suggest that the political realities reveal that the Comptroller General is free from influence by Congress. The Comptroller General heads the General Accounting Office (GAO), "an instrumentality of the United States Government independent of the executive departments," which was created by Congress in 1921 as part of the Budget and Accounting Act of 1921. Congress created the office because it believed that it "needed an officer, responsible to it alone, to check upon the application of public funds in accordance with appropriations."

It is clear that Congress has consistently viewed the Comptroller General as an officer of the Legislative Branch. The Reorganization Acts of 1945 and 1949, for example, both stated that the Comptroller General and the GAO are "a part of the legislative branch of the Government." Similarly, in the Accounting and Auditing Act of 1950, Congress required the Comptroller General to conduct audits "as an agent of the Congress."

Against this background we see no escape from the conclusion that because Congress has retained removal authority over the Comptroller General, he may not be entrusted with executive powers. . . .

Appellants suggest that the duties assigned to the Comptroller General in the Act are essentially ministerial and mechanical so that their performance does not constitute "execution of the law" in a meaningful sense. On the contrary, we view these functions as plainly entailing execution of the law in constitutional terms. Interpreting a law enacted by Congress to implement the legislative mandate is the very essence of "execution" of the law. . . . [T]he

Comptroller General must exercise judgment concerning facts that affect the application of the Act. He must also interpret the provisions of the Act to determine precisely what budgetary calculations are required. Decisions of that kind are typically made by officers charged with executing a statute.

. . . By placing the responsibility for execution of the Balanced Budget and Emergency Deficit Control Act in the hands of an officer who is subject to removal only by itself, Congress in effect has retained control over the execution of the Act and has intruded into the executive function. The Constitution does not permit such intrusion.

No one can doubt that Congress and the President are confronted with fiscal and economic problems of unprecedented magnitude, but "the fact that a given law or procedure is efficient, convenient, and useful in facilitating functions of government, standing alone, will not save it if it is contrary to the Constitution. Convenience and efficiency are not the primary objectives—or the hallmarks—of democratic government. . . ." *Chadha*.

We conclude that the District Court correctly held that the powers vested in the Comptroller General under s 251 violate the command of the Constitution that the Congress play no direct role in the execution of the laws. Accordingly, the judgment and order of the District Court are affirmed.

It is so ordered.

Justice WHITE, dissenting.

The Court's recognition of the legitimacy of legislation vesting "executive" authority in officers independent of the President does not imply derogation of the President's own constitutional authority . . . In determining whether a limitation on the President's power to remove an officer performing executive functions constitutes a violation of the constitutional scheme of separation of powers, a court must "focu[s] on the extent to which [such a limitation] prevents the Executive Branch from accomplishing its constitutionally assigned functions." . . . "Only where the potential for disruption is present must we then determine whether that impact is justified by an overriding need to promote objectives within the constitutional authority of Congress." . . .

It is evident (and nothing in the Court's opinion is to the contrary) that the powers exercised by the Comptroller General under the Gramm-Rudman-Hollings Act are not such that vesting them in an officer not subject to removal at will by the President would in itself improperly interfere with Presidential powers. Determining the level of spending by the Federal Government is not by nature a function central either to the exercise of the President's enumerated powers or to his general duty to ensure execution of the laws; rather, appropriating funds is a peculiarly legislative function, and one expressly committed to Congress by Art. I, s 9, which provides that "No Money shall be drawn from the Treasury, but in Consequence of Appropriations made by Law." In enacting Gramm-Rudman-Hollings, Congress has chosen to exercise this legislative power to establish the level of federal spending by providing a detailed set of criteria for reducing expenditures below the level of appropriations in the event that certain conditions are met. Delegating the execution of this legislation—that is, the power to apply the Act's criteria and make the required calculations—to an officer independent of the President's will does not deprive the President of any power that he would otherwise have or that is essential to the performance of the duties of his office. Rather, the result of such a delegation, from the standpoint of the President, is no different from the result of more traditional forms of appropriation: under either system, the level of funds available to the Executive Branch to carry out its duties is not within the President's discretionary control. . . . Given that the exercise of policy choice by the officer executing the statute would be inimical to Congress' goal in enacting "automatic" budget-cutting measures, it is eminently reasonable and proper for Congress to vest the budget-cutting authority in an officer who is to the greatest degree possible nonpartisan and independent of the President and his political agenda and who therefore may be relied upon not to allow his calculations to be colored by political considerations. Such a delegation deprives the President of no authority that is rightfully his.

If, as the Court seems to agree, the assignment of "executive" powers under Gramm-Rudman-Hollings to an officer not removable at will by the President would not in itself represent a violation of the constitutional scheme of separated powers, the question remains whether, as the Court concludes, the fact that the officer to whom Congress has delegated the authority to implement the Act is removable by a joint resolution of Congress should require invalidation of the Act. . . . I have no quarrel with the proposition that the powers exercised by the Comptroller under the Act may be characterized as "executive" in that they involve the interpretation and carrying out of the Act's mandate. I can also accept the general proposition that although Congress has considerable authority in designating the officers who are to execute legislation, the constitutional scheme of separated powers does prevent Congress from reserving an executive role for itself or for its "agents." I cannot accept, however, that the exercise of authority by an officer removable for cause by a joint resolution of Congress is analogous to the impermissible execution of the law by Congress itself, nor would I hold that the congressional role in the removal process renders the

Comptroller an "agent" of the Congress, incapable of receiving "executive" power.

The deficiencies in the Court's reasoning are apparent. First, the Court baldly mischaracterizes the removal provision when it suggests that it allows Congress to remove the Comptroller for "executing the laws in any fashion found to be unsatisfactory"; in fact, Congress may remove the Comptroller only for one or more of five specified reasons, which "although not so narrow as to deny Congress any leeway, circumscribe Congress' power to some extent by providing a basis for judicial review of congressional removal." Second, and more to the point, the Court overlooks or deliberately ignores the decisive difference between the congressional removal provision and the legislative veto struck down in *Chadha*: under the Budget and Accounting Act, Congress may remove the Comptroller only through a joint resolution, which by definition must be passed by both Houses and signed by the President. In other words, a removal of the Comptroller under the statute *satisfies the requirements of bicameralism and presentment laid down in Chadha*. . . .

That a joint resolution removing the Comptroller General would satisfy the requirements for legitimate legislative action laid down in *Chadha* does not fully answer the separation of powers argument, for it is apparent that even the results of the constitutional legislative process may be unconstitutional if those results are in fact destructive of the scheme of separation-of-powers. The question to be answered is whether the threat of removal of the Comptroller General for cause through joint resolution as authorized by the Budget and Accounting Act renders the Comptroller sufficiently subservient to Congress that investing him with "executive" power can be realistically equated with the unlawful retention of such power by Congress itself; more generally, the question is whether there is a genuine threat of "encroachment at the expense of the other." Common sense indicates that the existence of the removal provision poses no such threat to the principle of separation of powers.

The statute does not permit anyone to remove the Comptroller at will; removal is permitted only for specified cause, with the existence of cause to be determined by Congress following a hearing. Any removal under the statute would presumably be subject to post-termination judicial review to ensure that a hearing had in fact been held and that the finding of cause for removal was not arbitrary. These procedural and substantive limitations on the removal power militate strongly against the characterization of the Comptroller as a mere agent of Congress by virtue of the removal authority. . . . Removal authority limited in such a manner is more properly viewed as motivating adherence to a substantive standard established by law than

as inducing subservience to the particular institution that enforces that standard. That the agent enforcing the standard is Congress may be of some significance to the Comptroller, but Congress' substantively limited removal power will undoubtedly be less of a spur to subservience than Congress' unquestionable and unqualified power to enact legislation reducing the Comptroller's salary, cutting the funds available to his department, reducing his personnel, limiting or expanding his duties, or even abolishing his position altogether.

More importantly, the substantial role played by the President in the process of removal through joint resolution reduces to utter insignificance the possibility that the threat of removal will induce subservience to the Congress. . . . The requirement of Presidential approval obviates the possibility that the Comptroller will perceive himself as so completely at the mercy of Congress that he will function as its tool. If the Comptroller's conduct in office is not so unsatisfactory to the President as to convince the latter that removal is required under the statutory standard, Congress will have no independent power to coerce the Comptroller unless it can muster a two-thirds majority in both Houses. . . .

The practical result of the removal provision is not to render the Comptroller unduly dependent upon or subservient to Congress but to render him one of the most independent officers in the entire federal establishment. . . .

Realistic consideration of the nature of the Comptroller General's relation to Congress thus reveals that the threat to separation of powers conjured up by the majority is wholly chimerical. The power over removal retained by the Congress is not a power that is exercised outside the legislation, nor does it appear likely that it is a power that adds significantly to the influence Congress may exert over executive officers through other, undoubtedly constitutional exercises of legislative power and through the constitutionally guaranteed impeachment power. . . .

The majority's contrary conclusion rests on the rigid dogma that, outside of the impeachment process, any "direct congressional role in the removal of officers charged with the execution of the laws . . . is inconsistent with separation of powers." Reliance on such an unyielding principle to strike down a statute posing no real danger of aggrandizement of congressional power is extremely misguided and insensitive to our constitutional role. The wisdom of vesting "executive" powers in an officer removable by joint resolution may indeed be debatable—as may be the wisdom of the entire scheme of permitting an unelected official to revise the budget enacted by Congress—but such matters are for the most part to be worked out between the Congress and the President through the legislative process, which affords each branch ample opportunity to defend its interests. The Act vesting budget-cutting authority in the Comptroller General represents Congress' judgment that the delegation of such authority to counteract ever-mounting deficits is "necessary and proper" to the exercise of the powers granted the Federal Government by the Constitution; and the President's approval of the statute signifies his unwillingness to reject the choice made by Congress. Under such circumstances, the role of this Court should be limited to determining whether the Act so alters the balance of authority among the branches of government as to pose a genuine threat to the basic division between the lawmaking power and the power to execute the law. Because I see no such threat, I cannot join the Court in striking down the Act.

Notes/Queries/Readings

1. What problem does the majority find with the power of the comptroller general? Who, precisely, has lost power under this provision? If both Congress and the executive have approved the structure of the original act, why then should the judiciary be able to invalidate it?

2. How can the Court legitimately question what Congress and the president have determined to be "necessary and proper" to carry out the great ends of the Constitution? Must the Court do so in order to maintain a constitutionally limited government?

3. What sort of relationship among the branches of the federal government does Chief Justice Burger assume in the opinion of the Court? What about Justice White? How is each consistent with their respective opinions in *Chadha*? Which is more consistent with the conception of the powers of the federal government as articulated by Chief Justice Marshall?

4. Do the different opinions in *Bowsher* rest on different understandings about how the democratic process should work? Do they rest, instead, on different understandings about the nature and limits of constitutional change and the role of judges in responding to and overseeing that change?

Morrison v. Olson

487 U.S. 654, 108 S. Ct. 2597, 101 L. Ed. 2d 569 (1988)

The Ethics in Government Act of 1978 authorized a Special Division of the United States Court of Appeals for the District of Columbia to appoint an independent counsel to investigate and, if necessary, prosecute high-ranking governmental officials for violating federal criminal law. In this case, Theodore Olson, assistant attorney general, was accused of giving false and misleading testimony to a House subcommittee investigating the activities of the Environmental Protection Agency. In accordance with the act's provisions, the chairman of the House Judiciary Committee sent a report to the attorney general requesting that an independent counsel be appointed to investigate the charges against Olson. After an inquiry by the Justice Department, the attorney general applied to the Special Division for the appointment of an independent counsel.

When Alexia Morrison, the appointee, caused a federal grand jury to issue a subpoena for the production of certain documents, Olson moved to quash the subpoena on the grounds that the act's independent counsel provisions violated the Constitution, thus invalidating the pending proceeding. The district court upheld the act, but the court of appeals reversed, holding that the act violated the Constitution's appointment clause (Art. 2, s 2, cl. 2). Opinion of the Court: *Rehnquist*, Brennan, White, Marshall, Blackmun, Stevens, O'Connor. Dissenting opinion: *Scalia*. Not participating: Kennedy.

Chief Justice REHNQUIST delivered the opinion of the Court.

This case presents us with a challenge to the independent counsel provisions of the Ethics in Government Act of 1978. . . . We hold today that these provisions of the Act do not violate the Appointments Clause of the Constitution, Art. II, s 2, cl. 2, or the limitations of Article III, nor do they impermissibly interfere with the President's authority under Article II in violation of the constitutional principle of separation of powers.

The Appointments Clause of Article II reads as follows:

> The President shall nominate, and by and with the Advice and Consent of the Senate, shall appoint Ambassadors, other public Ministers and Consuls, Judges of the Supreme Court, and all other Officers of the United States, whose Appointments are not herein otherwise provided for, and which shall be established by Law: but the Congress may by Law vest the Appointment of such inferior Officers, as they think proper, in the President alone, in the Courts of Law, or in the Heads of Departments. (U.S. Const., Art. II, s 2, cl. 2.)

The line between "inferior" and "principal" officers is one that is far from clear, and the Framers provided little guidance into where it should be drawn. We need not attempt here to decide exactly where the line falls between the two types of officers, because in our view appellant clearly falls on the "inferior officer" side of that line. Several factors lead to this conclusion.

Comparative Note 4.5

[In 1969 Ireland's Oireachtas (parliament) authorized its Committee of Public Accounts to investigate the diversion of public money to the IRA in Northern Ireland. If the committee found that a witness had committed a crime, it was authorized to certify that fact to Ireland's High Court with the provision that "the High Court may, after such inquiry as it thinks proper to make, punish or take steps for the punishment of that person in like manner as if he had been guilty of contempt of the High Court."]

Article 34 of the Constitution provides that justice shall be administered in courts established by law by judges appointed in the manner prescribed by the Constitution. The Committee of Public Accounts is not a court and its members are not judges. The Constitution of Ireland is founded on the doctrine of the tripartite division of the powers of government . . . and for a statute to confer on a committee of the Legislature a power to try a criminal offense would be repugnant to the Constitution. Moreover, under the Constitution the Courts cannot be used as appendages or auxiliaries to enforce the purported convictions of other tribunals. The Constitution vests the judicial power of government solely in the Courts and reserves exclusively to the Courts the power to try persons on criminal charges. Trial, conviction and sentence are indivisible parts of the exercise of this power.

Source: *In Re Haughey* [1971] I.R. 231, at 150.

First, appellant is subject to removal by a higher Executive Branch official. Although appellant may not be "subordinate" to the Attorney General (and the President) insofar as she possesses a degree of independent discretion to exercise the powers delegated to her under the Act, the fact that she can be removed by the Attorney General indicates that she is to some degree "inferior" in rank and authority. Second, appellant is empowered by the Act to perform only certain, limited duties. An independent counsel's role is restricted primarily to investigation and, if appropriate, prosecution for certain federal crimes.

Third, appellant's office is limited in jurisdiction. Not only is the Act itself restricted in applicability to certain federal officials suspected of certain serious federal crimes, but an independent counsel can only act within the scope of the jurisdiction that has been granted by the Special Division pursuant to a request by the Attorney General. Finally, appellant's office is limited in tenure. There is concededly no time limit on the appointment of a particular counsel. Nonetheless, the office of independent counsel is "temporary" in the sense that an independent counsel is appointed essentially to accomplish a single task, and when that task is over the office is terminated, either by the counsel herself or by action of the Special Division. Unlike other prosecutors, appellant has no ongoing responsibilities that extend beyond the accomplishment of the mission that she was appointed for and authorized by the Special Division to undertake. In our view, these factors relating to the ideas of tenure, duration . . . and duties of the independent counsel, are sufficient to establish that appellant is an "inferior" officer in the constitutional sense.

This does not, however, end our inquiry under the Appointments Clause. Appellees argue that even if appellant is an "inferior" officer, the Clause does not empower Congress to place the power to appoint such an officer outside the Executive Branch. They contend that the Clause does not contemplate congressional authorization of "interbranch appointments," in which an officer of one branch is appointed by officers of another branch. The relevant language of the Appointments Clause is worth repeating. It reads: " . . . but the Congress may by Law vest the Appointment of such inferior Officers, as they think proper, in the President alone, in the courts of Law, or in the Heads of Departments." On its face, the language of this "excepting clause" admits of no limitation on interbranch appointments. Indeed, the inclusion of "as they think proper" seems clearly to give Congress significant discretion to determine whether it is "proper" to vest the appointment of, for example, executive officials in the "courts of Law." . . .

We do not mean to say that Congress' power to provide for interbranch appointments of "inferior officers" is unlimited. In addition to separation-of-powers concerns, which would arise if such provisions for appointment had the potential to impair the constitutional functions assigned to one of the branches, . . . Congress' decision to vest the appointment power in the courts would be improper if there was some "incongruity" between the functions normally performed by the courts and the performance of their duty to appoint. . . . Congress, of course, was concerned when it created the office of independent counsel with the conflicts of interest that could arise in situations when the Executive Branch is called upon to investigate its own high-ranking officers. If it were to remove the appointing authority from the Executive Branch, the most logical place to put it was in the Judicial Branch. In light of the Act's provision making the judges of the Special Division ineligible to participate in any matters relating to an independent counsel they have appointed, we do not think that appointment of the independent counsel by the court runs afoul of the constitutional limitation on "incongruous" interbranch appointments.

Appellees next contend that the powers vested in the Special Division by the Act conflict with Article III of the Constitution. We have long recognized that by the express provision of Article III, the judicial power of the United States is limited to "Cases" and "Controversies." As a general rule, we have broadly stated that "executive or administrative duties of a nonjudicial nature may not be imposed on judges holding office under Art. III of the Constitution." The purpose of this limitation is to help ensure the independence of the Judicial Branch and to prevent the Judiciary from encroaching into areas reserved for the other branches. . . .

. . . This said, we do not think that Congress may give the Division unlimited discretion to determine the independent counsel's jurisdiction. In order for the Division's definition of the counsel's jurisdiction to be truly "incidental" to its power to appoint, the jurisdiction that the court decides upon must be demonstrably related to the factual circumstances that gave rise to the Attorney General's investigation and request for the appointment of the independent counsel in the particular case.

We now turn to consider whether the Act is invalid under the constitutional principle of separation of powers. Two related issues must be addressed: The first is whether the provision of the Act restricting the Attorney General's power to remove the independent counsel to only those instances in which he can show "good cause," taken by itself, impermissibly interferes with the President's exercise of his constitutionally appointed functions. The second is whether, taken as a whole, the Act violates the separation of powers by reducing the President's ability to control the prosecutorial powers wielded by the independent counsel.

Two terms ago we had occasion to consider whether it was consistent with the separation of powers for Congress to pass a statute that authorized a Government official who is removable only by Congress to participate in what we found to be "executive powers." We held in *Bowsher* that "Congress cannot reserve for itself the power of removal of an officer charged with the execution of the laws except by impeachment." . . .

. . . [T]his case does not involve an attempt by Congress itself to gain a role in the removal of executive officials other than its established powers of impeachment and conviction. The Act instead puts the removal power squarely in the hands of the Executive Branch; an independent counsel may be removed from office, "only by the personal action of the Attorney General, and only for good cause." There is no requirement of congressional approval of the Attorney General's removal decision, though the decision is subject to judicial review. . . .

. . . We do not mean to suggest that an analysis of the functions served by the officials at issue is irrelevant. But the real question is whether the removal restrictions are of such a nature that they impede the President's ability to perform his constitutional duty, and the functions of the officials in question must be analyzed in that light.

Nor do we think that the "good cause" removal provision at issue here impermissibly burdens the President's power to control or supervise the independent counsel, as an executive official, in the execution of his or her duties . . . This is not a case in which the power to remove an executive official has been completely stripped from the President, thus providing no means for the President to ensure the "faithful execution" of the laws. Rather, because the independent counsel may be terminated for "good cause," the Executive, through the Attorney General, retains ample authority to assure that the counsel is competently performing his or her statutory responsibilities in a manner that comports with the provisions of the Act. . . .

The final question to be addressed is whether the Act, taken as a whole, violates the principle of separation of powers by unduly interfering with the role of the Executive Branch. . . .

We observe first that this case does not involve an attempt by Congress to increase its own powers at the expense of the Executive Branch. Unlike some of our previous cases, most recently *Bowsher v. Synar* [1986], this case simply does not pose a "dange[r] of congressional usurpation of Executive Branch functions." Indeed, with the exception of the power of impeachment—which applies to all officers of the United States—Congress retained for itself no powers of control or supervision over an independent counsel. . . .

Similarly, we do not think that the Act works any judicial usurpation of properly executive functions. . . .

Finally, we do not think that the Act "impermissibly undermine[s]" the powers of the Executive Branch or "disrupts the proper balance between the coordinate branches [y] prevent[ing] the Executive Branch from accomplishing its constitutionally assigned functions. It is undeniable that the Act reduces the amount of control or supervision that the Attorney General and, through him, the President exercises over the investigation and prosecution of a certain class of alleged criminal activity. The Attorney General is not allowed to appoint the individual of his choice; he does not determine the counsel's jurisdiction; and his power to remove a counsel is limited. Nonetheless, the Act does give the Attorney General several means of supervising or controlling the prosecutorial powers that may be wielded by an independent counsel. Most importantly, the Attorney General retains the power to remove the counsel for "good cause," a power that we have already concluded provides the Executive with substantial ability to ensure that the laws are "faithfully executed" by an independent counsel. No independent counsel may be appointed without a specific request by the Attorney General, and the Attorney General's decision not to request appointment if he finds "no reasonable grounds to believe that further investigation is warranted" is committed to his unreviewable discretion. The Act thus gives the Executive a degree of control over the power to initiate an investigation by the independent counsel. In addition, the jurisdiction of the independent counsel is defined with reference to the facts submitted by the Attorney General, and once a counsel is appointed, the Act requires that the counsel abide by Justice Department policy unless it is not "possible" to do so. Notwithstanding the fact that the counsel is to some degree "independent" and free from executive supervision to a greater extent than other federal prosecutors, in our view these features of the Act give the Executive Branch sufficient control over the independent counsel to ensure that the President is able to perform his constitutionally assigned duties.

In sum, we conclude today that it does not violate the Appointments Clause for Congress to vest the appointment of independent counsel in the Special Division; that the powers exercised by the Special Division under the Act do not violate Article III; and that the Act does not violate the separation-of-powers principle by impermissibly interfering with the functions of the Executive Branch. The decision of the Court of Appeals is therefore reversed.

Justice SCALIA, dissenting.

The principle of separation of powers is expressed in our Constitution in the first section of each of the first three Articles . . .

But just as the mere words of a Bill of Rights are not self-effectuating, the Framers recognized "[t]he insufficiency of a mere parchment delineation of the boundaries" to achieve the separation of powers. . . . The major "fortification" provided, of course, was the veto power. But in addition to providing fortification, the Founders conspicuously and very consciously declined to sap the Executive's strength in the same way they had weakened the Legislature: by dividing the executive power. . . .

That is what this suit is about. Power. The allocation of

power among Congress, the President, and the courts in such fashion as to preserve the equilibrium the Constitution sought to establish—so that "a gradual concentration of the several powers in the same department," can effectively be resisted. Frequently an issue of this sort will come before the Court clad, so to speak, in sheep's clothing: the potential of the asserted principle to effect important change in the equilibrium of power is not immediately evident, and must be discerned by a careful and perceptive analysis. But this wolf comes as a wolf.

If to describe this case is not to decide it, the concept of a government of separate and coordinate powers no longer has meaning. The Court devotes most of its attention to such relatively technical details as the Appointments Clause and the removal power, addressing briefly and only at the end of its opinion the separation of powers. As my prologue suggests, I think that has it backwards. . . .

The Court concedes that "[t]here is no real dispute that the functions performed by the independent counsel are 'executive',", though it qualifies that concession by adding "in the sense that they are law enforcement functions that typically have been undertaken by officials within the Executive Branch." The qualifier adds nothing but atmosphere. In what *other* sense can one identify "the executive Power" that is supposed to be vested in the President (unless it includes everything the Executive Branch is given to do) *except* by reference to what has always and everywhere—if conducted by government at all—been conducted never by the legislature, never by the courts, and always by the executive. There is no possible doubt that the independent counsel's functions fit this description. She is vested with the "full power and independent authority to exercise all investigative and prosecutorial functions and powers of the Department of Justice [and] the Attorney General." Governmental investigation and prosecution of crimes is a quintessentially executive function.

. . . [W]hether the statute before us deprives the President of exclusive control over that quintessentially executive activity: The Court does not, and could not possibly, assert that it does not. That is indeed the whole object of the statute. Instead, the Court points out that the President, through his Attorney General, has at least some control. That concession is alone enough to invalidate the statute, but I cannot refrain from pointing out that the Court greatly exaggerates the extent of that "some" Presidential control. "Most importan[t]" among these controls, the Court asserts, is the Attorney General's "power to remove the counsel for 'good cause.'" This is somewhat like referring to shackles as an effective means of locomotion. . . . [L]imiting removal power to "good cause" is an impediment to, not an effective grant of, Presidential control. We said that limitation was necessary with respect to members of the Federal

Trade Commission, which we found to be "an agency of the legislative and judicial departments," and "wholly disconnected from the executive department," because "it is quite evident that one who holds his office only during the pleasure of another, cannot be depended upon to maintain an attitude of independence against the latter's will." What we in *Humphrey's Executor* found to be a means of eliminating Presidential control, the Court today considers the "most importan[t]" means of assuring Presidential control. Congress, of course, operated under no such illusion when it enacted this statute, describing the "good cause" limitation as "protecting the independent counsel's ability to act independently of the President's direct control" since it permits removal only for "misconduct."

. . . Finally, the Court points out that the Act directs the independent counsel to abide by general Justice Department policy, except when not "possible." The exception alone shows this to be an empty promise. Even without that, however, one would be hard put to come up with many investigative or prosecutorial "policies" (other than those imposed by the Constitution or by Congress through law) that are absolute. Almost all investigative and prosecutorial decisions including the ultimate decision whether, after a technical violation of the law has been found, prosecution is warranted—involve the balancing of innumerable legal and practical considerations. . . . In sum, the balancing of various legal, practical, and political considerations, none of which is absolute, is the very essence of prosecutorial discretion. To take this away is to remove the core of the prosecutorial function, and not merely "some" Presidential control.

. . . It is not for us to determine, and we have never presumed to determine, how much of the purely executive powers of government must be within the full control of the President. The Constitution prescribes that they *all* are.

. . . While the separation of powers may prevent us from righting every wrong, it does so in order to ensure that we do not lose liberty. The checks against any branch's abuse of its exclusive powers are twofold: First, retaliation by one of the other branch's use of *its* exclusive powers: Congress, for example, can impeach the executive who willfully fails to enforce the laws; the executive can decline to prosecute under unconstitutional statutes; and the courts can dismiss malicious prosecutions. Second, and ultimately, there is the political check that the people will replace those in the political branches . . . who are guilty of abuse. Political pressures produced special prosecutors—for Teapot Dome and for Watergate, for example—long before this statute created the independent counsel.

As I indicated earlier, the basic separation-of-powers principles I have discussed are what give life and content to our jurisprudence concerning the President's power to appoint and remove officers. The same result of unconstitutionality is therefore plainly indicated by our case law in these areas.

. . . I think it preferable to look to the text of the Constitution and the division of power that it establishes. These demonstrate, I think, that the independent counsel is not an inferior officer because she is not subordinate to any officer in the Executive Branch [indeed, not even to the President]. . . .

To be sure, it is not a sufficient condition for "inferior" officer status that one be subordinate to a principal officer. . . . But it is surely a necessary condition for inferior officer status that the officer be subordinate to another officer.

Since our 1935 decision in *Humphrey's Executor v. United States*—which was considered by many at the time the product of an activist, anti-New Deal Court bent on reducing the power of President Franklin Roosevelt—it has been established that the line of permissible restriction upon removal of principal officers lies at the point at which the powers exercised by those officers are no longer purely executive. . . .

. . . By its shortsighted action today, I fear the Court has permanently encumbered the Republic with an institution that will do it great harm.

Worse than what it has done, however, is the manner in which it has done it. A government of laws means a government of rules. Today's decision on the basic issue of fragmentation of executive power is ungoverned by rule, and hence ungoverned by law. It extends into the very heart of our most significant constitutional function the "totality of the circumstances" mode of analysis that this Court has in recent years become fond of. Taking all things into account, we conclude that the power taken away from the President here is not really too much. The next time executive power is assigned to someone other than the President we may conclude, taking all things into account, that it is too much. That opinion, like this one, will not be confined by any rule. We will describe, as we have done today . . . the effects of the provision in question, and will authoritatively announce: "The President's need to control the exercise of the [subject officer's] discretion is so central to the functioning of the Executive Branch as to require complete control." This is not analysis; it is ad hoc judgment. And it fails to explain why it is not true that—as the text of the Constitution seems to require, as the Founders seemed to expect, and as our past cases have uniformly assumed—all purely executive power must be under the control of the President.

The ad hoc approach to constitutional adjudication has real attraction, even apart from its work-saving potential. It is guaranteed to produce a result, in every case, that will make a majority of the Court happy with the law. The law is, by definition, precisely what the majority thinks, taking all things into account, it ought to be. I prefer to rely upon the judgment of the wise men who constructed our system, and of the people who approved it, and of two centuries of history that have shown it to be sound. Like it or not, that judgment says, quite plainly, that "[t]he executive Power shall be vested in a President of the United States."

Notes/Queries/Readings

1. What difference does it make to the Court whether the independent counsel is a "principal" or "inferior" officer? How does the Court determine which powers are central to the functioning of the executive branch? Can the Court, in fact, make such a determination?

2. Which opinion comes closest to the approach taken by Justice Black in *Youngstown Sheet & Tube Co. v. Sawyer* (1952)? Which is closer to that of Justice Frankfurter? To that of Justice Jackson? Is the conception of separation of powers expressed by the Court in this case consistent with that of *Chadha* and *Bowsher*? What makes this case different? Is Justice Scalia's approach to separation of powers tenable in the modern administrative state?

3. In his dissent, Justice Scalia accused the majority of deciding this case not on the basis of rules but on the basis of its "ad hoc judgment." Do you agree? Is Justice Scalia correct to note that a decision that cannot ground itself in rules traced to the Constitution is a decision that cannot ground itself in law? Is the alternative, as Scalia suggests, to "rely upon the judgment of the wise men who constructed our system, and of the people who approved it, and of two centuries of history that have shown it to be sound"?

4. In *Myers v. United States*, 272 U.S. 52 (1926), the Court was called upon to decide the extent of the president's power to remove government officials. The statute re-

viewed provided that the president could remove postmasters appointed to a four-year term only with the advice and consent of the Senate. In one of the broadest readings of presidential power, Chief Justice Taft, writing for a majority of six justices, declared that the statute invaded the power of the executive. "The power of removal," wrote Taft, "is incident to the power of appointment, not to the power of advising and consenting to appointment." The power of removal derives from the president's duty, laid down in Article 2, to "take care that the laws be faithfully executed." The President's discretionary power to remove officials is absolute, for executive subordinates "must do his will." When "he loses confidence in the intelligence, ability, judgment or loyalty of any one of them, he must have the power to remove him without delay."

In two subsequent cases, however, the Court limited the President's removal power but without undermining the logic of *Myers*. In *Humphrey's Executor v. United States*, 295 U.S. 602 (1935), the Court held that Congress could limit the president's power to fire employees—such as the members of the Federal Trade Commission, an *independent* regulatory agency—not engaged in purely executive duties but acting "in part quasi-legislatively and in part quasi-judicially." And in *Wiener v. United States*, 357 U.S. 340 (1958), by a vote of nine to zero, the Court held that the president could not remove a member of the War Claims Commission because of the "intrinsic judicial character" of his function.

5. For a commentary on *Morrison*, see Stephen L. Carter, *The Independent Counsel Mess*, 102 Harvard Law Review 105 (1988). For more general treatment of the appointment process, see G. Calvin McKenzie, *The Politics of Presidential Appointments* (New York: Free Press, 1981).

United States v. Nixon
418 U.S. 683, 94 S. Ct. 3090, 41 L. Ed. 2d 1039 (1974)

In 1974 a federal grand jury indicted the attorney general and several presidential assistants for various offenses, including a conspiracy to defraud the United States and to obstruct justice. The grand jury also named President Richard Nixon as an unindicted co-conspirator. The special prosecutor caused the district court to issue a *subpoena duces tecum* directing the president to produce certain tape recordings and documents relating to his conversations with aides and advisors. The president released edited transcripts of several conversations, but refused to turn over other specified transcripts and papers. He moved to squash the subpoena, claiming that the dispute was a nonjusticiable dispute within the executive branch and that his confidential conversations within the White House

were privileged communications. The district court denied the motion, and the president appealed the decision to the court of appeals. At the request of the special prosecutor, the Supreme Court expedited the matter by granting a writ of certiorari before any judgment by the court of appeals. Opinion of the Court: *Burger*, Douglas, Brennan, Stewart, White, Marshall, Blackmun, Powell. Not participating: Rehnquist.

Mr. Chief Justice BURGER delivered the opinion of the Court.

Justiciability

In the District Court, the President's counsel argued that the court lacked jurisdiction to issue the *subpoena* because the matter was an intra-branch dispute between a subordinate and superior officer of the Executive Branch and hence not subject to judicial resolution. That argument has been renewed in this Court with emphasis on the contention that the dispute does not present a "case" or "controversy" which can be adjudicated in the federal courts. . . . Since the Executive Branch has exclusive authority and absolute discretion to decide whether to prosecute a case, it is contended that a President's decision is final in determining what evidence is to be used in a given criminal case. . . . The Special Prosecutor's demand for the items therefore presents, in the view of the President's counsel, a political question . . . since it involves a "textually demonstrable" grant of power under Art. II.

The mere assertion of a claim of an "intra-branch dispute," without more, has never operated to defeat federal jurisdiction; justiciability does not depend on such a surface inquiry. . . .

Our starting point is the nature of the proceeding for which the evidence is sought—here a pending criminal prosecution. . . . Under the authority of Art. II, s 2, Congress has vested in the Attorney General the power to conduct the criminal litigation of the United States Government. It has also vested in him the power to appoint subordinate officers to assist him in the discharge of his duties. Acting pursuant to those statutes, the Attorney General has delegated the authority to represent the United States in these particular matters to a Special Prosecutor with unique authority and tenure. The regulation gives the Special Prosecutor explicit power to contest the invocation of executive privilege in the process of seeking evidence deemed relevant to the performance of these specially delegated duties.

So long as this regulation is extant it has the force of law. . . . Here at issue is the production or nonproduction of specified evidence deemed by the Special Prosecutor to be relevant and admissible in a pending criminal case. It is sought by one official of the Executive Branch within the scope of his express authority; it is resisted by the Chief Executive on the ground of his duty to preserve the confidentiality of the communications of the President. Whatever the correct answer on the merits, these issues are "of a type which are traditionally justiciable." . . .

The Claim of Privilege

. . . [W]e turn to the claim that the subpoena should be quashed because it demands "confidential conversations between a President and his close advisors that it would be inconsistent with the public interest to produce." The first contention is a broad claim that the separation of powers doctrine precludes judicial review of a President's claim of privilege. The second contention is that if he does not prevail on the claim of absolute privilege, the court should

hold as a matter of constitutional law that the privilege prevails over the *subpoena duces tecum*.

In the performance of assigned constitutional duties each branch of the Government must initially interpret the Constitution, and the interpretation of its powers by any branch is due great respect from the others. The President's counsel, as we have noted, reads the Constitution as providing an absolute privilege of confidentiality for all Presidential communications. Many decisions of this Court, however, have unequivocally reaffirmed the holding of *Marbury v. Madison* [1803], that "(i)t is emphatically the province and duty of the judicial department to say what the law is."

In support of his claim of absolute privilege, the President's counsel urges two grounds, one of which is common to all governments and one of which is peculiar to our system of separation of powers. The first ground is the valid need for protection of communications between high Government officials and those who advise and assist them in the performance of their manifold duties; the importance of this confidentiality is too plain to require further discussion. Human experience teaches that those who expect public dissemination of their remarks may well temper candor with a concern for appearances and for their own interests to the detriment of the decision making process. Whatever the nature of the privilege of confidentiality of Presidential communications in the exercise of Art. II powers, the privilege can be said to derive from the supremacy of each branch within its own assigned area of constitutional duties. Certain powers and privileges flow from the nature of enumerated powers; the protection of the confidentiality of Presidential communications has similar constitutional underpinnings.

The second ground asserted by the President's counsel in support of the claim of absolute privilege rests on the doctrine of separation of powers. Here it is argued that the independence of the Executive Branch within its own sphere, insulates a President from a judicial subpoena in an ongoing criminal prosecution, and thereby protects confidential Presidential communications.

However, neither the doctrine of separation of powers, nor the need for confidentiality of high-level communications, without more, can sustain an absolute, unqualified Presidential privilege of immunity from judicial process under all circumstances. The President's need for complete candor and objectivity from advisers calls for great deference from the courts. However, when the privilege depends solely on the broad, undifferentiated claim of public interest in the confidentiality of such conversations, a confrontation with other values arises. Absent a claim of need to protect military, diplomatic, or sensitive national security secrets, we find it difficult to accept the argument that even

Comparative Note 4.6

[In the following extract, the Canadian Supreme Court rejected a high public official's claim to testimonial immunity. The official invoked the Crown privilege to protect the public interest. In this leading case, the Court explored the scope of the Crown privilege.]

Once the nature . . . of [the] documents or the reasons against its disclosure are shown, the question for the Court is whether they might, on any rational view . . . be such that the public interest requires that they should not be revealed; if they are capable of sustaining such an interest, and a Minister of the Crown avers its existence, then the Courts must accept his decision. On the other hand, if the facts . . . show that . . . no such interest can exist, then such a [ministerial] declaration . . . must . . . be disregarded. To eliminate the Courts in a function with which the tradition of the common law has invested them and to hold them subject to any opinion formed, rational or irrational, by a member of the Executive to the prejudice, it might be, of the lives of private individuals, is not in harmony with the basic conceptions of our polity. . . .

What is secured by attributing to the Courts this preliminary determination of possible prejudice is protection against Executive encroachments upon the administration of justice; and in the present trend of government, little can be more essential to the maintenance of individual security. In this important matter, to relegate the Courts to such a subserviency as is suggested would be to withdraw from them the confidence of independence and judicial appraisal that so far appear to have served well the organization of which we are the heirs.

SOURCE: *R. V. Snider* [1954] 4 D.L.R. 485–86.

---

the very important interest in confidentiality of Presidential communications is significantly diminished by production of such material for *in camera* inspection with all the protection that a district court will be obliged to provide.

The impediment that an absolute, unqualified privilege would place in the way of the primary constitutional duty of the Judicial Branch to do justice in criminal prosecutions would plainly conflict with the function of the courts under Art. III. In designing the structure of our Government and dividing and allocating the sovereign power among three co-equal branches, the Framers of the Constitution sought to provide a comprehensive system, but the separate powers were not intended to operate with absolute independence. . . . To read the Art. II powers of the President as providing an absolute privilege as against a subpoena essential to enforcement of criminal statutes on no more than a generalized claim of the public interest in confidentiality of nonmilitary and nondiplomatic discussions would upset the constitutional balance of "a workable government" and gravely impair the role of the courts under Art. III.

Since we conclude that the legitimate needs of the judicial process may outweigh Presidential privilege, it is necessary to resolve those competing interests in a manner that preserves the essential functions of each branch. The right and indeed the duty to resolve that question does not free the Judiciary from according high respect to the representations made on behalf of the President.

The expectation of a President to the confidentiality of his conversations and correspondence, like the claim of confidentiality of judicial deliberations, for example, has all the values to which we accord deference for the privacy of all citizens and, added to those values, is the necessity for protection of the public interest in candid, objective, and even blunt or harsh opinions in Presidential decision making. . . .

But this presumptive privilege must be considered in light of our historic commitment to the rule of law. . . . The ends of criminal justice would be defeated if judgments were to be founded on a partial or speculative presentation of the facts. The very integrity of the judicial system and public confidence in the system depend on full disclosure of all the facts, within the framework of the rules of evidence. To ensure that justice is done, it is imperative to the function of courts that compulsory process be available for the production of evidence needed either by the prosecution or by the defense.

In this case the President challenges a subpoena served on him as a third party requiring the production of materials for use in a criminal prosecution; he does so on the claim that he has a privilege against disclosure of confidential communications. He does not place his claim of privilege on the ground they are military or diplomatic secrets. As to these areas of Art. II duties the courts have traditionally shown the utmost deference to Presidential responsibilities. . . .

On the other hand, the allowance of the privilege to withhold evidence that is demonstrably relevant in a criminal trial would cut deeply into the guarantee of due process of law and gravely impair the basic function of the courts. A President's acknowledged need for confidentiality in the communications of his office is general in nature, whereas the constitutional need for production of relevant evidence in a criminal proceeding is specific and central to the fair adjudication of a particular criminal case in the administration of justice. Without access to specific facts a criminal prosecution may be totally frustrated. The President's broad interest in confidentiality of communications will not be vitiated by disclosure of a limited number of conversations preliminarily shown to have some bearing on the pending criminal cases.

We conclude that when the ground for asserting privilege as to subpoenaed materials sought for use in a criminal trial is based only on the generalized interest in confidentiality, it cannot prevail over the fundamental demands of due process of law in the fair administration of criminal justice. The generalized assertion of privilege must yield to the demonstrated, specific need for evidence in a pending criminal trial.

Affirmed.

Notes/Queries/Readings

1. The events surrounding this case were extraordinary. After President Nixon refused to turn over subpoenaed materials to special prosecutor Leon Jaworski in March 1974, a federal district court held a trial and eventually rejected Nixon's claim to executive privilege. The president appealed to the court of appeals, but before they could rule, the special prosecutor petitioned the Supreme Court to grant certiorari. The Supreme Court accepted Jaworski's request. The Court heard oral arguments in a special session on 8 July and handed down its opinion on 24 July. Less than a week after this decision, the House voted to impeach the President. On 9 August 1974, President Nixon resigned the presidency.

2. Was President Nixon insisting that the president has an independent authority to interpret the Constitution? Consider our discussion of judicial supremacy in chapter 3. Was President Nixon's claim unprecedented? Did the Court deny that the president has that authority?

3. The Court was careful to note that Nixon's claim of privilege did not ground itself in the need to protect sensitive information or national security. Would the Court have decided differently if the president had made such a claim? Would the presence of such claims strengthen the president's authority to interpret the Constitution to permit him to withhold such information? How should we weigh such a claim against a "demonstrated, specific need to evidence in a pending criminal trial"? Who should weigh such a claim? The Court suggested that the president's judgment must necessarily be influenced by his self-interest. Is that true of the Court's judgment as well?

4. For commentary on the case, see *Symposium*: United States v. Nixon, 22 University of California at Los Angeles Law Review 13 (1974) and Archibald Cox, *Presidential Privilege*, 122 University of Pennsylvania Law Review 1383 (1974). For more general discussions, see Raoul Berger, *Executive Privilege* (Cambridge: Harvard University Press, 1974) and Philip B. Kurland, *Watergate and the Constitution* (Chicago: University of Chicago Press, 1978).

Mistretta v. United States
488 U.S. 361, 109 S. Ct. 647, 102 L.Ed. 2d 714 (1989)

In 1984, Congress established the United States Sentencing Commission as an independent body within the judicial branch. In creating the Commission, Congress sought to eliminate the substantial disparity in the penalties federal judges were handing down for the same offenses, a problem caused by the broad sentencing discretion conferred on federal judges. The Commission was charged with the task of writing new criteria for the imposition of criminal sentences. The guidelines adopted required federal judges to justify deviations from them. The constitutionality of these guidelines was widely contested in federal district courts. Numerous courts upheld their validity, whereas many others declared them unconstitutional. Opinion of the Court: *Blackmun*, Rehnquist, Brennan (in part), White, Marshall, Stevens, O'Connor, Kennedy. Dissenting opinion: *Scalia*.

Justice BLACKMUN delivered the opinion of the Court.

Delegation of Power

Petitioner argues that in delegating the power to promulgate sentencing guidelines for every federal criminal offense to an independent Sentencing Commission, Congress has granted the Commission excessive legislative discretion in violation of the constitutionally based nondelegation doctrine. We do not agree.

The nondelegation doctrine is rooted in the principle of separation of powers that underlies our tripartite system of

Government. The Constitution provides that "[a]ll legislative Powers herein granted shall be vested in a Congress of the United States," U.S. Const., Art. I, s 1, and we long have insisted that "the integrity and maintenance of the system of government ordained by the Constitution" mandate that Congress generally cannot delegate its legislative power to another Branch. We also have recognized, however, that the separation-of-powers principle, and the nondelegation doctrine in particular, do not prevent Congress from obtaining the assistance of its coordinate Branches. In a passage now enshrined in our jurisprudence, Chief Justice Taft, writing for the Court, explained our approach to such cooperative ventures: "In determining what [Congress] may do in seeking assistance from another branch, the extent and character of that assistance must be fixed according to common sense and the inherent necessities of the government co-ordination." So long as Congress "shall lay down by legislative act an intelligible principle to which the person or body authorized to [exercise the delegated authority] is directed to conform, such legislative action is not a forbidden delegation of legislative power."

. . . The Act sets forth more than merely an "intelligible principle" or minimal standards. One court has aptly put it: "The statute outlines the policies which prompted establishment of the Commission, explains what the Commission should do and how it should do it, and sets out specific directives to govern particular situations."

Developing proportionate penalties for hundreds of different crimes by a virtually limitless array of offenders is precisely the sort of intricate, labor-intensive task for which delegation to an expert body is especially appropriate. Although Congress has delegated significant discretion to the Commission to draw judgments from its analysis of existing sentencing practice and alternative sentencing models, "Congress is not confined to that method of executing its policy which involves the least possible delegation of discretion to administrative officers." We have no doubt that in the hands of the Commission "the criteria which Congress has supplied are wholly adequate for carrying out the general policy and purpose" of the Act.

Separation of Powers

Having determined that Congress has set forth sufficient standards for the exercise of the Commission's delegated authority, we turn to Mistretta's claim that the Act violates the constitutional principle of separation of powers.

This Court consistently has given voice to, and has reaffirmed, the central judgment of the Framers of the Constitution that, within our political scheme, the separation of governmental powers into three coordinate Branches is essential to the preservation of liberty. Madison, in writing about the principle of separated powers, said: "No political truth is certainly of greater intrinsic value or is stamped with the authority of more enlightened patrons of liberty." *The Federalist* No. 47.

In applying the principle of separated powers in our jurisprudence, we have sought to give life to Madison's view of the appropriate relationship among the three coequal Branches. Accordingly, we have recognized, as Madison admonished at the founding, that while our Constitution mandates that "each of the three general departments of government [must remain] entirely free from the control or coercive influence, direct or indirect, of either of the others," the Framers did not require—and indeed rejected—the notion that the three Branches must be entirely separate and distinct. Madison, defending the Constitution against charges that it established insufficiently separate Branches, addressed the point directly. Separation of powers, he wrote, "doe[s] not mean that these [three] departments ought to have no *partial agency* in, or no *controul* over the acts of each other," but rather "that where the *whole* power of one department is exercised by the same hands which possess the *whole* power of another department, the fundamental principles of a free constitution, are subverted." *The Federalist* No. 47. Madison recognized that our constitutional system imposes upon the Branches a degree of overlapping responsibility, a duty of interdependence as well as independence the absence of which "would preclude the establishment of a Nation capable of governing itself effectively." . . .

In adopting this flexible understanding of separation of powers, we simply have recognized Madison's teaching that the greatest security against tyranny—the accumulation of excessive authority in a single Branch—lies not in a hermetic division among the Branches, but in a carefully crafted system of checked and balanced power within each Branch. "[T]he greatest security," wrote Madison, "against a gradual concentration of the several powers in the same department, consists in giving to those who administer each department, the necessary constitutional means, and personal motives, to resist encroachments of the others." *The Federalist* No. 51. Accordingly, as we have noted many times, the Framers "built into the tripartite Federal Government . . . a self-executing safeguard against the encroachment or aggrandizement of one branch at the expense of the other."

Location of the Commission

The Sentencing Commission unquestionably is a peculiar institution within the framework of our Government. Although placed by the Act in the Judicial Branch, it is not a court and does not exercise judicial power. . . . Our constitutional principles of separated powers are not violated, however, by mere anomaly or innovation. . . . [W]e observe that Congress' decision to create an independent rulemaking body to promulgate sentencing guidelines and to locate that body within the Judicial Branch is not unconstitutional unless Congress has vested in the Commission powers that are more appropriately performed by the other Branches or that undermine the integrity of the Judiciary.

. . . [A]lthough the judicial power of the United States is limited by express provision of Article III to "Cases" and "Controversies," we have never held, and have clearly disavowed in practice, that the Constitution prohibits Congress from assigning to courts or auxiliary bodies within the Judicial Branch administrative or rulemaking duties that, in the words of Chief Justice Marshall, are "necessary and proper . . . for carrying into execution all the judgments which the judicial department has power to pronounce." Because of their close relation to the central mission of the Judicial Branch, such extrajudicial activities are consonant with the integrity of the Branch and are not more appropriate for another Branch.

Given the consistent responsibility of federal judges to pronounce sentence within the statutory range established by Congress, we find that the role of the Commission in promulgating guidelines for the exercise of that judicial function bears considerable similarity to the role of this Court in establishing rules of procedure under the various enabling Acts. Such guidelines, like the Federal Rules of Criminal and Civil Procedure, are court rules—rules, to paraphrase Chief Justice Marshall's language in *Wayman*, for carrying into execution judgments that the Judiciary has the power to pronounce. Just as the rules of procedure bind judges and courts in the proper management of the cases before them, so the Guidelines bind judges and courts in the exercise of their uncontested responsibility to pass sentence in criminal cases. In other words, the Commission's functions, like this Court's function in promulgating procedural rules, are clearly attendant to a central element of the historically acknowledged mission of the Judicial Branch. . . .

Nor do the Guidelines, though substantive, involve a degree of political authority inappropriate for a nonpolitical Branch. Although the Guidelines are intended to have substantive effects on public behavior [as do the rules of procedure], they do not bind or regulate the primary conduct of the public or vest in the Judicial Branch the legislative responsibility for establishing minimum and maximum penalties for every crime. They do no more than fetter the discretion of sentencing judges to do what they have done for generations—impose sentences within the broad limits established by Congress. Given their limited reach, the special role of the Judicial Branch in the field of sentencing, and the fact that the Guidelines are promulgated by an independent agency and not a court, it follows that as a matter of "practical consequences" the location of the Sentencing Commission within the Judicial Branch simply leaves with the Judiciary what long has belonged to it.

In sum, since substantive judgment in the field of sentencing has been and remains appropriate to the Judicial Branch, and the methodology of rulemaking has been and remains appropriate to that Branch, Congress' considered decision to combine these functions in an independent Sentencing Commission and to locate that Commission within the Judicial Branch does not violate the principle of separation of powers.

Composition of the Commission

We now turn to petitioner's claim that Congress' decision to require at least three federal judges to serve on the Commission and to require those judges to share their authority with nonjudges undermines the integrity of the Judicial Branch.

The text of the Constitution contains no prohibition against the service of active federal judges on independent commissions such as that established by the Act. The Constitution does include an Incompatibility Clause applicable to national legislators:

> No Senator or Representative shall, during the Time for which he was elected, be appointed to any civil Office under the Authority of the United States, which shall have been created, or the Emoluments whereof shall have been encreased during such time; and no Person holding any Office under the United States, shall be a Member of either House during his Continuance in Office. U.S. Const., Art. I, s 6, cl. 2.

No comparable restriction applies to judges, and we find it at least inferentially meaningful that at the Constitutional Convention two prohibitions against plural officeholding by members of the Judiciary were proposed, but did not reach the floor of the Convention for a vote. Our inferential reading that the Constitution does not prohibit Article III judges from undertaking extrajudicial duties finds support in the historical practice of the Founders after ratification. . . . Subsequent history, moreover, reveals a frequent and continuing, albeit controversial, practice of extrajudicial service. . . .

In light of the foregoing history and precedent, we conclude that the principle of separation of powers does not absolutely prohibit Article III judges from serving on commissions such as that created by the Act. The judges serve on the Sentencing Commission not pursuant to their status and authority as Article III judges, but solely because of their appointment by the President as the Act directs. Such power as these judges wield as Commissioners is not judicial power; it is administrative power derived from the enabling legislation. Just as the nonjudicial members of the Commission act as administrators, bringing their experience and wisdom to bear on the problems of sentencing disparity, so too the judges, uniquely qualified on the subject of sentencing, assume a wholly administrative role upon entering into the deliberations of the Commission. In other words, the Constitution, at least as a *per se* matter, does not forbid judges to wear two hats; it merely forbids them to wear both hats at the same time.

Presidential Control

The Act empowers the President to appoint all seven members of the Commission with the advice and consent of the Senate. The Act further provides that the President shall make his choice of judicial appointees to the Commission after considering a list of six judges recommended by the Judicial Conference of the United States. The Act also grants the President authority to remove members of the Commission, although "only for neglect of duty or malfeasance in office or for other good cause shown."

Mistretta argues that this power of Presidential appointment and removal prevents the Judicial Branch from performing its constitutionally assigned functions. Although we agree with petitioner that the independence of the Judicial Branch must be "jealously guarded" against outside interference, and that, as Madison admonished at the founding, "neither of [the Branches] ought to possess directly or indirectly, an overruling influence over the others in the administration of their respective powers," *The Federalist* No. 48, we do not believe that the President's appointment and removal powers over the Commission afford him influence over the functions of the Judicial Branch or undue sway over its members.

In other words, since the President has no power to affect the tenure or compensation of Article III judges, even if the Act authorized him to remove judges from the Commission at will, he would have no power to coerce the judges in the exercise of their judicial duties. In any case, Congress did not grant the President unfettered authority to remove Commission members. Instead, precisely to ensure that they would not be subject to coercion even in the exercise of their nonjudicial duties, Congress insulated the members from Presidential removal except for good cause. Under these circumstances, we see no risk that the President's limited removal power will compromise the impartiality of Article III judges serving on the Commission and, consequently, no risk that the Act's removal provision will prevent the Judicial Branch from performing its constitu-

tionally assigned function of fairly adjudicating cases and controversies.

We conclude that in creating the Sentencing Commission—an unusual hybrid in structure and authority—Congress neither delegated excessive legislative power nor upset the constitutionally mandated balance of powers among the coordinate Branches. The Constitution's structural protections do not prohibit Congress from delegating to an expert body located within the Judicial Branch the intricate task of formulating sentencing guidelines consistent with such significant statutory direction as is present here. Nor does our system of checked and balanced authority prohibit Congress from calling upon the accumulated wisdom and experience of the Judicial Branch in creating policy on a matter uniquely within the ken of judges. Accordingly, we hold that the Act is constitutional.

The judgment of United States District Court for the Western District of Missouri is affirmed.

It is so ordered.

Justice SCALIA, dissenting.

While the products of the Sentencing Commission's labors have been given the modest name "Guidelines," they have the force and effect of laws, prescribing the sentences criminal defendants are to receive. A judge who disregards them will be reversed. I dissent from today's decision because I can find no place within our constitutional system for an agency created by Congress to exercise no governmental power other than the making of laws.

Petitioner's most fundamental and far-reaching challenge to the Commission is that Congress' commitment of such broad policy responsibility to any institution is an unconstitutional delegation of legislative power. It is difficult to imagine a principle more essential to democratic government than that upon which the doctrine of unconstitutional delegation is founded: Except in a few areas constitutionally committed to the Executive Branch, the basic policy decisions governing society are to be made by the Legislature. . . .

But while the doctrine of unconstitutional delegation is unquestionably a fundamental element of our constitutional system, it is not an element readily enforceable by the courts. Once it is conceded, as it must be, that no statute can be entirely precise, and that some judgments, even some judgments involving policy considerations, must be left to the officers executing the law and to the judges applying it, the debate over unconstitutional delegation becomes a debate not over a point of principle but over a question of degree. . . .

In short, I fully agree with the Court's rejection of petitioner's contention that the doctrine of unconstitutional delegation of legislative authority has been violated because of the lack of intelligible, congressionally prescribed standards to guide the Commission.

Precisely because the scope of delegation is largely uncontrollable by the courts, we must be particularly rigorous in preserving the Constitution's structural restrictions that deter excessive delegation. The major one, it seems to me, is that the power to make law cannot be exercised by anyone other than Congress, except in conjunction with the lawful exercise of executive or judicial power.

The whole theory of *lawful* congressional "delegation" is not that Congress is sometimes too busy or too divided and can therefore assign its responsibility of making law to someone else; but rather that a certain degree of discretion, and thus of lawmaking, *inheres* in most executive or judicial action, and it is up to Congress, by the relative specificity or generality of its statutory commands, to determine—up to a point—how small or how large that degree shall be. . . .

. . . Strictly speaking, there is *no* acceptable delegation of legislative power. As John Locke put it almost 300 years ago, "[t]he power of the *legislative* being derived from the people by a positive voluntary grant and institution, can be no other, than what the positive grant conveyed, which be-

ing only to make laws, and not to make *legislators*, the *legislative* can have no power to transfer their authority of making laws, and place it in other hands." Or as we have less epigrammatically said: "That Congress cannot delegate legislative power to the President is a principle universally recognized as vital to the integrity and maintenance of the system of government ordained by the Constitution." In the present case, however, a pure delegation of legislative power is precisely what we have before us. It is irrelevant whether the standards are adequate, because they are not standards related to the exercise of executive or judicial powers; they are, plainly and simply, standards for further legislation.

The lawmaking function of the Sentencing Commission is completely divorced from any responsibility for execution of the law or adjudication of private rights under the law. . . .

The delegation of lawmaking authority to the Commission is, in short, unsupported by any legitimating theory to explain why it is not a delegation of legislative power. To disregard structural legitimacy is wrong in itself—but since structure has purpose, the disregard also has adverse practical consequences. In this case, as suggested earlier, the

---

Comparative Note 4.7

[The Solicitors Act of 1954, an Irish statute, authorized a disciplinary committee of the Incorporated Law Society to investigate complaints against solicitors and, if it found the complaints justified, to punish the offending attorney by forbidding him or her to practice law and, if appropriate, to order restitution of any property or money involved. In the extract below, the Irish Supreme Court considered the validity of the committee's proceedings.]

"Justice shall be administered in courts established by law by judges appointed in the manner provided by the Constitution. . . ." The corollary must be that justice is not to be administered by persons who are not judges appointed in the manner provided by the Constitution, save in those cases specially excluded by other provisions of the Constitution . . . Here we are dealing with a tribunal which depends for its existence and its powers on a legislative act of the State. If the effect of such legislation is to confer the power to administer justice on persons who are not regularly appointed as judges it is by Article 34 unconstitutional, unless it can be brought within some of the saving provisions of the Constitution. . . . From none of the pro-

nouncements as to the nature of judicial power which have been quoted can a definition at once exhaustive and precise be extracted, and probably no such definition can be framed. The varieties and combinations of powers with which the legislature may equip a tribunal are infinite, and in each case the particular powers must be considered in their totality and separately to see if a tribunal so endowed is invested with powers of such nature and extent that their exercise is in effect administering that justice which appertains to the judicial organ, and which the constitution indicates is properly entrusted only to judges. . . .

The power to strike a solicitor off the rolls is a "disciplinary" and "punitive" power. . . . It is a sanction of such severity that in its consequences it may be much more serious than a term of imprisonment. . . . The imposition of a penalty, which has such consequences, would seem to demand from those who impose it the qualities of impartiality, independence and experience which are required for the holder of a judicial office who, under the criminal law, imposes a fine or short sentence of imprisonment.

SOURCE: *In Re Solicitors Act* [1960] I.R. 239.

consequence is to facilitate and encourage judicially un-controllable delegation. Until our decision last Term in *Morrison v. Olson* [1988] . . . , it could have been said that Congress could delegate lawmaking authority only at the expense of increasing the power of either the President or the courts. Most often, as a practical matter, it would be the President, since the judicial process is unable to conduct the investigations and make the political assessments essential for most policymaking. Thus, the need for delegation would have to be important enough to induce Congress to aggrandize its primary competitor for political power, and the recipient of the policymaking authority, while not Congress itself, would at least be politically accountable. . . .

By reason of today's decision, I anticipate that Congress will find delegation of its lawmaking powers much more attractive in the future. If rulemaking can be entirely unrelated to the exercise of judicial or executive powers, I foresee all manner of "expert" bodies, insulated from the political process, to which Congress will delegate various portions of its lawmaking responsibility. How tempting to create an expert Medical Commission (mostly M.D.'s, with perhaps a few Ph.D.'s in moral philosophy) to dispose of such thorny, "no-win" political issues as the withholding of life-support systems in federally funded hospitals, or the use of fetal tissue for research. This is an undemocratic precedent that we set—not because of the scope of the delegated power, but because its recipient is not one of the three Branches of Government. The only governmental power the Commission possesses is the power to make law; and it is not the Congress.

Today's decision follows the regrettable tendency of our recent separation-of-powers jurisprudence . . . , to treat the Constitution as though it were no more than a generalized prescription that the functions of the Branches should not be commingled too much—how much is too much to be determined, case-by-case, by this Court. The Constitution is not that. Rather, as its name suggests, it is a prescribed structure, a framework, for the conduct of government. In designing that structure, the Framers themselves considered how much commingling was, in the generality of things, acceptable, and set forth their conclusions in the document. That is the meaning of the statements concerning acceptable commingling made by Madison in defense of the proposed Constitution, and now routinely used as an excuse for disregarding it. When he said, as the Court correctly quotes, that separation of powers "d[oes] not mean that these [three] departments ought to have no partial agency in, or no controul over the acts of each other," quoting *The Federalist* No. 47, his point was that the commingling specifically provided for in the structure that he and his colleagues had designed—the Presidential veto over legislation, the Senate's confirmation of executive and

judicial officers, the Senate's ratification of treaties, the Congress' power to impeach and remove executive and judicial officers—did not violate a proper understanding of separation of powers. He would be aghast, I think, to hear those words used as justification for ignoring that carefully designed structure so long as, in the changing view of the Supreme Court from time to time, "too much commingling" does not occur. Consideration of the degree of commingling that a particular disposition produces may be appropriate at the margins, where the outline of the framework itself is not clear; but it seems to me far from a marginal question whether our constitutional structure allows for a body which is not the Congress, and yet exercises no governmental powers except the making of rules that have the effect of laws.

I think the Court errs, in other words, not so much because it mistakes the degree of commingling, but because it fails to recognize that this case is not about commingling, but about the creation of a new Branch altogether, a sort of juniorvarsity Congress. It may well be that in some circumstances such a branch would be desirable; perhaps the agency before us here will prove to be so. But there are many desirable dispositions that do not accord with the constitutional structure we live under. And in the long run the improvisation of a constitutional structure on the basis of currently perceived utility will be disastrous.

I respectfully dissent from the Court's decision, and would reverse the judgment of the District Court.

Notes/Queries/Readings

1. Is Justice Blackmun's discussion of Congress's power to delegate authority compatible with the decisions in *Schechter* (1935) and *Chadha* (1983)?

2. Is the Sentencing Commission any more or less "necessary and proper" than the National Bank upheld in *McCulloch v. Maryland* (1819)? How does the presence of federal judges on the commission complicate its constitutionality?

3. Does Justice Scalia's opinion give new life to the nondelegation doctrine? What do you make of his admission that "while the doctrine of unconstitutional delegation is unquestionably a fundamental element of our constitutional system, it is not an element readily enforceable in the courts"? Does this mean that the principle has no utility in judicial decisionmaking? Or does Scalia suggest that the principle, although not directly enforceable, should influence how the Court assesses separation of powers more generally? Is Scalia employing structuralism as a method of constitutional interpretation?

4. Comparative Notes 4.5 and 4.7 include extracts from majority opinions on the Irish Supreme Court. Would *Mistretta* have been decided the same way in Ireland?

Chapter 5

Federalism and State Regulation

he Constitution created a *federal* system of government different from any other in history. Recall that the Framers met in Philadelphia to repair the defects of the Articles of Confederation. The Articles had combined the thirteen original states into little more than a league of friendship presided over by a Congress made up of sovereign and equal governments. Congress itself could not enact laws: its power was limited to passing resolutions and making financial requisitions, but only with the consent of at least nine of the thirteen states. No executive or judiciary existed to enforce its authority on recalcitrant states. Congress also lacked the power to regulate interstate commerce, one of the main reasons for the summoning of a new constitutional convention. Finally, any amendment to the Articles of Confederation required the unanimous consent of all thirteen states; constitutional change was thus a virtual impossibility.

It is important to bear in mind that particular federal arrangements are always predicated on different visions of the good life and the polity. The Articles of Confederation flow from the view that popular government begins and ends at the local and state levels, that the people are the best keepers of their own liberty, that good government depends on active and virtuous citizens rooted in the values and interests of their communities, and that a distant government unconnected to these values and interests is the very definition of despotism. These were powerful arguments on behalf of the government created by the Articles of Confederation, and they would surface again and again in debates over the adoption of a new constitution.[1]

The movement for a new constitutional convention was driven by a perceived need to transform the Confederation into a stronger federal union. The Framers were initially divided over the nature of the new federalism they set out to create. Two plans contested for initial acceptance in the Convention. The first, known as the Virginia Plan, proposed a radical reconstruction of the governmental system under the Articles of Confederation. More

---

[1] For a defense of the Articles of Confederation see Merrill Jensen, *The Articles of Confederation: An Interpretation of the Social-Constitutional History of the American Revolution 1774–1781* (Madison: University of Wisconsin Press, 1948).

national than federal in design, the plan would have established a government of the union with vastly increased powers, including the authority to veto state statutes deemed incompatible with national laws. To reduce the influence of the smaller states, the plan also called for the creation of a bicameral legislature, one house of which would be based on popular representation. The larger states tended to agree with this plan. The New Jersey Plan, on the other hand, would retain the basic "federal" design of the Confederation but remedy its most glaring defects. Although Congress would remain a single house with equal state representation, it would be granted enforceable lawmaking authority in the fields of taxation and commerce. To reinforce and carry out these powers, the plan proposed the establishment of a national supreme court and an executive council—albeit a relatively weak one—chosen by Congress.[2] Small states generally supported the New Jersey proposal.

The draft constitution that emerged from the Convention contained compromises between the New Jersey and Virginia plans (as well as other compromises between the northern and southern states). The proposed new government consisted of three independent and separate branches that would exercise the authority, among other powers, to levy and collect taxes, to make law, and to enforce its policies. Federal law, like the Constitution itself, would be supreme law and bind the judges and officials of every state. The states, however, would retain a crucial role in the national political process. They would enjoy equal representation in the Senate, figure prominently in the election of the president, retain dispositive authority over the process of amending the Constitution,[3] and reserve to themselves all powers not given to the national government.

In the end, the Framers discarded the Articles of Confederation in defiance of the existing order of constitutional legality. Hoping to create "a more perfect union" that would avoid the potential tyranny of a unitary government as well as an arrangement that would lead to further anarchy among sovereign and independent states, they established a broadly based national government that allowed the states to continue to take charge of their own affairs. The Founders thought this system of divided authority would contribute to the preservation of a republican form of government while avoiding the evils of pure majority rule at the national level. The states, on the other hand, retained their traditional political identities while preserving their own distinctive cultures, values, and institutions (including slavery).

Yet no person living in 1789 could have predicted how the new federal constitution would operate in practice, for this new federalism lacked clarity. In *Federalist* 39, James Madison rejected the anti-Federalist charge that the Constitution created a strictly *national* government.[4] He claimed that the Constitution was both national and federal, and he proceeded to develop a five-fold classification based on these two features. In its *foundation*, wrote Madison, the Constitution was a federal act; in the *source* of governmental power, it was partly federal and partly national; in the *operation* of these powers, it was national, not federal; in the *extent* of these powers, it was

---

[2] For a discussion of these plans, see Jack N. Rakove, *Original Meanings* (Lincoln and London: University of Nebraska Press, 1996), 57–93.

[3] As for the amendatory process, the Founders revised the rule of unanimity laid down in the Articles of Confederation. Under Article 7 nine states would be sufficient to ratify the new Constitution; similarly, Article 5 provides for amendment by a vote of three-fourths of the states. For a general discussion of the Convention's proceedings see Richard B. Morris, *The Forging of the Union: 1781–1789* (New York: Harper & Row Publishers, 1987), 267–97.

[4] Patrick Henry, among the Constitution's most vehement opponents, charged in the Virginia ratifying convention that the new government would be "one great consolidated empire," a monster wholly "incompatible with the genius of [American] republicanism." See Philip B. Kurland and Ralph Lerner, *The Founders' Constitution*, vol. I (Chicago: The University of Chicago Press, 1989), 289.

federal, not national; and in the *manner* of the amendatory power, it was neither wholly federal nor entirely national.[5] Madison's scheme may have been clear to him, but different understandings of what is national and what is federal emerged in the various state ratifying conventions, just as they would in judicial interpretations of the Constitution in the years and decades ahead.

As for judicial interpretation, the question arose early on whether the Supreme Court should limit its review of congressional laws allegedly interfering with the rights of the states under the Tenth Amendment. The following discussion of *McCulloch v. Maryland* (1819) shows that Marshall's broad interpretation of federal power won the day over Maryland's narrow interpretation. Yet, as we shall see, the Supreme Court has reserved to itself the power to strike down federal laws if they are deemed to violate the Tenth Amendment. The counterargument holds, on the basis of representational theory, that the Supreme Court ought not to strike down national laws on federalism grounds. The Court should stay its hand in such cases, runs the argument, because all the states are fully represented in the Congress and consequently are unlikely to vote against their own corporate interests.[6] These two argument often—not always—run parallel with different methods of constitutional interpretation. For example, the "plain words" of the Tenth Amendment approach tends to support the states in their arguments against the federal government, whereas "structuralism" or the "fully represented" in Congress approach tends to support the view of federal supremacy.

Enumerated, Implied, and Reserved Powers

As Chief Justice John Marshall noted repeatedly in *McCulloch v. Maryland* [1819, reprinted later in the chapter], the national government is one of enumerated powers, whereas under the Tenth Amendment all other powers "not delegated to the United States by the Constitution, nor prohibited by it to the States, are reserved to the States respectively, or to the people."[7] This formal distribution of power has been the subject of interpretive disagreement throughout American history. The elusive boundary between federal and state power demanded by the Constitution's broad language would not permit any final definition. As Marshall emphasized in *McCulloch*, if the Constitution were "to endure for ages to come [and] to be adapted to the various *crises* of human affairs," the authority of the national government would have to be broadly construed. Marshall's approach prevailed over the long term. But as *New York v. United States* (1992, reprinted later in the chapter) and *U.S. Term Limits, Inc. v. Thornton* (1995, reprinted later in the chapter) show, the historic debate over the reach of federal and state authority continues unabated today.

Marshall's Nationalism

The Supreme Court's contribution to our understanding of the nation-state relationship may begin with Marshall's opinion in *McCulloch v. Maryland* (1819). In that case, Marshall sustained the constitutionality of the Second Bank of the United States. Per-

---

[5] *The Federalist* (New York: Barnes & Noble, 1996), 282–85.

[6] This argument is vigorously advanced in Jesse Choper, *Judicial Review and the National Political Process* (Chicago: The University of Chicago Press, 1984).

[7] In Madison's formulation, the proposed constitution would extend federal authority to "certain enumerated objects only, [leaving] to the several States a residual and inviolable sovereignty over all other objects." Supra note 5, at 285. Among the enumerated objects that the federal government would control were matters of national importance such as interstate and foreign commerce, monetary policy, weights and measures, foreign affairs, postal administration, and the maintenance of an army and navy.

haps *McCulloch*'s most notable feature is the theory of the federal union that Marshall advanced to defeat Maryland's claim that the Constitution represented a *compact* among sovereign and independent states. In his reading of the preamble, Marshall claimed that the Constitution "emanated" from "we the people of the United States" and not from an agreement among the states acting in their sovereign capacities. In rejecting the compact theory of the Constitution, Marshall concluded that "the government of the Union . . . is emphatically, and truly, a government of the people." Hence, no one state containing a fraction of the people can disassemble what all the people in the assembled Congress have ordained in a duly passed and promulgated statute.[8]

Marshall's "emanation" theory of the Constitution helped to expand and solidify the principle of national supremacy, but it was unnecessary to justify the theory of implied power for which *McCulloch* is so famous. By examining the words and structure of the Constitution, and aided by the magnetic force of his own rhetoric, Marshall set out to show that even in the absence of any express language conferring on the national government the power to incorporate a national bank, Congress was nevertheless empowered to do so. In one of Marshall's most unforgettable passages, he reminded the world that "it is a *constitution* we are expounding"—a document that limits itself to marking government's "great outlines" and "important objects." Among these important objects—or express powers—is the power to tax and borrow money "on the due execution of which the happiness and prosperity of the nation so vitally depends." Any government entrusted with these powers, said the Chief Justice, must have "ample means for their execution" so long as they consist with the letter and spirit of the Constitution.

Note Marshall's reference to the letter and *spirit* of the Constitution. Is there any significant limit to the judgment of an interpreter who feels required to appeal to the spirit—or, for that matter, the structure—of the Constitution in his or her search for an answer to a specific constitutional problem? The question ties in to our treatment of interpretive methodology in chapter 2. Yet Marshall had it both ways. The broad construction of federal power, he noted, was fully consistent with textualism, for the last in the list of powers expressly delegated to Congress in Article 1, Section 8, is that of making "all laws which shall be necessary and proper, for carrying into execution the foregoing powers, and all other powers vested by this constitution in the government of the United States, or in any department thereof." Maryland had argued for a strict interpretation of the clause (i.e., the means must be *absolutely* necessary to carry out an express power.) But Marshall parried that thrust by a broad interpretation of the "necessary and proper" clause—which included an expansive definition of the word "necessary"—an approach that reinforced his conclusion that the national bank was an appropriate means for Congress to carry out its taxing and borrowing power.

Having established the bank's validity, Marshall proceeded to declare unconstitutional Maryland's tax on the operations of the federal bank within its borders. No state, he wrote, is empowered to deploy its taxing authority for the purpose of undermining or destroying a federal instrumentality. In the course of his argument, Marshall conceded that the power to tax "is essential to the very existence of [a state] government" and may be exercised to the utmost extent over persons and property within the state. "The only security against the abuse of this power," said Marshall, "is found in the structure of [state] government itself." But a state's right to tax the federal government cannot validly be "given by the people of a particular State." This power can only

---

[8]Marshall was not the first to advance the emanation theory of the Constitution. He borrowed heavily from John Jay's opinion in *Chisholm v. Georgia*, 2 U.S. (Dall.) 419 (1793), discussed in chapter 3.

reside in "the people of the United States, [in] a government whose laws, made in pursuance of the constitution, are declared to be supreme and thus binding on all the states." Thus, *McCulloch* provided an early definition of the boundary between federal and state governments.

Dual Federalism and Judicial Dualism

By 1836, one year after Marshall's death, Roger B. Taney assumed the office of chief justice. Taney, an ardent opponent of the Bank of the United States and staunch defender of states' rights, presided over a Court which by now was dominated by appointees of Andrew Jackson. Since the Jacksonians were known to loathe the memory of Marshall, the old Federalists—now called Whigs—feared that the new appointees would proceed to dismantle the jurisprudential structure that Marshall had built over the previous three decades. To the surprise of the anti-Jacksonians, however, the Taney Court did not mount a constitutional revolution against the principles of Marshallian nationalism. Instead, the Taney Court vigorously affirmed the residual authority of the states—thus local majorities—to regulate their own internal affairs, a doctrinal focus that Marshall himself had sanctioned in *Gibbons v. Ogden* (1824, reprinted in chapter 6). *Gibbons* drew a bright line between interstate commerce, which Congress is empowered to regulate, and the "completely internal commerce of a state" which, Marshall proclaimed, "may be considered as reserved for the state itself" under its general police power. (See the upcoming section entitled "Local Power over Commerce.")

In its assertion of judicial power, the Taney Court was no less active than Marshall's Court. But the Court would now use its power on behalf of states' rights and local interests. Taney's Court won broad public support in sustaining the validity of local legislation designed to curtail private monopolies and provide for the public welfare.[9] But when the Court entered the slavery controversy, it was swept into the eye of a political hurricane. *Dred Scott v. Sandford* (1857), as we saw in chapter 3, was the first case since *Marbury* to declare an act of Congress unconstitutional, but *Dred Scott* invalidated a national law on the basis of a theory of dual sovereignty that Marshall had rejected in *McCulloch*. In proclaiming that the United States is a "union of states, sovereign and independent," Taney revived the compact theory of the Constitution. *Ableman v. Booth* (1859), decided two years after *Dred Scott*, plunged the Court into further disrepute. When compared to *Scott*, this amounted to what Robert McCloskey called a "peculiar transvaluation of values,"[10] for *Ableman* upheld the constitutionality of a federal law—the Fugitive Slave Act—and upbraided Wisconsin for defying it.[11]

While the Civil War abolished slavery and gave birth to the Fourteenth Amendment—which nullified the *Dred Scott* decision—it failed to erode the power of the

---

[9]See, for example, *Mayor of the City of New York v. Miln*, 36 U.S. (11 Pet.) 102 (1837) and *Charles River Bridge v. Warren*, 36 U.S. (11 Pet.) 420 (1837). See also the *License* Cases, 46 U.S. (5 How.) 504 (1847).

[10]Robert G. McCloskey, *The American Supreme Court*, 2d ed., Rev. by Sanford Levinson (Chicago: University of Chicago Press, 1994), 63. "Ableman, a Milwaukee editor, had assisted a fugitive slave to escape from federal custody, and was therefore arrested for violation of the national Fugitive Slave Law. The Wisconsin Supreme Court ordered him released on a writ of habeas corpus, and the order was obeyed. However, the national government then appealed to the Supreme Court of the United States, which held that the state courts had no business to interfere with the conduct of federal law and that the Fugitive Slave Law was constitutional." *Ibid.*

[11]*Ableman v. Booth*, 62 U.S. (21 How.) 506 (1959). The Fugitive Slave Act required the states to cooperate in returning runaway slaves to their states of origin.

Supreme Court in the American governmental process. *Texas v. White* (1869) and *The Slaughterhouse Cases* (1873) helped to revive dual federalism. *Texas* affirmed the principle of the Union's "perpetuity" and "indissolubility"—the position championed by Lincoln in his First Inaugural Address (see Appendix C)—while stating that "the Constitution in all its provisions, looks to an indestructible Union, composed of indestructible States."[12] The statement was ironic because *Texas*'s effect was to uphold the power of the national government to deprive the state of its representation in Congress and to place its people under military rule. Still, the phrase about "indestructible states" could be exploited in the future for the purpose of defending state sovereignty as much as the nation's supremacy, as Justice O'Connor's opinion in the 1992 opinion of *New York v. United States* (discussed later in the chapter) shows.

Even *Slaughterhouse* celebrated the "indestructibility" of the states by exhibiting a narrow view of national "privileges and immunities" within the meaning of the Fourteenth Amendment. As noted in much greater detail in chapter 8, the Fourteenth Amendment—and the Thirteenth and Fifteenth Amendments, as well—resulted in a revolutionary shift of power from the states to the national government. Yet, in declining to place the general rights of citizenship under the protection of the United States government—even in the face of what appeared to be the clear purpose of the Fourteenth Amendment—*Slaughterhouse* simply refused to tolerate "so great a departure from the structure and spirit of our institutions, when the effect is to fetter and degrade the State governments by subjecting them to the control of Congress [in matters] of the most ordinary and fundamental character."[13] One of the lessons of *Slaughterhouse* is that the interpreter of a constitutional provision may be as important, if not more so, than the writer.

The theory of dual federalism flourished between 1870 and 1937, particularly in a series of reciprocal tax immunity cases, as well as in the Supreme Court's rejection of congressional efforts to regulate such matters as manufacturing, agricultural production, labor management relations, and minimum wages and maximum hours of labor—to name just four examples. The intergovernmental tax cases stood for the principle that a state government and its instrumentalities were as immune from federal taxation as the federal government was from state taxation.[14] Beginning in 1905, however, the Court would steadily narrow state immunity by upholding federal taxes on various state enterprises.[15] The Court also nullified numerous federal laws for infringing upon state sovereignty, decisions easily reached by its narrow interpretation of the federal commerce power. By 1937, however, the Court found that it could no longer realistically hold to a theory of dual federalism within the context of changing economic conditions. The Court would now follow rather than resist the coalition of forces that would push the principle of national supremacy to its limits.

---

[12] In 1866, the postwar military government of Texas initiated an original action in the Supreme Court to reclaim federal bonds that the state had seized after seceding from the Union. The bondholders argued that since Texas was not then a *state* in any constitutional sense, Texas was disabled from invoking the Supreme Court's original jurisdiction. See *Texas v. White*, 74 (7 Wall.) 700 (1869).

[13] *The Slaughterhouse Cases*, 83 U.S. (16 Wall.) 36 (1873).

[14] See, e.g., *Collector v. Day*, 78 U.S. (11 Wall.) 113 (1871), holding that Congress could not tax the salary of a state judge.

[15] See, e.g., *South Carolina v. United States*, 199 U.S. 437 (1905), sustaining a federal tax on South Carolina's liquor-dispensing business; *Graves v. New York*, 306 U.S. 466 (1939), upholding a federal tax on the salaries of state officials; and *New York v. United States*, 326 U.S. 572 (1946), upholding a federal tax on New York's sale of bottled mineral water. By 1988, the Supreme Court had even found that interest earned on unregistered long-term state and local government bonds did not violate the Tenth Amendment.

The Revival of Implied Limits on Federal Power

As the previous discussion suggests, constitutional cases usually mirror the shifts that have taken place in the balance of power between federal and state governments. These shifts have occurred over very long periods of time. From the 1870s to 1936 the states managed their affairs as if they were as fully supreme in their own sphere of authority as the federal government was in its sphere. In the six decades since 1936, starting with the New Deal, the country witnessed a massive transfer of responsibility from the states to the national level. The Supreme Court endorsed this transfer—at first hesitantly but later willingly—by refusing to review the balance of power that the states and nation managed to forge in the political realm. It would be difficult to argue that the constitutional text dictated juridical theories of either dual federalism or national supremacy. Both theories seemed perfectly compatible with a text read in the light of changing social and economic circumstances. The judicial shift also represents changing understandings within the Court about the limits of judicial power and whether the Court shall oversee the relationship between states and the national government.

In the 1990s the pendulum began swinging back toward state power, both on and off the Court. The political shift toward decentralization found its most compelling symbol in a national law returning primary responsibility for welfare to the states, a development foreshadowed by the "new federalism" of the Reagan administration and the sweeping rebellion against centralized government that burst forth upon the nation in the early 1990s. Judicial signs of this change showed up even earlier in *National League of Cities v. Usery* (1976). The overruling of *Usery* nine years later in *Garcia v. San Antonio Metropolitan Transit Authority* (1985) was not enough to stop the justices from seriously rethinking aspects of American federalism thought to have been long settled. Landmark cases such as *New York v. United States* (1992, reprinted later in the chapter) and *U. S. Term Limits, Inc. v. Thornton* (1996, reprinted later in the chapter) echoed the clarion call of a budding states' rights movement.[16]

New York featured a challenge to a federal statute that made the states accountable for the disposal of radioactive wastes produced within their borders. In revisiting the Tenth Amendment, the Court found that while Congress may employ various *incentives* to encourage the states to meet federal guidelines in disposing of waste material, it may not *compel* them to adopt a particular waste disposal system. Even while accepting a broad view of Congress's power under the commerce and spending clauses, *New York* rings with the language of states' rights. Like *Thornton*, *New York* recalls the debates over state sovereignty in the Philadelphia and state ratifying conventions. *New York* also contains echoes from the words and phrases of constitutional cases going back to the nation's beginning, an example of which is the refrain in *Texas v. White* (1869) that the United States is "an indestructible Union, composed of *indestructible states*" (emphasis added).

The decision in *Thornton*, on the other hand, seemed to be a setback for the states' rights movement. It declared unconstitutional an amendment to Arkansas' constitution limiting the number of terms that members of the state's congressional delegation could serve. Adopted directly by the voters, the amendment limited members of the House to three terms (six years) and members of the Senate to two terms (twelve

---

[16]*Usery* (1976) and *Garcia* (1985) are reprinted in chapter 6. *Gregory v. Ashcroft* (1991), *United States v. Lopez* (1995), and *Seminole Tribe of Florida v. Florida* (1996) are just a few of the "decentralizing" cases that might have been mentioned along with *New York* (1992) and *Thornton* (1996). Chapter 6 also reprints and discusses the *Lopez* case. For a discussion of *Seminole Tribe*, see the introduction to chapter 3.

years). By a five to four vote, the Court nullified these provisions under constitutional clauses (Art. 1, sec. 2, cl. 1 and Art. 1, sec. 3, cl. 3), which base eligibility for service in Congress on age, citizenship, and residency. "The right to choose representatives," declared the five justices in the majority, "belongs not to the States, but to the people," for "the Constitution creates a uniform national body representing the interests of a single people." Thus, neither Congress nor the states may alter or add to the criteria for service in the House or Senate except through a constitutional amendment.

For present purposes, however, *Thornton* is less notable for its nationlist outcome than for the debate inside the Court over the nature of the federal union. The justices staged a reenactment of the old conflict between the Federalists and anti-Federalists involving many of the interpretive and normative questions highlighted in this casebook. Relying on its decision in *Powell v. McCormack* (1969),[17] the Court started out with a detailed analysis of the original history and text of the qualification clauses. When considered in light of "the basic principles of our democratic system"—as validated in the majority's mind by congressional experience, state practice, and the Constitution's structure—these clauses compel the conclusion that the stated qualifications may not be changed in the absence of a constitutional amendment. The justices in the minority, on the other hand, countered with their own interpretation of the Constitution's structure and democratic principles. They found that in the absence of any constitutional language preventing the states from adopting additional standards of eligibility on congressional candidates, the *people* of the various states are entitled to prescribe standards as they wish. The dissenters dusted off cases such as *McCulloch v. Maryland* (1819) and *Gibbons v. Ogden* (1824) in an effort to reveal their essential meaning for rediscovering the proper line between federal and state authority today. And no fewer than four justices appear to have adopted a modified version of the compact theory when they insisted that the federal government created by the Constitution represents an agreement of the people *of the states* and not, as Marshall insisted, an emanation of the people of the *United States*. The Court seems to be back where it started two hundred years ago, which is perhaps a way of saying that Americans are united by their common embrace of a document whose principles lend themselves to perpetual disagreement in interpretation.

Local Power over Commerce

The cases discussed in this subsection stand on their own, but they are best read in light of *Gibbons v. Ogden* (1824) and the commerce clause cases concerning congressional power (see chapter 6.) *Gibbons*, it may suffice to note, invoked the Constitution's supremacy clause to strike down New York's state-granted steamboat monopoly because it clashed with a federal licensing statute regulating trade and transportation in the coastal waters of the United States. However, the cases discussed later in this chapter, unlike *Gibbons*, involve judicial challenges to state laws in the absence of any conflicting or parallel national legislation—that is, when the federal commerce power remains unexercised or lies in its so-called "dormant" or negative state. One compelling issue is whether the negative or dormant commerce clause authorizes the federal judiciary to nullify state legislation affecting commerce. (After all, it is sometimes remarked, the Constitution empowers Congress, not the courts, to regulate commerce.) In addition, as we shall see, the cases raise critical issues of democratic theory.

---

[17] *Powell v. McCormack*, 395 U.S. 486 (1969).

Arizona v. Southern Pacific Co. (1945) illustrates problems of judicial roles and democratic theory. Out of a legitimate concern for public safety, the state passed a law limiting the length of trains passing over its territory. States pass laws of this kind all the time, usually for a legitimate public purpose. Other examples are laws or ordinances punishing fraudulent business practices, enacting speed limits on public highways, prohibiting the sale of harmful products, and protecting the privacy of home owners against door-to-door sales pitches. As with the train-length statute, there is often no federal legislation on these issues. This absence of regulation might be taken as a sign that Congress does not want to deal with them or prefers that they be handled by the states, even though Congress could, at any time, enter the field and pass supervening legislation.

The *Arizona* Court found that the state's train-length law constituted an excessive burden on interstate commerce and thus violated the negative commerce clause. Dissenting, Justice Black made the case for judicial abstention on grounds of democratic theory. Judicial review of Arizona's law—and statutes like it—he suggested, turns the Court into a "superlegislature" by enmeshing it in public policy and factual issues concerning which it has little or no competence. "A century and a half of constitutional history and government admonishes this Court," he wrote, "to leave that choice to the elected legislative representatives or the people themselves, where it properly belongs on democratic principles and the requirements of efficient government." He might also have emphasized the argument cited earlier in this chapter: if state law does burden commerce excessively, Congress is able to enact corrective legislation. In that case, a national majority would validly replace the decision of a local majority without any outside interference by an electorally unaccountable judiciary.

Black's theory of popular democracy is compelling, but it also invites misgivings equally rooted in democratic theory, as *City of Philadelphia v. New Jersey* (1978, reprinted later in the chapter) suggests. It also overlooks the complicated history of negative commerce clause analysis as represented by *Gibbons v. Ogden* and *Cooley v. Board of Wardens* (1857, reprinted later in the chapter) as well as modern cases like *Arizona v. Southern Pacific.*

We will begin with a brief history. Two theories of the commerce clause contested for judicial approval at the time of *Gibbons.* One theory—the exclusive power theory—held that the affirmative grant of power to the national government to regulate interstate commerce was intended to give Congress sole authority over the nation's commercial life, banishing the state from any regulation of this realm. The other—the concurrent power theory—held that the states enjoyed coextensive authority with Congress to regulate all aspects of commerce within their borders not expressly denied to them by the Constitution. For practical reasons, *Gibbons* rejected both positions: the first because Congress could not be expected—and might not want—to regulate all aspects of interstate commerce, the second because the idea of a common market implicit in the commerce clause could easily be thwarted by varying state regulations. The exclusive power theory, it was argued in some circles, would have disabled the states from regulating aspects of commerce in the public interest in the event of any congressional refusal to deal with a local threat to commerce. On the other hand, giving the states a free hand to regulate their internal commerce might have led to the kind of "balkanized" economy that the commerce clause was designed to prevent. (Whether this reasoning accorded with reality is a question that deserves more attention than it has received.)

Gibbons broadly interpreted the federal commerce power to include the regulation of navigation within a state if it embraced the transportation of goods and persons across state lines. At the same time, however, Marshall affirmed the state's right to control its exclusively internal commerce and even to police the importation of goods from other states when necessary to protect the health and welfare of its people. Marshall drew a bright line between the federal commerce power and the state's police power—the general power to enact laws for the safety, comfort, and well being of the members of society. In short, the nature of the power exercised would determine its validity: only Congress could exercise the commerce power, only the states could exercise the police power. Once it was determined that New York had regulated interstate commerce—a federal prerogative—in violation of a federal statute, the case was at an end.

The question *Gibbons* left open is whether, in the absence of federal law, the states may regulate aspects of commerce that Congress could regulate through legislation. This question is at the heart of *Cooley v. Board of Wardens* (1857) and ultimately all negative commerce clause cases. *Cooley* showed that *Gibbons* did not determine what aspects of commerce the states may regulate when Congress's power remains unexercised, a silence that arms the Court with an enormous interpretive range as well as potential for doctrinal development. Accordingly, *Cooley*'s analytical focus shifted from an emphasis on the origin of the power exercised—i.e., the commerce power or the police power—to the nature of the particular subject regulated. The Court in *Cooley* found that the states may regulate a subject of interstate commerce in the silence of Congress when the subject lends itself to diverse legislation at the local level. But if the nature of the subject is one that requires a uniform system of regulation throughout the nation, only Congress can legislate on it. This has become known as the *Cooley* rule.

Arizona and *Philadelphia* continued the elusive search for the limits on state power over commerce when Congress's power remains dormant. Because in many situations *Cooley* provided no guidance on which subjects of commerce required uniform regulation, its rule was as defective as *Gibbons* in divining these limits. *Arizona* represents the modern balancing—or doctrinal—approach to dormant commerce clause analysis. The Court seeks now to weigh the benefits of legitimate—and in this case nondiscriminatory—state legislation against the burden it imposes on interstate commerce. If in the Court's judgment the burden on commerce is excessive relative to the local benefit, the state law will usually be struck down.[18] Furthermore, if a state law discriminates directly against interstate commerce by a regulatory—or tax—measure that prefers local over out-of-state businesses or markets, it is presumptively unconstitutional. Under this broad formula, the Court will strike the regulation unless the state can show that the public purpose advanced by the statute could not have been promoted by some other means with a lesser impact on commerce. Whether the Supreme Court is more competent to make such an empirical judgment than a state legislature would seem to be an open question.

From the perspective of democratic theory, however, discriminatory state legislation is constitutionally objectionable because out-of-state concerns lack representation in the legislature, thus putting them at a competitive disadvantage. In short, the

---

[18] *Pike v. Bruce Church, Inc.*, which involved an Arizona law requiring certain fruits to be crated and packaged according to the state's standards before being shipped out of state, includes this classic statement of the Court's present analytical approach: "Where the [local] statute regulates even-handedly to effectuate a legitimate local public interest, and its effects on interstate commerce are only incidental, it will be upheld unless the burden imposed on such commerce is clearly excessive in relation to the putative local benefits. . . . If a legitimate local purpose is found, then the question becomes one of degree. And the extent of the burden that will be tolerated will of course depend on the nature of the local interest involved, and on whether it could be promoted as well with a lesser impact on interstate activities." See 397 U.S. 137 (1970).

Court will use its power to oversee the state legislative process to guard against discrimination without representation. But as *Dean Milk Company v. City of Madison* shows,[19] even these cases divide the Court. *Dean Milk* involved a Madison, Wisconsin ordinance that prohibited the sale of milk in the city unless it was pasteurized and bottled at approved plants within five miles of the city's center. A majority of the justices concluded that the statute discriminated against an Illinois milk producer simply because its pasteurization plants were located outside Wisconsin. The Court recognized the valid public purpose behind the ordinance but found that Madison could have protected its citizens against contaminated milk by a less restrictive means. Justice Black, along with Justices Douglas and Minton, disagreed with the Court's reasoning and judgment. Finding that Dean Milk could easily have complied with Madison's ordinance without excessive expense or strain, he deplored this judicial interference "merely because the Court believes that alternative milk-inspection methods might insure the cleanliness and healthfulness of Dean's Illinois milk."

The Court's characterization of New Jersey's Waste Control Act as discriminatory in *City of Philadelphia v. New Jersey* (1978) also poses difficult questions of fact and value. It also shows more clearly the close relations between issues of policy and constitutionality. Apart from Justice Rehnquist's dissent—which is mainly a doctrinal disagreement with the majority—the case prompts inquiry into the costs and benefits of the state statute. How does the Court measure the burdens on out-of-state waste producers and in-state landfill operators against the benefits falling to out-of-state landfill operators and in-state waste producers? What is the degree of the burden on interstate commerce relative to New Jersey's interest in protecting its environment? Equally crucial is whether the continuing availability of New Jersey landfills resulting from *Philadelphia* will postpone the development of new waste disposal technologies in northeastern urban centers. On the other hand, might the Court's ruling have prompted Congress to substitute its own rules on waste disposal for those of the states? (The national government did eventually get into the picture, as we saw earlier in the case of *New York v. United States*.)

Preemption and Comity

Preemption

Dormant commerce clause analysis attempts to determine whether a state law conflicts with the commerce clause of the Constitution. The issue posed in *Pacific Gas & Electric v. Energy Resources* (1983, reprinted later in the chapter), however, is a related one: when and under what circumstances should federal law supercede (preempt) state law on the same subject? One can think of numerous issues over which both the nation and the state have concurrent authority. Speed limit laws provide an example. Suppose in the interest of highway safety and fuel conservation, Congress passes a national speed limit law of sixty-five miles an hour on all interstate highways. (Surely Congress possesses that power under the commerce clause.) Suppose in turn that a state promulgates a fifty-five mile limit on such highways within its borders, an exercise of the local police power the legitimacy and substantiality of which is beyond dispute. Finally, suppose a trucking company challenges the state's speed limit on the ground that the federal regulation supercedes the state rule. The company, by the way, might also allege that the state rule violates the commerce clause. Who wins in such a case?

---

[19] 340 U.S. 349 (1951).

As *Pacific Gas* shows, who wins depends largely on the purpose behind the federal legislation. If Congress makes clear its purpose to legislate *exclusively* on a given subject, then the states are barred from enforcing their own rules on that subject. On the other hand, even conflicting state legislation may be enforced if Congress expressly permits it. If, however, Congress's intent is unclear, the Court will usually examine the structure and purpose of the federal statute to see whether it preempts a parallel state law.

Well-established judicial doctrines are available for determining whether federal preemption obtains in a specific situation. One is whether the scheme of federal regulation is so *pervasive* as to exclude by implication any coextensive state regulation. Another doctrine is whether the federal interest in a given subject is so *dominant* as to exclude the enforcement of the state legislation. Finally, state law is preempted if it cannot be enforced without simultaneously violating federal law. In *Pacific Gas*, the Court concluded that the Atomic Energy Act preempts all state safety regulations dealing with the construction and operation of nuclear power plants, but that California's moratorium on the certification of nuclear power plants was not preempted because economic rather than safety concerns were at the basis of the state statute.[20] Perhaps what this and similar decisions show is the importance of constitutional structure in facilitating collaboration between national and state government.

Federal-State Comity

Most disputes between state and federal governments do not end in litigation before the Supreme Court. The cases featured in this chapter may therefore misrepresent the character of federal-state relationships in the United States. In all areas of public policy, most of these relationships are cooperative rather than conflictual. When conflicts do occur, they are usually resolved by negotiation and compromise. Teamwork, as suggested, is the *modus operandi*, particularly in such fields as education, crime control, road building, airport construction, environmental protection, and the development of nuclear power. Perhaps the most prominent examples of such cooperation are federal grants-in-aid to the states for the purpose of assisting them in caring for the needs of the poor, the disabled, and the unemployed. A full description of these cooperative federal-state arrangements in the United States would fill a large volume.

Where the Supreme Court has had to *insist* on federal-state cooperation—or comity—is in the area of judicial relations. Judicial federalism, as it is sometimes called, requires the federal courts to abstain from interfering with pending state judicial proceedings even when they involve allegations of a constitutional violation. A federal lawsuit to stop a prosecution in a state court is a serious matter. Accordingly, *Younger*

---

[20] A more recent preemption case involved several 1986 amendments to the Occupational Safety and Health Act (OSHA), directing the secretary of labor to promulgate federal standards for licensing workers who handle hazardous wastes. In 1988, the Illinois legislature enacted a licensing statute of its own for such workers and their supervisors. In addition to adopting training standards similar to the federal regulation, Illinois required applicants for a hazardous waste crane operator's permit to submit a certified record showing that they had operated the equipment to be used in hazardous waste handling for a minimum of 4,000 hours. A waste disposal trade association asked a federal court for a declaratory judgment that OSHA preempted the Illinois statute. After examining the structure and purpose of OSHA, the Supreme Court concluded that without the secretary of labor's approval of a supplementary state plan, the federal statute preempts all of the state's safety and health standards on the issue of hazardous waste disposal, whether or not they conflict with the federal standards. See *Gade v. National Solid Wastes Management Association*, 505 U.S. 88 (1992).

v. Harris (1971, reprinted later in the chapter) laid down the doctrine of abstention. Prior to *Younger*, federal courts often issued injunctions, especially in criminal cases, to halt state court proceedings. Federal courts would intervene on the grounds that state courts were prosecuting defendants under unconstitutional statutes.[21] This practice caused a great deal of friction between federal and state courts; state judges resented the assumption that they could not be trusted to protect rights secured by the United States Constitution. Rejecting the assumption behind the practice, Justice Black invoked the principle of "comity" to limit the ability of federal courts to interfere with state criminal proceedings. In Black's view, this was a constitutional requirement stemming from "a proper respect for state functions" and the principles of "our federalism."[22]

The Court did not, however, limit the abstention doctrine to injunctions in pending criminal trials. The doctrine has since been applied to civil proceedings in state courts, to declaratory judgments in pending state cases, to injunctions against state and local executive officials, and to state administrative proceedings if important state interests are at stake.[23] We may note in passing that these rulings supplement the Anti-Injunction Act of 1948, which provides that federal courts may not grant an injunction to stay proceedings in a state court unless they are expressly authorized to do so by an act of Congress. What *Younger* and its progeny have done is to create a separate and independent barrier to federal court injunctions rooted in the constitutional principle of comity.

Comity is a cherished constitutional value because it has to do with our preferred understanding about the nature of politics. Politics is—or should be—a cooperative enterprise, one that resolves disagreement through compromise or the harmonization of interests rather than by edict or judicial decree. The object of politics, which is built into the architecture of the Constitution, is political integration, which comes about through trust and mutual accommodation. This seems to be what the Supreme Court is telling Americans when it decides cases such as *Younger*.

Interstate Comity

Several provisions of the Constitution require the states to treat each other with courtesy and comity to create solidarity and friendship among the states. These provisions include the full faith and credit clause, the privileges and immunities clause, and the extradition clause, all of which appear in Article 4 of the Constitution. (The fugitive slave clause, which required the states to return escaped slaves to their states of origin on the demand of their owners, was repealed by the Thirteenth Amendment.) The full faith and credit clause, which obliges each state to recognize the "public acts, records, and judicial proceedings of every other state," is mentioned here because it

---

[21] The case of *Dombrowski v. Pfister*, 380 U.S. 479 (1965), which Justice Black frequently cites, held that federal courts were empowered to enjoin state court prosecutions under overbroad statutes violative of the First Amendment. Erwin Chemerinsky writes: "Following *Dombrowski*, hundreds of cases were filed in federal courts seeking injunctions of state court proceedings." See *Federal Jurisdiction*, 2d ed. (Boston: Little, Brown and Company, 1994), 718. *Younger* sought to stop this process.

[22] There are of course exceptions to the *Younger* rule. As Justice Stewart remarked in his concurring opinion, the *Younger* rule would not apply where the continuance of the state proceeding would pose a threat of irreparable injury "both great and immediate." 401 U. S. 37, 56 (1965) Such a threat might be present in the face of a statute that is clearly unconstitutional or in the presence of a judge or jury who are clearly biased.

[23] See *Samuels v. Mackell*, 401 U.S. 66 (1971), *Penzoil Co. v. Texaco, Inc.*, 481 U.S. 1 (1987), and *Ohio Civil Rights Comm'n. v. Dayton Christian Schools*, 477 U.S. 619 (1986).

has been invoked recently in connection with same-sex marriages. If a state grants a marriage license to a gay or lesbian couple, must that license be recognized by a state that refuses to permit such unions? (This issue, incidentally, is likely to be litigated in light of the Defense of Marriage Act, passed by Congress in 1996.)

The notion of "comity" also stands in the background of constitutional provisions on interstate relations. Comity, however, implies courtesy, deference, and mutual respect rather than obligation. The purpose of the provisions mentioned in the previous paragraph was to foster solidarity among the states, and it was expected that this would occur voluntarily. Yet the principle of comity does strain against a persistent fear in the United States that *too much* accommodation among the states threatens national unity, a fear reflected in the founding debates, in the constitutional structure (e.g., the supremacy clause and the Fourteenth Amendment), and in cases like *Cohens v. Virginia* (1821) and *McCulloch v. Maryland* (1819).

The case reprinted in this chapter—*Baldwin v. Montana Fish and Game Commission* (1978)—deals with the privileges and immunities clause of Article 4. The clause provides that "the citizens of each state shall be entitled to all privileges and immunities of citizens in the several states." (The term "citizen" has been held to include any legal resident of a state.) A simple example of the comity required by the clause will suffice. If Wisconsin allows its own citizens to buy and sell scarce property around its northern lakes, it must extend this privilege to any resident of Illinois or New York. Even though Wisconsin would like to reserve these choice lands for its own residents and keep the price of such property from skyrocketing because of the invasion of wealthy out-of-state residents who are buying up these properties, to deny nonresidents the right to purchase land would be unconstitutional. Similarly, Wisconsin could not refuse a sturgeon fishing license to out-of-state residents while licensing its own residents to spear sturgeon during the one month—February—in which such fishing is allowed. If it wished, the state could probably ban sturgeon fishing altogether for the purpose of conserving the sturgeon population, but the policy would have to be applied equally to all persons.

In *Baldwin*, however, Montana did not deny a game license to out-of-state residents; the state simply charged them more for it. The case is important for its clarification of the nature and scope of the privileges and immunities clause. The Court divided over the constitutionality of Montana's elk-hunting license policy, but all the justices agreed that the states are permitted to favor their own citizens with respect to privileges such as voting and running for political office. Another good example of a privilege a state may deny to an out-of-state resident is the right to attend its institutions of higher education. Even if out-of-state students are accepted, as they are, for example, at distinguished state universities in states such as Michigan, Wisconsin, California, or Virginia, the state may impose substantially higher tuition rates on out-of-state residents. As the standard of judgment mentioned by Justice Brennan in his *Baldwin* dissent would seem to suggest, this practice is probably justified by the fact that it advances a substantial state interest, namely, that of preserving its limited educational resources for its own residents whose taxes and sacrifices have made these resources possible.

Another problem of interstate comity to reach the Supreme Court in recent years stems from state residency requirements related to employment. *New Hampshire v. Piper* (1985) illustrates the problem. Piper, a resident of Vermont, was allowed to take New Hampshire's bar examination and passed. But because he resided in Vermont, he was not permitted to practice law in New Hampshire. The Court struck down the state rule and reaffirmed the well-settled principle that "one of the privileges which the [privileges and immunities] clause guarantees to citizens of State A is that of doing business in State B on terms of substantial equality with the citizens of that State." [24] As the Court noted in *Baldwin* and reemphasized in *Piper*, the pursuit of a common calling is among the most fundamental of the privileges protected by the clause. Indeed, like the right of Americans to travel from state to state without being hindered by local barriers, [25] the privileges and immunities clause was intended to bind the nation together in a single unit.

Comparative Perspectives

Established federal systems with which the United States can be compared are Canada, Germany, Australia, Switzerland, and—at the transnational level—the European Union. Each of these systems embodies common features that define the core of a *federal* union: they divide power between central and state or regional governments; they provide for institutions within which state or regional governments share in making national policy; and they establish a tribunal to resolve ordinary disputes and conflicts between levels of government. [26] These federal systems, however, vary considerably. All were designed to balance unity and diversity, but each has roots in a different set of historical circumstances. For example, Canada's federation emerged from a previously unitary system, whereas Germany returned to its own pre-1933 federal models after a stormy period of unitary rule. The United States, like Australia and Switzerland, aggregated previously independent political units. The European Union, on the other hand, is in the process of merging independent nation-states into a more perfect federal union.

The governing institutions of these federal systems differ as much as their origins. The United States is a presidential system, others are parliamentary. In Germany, state administrative agencies carry out "as a matter of their own concern" laws enacted by the national government, whereas the United States has created a huge federal bureaucracy, parallel to that of the states, to execute its own laws. In each federal system the states or regions also differ in their mode of representation at the national level and the degree to which, as independent units, they are allowed to shape national policy. The structure of the judiciary is also important because it affects the relationship between federal and state courts. For example, Germany's unified judicial system, as noted in chapter 1, contrasts sharply with the dual court sytem in the United States. One advantage of a unified judiciary is that it avoids federal-state judicial feuds such as those that erupted in *Martin v. Hunter's Lessee* (1816), and *Cohens v. Virginia* (1821). [27]

These federal systems could also be compared for the contribution each has made to those values federalism is often cited as serving—to wit, self-government, civic participation, economic prosperity, and the containment of divisions based on racial, ethnic, linguistic, and religious causes—but this would carry us far afield. A more

---

[24] *New Hampshire v. Piper*, 470 U.S. 274, 280. See also *Supreme Court of Virginia v. Friedman*, 487 U.S. 59 (1988).

[25] See *Shapiro v. Thompson*, 394 U.S. 618 (1969).

[26] As A.V. Dicey once observed, "Federalism means legalism [and] the prevalence of a spirit of legality among the people [and thus] judges [are] not only the guardians but also at a given moment the masters of the Constitution." *Introduction to the Study of the Law and of the Constitution*, 9th ed. (E.C.S. Wade, 1939), 173–75.

[27] There is also less chance of conflicts between federal and state courts in Canada because the Canadian Supreme Court is a general court of appeal for all matters of provincial and local law as well as for cases arising under the Canadian Charter of Rights and Liberties.

useful account would focus on legal and constitutional issues already discussed in this chapter. In the overview to follow, we deal mainly with Canada and Germany.

We may begin by looking at the impact of constitutional text on the evolution of federal systems. Constitutions do not always operate as their designers intended, and all too often hastily drafted constitutional blueprints do not match actual political conditions. In several systems, federalism has evolved in directions that belie the formal division of power between levels of government. Canadian federalism, for example, has not functioned as the unifying force that might have been expected from the original constitution—i.e., the British North American Act of 1867. In Germany, the house in which the states (*Länder*) are corporately represented has evolved into a more powerful body than the constitutional text originally prescribed. In the United States, too, as this chapter has shown, the divide between enumerated and reserved powers has been replaced with cooperative arrangements and the exercise of concurrent power by state and federal governments in many areas of public policy.

Practical politics and historical necessity have produced many of these changes, yet the role of judicial review should not be underestimated. The increasing power of the German Bundesrat—i.e., the Council of State Governments—owes much to decisions of the Federal Constitutional Court. The strong centralist vision of John Marshall is also crucial to an understanding of contemporary federalism in the United States. The Canadian Supreme Court, by contrast, took a much narrower view of national power over trade and commerce, as opposed to its broad interpretation of provincial powers over civil rights and property, the effect of which hampered the national government's effort to regulate the economy. In the hands of the American Supreme Court, the Fourteenth Amendment developed into a powerful tool for nationalizing basic rights and liberties (see chapter 8), whereas the nationalization of such rights in Canada has moved forward in limited ways under the 1982 Charter of Rights and Liberties. None of these developments was inevitable, for different scenarios might have been scripted under different sets of judicial interpreters.

Under Germany's system of administrative federalism, the national government monopolizes the field of policymaking, while the states dominate the implementation of policy. In an effort to protect and fortify the few powers reserved to the states, the Federal Constitutional Court has narrowly interpreted the catalogue of exclusive and concurrent powers conferred on the national government. This approach, unlike the American one, leaves little room for a jurisprudence of implied powers. For example, in 1962, the Constitutional Court struck down a federal law regulating the use of explosives because the statute could not be justified under the national government's concurrent power over "economic affairs." The statute had more to do with maintaining order and security, said the Court, than with furthering economic objectives. Ten years later, however, parliament amended the Basic Law to include "weapons and explosives" among the federal government's concurrent powers.

This episode is instructive when compared with similar conflicts in the United States. First, the Constitutional Court reserves for itself the power to declare with finality any and all constitutional disputes between nation and state, even those arising out of a federal law that arguably regulates the economy. We are reminded once again that all provisions of Germany's Basic Law are judicially enforceable. Second, and in sharp contrast to the teaching of the United States Supreme Court in *Garcia v. San Antonio Metropolitan District* (see chapter 6), the Court does not regard the *Länder*'s participation in the passage of such a law as a reason for deferring to parliament's judgment about its constitutionality. Finally, it is easier in Germany to correct a "misjudgment" of the Constitutional Court by amending the Basic Law. Amending the Basic Law is difficult—it requires a two-thirds vote of all members of the Bundestag and Bundesrat—but it is not the impossible hurdle that often prevails in the United States.

Amendments of the kind mentioned in the previous paragraph seem to be a reasonable way of reconciling judicial review with political democracy.

American judicial doctrines on federalism may be compared with still other features of German and Canadian constitutional law. In each of these systems the supremacy or paramountcy of federal law has been firmly established. In the absence of federal legislation, the German and Canadian high courts are not as likely to interfere with state legislation as is the U.S. Supreme Court. But when the German government chooses to exercise one of its many concurrent powers, then federal law preempts state law altogether. In Canada, on the other hand, concurrent legislation is likely to be sustained so long as no direct conflict exists between national and provincial legislation. But in the absence of national legislation, the Canadian Supreme Court is less apt to strike down provincial legislation merely because the field could otherwise be occupied by the national government. Similarly, Canadians seldom speak of a "dormant commerce clause." In an early case, Canada's Supreme Court ruled that in the absence of national legislation over the fire insurance business, which parliament could clearly regulate as a trade, Ontario was authorized to impose its own regulation, as being a civil rights matter within provincial jurisdiction, so long as the regulation affected only the commerce of the province.[28] This remains generally the case today.

An interesting debate taking shape in Canada is whether one level of government is constitutionally permitted to delegate its power to another level "as a device for realizing social and economic policies which neither the Parliament of Canada nor the provincial legislatures can implement on their own."[29] The Supreme Court has made it clear that the delegation doctrine as applied to administrative agencies does not apply to the question of whether one government may delegate power to another government. The advantage of such an exchange of legislative power is the flexibility it brings to the Constitution. As we saw in chapter 4, any such interchange of legislative power would be constitutionally suspect in the United States. Over the objection of many Canadian constitutional scholars, the Canadian Supreme Court has ruled that such delegations are unconstitutional, but it has tempered this view by suggesting that either parliament or a provincial legislature may "lend" one of its powers to the other in future legislation so long as the latter is not exercising power that it lacks under the Constitution. (The Australian Constitution explicitly permits a state legislature to delegate its authority to the national government.)

German federal constitutionalism, on the other hand, has sought to protect state interests in ways that differ from American constitutional case law. First, the Federal Constitutional Court has sought to protect both federal and state interests by frequently invoking the unwritten principle of federal comity (*Bundesteue*), a principle it has inferred from the various structures and relationships created by the Basic Law. (At least one-third of the 146 articles in the Basic Law deal with federal-state relations, financial and otherwise.) According to this principle, federal and state governments owe their loyalty to the federal union and are thus obligated to respect the rightful prerogatives of each other as integral parts of this union.

In the famous *Television Case* of 1961, for example, the Court nullified the national government's effort to create a federally operated television station, arguing that it had offended the principle of comity by not consulting with all *Länder* governments before proceeding with the creation of a new channel, particularly since the *Länder* are responsible for education and culture. The doctrine of comity was used against the *Länder*, on the other hand, in the *Atomic Referenda Cases* (1958). In the late 1950s,

---

[28] See Neil Finkelstein, *Laskin's Canadian Constitutional Law*, 5th ed. (Toronto: Carswell, 1986), 418.

[29] *Ibid*., 42.

the ruling Christian Democrats agreed to equip the German Army with tactical nuclear weapons. Several cities and states controlled by the Social Democrats planned to hold advisory referenda on the issue in the expectation of a negative popular vote that would embarass the national government. The Court nullified the planned referenda because they showed a lack of state respect for the national government's exclusive responsibility for military affairs.[30] It is hard to imagine such a decision by the American Supreme Court.

In two other areas of constitutional adjudication discussed in greater detail in chapter 6, the Constitutional Court has departed substantially from prevailing doctrine in the United States. First, in subsidizing programs such as urban renewal through grants-in-aid to the *Länder*, the national government may not encroach on the substantive powers of the *Länder* or local communities or interfere with the right of the *Länder* to administer federal financial programs "as a matter of their own concern" within the meaning of these terms as used in the Basic Law.[31] Under equivalent decisions of the Supreme Court, Congress's spending power has a much longer reach. (See *South Dakota v. Dole* in chapter 6.)

Finally, the Constitutional Court has defended the so-called "core functions" (*Kernbereich*) of local government against both federal and state encroachment. In a recent case, the Court nullified a provision of the Waste Disposal Act of 1972, enacted under the federation's concurrent powers, because it deprived a local community of its responsibility over waste disposal, thus offending the community's constitutional right to self-government.[32] The *Kernbereich* theory echoes the federalism controversy in the United States triggered by *National League of Cities v. Usery* (1976) and *Garcia v. San Antonio Metropolitan District* (1985), both of which are discussed in the next chapter. In *Garcia*, the Supreme Court gave up on trying to defend the states against the federal displacement of their "traditional" governmental functions. Any such determination, said the Court, would be arbitrary, for no principled standards exist for determining what is or is not a traditional function of state or local government. Hence, declared the Court, the states must look to the political process and not to the judiciary in defense of their traditional functions. It is difficult to imagine a similar decision by the Federal Constitutional Court. Perhaps the Basic Law's text encourages an active judicial role here as in most other areas of German constitutional law. After all, Article 28 (2) grants local governments explicit protection, whereas the American Tenth Amendment erects no textual barrier against displacing state authority when the national government has validly exercised one of its enumerated powers.

The Canadian Supreme Court has also played a vigilant role in monitoring the division of powers between the dominion government and the various provinces. This role has expanded measurably in recent decades with the "veritable explosion," as one study noted,[33] of constitutional litigation involving disputes between the two levels of government. The study reported that between 1975 and 1983 the Supreme Court decided no fewer than seventy-eight cases dealing with such disputes. As in the United States, the Supreme Court handed down victories almost uniformly to the federal (i.e., dominion) government, but the Court's perspective became less nationalistic after 1975. In 1977, for the first time since 1949, the Court unanimously invalidated

[30] See Donald P. Kommers, *The Constitutional Jurisprudence of the Federal Republic of Germany*, 2d ed. (Durham: Duke University Press, 1997), 76–78.

[31] See *Financial Subsidies Case* (1975), Ibid., 93–96.

[32] Ibid., 106–107.

[33] See Peter H. Russell *et al.*, *Federalism and the Charter* (Ottawa: Carleton University Press, 1990), 8.

part of a federal Trade Marks Act establishing a national fair business code.[34] Foreshadowing this decision was the Court's 1976 decision in which five of the nine justices held that the national government's general power "to make laws for the peace, order, and good government of Canada" did not include general anti-inflationary legislation—outside the context of a national emergency—extending to the "control and regulation of local trade and of commodity pricing and of profit margins in the provincial sector."[35]

Leading Canadian scholars have noted that earlier provincial attacks on the Court for its pro-national decisions "put pressure on the justices to demonstrate their legitimacy as trustworthy arbiters of federal-provincial disputes."[36] The Court thus began to strike a noteworthy balance in adjudicating federalism issues, "a balance highlighted in its decision in *Patriation Reference*."[37] The issue in *Patriation* was whether the national government could, as the prime minister (Pierre Trudeau) insisted, unilaterally request the British Parliament to amend the 1867 Constitution. The Court held that customary constitutional practice required "a substantial degree of provincial consent" for federal requests to the British Parliament to amend the Constitution. Even though the national government was not *constitutionally required* to seek provincial support of its request, it nevertheless bowed to the Court's judgment by taking steps to insure substantial federal-provincial agreement on patriation.[38]

Canadian federalism, needless to say, is buffeted by problems of unity that defy comparison with the United States today. It is nevertheless instructive to observe that the Canadian Supreme Court, like Germany's Federal Constitutional Court, takes seriously the federal-state relationship as laid down in the Constitution. The U.S. Supreme Court's view that state challenges to federal law are to be settled in the political realm is unacceptable in Canada and Germany. As we shall see in chapter 6, however, the U.S. Supreme Court is deeply divided on the question of the Court's role in federal-state conflicts. With decisions such as *Lopez v. United States*, the Court may be inching toward the Canadian and German visions of the judicial role.

Selected Bibliography

Berger, Raoul. *Federalism: The Founders' Design*. Norman: University of Oklahoma Press, 1987.

Blair, Philip M. *Federalism and Judicial Review in West Germany*. Oxford: Clarendon Press, 1981.

Conference on Constitutional Federalism (symposium issue), 8 The American University Journal of International Law and Policy, 375–454 (Winter/Spring, 1992/1993).

Corwin, Edward A. *The Passing of Dual Federalism,* 36 Virginia Law Review 1 (1950).

Diamond, Martin. *Democracy and the Federalist: A Reconsideration of the Framers' Intent,* American Political Science Review 64 (1959).

Elazar, Daniel J. *Exploring Federalism*. Tuscaloosa: University of Alabama Press, 1986.

Elazar, Daniel J., *Federalism vs. Decentralization: The Drift from Authenticity*, 6 Publius 9–19 (1976).

Finn, John E. *Federalism in Perpetuity: West German and United States Federalism in Comparative Perspective*, 22 New York University Journal of International Law and Politics 1 (1989).

Kommers, Donald P. "Federalism and European Integration: A Commentary." In Mauro Cappelletti *et al. Integration Through Law: European and the American Federal Experience*, vol. 1, Book 1. Berlin: Walter de Gruyter, 1986, 603–16.

[34] *McDonald v. Vapor Canada Ltd.* [1977] 2 S.C.R. 134.

[35] Reference *Re Anti-Inflation Act* [1976] 2 S.C.R. 373. The quote is from the opinion of Justice Beetz, with whom four justices concurred.

[36] See Russell, supra note 33, at 9.

[37] *Ibid.*

[38] *Ibid.*, 706–11. *Patriation Reference* is reprinted at pages 711–59.

McConnell, Michael W. *Federalism: Evaluating the Founders' Design*, 54 University of Chicago Law Review 1484 (1987).

McWhinney, Edward *et al. Federalism in-the-Making: Contemporary Canadian and German Constitutionalism, National and Transnational.* Dordrecht, The Netherlands: Martinus Nijhoff Publishers, 1992.

McWhinney, Edward. *Comparative Federalism*, 2d ed. Toronto: University of Toronto Press, 1965.

Merritt, Deborah Jones. *The Guarantee Clause and State Autonomy: Federalism for a Third Century*, 88 Columbia Law Review 1 (1988).

Rakove, Jack N. *Original Meanings: Politics and Ideas in the Making of the Constitution.* New York: Alfred A. Knopf, Inc., 1996. See chap. 7 on federalism, 161–202.

Redish, Martin H. *Abstention, Separation of Powers, and the Limits of the Judicial Function*, 94 Yale Law Journal 71 (1984).

Schmidhauser, John. *The Supreme Court as Final Arbiter in Federal-State Relations, 1789–1957.* Chapel Hill: University of North Carolina Press, 1958.

Taylor, Charles. *Reconciling the Solitudes: Essays on Canadian Federalism and Nationalism.* Montreal: McGill-Queens University Press, 1993.

Vipond, Robert. *Constitutional Politics and the Legacy of the Provincial Rights Movement in Canada,* 18 Canadian Journal of Political Science 495 (1985).

Zuckert, Michael P. *Federalism and the Founding: Toward a Reinterpretation of the Constitutional Convention,* 48 Review of Politics 166 (1986).

McCulloch v. State of Maryland

17 U.S. 316, 4 Wheat. 316, 4 L. Ed. 579 (1819)

In 1816 Congress incorporated the Bank of the United States, which in 1817 established a branch in Baltimore. In 1818 the Maryland legislature passed an act imposing a tax on all banks or branches in Maryland not chartered by the state legislature. James McCulloch, a cashier at the Baltimore branch of the Second National Bank, refused to pay the tax. A Maryland trial court upheld the state's right to collect the tax, and the state court of appeals affirmed. Opinion of the Court: *Marshall*, Washington, Johnson, Livingston, Todd, Duvall, Story.

MARSHALL, Ch. J., delivered the opinion of the Court.

In the case now to be determined, the defendant, a sovereign state, denies the obligation of a law enacted by the legislature of the Union, and the plaintiff, on his part, contests the validity of an act which has been passed by the legislature of that state. The constitution of our country, in its most interesting and vital parts, is to be considered; the conflicting powers of the government of the Union and of its members, as marked in that constitution, are to be discussed; and an opinion given, which may essentially influence the great operations of the government. No tribunal can approach such a question without a deep sense of its importance, and of the awful responsibility involved in its decision. But it must be decided peacefully, or remain a source of hostile legislation, perhaps of hostility of a still more serious nature; and if it is to be so decided, by this tribunal alone can the decision be made. On the supreme court of the United States has the constitution of our country devolved this important duty.

The first question made in the cause is—has congress power to incorporate a bank? It has been truly said, that this can scarcely be considered as an open question, entirely unprejudiced by the former proceedings of the nation respecting it. The principle now contested was introduced at a very early period of our history, has been recognised by many successive legislatures, and has been acted upon by the judicial department, in cases of peculiar delicacy, as a law of undoubted obligation.

In discussing this question [of the federal bank's validity], the counsel for the state of Maryland have deemed it of some importance, in the construction of the constitution, to consider that instrument, not as emanating from the people, but as the act of sovereign and independent states. The powers of the general government, it has been said, are delegated by the states, who alone are truly sovereign; and must be exercised in subordination to the states, who alone possess supreme dominion. It would be difficult to sustain this proposition. The convention which framed the constitution was indeed elected by the state legislatures. But the instrument, when it came from their hands . . . was reported to the then existing congress of the United States, with a request that it might "be submitted to a convention of delegates, chosen in each state by the people thereof . . . for their assent and ratification." This mode of proceeding was adopted [and] the instrument was submitted to the *people.* They acted upon it in the only manner in which they can act safely, effectively and wisely, on such a subject, by assembling in convention. It is true, they assembled in their several states—and where else should they have assembled? No political dreamer was ever wild enough to think of breaking down the lines which separate the states, and of compounding the American people into one common mass. Of consequence, when they act, they act in their states. But the measures they adopt do not, on that account, cease to be the measures of the people themselves, or become measures of the state governments.

. . . The government [of the United States therefore] proceeds directly from the people; is "ordained and established," in the name of the people; and is declared to be ordained, "in order to form a more perfect union, establish justice, insure domestic tranquillity, and secure the blessings of liberty to themselves and to their posterity."

. . . The government of the Union, then (whatever may be the influence of this fact on the case), is emphatically and truly, a government of the people. In form, and in substance, it emanates from them. Its powers are granted by them, and are to be exercised directly on them, and for their benefit.

This government is acknowledged by all, to be one of enumerated powers. The principle, that it can exercise only the powers granted to it, would seem too apparent . . . ; that principle is now universally admitted. But the question respecting the extent of the powers actually granted, is perpetually arising, and will probably continue to arise, so long as our system shall exist. In discussing these questions, the conflicting powers of the general and state governments must be brought into view, and the supremacy of their respective laws, when they are in opposition, must be settled.

If any one proposition could command the universal assent of mankind, we might expect it would be this—that the government of the Union, though limited in its powers, is supreme within its sphere of action. This would seem to result, necessarily, from its nature. It is the government of all; its powers are delegated by all; it represents all, and acts for all. Though any one state may be willing to control its operations, no state is willing to allow others to control them. The nation, on those subjects on which it can act, must necessarily bind its component parts. But this question is not left to mere reason: the people have, in express terms, decided it, by saying, "this constitution, and the laws of the United States, which shall be made in pursuance thereof, shall be the supreme law of the land," and by requiring that the members of the state legislatures, and the officers of the executive and judicial departments of the states, shall take the oath of fidelity to it. The government of the United States, then, though limited in its powers, is supreme; and its laws, when made in pursuance of the constitution, form the supreme law of the land, "any thing in the constitution or laws of any state to the contrary notwithstanding."

Among the enumerated powers, we do not find that of establishing a bank or creating a corporation. But there is no phrase in the instrument which, like the articles of confederation, excludes incidental or implied powers; and which requires that everything granted shall be expressly and minutely described. Even the 10th amendment, which was framed for the purpose of quieting the excessive jealousies which had been excited, omits the word "expressly," and declares only, that the powers "not delegated to the United States, nor prohibited to the states, are reserved to the states or to the people;" thus leaving the question, whether the particular power which may become the subject of contest, has been delegated to the one government, or prohibited to the other, to depend on a fair construction of the whole instrument. The men who drew and adopted this amendment had experienced the embarrassments resulting from the insertion of this word in the articles of confederation, and probably omitted it, to avoid those embarrassments. A constitution, to contain an accurate detail of all the subdivisions of which its great powers will admit, and of all the means by which they may be carried into execution, would partake of the prolixity of a legal code, and could scarcely be embraced by the human mind. It would, probably, never be understood by the public. Its nature, therefore, requires, that only its great outlines should be marked, its important objects designated, and the minor ingredients which compose those objects, be deduced from the nature of the objects themselves. That this idea was entertained by the framers of the American constitution, is not only to be inferred from the nature of the instrument, but from the language. Why else were some of the limitations, found in the 9th section of the 1st article, introduced? It is also, in some degree, warranted, by their having omitted to use any restrictive term which might prevent its receiving a fair and just interpretation. In considering this question, then, we must never forget that it is a *constitution* we are expounding.

Although, among the enumerated powers of government, we do not find the word "bank" or "incorporation," we find the great powers, to lay and collect taxes; to borrow money; to regulate commerce; to declare and conduct a war; and to raise and support armies and navies. The sword and the purse, all the external relations, and no inconsiderable portion of the industry of the nation, are intrusted to its government. It can never be pretended, that these vast powers draw after them others of inferior importance, merely because they are inferior. Such an idea can never be advanced. But it may with great reason be contended, that a government, intrusted with such ample powers, on the due execution of which the happiness and prosperity of the nation so vitally depends, must also be intrusted with ample means for their execution. The power being given, it is the interest of the nation to facilitate its execution. It can never be their interest, and cannot be presumed to have been their intention, to clog and embarrass its execution, by withholding the most appropriate means. Throughout this vast republic, from the St. Croix to the Gulf of Mexico, from the Atlantic to the Pacific, revenue is to be collected and expended, armies are to be marched and supported. The exigencies of the nation may require, that the treasure raised in the north should be transported

Comparative Note 5.1

Sec. 91. It shall be lawful for the Queen, by and with the advice and consent of the Senate and House of Commons, to make Laws for the peace, order, and good government of Canada, in relation to all matters not coming within the classes of subjects by this Act assigned exclusively to the legislatures of the provinces; . . . [T]he exclusive legislative authority of the parliament of Canada extends to . . .

2. The regulation of trade and commerce
3. The raising of money by any mode or system of taxation. . . .
4. The borrowing of money on the public credit. . . .
9. Beacons, buoys, lighthouses, and Sable Island.
10. Navigation and shipping. . . .
11. Sea coast and inland fisheries. . . .
16. Savings banks. . . .
26. Marriage and divorce.
27. The criminal law, except the constitution of

courts of criminal jurisdiction, but including the procedure in criminal matters. . . .

Sec. 92. In each province the legislature may exclusively make laws in relation to matters coming within the classes of subject next hereinafter enumerated; that is to say,—

2. Direct taxation within the province in order to raise revenue for provincial purposes.
3. The borrowing of money on the sole credit of the province. . . .
11. The incorporation of companies with provincial objects. . . .
12. The solemnization of marriage in the province.
13. Property and civil rights in the province. . . .
14. The administration of justice in the province, including the Constitution, maintenance, and organization of provincial courts, . . .
16. Generally all matters of a merely local or private nature in the province.

Source: Constitution Act, 1867 (Canada).

---

to the south, that raised in the east, conveyed to the west, or that this order should be reversed. Is that construction of the constitution to be preferred, which would render these operations difficult, hazardous and expensive? Can we adopt that construction (unless the words imperiously require it), which would impute to the framers of that instrument, when granting these powers for the public good, the intention of impeding their exercise, by withholding a choice of means? If, indeed, such be the mandate of the constitution, we have only to obey; but that instrument does not profess to enumerate the means by which the powers it confers may be executed; nor does it prohibit the creation of a corporation, if the existence of such a being be essential, to the beneficial exercise of those powers. It is, then, the subject of fair inquiry, how far such means may be employed.

It is not denied, that the powers given to the government imply the ordinary means of execution. That, for example, of raising revenue, and applying it to national purposes, is admitted to imply the power of conveying money from place to place, as the exigencies of the nation may require, and of employing the usual means of conveyance. But it is denied, that the government has its choice of means; or, that it may employ the most convenient means, if, to employ them, it be necessary to erect a corporation.

The power of creating a corporation, though appertaining to sovereignty, is not, like the power of making war, or levying taxes, or of regulating commerce, a great substantive and independent power, which cannot be implied as incidental to other powers, or used as a means of executing them. It is never the end for which other powers are exercised, but a means by which other objects are accomplished.

But the constitution of the United States has not left the right of congress to employ the necessary means, for the execution of the powers conferred on the government, to general reasoning. To its enumeration of powers is added, that of making "all laws which shall be necessary and proper, for carrying into execution the foregoing powers, and all other powers vested by this constitution, in the government of the United States, or in any department thereof." The counsel for the state of Maryland have urged various arguments, to prove that this clause, though, in terms, a grant of power, is not so, in effect; but is really restrictive of the general right, which might otherwise be implied, of selecting means for executing the enumerated powers. . . .

[T]he argument on which most reliance is placed, is drawn from the peculiar language of this clause. Congress is not empowered by it to make all laws, which may have relation to the powers conferred on the government, but such only as may be "necessary and proper" for carrying them into execution. The word "necessary" is considered as controlling the whole sentence, and as limiting the right to pass laws for the execution of the granted powers, to such as are indispensable, and without which the power would be nugatory. That it excludes the choice of means, and leaves to congress, in each case, that only which is most direct and simple.

Is it true, that this is the sense in which the word "necessary" is always used? Does it always import an absolute physical necessity, so strong, that one thing to which another may be termed necessary, cannot exist without that other? We think it does not. If reference be had to its use, in the common affairs of the world, or in approved authors, we find that it frequently imports no more than that one thing is convenient, or useful, or essential to another. To employ the means necessary to an end, is generally understood as employing any means calculated to produce the end, and not as being confined to those single means, without which the end would be entirely unattainable. Such is the character of human language, that no word conveys to the mind, in all situations, one single definite idea; and nothing is more common than to use words in a figurative sense. Almost all compositions contain words, which, taken in their rigorous sense, would convey a meaning different from that which is obviously intended. It is essential to just construction, that many words which import something excessive, should be understood in a more mitigated sense—in that sense which common usage justifies. The word "necessary" is of this description. It has not a fixed character, peculiar to itself. It admits of all degrees of comparison; and is often connected with other words, which increase or diminish the impression the mind receives of the urgency it imports. A thing may be necessary, very necessary, absolutely or indispensably necessary. To no mind would the same idea be conveyed by these several phrases. The comment on the word is well illustrated by the passage cited at the bar, from the 10th section of the 1st article of the constitution. It is, we think, impossible to compare the sentence which prohibits a state from laying "imposts, or duties on imports or exports, except what may be absolutely necessary for executing its inspection laws," with that which authorizes congress "to make all laws which shall be necessary and proper for carrying into execution" the powers of the general government, without feeling a conviction, that the convention understood itself to change materially the meaning of the word "necessary," by prefixing the word "absolutely." This word, then, like others, is used in various senses; and, in its construction, the subject, the context, the intention of the person using them, are all to be taken into view.

Let this be done in the case under consideration. The subject is the execution of those great powers on which the welfare of a nation essentially depends. It must have been the intention of those who gave these powers, to insure, so far as human prudence could insure, their beneficial execution. This could not be done, by confiding the choice of means to such narrow limits as not to leave it in the power of congress to adopt any which might be appropriate, and which were conducive to the end. This provision is made in a constitution, intended to endure for ages to come, and consequently, to be adapted to the various *crises* of human affairs. To have prescribed the means by which government should, in all future time, execute its powers, would have been to change, entirely, the character of the instrument, and give it the properties of a legal code. It would have been an unwise attempt to provide, by immutable rules, for exigencies which, if foreseen at all, must have been seen dimly, and which can be best provided for as they occur. To have declared, that the best means shall not be used, but those alone without which the power given would be nugatory, would have been to deprive the legislature of the capacity to avail itself of experience, to exercise its reason, and to accommodate its legislation to circumstances. If we apply this principle of construction to any of the powers of the government, we shall find it so pernicious in its operation that we shall be compelled to discard it.

Take, for example, the power "to establish post-offices and post-roads." This power is executed, by the single act of making the establishment. But, from this has been inferred the power and duty of carrying the mail along the post-road, from one post-office to another. And from this implied power, has again been inferred the right to punish those who steal letters from the post-office, or rob the mail. It may be said, with some plausibility, that the right to carry the mail, and to punish those who rob it, is not indispensably necessary to the establishment of a post-office and post-road. This right is indeed essential to the beneficial exercise of the power, but not indispensably necessary to its existence. So, of the punishment of the crimes of stealing or falsifying a record or process of a court of the United States, or of perjury in such court. To punish these offences, is certainly conducive to the due administration of justice. But courts may exist, and may decide the causes brought before them, though such crimes escape punishment.

If this limited construction of the word "necessary" must be abandoned, in order to punish, whence is derived the rule which would reinstate it, when the government would carry its powers into execution, by means not vindictive in their nature? If the word "necessary" means "needful," "requisite," "essential," "conducive to," in order to let in the power of punishment for the infraction of law; why is it not equally comprehensive, when required to authorize the use of means which facilitate the execution of the powers of government without the infliction of punishment?

But the argument which most conclusively demonstrates the error of the construction contended for by the counsel for the state of Maryland, is founded on the intention of the convention, as manifested in the whole clause. . . . As little can it be required to prove, that in the absence of this clause, congress would have some choice of means. That it might employ those which, in its judgment, would most advantageously effect the object to be accomplished. That any means adapted to the end, any means which tended directly to the execution of the constitutional powers of the government, were in themselves constitutional. This clause, as construed by the state of Maryland, would abridge, and almost annihilate, this useful and necessary right of the legislature to select its means. That this could not be intended, is, we should think, had it not been already controverted, too apparent for controversy.

We think so for the following reasons: 1st. The clause is placed among the powers of congress, not among the limitations on those powers. Its terms purport to enlarge, not to diminish the powers vested in the government. It purports to be an additional power, not a restriction on those already granted. No reason has been, or can be assigned, for thus concealing an intention to narrow the discretion of the national legislature, under words which purport to enlarge it. The framers of the constitution wished its adoption, and well knew that it would be endangered by its strength, not by its weakness. Had they been capable of using language which would convey to the eye one idea, and, after deep reflection, impress on the mind, another, they would rather have disguised the grant of power, than its limitation. If, then, their intention had been, by this clause, to restrain the free use of means which might otherwise have been implied, that intention would have been inserted in another place, and would have been expressed in terms resembling these. "In carrying into execution the foregoing powers, and all others," &c. "No laws shall be passed but such as are necessary and proper." Had the intention been to make this clause restrictive, it would unquestionably have been so in form as well as in effect.

We admit, as all must admit, that the powers of the government are limited, and that its limits are not to be transcended. But we think the sound construction of the constitution must allow to the national legislature that discretion, with respect to the means by which the powers it confers are to be carried into execution, which will enable that body to perform the high duties assigned to

it, in the manner most beneficial to the people. Let the end be legitimate, let it be within the scope of the constitution, and all means which are appropriate, which are plainly adapted to that end, which are not prohibited, but consist with the letter and spirit of the constitution, are constitutional.

. . . Should congress, in the execution of its powers, adopt measures which are prohibited by the constitution; or should congress, under the pretext of executing its powers, pass laws for the accomplishment of objects not intrusted to the government; it would become the painful duty of this tribunal, should a case requiring such a decision come before it, to say, that such an act was not the law of the land. But where the law is not prohibited, and is really calculated to effect any of the objects intrusted to the government, to undertake here to inquire into the decree of its necessity, would be to pass the line which circumscribes the judicial department, and to tread on legislative ground. This court disclaims all pretensions to such a power.

After the most deliberate consideration, it is the unanimous and decided opinion of this court, that the act to incorporate the Bank of the United States is a law made in pursuance of the constitution, and is a part of the supreme law of the land.

It being the opinion of the court, that the act incorporating the bank is constitutional; and that the power of establishing a branch in the state of Maryland might be properly exercised by the bank itself, we proceed to inquire.

2. Whether the state of Maryland may, without violating the constitution, tax that branch?

. . . [T]he very terms of this argument admit, that the sovereignty of the state, in the article of taxation itself, is subordinate to, and may be controlled by the constitution of the United States. How far it has been controlled by that instrument, must be a question of construction. In making this construction, no principle, not declared, can be admissible, which would defeat the legitimate operations of a supreme government. It is of the very essence of supremacy, to remove all obstacles to its action within its own sphere, and so to modify every power vested in subordinate governments, as to exempt its own operations from their own influence. This effect need not be stated in terms. It is so involved in the declaration of supremacy, so necessarily implied in it, that the expression of it could not make it more certain. We must, therefore, keep it in view, while construing the constitution.

The argument on the part of the state of Maryland, is, not that the states may directly resist a law of congress, but that they may exercise their acknowledged powers upon it, and that the constitution leaves them this right, in the confidence that they will not abuse it.

Before we proceed to examine this argument, and to subject it to the test of the constitution, we must be permitted to bestow a few considerations on the nature and extent of this original right of taxation, which is acknowledged to remain with the states. It is admitted that the power of taxing the people and their property is essential to the very existence of government, and may be legitimately exercised on the objects to which it is applicable, to the utmost extent to which the government may chuse to carry it. The only security against the abuse of this power, is found in the structure of the government itself. In imposing a tax the legislature acts upon its constituents. This is in general a sufficient security against erroneous and oppressive taxation.

The people of a state, therefore, give to their government a right of taxing themselves and their property, and as the exigencies of government cannot be limited, they prescribe no limits to the exercise of this right, resting confidently on the interest of the legislator, and on the influence of the constituents over their representative, to guard them against its abuse. But the means employed by the government of the Union have no such security, nor is the right of a state to tax them sustained by the same theory. Those means are not given by the people of a particular state, not given by the constituents of the legislature, which claim the right to tax them, but by the people of all the states. They are given by all, for the benefit of all—and upon theory, should be subjected to that government only which belongs to all.

The sovereignty of a state extends to every thing which exists by its own authority, . . . but does it extend to those means which are employed by congress to carry into execution powers conferred on that body by the people of the United States? We think it demonstrable that it does not. Those powers are not given by the people of a single state. They are given by the people of the United States, to a government whose laws, made in pursuance of the constitution, are declared to be supreme. Consequently, the people of a single state cannot confer a sovereignty which will extend over them.

That the power to tax involves the power to destroy; that the power to destroy may defeat and render useless the power to create; that there is a plain repugnance in conferring on one government a power to control the constitutional measures of another, which other, with respect to those very measures, is declared to be supreme over that which exerts the control, are propositions not to be denied. But all inconsistencies are to be reconciled by the magic of the word confidence. Taxation, it is said, does

not necessarily and unavoidably destroy. To carry it to the excess of destruction, would be an abuse, to presume which, would banish that confidence which is essential to all government. But is this a case of confidence? Would the people of any one state trust those of another with a power to control the most insignificant operations of their state government? We know they would not. Why, then, should we suppose, that the people of any one state should be willing to trust those of another with a power to control the operations of a government to which they have confided their most important and most valuable interests? In the legislature of the Union alone, are all represented. The legislature of the Union alone, therefore, can be trusted by the people with the power of controlling measures which concern all, in the confidence that it will not be abused. This, then, is not a case of confidence, and we must consider it is as it really is.

If we apply the principle for which the counsel for the State of Maryland contends, to the constitution generally, we shall find it capable of changing totally the character of that instrument. We shall find it capable of arresting all the measures of the government, and of prostrating it at the foot of the states. The American people have declared their constitution and the laws made in pursuance thereof, to be supreme; but this principle would transfer the supremacy, in fact, to the states.

The question is, in truth, a question of supremacy; and if the right of the states to tax the means employed by the general government be conceded, the declaration that the constitution, and the laws made in pursuance thereof, shall be the supreme law of the land, is empty and unmeaning declamation.

It has also been insisted, that, as the power of taxation in the general and state governments is acknowledged to be concurrent, every argument which would sustain the right of the general government to tax banks chartered by the states, will equally sustain the right of the states to tax banks chartered by the general government. But the two cases are not on the same reason. The people of all the states have created the general government, and have conferred upon it the general power of taxation. The people of all the states, and the states themselves, are represented in congress, and, by their representatives, exercise this power. When they tax the chartered institutions of the states, they tax their constituents; and these taxes must be uniform. But when a state taxes the operations of the government of the United States, it acts upon institutions created, not by their own constituents, but by people over whom they claim no control. It acts upon the measures of a government created by others as well as themselves, for the benefit of others in common with themselves. The

Comparative Note 5.2

In Germany's federal state, the unwritten constitutional principle of comity . . . governs all constitutional relationships between the nation as a whole and its [constituent] states as well as relationship among the states. From this principle there follows a number of legal obligations rooted in the Constitution. In considering the constitutionality of the so-called horizontal financial adjustment, this Court said: "the federal principle [of comity] by its nature creates not only rights but obligations. One of these obligations consists in financially strong states having to give assistance within certain limits to financially weaker states. . . ." This legal restraint, derived from the concept of loyalty to the [federal] union, becomes even more evident in the exercise of legislative powers: "If the effects of a law are not limited to the territory of a state, the state legislature must show consideration for the interests of the federation and the other states. . . .

The rule of comity also governs the procedure and style of the negotiations required in the constitutional relationship between the federation and its members as well as between the states. In the Federal Republic of Germany all states have the same constitutional status; they are states entitled to equal treatment when dealing with the federation. Whenever the federation tries to achieve a constitutionally relevant agreement in a matter in which all states are interested and participating, the obligation to act in a profederal manner prohibits the federation from trying to "divide and conquer;" that is, from attempting to divide the states, to seek an agreement with only some of them and then force the others to join. In negotiations that concern all the states, that principle also prohibits the federal government from treating state governments differently because of their party orientation and, in particular, from inviting to politically decisive discussions only representatives from those state governments politically close to the federal government and excluding state governments which are close to opposition parties in the federal parliament.

SOURCE: *Television I Case* [1961], German Federal Constitutional Court, in Kommers, *Constitutional Jurisprudence*, 69.

---

difference is that which always exists, and always must exist, between the action of the whole on a part, and the action of a part on the whole—between the laws of a government declared to be supreme, and those of a government which, when in opposition to those laws, is not supreme.

The court has bestowed on this subject its most deliberate consideration. The result is a conviction that the states have no power, by taxation or otherwise, to retard, impede, burden, or in any manner control, the operations of the constitutional laws enacted by congress to carry into execution the powers vested in the general government. This is, we think, the unavoidable consequence of that supremacy which the constitution has declared. We are unanimously of opinion, that the law passed by the legislature of Maryland, imposing a tax on the Bank of the United States, is unconstitutional and void.

Notes/ Queries/ Readings

1. What theory of the Constitution is at the basis of Marshall's opinion? Identify the competing theory advanced by Maryland. Which theory is most defensible in the light of the historical record?

2. Chief Justice Marshall justified his reading of the necessary and proper clause in part on the specific location of the clause in the larger text—it is significant, he concluded, that the clause appears in that section of Article 1 that grants rather than limits legislative power. Was this use of structuralism as a method of constitutional interpretation appropriate? Is structuralism an especially apt method of interpretation in cases concerning federalism? Why or why not? See Charles Black, *Structure and Relationship in Constitutional Law* (Baton Rouge: Louisiana State University Press, 1969).

3. Justice Frankfurter once said that Marshall's claim that "it is a *constitution* we are expounding" is the single most important utterance in the literature of constitutional law—most important because "most comprehensive and most comprehending." See *John Marshall and the Judicial Function*, 69 Harvard Law Review 217, 219 (1955). Do you agree?

4. Suppose Marshall decided this case under the terms of the Canadian Constitution as set forth in Comparative Note 5.1. Would the result be the same?

5. In discussing the issue of taxation, Marshall rejected Maryland's claim that the possibility of abuse should be combated through "confidence." Isn't confidence just

another word for comity? Did the Court do damage to the principle of comity when it concluded that trust was an insufficient guarantee? See Comparative Note 5.2 for a perspective on comity between levels of government.

6. Does Marshall's definition of the word "necessary" fit with common usage of the term? It is plausible? What notion of original intent lies behind this interpretation? Do the examples he uses make his point about Congress's power to create a national bank? Should we read the words of the constitutional text differently from how we define those words in our everyday life? Did the Framers intend for us to read the Constitution this way? How do we know? See Laurence H. Tribe and Michael C. Dorf, *On Reading the Constitution* (Cambridge: Harvard University Press, 1991).

7. Marshall noted that Congress had twice debated the constitutionality of a national bank and on both occasions Congress voted to establish the bank, which in his view argued for its validity. But Congress also debated the constitutionality of the Judiciary Act of 1789, section 13 of which Marshall struck down in *Marbury v. Madison*. Was Marshall being inconsistent?

8. What conclusion did Marshall draw from the fact that the states are represented in Congress? How much would his case be hurt if at that time, as now, senators were directly elected by the people, rather than appointed by state legislatures? Is the mere fact of state representation in Congress sufficient to uphold the balance of power between state and federal governments? What role should the judiciary play in maintaining the federal balance? Does the Tenth Amendment demand that the Court play such a role?

9. Consider this comment on *McCulloch* made in 1828 by one of Marshall's critics:

[The reader] will find that the government has been fundamentally altered by . . . the opinion—that instead of being any longer one of enumerated powers and a circumscribed sphere, as it was beyond all doubt intended to be, it knows absolutely no bounds but the will of a majority of Congress. . . . He will find that [an] extraordinary revolution has been brought about, in a good degree by the Supreme Court of the United States—very innocently, no doubt, and with commanding ability in argument—and thus given authority and currency to such canons of interpretation, as necessarily lead to these extravagant results.

Do you agree with this description of *McCulloch* as a constitutional revolution? Do you agree with his statement that the federal government should be one of "enumerated powers and a circumscribed sphere," and not one merely dependent on the will of majority in Congress? How would Marshall respond?

10. What would the implications be—practically, politically and theoretically—on the operation of the federal government had Maryland's arguments prevailed? Could such a constrained national government have survived then? Could it survive today?

11. Marshall's decision in *McCulloch* met severe criticism, especially in the South. It met such opposition in Marshall's home state of Virginia that he took to writing, under pseudonyms, a series of newspaper articles justifying his opinion. Marshall's articles, as well as several prominent attacks on his opinions, are collected in Gerald Gunther, *John Marshall's Defense of* McCulloch v. Maryland (Stanford, Calif.: Stanford University, 1969). For additional reading, see Bray Hammond, *Banks and Politics in America from the Revolution to the Civil War* (Princeton, N.J.: Princeton University Press, 1957.)

New York v. United States

505 U.S. 144, 112 S. Ct. 2408, 120 L. Ed. 2d 120 (1992)

In 1985 Congress enacted the Low-Level Radioactive Waste Policy Amendments Act to deal with the scarcity of disposal sites for low-level radioactive waste. The act embodied a compromise between "sited" and "unsited" states. States having low-level radioactive waste disposal sites agreed to accept such wastes from unsited states for another seven years, while unsited states agreed to end their reliance on the sited states by 1992. The law contained three incentives to induce states to comply. The first was monetary: states with sites were allowed to impose a-surcharge on waste received from other states. The second was an access incentive: sited states could increase the cost of access to their sites and eventually deny access to these sites entirely. The third was a negative "take title" provision: after seven years, states failing to provide for the disposal of internally generated waste by a specific date must, upon request of the waste's generator or owner, take possession of the waste and become liable for damages incurred by the generator or owner because of the state's failure to take prompt possession. New York sought a declaratory judgment that the act violated the Tenth Amendment. The District Court dismissed the suit and the U.S. Court of Appeals affirmed. Opinion of the Court: *O'Connor*, Kennedy, Rehnquist, Scalia, Souter, Thomas.

Concurring in part and dissenting in part: *White*, Blackmun, *Stevens*.

Justice O'CONNOR delivered the opinion of the Court.

These cases implicate one of our Nation's newest problems of public policy and perhaps our oldest question of constitutional law. The public policy issue involves the disposal of radioactive waste. . . . The constitutional question is as old as the Constitution: It consists of discerning the proper division of authority between the Federal Government and the States. We conclude that while Congress has substantial power under the Constitution to encourage the States to provide for the disposal of the radioactive waste generated within their borders, the Constitution does not confer upon Congress the ability simply to compel the States to do so. We therefore find that only two of the Act's three provisions at issue are consistent with the Constitution's allocation of power to the Federal Government.

In 1788, in the course of explaining to the citizens of New York why the recently drafted Constitution provided for federal courts, Alexander Hamilton observed: "The erection of a new government, whatever care or wisdom may distinguish the work, cannot fail to originate questions of intricacy and nicety; and these may, in a particular manner, be expected to flow from the establishment of a constitution founded upon the total or partial incorporation of a number of distinct sovereignties." *The Federalist*, No. 82. Hamilton's prediction has proved quite accurate. While no one disputes the proposition that "[t]he Constitution created a Federal Government of limited powers," and while the Tenth Amendment makes explicit that "[t]he powers not delegated to the United States by the Constitution, nor prohibited by it to the States, are reserved to the States respectively, or to the people"; the task of ascertaining the constitutional line between federal and state power has given rise to many of the Court's most difficult and celebrated cases. At least as far back as *Martin v. Hunter's Lessee* [1816] the Court has resolved questions "of great importance and delicacy" in determining whether particular sovereign powers have been granted by the Constitution to the Federal Government or have been retained by the States.

These questions can be viewed in either of two ways. In some cases the Court has inquired whether an Act of Congress is authorized by one of the powers delegated to Congress in Article I of the Constitution. In other cases the Court has sought to determine whether an Act of Congress invades the province of state sovereignty reserved by the Tenth Amendment. In a case like this one, involving the division of authority between federal and state governments, the two inquiries are mirror images of each other. If a power is delegated to Congress in the Constitution, the Tenth Amendment expressly disclaims any reservation of that power to the States; if a power is an attribute of state sovereignty reserved by the Tenth Amendment, it is necessarily a power the Constitution has not conferred on Congress.

It is in this sense that the Tenth Amendment "states but a truism that all is retained which has not been surrendered." As Justice Story put it, "[t]his amendment is a mere affirmation of what, upon any just reasoning, is a necessary rule of interpreting the constitution. Being an instrument of limited and enumerated powers, it follows irresistibly, that what is not conferred, is withheld, and belongs to the state authorities." This has been the Court's consistent understanding: "The States unquestionably do retai[n] a significant measure of sovereign authority . . . to the extent that the Constitution has not divested them of their original powers and transferred those powers to the Federal Government." *Garcia v. San Antonio Metropolitan Transit Authority* [1985, reprinted in chapter 6].

Congress exercises its conferred powers subject to the limitations contained in the Constitution. Thus, for example, under the Commerce Clause Congress may regulate publishers engaged in interstate commerce, but Congress is constrained in the exercise of that power by the First Amendment. The Tenth Amendment likewise restrains the power of Congress, but this limit is not derived from the text of the Tenth Amendment itself, which, as we have discussed, is essentially a tautology. Instead, the Tenth Amendment confirms that the power of the Federal Government is subject to limits that may, in a given instance, reserve power to the States. The Tenth Amendment thus directs us to determine, as in this case, whether an incident of state sovereignty is protected by a limitation on an Article I power.

The benefits of this federal structure have been extensively cataloged elsewhere, but they need not concern us here. Our task would be the same even if one could prove that federalism secured no advantages to anyone. It consists not of devising our preferred system of government, but of understanding and applying the framework set forth in the Constitution. "The question is not what power the Federal Government ought to have but what powers in fact have been given by the people."

The actual scope of the Federal Government's authority with respect to the States has changed over the years, but the constitutional structure underlying and limiting that authority has not. In the end, just as a cup may be half empty or half full, it makes no difference whether one views the question at issue in this case as one of ascertaining the limits of the power delegated to the Federal Government under the affirmative provisions of the Constitution or one of discerning the core of sovereignty retained by the States under the Tenth Amendment. Either way, we must determine whether any of the three challenged provisions of the Low-Level Radioactive Waste Amendments of 1985 oversteps the boundary between federal and state authority. Petitioners do not contend that Congress lacks the power to regulate the disposal of low level radioactive waste. . . . Petitioners likewise do not dispute that under the Supremacy Clause Congress could, if it wished, pre-empt state radioactive waste regulation. Petitioners contend only that the Tenth Amendment limits the power of Congress to regulate in the way it has chosen. Rather than addressing the problem of waste disposal by directly regulating the generators and disposers of waste, petitioners argue, Congress has impermissibly directed the States to regulate in this field.

Most of our recent cases interpreting the Tenth Amendment have concerned the authority of Congress to subject state governments to generally applicable laws. The Court's jurisprudence in this area has traveled an unsteady path. . . . This litigation instead concerns the circumstances under which Congress may use the States as implements of regulation; that is, whether Congress may direct or otherwise motivate the States to regulate in a particular field or a particular way. Our cases have established a few principles that guide our resolution of the issue.

As an initial matter, Congress may not simply "commandee[r] the legislative processes of the States by directly compelling them to enact and enforce a federal regulatory program."

While Congress has substantial powers to govern the Nation directly, including in areas of intimate concern to the States, the Constitution has never been understood to confer upon Congress the ability to require the States to govern according to Congress' instructions. The Court has been explicit about this distinction. "Both the States and the United States existed before the Constitution. The people, through that instrument, established a more perfect union by substituting a national government, acting, with ample power, directly upon the citizens, instead of the Confederate government, which acted with powers, greatly restricted, only upon the States." . . .

Indeed, the question whether the Constitution should permit Congress to employ state governments as regulatory agencies was a topic of lively debate among the Framers. Under the Articles of Confederation, Congress lacked the authority in most respects to govern the people directly. . . .

The inadequacy of this governmental structure was responsible in part for the Constitutional Convention. . . . In the end, the Convention opted for a Constitution in which Congress would exercise its legislative authority directly over individuals rather than over States.

In providing for a stronger central government, therefore, the Framers explicitly chose a Constitution that confers upon Congress the power to regulate individuals, not States.

This is not to say that Congress lacks the ability to encourage a State to regulate in a particular way, or that Congress may not hold out incentives to the States as a method of influencing a State's policy choices. Our cases have identified a variety of methods, short of outright coercion, by which Congress may urge a State to adopt a legislative program consistent with federal interests. Two of these methods are of particular relevance here.

First, under Congress' spending power, "Congress may attach conditions on the receipt of federal funds." *South Dakota v. Dole* [1987, reproduced in chapter 6] was one such case: The Court found no constitutional flaw in a federal statute directing the Secretary of Transportation to withhold federal highway funds from States failing to adopt Congress' choice of a minimum drinking age.

Second, where Congress has the authority to regulate private activity under the Commerce Clause, we have recognized Congress' power to offer States the choice of regulating that activity according to federal standards or having state law pre-empted by federal regulation. This arrangement, which has been termed "a program of cooperative federalism," is replicated in numerous federal statutory schemes. . . .

By either of these methods, as by any other permissible method of encouraging a State to conform to federal policy choices, the residents of the State retain the ultimate decision as to whether or not the State will comply. If a State's citizens view federal policy as sufficiently contrary to local interests, they may elect to decline a federal grant. If state residents would prefer their government to devote its attention and resources to problems other than those deemed important by Congress, they may choose to have the Federal Government rather than the State bear the expense of a federally mandated regulatory program, and supplement that program to the extent state law is not pre-empted. Where Congress encourages state regulation rather than compelling it, state governments remain responsive to the local electorate's preferences; state officials remain accountable to the people.

By contrast, where the Federal Government compels States to regulate, the accountability of both state and federal officials is diminished. If the citizens of New York, for example, do not consider that making provision for the disposal of radioactive waste is in their best interest, they may elect state officials who share their view. That view can always be pre-empted under the Supremacy Clause if it is contrary to the national view, but in such a case it is the Federal Government that makes the decision in full view of the public, and it will be federal officials that suffer the consequences if the decision turns out to be detrimental or unpopular. But where the Federal Government directs the States to regulate, it may be state officials who will bear the brunt of public disapproval, while the federal officials who devised the regulatory program may remain insulated from the electoral ramifications of their decision. Accountability is thus diminished when, due to federal coercion, elected state officials cannot regulate in accordance with the views of the local electorate in matters not pre-empted by federal regulation.

With these principles in mind, we turn to the three challenged provisions of the Low-Level Radioactive Waste Policy Amendments Act of 1985.

The Act's first set of incentives, in which Congress has conditioned grants to the States upon the States' attainment of a series of milestones, is thus well within the authority of Congress under the Commerce and Spending Clauses. Because the first set of incentives is supported by affirmative constitutional grants of power to Congress, it is not inconsistent with the Tenth Amendment.

In the second set of incentives, Congress has authorized States and regional compacts with disposal sites gradually to increase the cost of access to the sites, and then to deny access altogether, to radioactive waste generated in States that do not meet federal deadlines. As a simple regulation, this provision would be within the power of Congress to authorize the States to discriminate against interstate commerce. Where federal regulation of private activity is within the scope of the Commerce Clause, we have recognized the ability of Congress to offer States the choice of regulating that activity according to federal standards or having state law pre-empted by federal regulation.

This is the choice presented to nonsited States by the Act's second set of incentives: States may either regulate the disposal of radioactive waste according to federal standards by attaining local or regional self-sufficiency, or their residents who produce radioactive waste will be subject to federal regulation authorizing sited States and regions to deny access to their disposal sites. The affected States are not compelled by Congress to regulate, because any burden caused by a State's refusal to regulate will fall on those who generate waste and find no outlet for its disposal, rather than on the State as a sovereign. A State whose citizens do not wish it to attain the Act's milestones may devote its attention and its resources to issues its citizens deem more worthy; the choice remains at all times with the residents of the State, not with Congress. The State need not expend any funds, or participate in any federal program, if local residents do not view such expenditures or participation as worthwhile. Nor must the State abandon the field if it does not accede to federal direction; the State

may continue to regulate the generation and disposal of radioactive waste in any manner its citizens see fit.

The Act's second set of incentives thus represents a conditional exercise of Congress' commerce power, along the lines of those we have held to be within Congress' authority. As a result, the second set of incentives does not intrude on the sovereignty reserved to the States by the Tenth Amendment.

The take title provision is of a different character. This third so-called "incentive" offers States, as an alternative to regulating pursuant to Congress' direction, the option of taking title to and possession of the low level radioactive waste generated within their borders and becoming liable for all damages waste generators suffer as a result of the States' failure to do so promptly. In this provision, Congress has crossed the line distinguishing encouragement from coercion.

The take title provision offers state governments a "choice" of either accepting ownership of waste or regulating according to the instructions of Congress. Respondents do not claim that the Constitution would authorize Congress to impose either option as a freestanding requirement. On one hand, the Constitution would not permit Congress simply to transfer radioactive waste from generators to state governments. Such a forced transfer, standing alone, would in principle be no different than a congressionally compelled subsidy from state governments to radioactive waste producers. The same is true of the provision requiring the States to become liable for the generators' damages. Standing alone, this provision would be indistinguishable from an Act of Congress directing the States to assume the liabilities of certain state residents. Either type of federal action would "commandeer" state governments into the service of federal regulatory purposes, and would for this reason be inconsistent with the Constitution's division of authority between federal and state governments. On the other hand, the second alternative held out to state governments—regulating pursuant to Congress' direction—would, standing alone, present a simple command to state governments to implement legislation enacted by Congress. As we have seen, the Constitution does not empower Congress to subject state governments to this type of instruction.

Because an instruction to state governments to take title to waste, standing alone, would be beyond the authority of Congress, and because a direct order to regulate, standing alone, would also be beyond the authority of Congress, it follows that Congress lacks the power to offer the States a choice between the two. Unlike the first two sets of incentives, the take title incentive does not represent the conditional exercise of any congressional power enumerated in the Constitution. In this provision, Congress has not held out the threat of exercising its spending power or its commerce power; it has instead held out the threat, should the States not regulate according to one federal instruction, of simply forcing the States to submit to another federal instruction. A choice between two unconstitutionally coercive regulatory techniques is no choice at all. Either way, "the Act commandeers the legislative processes of the States by directly compelling them to enact and enforce a federal regulatory program," an outcome that has never been understood to lie within the authority conferred upon Congress by the Constitution.

The take title provision appears to be unique. No other federal statute has been cited which offers a state government no option other than that of implementing legislation enacted by Congress. Whether one views the take title provision as laying outside Congress' enumerated powers, or as infringing upon the core of state sovereignty reserved by the Tenth Amendment, the provision is inconsistent with the federal structure of our Government established by the Constitution.

Respondents raise a number of objections to this understanding of the limits of Congress' power. . . . [They] note that the Act embodies a bargain among the sited and unsited States, a compromise to which New York was a willing participant and from which New York has reaped much benefit. Respondents then pose what appears at first to be a troubling question: How can a federal statute be found an unconstitutional infringement of state sovereignty when state officials consented to the statute's enactment?

The answer follows from an understanding of the fundamental purpose served by our Government's federal structure. The Constitution does not protect the sovereignty of States for the benefit of the States or state governments as abstract political entities, or even for the benefit of the public officials governing the States. To the contrary, the Constitution divides authority between federal and state governments for the protection of individuals. State sovereignty is not just an end in itself: "Rather, federalism secures to citizens the liberties that derive from the diffusion of sovereign power." "Just as the separation and independence of the coordinate branches of the Federal Government serves to prevent the accumulation of excessive power in any one branch, a healthy balance of power between the States and the Federal Government will reduce the risk of tyranny and abuse from either front."

Where Congress exceeds its authority relative to the States, therefore, the departure from the constitutional plan cannot be ratified by the "consent" of state officials. An analogy to the separation of powers among the Branches of the Federal Government clarifies this point. The Constitution's division of power among the three Branches is violated where one Branch invades the territory of another, whether or not the encroached-upon Branch approves the encroachment. In *INS v. Chadha* [1983], we held that the legislative veto violated the constitutional requirement that legislation be presented to the President, despite Presidents' approval of hundreds of statutes containing a legislative veto provision. The constitutional authority of Congress cannot be expanded by the "consent" of the governmental unit whose domain is thereby narrowed, whether that unit is the Executive Branch or the States.

State officials thus cannot consent to the enlargement of the powers of Congress beyond those enumerated in the Constitution. Indeed, the facts of these cases raise the possibility that powerful incentives might lead both federal and state officials to view departures from the federal structure to be in their personal interests. Most citizens recognize the need for radioactive waste disposal sites, but few want sites near their homes. As a result, while it would be well within the authority of either federal or state officials to choose where the disposal sites will be, it is likely to be in the political interest of each individual official to avoid being held accountable to the voters for the choice of location. If a federal official is faced with the alternatives of choosing a location or directing the States to do it, the official may well prefer the latter, as a means of shifting responsibility for the eventual decision. If a state official is faced with the same set of alternatives—choosing a location or having Congress direct the choice of a location—the state official may also prefer the latter, as it may permit the avoidance of personal responsibility. The interests of public officials thus may not coincide with the Constitution's intergovernmental allocation of authority. Where state officials purport to submit to the direction of Congress in this manner, federalism is hardly being advanced.

Some truths are so basic that, like the air around us, they are easily overlooked. Much of the Constitution is concerned with setting forth the form of our government, and the courts have traditionally invalidated measures deviating from that form. The result may appear "formalistic" in a given case to partisans of the measure at issue, because such measures are typically the product of the era's perceived necessity. But the Constitution protects us from our own best intentions: It divides power among sovereigns and among branches of government precisely so that we may resist the temptation to concentrate power in one location as an expedient solution to the crisis of the day. The shortage of disposal sites for radioactive waste is a pressing national problem, but a judiciary that licensed extraconstitutional government with each issue of comparable gravity would, in the long run, be far worse.

States are not mere political subdivisions of the United States. State governments are neither regional offices nor administrative agencies of the Federal Government. The positions occupied by state officials appear nowhere on the Federal Government's most detailed organizational chart. The Constitution instead "leaves to the several States a residuary and inviolable sovereignty," reserved explicitly to the States by the Tenth Amendment.

Whatever the outer limits of that sovereignty may be, one thing is clear: The Federal Government may not compel the States to enact or administer a federal regulatory program. The Constitution permits both the Federal Government and the States to enact legislation regarding the disposal of low-level radioactive waste. The Constitution enables the Federal Government to pre-empt state regulation contrary to federal interests, and it permits the Federal Government to hold out incentives to the States as a means of encouraging them to adopt suggested regulatory schemes. It does not, however, authorize Congress simply to direct the States to provide for the disposal of the radioactive waste generated within their borders. While there may be many constitutional methods of achieving regional self-sufficiency in radioactive waste disposal, the method Congress has chosen is not one of them. The judgment of the Court of Appeals is accordingly

Affirmed in part and reversed in part.

Justice WHITE, with whom Justice BLACKMUN and Justice STEVENS join, concurring in part and dissenting in part.

It is clear, therefore, that even under the precedents selectively chosen by the Court, its analysis of the take title provision's constitutionality in these cases falls far short of being persuasive. . . . Where it addresses this aspect of respondents' argument, the Court tacitly concedes that a failing of the political process cannot be shown in these cases because it refuses to rebut the unassailable arguments that the States were well able to look after themselves in the legislative process that culminated in the 1985 Act's passage. Indeed, New York acknowledges that its "congressional delegation participated in the drafting and enactment of both the 1980 and the 1985 Acts." The Court rejects this process-based argument by resorting to generalities and platitudes about the purpose of federalism being to protect individual rights.

Ultimately, I suppose, the entire structure of our federal constitutional government can be traced to an interest in establishing checks and balances to prevent the exercise of tyranny against individuals. But these fears seem extremely far distant to me in a situation such as this. We face a crisis of national proportions in the disposal of low-level radioactive waste, and Congress has acceded to the wishes of the States by permitting local decision making rather than imposing a solution from Washington. New York itself participated and supported passage of this legislation at both the gubernatorial and federal representative levels, and then enacted state laws specifically to comply with the deadlines and timetables agreed upon by the States in the 1985 Act. For me, the Court's civics lecture has a decidedly hollow ring at a time when action, rather than rhetoric, is needed to solve a national problem.

The ultimate irony of the decision today is that in its formalistically rigid obeisance to "federalism," the Court gives Congress fewer incentives to defer to the wishes of state officials in achieving local solutions to local problems. This legislation was a classic example of Congress acting as arbiter among the States in their attempts to accept responsibility for managing a problem of grave import. The States urged the National Legislature not to impose from Washington a solution to the country's low-level radioactive waste management problems. Instead, they sought a reasonable level of local and regional autonomy consistent

Comparative Note 5.3

There can be no doubt that judicial review permits, indeed requires, nonelected judges to make decisions of great political significance. Yet Canada's adoption of the Charter of Rights in 1982 was a conscious decision to increase the scope of judicial review. It is hard to say whether public acceptance of judicial review flows from a belief in the myth of "a strict and complete legalism," or whether people really are content that some political choices be made by judges. It seems to me, however, that the judges' lack of democratic accountability, coupled with the limitations inherent in the adversarial judicial process, dictates that the appropriate posture for the courts in the distribution of powers (or federalism) cases is one of restraint: the legislative decision should be overridden only where its invalidity is clear. There should be, in other words, a presumption of constitutionality. In this way a proper respect is paid to the legislators, and the danger of covert (albeit unconscious) imposition of judicial policy preferences is minimized.

SOURCE: Peter W. Hogg, *Canadian Constitutional Law*, 3d ed. (Toronto: Carswell, 1992), 122–23.

with Art. I, s 10, cl. 3, of the Constitution. By invalidating the measure designed to ensure compliance for recalcitrant States, such as New York, the Court upsets the delicate compromise achieved among the States and forces Congress to erect several additional formalistic hurdles to clear before achieving exactly the same objective. Because the Court's justifications for undertaking this step are unpersuasive to me, I respectfully dissent.

Notes/Queries/Readings

1. What provisions of the statute at issue in this case does the Court unanimously find to be legitimate? In what ways are these provisions consistent with the standards set forth in *South Dakota v. Dole* (1987; see chapter 6)? According to the majority, why are these provisions allowable from the perspective of democratic accountability?

2. How does Justice O'Connor interpret the significance of the Tenth Amendment in this case? How might the result in this case reassert the power of state governments? In what ways is the majority's analysis similar to that of the dissent in *U.S. Term Limits v. Thornton*? (Four of the six justices in the majority in *New York v. United States* were in the minority in *Thornton*.)

3. Should it matter constitutionally that the New York state government supported this regulation, and the state's congressional delegation voted overwhelmingly for it? Is New York merely trying to get all the benefits of the legislation with none of the costs? Besides the state government, who exactly is hurt by the take title provision? What is the purpose of the federal nature of our government? Who ultimately is it designed to protect?

4. Do you agree with Justice White's opinion that the majority view is a "formalistically rigid obeisance to 'federalism.'" Compare his opinion with his dissent in *INS v. Chadha*.

5. Is the Tenth Amendment, as Justice O'Connor concluded, "essentially a tautology"? Why? If it is not a tautology, how are judges to give it a principled meaning?

6. Consider the comment of Professor Hogg in Comparative Note 5.3. Is his perspective with respect to the power of Canadian judges consistent with the Supreme Court's view of its power in federalism and separation of powers cases?

7. For additional reading, see Martin H. Redish, *Doing it with Mirrors:* New York v. United States *and Constitutional Limitations on Federal Power to Require State Legislation*, 21 Hastings Constitutional Law Quarterly 593 (1994).

U.S. Term Limits, Inc. v. Thornton
514 U.S. 779, 115 S. Ct. 1842, 131 L. Ed. 2d 881 (1995)

In 1992, the voters of Arkansas approved Amendment 73 to their state constitution. The amendment prohibited a candidate for Congress from appearing on the ballot if the candidate had already served three terms in the House or two terms in the Senate. Candidates who had served the stated number of terms were not disqualified from running but could only receive "write-in" votes. An Arkansas trial court found that the amendment violated the qualifications clause of Article 1 of the federal Constitution, and the state supreme court affirmed. Opinion of the Court: *Stevens*, Kennedy, Souter, Ginsberg, Breyer. Concurring opinion: *Kennedy*. Dissenting opinion: *Thomas*, Rehnquist, O'Connor, Scalia.

Justice STEVENS delivered the opinion of the Court.

. . . The constitutionality of Amendment 73 depends critically on the resolution of two distinct issues. The first is whether the Constitution forbids States from adding to or altering the qualifications specifically enumerated in the Constitution. The second is, if the Constitution does so forbid, whether the fact that Amendment 73 is formulated as a ballot access restriction rather than as an outright disqualification is of constitutional significance. Our resolution of these issues draws upon our prior resolution of a related but distinct issue: whether Congress has the power to add to or alter the qualifications of its Members.

Petitioners argue that whatever the constitutionality of additional qualifications for membership imposed by Congress, the historical and textual materials discussed in *Powell* [*v. McCormack* (1969)] do not support the conclusion that the Constitution prohibits additional qualifications imposed by States. In the absence of such a constitutional prohibition, petitioners argue, the Tenth Amendment and the principle of reserved powers require that States be allowed to add such qualifications.

Petitioners argue that the Constitution contains no express prohibition against state-added qualifications, and that Amendment 73 is therefore an appropriate exercise of a State's reserved power to place additional restrictions on the choices that its own voters may make. We disagree for two independent reasons. First, we conclude that the power to add qualifications is not within the "original powers" of the States, and thus is not reserved to the States by the Tenth Amendment. Second, even if States possessed some original power in this area, we conclude that the Framers intended the Constitution to be the exclusive source of qualifications for members of Congress, and that the Framers thereby "divested" States of any power to add qualifications.

Contrary to petitioner's assertions, the power to add qualifications is not part of the original powers of sovereignty that the Tenth Amendment reserved to the States. Petitioner's Tenth Amendment argument misconceives the nature of the right at issue because that Amendment could only "reserve" that which existed before. As Justice Story recognized, "the states can exercise no powers whatsoever, which exclusively spring out of the existence of the national government, which the constitution does not delegate to them. . . . No state can say that it has reserved what it never possessed."

Each member of Congress is "an officer of the union, deriving his powers and qualifications from the Constitution, and neither created by, dependent upon, nor controllable by, the states. Those officers owe their existence and function to the united voice of the whole, not a portion, of the people." Representatives and Senators are as much officers of the entire nation as is the President. States thus "have just as much right, and no more, to prescribe new qualifications for a representative, as they have for a president. . . . It is no original prerogative of state power to appoint a representative, a senator, or a president for the union."

We believe that the Constitution reflects the Framers' general agreement with the approach later articulated by Justice Story. For example, Art. I, s. 5, cl. 1 provides: "Each House shall be the Judge of the Elections, Returns and Qualifications of its own Members." The text of the Constitution thus gives the representatives of all the people the final say in judging the qualifications of the representatives of any one State. For this reason, the dissent falters when it states that "the people of Georgia have no say over whom the people of Massachusetts select to represent them in Congress."

Two other sections of the Constitution further support our view of the Framers' vision. First, consistent with Story's view, the Constitution provides that the salaries of representatives should "be ascertained by Law, and paid out of the Treasury of the United States," Art. I, s. 6, rather than by individual States. The salary provisions reflect the view that representatives owe their allegiance to the people, and not to States. Second, the provisions governing elections reveal the Framers' understanding that powers over the election of federal officers had to be delegated to, rather than reserved by, the States. It is surely no coincidence that the context of federal elections provides one of the few areas in which the Constitution expressly requires action by the States, namely that "the Times, Places and Manner of holding Elections for Senators and Representatives, shall be prescribed in each State by the legislature thereof." This duty parallels the duty under Article II

that "Each State shall appoint, in such Manner as the Legislature thereof may direct, a Number of Electors." Art II., s. 1, cl. 2. These Clauses are express delegations of power to the States to act with respect to federal elections.

In short, as the Framers recognized, electing representatives to the National Legislature was a new right, arising from the Constitution itself. The Tenth Amendment thus provides no basis for concluding that the States possess reserved power to add qualifications to those that are fixed in the Constitution. Instead, any state power to set the qualifications for membership in Congress must derive not from the reserved powers of state sovereignty, but rather from the delegated powers of national sovereignty. In the absence of any constitutional delegation to the States of power to add qualifications to those enumerated in the Constitution, such a power does not exist.

Even if we believed that States possessed as part of their original powers some control over congressional qualifications, the text and structure of the Constitution, the relevant historical materials, and, most importantly, the "basic principles of our democratic system" all demonstrate that the Qualifications Clauses were intended to preclude the States from exercising any such power and to fix as exclusive the qualifications in the Constitution.

The Convention and Ratification Debates

The available affirmative evidence indicates the Framers' intent that States have no role in the setting of qualifications. In *Federalist Paper* No. 52, dealing with the House of Representatives, Madison addressed the "qualifications of the electors and the elected." Madison first noted the difficulty in achieving uniformity in the qualifications for electors, which resulted in the Framers' decision to require only that the qualifications for federal electors be the same as those for state electors. Madison argued that such a decision "must be satisfactory to every State, because it is comfortable to the standard already established, or which may be established, by the State itself."

The provisions in the Constitution governing federal elections confirm the Framers' intent that States lack power to add qualifications. The Framers feared that the diverse interests of the States would undermine the National Legislature, and thus they adopted provisions intended to minimize the possibility of state interference with federal elections. For example, to prevent discrimination against federal electors, the Framers required in Art. I, s. 2, cl. 1, that the qualifications for federal electors be the same as those for state electors. As Madison noted, allowing States to differentiate between the qualifications for state and federal electors "would have rendered too dependent on the State governments that branch of the federal government which ought to be dependent on the people alone." *The Federalist* No. 52. Similarly, in Art. I, s. 4, cl. 1, though giving the States the freedom to regulate the "Times, Places and Manner of holding Elections," the Framers created a safeguard against state abuse by giving Congress the power to "by Law make or alter such Regulations." The Convention debates make clear that the Framers' overriding concern was the potential for States' abuse of the power to set the "Times, Places and Manner" of elections. Madison noted that "it was impossible to foresee all the abuses that might be made of the discretionary power."

In light of the Framers' evident concern that States would try to undermine the National Government, they could not have intended States to have the power to set qualifications. Indeed, one of the more anomalous consequences of petitioners' argument is that it accepts federal supremacy over the procedural aspects of determining the times, places, and manner of elections while allowing the states carte blanche with respect to the substantive qualifications for membership in Congress.

We also find compelling the complete absence in the ratification debates of any assertion that States had the power to add qualifications. In those debates, the question whether to require term limits, or "rotation," was a major source of controversy. The draft of the Constitution that was submitted contained no provision for rotation. . . .

Regardless of which side has the better of the debate over rotation, it is most striking that nowhere in the extensive ratification debates have we found any statement by either a proponent or an opponent of rotation that the draft constitution would permit States to require rotation for the representatives of their own citizens. If the participants in the debate had believed that the States retained the authority to impose term limits, it is inconceivable that the Federalists would not have made this obvious response to the arguments of the pro-rotation forces. The absence in an otherwise freewheeling debate of any suggestion that States had the power to impose additional qualifications unquestionably reflects the Framers' common understanding that States lacked that power.

In short, if it had been assumed that States could add additional qualifications, that assumption would have provided the basis for a powerful rebuttal to the arguments being advanced. The failure of intelligent and experienced advocates to utilize this argument must reflect a general agreement that its premise was unsound, and that the power to add qualifications was one that the Constitution denied the States.

Democratic Principles

Our conclusion that States lack the power to impose qualifications vindicates the same "fundamental principle of our representative democracy" that we recognized in *Powell*, namely that "the people should choose whom they please to govern them. . . ." Additional qualifications pose the same obstacle to open elections whatever their source. The egalitarian ideal, so valued by the Framers, is thus compromised to the same degree by additional qualifications imposed by States as by those imposed by Congress.

Similarly, we believe that state-imposed qualifications, as much as congressionally imposed qualifications, would undermine the second critical idea recognized in *Powell*: that an aspect of sovereignty is the right of the people to vote for whom they wish. Again, the source of the qualification is of little moment in assessing the qualification's restrictive impact.

Finally, state-imposed restrictions, unlike the congressionally imposed restrictions at issue in *Powell*, violate a third idea central to this basic principle: that the right to choose representatives belongs not to the States, but to the people.

Consistent with these views, the constitutional structure provides for a uniform salary to be paid from the national treasury, allows the States but a limited role in federal elections, and maintains strict checks on state interference with the federal election process. The Constitution also provides that the qualifications of the representatives of each State will be judged by the representatives of the entire Nation. The Constitution thus creates a uniform national body representing the interests of a single people.

Permitting individual States to formulate diverse qualifications for their representatives would result in a patchwork of state qualifications, undermining the uniformity and the national character that the Framers envisioned and sought to ensure. *McCulloch v. Maryland* [1819], ("Those means are not given by the people of a particular State, not given by the constituents of the legislature, . . . but by the people of all the States. They are given by all, for the benefit of all—and upon theory should be subjected to that government only which belongs to all"). Such a patchwork would also sever the direct link that the Framers found so critical between the National Government and the people of the United States.

State Practice

. . . The Articles of Confederation contained a provision for term limits. As we have noted, some members of the Convention had sought to impose term limits for Members of Congress. In addition, many States imposed term limits on state officers, four placed limits on delegates to the Continental Congress, and several States voiced support for term limits for Members of Congress. Despite this widespread support, no State sought to impose any term limits on its own federal representatives. Thus, a proper assessment of contemporaneous state practice provides further persuasive evidence of a general understanding that the qualifications in the Constitution were unalterable by the States.

In sum, the available historical and textual evidence, read in light of the basic principles of democracy underlying the Constitution and recognized by this Court in *Powell*, reveal the Framers' intent that neither Congress nor the States should possess the power to supplement the exclusive qualifications set forth in the text of the Constitution.

Petitioners argue that, even if States may not add qualifications, Amendment 73 is constitutional because it is not such a qualification, and because Amendment 73 is a permissible exercise of state power to regulate the "Times, Places and Manner of Holding Elections." We reject these contentions.

In our view, Amendment 73 is an indirect attempt to accomplish what the Constitution prohibits Arkansas from accomplishing directly. As the plurality opinion of the Arkansas Supreme Court recognized, Amendment 73 is an "effort to dress eligibility to stand for Congress in ballot access clothing," because the "intent and the effect of Amendment 73 are to disqualify congressional incumbents from further service." . . .

It is not our province to resolve this longstanding debate.

We are, however, firmly convinced that allowing the several States to adopt term limits for congressional service would effect a fundamental change in the constitutional framework. Any such change must come not by legislation adopted either by Congress or by an individual State, but rather—as have other important changes in the electoral process—through the Amendment procedures set forth in Article V. The Framers decided that the qualifications for service in the Congress of the United States be fixed in the Constitution and be uniform throughout the Nation. That decision reflects the Framers' understanding that Members of Congress are chosen by separate constituencies, but that they become, when elected, servants of the people of the United States. They are not merely delegates appointed by separate, sovereign States; they occupy offices that are integral and essential components of a single National Government. In the absence of a properly passed constitutional amendment, allowing individual States to craft their own qualifications for Congress would thus erode the structure envisioned by the Framers, a structure that was designed, in the words of the Preamble to our Constitution, to form a "more perfect Union."

The judgment is affirmed.

It is so ordered.

Justice THOMAS, with whom The Chief Justice, Justice O'CONNOR, and Justice SCALIA join, dissenting.

It is ironic that the Court bases today's decision on the right of the people to "choose whom they please to govern them." Under our Constitution, there is only one State whose people have the right to "choose whom they please" to represent Arkansas in Congress. The Court holds, however, that neither the elected legislature of that State nor the people themselves (acting by ballot initiative) may prescribe any qualifications for those representatives. The majority therefore defends the right of the people of Arkansas to "choose whom they please to govern them" by invalidating a provision that won nearly 60% of the votes cast in a direct election and that carried every congressional district in the State.

I dissent. Nothing in the Constitution deprives the people of each State of the power to prescribe eligibility requirements for the candidates who seek to represent them in Congress. The Constitution is simply silent on this question. And where the Constitution is silent, it raises no bar to action by the States or the people.

Because the majority fundamentally misunderstands the notion of "reserved" powers, I start with some first principles. Contrary to the majority's suggestion, the people of the States need not point to any affirmative grant of power in the Constitution in order to prescribe qualifications for their representatives in Congress, or to authorize their elected state legislators to do so . . . When they adopted the Federal Constitution, of course, the people of each State surrendered some of their authority to the United States (and hence to entities accountable to the people of other States as well as to themselves). . . . In each State, the remainder of the people's powers—"the powers not delegated to the United States by the Constitution, nor prohibited by it to the States," Amdt. 10—are either delegated to the state government or retained by the people. . . . The Federal Government and the States thus face different default rules: where the Constitution is silent about the exercise of a particular power—that is, where the Constitution does not speak either expressly or by necessary implication—the Federal Government lacks that power and the States enjoy it.

These basic principles are enshrined in the Tenth Amendment, which declares that all powers neither delegated to the Federal Government nor prohibited to the States "are reserved to the States respectively, or to the people." . . . [T]he Amendment does make clear that powers reside at the state level except where the Constitution removes them from that level . . .

Any ambiguity in the Tenth Amendment's use of the phrase "the people" is cleared up by the body of the Constitution itself. Article I begins by providing that the Congress of the United States enjoys "all legislative Powers herein granted," s. 1, and goes on to give a careful enumeration of Congress' powers, s. 8. It then concludes by enumerating certain powers that are *prohibited* to the

States. The import of this structure is the same as the import of the Tenth Amendment: if we are to invalidate Arkansas' Amendment 73, we must point to something in the Federal Constitution that deprives the people of Arkansas of the power to enact such measures.

The majority begins by announcing an enormous and untenable limitation on the principle expressed by the Tenth Amendment. According to the majority, the States possess only those powers that the Constitution affirmatively grants to them or that they enjoyed before the Constitution was adopted; the Tenth Amendment "could only 'reserve' that which existed before." . . . The majority's essential logic is that the state governments could not "reserve" any powers that they did not control at the time the Constitution was drafted. But it was not the state governments that were doing the reserving. The Constitution derives its authority instead from the consent of *the people* of the States. Given the fundamental principle that all governmental powers stem from the people of the States, it would simply be incoherent to assert that the people of the States could not reserve any powers that they had not previously controlled.

The majority also sketches out what may be an alternative (and narrower) argument. Again citing Story, the majority suggests that it would be inconsistent with the notion of "national sovereignty" for the States or the people of the States to have any reserved powers over the selection of Members of Congress. The majority apparently reaches this conclusion in two steps. First, it asserts that because Congress as a whole is an institution of the National Government, the individual Members of Congress "owe primary allegiance not to the people of a State, but to the people of the Nation." Second, it concludes that because each Member of Congress has a nationwide constituency once he takes office, it would be inconsistent with the Framers' scheme to let a single state prescribe qualifications for him.

. . . [W]hile the majority is correct that the Framers expected the selection process to create a "direct link" between members of the House of Representatives and the people, the link was between the Representatives from each State and the people of that State; the people of Georgia have no say over whom the people of Massachusetts select to represent them in Congress. This arrangement must baffle the majority, whose understanding of Congress would surely fit more comfortably within a system of nationwide elections. But the fact remains that when it comes to the selection of Members of Congress, the people of each State have retained their independent political identity. As a result, there is absolutely nothing strange about the notion that the people of the states or their state legislature possess "reserved" powers in this area.

In a final effort to deny that the people of the States enjoy "reserved" powers over the selection of their representatives in Congress, the majority suggests that the Constitution expressly delegates to the States certain powers over congressional elections. Such delegations of power, the majority argues, would be superfluous if the people of the States enjoyed reserved powers in this area.

Only one constitutional provision—the Times, Places and Manner Clause of Article I, s. 4—even arguably supports the majority's suggestion. It reads:

"The Times, Places and Manner of holding Elections for Senators and Representatives, shall be prescribed in each State by the Legislature thereof; but the Congress may at any time by Law make or alter such Regulations, except as to the Places of chusing Senators."

Contrary to the majority's assumption, however, this Clause does not delegate any authority to the States. Instead, it simply imposes a duty upon them. The majority gets it exactly right: by specifying that the state legislatures "shall" prescribe the details necessary to hold congressional elections, the Clause "expressly requires action by the States." This command meshes with one of the principal purposes of Congress' "make or alter" power: to ensure that the States hold congressional elections in the first place, so that Congress continues to exist.

I take it to be established, then, that the people of Arkansas do enjoy "reserved" powers over the selection of their representatives in Congress. Purporting to exercise those reserved powers, they have agreed among themselves that the candidates covered by s. 3 of Amendment 73—those whom they have already elected to three or more terms in the House of Representatives or to two or more terms in the Senate—should not be eligible to appear on the ballot for reelection, but should none the less be returned to Congress if enough voters are sufficiently enthusiastic about their candidacy to write in their names. Whatever one might think of the wisdom of this arrangement, we may not override the decision of the people of Arkansas unless something in the Federal Constitution deprives them of the power to enact such measures.

The majority settles on "the Qualifications Clauses" as the constitutional provisions that Amendment 73 violates.

The Qualifications Clauses do prevent the individual States from abolishing all eligibility requirements for Congress.

If the people of a State decide that they would like their representatives to possess additional qualifications, however, they have done nothing to frustrate the policy behind the Qualifications Clauses. Anyone who possesses all of the constitutional qualifications, plus some qualifications required by state law, still has all of the federal qualifications. Accordingly, the fact that the Constitution specifies .

certain qualifications that the Framers deemed necessary to protect the competence of the National Legislature does not imply that it strips the people of the individual States of the power to protect their own interests by adding other requirements for their own representatives.

The majority responds that "a patchwork of state qualifications" would "undermine the uniformity and the national character that the Framers envisioned and sought to ensure." Yet the Framers thought it perfectly consistent with the "national character" of Congress for the Senators and Representatives from each State to be chosen by the legislature or the people of that State. The majority never explains why Congress' fundamental character permits this state-centered system, but nonetheless prohibits the people of the States and their state legislatures from setting any eligibility requirements for the candidates who seek to represent them.

In discussing the ratification period, the majority stresses two principal data. One of these pieces of evidence is no evidence at all—literally. The majority devotes considerable space to the fact that the recorded ratification debates do not contain any affirmative statement that the States can supplement the constitutional qualifications. For the majority, this void is "compelling" evidence that "unquestionably reflects the Framers' common understanding that States lacked that power." The majority reasons that delegates at several of the ratifying conventions attacked the Constitution for failing to require Members of Congress to rotate out of office. If supporters of ratification had believed that the individual States could supplement the constitutional qualifications, the majority argues, they would have blunted these attacks by pointing out that rotation requirements could still be added State by State.

But the majority's argument cuts both ways. The recorded ratification debates also contain no affirmative statement that the States cannot supplement the constitutional qualifications. While ratification was being debated, the existing rule in America was that the States could prescribe eligibility requirements for their delegates to Congress, even though the Articles of Confederation gave Congress itself no power to impose such qualifications. If the Federal Constitution had been understood to deprive the States of this significant power, one might well have expected its opponents to seize on this point in arguing against ratification.

The fact is that arguments based on the absence of recorded debate at the ratification conventions are suspect, because the surviving records of those debates are fragmentary. If one concedes that the absence of relevant records from the ratification debates is not strong evidence for either side, then the majority's only significant piece of evidence from the ratification period is *Federalist* No. 52.

Contrary to the majority's assertion, however, this essay simply does not talk about "the lack of state control over the qualifications of the elected," whether "explicitly" or otherwise.

It is true that *Federalist* No. 52 contrasts the Constitution's treatment of the qualifications of voters in elections for the House of Representatives with its treatment of the qualifications of the Representatives themselves. As Madison noted, the Framers did not specify any uniform qualifications for the franchise in the Constitution; instead, they simply incorporated each State's rules about eligibility to vote in elections for the most numerous branch of the state legislature. By contrast, Madison continued, the Framers chose to impose some particular qualifications that all members of the House had to satisfy. But while Madison did say that the qualifications of the elected were "more susceptible of uniformity" than the qualifications of electors, *Federalist* No. 52, he did not say that the Constitution prescribes anything but uniform minimum qualifications for congressmen. That, after all, is more than it does for congressional electors.

It is radical enough for the majority to hold that the Constitution implicitly precludes the people of the States from prescribing any eligibility requirements for the congressional candidates who seek their votes. This holding, after all, does not stop with negating the term limits that many States have seen fit to impose on their Senators and Representatives. Today's decision also means that no State may disqualify congressional candidates whom a court has found to be mentally incompetent, who are currently in prison, or who have past vote-fraud convictions.

In order to invalidate s. 3 of Amendment 73, however, the majority must go farther. The bulk of the majority's analysis—like Part II of my dissent—addresses the issues that would be raised if Arkansas had prescribed "genuine, unadulterated, undiluted term limits." But as the parties have agreed, Amendment 73 does not actually create this kind of disqualification. It does not say that covered candidates may not serve any more terms in Congress if reelected, and it does not indirectly achieve the same result by barring those candidates from seeking reelection. It says only that if they are to win reelection, they must do so by write-in votes. One might think that this is a distinction without a difference. As the majority notes, "[t]he uncontested data submitted to the Arkansas Supreme Court" show that write-in candidates have won only six congressional elections in this century. But while the data's accuracy is indeed "uncontested," petitioners filed an equally uncontested affidavit challenging the data's relevance. As political science professor James S. Fay swore to the Arkansas Supreme Court, "most write-in candidacies in the past have been waged by fringe candidates, with little public support and extremely low name identification." [I]n modern times only two incumbent Congressmen have ever sought reelection as write-in candidates. One of them was Dale Alford of Arkansas, who had first entered the House of Representatives by winning 51% of the vote as a write-in candidate in 1958; Alford then waged a write-in campaign for reelection in 1960, winning a landslide 83% of the vote against an opponent who enjoyed a place on the ballot. The other incumbent write-in candidate was Philip J. Philbin of Massachusetts, who—despite losing his party primary and thus his spot on the ballot—won 27% of the vote in his unsuccessful write-in candidacy. . . . [T]hese results—coupled with other examples of successful write-in campaigns, such as Ross Perot's victory in North Dakota's 1992 Democratic presidential primary—"demonstrate that when a write-in candidate is well-known and well-funded, it is quite possible for him or her to win an election."

. . . [T]oday's decision reads the Qualifications Clauses to impose substantial implicit prohibitions on the States and the people of the States. I would not draw such an expansive negative inference from the fact that the Constitution requires Members of Congress to be a certain age, to be inhabitants of the States that they represent, and to have been United States citizens for a specified period. Rather, I would read the Qualifications Clauses to do no more than what they say. I respectfully dissent.

Notes/Queries/Readings

1. How does Justice Stevens apply the principle of *Powell* to *Thornton*? What reading of the Constitution and conception of national/state relations does he advance in *Thornton*?

2. What significance should historical practice have on current evaluations of whether an action is constitutional? Are the historical studies in each opinion merely selective and used to support the justices' pre-existing readings of the Constitution's text and structure? Or are they used to support their intellectual or personal predilections?

3. All the opinions appeal in some way to Chief Justice Marshall's articulation of federal-state relations in *McCulloch*. Which opinion most closely approximates the spirit of Marshall's argument? Should this matter?

4. Which account seems to fit best with what you know about the behavior of Congress's members—that they serve the nation as a whole or that they consider themselves accountable only to their electoral constituency? Which account best explains the behavior of voters? Should we make constitutional arguments from such observations of political practice? Why or why not?

5. In his dissent, Justice Thomas argued that the national government and the states "face different default rules." Why? Are these different default rules a consequence of the constitutional text? Of constitutional theory? Of judicial interpretation?

6. Justice Thomas writes: "If we are to invalidate Arkansas' Amendment 73, we must point to something in the Federal Constitution that deprives the people of Arkansas of the power to enact such measures." Do you agree?

7. The majority insists that the Constitution derives its authority from the people *of the nation*, whereas the dissent insists that it derives its authority from the people *of the states*. Is this mere quibbling or is something very critical at stake here?

8. For reading on *Thornton*, see Chris Marks, U.S. Terms Limits, Inc. v. Thornton *and* United States v. Lopez: *The Supreme Court Resuscitates the Tenth Amendment,* 68 Colorado Law Review 541 (1997) and Lynn A. Baker, *They the People: A Comment on* U.S. Terms Limits, Inc. v. Thornton, 38 Arizona Law Review 859 (1996). On the topic of term limits more generally, see Bernard Grofman, ed., *Legislative Term Limits: Public Choice and Legislative Representation* (Cambridge: Cambridge University Press, 1996).

Younger v. Harris
401 U.S. 37; 91 S. Ct. 746, 27 L. Ed. 2d 669 (1971)

John Harris, Jr. was indicted in California for violating the state's Criminal Syndicalism Act. The act punished personal conduct that "advocates, teaches or aids and abets criminal syndicalism or the . . . propriety of . . . any unlawful method of terrorism as a means of accomplishing a change in industrial ownership or control, or effecting any political change." Harris was prosecuted under the act for advocating the abolition of capitalism and replacing it with socialism. Claiming that the state law violated his right to freedom of speech under the First Amendment, Harris filed suit in federal district court to enjoin the state prosecutor from proceeding with trial. A three-judge panel held the law invalid as a violation of the First Amendment and enjoined the prosecution. Opinion of the Court: *Black*, Blackmun, Burger, Harlan, Stewart. Concurring opinions: *Stewart*, Harlan, *Brennan*, Marshall, White. Dissenting opinion: *Douglas*.

Mr. Justice BLACK delivered the opinion of the Court.

A federal lawsuit to stop a prosecution in a state court is a serious matter.

Since the beginning of this country's history Congress has, subject to few exceptions, manifested a desire to permit state courts to try state cases free from interference by federal courts.

The precise reasons for this longstanding public policy against federal court interference with state court proceedings have never been specifically identified but the primary sources of the policy are plain. One is the basic doctrine of equity jurisprudence that courts of equity should not act, and particularly should not act to restrain a criminal prosecution, when the moving party has an adequate remedy at law and will not suffer irreparable injury if denied equitable relief. The doctrine . . . is . . . important under our Constitution, in order to prevent erosion of the role of the jury and avoid a duplication of legal proceedings and legal sanctions where a single suit would be adequate to protect the rights asserted. This underlying reason for restraining courts of equity from interfering with criminal prosecutions is reinforced by an even more vital consideration, the notion of "comity," that is, a proper respect for state functions, a recognition of the fact that the entire country is made up of a Union of separate state governments, and a continuance of the belief that the National Government will fare best if the States and their institutions are left free to perform their separate functions in their separate ways. This, perhaps for lack of a better and clearer

way to describe it, is referred to by many as "Our Federalism," and one familiar with the profound debates that ushered our Federal Constitution into existence is bound to respect those who remain loyal to the ideals and dreams of "Our Federalism." The concept does not mean blind deference to "States' Rights" any more than it means centralization of control over every important issue in our National Government and its courts. The Framers rejected both these courses. What the concept does represent is a system in which there is sensitivity to the legitimate interests of both State and National Governments, and in which the National Government, anxious though it may be to vindicate and protect federal rights and federal interests, always endeavors to do so in ways that will not unduly interfere with the legitimate activities of the States. It should never be forgotten that this slogan, "Our Federalism," born in the early struggling days of our Union of States, occupies a highly important place in our Nation's history and its future.

This is where the law stood when the Court decided *Dombrowski v. Pfister* [1965] and held that an injunction against the enforcement of certain state criminal statutes could properly issue under the circumstances presented in that case. In *Dombrowski*, unlike many of the earlier cases

---

Comparative Note 5.4

[In this case, Canada's Supreme Court had to decide whether the federal Combines Investigation Act giving the federal attorney general control of prosecutions under the act was within federal jurisdiction. The constitutional provisions cited in the following extract appear in Comparative Note 5.1 (p. 188).]

THE CHIEF JUSTICE— . . . Language and logic inform constitutional interpretation, and they are applicable in considering the alleged reach of s. 92 (14) and the allegedly correlative limitation of criminal procedure in s. 91 (27). I find it difficult, indeed impossible, to read s. 92 (14) as not only embracing prosecutorial authority respecting the enforcement of federal criminal law but diminishing the *ex facie* impact of s. 91 (27) which includes procedure in criminal matters. As a matter of language, there is nothing in s. 92 (14) which embraces prosecutorial authority in respect of federal criminal matters. Section 92 (14) grants jurisdiction over the administration of justice, including procedure in civil matters and including also the constitution, maintenance and organization of civil and criminal

provincial courts. The section thus narrows the scope of the criminal law power under s. 91, but only with respect to what is embraced within "the Constitution, Maintenance, and Organization of Provincial Courts . . . of Criminal Jurisdiction." By no stretch of language can these words be construed to include jurisdiction over the conduct of criminal prosecutions. Moreover, as a matter of conjunctive assessment of the two constitutional provisions, the express inclusion of procedure in civil matters in provincial Courts points to an express provincial exclusion of procedure in criminal matters specified in s. 91 (27). . . .

It must be remembered that s. 92 (14) is a grant of legislative power and if it gave the provinces legislative authority over the conduct of criminal prosecutions, then federal legislation conferring prosecutorial authority on either provincial or federal Attorneys General would be *ultra vires*. It cannot be argued that Parliament confers prosecutorial authority only with the consent of the provinces, for this would involve an unconstitutional delegation of legislative power.

SOURCE: *Attorney General of Canada v. Canadian National Transportation.* In the Supreme Court of Canada [1983] 2 S.C.R. 206.

denying injunctions, the complaint made substantial allegations that: "the threats to enforce the statutes against appellants are not made with any expectation of securing valid convictions, but rather are part of a plan to employ arrests, seizures, and threats of prosecution under color of the statutes to harass appellants and discourage them and their supporters from asserting and attempting to vindicate the constitutional rights of Negro citizens of Louisiana."

These circumstances, as viewed by the Court sufficiently establish the kind of irreparable injury, above and beyond that associated with the defense of a single prosecution brought in good faith, that had always been considered sufficient to justify federal intervention.

The District Court, however, thought that the *Dombrowski* decision substantially broadened the availability of injunctions against state criminal prosecutions and that under that decision the federal courts may give equitable relief, without regard to any showing of bad faith or harassment, whenever a state statute is found "on its face" to be vague or overly broad, in violation of the First Amendment. We recognize that there are some statements in the *Dombrowski* opinion that would seem to support this argument. But, as we have already seen, such statements were unnecessary to the decision of that case, because the Court found that the plaintiffs had alleged a basis for equitable relief under the long-established standards. In addition, we do not regard the reasons adduced to support this position as sufficient to justify such a substantial departure from the established doctrines regarding the availability of injunctive relief. It is undoubtedly true, as the Court stated in *Dombrowski*, that "(a) criminal prosecution under a statute regulating expression usually involves imponderables and contingencies that themselves may inhibit the full exercise of First Amendment freedoms." But this sort of "chilling effect," as the Court called it, should not by itself justify federal intervention.

Beyond all this is another more basic consideration. Procedures for testing the constitutionality of a statute "on its face" in the manner apparently contemplated by *Dombrowski*, and for then enjoining all action to enforce the statute until the State can obtain court approval for a modified version, are fundamentally at odds with the function of the federal courts in our constitutional plan. The power and duty of the judiciary to declare laws unconstitutional is in the final analysis derived from its responsibility for resolving concrete disputes brought before the courts for decision; a statute apparently governing a dispute cannot be applied by judges, consistently with their obligations under the Supremacy Clause, when such an application of the statute would conflict with the Constitution. But this vital responsibility, broad as it is, does not amount to an unlimited power to survey the statute books and pass judgment on laws before the courts are called upon to enforce them. Ever since the Constitutional Convention rejected a proposal for having members of the Supreme Court render advice concerning pending legislation it has been clear that, even when suits of this kind involve a "case or controversy" sufficient to satisfy the requirements of Article III of the Constitution, the task of analyzing a proposed statute, pinpointing its deficiencies, and requiring correction of these deficiencies before the statute is put into effect, is rarely if ever an appropriate task for the judiciary. . . . In light of this fundamental conception of the Framers as to the proper place of the federal courts in the governmental processes of passing and enforcing laws, it can seldom be appropriate for these courts to exercise any such power of prior approval or veto over the legislative process.

For these reasons, fundamental not only to our federal system but also to the basic functions of the Judicial Branch of the National Government under our Constitution, we hold that the *Dombrowski* decision should not be regarded as having upset the settled doctrines that have always confined very narrowly the availability of injunctive relief against state criminal prosecutions. We do not think that opinion stands for the proposition that a federal court can properly enjoin enforcement of a statute solely on the basis of a showing that the statute "on its face" abridges First Amendment rights.

The judgment of the District Court is reversed, and the case is remanded for further proceedings not inconsistent with this opinion.

Reversed.

Notes/Queries/Readings

1. How does Justice Black envision comity in terms of "Our Federalism"? What does his interpretation of the idea presume about our federal structure? Compare the notion of comity set forth in *Younger* and that advanced by the Federal Constitutional Court in Comparative Note 5.2 (p. 192). Could the German notion of comity be easily transplanted into American constitutional law?

2. Where is the idea of federalism articulated in the Constitution, according to Black? How does he know what the "ideals and dreams" of the Founders are?

3. What precisely is Black's theory of federalism? Can it be defined by any objective or absolute rule? If he proposes a balancing test, how is this balance to be struck? Can the text of the Constitution provide any guidance in solving this problem? What conception of the political community is embodied in Black's opinion? Compare Black's perspective with that of Chief Justice Laskin in Comparative Note 5.4 (p. 206). Does the Canadian perspective as articulated here leave any room for federal-state comity?

Pacific Gas and Electric Company v. State Energy Resources Conservation & Development Commission

461 U.S. 190, 103 S. Ct. 1713, 75 L. Ed. 2d 752 (1983)

A California statute conditions the construction of nuclear power plants on findings by the State Energy Resources Conservation and Development Commission that adequate storage facilities and means of disposal are available for nuclear waste. The statute also imposes a moratorium on the certification of new nuclear plants until the Energy Commission "finds that there has been developed and that the United States through its authorized agency has approved and there exists a demonstrated technology or means for the disposal of high-level nuclear waste." Pacific Gas and Electric Company and the Southern California Edison Company filed an action in federal district court claiming that these state provisions are invalid under the supremacy clause because they are preempted by the Federal Atomic Energy Act. The district court ruled in favor of the companies. The court of appeals held that the nuclear moratorium provisions in question were not preempted. Opinion of the Court: *White*, Burger, Brennan, Marshall, Powell, Rehnquist, O'Connor. Concurring opinion (in part): *Blackmun*, Stevens.

Justice WHITE delivered the opinion of the Court.

It is well-established that within Constitutional limits Congress may preempt state authority by so stating in express terms. . . . Absent explicit preemptive language, Congress' intent to supercede state law altogether may be found from a "scheme of federal regulation so pervasive as to make reasonable the inference that Congress left no room to supplement it," "because the Act of Congress may touch a field in which the federal interest is so dominant that the federal system will be assumed to preclude enforcement of state laws on the same subject," or because "the object sought to be obtained by the federal law and the character of obligations imposed by it may reveal the same purpose." Even where Congress has not entirely displaced state regulation in a specific area, state law is preempted to the extent that it actually conflicts with federal law. Such a conflict arises when "compliance with both federal and state regulations is a physical impossibility," . . . or where state law "stands as an obstacle to the accomplishment and execution of the full purposes and objectives of Congress."

Petitioners, the United States, and supporting amici, present three major lines of argument as to why [the state's action] is preempted. First, they submit that the statute—because it regulates construction of nuclear plants and because it is allegedly predicated on safety concerns—ignores the division between federal and state authority created by the Atomic Energy Act, and falls within the field that the federal government has preserved for its own exclusive control. Second, the statute, and the judgments that underlie it, conflict with decisions concerning the nuclear waste disposal issue made by Congress and the Nuclear Regulatory Commission [NRC]. Third, the California statute frustrates the federal goal of developing nuclear technology as a source of energy. We consider each of these contentions in turn.

. . . [F]rom the passage of the Atomic Energy Act in 1954, through several revisions, and to the present day, Congress has preserved the dual regulation of nuclear-powered electricity generation: the federal government maintains complete control of the safety and "nuclear" aspects of energy generation; the states exercise their traditional authority over the need for additional generating capacity, the type of generating facilities to be licensed, land use, rate-making, and the like.

The above is not particularly controversial. But deciding how [the statute] is to be construed and classified is a more difficult proposition. At the outset, we emphasize that the statute does not seek to regulate the construction or operation of a nuclear powerplant. It would clearly be impermissible for California to attempt to do so, for such regulation, even if enacted out of non-safety concerns, would nevertheless directly conflict with the NRC's exclusive authority over plant construction and operation. Respondents appear to concede as much. Respondents do broadly argue, however, that although safety regulation of nuclear plants by states is forbidden, a state may completely prohibit new construction until its safety concerns are satisfied by the federal government. We reject this line of reasoning. State safety regulation is not preempted only when it conflicts with federal law. Rather, the federal government has occupied the entire field of nuclear safety concerns, except the limited powers expressly ceded to the states. When the federal government completely occupies a given field or an identifiable portion of it, as it has done here, the test of preemption is whether "the matter on which the state asserts the right to act is in any way regulated by the Federal Act." A state moratorium on nuclear construction grounded in safety concerns falls squarely within the prohibited field.

That being the case, it is necessary to determine whether there is a non-safety rationale for [the statute]. . . .

Although these specific indicia of California's intent in enacting [the statute] are subject to varying interpretation, there are two further reasons why we should not become embroiled in attempting to ascertain California's true motive. First, inquiry into legislative motive is often an unsatisfactory venture. What motivates one legislator to vote for a statute is not necessarily what motivates scores of others to enact it. Second, it would be particularly pointless for us to engage in such inquiry here when it is clear that the states have been allowed to retain authority over the need for electrical generating facilities easily sufficient to permit a state so inclined to halt the construction of new nuclear plants by refusing on economic grounds to issue certificates of public convenience in individual proceedings. In these circumstances, it should be up to Congress to determine whether a state has misused the authority left in its hands.

Therefore, we accept California's avowed economic purpose as the rationale for enacting [the statute]. Accordingly, the statute lies outside the occupied field of nuclear safety regulation.

Petitioners' second major argument concerns federal regulation aimed at the nuclear waste disposal problem itself. It is contended that [the statute] conflicts with federal regulation of nuclear waste disposal, with the NRC's decision that it is permissible to continue to license reactors, notwithstanding uncertainty surrounding the waste disposal problem, and with Congress' recent passage of legislation directed at that problem.

The NRC's *imprimatur*, however, indicates only that it is safe to proceed with such plants, not that it is economically wise to do so. Because the NRC order does not and could not compel a utility to develop a nuclear plant, compliance with both it and [the statute] is possible. Moreover, because the NRC's regulations are aimed at insuring that plants are safe, not necessarily that they are economical, [the statute] does not interfere with the objective of the federal regulation.

Nor has California sought through [the statute] to impose its own standards on nuclear waste disposal. The statute accepts that it is the federal responsibility to develop and license such technology. As there is no attempt on California's part to enter this field, one which is occupied by the federal government, we do not find [the statute] preempted any more by the NRC's obligations in the waste disposal field than by its licensing power over the plants themselves.

Finally, it is strongly contended that [the statute] frustrates the Atomic Energy Act's purpose to develop the commercial use of nuclear power. It is well established that state law is preempted if it "stands as an obstacle to the accomplishment of the full purposes and objectives of Congress."

There is little doubt that a primary purpose of the Atomic Energy Act was, and continues to be, the promotion of nuclear power. The Act itself states that it is a program "to encourage widespread participation in the development and utilization of atomic energy for peaceful purposes to the maximum extent consistent with the common defense and security and with the health and safety of the public." The House and Senate Reports confirmed

---

Comparative Note 5.5

[For the content of Sections 91 and 92 of the Canadian Constitution, see Comparative Note 5.1 (p. 188).]

. . . "subjects which in one aspect and for one purpose fall within s. 92, may in another aspect and for another purpose fall within s. 91."

It follows from this theory that two relatively similar rules or sets of rules may validly be found, one in legislation within the exclusive federal jurisdiction, and the other in legislation within exclusive provincial jurisdiction, because they are enacted for different purposes and in different legislative contexts which give them distinct constitutional characterizations.

Thus the prohibition from driving a motor vehicle imposed following a conviction for driving while intoxicated may be the penalty for a criminal offense, validly enacted by Parliament, just as the suspension of a driving licence may be validly prescribed by a province for highway safety reasons.

• • •

Similarly, rules regarding "insider trading" may be regarded as belonging to corporate law within exclusive federal jurisdiction in the case of federally-incorporated companies and as regulation of trade in securities within exclusive provincial jurisdiction, applicable to federally-incorporated companies, provided the latter are not singled out and their essential powers are not impaired.

So too public nudity may be prohibited by Parliament in a criminal law context, and also be the subject of provincial regulation of entertainment in public houses operated under a provincial licence.

SOURCE: *Bell Canada v. Quebec*. In the Supreme Court of Canada [1988] 1 S.C.R. 749.

that it was "a major policy goal of the United States" that the involvement of private industry would "speed the further development of the peaceful uses of atomic energy." The same purpose is manifest in the passage of the Price-Anderson Act, which limits private liability from a nuclear accident. The Act was passed "in order to protect the public and to encourage the development of the atomic energy industry . . . ".

The Court of Appeals' suggestion that legislation since 1974 has indicated a "change in congressional outlook" is unconvincing.

The Court of Appeals is right, however, that the promotion of nuclear power is not to be accomplished "at all costs." The elaborate licensing and safety provisions and the continued preservation of state regulation in traditional areas belie that. Moreover, Congress has allowed the States to determine—as a matter of economics—whether a nuclear plant vis-a-vis a fossil fuel plant should be built. The decision of California to exercise that authority does not, in itself, constitute a basis for preemption. Therefore, while the argument of petitioners and the United States has considerable force, the legal reality remains that Congress has left sufficient authority in the states to allow the development of nuclear power to be slowed or even stopped for economic reasons. Given this statutory scheme, it is for Congress to rethink the division of regulatory authority in light of its possible exercise by the states to undercut a federal objective. The courts should not assume the role which our system assigns to Congress.

The judgment of the Court of Appeals is

Affirmed.

Mr. Justice BLACKMUN, with whom Mr. Justice STEVENS joins, concurring in part and concurring in the judgment.

I join the Court's opinion, except to the extent it suggests that a State may not prohibit the construction of nuclear power plants if the State is motivated by concerns about the safety of such plants.

. . . The Atomic Energy Act's twin goals were to promote the development of a technology and to ensure the safety of that technology. Although that Act reserves to the NRC decisions about how to build and operate nuclear plants, the Court reads too much into the Act in suggesting that it also limits the States' traditional power to decide what types of electric power to utilize. Congress simply has made the nuclear option available, and a State may decline that option for any reason. Rather than rest on the elusive test of legislative motive, therefore, I would conclude that the decision whether to build nuclear plants remains with the States. In my view, a ban on construction of nuclear power plants would be valid even if its authors were motivated by fear of a core meltdown or other nuclear catastrophe.

Notes/Queries/Readings

1. Does Justice White's analysis of the problem of comity differ from that of Justice Black in *Younger*?

2. What is the majority's vision of the nature of the *federal* union? What regulatory power does it allow the states over subjects on which Congress is also permitted to legislate? How might the text or the structure of the Constitution support Justice White's view?

3. Are the conditions of federal preemption mentioned at the outset of White's opinion consistent with the idea of the states as independent entities within a federal union?

4. Does the concurring opinion differ in its analysis? Does it allow for a greater state role in regulation?

5. Compare the reasoning of *Pacific Gas* with the statement of the Canadian Supreme Court in Comparative Note 5.5 (p. 209). Are the Canadian and American views on the doctrine of preemption compatible with one another?

Cooley v. Board of Wardens
53 U.S. 299, 12 How. 299, 13 L. Ed. 996 (1851)

In *Gibbons v. Ogden, infra,* p. 236, the Supreme Court held that a state could not exercise its power over local commerce in such a way as to interfere with the regulation by Congress of commerce among the states. But suppose Congress declines to regulate an aspect of local commerce. May a state then regulate that commerce even if it affects commerce that could otherwise be regulated by Congress? That is the issue here. In 1789, Congress placed the administration of harbors and ports under state control until national legislation could be enacted. In the absence of further legislation, Pennsylvania passed a law that required all ships entering or leaving the port of Philadelphia either to hire a local pilot or pay a fine of one-half the pilotage fee. Cooley was fined for not hiring a local pilot. He refused to pay, claiming that the state law impermissibly restrained interstate commerce. The lower courts ruled against Cooley. Opinion of the Court: *Curtis,* Taney, Catron, McKinley, Nelson, Grier. Concurring opinion: *Daniel.* Dissenting opinion: *McLean,* Wayne.

Mr. Justice CURTIS delivered the opinion of the Court.

That the power to regulate commerce includes the regulation of navigation, we consider settled. And when we look to the nature of the service performed by pilots, to the relations which that service and its compensations bear to navigation between the several states, and between the ports of the United States and foreign countries, we are brought to the conclusion, that the regulation of the qualifications of pilots, of the modes and times of offering and rendering their services, of the responsibilities which shall rest upon them, of the powers they shall possess, of the compensation they may demand, and of the penalties by which their rights and duties may be enforced, do constitute regulations of navigation, and consequently of commerce, within the just meaning of this clause of the Constitution.

It becomes necessary, therefore, to consider whether this law of Pennsylvania, being a regulation of commerce, is valid.

. . . [W]e are brought directly and unavoidably to the consideration of the question, whether the grant of the commercial power to Congress, did *per se* deprive the states of all power to regulate pilots. This question has never been decided by this court, nor, in our judgment, has any case depending upon all the considerations which must govern this one, come before this court. The grant of commercial power to Congress does not contain any terms which expressly exclude the states from exercising an authority over its subject-matter. If they are excluded it must be because the nature of the power, thus granted to Congress, requires that a similar authority should not exist in the states. If it were conceded on the one side, that the nature of this power, like that to legislate for the District of Columbia, is absolutely and totally repugnant to the existence of similar power in the states, probably no one would deny that the grant of the power to Congress, as effectually and perfectly excludes the states from all future legislation on the subject, as if express words had been used to exclude them. And on the other hand, if it were admitted that the existence of this power in Congress, like the power of taxation, is compatible with the existence of a similar power in the states, then it would be in conformity with the contemporary exposition of the Constitution (*Federalist*, No. 32), and with the judicial construction, given from time to time by this court, after the most deliberate consideration, to hold that the mere grant of such a power to Congress, did not imply a prohibition on the states to exercise the same power; that it is not the mere existence of such a power, but its exercise by Congress, which may be incompatible with the exercise of the same power by the states, and that the states may legislate in the absence of congressional regulations.

A majority of the court are of opinion that a regulation of pilots is a regulation of commerce, within the grant to Congress of the commercial power, contained in the third clause of the eighth section of the first article of the Constitution.

The diversities of opinion, therefore, which have existed on this subject, have arisen from the different views taken of the nature of this power. But when the nature of a power like this is spoken of, when it is said that the nature of the power requires that it should be exercised exclusively by Congress, it must be intended to refer to the subjects of that power, and to say they are of such a nature as to require exclusive legislation by Congress. Now the power to regulate commerce, embraces a vast field, containing not only many, but exceedingly various subjects, quite unlike in their nature; some imperatively demanding a single uniform rule, operating equally on the commerce of the United States in every port; and some, like the subject now in question, as imperatively demanding that diversity, which alone can meet the local necessities of navigation.

Either absolutely to affirm, or deny that the nature of this power requires exclusive legislation by Congress, is to lose sight of the nature of the subjects of this power, and to assert concerning all of them, what is really applicable but to a part. Whatever subjects of this power are in their nature national, or admit only of one uniform system, or plan of regulation, may justly be said to be of such a nature as to require exclusive legislation by Congress. That this cannot be affirmed of laws for the regulation of pilots and pilotage is plain. The act of 1789 contains a clear and authoritative declaration by the first Congress, that the nature of this subject is such, that until Congress should find it necessary to exert its power, it should be left to the legislation of the states; that it is local and not national; that it is likely to be the best provided for, not by one system, or plan of regulations, but by as many as the legislative discretion of the several states should deem applicable to the local peculiarities of the ports within their limits.

Viewed in this light, so much of this act of 1789 as declares that pilots shall continue to be regulated "by such laws as the states may respectively hereafter enact for that purpose," instead of being held to be inoperative, as an attempt to confer on the states a power to legislate, of which the Constitution had deprived them, is allowed an appropriate and important signification. It manifests the understanding of Congress, at the outset of the government, that the nature of this subject is not such as to require its exclusive legislation. The practice of the states, and of the national government, has been in conformity with this declaration, from the origin of the national government to this time; and the nature of the subject when examined, is such as to leave no doubt of the superior fitness and propriety, not to say the absolute necessity, of different systems of regulation, drawn from local knowledge and experience, and confined to local wants. How then can we say, that by the mere grant of power to regulate commerce, the states are deprived of all the power to legislate on this subject, because from the nature of the power the legislation of Congress must be exclusive. This would be to affirm that the nature of the power is in any case, something different from the nature of the subject to which, in such case, the power extends, and that the nature of the power necessarily demands, in all cases, exclusive legislation by Congress, while the nature of one of the subjects of that power, not only does not require such exclusive legislation, but may be best provided for by many different systems enacted by the states, in conformity with the circumstances of the ports within their limits. In construing an instrument designed for the formation of a government, and in determining the extent of one of its important grants of power to legislate, we can make no such distinction between the nature of the power and the nature of the subject on which that power was intended practically to operate, nor consider the grant more extensive by affirming of the power, what is not true of its subject now in question.

It is the opinion of a majority of the court that the mere grant to Congress of the power to regulate commerce, did not deprive the states of power to regulate pilots, and that although Congress has legislated on this subject, its legislation manifests an intention, with a single exception, not to regulate this subject, but to leave its regulation to the several states. To these precise questions, which are all we are called on to decide, this opinion must be understood to be confined. It does not extend to the question what other subjects, under the commercial power, are within the exclusive control of Congress, or may be regulated by the states in the absence of all congressional legislation; nor to the general question, how far any regulation of a subject by Congress, may be deemed to operate as an exclusion of all legislation by the states upon the same subject. We decide the precise questions before us, upon what we deem sound principles, applicable to this particular subject in the state in which the legislation of Congress has left it. We go no further.

We are of opinion that this state law was enacted by virtue of a power, residing in the state to legislate; that it is not in conflict with any law of Congress; that it does not interfere with any system which Congress has established by making regulations, or by intentionally leaving individuals to their own unrestricted action; that this law is therefore valid, and the judgment of the Supreme Court of Pennsylvania in each case must be affirmed.

Notes/Queries/Readings

1. Read *Gibbons v. Ogden* in chapter 6. Can *Cooley* be reconciled with *Gibbons*?

2. Should the fact that Congress expressly allowed states to impose their own regulations matter constitutionally—i.e., was the congressional statute itself unconstitutional? Does the existence of these different standards place too great a burden on interstate commerce? Or does it merely signal that Congress felt that "local peculiarities," best known by state governments, must be taken into account?

3. Would Pennsylvania's regulations have violated the commerce clause if Congress had not explicitly permitted the states to have different standards? Should Congress have the power to delegate regulation of interstate commerce to the states?

4. Should the absence of congressional guidance mean that states can act as they wish? Or could it mean that Congress thinks the activity should not be regulated, and it implicitly prohibits the states from enacting such regulations? For further reading see Laurence Tribe, *Toward a Syntax of the Unsaid: Construing the Sounds of Congressional and Constitutional Silence*, 57 Indiana Law Journal 515 (1982).

5. What conception of local and state community is implied in the majority opinion? Is the existence of many different standards in many different states destructive of national economic unity? Of local community? Why should we even consider the nation to comprise a single economic unit?

Southern Pacific Company v. State of Arizona

325 U.S. 761, 65 S. Ct. 1515, 89 L. Ed. 1915 (1945)

Arizona's Train Limit Law of 1912 made it unlawful for any person or corporation to operate within the state a railroad train with more than fourteen passenger cars or more than seventy freight cars. The law was a safety measure de-

signed to prevent accidents owing to the "slack action" of cars on long trains. In 1940 Arizona sued the Southern Pacific Company for its repeated violations of the law. The company admitted the offenses but maintained that the law violated the Constitution. The trial court ruled in favor of the company, but the state supreme court reversed. Opinion of the Court: *Stone*, Reed, Frankfurter, Murphy, Jackson, Burton. Concurring opinion: *Rutledge*. Dissenting opinions: *Black*, Douglas.

**Mr. Chief Justice STONE delivered
the opinion of the Court.**

Congress, in enacting legislation within its constitutional authority over interstate commerce, will not be deemed to have intended to strike down a state statute designed to protect the health and safety of the public unless its purpose to do so is clearly manifested, or unless the state law, in terms or in its practical administration, conflicts with the Act of Congress, or plainly and palpably infringes its policy.

Although the commerce clause conferred on the national government power to regulate commerce, its possession of the power does not exclude all state power of regulation. . . . [I]t has been recognized that, in the absence of conflicting legislation by Congress, there is a residuum of power in the state to make laws governing matters of local concern which nevertheless in some measure affect interstate commerce or even, to some extent, regulate it. Thus the states may regulate matters which, because of their number and diversity, may never be adequately dealt with by Congress. When the regulation of matters of local concern is local in character and effect, and its impact on the national commerce does not seriously interfere with its operation, and the consequent incentive to deal with them nationally is slight, such regulation has been generally held to be within state authority.

But ever since *Gibbons v. Ogden* [1824], the states have not been deemed to have authority to impede substantially the free flow of commerce from state to state, or to regulate those phases of the national commerce which, because of the need of national uniformity, demand that their regulation, if any, be prescribed by a single authority.

In the application of these principles some enactments may be found to be plainly within and others plainly without state power. But between these extremes lies the infinite variety of cases in which regulation of local matters may also operate as a regulation of commerce, in which reconciliation of the conflicting claims of state and national power is to be attained only by some appraisal and accommodation of the competing demands of the state and national interests involved.

Hence the matters for ultimate determination here are the nature and extent of the burden which the state regulation of interstate trains, adopted as a safety measure, imposes on interstate commerce, and whether the relative weights of the state and national interests involved are such as to make inapplicable the rule, generally observed, that the free flow of interstate commerce and its freedom from local restraints in matters requiring uniformity of regulation are interests safeguarded by the commerce clause from state interference.

The findings show that the operation of long trains, that is trains of more than fourteen passenger and more than seventy freight cars, is standard practice over the main lines of the railroads of the United States, and that, if the length of trains is to be regulated at all, national uniformity in the regulation adopted, such as only Congress can prescribe, is practically indispensable to the operation of an efficient and economical national railway system. On many railroads passenger trains of more than seventy cars are operated, and on some systems freight trains are run ranging from one hundred and twenty-five to one hundred and sixty cars in length. Outside of Arizona, where the length of trains is not restricted, appellant runs a substantial proportion of long trains. In 1939 on its comparable route for through traffic through Utah and Nevada from 66 to 85% of its freight trains were over 70 cars in length and over 43% of its passenger trains included more than fourteen passenger cars.

In Arizona, approximately 93% of the freight traffic and 95% of the passenger traffic is interstate. Because of the Train Limit Law appellant is required to haul over 30% more trains in Arizona than would otherwise have been necessary. The record shows a definite relationship between operating costs and the length of trains, the increase in length resulting in a reduction of operating costs per car. The additional cost of operation of trains complying with the Train Limit Law in Arizona amounts for the two railroads traversing that state to about $1,000,000 a year. The reduction in train lengths also impedes efficient operation. More locomotives and more manpower are required; the necessary conversion and reconversion of train lengths at terminals and the delay caused by breaking up and remaking long trains upon entering and leaving the state in order to comply with the law, delays the traffic and diminishes its volume moved in a given time, especially when traffic is heavy.

The unchallenged findings leave no doubt that the Arizona Train Limit Law imposes a serious burden on the interstate commerce conducted by appellant. It materially impedes the movement of appellant's interstate trains through that state and interposes a substantial obstruction to the national policy proclaimed by Congress, to promote adequate, economical and efficient railway transportation service. . . . Enforcement of the law in Arizona, while train lengths remain unregulated or are regulated by varying standards in other states, must inevitably result in an impairment of uniformity of efficient railroad operation because the railroads are subjected to regulation which is not uniform in its application. Compliance with a state statute limiting train lengths requires interstate trains of a length lawful in other states to be broken up and reconstituted as they enter each state according as it may impose varying limitations upon train lengths. The alternative is for the carrier to conform to the lowest train limit restriction of any of the states through which its trains pass, whose laws thus control the carriers' operations both within and without the regulating state.

If one state may regulate train lengths, so may all the others, and they need not prescribe the same maximum limitation. The practical effect of such regulation is to control train operations beyond the boundaries of the state exacting it because of the necessity of breaking up and reassembling long trains at the nearest terminal points before entering and after leaving the regulating state. The serious impediment to the free flow of commerce by the local regulation of train lengths and the practical necessity that such regulation, if any, must be prescribed by a single body having a nation-wide authority are apparent.

The trial court found that the Arizona law had no reasonable relation to safety, and made train operation more dangerous.

The principal source of danger of accident from increased length of trains is the resulting increase of "slack action" of the train. Slack action is the amount of free movement of one car before it transmits its motion to an adjoining coupled car.

. . . The length of the train increases the slack since the slack action of a train is the total of the free movement between its several cars. The amount of slack action has some effect on the severity of the shock of train movements, and on freight trains sometimes results in injuries to operatives, which most frequently occur to occupants of the caboose. The amount and severity of slack action, however, are not wholly dependent upon the length of train, as they may be affected by the mode and conditions of operation as to grades, speed, and load.

. . . The accident rate in Arizona is much higher than on comparable lines elsewhere, where there is no regulation of length of trains. The record lends support to the trial court's conclusion that the train length limitation increased rather than diminished the number of accidents. This is shown by comparison of appellant's operations in Arizona with those in Nevada, and by comparison of operations of appellant and of the Santa Fe Railroad in Arizona with those of the same roads in New Mexico, and by like comparison between appellant's operations in Arizona and operations throughout the country.

We think, as the trial court found, that the Arizona Train Limit Law, viewed as a safety measure, affords at most slight and dubious advantage, if any, over unregulated train lengths. . . . Its undoubted effect on the commerce is the regulation, without securing uniformity, of the length of trains operated in interstate commerce, which lack is it-self a primary cause of preventing the free flow of commerce by delaying it and by substantially increasing its cost and impairing its efficiency.

Here we conclude that the state does go too far. Its regulation of train lengths, admittedly obstructive to interstate train operation, and having a seriously adverse effect on transportation efficiency and economy, passes beyond what is plainly essential for safety since it does not appear that it will lessen rather than increase the danger of accident. Its attempted regulation of the operation of interstate trains cannot establish nation-wide control such as is essential to the maintenance of an efficient transportation system, which Congress alone can prescribe. The state interest cannot be preserved at the expense of the national interest by an enactment which regulates interstate train lengths without securing such control, which is a matter of national concern. To this the interest of the state here asserted is subordinate.

. . . Here examination of all the relevant factors makes it plain that the state interest is outweighed by the interest of the nation in an adequate, economical and efficient railway transportation service, which must prevail.

Mr. Justice BLACK, dissenting.

In *Hennington v. Georgia* [1896], a case which involved the power of a state to regulate interstate traffic, this Court said: "The whole theory of our government, federal and state, is hostile to the idea that questions of legislative authority may depend . . . upon opinions of judges as to the wisdom or want of wisdom in the enactment of laws under powers clearly conferred upon the legislature." What the Court decides today is that it is unwise governmental policy to regulate the length of trains. I am therefore constrained to note my dissent.

. . . [T]he "findings" of the state court do not authorize today's decision. That court did not find that there is no unusual danger from slack movements in long trains. It did decide on disputed evidence that the long train "slack movement" dangers were more than offset by prospective dangers as a result of running a larger number of short trains, since many people might be hurt at grade crossings. There was undoubtedly some evidence before the state court from which it could have reached such a conclusion. There was undoubtedly as much evidence before it which would have justified a different conclusion.

Under those circumstances, the determination of whether it is in the interest of society for the length of trains to be governmentally regulated is a matter of public policy. Someone must fix that policy—either the Congress, or the state, or the courts. A century and a half of constitutional history and government admonishes this Court to leave that choice to the elected legislative representatives of the people themselves, where it properly belongs both on democratic principles and the requirements of efficient government.

When we finally get down to the gist of what the Court today actually decides, it is this: Even though more railroad employees will be injured by "slack action" movements on long trains than on short trains, there must be no regulation of this danger in the absence of "uniform regulations." That means that no one can legislate against this danger except the Congress; and even though the Congress is perfectly content to leave the matter to the different state legislatures, this Court, on the ground of "lack of uniformity," will require it to make an express avowal of that fact before it will permit a state to guard against that admitted danger.

We are not left in doubt as to why, as against the potential peril of injuries to employees, the Court tips the scales on the side of "uniformity." For the evil it finds in a lack of uniformity is that it (1) delays interstate commerce, (2) increases its cost and (3) impairs its efficiency. All three of these boil down to the same thing, and that is that running shorter trains would increase the cost of railroad operations. The "burden" on commerce reduces itself to mere cost because there was no finding, and no evidence to support a finding, that by the expenditure of sufficient sums of money, the railroads could not enable themselves to carry goods and passengers just as quickly and efficiently with short trains as with long trains. Thus the conclusion that a

requirement for long trains will "burden interstate commerce" is a mere euphemism for the statement that a requirement for long trains will increase the cost of railroad operations. . . .

. . . I would affirm the judgment of the Supreme Court of Arizona.

Notes/Queries/Readings

1. This case seems to present a classic conflict between the principles of judicial supremacy and democracy. Would the result have been different had the Supreme Court heeded the advice contained in Comparative Note 5.3?

2. Was the state's interest in public safety accorded sufficient weight in this case? How is the legitimate state interest in safety to be balanced against the burden on interstate commerce?

3. Does the text or the structure of the Constitution provide any guidance to how this balance should be carried out? Is any balancing test necessarily a subjective product of the will of a majority of justices? Is such balancing nonetheless necessary?

4. Are Justice Black's objections effectively met by the majority? How closely would he examine state justifications for economic regulation? Is his reasoning more consistent with the concept of federalism?

City of Philadelphia v. New Jersey
437 U.S. 617, 98 S. Ct. 2531, 57 L. Ed. 2d 475 (1978)

A New Jersey statute prohibited the importation of most solid or liquid waste that originated or was collected outside the state. Operators of private landfills in New Jersey and several cities with contracts with these operators challenged the statute, claiming that it discriminated against interstate commerce. The Supreme Court of New Jersey upheld the law. Opinion of the Court: *Stewart*, Brennan, White, Marshall, Blackmun, Powell, Stevens. Dissenting opinion: *Rehnquist*, Burger.

Mr. Justice STEWART delivered the opinion of the Court.

Before it addressed the merits of the appellants' claim, the New Jersey Supreme Court questioned whether the interstate movement of those wastes banned by ch. 363 is "commerce" at all within the meaning of the Commerce Clause. Any doubts on that score should be laid to rest at the outset.

The state court expressed the view that there may be two definitions of "commerce" for constitutional purposes. When relied on "to support some exertion of federal control or regulation," the Commerce Clause permits "a very sweeping concept" of commerce. But when relied on "to strike down or restrict state legislation," that Clause and the term "commerce" have a "much more confined . . . reach."

We think the state court misread our cases, and thus erred in assuming that they require a two-tiered definition of commerce. In saying that innately harmful articles "are not legitimate subjects of trade and commerce," the *Bowman* Court [referring to *Bowman v. Chicago & Northwestern R. Co.* (1888)] was stating its conclusion, not the starting point of its reasoning. All objects of interstate trade merit Commerce Clause protection; none is excluded by definition at the outset. . . . [T]he Court [has] held simply that because the articles' worth in interstate commerce was far outweighed by the dangers inhering in their very movement, States could prohibit their transportation across state lines. Hence, we reject the state court's suggestion that the banning of "valueless" out-of-state wastes by ch. 363 implicates no constitutional protection. Just as Congress has power to regulate the interstate movement of these wastes,

States are not free from constitutional scrutiny when they restrict that movement.

Although the Constitution gives Congress the power to regulate commerce among the States, many subjects of potential federal regulation under that power inevitably escape congressional attention "because of their local character and their number and diversity." In the absence of federal legislation, these subjects are open to control by the States so long as they act within the restraints imposed by the Commerce Clause itself. The bounds of these restraints appear nowhere in the words of the Commerce Clause, but have emerged gradually in the decisions of this Court giving effect to its basic purpose. . . .

The opinions of the Court through the years have reflected an alertness to the evils of "economic isolation" and protectionism, while at the same time recognizing that incidental burdens on interstate commerce may be unavoidable when a State legislates to safeguard the health and safety of its people. Thus, where simple economic protectionism is effected by state legislation, a virtually *per se* rule of invalidity has been erected. . . .

The crucial inquiry, therefore, must be directed to determining whether ch. 363 is basically a protectionist measure, or whether it can fairly be viewed as a law directed to legitimate local concerns, with effects upon interstate commerce that are only incidental.

The New Jersey law at issue in this case falls squarely within the area that the Commerce Clause puts off limits to state regulation. On its face, it imposes on out-of-state commercial interests the full burden of conserving the State's remaining landfill space.

The appellees argue that not all laws which facially discriminate against out-of-state commerce are forbidden protectionist regulations. In particular, they point to quarantine laws, which this Court has repeatedly upheld even though they appear to single out interstate commerce for special treatment.

It is true that certain quarantine laws have not been considered forbidden protectionist measures, even though they were directed against out-of-state commerce. But those quarantine laws banned the importation of articles such as diseased livestock that required destruction as soon as possible because their very movement risked contagion and other evils. Those laws thus did not discriminate against interstate commerce as such, but simply prevented traffic in noxious articles, whatever their origin.

The New Jersey statute is not such a quarantine law. There has been no claim here that the very movement of waste into or through New Jersey endangers health, or that waste must be disposed of as soon and as close to its point of generation as possible. The harms caused by waste are said to arise after its disposal in landfill sites, and at that point, as New Jersey concedes, there is no basis to distinguish out-of-state waste from domestic waste. If one is inherently harmful, so is the other. Yet New Jersey has banned the former while leaving its landfill sites open to the latter. The New Jersey law blocks the importation of waste in an obvious effort to saddle those outside the State with the entire burden of slowing the flow of refuse into New Jersey's remaining landfill sites. That legislative effort is clearly impermissible under the Commerce Clause of the Constitution.

Today, cities in Pennsylvania and New York find it expedient or necessary to send their waste into New Jersey for disposal, and New Jersey claims the right to close its borders to such traffic. Tomorrow, cities in New Jersey may find it expedient or necessary to send their waste into Pennsylvania or New York for disposal, and those States might then claim the right to close their borders. The Commerce Clause will protect New Jersey in the future, just as it protects her neighbors now, from efforts by one State to isolate itself in the stream of interstate commerce from a problem shared by all. The judgment is

Reversed.

Mr. Justice REHNQUIST, with whom the Chief Justice joins, dissenting.

The question presented in this case is whether New Jersey must also continue to receive and dispose of solid waste from neighboring States, even though these will inexorably increase the health problems discussed above. The Court answers this question in the affirmative. New Jersey must either prohibit all landfill operations, leaving itself to cast about for a presently nonexistent solution to the serious problem of disposing of the waste generated within its own borders, or it must accept waste from every portion of the United States, thereby multiplying the health and safety problems which would result if it dealt only with such wastes generated within the State. Because past precedents establish that the Commerce Clause does not present appellees with such a Hobson's choice, I dissent.

. . . Under [prior cases], New Jersey may require germ-infected rags or diseased meat to be disposed of as best as possible within the State, but at the same time prohibit the importation of such items for disposal at the facilities that are set up within New Jersey for disposal of such material generated within the State. The physical fact of life that New Jersey must somehow dispose of its own noxious items does not mean that it must serve as a depository for those of every other State. Similarly, New Jersey should be free under our past precedents to prohibit the importation of solid waste because of the health and safety problems that such waste poses to its citizens. The fact that New Jersey continues to, and indeed must continue to, dispose of its own solid waste does not mean that New Jersey may not prohibit the importation of even more solid waste into the State. I simply see no way to distinguish solid waste, on the record of this case, from germ-infected rags, diseased meat, and other noxious items.

. . . According to the Court, the New Jersey law is distinguishable from these other laws, and invalid, because the concern of New Jersey is not with the movement of solid waste but with the present inability to safely dispose of it once it reaches its destination.

. . . [T]he Court implies that the challenged laws must be invalidated because New Jersey has left its landfills open to domestic waste. But, as the Court notes, this Court has repeatedly upheld quarantine laws "even though they appear to single out interstate commerce for special treatment." The fact that New Jersey has left its landfill sites open for domestic waste does not, of course, mean that solid waste is not innately harmful. Nor does it mean that New Jersey prohibits importation of solid waste for reasons other than the health and safety of its population. New Jersey must out of sheer necessity treat and dispose of its solid waste in some fashion, just as it must treat New Jersey cattle suffering from hoof-and-mouth disease. It does not follow that New Jersey must, under the Commerce Clause, accept solid waste or diseased cattle from outside its borders and thereby exacerbate its problems.

The Supreme Court of New Jersey expressly found that ch. 363 was passed "to preserve the health of New Jersey residents by keeping their exposure to solid waste and landfill areas to a minimum." The Court points to absolutely no evidence that would contradict this finding by the New Jersey Supreme Court. Because I find no basis for distinguishing the laws under challenge here from our past cases upholding state laws that prohibit the importation of items that could endanger the population of the State, I dissent.

Notes/Queries/Readings

1. What interest does New Jersey claim its regulation advances? Did the Court recognize this interest as legitimate? Why, then, did the Court strike down the law?

2. How does the Court connect the impact of this legislation to the commerce clause? How does the Court show that the New Jersey legislation produces an unconstitutional "economic isolation"? What would be the effect of allowing such legislation according to the majority's claim?

3. Why does Justice Rehnquist assert that the majority opinion offers the state a Hobson's choice? If the regulation were strictly motivated by a concern about waste, why were no restrictions placed on the in-state production and disposal of waste?

4. On the other hand, consider the broader policy implications of *Philadelphia*. Would a decision for New Jersey have prompted Philadelphia or Pennsylvania to develop new technologies of waste disposal? Might a decision for New Jersey have also prompted Congress to deal more readily with the neglected problem of waste disposal nationwide? Might the Court's fixation on "legal" federalism in *Philadelphia* have inhibited the development of a "democratic" solution to the problem of waste disposal in America?

5. For reading on this case, see Stanley E. Cox, *Burying Misconceptions about Trash and Commerce: Why It Is Time to Dump* Philadelphia v. New Jersey, 95 Dickenson Law Review 131 (1990) and David Pomper, *Recycling* Philadelphia v. New Jersey: *The Dormant Commerce Clause, Postindustrial "Natural" Resources, and the Solid Waste Crisis*, 137 University of Pennsylvania Law Review 1309 (1989).

Baldwin v. Fish and Game Commission of Montana

436 U.S. 371, 98 S. Ct. 1852, 56 L. Ed. 2d 354 (1978)

Montana residents were able to purchase a state elk-hunting license for $9 a year, while out-of-state residents who wanted to hunt elk in Montana were required to purchase a combination hunting and fishing license for $225 a year. A group of hunters from Minnesota, who had previously hunted elk in Montana, challenged the constitutionality of Montana's licensing scheme under the privileges and immunities clause of Article 4, sec. 2. A three-judge federal district court denied relief. Opinion of the Court: *Blackmun*, Burger, Powell, Rehnquist, Stevens, Stewart. Concurring opinion: *Burger*. Dissenting opinion: *Brennan*, Marshall, *White*.

Mr. Justice BLACKMUN delivered the opinion of the Court.

Appellants strongly urge here that the Montana licensing scheme for the hunting of elk violates the Privileges and Immunities Clause of Art. IV, s 2, of our Constitution. That Clause is not one the contours of which have been precisely shaped by the process and wear of constant litigation and judicial interpretation over the years since 1789. . . . We are, nevertheless, not without some pronouncements by this Court as to the Clause's significance and reach.

When the Privileges and Immunities Clause has been applied to specific cases, it has been interpreted to prevent a State from imposing unreasonable burdens on citizens of other States in their pursuit of common callings within the State, in the ownership and disposition of privately held property within the State, and in access to the courts of the State.

It has not been suggested, however, that state citizenship or residency may never be used by a State to distinguish among persons. Suffrage, for example, always has been understood to be tied to an individual's identification with a particular State. No one would suggest that the Privileges and Immunities Clause requires a State to open its polls to a person who declines to assert that the State is the only one where he claims a right to vote. The same is true as to qualification for an elective office of the State. Nor must a State always apply all its laws or all its services equally to anyone, resident or nonresident, who may request it so to do. Some distinctions between residents and nonresidents merely reflect the fact that this is a Nation composed of individual States, and are permitted; other distinctions are prohibited because they hinder the formation, the purpose, or the development of a single Union of those States. Only with respect to those "privileges" and "immunities" bearing upon the vitality of the Nation as a single entity must the State treat all citizens, resident and nonresident, equally. Here we must decide into which category falls a distinction with respect to access to recreational big-game hunting.

Many of the early cases embrace the concept that the States had complete ownership over wildlife within their boundaries, and, as well, the power to preserve this bounty for their citizens alone. It was enough to say "that in regulating the use of the common property of the citizens of [a] state, the legislature is [not] bound to extend to the citizens of all the other states the same advantages as are secured to their own citizens." *Corfield v. Coryell* [1825]. It appears to have been generally accepted that although the States were obligated to treat all those within their territory equally in most respects, they were not obliged to share those things they held in trust for their own people. In *Corfield*, Mr. Justice Washington, sitting as Circuit Justice, although recognizing that the States may not interfere with the "right of a citizen of one state to pass through, or to reside in any other state, for purposes of trade, agriculture, professional pursuits, or otherwise; to claim the benefit of the writ of habeas corpus; to institute and maintain actions of any kind in the courts of the state;

to take, hold and dispose of property, either real or personal," nonetheless concluded that access to oyster beds determined to be owned by New Jersey could be limited to New Jersey residents. This holding, and the conception of state sovereignty upon which it relied, formed the basis for similar decisions during later years of the 19th century.

In more recent years, however, the Court has recognized that the States' interest in regulating and controlling those things they claim to "own," including wildlife, is by no means absolute. States may not compel the confinement of the benefits of their resources, even their wildlife, to their own people whenever such hoarding and confinement impedes interstate commerce.

Appellants contend that the doctrine on which *Corfield* relied has no remaining vitality. We do not agree. . . . The fact that the State's control over wildlife is not exclusive and absolute in the face of federal regulation and certain federally protected interests does not compel the conclusion that it is meaningless in their absence.

Appellants have demonstrated nothing to convince us that we should completely reject the Court's earlier decisions. In his opinion in *Coryell*, Mr. Justice Washington, although he seemingly relied on notions of "natural rights" when he considered the reach of the Privileges and Immunities Clause, included in his list of situations, in which he believed the States would be obligated to treat each other's residents equally, only those where a nonresident sought to engage in an essential activity or exercise a basic right. He himself used the term "fundamental," in the modern as well as the "natural right" sense. . . . With respect to such basic and essential activities, interference with which would frustrate the purposes of the formation of the Union, the States must treat residents and nonresidents without unnecessary distinctions.

Does the distinction made by Montana between residents and nonresidents in establishing access to elk hunting threaten a basic right in a way that offends the Privileges and Immunities Clause? Merely to ask the question seems to provide the answer. . . . Elk hunting by nonresidents in Montana is a recreation and a sport. In itself—wholly apart from license fees—it is costly and obviously available only to the wealthy nonresident or to the one so taken with the sport that he sacrifices other values in order to indulge in it and to enjoy what it offers. It is not a means to the nonresident's livelihood. The mastery of the animal and the trophy are the ends that are sought; appellants are not totally excluded from these. The elk supply, which has been entrusted to the care of the State by the people of Montana, is finite and must be carefully tended in order to be preserved.

Appellants' interest in sharing this limited resource on more equal terms with Montana residents simply does not fall within the purview of the Privileges and Immunities Clause. Equality in access to Montana elk is not basic to the maintenance or well-being of the Union. . . . We do not decide the full range of activities that are sufficiently basic to the livelihood of the Nation that the States may not interfere with a nonresident's participation therein without similarly interfering with a resident's participation. Whatever rights or activities may be "fundamental" under the Privileges and Immunities Clause, we are persuaded, and hold, that elk hunting by nonresidents in Montana is not one of them.

Mr. Chief Justice BURGER, concurring.

In joining the Court's opinion, I write separately only to emphasize the significance of Montana's special interest in its elk population and to point out the limits of the Court's holding.

The doctrine that a State "owns" the wildlife within its borders as trustee for its citizens is admittedly a legal anachronism of sorts. . . . But, as noted in the Court's opinion, and contrary to the implications of the dissent, the doctrine is not completely obsolete. It manifests the State's special interest in regulating and preserving wildlife for the benefit of its citizens.

[This Court has] made clear that the Privileges and Immunities Clause does not prevent a State from preferring its own citizens in granting public access to natural resources in which they have a special interest.

It is the special interest of Montana citizens in its elk that permits Montana to charge nonresident hunters higher license fees without offending the Privileges and Immunities Clause. The Court does not hold that the Clause permits a State to give its residents preferred access to recreational activities offered for sale by private parties. Indeed it acknowledges that the Clause requires equality with respect to privileges "bearing upon the vitality of the Nation as a single entity." It seems clear that those basic privileges include "all the privileges of trade and commerce" which were protected in the fourth article of the Articles of Confederation. The Clause assures noncitizens the opportunity to purchase goods and services on the same basis as citizens; it confers the same protection upon the buyer of luxury goods as upon the buyer of bread.

Mr. Justice BRENNAN, with whom Mr. Justice WHITE and Mr. Justice MARSHALL join, dissenting.

Far more troublesome than the Court's narrow holding— elk hunting in Montana is not a privilege or immunity entitled to protection under Art. IV, s. 2, cl. 1, of the Constitution—is the rationale of the holding that Montana's elk- hunting licensing scheme passes constitutional muster. The Court concludes that because elk hunting is not a "basic and essential activit[y], interference with which would frustrate the purposes of the formation of the Union," . . . the Privileges and Immunities Clause of Art. IV, s. 2—"The Citizens of each State shall be entitled to all Privileges and Immunities of Citizens in the several States"— does not prevent Montana from irrationally, wantonly, and even invidiously discriminating against nonresidents seeking to enjoy natural treasures it alone among the 50 States possesses. I cannot agree that the Privileges and Immunities Clause is so impotent a guarantee that such discrimination remains wholly beyond the purview of that provision.

I think the time has come to confirm explicitly that which has been implicit in our modern privileges and immunities decisions, namely that an inquiry into whether a given right is "fundamental" has no place in our analysis of whether a State's discrimination against nonresidents— who "are not represented in the [discriminating] State's legislative halls,"—violates the Clause. Rather, our primary concern is the State's justification for its discrimination. . . . [A] State's discrimination against nonresidents is permissible where (1) the presence or activity of nonresidents is the source or cause of the problem or effect with which the State seeks to deal, and (2) the discrimination practiced against nonresidents bears a substantial relation to the problem they present.

It is clear that under a proper privileges and immunities analysis Montana's discriminatory treatment of nonresident big-game hunters in this case must fall. . . . There are three possible justifications for charging nonresident elk hunters an amount at least 7.5 times the fee imposed on resident big-game hunters. The first is conservation. . . . [T]here is nothing in the record to indicate that the influx of nonresident hunters created a special danger to Montana's elk or to any of its other wildlife species.

Moreover, if Montana's discriminatorily high big-game license fee is an outgrowth of general conservation policy to discourage elk hunting, this too fails as a basis for the licensing scheme. Montana makes no effort similarly to inhibit its own residents.

The second possible justification for the fee differential . . . is a cost justification. . . . The licensing scheme, appellants contend, is simply an attempt by Montana to shift the costs of its conservation efforts, however commendable they may be, onto the shoulders of nonresidents who are powerless to help themselves at the ballot box. The District Court agreed, finding that "[o]n a consideration of [the] evidence . . . and with due regard to the presumption of constitutionality . . . the ratio of 7.5 to 1 cannot be justified on any basis of cost allocation." . . . Montana's attempt to cost-justify its discriminatory licensing practices thus fails under the second prong of a correct privileges

220 Part Two   Intergovernmental Powers and Relationships

and immunities analysis—that which requires the discrimination a State visits upon nonresidents to bear a substantial relation to the problem or burden they pose.

The third possible justification for Montana's licensing scheme, . . . is actually no justification at all, but simply an assertion that a State "owns" the wildlife within its borders in trust for its citizens and may therefore do with it what it pleases.

In unjustifiably discriminating against nonresident elk hunters, Montana has not "exercised its police power in conformity with the . . . Constitution." The State's police power interest in its wildlife cannot override the appellants' constitutionally protected privileges and immunities right. I respectfully dissent and would reverse.

Notes/Queries/Readings

1. How does the Court distinguish between interests that are "fundamental" under the privileges and immunities clause and those that are not? Does the Constitution offer any guidance? Does the privileges and immunities clause protect only those activities or resources that are "basic to the maintenance or well-being of the Union"?

2. Does the distinction between fundamental and nonfundamental interests in fact elevate local or parochial definitions of community over a national definition of community?

3. Could Montana under *Baldwin* exclude nonresidents altogether from hunting elk within the state?

Chapter 6

Congressional Powers

*T*he fundamental defect of the Confederation, wrote Alexander Hamilton in 1780, "is a want of power in Congress."[1] He argued that "Congress should have complete sovereignty in all that relates to war, peace, trade, finance, and to the management of foreign affairs."[2] For the purpose of creating "a more perfect union," and over the strong objections of the anti-Federalists, Article 1 confered upon the national government primary—but not complete—authority over these realms of public policy. Article 1 incorporates most of Congress's powers and in terms noticeably more specific than those conferred on the judiciary (Article 3) or the executive branch (Article 2). Yet, as the cases in this chapter illustrate, the scope and range of these powers remain disputed. The dispute, of course, relates to our discussion in chapter 2 of the necessity (i.e., the "why and what") of constitutional interpretation.

Among the most disputed of Congress's powers is its authority "to regulate commerce . . . among the several states," commonly called the power to regulate interstate commerce. This clause has played an important role in binding the nation together as an integrated economic unit, but it has also been critical in determining the extent of congressional power generally. Over the decades, however, the commerce clause has been subject to broad and narrow interpretation. These varying interpretations have often corresponded to the ebb and flow of American economic and political development. The Court's abrupt change in direction in *NLRB v. Jones & Laughlin Steel Corporation* (1937, reprinted later in the chapter) is one prominent example of these cycles of change. The decision should be viewed against the backdrop of the growth in multistate corporate enterprise as well as within the context of the 1936 presidential election and Roosevelt's plan to pack the Supreme Court with justices favorable to the New Deal. *United States v. Lopez* (1995, reprinted later in the chapter) is the most recent turning point in the interpretation of federal power under the commerce clause. *Lopez* commands our attention because it resurrects and reenacts the debates among the Consti-

---

[1] Letter from Alexander Hamilton to James Duane, 3 September 1780 in Philip B. Kurland and Ralph Lerner, eds., *The Founder's Constitution* (Chicago: University of Chicago Press, 1987) I: 150.

[2] *Ibid.*, 153.

tution's Framers over the allocation of national and state authority. The case also fixes our attention on another of our themes, the tension between judicial review and democracy in America.

Regulating Interstate Commerce

The commerce clause raises several interpretive and normative questions. How, for example, is commerce to be defined? What constitutes commerce among the several states? What are the proper functions and powers of the state and federal governments under this clause? Does the change and growth of the nation's increasingly capitalist, commercial economy require a change in traditional ideas of which governmental structures have the power to regulate commerce? What weight should original intent, current values, or modern conditions of trade have in construing the commerce clause? Should constitutional interpreters hold fast to the more restrictive founding idea of what constitutes commerce among the states so as to avoid one of the Founders' fears, namely, a tyrannical national government? (The Founders, for their part, also feared the impotence of the Articles of Confederation.) Should they take account of a changing interdependent national economy that affects more than one state? If the states do not possess enough power to control commercial activities implicating more than a single state, should control then pass to the federal government? Should federal power extend to noncommercial activities with only an indirect or remote relationship to commerce?

Overlapping these queries are broader questions of democratic theory. When is it proper for the judicial branch to override decisions on commercial or economic matters forged in the national political process? Scholars such as Jesse Choper have argued that because the states play such a significant role in the composition and selection of the national government, the federal courts should not decide constitutional questions respecting the ultimate power of the national government relative to the states.[3] Would the same consideration apply when political majorities at the state level enact legislation impinging on commerce when no conflicting federal law exists? Should the federal courts interdict such laws merely because they independently conclude that a state has regulated interstate trade in violation of the commerce clause itself? Finally, how much responsibility under the Constitution do Congress and the Court have in assuring that the exercise of the commerce power does not interfere with the reserved powers of the states?

Marshall's Textualism

All treatments of the commerce clause begin with John Marshall's interpretation of its meaning in the seminal case of *Gibbons v. Ogden* (1824, reprinted later in the chapter). His *Gibbons* opinion, like that of *McCulloch v. Maryland*, belongs in the pantheon of great essays on American federalism. Its ruling—that New York's state-granted steamboat monopoly was unconstitutional because it conflicted with a federal coasting statute—is less important for present purposes than its definition of commerce and the scope of the power to regulate it. Commerce, Marshall declared, comprehends not only navigation between the ports of different states—the specific activity at issue in *Gibbons*—but "every species of commercial intercourse." As long as any aspect of commerce implicates or involves more than one state, such as trans-

---

[3]Jesse Choper, *Judicial Review and the National Political Process: A Functional Reconsideration of the Role of the Supreme Court* (Chicago: University of Chicago Press, 1980), 2.

portation or the exchange of commodities across state lines, Congress may regulate it, according to Marshall. The power to *regulate*, however, is equally broad. "This power, like all others vested in congress," wrote Marshall, "is complete in itself, may be exercised to its utmost extent, and acknowledges no limitations, other than are prescribed in the constitution." Marshall conceded, as in *McCulloch*, that the national government is "limited to specified objects," but the power to regulate those objects—interstate commerce being one of them—is "vested in congress as absolutely as it would be in a single [unitary] government."

Marshall's doctrine of national supremacy with respect to the clauses of Article 1 was not meant to deprive the states of their rightful authority over their internal affairs. Whereas commerce *among* the states is clearly subject to congressional legislation, commerce *within* the states, said Marshall, is subject to state regulation. Marshall also conceded that the state's police power extends to "inspection laws, quarantine laws, and health laws of every description" even though they "may have . . . considerable influence on commerce." It was Justice William Johnson, not Marshall, who in *Gibbons* posited Congress's exclusive authority over commerce and denied any significant difference between commerce among and within the states. This power, in Johnson's words, "can reside but in one potentate; and hence, the grant of this power carries with it the whole subject, leaving nothing for the state to act upon."

Marshall's disagreement with Johnson may have been more political than jurisprudential. Against the backdrop of a fierce national debate over the slave trade, Marshall seemed unwilling to make any grand doctrinal pronouncement on the full scope of federal or state authority over commerce. Any such pronouncement might have stoked the flames of the emerging national conflict over slavery and exposed the Supreme Court to political retaliation. (Southerners would have reacted bitterly to any decision giving Congress sweeping power over commerce; such power would have validated Congress's control of the slave trade within and among the states.) It was sufficient for the purpose at hand simply to strike down New York's law because it contravened a federal statute on the same subject. Judicial pragmatism was the order of the day, and future generations would have to work out, often in an equally pragmatic way, the implications of the middle road that Marshall sought to map out between Johnson's nationalism and state claims to concurrent authority over commerce.

Post-*Gibbons* Checks on National Power

When Roger Brooke Taney, a Jacksonian Democrat, became Chief Justice in 1836, many thought that he would proceed to demolish the constitutional edifice of judicial sovereignty and federal supremacy that Marshall had so deftly constructed. But Taney held firmly to the principle of judicial review and only refined the jurisprudence of federal supremacy. Taney, whose tenure lasted until his death in 1864, presided over the Supreme Court when the states were vigorously reacting to the challenges and evils of preindustrial capitalism. (For additional details see chapter 9.) Although his Court sustained many local regulations of business and commerce in ways that Marshall would not have approved, it left intact the basic structure of Marshall's nation-state jurisprudence. As for judicial review, Taney built on Marshall's gains, performing so well "that not even the monumental indiscretion of the *Dred Scott* decision could quite destroy the judicial imperium."[4] Together with the modifications in the field of federal-state relations, Taney's decisions set the stage for the era of judicial vigilance in support of capitalism and free enterprise.

---

[4] Robert G. McCloskey, *The American Supreme Court*, rev. by Sanford Levinson (Chicago: University of Chicago Press, 1994), 56.

Later in the nineteenth and well into the twentieth century, the Supreme Court returned to the dual federalism implicit in the states' rights account of the Constitution. It often used the commerce clause as a weapon to limit the ability of the federal government to regulate the national economy. These years corresponded roughly with the gilded age of American politics.[5] The gospel of wealth ruled the land, businessmen equated freedom with absolute liberty in the economic realm, and judges protected the rights of contract and property with a vengeance. Between 1888 and 1937, the federal judiciary itself zealously defended *laissez faire* capitalism and corporate autonomy. (See chapter 9.) The constitutionalism of economic liberty that reached its zenith in *Lochner v. New York* (1905), which restricted state power, found echoes in commerce clause cases such as *United States v. E. C. Knight* (1895, reprinted later in the chapter) and its progeny. The tension between federal and state authority was most acute here as the Court narrowed the scope of national authority in the interest of state sovereignty. (In *E. C. Knight*, the Court held that national regulatory power did not extend to "local" activities such as manufacturing or production.)

At the same time, however, we observe strong countervailing trends in support of a more magnanimous view of the commerce power. *Champion v. Ames* (1903, reprinted later in the chapter) initiated one of these trends. Known as the *Lottery Case*, *Champion* sustained a federal statute that had little to do with interstate commerce. Rather, it was designed to achieve a police power purpose in support of state efforts to suppress disfavored activities, here gambling, having no immediate relationship to commerce. The Court ruled that Congress could assist the states in rooting out certain viruses threatening national morals by blocking their entrance into the bloodstream of interstate commerce. "As a state may, for the purpose of guarding the morals of its own people, forbid all sales of lottery tickets within its limits," the Court declared, "so Congress, for the purpose of guarding the people of the United States against the 'widespread pestilence of lotteries,' and to protect the commerce which concerns all the states, may prohibit the carrying of lottery tickets from one state to another." In the years ahead, the Supreme Court would rely on *Champion* to sustain congressional efforts to keep the channels of commerce free of other "pollutants" such as prostitution, pornography, adulterated foods, and misbranded products.[6] In all these cases, the impetus for regulation had more to do with the police power than with the regulation of commerce.

Two other lines of authority helped to counterbalance the dual federalism implicit in decisions such as *E. C. Knight*. One line begins with the so-called *Shreveport* case,[7] in which the Supreme Court sustained an order requiring the Texas Railroad Commission to bring its intrastate shipment rates into line with higher interstate rates fixed by the Interstate Commerce Commission. By this time, trains had transformed the nation into a single economic unit. They were common instruments of interstate traffic and were so closely and substantially related to intrastate rail shipments, declared the Court, that Congress could regulate the latter when necessary to protect the former against local discriminatory ratemaking. *Swift & Co. v. United States* (1905), on the other hand, marks the start of a related line of authority.[8] *Swift* sustained the federal

---

[5] See Ralph Henry Gabriel, *The Course of American Democratic Thought* (New York: Greenwood Press, 1986), chap. 13, 151–69.

[6] See *Hoke v. United States*, 227 U.S. 308 (1913) and *Hippolite Egg Co. v. United States*, 220 U.S. 45 (1911), which have also been applied to immoral activity of a noncommercial kind. See *Caminetti v. United States*, 242 U.S. 470 (1917) and *Cleveland v. United States*, 329 U.S. 14 (1946).

[7] *Houston, East and West Texas Ry. v. United States*, 234 U.S. 342 (1914).

[8] See 196 U.S. 375 (1905) and *Stafford v. Wallace*, 258 U.S. 495 (1922).

Chapter 6   Congressional Powers

regulation of transactions in the stockyards of Chicago and other midwestern cities, since the cattle shipped in from out of state and slaughtered there were still in the stream of commerce. The meats processed and packaged in the stockyards were to be shipped and sold to dealers and consumers in still other states. Accordingly, Congress could regulate the sales practices of stockyard dealers so as to immunize the interstate market against local monopolies.

E. C. Knight, for its part, is prototypical of those pre-1937 cases that disabled the national government from dealing with the abuses of an unregulated market economy, just as they represented a return to what was thought to be the original vision of the Constitution's Framers. The sugar monopoly at issue in *Knight* could not be regulated by Congress because manufacturing was declared a local activity unrelated to the exchange of commodities in interstate commerce. In addition, the monopoly's effect on interstate commerce was considered to be indirect rather than direct and thus also outside the compass of congressional control. The Court reached a similar conclusion in *Hammer v. Dagenhart* (1918, reprinted later in the chapter). Congress sought to strike at the evil of child labor by prohibiting the interstate transportation of goods produced by underage children. The Court labored to distinguish this case from *Champion*, arguing that the particular goods involved here, unlike lottery tickets, were harmless. In any event, the evil sought to be eliminated—i.e, the exploitation of children—was strictly local and thus subject to the exclusive jurisdiction of the state.

The Supreme Court carried this originalist reasoning to new heights in *Carter v. Carter Coal Co.* (1936).[9] The Bituminous Coal Conservation Act of 1935 was one of several New Deal measures designed to rebuild and stabilize the American economy in a period of industrial crisis. It sought to regulate wages and hours of work in the nation's coal mines. Despite the importance of coal to the national economy, the Court nullifed the act because the *production* of coal, like labor relations in the coal industry, was a local activity with no more than an *indirect* effect on commerce. The Court implied that if the effect on commerce had been *direct*, the activity would be subject to congressional regulation. Insensitive to considerations of degree, the Court announced that if one ton of coal can be said to have but an indirect effect on commerce, the effect does not become direct by multiplying the tonnage. With this decision, like several others handed down in 1935 and 1936, the Supreme Court cut the heart out of President Roosevelt's program of economic recovery.[10]

Carter raises serious questions about the relationship between institutional competence and the structural design of the Constitution. Jesse Choper has urged the Supreme Court to regard as nonjusticiable federal-state conflicts grounded on the argument that federal law violates "states' rights." These disputes, he asserts, raise "issues of practicability" and "effectiveness of governmental levels" and thus should be resolved by the political branches. He writes: "Whatever the [judiciary's] special competence in adjudicating disputes over individual rights, when the fundamental constitutional issue turns on the relative competence of different levels of government to deal with societal problems, the courts are no more inherently capable of correct judgment than are the companion federal branches." Indeed, he continues, "the judiciary may well be less capable than the national legislature or executive in such inquiries,

---

[9] 298 U.S. 238 (1936).

[10] See, for example, *Schechter Poultry Corp. v. United States*, 295 U.S. 495 (1935); *United States v. Butler*, 297 U.S. 1 (1936); and *Railroad Retirement Board v. Alton R.R.*, 295 U.S. 330 (1935). These cases nullified, respectively, the National Industrial Recovery Act, the Agricultural Adjustment Act, and the Railroad Retirement Act.

given both the highly pragmatic nature of federal-state questions and the forceful representation of the states in the national political process."[11] The theory of democracy that inheres in many of the post-Civil War amendments to the Constitution would support Choper's view. It is a view that won the Court over in *Garcia v. San Antonio Metropolitan Transit Authority* (1985, reprinted later in the chapter).

In any event, the Supreme Court, largely in response to public criticism and President Roosevelt's well known court-packing plan, changed its mind and proceeded to uphold the validity of the nation's economic recovery program. The switch occurred when the Court decided to uphold the National Labor Relations Act in *NLRB v. Jones & Laughlin Steel Corp.* (1937, reprinted later in the chapter).[12] Far more sensitive than *Carter* to matters of degree, *NLRB* found that the unfair labor practices regulated by the federal law interrupted commerce so greatly as to burden it *directly*. While *NLRB* adhered to the analytical pattern of the Court's pre-1937 cases, it soon became clear that the line between local and national would no longer hold up in an increasingly complex economy. It was swiftly abandoned, along with the direct-indirect standard. Now Congress could regulate *any* local activity having a substantial economic effect on interstate commerce.

Wickard v. Filburn (1942, reprinted later in the chapter) took a giant step forward by allowing Congress to reach even the trivial actions of a single farmer if these actions, taken cumulatively with those of many others similarly situated, have a substantial impact on interstate commerce. In an effort to stabilize the agricultural economy, the Agricultural Adjustment Act of 1938 established a national acreage allotment for wheat and penalized farmers for growing wheat in excess of their assigned quotas. Filburn, a small Ohio farmer, planted wheat in excess of his allotment but used the excess for his own family. Nevertheless, the Court sustained the fine levied against him because even the personal consumption of the wheat grown on one's own property would affect the marketing of wheat generally. The Agricultural Adjustment Act was thus a valid exercise of the commerce power. *Wickard* pushed the commerce power to its limits, for almost any local economic activity seemed open to regulation under its logic.

Heart of Atlanta Motel v. United States (1964, reprinted later in the chapter), also represents a major expansion of the commerce power. *Wickard*, as noted, involved congressional regulation of economic activity. *Heart of Atlanta*, by contrast, validated the use of the commerce power for the purpose of achieving a social end, namely, the prohibition of racial discrimination. Title II of the Civil Rights Act of 1964 bans racial discrimination in public accommodations related to interstate commerce. That this section of the Civil Rights Act of 1964 sought to deal with a moral wrong, said the Court, does not invalidate the enactment if Congress has rational grounds for believing that racial discrimination "has a disruptive effect on commercial intercourse." Even conceding that the hotel operation was purely local, "if it is interstate commerce that feels the pinch," said the Court, "it does not matter how local the operation that applies the squeeze."[13] But Congress had no hard data on the magnitude of the pinch. Anecdotal evidence of racial discrimination in motels along interstate highways was sufficient to supply the rational basis for the law's passage.

---

[11]Jesse Choper, *The Scope of National Power vis-a-vis the State: The Dispensability of Judicial Review*, 86 Yale Law Journal 1556–57 (1977).

[12]*NLRB* was foreshadowed a month earlier by *West Coast Hotel Co. v. Parrish* [1937] in which the Court by the same vote sustained a state minimum wage law for women and children. It thus overruled *Adkins v. Children's Hospital* [1923], 261 U.S. 525, a decision which had nullified a similar statute because it violated freedom of contract.

[13]379 U.S. 241, 258 (1964).

Katzenbach v. McClung (1964) extended the application of the Civil Rights Act to Ollie's Barbecue, a family-owned restaurant located within the city of Birmingham, Alabama, some distance from an interstate highway. Nevertheless, Olie's Barbecue was reachable through the federal commerce power because forty-six percent of the meat the restaurant sold to local customers "was bought from a local supplier who had procured it from outside the state."[14] After *Wickard*, *Atlanta*, and *McClung*, the reach of congressional power under the commerce clause seemed nearly unlimited.

New-Found Limits on Congressional Power

On 24 June 1976 by a five to four vote, the Supreme Court struck down a federal statute that extended the maximum hours and minimum wage provisions of the Fair Labor Standards Act (FLSA) to most state and local employees. *National League of Cities v. Usery* (1976, reprinted later in this chapter), wrote Justice Brennan in dissent, "repudiates principles governing judicial interpretation of our Constitution settled since the time of Chief Justice John Marshall."[15] Not since 1936 had the Supreme Court found unconstitutional an exercise of the federal commerce power. The story of *Usery* and its repudiation just nine years later in *Garcia v. San Antonio Metropolitan Transit Authority* (1985, reprinted later in this chapter) is a fascinating tale of doctrinal warfare on the Supreme Court. But the dispute also triggered a fierce debate over the constitutional role of the federal judiciary in commerce clause cases. The highlights of the dispute are worth examining, and we will do so by retracing the path of the four cases in table 6.1.

TABLE 6.1 *Alignment on the Supreme Court*

Wirtz (1968)		*Fry* (1975)		*Usery* (1976)		*Garcia* (1985)	
Harlan	+	Marshall	+	Rehnquist	+	Blackmun	+
Black	+	Burger	+	Burger	+	Brennan	+
Brennan	+	Brennan	+	Powell	+	White	+
White	+	White	+	Stewart	+	Marshall	+
Fortas	+	Blackmun	+	Blackmun	+	Stevens	+
Warren	+	Powell	+	Brennan	−	Powell	−
Douglas	−	Stewart	+	White	−	Burger	−
Stewart	−	Douglas	x	Marshall	−	O'Connor	−
Marshall	o	Rehnquist	−	Stevens	−	Rehnquist	−

Legend: + = in the majority; − = in dissent; o = nonparticipating; x = review improvidently granted.

The Rise and Fall of a Constitutional Doctrine

Congress's power clearly extends to nonstate activities and private businesses affecting or affected by interstate commerce. But may Congress subject a state to the same legislation applicable to private parties? The Supreme Court had already answered this question in 1936. *United States v. California* had ruled that a state-owned railroad running between two points within a single state is subject to the terms of the Federal Safety Appliance Act.[16] Whether state-run or not, said the Court, the railroad is a common carrier engaged in interstate trade and thus subject to congressional regulation. In contrast, the state argued that by regulating the railroad it was performing a public function in its sovereign capacity as a state; accordingly, the railroad lay outside the

---

[14] 379 U.S. 294, 296 (1964).

[15] 426 U.S. 833, 857 (1976).

[16] 297 U.S. 275.

scope of federal control. Relying on *Shreveport* and the *Stockyard* cases, the Court noted simply that a state—no less than an individual—is within Congress's reach when its activity affects interstate commerce. Chief Justice Stone, speaking for the Court, dismissed the state's "sovereignty" argument by asserting that "the sovereign power of the state is necessarily diminished to the extent of the grant of power to the Federal Government in the Constitution."[17]

When *Maryland v. Wirtz* (1968) was decided, Stone's view seemed solidly entrenched in American law.[18] But Maryland and twenty-seven other states challenged the validity of congressional amendments extending the Fair Labor Standards Act (FLSA) to employees of state hospitals and public schools. A 1941 decision had overruled *Hammer v. Dagenhart* (1918)[19]—a case that struck down a federal statute (Federal Child Labor Act) prohibiting the shipment in interstate commerce of goods produced in factories that employed children under the age of fourteen—and upheld the FLSA as a valid means of curtailing the industrial strife that often interferes with the free flow of commerce. But could the FLSA be amended to reach *state* employees? For six of the *Wirtz* justices, the answer was an easy "yes." Because the commerce power is plenary, as Chief Justice Marshall insisted in *Gibbons v. Ogden* (1824), regulations affecting interstate commerce may cover *any* enterprise, activity, or employee related to commerce. In short, as in other post-1937 cases, the *Wirtz* Court conferred constitutional status on its vision of the national economy as an organic unity.

Seven years later, in *Fry v. United States* (1975),[20] the Supreme Court relied on *Wirtz* to sustain a special program of wage and salary controls that applied to government employees as well as workers in the private economy. (Congress enacted the Economic Stabilization Act of 1970 during an economic crisis.) *Fry*'s most notable feature, however, was Justice Rehnquist's lone dissent. Already known for his strong views in favor of state sovereignty, Rehnquist drew upon dual federalist lines of thought in several old federal tax cases to mount a skillful assault on the doctrinal basis of *Wirtz*. Rehnquist had dramatically shifted the Court's interpretive perspective. The question for him was not whether Article 1 had authorized this exercise of the federal commerce power, but rather whether Congress had invaded a province of state sovereignty under the Tenth Amendment. He was even able to draw support from the liberal Justice William O. Douglas, whose dissent in *Wirtz* had labeled FLSA's application to state employees as "a serious invasion of state sovereignty . . . [in]consistent with our constitutional federalism."[21]

Rehnquist's opinion set the stage for the equally dramatic reversal of *Wirtz* in *Usery*. Even allowing for the different circumstances behind *Fry* and *Usery*, it was amazing to find Rehnquist's lone dissent in 1975 carrying the day in 1976. Congress had amended the FLSA once again, now to extend its reach to nearly all employees of the states and their political subdivisions. Rehnquist did not deny that the wages and hours of state employees affected interstate commerce. In his view, however, the legislation was directed against the "States as States," displacing them "in areas of [their] traditional governmental functions," thus violating the Tenth Amendment. The decision had potentially revolutionary implications, and from the scathing words of Justice Brennan's dissent, it was clear that the majority opinion had profoundly influenced the Court's commerce clause jurisprudence.

---

[17] *Ibid.*, at 184.

[18] 392 U.S. 183 (1968).

[19] *United States v. Darby*, 312 U.S. 100 (1941).

[20] 421 U.S. 542 (1975).

[21] 392 U.S. 183, 201.

Overlaying the doctrinal division on the *Usery* Court was the equally intense conflict among the justices over the role of the judiciary in federal commerce clause cases. Justice Brennan rebuked the majority for its "patent usurpation of the role reserved for the political process." Worse, he wrote, is "the startling restructuring of our federal system, and the role . . . create[d] therein for the federal judiciary." Justice Blackmun, on the other hand, was unwilling to read the majority opinion "so despairingly"—as if the Court had reverted to the conceptual reasoning of its pre-1937 jurisprudence. He stressed what he thought was the Court's attempt to balance state and federal interests. His own view was that the Court had merely concluded in the particular circumstances of *Usery* that the state's vital interest in structuring the wages of its employees outweighed the asserted national interest in setting those wages. Blackmun tried to soothe the dissenters by suggesting that with respect to federal environmental legislation, for example, the balance of interests would favor the federal government.

Nevertheless, as might have been anticipated, *Usery* triggered scores of constitutional challenges against other federal laws regulating various kinds of state activities, enterprises, or functions. In each of the cases reaching the Supreme Court, the federal act was sustained, with Blackmun almost always providing the deciding vote to sustain it. Blackmun seemed determined to confine *Usery* to its particular facts, concluding in those other instances that the activity in question failed to qualify as a "traditional governmental function" worthy of protection under the Tenth Amendment.[22] Finally, frustrated by its inability to clearly distinguish traditional from nontraditional state functions—an uncertainty reflected by the inconsistent results among the lower federal courts on this question—the Court gave up altogether in *Garcia*, consigning *Usery* to the grave just nine years after its birth. Unsurprisingly, it was Justice Blackmun who provided the fifth vote to overrule *Usery*.

The doctrinal results in *Usery* and *Garcia* demonstrate how the method of structural interpretation can yield different outcomes. As for *Garcia*, however, the result seems less important than the tension it reflects between democracy and judicial review. Because the states are represented in the structure of the federal government, one side argues, the federal judiciary need not be called upon to protect the vital interests of the states against the majoritarian decisions of Congress. The other side argues that close judicial vigilance of these decisions is important lest a "nationalistic" Congress be allowed to intrude into the vital core of state sovereignty. On this view, the vigorous exercise of judicial oversight may help to protect local majorities against invasion by the national government.

Lopez v. United States (1995, reprinted later in the chapter) also raises issues of democratic theory and federalism. *Usery* eventually became a temporary departure from the extension of the federal commerce power. *Lopez*, on the other hand, was a constitutional change of major importance. For the first time in sixty years, a general law enacted by Congress under the commerce clause failed to receive the Court's approval. Writing for a five to four majority, as he had in *Usery*, Chief Justice Rehnquist invalidated the Gun-Free School Zones Act of 1990, which had made it a federal offense "for any individual knowingly to possess a firearm at a place that [he] knows, or has reasonable cause to believe, is a school zone." Until *Lopez*, it was established doctrine that Congress could regulate any intrastate activity having a substantial effect

---

[22]See, for example, *Hodel v. Virginia Surface Mining Association*, 452 U.S. 264 (1981) upholding a federal statute regulating a state-owned strip mining operation; *Federal Energy Regulatory Commission v. Mississippi*, 456 U.S. 742 (1982) upholding a federal utility regulatory act; and *EEOC v. Wyoming*, 460 U.S. 226 (1983) sustaining a federal age discrimination in employment act over a law on mandatory retirement for state employees.

on commerce. Indeed, this doctrine had long provided a vehicle for federalizing intrastate crime as a means of cutting down on interstate criminal activity.[23] Any such law would receive the Court's blessing if it could be found that Congress had a rational basis for believing that such a law affected interstate commerce. At least with regard to criminal activity, *Lopez* seemed resolved to halt any further conversion of the commerce clause into "a general police power of the sort retained by the States." The "gun-possession" law was struck down because in the majority's judgment, Congress had regulated a purely local activity on the pretext of regulating commerce.

Thus the originalist doctrinal distinction between national and local was brought back to life. Chief Justice Rehnquist, however, claimed that it had never died, and in support of his claim he appealed to *Gibbons* and most of the cases discussed in this introduction. The justices in the minority, citing and reviewing the same cases, saw the "gun-possession" statute as a measure rationally related to the interstate gun market and thus to interstate commerce and subject to congressional regulation. We may doubt whether constitutional doctrine as such yields any right answer to the question *Lopez* poses. One commentator has described the majority opinion as an effort to return to an "originalist" reading of the Constitution—"an act of interpretive fidelity," as he put it—whereas the minority opinion represents a "textualist" account that seeks an "understanding of the [Constitution] that is most compelling in the current context."[24] American constitutionalism illustrates the cycles between the two approaches, and *Lopez* may mark the start of another "originalist" cycle. (Alternatively, like *National League of Cities*, *Lopez* could be destined for a short life.) In the end, these cycles seem driven by a still larger vision of the social economy. One vision— the originalist—sees the economy in territorial terms where state and national interests are discernible and distinguishable, whereas the textualist vision—in the sense used here—envisions the economy as a single organic unit that defies any such division. The same tensions, we shall find, are at work in the interpretation of the power to tax and spend.

Taxing and Spending Powers

Levying taxes is a government's most awesome—and fearsome—power. In the United States it even exceeds the reach of the commerce power. The power to regulate commerce, as *Lopez* instructs, must have *some* connection to interstate traffic or activity. The taxing and spending power, by contrast, may touch any object or activity, local or not, so long as the taxes are imposed uniformly throughout the nation and the spending serves the general welfare. In addition to this rule of uniformity, the Constitution prohibits any tax on exports and provides that direct taxes can only be apportioned among the states according to population. The "direct" tax clause was rendered a virtual nullity when the Sixteenth Amendment, ratified in 1913, empowered Congress "to lay and collect taxes on incomes, from whatsoever source, without apportionment among the several States."[25]

Apart from the limits just mentioned, Article 1, Section 8, clause 1, confers on Congress the general power "to lay and collect taxes [and] pay the debts and provide for the common defense and general welfare of the United States" (Article 1, Section 8).

---

[23] See, e.g., *Perez v. United States*, 402 U.S. 146 (1971), which sustained provisions of the Consumer Credit Protection Act prohibiting purely intrastate "loan sharking" activity.

[24] Lawrence Lessig, *Translating Federalism:* Lopez v. United States, 1995 The Supreme Court Review 126–28 (1996).

[25] The Sixteenth Amendment was ratified in the aftermath of *Pollock v. Farmer's Loan & Trust Company*, 157 U.S. 429 (1895), which invalidated a federal tax on real estate as an unapportioned direct tax.

This power has constituted a weapon that rivals the commerce clause in its contribution to the expansion of federal authority in our time. In reviewing the exercise of this power, the Supreme Court would wrestle once again with the perennial tension between democracy and constitutionalism, as well as the competing claims of nation and state.

This tension surfaced early on in *Bailey v. Drexel Furniture Company* (1922), which nullifed a federal tax on factories employing children.[26] The question was whether a federal tax could be justified if its effect and purpose were palpably regulatory rather than fiscal. The *Bailey* Court answered in the negative. The main purpose of the statute, said the Court, was not to raise revenue but to stop the employment of children. Additionally, as in *Hammer v. Dagenbart*, the Court found that the regulation of employment was a state function within the reservations of the Tenth Amendment.

From 1937 to the present, however, the Court would revert to the spirit of some of its pre-*Bailey* decisions by deferring to Congress's judgment on the need for federal tax legislation. As in *McCray v. United States* (1904),[27] which upheld a federal excise tax on oleomargarine colored like butter, the Court would refuse to inquire into the existence of some hidden regulatory motive. A federal tax statute would be valid if, on its face, it levied a tax no matter what the degree of its effect in discouraging certain practices or activities. In *United States v. Kabriger* (1953, reprinted later in the chapter), for example, the Court sustained a federal excise tax on gambling—designed clearly to penalize the business of wagering—because *objectively* it qualified as a tax measure that produced revenue. "Unless there are provisions, extraneous to any tax need," said the Supreme Court, "courts are without authority to limit the exercise of the taxing power." A lawful power could of course be exerted for an unlawful purpose, but "under our constitutional system," as the *McCray* Court said, the remedy for such abuses of power lies not with the judiciary but with the people.

Congress, as noted, may tax and spend "for the general welfare." The meaning of the general welfare clause has been vigorously debated ever since James Madison and Alexander Hamilton locked horns over its scope. Madison, taking the narrow view, maintained that the taxing and spending power could only be used to accomplish the specific objectives enumerated in the Constitution. Hamilton, taking the broader view, held that the clause served as an independent source of federal power. In short, Hamilton maintained, Congress could tax and spend for any purpose so long as by doing so it advanced the general welfare. In *United States v. Butler* (1936, reprinted later in the chapter), the Supreme Court accepted Hamilton's expansive view. Still in its pre-New Deal "dual federalist" mode, the *Butler* Court struck down Congress's attempt to limit agricultural output by paying farmers to take acreage out of production with funds derived from a tax on food processors. The tax was invalid, ruled the Court, because the money was being spent not for the general welfare but for a local purpose, namely production, wholly within the jurisdiction of the states.

Butler also featured the often quoted dissenting opinion of Justice Stone, who reminded his brothers of an important principle of judicial review that he thought the majority had ignored. Courts, he wrote, "are only concerned with the power to enact statutes, not with their wisdom," and that "for the removal of unwise [legislation] appeal lies not the courts but to the ballot box and to the processes of democratic government." (As noted in chapter 10, Stone would offer a different theory of judicial review in cases involving racial discrimination or affecting individual rights and

---

[26] 259 U.S. 20 (1922).

[27] 195 U.S. 27 (1904). See also *United States v. Doremus*, 249 U.S. 86 (1919) upholding the Narcotic Drug Act, which imposed a special tax on the manufacture or sale of opium or coca leaves or their derivatives.

liberties.) The Court eventually came around to Stone's position. Except for the reservation laid out in *South Dakota v. Dole* (1987), the Court no longer regards the Tenth Amendment as a significant limit on the spending power. In addition, the Court has given up on any independent attempt to define the "general welfare;" it defers instead to Congress's determination about what the general welfare includes.

Today the spending power justifies a wide variety of federal programs ranging from highway construction to Medicare and caring for the poor. In fact, Congress has used the spending power to influence the policies and practices of local governments as well as private establishments. Congress does so by attaching conditions to the receipt of federal money. For example, a public or private university may be denied federal funds if it discriminates on the basis of race in any of its programs or activities.[28] Indeed, they may be required to meet specified affirmative action goals in the hiring of women and minorities as a condition for continuing to receive federal funds.

South Dakota v. Dole (1987, reprinted later in the chapter) is one of the most recent challenges to the exercise of the spending power. Here the question was whether Congress could withhold a percentage of the highway funds to which a state would be entitled if the legislature of that state failed to adopt a minimum drinking age law. Thus, the main question before the Court was whether Congress could regulate indirectly through the spending power what it could not regulate directly under its enumerated authority. Chief Justice Rehnquist, writing for the majority, sustained the federal statute because the means chosen to deal with the problem of highway safety "were reasonably calculated to advance the general welfare." The new wrinkle in *Dole* seemed to be the Court's willingness, at least at the edges of constitutional legality, to decide for itself what, in fact, advances the general welfare. *Dole* also revived the Tenth Amendment. The opinion made clear, and Justice O'Connor argued even more forcefully in dissent, that while Congress may use the power of the purse to induce the states to adopt policies they would otherwise reject, it may not compel them to adopt such policies. If they succumb to the allure of federal dollars, they must abide by the conditions Congress imposes. But the states must be left with the option of rejecting federal funding in the interest of their reserved powers.

Additional Congressional Powers

Congress possesses a large number of powers outside of Article 1. For example, various amendments to the Constitution, including the Reconstruction Amendments, empower Congress to enforce their mandates by appropriate legislation. In addition, Article 3 works in conjunction with Article 1, Section 8, clause 9 by authorizing Congress to create a system of inferior federal courts. Article 4 gives Congress the right to make rules for territories and property belonging to the United States, while Article 2 empowers the Senate to participate in the important treaty-making process discussed in the next chapter. Finally, as already noted, the Sixteenth Amendment confers on Congress the power to lay and collect taxes on incomes.

Comparative Perspectives

Since the United States has a federal constitution, common sense dictates that it be compared with other federal systems. In this brief comparative note, we confine our attention to Canada and Germany. The constitutions of these nations divide authority

---

[28] See *Bob Jones University v. United States*, 461 U.S. 574 (1983).

between nation and state and grant the judiciary the authority to resolve conflicts between levels of government. In addition, each constitution includes words and phrases similar to the American commerce clause. Finally, as several of the comparative notes in the cases reproduced later show, the content of the commerce power depends as much on judicial interpretation of the text as on the text of the constitution itself.

According to Section 91 of the Canadian Constitution, as shown in Comparative Note 6.1, "the exclusive Legislative Authority of the Parliament of Canada extends to . . . the Regulation of Trade and Commerce."[29] Section 91 lists twenty-eight other subjects or topics over which the national government has exclusive jurisdiction while the provinces enjoy equally exclusive jurisdiction over other specified classes of subjects. The dominion or national government, however, is not confined to its enumerated powers; Parliament is empowered "to make laws for the peace, order, and good government of Canada in relation to all matters not coming . . . [within the exclusive jurisdiction of the] Provinces." Thus, under the Canadian Constitution, unlike the American, the national government is one of reserved powers, whereas the states (provinces) are confined to their delegated powers.

What is so interesting about the Canadian commerce power and other powers— such as the power to raise and spend money—that Section 91 gives the dominion government is that the Canadian founders set out deliberately to correct what they saw as a weakness in the U.S. Constitution—a system of divided power that left too much sovereignty to the states, thus planting the seeds of the Civil War. John Macdonald, often regarded as Canada's Alexander Hamilton, observed that "the primary error at the formation of [the U.S.] constitution was that each state reserved for itself all sovereign rights, save the small portion delegated. We must reverse this process by strengthening the General Government and conferring on the [provinces] only such power as may be required for local purposes."[30] But in an ironic twist of fate, the judiciary of each country read the commerce power of its respective constitution in a way that seemed to contradict the terms of the original text.

Whereas the American Supreme Court turned a strong federal instrument into one possessing unitary features, the Canadian Supreme Court turned the centralizing language of its Constitution into something resembling a dual federalist system. Although in recent decades the Canadian Supreme Court has expanded the meaning of "trade and commerce," it often construes these terms to the advantage of the provinces. Canadian laws dealing with agriculture, fair competition, and food and drug standards that would have been sustained under the American commerce power have been invalidated as *ultra vires* under Canada's trade and commerce power.[31] Another prominent example is the field of labor- management relations, an area judicially seen in Canada as a matter relating to "property and civil rights," subjects within the exclusive jurisdiction of the provinces.[32] The term "trade" in the trade and commerce clause

---

[29] Constitution Act, 1867, Section 91 (2) (formerly, the British North American Act, 1867).

[30] Quoted in Alexander Smith, *The Commerce Power in Canada and the United States* (Toronto: Butterworths, 1963), 15.

[31] See, for example, federal statutes establishing a grading system for agricultural products in *Dominion Stores v. The Queen*, 1 S.C.R. 844 (1980), setting national standards on the composition and quality of goods in *Labatt Breweries of Can. Ltd. v. A.G. Can*, 1 S.C.R. 914 (1980), and regulating unfair business practices and providing a civil remedy for engaging in such practice in *McDonald v. Vapor Canada*, 2 S.C.R. 134 (1977).

[32] See *Northern Telecom Ltd. v. Communications Workers of Canada*, 1 S.C.R. 115 (1980). National power over employee-employer relations extends only to those industries or enterprises—e.g., banks, inland fisheries, and the postal service—falling within the dominion's exclusive jurisdiction.

has also been given a narrowing construction; the Court sanctions national legislation that is concerned with trade in general and throughout the country, but not laws that regulate a single trade within a province or even throughout the country. Similarly, the term "regulate," unlike Chief Justice Marshall's broad definition, permits only a *regulatory* scheme overseen by a national regulatory agency. Accordingly, as Comparative Note 6.6 (p. 255) suggests, the power to regulate trade and commerce does not support a national law to discourage an unfair business practice through a civil damage suit brought by a private party. These examples show that, in Canada, provincial rights serve as a significant limit on the national trade and commerce power. By contrast, in the United States—with possibly the single exception of *Lopez*—the reserved power clause of the Tenth Amendment has ceased to be a limit on the national commerce power.

How does one explain the differing constructions of the Canadian and American commerce clauses? By the intent of the Framers? We have seen that intent was basically ignored in both countries. By the constitutional text? One could argue that Canada has been more faithful to the constitutional text in as much as it expressly confers on the provinces jurisdiction over "all Matters of a merely local or private Nature in the Province."[33] This provision, however, determines the meaning of trade and commerce no more or less than any other subject contained within the sphere of provincial powers. Consider whether the different doctrinal approaches of the two tribunals simply represent pragmatic judgments about how to balance state and federal authority. Are their respective doctrinal formulations driven by independent judicial images of how a federal system ought to operate? Such images, however, are not fixed in time or space, and even on the same tribunal the judicial image is rarely unanimous. Just as American dissenting opinions offer highly federalized views of the nation-state relationship, Canadian dissenting opinions offer highly centralized views of that relationship, perhaps suggesting far more indeterminacy in constitutional interpretation than many textualists would be willing to admit.

In recent years, Canada has made some attempts to move away from its version of "dual federalism." The Charlottetown Agreement (1992), for example, included a passage committing Canada to the preservation and development of its social and economic union. This provision might have given new life to the trade and commerce clause, especially when viewed in light of Section 121 of the Constitution Act of 1867, which provides for a common market. (Section 121 reads: "All Articles of Growth, Produce, or Manufacture of any one of the Provinces shall, from and after the Union, be admitted free into each of the other Provinces.") Two years earlier, Justice La Forest of the Canadian Supreme Court wrote, "The concept of Canada as a single country comprising what one would now call a common market was basic to the [original] Confederation arrangements, and the drafters of the *British North American Act* attempted to pull down the existing internal barriers that restricted movement within the country."[34] Canadians, however, rejected the Charlottetown Agreement in a national referendum and, as one Canadian scholar notes, "the full impact of s. 121 on presently existing trade barriers, and its relation to the Trade and Commerce power has yet to be developed by the courts."[35]

In Germany's Basic Law, we find that there is no general commerce power as in the United States and Canadian constitutions, but rather a catalogue of subjects that embrace activities such as transportation, labor relations, and the marketing of food, drink, and tobacco. Perhaps the advantage of a twentieth-century constitution such as

---

[33] Can. Const. Act, 1967, sec. 92 (16).

[34] *Black v. Law Society of Alberta*, 1 S.C.R. 591, at 609 (1989).

[35] Joseph Eliot Magnet, *Constitutional law of Canada* (Cowansville, Quebec: Yvon Blais Inc., 1993), 304.

the Basic Law is that it specifies those subjects and activities of commerce that the national government is empowered to regulate, either exclusively or concurrently. These subjects include telecommunications, federal railroads, labor relations, agricultural production, air transportation, the free movement and exchange of goods, the production and utilization of nuclear energy, the construction and maintenance of long distance highways, and economic matters relating to mining, industry, crafts, commerce, banking, stock exchanges, and private insurance. While these terms require interpretation no less than the more general words and phrases of the Basic Law, the textual detail seems to provide the Constitutional Court with more guidance in defining the nature and scope of national power than does the American or Canadian constitution.

The prolixity of the Basic Law may account for the highly active judicial role, as noted in chapter 5, in defining the boundary between national and state authority. Because the national government enjoys such a monopoly of policymaking power, the Federal Constitutional Court seems determined to protect and fortify those powers that have been reserved to the states. For example, in one of its most notable decisions, the Court declared unconstitutional the creation of a national television station because it invaded the states' reserved power over cultural affairs, notwithstanding the national government's exclusive jurisdiction over "telecommunications." As one observer of the Constitutional Court has noted, "the German approach contrasts sharply with Justice Stone's familiar insistence that the tenth amendment's reservation to the states of all powers not granted to the federal government was a mere 'truism.'"[36]

In shifting the scene to the power to tax and spend, we find that the Basic Law, like many other modern constitutions and unlike the United States Constitution, devotes numerous provisions to the field of public finance. Most of these provisions are devoted to the apportionment of revenue between the national and state governments. For present purposes, it is sufficient to note that the national government has exclusive authority over export and import taxes. In addition, Article 106 of the Basic Law reserves several tax sources to the national government, among them customs duties, certain excise taxes, and income and corporation surtaxes. As in the United States, tax statutes may be enacted for social purposes not directly related to the production of revenue.

The spending power of the national government, while broad, is nevertheless more limited than in the United States, at least where grants in aid to states and localities are concerned. In the *Financial Subsidies Case* (1976), for example, the Court reviewed Bavaria's complaint that an urban renewal program interfered with the state's autonomy. Summarizing this and another constitutional case, David P. Currie writes:

> . . . *[I]n order to preserve state autonomy, the Court continued, implementation of the grant program must be left essentially to the states. The Federation might spend money to rebuild cities, but the Länder must be free to determine where and how to do it. Since the urban renewal law could be construed to leave the choice of individual projects principally to the states, it was upheld; a second program that did not meet this requirement was struck down the next year. Thus, unlike the modern Supreme Court, the German court polices federal spending to prevent usurpation of state or local authority by the attachment of conditions to the enjoyment of largesse.*"[37]

---

[36] David P. Currie, *The Constitution of the Federal Republic of Germany* (Chicago: University of Chicago Press, 1994), 38.

[37] *Ibid.*, 58.

The relative activism of Germany's Federal Constitutional Court in this field also contrasts with the Supreme Court's relatively restrained position in *South Dakota v. Dole* (1987). It is probable that *Dole*, like *Garcia v. San Antonio Metropolitan Transit Authority* (1985) would have been decided differently in the hands of the Federal Constitutional Court.

Selected Bibliography

Barber, Sotirios A. *On What the Constitution Means*. Baltimore: Johns Hopkins University Press, 1984. Chap. 4.

Choper, Jesse H. *Judicial Review and the National Political Process: A Functional Reconsideration of the Role of the Supreme Court*. Chicago: University of Chicago Press, 1980.

Corwin, Edward S. "The Passing of Dual Federalism." In Robert G. McCloskey, ed., *Essays in Constitutional Law*. New York: Vintage, 1957.

———. *The Commerce Power Versus States Rights*. Princeton, N.J.: Princeton University Press, 1936.

Epstein, Richard A. *The Proper Scope of the Commerce Power*, 73 Virginia Law Review 1387 (1987).

The Federalist, Nos. 30–36, 41–42, 56.

Frankfurter, Felix. *The Commerce Clause Under Marshall, Taney, and Waite*. Chapel Hill, N.C.: University of North Carolina Press, 1937.

MacDonald, Vincent C. *The Constitution in a Changing World*, 26 Canadian Bar Review 21 (1948).

McCoy, Thomas R., and Barry Friedmann. *Conditional Spending: Federalism's Trojan Horse*, 1988 Supreme Court Review 85–128 (1988).

Smith, Alexander. *The Commerce Power in Canada and the United States*. Toronto: Butterworth & Co. Ltd., 1963.

Gibbons v. Ogden
22 U.S. 1 (9 Wheat). 1, 6 L. Ed. 23 (1824)

In 1808 Robert Fulton and Robert R. Livingston, pioneers in the development of the steamboat, received from the New York legislature an exclusive right to operate steamboats on the state's streams and waters. Later Aaron Ogden secured from Fulton and Livingston the exclusive right to engage in steam navigation across the Hudson River between New York and New Jersey. Thomas Gibbons, however, was navigating a steamboat of his own on the same waters with a license secured under the Federal Coasting Act of 1893. Ogden sued Gibbons under the steamboat monopoly law. The New York courts upheld Ogden's claim and the New York statute. Opinion of the Court: *Marshall*, Todd, Duval, Story, Thompson. Concurring opinion: *Johnson*.

Mr. Chief Justice MARSHALL delivered the opinion of the Court.

The state of New York maintains the constitutionality of these laws; and their legislature, their council of revision, and their judges, have repeatedly concurred in this opinion. It is supported by great names—by names which have all the titles to consideration that virtue, intelligence and office can bestow. No tribunal can approach the decision of this question without feeling a just and real respect for that opinion which is sustained by such authority; but it is the province of this court, while it respects, not to bow to it implicitly; and the judges must exercise, in the examination of the subject, that understanding which Providence has bestowed upon them, with that independence which the people of the United States expect from this department of the government.

As preliminary to the very able discussions of the constitution, which we have heard from the bar, and as having some influence on its construction, reference has been made to the political situation of these States, anterior to its formation. It has been said, that they were sovereign, were completely independent, and were connected with each other only by a league. This is true. But, when these allied sovereigns converted their league into a government, when they converted their Congress of Ambassadors, deputed to deliberate on their common concerns, and to recommend measures of general utility, into a Legislature, empowered to enact laws on the most interesting subjects, the whole character in which the States appear, underwent a change, the extent of which must be determined by a fair consideration of the instrument by which that change was effected.

This instrument contains an enumeration of powers expressly granted by the people to their government. It has been said, that these powers ought to be construed strictly. But why ought they to be so construed? Is there one sentence in the constitution which gives countenance to this rule? In the last of the enumerated powers, that which grants, expressly, the means for carrying all others into execution, Congress is authorized "to make all laws which shall be necessary and proper" for the purpose. But this limitation on the means which may be used, is not extended to the powers which are conferred; nor is there one sentence in the constitution, which has been pointed out by the gentlemen of the bar, or which we have been able to discern, that prescribes this rule. We do not, therefore, think ourselves justified in adopting it. What do gentlemen mean, by a strict construction? If they contend only against that enlarged construction, which would extend words beyond their natural and obvious import, we might question the application of the term, but should not controvert the principle. If they contend for that narrow construction which, in support of some theory not to be found in the constitution, would deny to the government those powers which the words of the grant, as usually understood, import, and which are consistent with the general views and objects of the instrument; for that narrow construction, which would cripple the government, and render it unequal to the object for which it is declared to be instituted, and to which the powers given, as fairly understood, render it competent; then we cannot perceive the propriety of this strict construction, nor adopt it as the rule by which the constitution is to be expounded. . . .

The words are, "Congress shall have power to regulate commerce with foreign nations, and among the several States, and with the Indian tribes."

The subject to be regulated is commerce; and our constitution being, as was aptly said at the bar, *one of enumeration, and not of definition*, to ascertain the extent of the power, it becomes necessary to settle the meaning of the word. The counsel for the appellee would limit it to traffic, to buying and selling, or the interchange of commodities, and do not admit that it comprehends navigation. This would restrict a general term, applicable to many objects, to one of its significations. Commerce, undoubtedly, is traffic, but it is something more: it is intercourse. It describes the commercial intercourse between nations, and parts of nations, in all its branches, and is regulated by prescribing rules for carrying on that intercourse. The mind can scarcely conceive a system for regulating commerce between nations, which shall exclude all laws concerning navigation, which shall be silent on the admission of the vessels of the one nation into the ports of the other, and be confined to prescribing rules for the conduct of individuals, in the actual employment of buying and selling, or of barter.

If commerce does not include navigation, the government of the Union has no direct power over that subject, and can make no law prescribing what shall constitute American vessels, or requiring that they shall be navigated by American seamen. Yet this power has been exercised from the commencement of the government, has been exercised with the consent of all, and has been understood by all to be a commercial regulation. All America understands, and has uniformly understood, the word "commerce," to comprehend navigation. It was so understood, and must have been so understood, when the constitution was framed. The power over commerce, including navigation, was one of the primary objects for which the people of America adopted their government, and must have been contemplated in forming it. The convention must have used the word in that sense, because all have understood it in that sense; and the attempt to restrict it comes too late.

The word used in the constitution, then, comprehends, and has been always understood to comprehend, navigation within its meaning; and a power to regulate navigation, is as expressly granted, as if that term had been added to the word "commerce." To what commerce does this power extend? The constitution informs us, to commerce "with foreign nations, and among the several States, and with the Indian tribes." It has, we believe, been universally admitted, that these words comprehend every species of commercial intercourse between the United States and foreign nations. No sort of trade can be carried on between this country and any other, to which this power does not extend. . . .

If this be the admitted meaning of the word, in its application to foreign nations, it must carry the same meaning throughout the sentence, and remain a unit, unless there be some plain intelligible cause which alters it. The subject to which the power is next applied, is to commerce "among the several States." The word "among" means intermingled with. A thing which is among others, is intermingled with them. Commerce among the States, cannot stop at the external boundary line of each State, but may be introduced into the interior. It is not intended to say that these words comprehend that commerce, which is completely internal, which is carried on between man and man in a State, or between different parts of the same State, and which does not extend to or affect other States. Such a power would be inconvenient, and is certainly unnecessary.

Comprehensive as the word "among" is, it may very properly be restricted to that commerce which concerns more States than one. The phrase is not one which would probably have been selected to indicate the completely interior traffic of a State, because it is not an apt phrase for that purpose; and the enumeration of the particular classes of commerce, to which the power was to be extended, would not have been made, had the intention been to extend the power to every description. The enumeration presupposes something not enumerated; and that something, if we regard the language or the subject of the sentence,

Comparative Note 6.1

U.S. Constitution, art. 1, sec. 8, cl. 3

The Congress shall have the power to regulate commerce . . . among the several states.

Commonwealth of Australia Constitution Act (1900)

Sec. 51. The Parliament shall . . . have power to make laws for the peace, order, and good government of the Commonwealth with respect to:

(i.) Trade and commerce with other countries, and among the States . . .

(ii.) Taxation; but so as not to discriminate between states or parts of states.

Sec. 92. On the imposition of uniform duties of customs, trade, commerce, and intercourse among the states, whether by means of internal carriage or ocean navigation, shall be absolutely free. . . .

Constitution Act, 1867 (Canada)

Sec. 91. . . . [E]xclusive legislative authority of the Parliament of Canada extends to all matters coming within the classes of subjects next hereinafter enumerated; that is to say . . . 2. The regulation of trade and commerce.

Basic Law of the Federal Republic of Germany (1949)

Art. 73. The Federation shall have exclusive power in respect of: . . .

5. unity of customs and trading area [and] free movement of goods, . . .

6. air transport;

6a. the operation of railways wholly or majority-owned by the Federation, the construction, maintenance and operation of the infrastructure of the federal railways . . .

Art. 74. The Federation shall have concurrent legislative power over. . . .

11. economic affairs (mining, industry, energy, crafts and trades, commerce, banking, the stock exchange system and private insurance);

12. labor relations, including . . . industrial safety . . . as well as social security and unemployment insurance; . . .

16. measures to prevent abuse of economic power;

17. promotion of agricultural production and forestry; . . .

22. road traffic, motor transport, construction and maintenance of roads for long-distance traffic. . . .

---

must be the exclusively internal commerce of a State. The genius and character of the whole government seem to be, that its action is to be applied to all the external concerns of the nation, and to those internal concerns which affect the States generally; but not to those which are completely within a particular State, which do not affect other States, and with which it is not necessary to interfere, for the purpose of executing some of the general powers of the government. The completely internal commerce of a State, then, may be considered as reserved for the State itself.

But, in regulating commerce with foreign nations, the power of Congress does not stop at the jurisdictional lines of the several States. It would be a very useless power, if it could not pass those lines. The commerce of the United States with foreign nations, is that of the whole United States. Every district has a right to participate in it. The deep streams which penetrate our country in every direction, pass through the interior of almost every State in the Union, and furnish the means of exercising this right. If Congress has the power to regulate it, that power must be exercised whenever the subject exists. If it exists within the States, if a foreign voyage may commence or terminate at a port within a State, then the power of Congress may be exercised within a State.

This principle is, if possible, still more clear, when applied to commerce "among the several States." They either join each other, in which case they are separated by a mathematical line, or they are remote from each other, in which case other States lie between them. What is commerce "among" them; and how is it to be conducted? Can a trading expedition between two adjoining States, commence and terminate outside of each? And if the trading intercourse be between two States remote from each other, must it not commence in one, terminate in the other, and probably pass through a third? . . . The power of Congress, then, whatever it may be, must be exercised within the territorial jurisdiction of the several States. . . .

We are now arrived at the inquiry—What is this power? It is the power to regulate; that is, to prescribe the rule by which commerce is to be governed. This power, like all others vested in Congress, is complete in itself, may be exercised to its utmost extent, and acknowledges no limitations, other than are prescribed in the constitution. These are expressed in plain terms, and do not affect the questions which arise in this case, or which have been discussed at the bar. If, as has always been understood, the sovereignty of Congress, though limited to specified objects, is plenary as to those objects, the power over commerce with foreign nations, and among the several States, is vested in Congress as absolutely as it would be in a single government, having in its constitution the same restrictions on the exercise of the power as are found in the constitution of the United States. The wisdom and the discretion of Congress, their identity with the people, and the influence which their constituents possess at elections, are, in this, as in many other instances, as that, for example, of declaring war, the sole restraints on which they have relied, to secure them from its abuse. They are the restraints on which the people must often rely, solely, in all representative governments.

But it has been urged with great earnestness, that, although the power of Congress to regulate commerce with foreign nations, and among the several States, be co-extensive with the subject itself, and have no other limits than are prescribed in the constitution, yet the States may severally exercise the same power, within their respective jurisdictions. . . .

The grant of the power to lay and collect taxes is, like the power to regulate commerce, made in general terms, and has never been understood to interfere with the exercise of the same power by the State; and hence has been drawn an argument which has been applied to the question under consideration. But the two grants are not, it is conceived, similar in their terms or their nature. Although many of the powers formerly exercised by the States, are transferred to the government of the Union, yet the State governments remain, and constitute a most important part of our system. The power of taxation is indispensable to their existence, and is a power which, in its own nature, is capable of residing in, and being exercised by, different authorities at the same time. We are accustomed to see it placed, for different purposes, in different hands. Taxation is the simple operation of taking small portions from a perpetually accumulating mass, susceptible of almost infinite division; and a power in one to take what is necessary for certain purposes, is not, in its nature, incompatible with a power in another to take what is necessary for other purposes. Congress is authorized to lay and collect taxes, to pay the debts, and provide for the common defence and general welfare of the United States. This does not interfere with the power of the States to tax for the support of their own governments; nor is the exercise of that power by the States, an exercise of any portion of the power that is granted to the United States. In imposing taxes for State purposes, they are not doing what Congress is empowered to do. Congress is not empowered to tax for those

purposes which are within the exclusive province of the States. When, then, each government exercises the power of taxation, neither is exercising the power of the other. But, when a State proceeds to regulate commerce with foreign nations, or among the several States, it is exercising the very power that is granted to Congress, and is doing the very thing which Congress is authorized to do. There is no analogy, then, between the power of taxation and the power of regulating commerce.

In discussing the question, whether this power is still in the States, in the case under consideration, we may dismiss from it the inquiry, whether it is surrendered by the mere grant to Congress, or is retained until Congress shall exercise the power. We may dismiss that inquiry, because it has been exercised, and the regulations which Congress deemed it proper to make, are now in full operation. The sole question is, can a State regulate commerce with foreign nations and among the States, while Congress is regulating it?

But, the inspection laws are said to be regulations of commerce, and are certainly recognised in the constitution, as being passed in the exercise of a power remaining with the States. That inspection laws may have a remote and considerable influence on commerce, will not be denied; but that a power to regulate commerce is the source from which the right to pass them is derived, cannot be admitted. The object of inspection laws, is to improve the quality of articles produced by the labour of a country; to fit them for exportation; or, it may be, for domestic use. They act upon the subject before it becomes an article of foreign commerce, or of commerce among the States, and prepare it for that purpose. They form a portion of that immense mass of legislation, which embraces every thing within the territory of a State, not surrendered to the general government: all which can be most advantageously exercised by the States themselves. Inspection laws, quarantine laws, health laws of every description, as well as laws for regulating the internal commerce of a State, and those which respect turnpike roads, ferries [and so forth] are component parts of this mass.

No direct general power over these objects is granted to Congress; and, consequently, they remain subject to State legislation. If the legislative power of the Union can reach them, it must be for national purposes; it must be where the power is expressly given for a special purpose, or is clearly incidental to some power which is expressly given. It is obvious, that the government of the Union, in the exercise of its express powers, that, for example, of regulating commerce with foreign nations and among the States, may use means that may also be employed by a State, in the exercise of its acknowledged powers; that, for example, of regulating commerce within the State. . . .

In our complex system, presenting the rare and difficult scheme of one general government, whose action extends over the whole, but which possesses only certain enumerated powers; and of numerous state governments, which retain and exercise all powers not delegated to the Union, contests respecting power must arise. Were it even otherwise, the measures taken by the respective governments to execute their acknowledged powers, would often be of the same description, and might, sometimes, interfere. This, however, does not prove that the one is exercising, or has a right to exercise, the powers of the other.

Since, however, in exercising the power of regulating their own purely internal affairs, whether of trading or police, the States may sometimes enact laws, the validity of which depends on their interfering with, and being contrary to, an act of Congress passed in pursuance of the constitution, the Court will enter upon the inquiry, whether the laws of New York, as expounded by the highest tribunal of that State, have, in their application to this case, come into collision with an act of Congress, and deprived a citizen of a right to which that act entitles him. Should this collision exist, it will be immaterial whether those laws were passed in virtue of a concurrent power "to regulate commerce with foreign nations and among the several States," or, in virtue of a power to regulate their domestic trade and police. In one case and the other, the acts of New York must yield to the law of Congress; and the decision sustaining the privilege they confer, against a right given by a law of the Union, must be erroneous.

This opinion has been frequently expressed in this Court, and is founded, as well on the nature of the government as on the words of the constitution. In argument, however, it has been contended, that if a law passed by a State, in the exercise of its acknowledged sovereignty, comes into conflict with a law passed by Congress in pursuance of the constitution, they affect the subject, and each other, like equal opposing powers.

But the framers of our constitution foresaw this state of things, and provided for it, by declaring the supremacy not only of itself, but of the laws made in pursuance of it. The nullity of any act, inconsistent with the constitution, is produced by the declaration, that the constitution is the supreme law. The appropriate application of that part of the clause which confers the same supremacy on laws and treaties, is to such acts of the State Legislatures as do not transcend their powers, but, though enacted in the execution of acknowledged State powers, interfere with, or are contrary to the laws of Congress, made in pursuance of the constitution, or some treaty made under the authority of the United States. In every such case, the act of Congress, or the treaty, is supreme; and the law of the State, though

enacted in the exercise of powers not controverted, must yield to it. . . .

But all inquiry into this subject seems to the Court to be put completely at rest, by the act already mentioned, entitled, "An act for the enrolling and licensing of steam boats."

This act authorizes a steam boat employed, or intended to be employed, only in a river or bay of the United States, owned wholly or in part by an alien, resident within the United States, to be enrolled and licensed as if the same belonged to a citizen of the United States.

This act demonstrates the opinion of Congress, that steam boats may be enrolled and licensed, in common with vessels using sails. They are, of course, entitled to the same privileges, and can no more be restrained from navigating waters, and entering ports which are free to such vessels, than if they were wafted on their voyage by the winds, instead of being propelled by the agency of fire. The one element may be as legitimately used as the other, for every commercial purpose authorized by the laws of the Union; and the act of a State inhibiting the use of either to any vessel having a license under the act of Congress, comes, we think, in direct collision with that act.

Mr. Justice JOHNSON, concurring.

In attempts to construe the constitution, I have never found much benefit resulting from the inquiry, whether the whole; or any part of it, is to be construed strictly or liberally. The simple, classical, precise, yet comprehensive language in which it is couched, leaves, at most, but very little latitude for construction; and when its intent and meaning are discovered, nothing remains but to execute the will of those who made it, in the best manner to effect the purposes intended. The great and paramount purpose was, to unite the mass of wealth and power, for the protection of the humblest individual; his rights, civil and political, his interests and prosperity, are the sole end; the rest are nothing but the means. . . .

The history of the times will . . . sustain the opinion, that the grant of power over commerce, if intended to be commensurate with the evils existing, and the purpose of remedying those evils, could be only commensurate with the power of the states over the subject. . . .

. . . But what was that power? The states were, unquestionably, supreme; and each possessed that power over commerce, which is acknowledged to reside in every sovereign state. . . . The power of a sovereign state over commerce, therefore, amounts to nothing more than a power to limit and restrain it at pleasure. And since the power to prescribe the limits to its freedom, necessarily implies the power to determine what shall remain unrestrained, it follows, that the power must be exclusive: it can reside but in one potentate; and hence, the grant of this power carries with it the whole subject, leaving nothing for the state to act upon.

Notes/Queries/Readings

1. In chapter 2 we described competing approaches to constitutional interpretation, such as originalism, textualism, structuralism, and prudentialism. Which of these approaches does Marshall follow in *Gibbons*? Is this case really a debate over the meaning of the words in the Constitution or is some larger value or theory at work here?

2. Consult the constitutional provisions of the four federal systems in Comparative Note 6.1 on page 238. Would Marshall have had an easier time justifying the result in *Gibbons* under the foreign constitutions? What does Marshall's opinion say about the determinacy or indeterminacy of a constitutional text?

3. What limits, if any, does Marshall impose on Congress's power to regulate commerce? Are they similar to—or different from—the limits on federal power articulated in *McCulloch* (chapter 5)?

4. How does Justice Johnson's analysis of federal power under the commerce clause differ from Marshall's? Whose opinion is the most persuasive? Does Marshall's vision of the nature of the national political community differ from Johnson's? In what way?

5. The Court wrote that the definition of the word "commerce" must include navigation because it was so understood when the Constitution was written. Does this appeal to original understanding sufficiently account for the great commercial and industrial change that had occurred between the framing and 1824, when *Gibbons* was decided?

6. The Court also wrote that "all America understands, and has uniformly understood, the word 'commerce,' to comprehend navigation." Should the definition of constitutional terms depend upon popular understanding of those terms? Why or why not?

7. For additional reading, see Felix Frankfurter, *The Commerce Clause Under Marshall, Taney, and Waite* (Chapel Hill, N.C.: University of North Carolina Press, 1937).

United States v. E. C. Knight Co.
156 U.S. 1, 15 S. Ct. 249, 39 L. Ed. 325 (1895)

The American Sugar Refining Company, which purchased the stock of E. C. Knight and three other companies in Philadelphia, obtained control over the bulk of the nation's sugar refining business. The U.S. government sued E. C. Knight and the other companies for violating the Sherman Anti-Trust Act of 1890. The act made it illegal to monopolize or restrain interstate commerce by means of any contract, combination, or conspiracy. The lower federal courts refused to cancel the agreements, holding that the activity engaged in by the companies did not constitute interstate commerce. The Supreme Court did not strike the statute, but interpreted its reach narrowly so as to save it. Opinion of the Court: *Fuller*, Field, Gray, Brewer, Brown, Shiras, White, Peckham. Dissenting opinion: *Harlan*.

Mr. Chief Justice FULLER delivered the opinion of the Court.

The fundamental question is whether, conceding that the existence of a monopoly in manufacture is established by the evidence, that monopoly can be directly suppressed under the act of Congress in the mode attempted by this bill.

It cannot be denied that the power of a state to protect the lives, health, and property of its citizens, and to preserve good order and the public morals, "the power to govern men and things within the limits of its dominion," is a power originally and always belonging to the States, not surrendered by them to the general government, nor directly restrained by the constitution of the United States, and essentially exclusive. . . . The Constitution does not provide that interstate commerce shall be free, but, by the grant of this exclusive power to regulate it, it was left free, except as Congress might impose restraints. Therefore it has been determined that the failure of Congress to exercise this exclusive power in any case is an expression of its will that the subject shall be free from restrictions or impositions upon it by the several States, and if a law passed by a State in the exercise of its acknowledged powers comes into conflict with that will, the Congress and the State cannot occupy the position of equal opposing sovereignties, because the constitution declares its supremacy, and that of the laws passed in pursuance thereof; and that which is not supreme must yield to that which is supreme. . . . That which belongs to commerce is within the jurisdiction of the United States, but that which does not belong to commerce is within the jurisdiction of the police power of the State.

The argument is that the power to control the manufacture of refined sugar is a monopoly over a necessary of life, to the enjoyment of which by a large part of the population of the United States interstate commerce is indispensable, and that, therefore, the general government, in the exercise of the power to regulate commerce, may repress such monopoly directly, and set aside the instruments which have created it. But this argument cannot be confined to necessaries of life merely, and must include all articles of general consumption. Doubtless the power to control the manufacture of a given thing involves, in a certain sense, the control of its disposition, but this is a secondary, and not the primary, sense; and, although the exercise of that power may result in bringing the operation of commerce into play, it does not control it, and affects it only incidentally and indirectly. Commerce succeeds to manufacture, and is not a part of it. The power to regulate commerce is the power to prescribe the rule by which commerce shall be governed, and is a power independent of the power to suppress monopoly. But it may operate in repression of monopoly whenever that comes within the rules by which commerce is governed, or whenever the transaction is itself a monopoly of commerce.

It is vital that the independence of the commercial power and of the police power, and the delimitation between them, however sometimes perplexing, should always be recognized and observed, for, while the one furnishes the strongest bond of union, the other is essential to the preservation of the autonomy of the States as required by our dual form of government; and acknowledged evils, however grave and urgent they may appear to be, had better be borne, than the risk be run, in the effort to suppress them, of more serious consequences by resort to expedients of even doubtful constitutionality.

It will be perceived how far-reaching the proposition is that the power of dealing with a monopoly directly may be exercised by the general government whenever interstate or international commerce may be ultimately affected. The regulation of commerce applies to the subjects of commerce, and not to matters of internal police. Contracts to buy, sell, or exchange goods to be transported among the several States, the transportation and its instrumentalities, and articles bought, sold, or exchanged for the purposes of such transit among the States, or put in the way of transit, may be regulated; but this is because they form part of interstate trade or commerce. The fact that an article is manufactured for export to another State does not of itself make it an article of interstate commerce, and the intent of the manufacturer does not determine the time when the article or product passes from the control of the State and belongs to commerce. . . .

Contracts, combinations, or conspiracies to control domestic enterprise in manufacture, agriculture, mining, production in all its forms, or to raise or lower prices or wages, might unquestionably tend to restrain external as well as domestic trade, but the restraint would be an indirect result, however inevitable, and whatever its extent, and such result would not necessarily determine the object of the contract, combination, or conspiracy.

. . . Slight reflection will show that, if the national power extends to all contracts and combinations in manufacture, agriculture, mining, and other productive industries, whose ultimate result may affect external commerce, comparatively little of business operations and affairs would be left for state control.

It was in the light of well-settled principles that the act of July 2, 1890, was framed. Congress did not attempt thereby to assert the power to deal with monopoly directly as such. . . . [W]hat the law struck at was combinations, contracts, and conspiracies to monopolize trade and com-

---

Comparative Note 6.2

[In this case Chief Justice Dixon handed down an influential opinion interpreting Sec. 51 (i) of the Australian Constitution. For the text of Sec. 51 (i) see Comparative Note 6.1.]

The distinction which is drawn between inter-State trade and the domestic trade of a State for the purpose of the power conferred upon the Parliament by s. 51 (i) to make laws with respect to trade and commerce with other countries and among the States may well be considered artificial and unsuitable to modern times. But it is a distinction adopted by the Constitution and it must be observed however much inter-dependence may now exist between the two divisions of trade and commerce which the Constitution thus distinguishes. A legislative power, however, with respect to any subject matter contains within itself authority over whatever is incidental to the subject matter of the power and enables the legislature to include within laws made in pursuance of the power provisions which can only be justified as ancillary or incidental. But even in the application of this principle . . . the distinction which the Constitution makes between the two branches of trade and commerce must be maintained.

SOURCE: *Wragg v. New South Wales* (1953), 88 C.L.R. 353.

merce among the several States or with foreign nations; but the contracts and acts of the defendants related exclusively to the acquisition of the Philadelphia refineries and the business of sugar refining in Pennsylvania, and bore no direct relation to commerce between the States or with foreign nations. The object was manifestly private gain in the manufacture of the commodity, but not through the control of interstate or foreign commerce. It is true that the bill alleged that the products of these refineries were sold and distributed among the several states, and that all the companies were engaged in trade or commerce with the several states and with foreign nations; but this was no more than to say that trade and commerce served manufacture to fulfill its function. Sugar was refined for sale, and sales were probably made at Philadelphia for consumption, and undoubtedly for resale by the first purchasers throughout Pennsylvania and other states, and refined sugar was also forwarded by the companies to other states for sale. Nevertheless it does not follow that an attempt to monopolize, or the actual monopoly of, the manufacture was an attempt, whether executory or consummated, to monopolize commerce, even though, in order to dispose of the product, the instrumentality of commerce was necessarily invoked. There was nothing in the proofs to indicate any intention to put a restraint upon trade or commerce, and the fact, as we have seen, that trade or commerce might be indirectly affected, was not enough to entitle complainants to a decree. . . .

Decree affirmed.

Mr. Justice HARLAN, dissenting.

The court holds it to be vital in our system of government to recognize and give effect to both the commercial power of the nation and the police powers of the States, to the end that the Union be strengthened, and the autonomy of the States preserved. In this view I entirely concur. Undoubtedly, the preservation of the just authority of the States is an object of deep concern to every lover of his country. No greater calamity could befall our free institutions than the destruction of that authority, by whatever means such a result might be accomplished. . . . But it is equally true that the preservation of the just authority of the general government is essential as well to the safety of the States as to the attainment of the important ends for which that government was ordained by the people of the United States; and the destruction of *that* authority would be fatal to the peace and well-being of the American people. The Constitution, which enumerates the powers committed to the nation for objects of interest to the people of all the States, should not, therefore, be subjected to an interpretation so rigid, technical, and narrow that those objects cannot be accomplished. . . .

Congress is invested with power to regulate commerce with foreign nations and among the several states. . . . It is the settled doctrine of this court that interstate commerce embraces something more than the mere physical transportation of articles of property, and the vehicles or vessels by which such transportation is effected. . . . It includes the purchase and sale of articles that are intended to be transported from one State to another,—every species of commercial intercourse among the states and with foreign nations.

If it be true that a *combination* of corporations or individuals may, so far as the power of congress is concerned, subject interstate trade, in any of its stages, to unlawful restraints, the conclusion is inevitable that the Constitution has failed to accomplish one primary object of the Union, which was to place commerce *among the States* under the control of the common government of all the people, and thereby relieve or protect it against burdens or restrictions imposed, by whatever authority, for the benefit of particular localities or special interests.

The fundamental inquiry in this case is, what, in a legal sense, is an unlawful restraint of trade? . . .

In my judgment, the citizens of the several States composing the Union are entitled of right to buy goods in the State where they are manufactured, or in any other State, without being confronted by an illegal combination whose business extends throughout the whole country, which, by the law everywhere, is an enemy to the public interests, and which prevents such buying, except at prices arbitrarily fixed by it. . . . Whatever improperly obstructs the free course of interstate intercourse and trade, as involved in the buying and selling of articles to be carried from one State to another, may be reached by Congress under its authority to regulate commerce among the states. The exercise of that authority so as to make trade among the states in all recognized articles of commerce absolutely free from unreasonable or illegal restrictions imposed by combinations is justified by an express grant of power to congress, and would redound to the welfare of the whole country. I am unable to perceive that any such result would imperil the autonomy of the states, especially as that result cannot be attained through the action of any one State.

Notes/Queries/Readings

1. Chief Justice Fuller wrote that "Commerce succeeds to manufacture and is not a part of it." Where does this distinction come from? Is it implicit in the definition of commerce? Does Fuller trace it to the intent of the Founders or to the original understanding of the commerce clause? Is it a necessary consequence of the Tenth Amendment or of federalism itself?

2. Is Fuller's argument compatible with Marshall's reasoning in *Gibbons*? (Marshall had acknowledged the state's police power jurisdiction over its internal affairs.)

3. Compare the reasoning of *E. C. Knight* with the extract in Comparative Note 6.2 (p. 242), where Chief Justice Dixon restricts the power of the national government under Section 51 (i) of the Australian Constitution. (See Comparative Note 6.1 on p. 238 for the text of Section 51. [i].) What do the two decisions—i.e., *E. C. Knight* and *Wragg*—tell us about the nature of the interpretive process? (In *James v. Commonwealth*, 55 C.L.R. 1 [1936], the privy council also restricted the Australian national government's power over trade and commerce under Section 92 of the Constitution. See text of Section 92 in Comparative Note 6.1. *James* invalidated a commonwealth statute that limited the quantity of dried fruit that could be marketed nationwide. By striking the statute, the privy council conferred on the states the effective power to decide what amount of dried fruit could be marketed in Australia.)

4. Is Justice Harlan's interpretation of the commerce clause more firmly based in the Constitution? What does he see as the purpose of the clause? Of the Constitution as a whole? What place would he allow for democratic regulation of individual and corporate property?

5. Should the economic changes that took place in the one hundred years between the ratification of the Constitution and this case influence how the commerce clause should be interpreted? Why or why not?

6. For additional reading on the doctrine of dual federalism, see Edward S. Corwin, "The Passing of Dual Federalism," in Robert G. McCloskey, ed., *Essays in Constitutional Law* (New York: Knopf, 1962).

Champion v. Ames
188 U.S. 321, 23 S. Ct. 321, 47 L. Ed. 492 (1903)

In 1895 Congress passed a statute that prohibited the shipment of lottery tickets in interstate commerce or through the U.S. mail. W. F. Champion was arrested and held for trial in federal district court for having used the Wells-Fargo Express Company to ship a package containing lottery tickets issued by the Pan-American Lottery Company. He then sued out a writ of habeas corpus against a U.S. Marshall on the ground that the act under which he was to be tried was unconstitutional and void. Opinion of the Court: *Harlan*, Holmes, McKenna, White, Brown. Dissenting opinion: *Fuller*, Brewer, Shiras, Peckham.

Mr. Justice HARLAN delivered the opinion of the court.

The appellant insists that the carrying of lottery tickets from one State to another State by an express company engaged in carrying freight and packages from State to State, although such tickets may be contained in a box or package, does not constitute, and cannot by any act of Congress be legally made to constitute, *commerce* among the States within the meaning of the clause of the Constitution of the United States providing that Congress shall have power "to regulate commerce with foreign nations, and among the several states, and with the Indian tribes"; consequently, that Congress cannot make it an offense to cause such tickets to be carried from one State to another.

The Government insists that express companies, when engaged, for hire, in the business of transportation from one State to another, are instrumentalities of commerce among the States; that the carrying of lottery tickets from one State to another is commerce which Congress may regulate; and that as a means of executing the power to regulate interstate commerce Congress may make it an offense against the United States to cause lottery tickets to be carried from one State to another.

The questions presented by these opposing contentions are of great moment, and are entitled to receive, as they have received, the most careful consideration.

What is the import of the word "commerce" as used in the Constitution? It is not defined by that instrument. Undoubtedly, the carrying from one State to another by independent carriers of things or commodities that are ordinary subjects of traffic, and which have in themselves a recognized value in money, constitutes interstate commerce. But does not commerce among the several States include something more? Does not the carrying from one State to another, by independent carriers, of lottery tickets that entitle the holder to the payment of a certain amount of money therein specified also constitute commerce among the States?

The leading case under the commerce clause of the Constitution is *Gibbons v. Ogden* [1824]. Referring to that clause, Chief Justice Marshall said: "The subject to be regulated is commerce; and our Constitution being, as was aptly said at the bar, one of enumeration, and not of definition, to ascertain the extent of the power it becomes necessary to settle the meaning of the word. . . . Commerce, undoubtedly, is traffic, but it is something more; it is intercourse. It describes the commercial intercourse between nations and parts of nations, in all its branches, and is regulated by prescribing rules for carrying on that intercourse. . . ."

Again: "We are now arrived at the inquiry,—What is this power? It is the power to regulate; that is, to prescribe the rule by which commerce is to be governed. This power, like all others vested in Congress, is complete in itself, may be exercised *to its utmost extent*, and acknowledges *no limitations, other than are prescribed in the Constitution.*" . . .

This reference to prior adjudications could be extended if it were necessary to do so. The cases cited . . . show that commerce among the States embraces navigation, intercourse, communication, traffic, the transit of persons, and the transmission of messages by telegraph. They also show that the power to regulate commerce among the several states is vested in Congress as absolutely as it would be in a single government, having in its constitution the same restrictions on the exercise of the power as are found in the Constitution of the United States; that such power is plenary, complete in itself, and may be exerted by Congress to its utmost extent, subject *only* to such limitations as the Constitution imposes upon the exercise of the powers granted by it; and that in determining the character of the regulations to be adopted Congress has a large discretion which is not to be controlled by the courts, simply because, in their opinion, such regulations may not be the best or most effective that could be employed.

We come, then, to inquire whether there is any solid foundation upon which to rest the contention that Congress may not regulate the carrying of lottery tickets from one State to another, at least by corporations or companies whose business it is, for hire, to carry tangible property from one State to another. We are of opinion that lottery tickets are subjects of traffic, and therefore are subjects of commerce, and the regulation of the carriage of such tickets from State to State, at least by independent carriers, is a regulation of commerce among the several States. But it is said that the statute in question does not regulate the carrying of lottery tickets from State to State, but by punishing those who cause them to be so carried Congress in effect prohibits such carrying; that in respect of the carrying from one State to another of articles or things that are, in fact, or according to usage in business, the subjects of commerce, the authority given Congress was not to *prohibit*, but only to *regulate.* . . .

If a State, when considering legislation for the suppression of lotteries within its own limits, may properly take into view the evils that inhere in the raising of money, in that mode, why may not Congress, invested with the power to regulate commerce among the several States, provide that such commerce shall not be polluted by the carrying of lottery tickets from one State to another? In this connection it must not be forgotten that the power of Congress to regulate commerce among the States is plenary, is complete in itself, and is subject to no limitations except such as may be found in the Constitution. What provision in that instrument can be regarded as limiting the exercise of the power granted? . . . If it be said that the act of 1895 is inconsistent with the Tenth Amendment, reserving to the States respectively, or to the people, the powers not delegated to the United States, the answer is that the power to regulate commerce among the states has been expressly delegated to Congress.

Besides, Congress, by that act, does not assume to interfere with traffic or commerce in lottery tickets carried on exclusively within the limits of any State, but has in view only commerce of that kind among the several States. It has not assumed to interfere with the completely internal affairs of any State, and has only legislated in respect of a matter which concerns the people of the United States. As a State may, for the purpose of guarding the morals of its own people, forbid all sales of lottery tickets within its limits, so Congress, for the purpose of guarding the people of the United States against the "widespread pestilence of lotteries" and to protect the commerce which concerns all the States, may prohibit the carrying of lottery tickets from one State to another. In legislating upon the subject of the traffic in lottery tickets, as carried on through interstate commerce, Congress only supplemented the action of those States—perhaps all of them—which, for the protection of the public morals, prohibit the drawing of lotteries, as well as the sale or circulation of lottery tickets, within their respective limits. It said, in effect, that it would not permit the declared policy of the States, which sought to protect their people against the mischiefs of the lottery business, to be overthrown or disregarded by the agency of interstate commerce. We should hesitate long before adjudging that an evil of such appalling character, carried on through interstate commerce, cannot be met and crushed by the only power competent to that end. . . .

It is said, however, that if, in order to suppress lotteries carried on through interstate commerce, Congress may exclude lottery tickets from such commerce, that principle leads necessarily to the conclusion that Congress may arbitrarily exclude from commerce among the States any article, commodity, or thing, of whatever kind or nature, or however useful or valuable, which it may choose, no matter with what motive, to declare shall not be carried from one State to another. It will be time enough to consider the constitutionality of such legislation when we must do so. The present case does not require the court to declare the full extent of the power that Congress may exercise in the regulation of commerce among the States. We may, however, repeat, in this connection, what the court has heretofore said, that the power of Congress to regulate commerce among the States, although plenary, cannot be deemed arbitrary, since it is subject to such limitations or restrictions as are prescribed by the Constitution. . . .

The whole subject is too important, and the questions suggested by its consideration are too difficult of solution, to justify any attempt to lay down a rule for determining in advance the validity of every statute that may be enacted under the commerce clause. We decide nothing more in the present case than that lottery tickets are subjects of traffic among those who choose to sell or buy them; that the carriage of such tickets by independent carriers from one State to another is therefore interstate commerce; that under its power to regulate commerce among the several States Congress—subject to the limitations imposed by the Constitution upon the exercise of the powers granted—has plenary authority over such commerce, and may prohibit the carriage of such tickets from State to State; and that legislation to that end, and of that character, is not inconsistent with any limitation or restriction imposed upon the exercise of the powers granted to Congress.

The judgment is affirmed.

Mr. Chief Justice FULLER, dissenting.

The power of the State to impose restraints and burdens on persons and property in conservation and promotion of the public health, good order, and prosperity is a power originally and always belonging to the States, not surrendered by them to the General Government, nor directly restrained by the Constitution of the United States, and essentially exclusive, and the suppression of lotteries as a harmful business falls within this power, commonly called, of police.

It is urged, however, that because Congress is empowered to regulate commerce between the several States, it, therefore, may suppress lotteries by prohibiting the carriage of lottery matter. Congress may, indeed, make all laws necessary and proper for carrying the powers granted to it into execution, and doubtless an act prohibiting the carriage of lottery matter would be necessary and proper to the execution of a power to suppress lotteries; but that power belongs to the States and not to Congress. To hold that Congress has general police power would be to hold that it may accomplish objects not intrusted to the General Government, and to defeat the operation of the Tenth Amendment, declaring that "the powers not delegated to the United States by the Constitution, nor prohibited by it to the states, are reserved to the states respectively, or to the people." . . .

. . . To say that the mere carrying of an article which is not an article of commerce in and of itself nevertheless becomes such the moment it is to be transported from one State to another, is to transform a non-commercial article into a commercial one simply because it is transported. I cannot conceive that any such result can properly follow. It would be to say that everything is an article of commerce the moment it is taken to be transported from place to place, and of interstate commerce if from State to State. An invitation to dine, or to take a drive, or a note of introduction, all become articles of commerce under the ruling in this case, by being deposited with an express company for transportation. This in effect breaks down all the differences between that which is, and that which is not, an article of commerce, and the necessary consequence is to take from the States all jurisdiction over the subject so far as interstate communication is concerned. It is a long step in the direction of wiping out all traces of State lines, and the creation of a centralized government.

Does the grant to Congress of the power to regulate interstate commerce impart the absolute power to prohibit it?

The power to prohibit the transportation of diseased animals and infected goods over railroads or on steamboats is an entirely different thing, for they would be in themselves injurious to the transaction of interstate commerce, and, moreover, are essentially commercial in their nature. And the exclusion of diseased persons rests on different ground, for nobody would pretend that persons could be kept off the trains because they were going from one State to another to engage in the lottery business. However enticing that business may be, we do not understand these pieces of paper themselves can communicate bad principles by contact.

In my opinion the act in question in the particular under consideration is invalid, and the judgments below ought to be reversed.

Notes/Queries/Readings

1. Is the use of federal power at issue in *Champion* consistent with Chief Justice Marshall's analysis in *Gibbons*? How is *Champion* to be squared with *E. C. Knight*? Has the commerce clause been used here as a pretext to regulate a subject unrelated to commerce? What other provisions of the Constitution might support the exercise of the federal power that has been exercised here? Would the Preamble be of any help?

2. There seems little doubt that the congressional legislation at issue in *Champion* was in the national interest. Does the Constitution, however, confer on the federal government the power to regulate matters in the national interest? If so, what function does the Tenth Amendment serve?

3. In his opinion for the Court, Justice Harlan noted that the plenary power of Congress to regulate commerce is not arbitrary because "it is subject to such limitations or restrictions as are prescribed by the Constitution." What are those limits?

4. For additional reading, see Robert E. Cushman, *The National Police Power Under the Commerce Clause of the Constitution,* 3 Minnesota Law Review 289 (1919).

Hammer v. Dagenhart
247 U.S. 251, 38 S. Ct. 529, 62 L. Ed. 1101 (1918)

The Federal Child Labor Act of 1916 prohibited the transportation in interstate commerce of products made in any mill, factory, or manufacturing establishment in which children under fourteen years of age were employed or in which children between fourteen and sixteen were employed to work more than eight hours a day or more than six days a week. Dagenhart brought suit on behalf of himself and his two minor sons who were employed in a North Carolina cotton mill. The government appealed when the federal district court struck down the statute. Opinion of the Court: *Day*, White, VanDevanter, Pitney, McReynolds. Dissenting opinion: *Holmes*, McKenna, Brandeis, Clarke.

Mr. Justice DAY delivered the opinion of the Court.

The controlling question for decision is: Is it within the authority of Congress in regulating commerce among the States to prohibit the transportation in interstate commerce of manufactured goods, the product of a factory in which, within thirty days prior to their removal therefrom, children under the age of fourteen have been employed or permitted to work, or children between the ages of fourteen and sixteen years have been employed or permitted to work more than eight hours in any day, or more than six days in any week, or after the hour of 7 o'clock p. m., or before the hour of 6 o'clock a. m.?

The power essential to the passage of this act, the government contends, is found in the commerce clause of the Constitution which authorizes Congress to regulate commerce with foreign nations and among the States.

In *Gibbons v. Ogden*, Chief Justice Marshall, speaking for this court, and defining the extent and nature of the commerce power, said, "It is the power to regulate, that is, to prescribe the rule by which commerce is to be governed." In other words, the power is one to control the means by which commerce is carried on, which is directly the contrary of the assumed right to forbid commerce from moving and thus destroy it as to particular commodities. But it is insisted that adjudged cases in this court [e.g., *Champion v. Ames*] establish the doctrine that the power to regulate given to Congress incidentally includes the authority to prohibit the movement of ordinary commodities and

therefore that the subject is not open for discussion. The cases demonstrate the contrary. They rest upon the character of the particular subjects dealt with and the fact that the scope of governmental authority, state or national, possessed over them is such that the authority to prohibit is as to them but the exertion of the power to regulate.

In [earlier cases] the use of interstate transportation was necessary to the accomplishment of harmful results. In other words, although the power over interstate transportation was to regulate, that could only be accomplished by prohibiting the use of the facilities of interstate commerce to effect the evil intended.

This element is wanting in the present case. The thing intended to be accomplished by this statute is the denial of the facilities of interstate commerce to those manufacturers in the states who employ children within the prohibited ages. The act in its effect does not regulate transportation among the States, but aims to standardize the ages at which children may be employed in mining and manufacturing within the States. The goods shipped are of themselves harmless. The act permits them to be freely shipped after thirty days from the time of their removal from the factory. When offered for shipment, and before transportation begins, the labor of their production is over, and the mere fact that they were intended for interstate commerce transportation does not make their production subject to federal control under the commerce power.

Over interstate transportation, or its incidents, the regulatory power of Congress is ample, but the production of articles, intended for interstate commerce, is a matter of local regulation. If it were otherwise, all manufacture intended for interstate shipment would be brought under federal control to the practical exclusion of the authority of the States, a result certainly not contemplated by the framers of the Constitution when they vested in Congress the authority to regulate commerce among the States.

It is further contended that the authority of Congress may be exerted to control interstate commerce in the shipment of childmade goods because of the effect of the circulation of such goods in other States where the evil of this class of labor has been recognized by local legislation, and the right to thus employ child labor has been more rigorously restrained than in the State of production. In other words, that the unfair competition, thus engendered, may

Comparative Note 6.3

[The Industrial Disputes Act of 1907 was designed to deal with work stoppages and labor disputes in some of Canada's most vital industries. The act was regarded as "emergency" legislation enacted pursuant to the Canadian government's power "to make laws for the peace, order and good government of Canada." The privy council declared the act invalid as a violation of the Constitution (i.e., the British North American Act, 1867).]

Whatever else may be the effect of this enactment, it is clear that it is one which could have been passed, so far as any Province was concerned, by the Provincial Legislature under the powers concerned by s. 92 of the [Constitution]. For its provisions were concerned directly with the civil rights of both employers and employed in the Province. . . . The Dominion parliament has, under the initial words of s. 91, a general power to make laws for Canada. But these laws are not to relate to the classes of subjects assigned to the Provinces by s. 92, unless their enactment falls under heads specifi-

cally assigned to the Dominion Parliament by the enumeration in s. 91. . . .

. . . [T]he invocation of the specific power in s. 91 to regulate trade and commerce [does not] assist the Dominion contention. . . . [We cannot accept] the general principle that the mere fact that Dominion legislation is for the general advantage of Canada, or is such that it will meet a mere want which is felt throughout the Dominion, renders it competent if it cannot be brought within the heads enumerated specifically in s. 91. . . . No doubt there may be cases arising out of some extraordinary peril to the national life of Canada, as a whole, such as the cases arising out of a war, where legislation is required of an order that passes beyond the heads of exclusive Provincial competency. Such cases may be dealt with under the words at the commencement of s. 91, conferring general powers in relation to peace, order, and good government, simply because such cases are not otherwise provided for. But instances of this . . . are highly exceptional.

SOURCE: *Toronto Electric Commissioners v. Snider*, In the Privy Council [1925] A.C. 396; II Olmstead 394.

be controlled by closing the channels of interstate commerce to manufacturers in those States where the local laws do not meet what Congress deems to be the more just standard of other States.

There is no power vested in Congress to require the States to exercise their police power so as to prevent possible unfair competition. Many causes may co-operate to give one State, by reason of local laws or conditions, an economic advantage over others. The commerce clause was not intended to give to Congress a general authority to equalize such conditions. . . .

The grant of power of Congress over the subject of interstate commerce was to enable it to regulate such commerce, and not to give it authority to control the States in their exercise of the police power over local trade and manufacture.

The grant of authority over a purely federal matter was not intended to destroy the local power always existing and carefully reserved to the States in the Tenth Amendment to the Constitution.

A statute must be judged by its natural and reasonable effect. The control by Congress over interstate commerce cannot authorize the exercise of authority not entrusted to it by the Constitution. The maintenance of the authority of the States over matters purely local is as essential to the

preservation of our institutions as is the conservation of the supremacy of the federal power in all matters entrusted to the Nation by the federal Constitution.

In interpreting the Constitution it must never be forgotten that the Nation is made up of States to which are entrusted the powers of local government. And to them and to the people the powers not expressly delegated to the National Government are reserved. . . . To sustain this statute would not be in our judgment a recognition of the lawful exertion of congressional authority over interstate commerce, but would sanction an invasion by the federal power of the control of a matter purely local in its character, and over which no authority has been delegated to Congress in conferring the power to regulate commerce among the States.

In our view the necessary effect of this act is, by means of a prohibition against the movement in interstate commerce of ordinary commercial commodities to regulate the hours of labor of children in factories and mines within the States, a purely state authority. Thus the act in a two-fold sense is repugnant to the Constitution. It not only transcends the authority delegated to Congress over commerce but also exerts a power as to a purely local matter to which the federal authority does not extend. The far reaching result of upholding the act cannot be more plainly indicated than by pointing out that if Congress can thus regulate matters entrusted to local authority by prohibition of the movement of commodities in interstate commerce, all freedom of commerce will be at an end, and the power of the States over local matters may be eliminated, and thus our system of government be practically destroyed.

For these reasons we hold that this law exceeds the constitutional authority of Congress. It follows that the decree of the District Court must be

Affirmed.

Mr. Justice HOLMES, dissenting.

The first step in my argument is to make plain what no one is likely to dispute—that the statute in question is within the power expressly given to Congress if considered only as to its immediate effects and that if invalid it is so only upon some collateral ground. The statute confines itself to prohibiting the carriage of certain goods in interstate or foreign commerce. Congress is given power to regulate such commerce in unqualified terms. It would not be argued today that the power to regulate does not include the power to prohibit. Regulation means the prohibition of something, and when interstate commerce is the matter to be regulated I cannot doubt that the regulation may prohibit any part of such commerce that Congress sees fit to forbid. . . .

The question then is narrowed to whether the exercise of its otherwise constitutional power by Congress can be pronounced unconstitutional because of its possible reaction upon the conduct of the States in a matter upon which I have admitted that they are free from direct control. I should have thought that that matter had been disposed of so fully as to leave no room for doubt. I should have thought that the most conspicuous decisions of this Court had made it clear that the power to regulate commerce and other constitutional powers could not be cut down or qualified by the fact that it might interfere with the carrying out of the domestic policy of any State.

The notion that prohibition is any less prohibition when applied to things now thought evil I do not understand. But if there is any matter upon which civilized countries have agreed—far more unanimously than they have with regard to intoxicants and some other matters over which this country is now emotionally aroused—it is the evil of premature and excessive child labor. I should have thought that if we were to introduce our own moral conceptions where in my opinion they do not belong, this was preeminently a case for upholding the exercise of all its powers by the United States.

But I had thought that the propriety of the exercise of a power admitted to exist in some cases was for the consideration of Congress alone and that this Court always had disavowed the right to intrude its judgment upon questions of policy or morals. It is not for this Court to pronounce when prohibition is necessary to regulation if it ever may be necessary—to say that it is permissible as against strong drink but not as against the product of ruined lives.

The act does not meddle with anything belonging to the States. They may regulate their internal affairs and their domestic commerce as they like. But when they seek to send their products across the State line they are no longer within their rights. If there were no Constitution and no Congress their power to cross the line would depend upon their neighbors. Under the Constitution such commerce belongs not to the States but to Congress to regulate. It may carry out its views of public policy whatever indirect effect they may have upon the activities of the States. Instead of being encountered by a prohibitive tariff at her boundaries the State encounters the public policy of the United States which it is for Congress to express. The public policy of the United States is shaped with a view to the benefit of the nation as a whole. If, as has been the case within the memory of men still living, a State should take a different view of the propriety of sustaining a lottery from that which generally prevails, I cannot believe that the fact would require a different decision from that reached in *Champion v. Ames.* Yet in that case it would be said with quite as much force as in this that Congress was attempting to intermeddle with the State's domestic affairs. The national welfare as understood by Congress may require a different attitude within its sphere from that of some self-seeking State. It seems to me entirely constitutional for Congress to enforce its understanding by all the means at its command.

Notes/Queries/Readings

1. Justice Day wrote that to the states and the people "the powers not expressly delegated to the national government are reserved." Is this what the Tenth Amendment actually says? The Founders consciously omitted the word "expressly" when they drafted the amendment. Does adding it change anything? Would it affect the relationship between the Tenth Amendment and the necessary and proper clause?

2. In its effort to distinguish this case from others, the Court distinguished between evil and nonevil products. Is the distinction fairly traceable to the commerce clause or to the Constitution more generally?

3. Justice Day also distinguished between local manufacture and interstate shipping. Is this distinction implicit in the commerce clause? In the Tenth Amendment? In dual federalism?

4. Can the Court's opinion in *Hammer* be reconciled with the decision in *E. C. Knight*? How? Can it be squared with the Court's opinion in *Champion*?

5. Holmes remarked that "this Court always had disavowed the right to intrude [on Congress's] judgment upon questions of policy or morals." Did the Court ignore its disavowal in *Hammer*? When does the Court cross the line from constitutional interpretation to ordinary policymaking? Is it possible to clearly distinguish the two?

6. *Hammer v. Dagenhart* was overruled by *United States v. Darby*, 312 U.S. 100 (1941). *Hammer* is nevertheless important because it showed how narrowly the Supreme Court interpreted the scope of Congress's power over interstate commerce at the time of the decision. *Hammer* should also be seen in tandem with numerous decisions of the Supreme Court that struck down congressional statutes designed to deal with the economic depression of the 1930s. Notable among these cases was *Schechter Poultry Corp. v. United States* (1935), a case we have already visited in regard to the doctrine of nondelegation (see chapter 4). But *Schechter* also struck down the National Industrial Recovery Act for exceeding Congress's power under the commerce clause. The Court acknowledged "the grave national crisis with which Congress was confronted," but went on to say that "[e]xtraordinary conditions do not create or enlarge constitutional power." The Court continued:

> The Constitution established a national government with powers deemed to be adequate, as they have proved to be both in war and peace, but these powers of the national government are limited by the constitutional grants. Those who act under these grants are not at liberty to transcend the imposed limits because they believe that more or different power is necessary. Such assertions of extraconstitutional authority were anticipated and precluded by the explicit terms of the Tenth Amendment."

Are the terms of the Tenth Amendment as explicit as the Court suggests?

7. Compare *Hammer* to the Privy Council decision in Comparative Note 6.3 (p. 248) Do *Hammer* and *Snider* follow the same approach to constitutional interpretation?

National Labor Relations Board v. Jones & Laughlin Steel Corporation
301 U.S. 1, 57 S. Ct. 615, 81 L. Ed. 893 (1937)

The National Labor Relations Act of 1935 gave employees the right to organize unions and to bargain collectively through representatives of their own choosing. It established the National Labor Relations Board (NLRB) to investigate and prevent specified "unfair labor practices" that affect interstate commerce. The declared policy behind the law was to eliminate the sources of obstruction to the free flow of commerce, among them the refusal by employers to recognize unions or to accept collective bargaining.

The NLRB investigated charges of anti-union activity against the Jones and Laughlin Steel Corporation, the fourth largest producer of steel in the United States. The corporation was charged with dismissing union officials and discriminating against union members in its hiring and tenure policies. The NLRB sustained the charges and ordered the corporation to cease and desist from its discriminatory activity. The Board petitioned the circuit court of appeals to enforce the order when Jones and Laughlin failed to comply. The court denied the petition, holding the NLRB's order beyond the scope of federal power. Opinion of the Court: *Hughes*, Brandeis, Stone, Roberts, Cardozo. Dissenting opinion: *McReynolds*, VanDevanter, Sutherland, Butler.

Mr. Chief Justice HUGHES delivered the opinion of the Court.

First. The Scope of the Act.—The act is challenged in its entirety as an attempt to regulate all industry, thus invading the reserved powers of the States over their local concerns. It is asserted that the references in the Act to interstate and foreign commerce are colorable at best; that the Act is not a true regulation of such commerce or of matters which directly affect it, but on the contrary has the fundamental object of placing under the compulsory supervision of the federal government all industrial labor relations within the nation. . . .

The grant of authority to the Board does not purport to extend to the relationship between all industrial employees and employers. Its terms do not impose collective bargaining upon all industry regardless of effects upon interstate or foreign commerce. It purports to reach only what may be deemed to burden or obstruct that commerce and, thus qualified, it must be construed as contemplating the exercise of control within constitutional bounds. It is a familiar principle that acts which directly burden or obstruct interstate or foreign commerce, or its free flow, are within the reach of the congressional power. Acts having that effect are not rendered immune because they grow out of labor disputes. It is the effect upon commerce, not the source of the injury, which is the criterion. Whether or not particular action does affect commerce in such a close and intimate fashion as to be subject to federal control, and hence to lie within the authority conferred upon the Board, is left by the statute to be determined as individual cases arise. . . .

Second. The unfair labor practices in question. . . .

. . . [I]n its present application, the statute goes no further than to safeguard the right of employees to self-organization and to select representatives of their own choosing for collective bargaining or other mutual protection without restraint or coercion by their employer.

That is a fundamental right. Employees have as clear a right to organize and select their representatives for lawful purposes as the respondent has to organize its business and select its own officers and agents. Discrimination and coercion to prevent the free exercise of the right of employees to self-organization and representation is a proper subject for condemnation by competent legislative authority. . . . Hence the prohibition by Congress of interference with the selection of representatives for the purpose of negotiation and conference between employers and employees, "instead of being an invasion of the constitutional right of either, was based on the recognition of the rights of both." . . .

Third. The application of the Act to Employees Engaged in Production.— The Principle Involved.—Respondent says that, whatever may be said of employees engaged in interstate commerce, the industrial relations and activities in the manufacturing department of respondent's enterprise are not subject to federal regulation. The argument rests upon the proposition that manufacturing in itself is not commerce.

. . . The congressional authority to protect interstate commerce from burdens and obstructions is not limited to transactions which can be deemed to be an essential part of a "flow" of interstate or foreign commerce. Burdens and obstructions may be due to injurious action springing from other sources. . . . Although activities may be intrastate in character when separately considered, if they have such a close and substantial relation to interstate commerce that their control is essential or appropriate to protect that commerce from burdens and obstructions, Congress cannot be denied the power to exercise that control. Undoubtedly the scope of this power must be considered in the light of our dual system of government and may not be extended so as to embrace effects upon interstate commerce so indirect and remote that to embrace them, in view of our complex society, would effectually obliterate the distinction between what is national and what is local and create a completely centralized government. The question is necessarily one of degree. . . .

It is thus apparent that the fact that the employees here concerned were engaged in production is not determinative. The question remains as to the effect upon interstate commerce of the labor practice involved. . . .

Fourth. Effects of the Unfair Labor Practice in Respondent's Enterprise.—Giving full weight to respondent's contention with respect to a break in the complete continuity of the "stream of commerce" by reason of respondent's manufacturing operations, the fact remains that the stoppage of those operations by industrial strife would have a most serious effect upon interstate commerce. In view of respondent's far-flung activities, it is idle to say that the effect would be indirect or remote. It is obvious that it would be immediate and might be catastrophic. We are asked to shut our eyes to the plainest facts of our national life and to deal with the question of direct and indirect effects in an intellectual vacuum. Because there may be but indirect and remote effects upon interstate commerce in connection with a host of local enterprises throughout the country, it does not follow that other industrial activities do not have such a close and intimate relation to interstate commerce as to make the presence of industrial strife a matter of the most urgent national concern. When industries organize themselves on a national scale, making their relation to interstate commerce the dominant factor in their activities, how can it be maintained that their industrial labor relations constitute a forbidden field into which Congress may not enter when it is necessary to protect interstate commerce from the paralyzing consequences of industrial war? We have often said that interstate commerce itself is a practical conception. It is equally true that interferences with that commerce must be appraised by a judgment that does not ignore actual experience.

Experience has abundantly demonstrated that the recognition of the right of employees to self-organization and to have representatives of their own choosing for the purpose of collective bargaining is often an essential condition of industrial peace. Refusal to confer and negotiate has been one of the most prolific causes of strife. This is such an outstanding fact in the history of labor disturbances that it is a proper subject of judicial notice and requires no citation of instances. . . .

Our conclusion is that the order of the Board was within its competency and that the act is valid as here applied. The judgment of the Circuit Court of Appeals is reversed and the cause is remanded for further proceedings in conformity with this opinion. It is so ordered.

Reversed and remanded.

Mr. Justice McREYNOLDS delivered the following dissenting opinion.

. . . Six District Courts, on the authority of *Schechter's* and *Carter's* Cases, have held that the Board has no authority to regulate relations between employers and employees engaged in local production. No decision or judicial opinion to the contrary has been cited, and we find none. Every

Comparative Note 6.4

The interpretive problem for Canada lay in the accommodation of the federal power over "the regulation of trade and commerce" (s. 91 [2]) with the provincial power over "property and civil rights in the province" (s. 92 [13]). On the face of it, these powers appear to overlap. Trade and commerce is carried on by means of contracts which give rise to "civil rights" over "property." However, the courts, by a process of "mutual modification," have narrowed the two classes of subjects so as to eliminate the overlapping and make each power exclusive. The leading case is *Citizens' Insurance Co. v. Parsons* (1881), in which the issue was the validity of a provincial statute which stipulated that certain conditions were to be included in all fire insurance policies entered into in the province. The Privy Council . . . held that the statute was a valid law in relation to property and civil rights in the province. It did not come within the federal trade and commerce power, because that power should be read as not including "the power to regulate by legislation the contracts of a particular business or trade, such as the business of fire insurance in a single province." What the phrase "the regulation of trade and commerce" did include was "political arrangements in regard to trade requiring the sanction of Parliament, regulations of trade in matters of inter-provincial concern, and it may be that they would include general regulation of trade affecting the whole dominion.

Source: Hogg, *Constitutional Law of Canada*, 522.

consideration brought forward to uphold the act before us was applicable to support the acts held unconstitutional in causes decided within two years. And the lower courts rightly deemed them controlling.

Any effect on interstate commerce by the discharge of employees shown here would be indirect and remote in the highest degree, as consideration of the facts will show. In [this case] ten men out of ten thousand were discharged; in the other cases only a few. The immediate effect in the factory may be to create discontent among a reducing production, which ultimately may reduce the volume of goods moving in interstate commerce. By this chain of indirect and progressively remote events we finally reach the evil with which it is said the legislation under consideration undertakes to deal. A more remote and indirect interference with interstate commerce or a more definite invasion of the powers reserved to the states is difficult, if not impossible, to imagine. . . . The Constitution still recognizes the existence of states with indestructible powers; the Tenth Amendment was supposed to put them beyond controversy.

We are told that Congress may protect the "stream of commerce" and that one who buys raw material without the state, manufactures it therein, and ships the output to another state is in that stream. Therefore it is said he may be prevented from doing anything which may interfere with its flow. . . . There is no ground on which reasonably to hold that refusal by a manufacturer, whose raw materials come from states other than that of his factory and whose products are regularly carried to other states, to bargain collectively with employees in his manufacturing plant, directly affects interstate commerce. . . . Whatever effect any cause of discontent may ultimately have upon commerce is far too indirect to justify congressional regulation. . . .

That Congress has power by appropriate means, not prohibited by the Constitution, to prevent direct and material interference with the conduct of interstate commerce is settled doctrine. But the interference struck at must be direct and material, not some mere possibility contingent on wholly uncertain events; and there must be no impairment of rights guaranteed. A state by taxation on property may indirectly but seriously affect the cost of transportation; it may not lay a direct tax upon the receipts from interstate transportation. The first is an indirect effect, the other direct. . . .

The things inhibited by the Labor Act relate to the management of a manufacturing plant—something distinct from commerce and subject to the authority of the state. And this may not be abridged because of some vague possibility of distant interference with commerce. . . .

It seems clear to us that Congress has transcended the powers granted.

Notes/Queries/Readings

1. The respondent argued that manufacturing is not commerce. How did the Court respond to this distinction? Was its reading of the commerce clause influenced by national economic conditions?

2. Is Chief Justice Hughes's opinion consistent with the Court's approach in *E. C. Knight*?

3. *Jones & Laughlin* was a turning point in the Supreme Court's commerce clause jurisprudence. From then on the Court rarely questioned Congress's exercise of the com-

merce power. In Canada, however, the Supreme Court and Privy Council would continue to hold fast to its restricted view not only of the Dominion's power over trade and commerce but of its residual power to make laws for the peace, order, and good government of Canada. (See Comparative Note 6.5.) What explains the different approaches of the two courts? Is it plausible that in 1937 the U.S. Supreme Court might have taken the more restrictive view of federal power and the Canadian Supreme Court the

broader view? (For the relevant Canadian constitutional provisions see Comparative Note 6.1 at p. 238.) If so, what does this tell you about the process of constitutional interpretation?

4. For additional reading see William M. Wiecek, *Liberty Under Law: The Supreme Court in American Life* (Baltimore: Johns Hopkins University Press, 1988) and Richard C. Cortner, *The Wagner Act Cases* (Knoxville: University of Tennessee Press, 1964).

Wickard v. Filburn

317 U.S. 111, 63 S. Ct. 82, 87 L. Ed. 122 (1942)

The Agricultural Adjustment Act of 1938 limited the amount of acreage that individual farmers could devote to the production of wheat. The act, which purported to be a regulation of interstate commerce, was designed to stabilize the price of wheat in the national market. Filburn, an Ohio farmer, was fined for raising wheat in excess of the quota allotted to him under the act. He defended himself on the grounds that the excess wheat he had grown on his farm was for his own home consumption and not intended for shipment in interstate commerce. The government appealed after a federal district court had enjoined the collec-

tion of the fine. Opinion of the Court: *Jackson*, Stone, Roberts, Black, Reed, Frankfurter, Douglas, Murphy, Byrnes.

**Mr. Justice JACKSON delivered
the opinion of the Court.**

It is urged that under the Commerce Clause of the Constitution, Article I, s 8, clause 3, Congress does not possess the power it has in this instance sought to exercise. The question would merit little consideration since our decision in *United States v. Darby* [1941] . . . , sustaining the federal power to regulate production of goods for commerce, except for the fact that this Act extends federal regulation to production not intended in any part for commerce but wholly for consumption on the farm. . . .

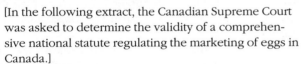

Comparative Note   6.5

[In the following extract, the Canadian Supreme Court was asked to determine the validity of a comprehensive national statute regulating the marketing of eggs in Canada.]

[This case] concern[s] the validity of the egg producers quota regulations. In my view, the control of production, whether agricultural or industrial, is *prima facie* a local matter, a matter of provincial jurisdiction. Egg farms, if I may use this expression to designate the kind of factories in which feed is converted into eggs and fowl, are local undertakings subject to provincial jurisdiction under s. 92 (10) of the *British North American Act, 1867*, unless they are considered as within the scope of "agriculture" in which case, by virtue of s. 95, the jurisdiction is provincial subject to the overriding authority of Parliament. In my view, *Carnation Co. Ltd. v. Quebec Agricultural Marketing Board* (1968) is conclusive in favour of provincial jurisdiction over undertakings where primary agricultural products

are transformed into other food products. In that case, the major portion of the production was shipped outside the Province. In view of the reasons given, the conclusion could not have been different even if the whole production had been going into extra-provincial trade.

• • •

We are not called upon to decide in the present case whether the federal Parliament could assume control over egg farms devoted exclusively to the production of eggs for extra-provincial trade. Under the present circumstances such farms are, like any other farms, local undertakings subject to provincial authority, irrespective of the destination of their output. . . . That does not mean that such power is unlimited, a Province cannot control extra-provincial trade . . . However, "Marketing" does not include production and, therefore, provincial control of production is *prima facie* valid.

SOURCE: *Reference Re Agricultural Products Marketing Act.* In the Supreme Court of Canada [1978] 2 S.C.R. 1198, 84 D.L.R. (3rd) 257.

Appellee says that this is a regulation of production and consumption of wheat. Such activities are, he urges, beyond the reach of Congressional power under the Commerce Clause, since they are local in character, and their effects upon interstate commerce are at most "indirect." In answer the Government argues that the statute regulates neither production nor consumption, but only marketing; and, in the alternative, that if the Act does go beyond the regulation of marketing it is sustainable as a "necessary and proper" implementation of the power of Congress over interstate commerce.

Whether the subject of the regulation in question was "production," "consumption," or "marketing" is . . . not material for purposes of deciding the question of federal power before us. That an activity is of local character may help in a doubtful case to determine whether Congress intended to reach it. The same consideration might help in determining whether in the absence of Congressional action it would be permissible for the state to exert its power on the subject matter, even though in so doing it to some degree affected interstate commerce. But even if appellee's activity be local though it may not be regarded as commerce, it may still, whatever its nature, be reached by Congress if it exerts a substantial economic effect on interstate commerce and this irrespective of whether such effect is what might at some earlier time have been defined as "direct" or "indirect."

The effect of consumption of homegrown wheat on interstate commerce is due to the fact that it constitutes the most variable factor in the disappearance of the wheat crop. Consumption on the farm where grown appears to vary in an amount greater than 20 per cent of average production. The total amount of wheat consumed as food varies but relatively little, and use as seed is relatively constant.

The maintenance by government regulation of a price for wheat undoubtedly can be accomplished as effectively by sustaining or increasing the demand as by limiting the supply. The effect of the statute before us is to restrict the amount which may be produced for market and the extent as well to which one may forestall resort to the market by producing to meet his own needs. That appellee's own contribution to the demand for wheat may be trivial by itself is not enough to remove him from the scope of federal regulation where, as here, his contribution, taken together with that of many others similarly situated, is far from trivial.

It is well established by decisions of this Court that the power to regulate commerce includes the power to regulate the prices at which commodities in that commerce are dealt in and practices affecting such prices. One of the primary purposes of the Act in question was to increase the market price of wheat and to that end to limit the volume thereof that could affect the market. It can hardly be denied that a factor of such volume and variability as home-consumed wheat would have a substantial influence on price and market conditions. . . . This record leaves us in no doubt that Congress may properly have considered that wheat consumed on the farm where grown, if wholly outside the scheme of regulation, would have a substantial effect in defeating and obstructing its purpose to stimulate trade therein at increased prices.

It is said, however, that this Act, forcing some farmers into the market to buy what they could provide for themselves, is an unfair promotion of the markets and prices of specializing wheat growers. It is of the essence of regulation that it lays a restraining hand on the self-interest of the regulated and that advantages from the regulation commonly fall to others. The conflicts of economic interest between the regulated and those who advantage by it are wisely left under our system to resolution by the Congress under its more flexible and responsible legislative process. Such conflicts rarely lend themselves to judicial determination. And with the wisdom, workability, or fairness, of the plan of regulation we have nothing to do.

Reversed.

Notes/Queries/Readings

1. Is Justice Jackson's argument in favor of the regulatory statute in *Wickard* merely a "pretext" for the regulation of activity reserved exclusively to the states?

2. Are there any limitations on the exercise of the commerce power after *Wickard*? Compare Jackson's opinion with the Canadian Supreme Court's decision in Comparative Note 6.5. Might the U.S. Supreme Court have plausibly advanced a similar argument against federal regulation in *Wickard*?

3. Should the Tenth Amendment constitute a bar to the kind of federal regulation imposed in *Wickard*? In this connection, see *United States v. Darby* (1941), decided shortly before *Wickard*. In *Darby*, Justice Stone asserted that the Tenth Amendment "states but a truism that all is retained which has not been surrendered. There is nothing in the history of its adoption to suggest that it was more than declaratory of the relationship between the national and state governments as it had been established by the Constitution before the Amendment." Do you agree?

4. The Court claimed that it had nothing to do with whether the regulation in this case was wise, workable, or fair. Is this disinterest a constitutional mandate? Is it grounded in an understanding about the nature and limits of judicial authority in a constitutional democracy?

5. Is it possible to square the Court's claim of disinterest with its earlier observation that the cumulative effects of personal wheat consumption might have a "substantial" impact on interstate commerce?

Heart of Atlanta Motel, Inc. v. United States

379 U.S. 241, 85 S. Ct. 348, 13 L. Ed. 2d 258 (1964)

The Civil Rights Act of 1964 prohibited discrimination based on race, color, religion, or national origin in public accommodations whose operations affect interstate commerce. The Heart of Atlanta Motel, which was readily accessible to interstate highways and seventy-five percent of whose guests were from states other than Georgia, refused to comply with the statute. The motel sought a declaratory judgment, claiming that the public accommodations section (Title II) of the act violated the Constitution. A three-judge federal district court upheld the section as a legitimate exercise of the federal commerce power. Opinion of the Court: *Clark*, Warren, Black, Douglas, Harlan, Brennan, Stewart, White, Goldberg. Concurring opinions: *Black, Douglas*.

Mr. Justice CLARK delivered the opinion of the Court.

It is admitted that the operation of the motel brings it within the provisions of s 201(a) of the Act and that appellant refused to provide lodging for transient Negroes because of their race or color and that it intends to continue that policy unless restrained.

The sole question posed is, therefore, the constitutionality of the Civil Rights Act of 1964 as applied to these facts. The legislative history of the Act indicates that Congress based the Act on s 5 and the Equal Protection Clause of the Fourteenth Amendment as well as its power to regulate interstate commerce under Art. I, s 8, cl. 3, of the Constitution. . . .

While the Act as adopted carried no congressional findings the record of its passage through each house is replete with evidence of the burdens that discrimination by race or color places upon interstate commerce. This testimony included the fact that our people have become increasingly mobile with millions of people of all races traveling from State to State; that Negroes in particular have been the subject of discrimination in transient accommodations, having to travel great distances to secure the same; that often they have been unable to obtain accommodations and have had to call upon friends to put them up overnight, and that these conditions had become so acute as to require the listing of available lodging for Negroes in a special guidebook which was itself "dramatic testimony to the difficulties" Negroes encounter in travel. . . . This testimony indicated a qualitative as well as quantitative effect on interstate travel

Comparative Note 6.6

[Section 7(e) of Canada's Federal Trade Marks Act proscribed misleading and anti-social business practices and provided for both civil and criminal remedies for its violation. The main issue here is whether this is a valid exercise of the "trade and commerce" power under s. 91 (2). In declaring the provisions at issue unconstitutional, Chief Justice Laskin identifies the conditions that any federal act enacted pursuant to s. 91 (2) must fulfill.]

The plain fact is that s. 7 (e) is not a regulation, nor is it concerned with trade as a whole nor with general trade and commerce. In a loose sense every legal prescription is regulatory, even the prescriptions of the *Criminal Code*, but I do not read s. 91 (2) as in itself authorizing federal legislation that merely creates a statutory tort, enforceable by private action, and applicable, as here, to the entire range of business relationships in any activity, whether the activity be itself within or beyond federal legislative authority.

What is evident here is that the Parliament of Canada has simply extended or intensified existing common and civil law delictual liability by statute which at the same time has prescribed the usual civil remedies open to an aggrieved person. The Parliament of Canada can no more acquire legislative jurisdiction by supplementing existing tort liability, cognizable in provincial Courts as reflective of provincial competence, than the provincial Legislatures can acquire legislative jurisdiction by supplementing the federal criminal law.

. . . The provision is not directed to trade but to the ethical conduct of persons engaged in trade or in business, and, in my view, such a detached provision cannot survive alone unconnected to a general regulatory scheme to govern trading relations going beyond merely local concern. Even on the footing of being concerned with practices in the conduct of trade, its private enforcement by civil action gives it a local cast because it is as applicable in its terms to local or intra-provincial competitors as it is to competitors in inter-provincial trade.

SOURCE: *MacDonald v. Vapour Can. Ltd*. In the Supreme Court of Canada [1977] 2 S.C.R. 134.

by Negroes. The former was the obvious impairment of the Negro traveler's pleasure and convenience that resulted when he continually was uncertain of finding lodging. As for the latter, there was evidence that this uncertainty stemming from racial discrimination had the effect of discouraging travel on the part of a substantial portion of the Negro community. . . . [T]he voluminous testimony presents overwhelming evidence that discrimination by hotels and motels impedes interstate travel.

That Congress was legislating against moral wrongs in many of these areas rendered its enactments no less valid. In framing Title II of this Act Congress was also dealing with what it considered a moral problem. But that fact does not detract from the overwhelming evidence of the disruptive effect that racial discrimination has had on commercial intercourse. It was this burden which empowered Congress to enact appropriate legislation, and, given this basis for the exercise of its power, Congress was not restricted by the fact that the particular obstruction to interstate commerce with which it was dealing was also deemed a moral and social wrong.

It is said that the operation of the motel here is of a purely local character. But, assuming this to be true, "[i]f it is interstate commerce that feels the pinch, it does not matter how local the operation which applies the squeeze." . . . Thus the power of Congress to promote interstate commerce also includes the power to regulate the local incidents thereof, including local activities in both the States of origin and destination, which might have a substantial and harmful effect upon that commerce. One need only examine the evidence which we have discussed above to see that Congress may—as it has—prohibit racial discrimination by motels serving travelers, however "local" their operations may appear.

We, therefore, conclude that the action of the Congress in the adoption of the Act as applied here to a motel which concededly serves interstate travelers is within the power granted it by the Commerce Clause of the Constitution, as interpreted by this Court for 140 years. It may be argued that Congress could have pursued other methods to eliminate the distinctions it found in interstate commerce caused by racial discrimination. But this is a matter of policy that rests entirely with the Congress not with the courts. How obstructions in commerce may be removed—what means are to be employed—is within the sound and exclusive discretion of the Congress. It is subject only to one caveat—that the means chosen by it must be reasonably adapted to the end permitted by the Constitution. We cannot say that its choice here was not so adapted. The Constitution requires no more.

Affirmed.

Mr. Justice BLACK, concurring.

[In the following extract Justice Black refers to "Ollie's Barbecue," a restaurant located in a residential section of Birmingham, Alabama, some distance away from the nearest interstate highway. This restaurant was also charged with violating the public accommodations section of the Civil Rights Act. In *Katzenbach v. McClung*, 379 U.S. 294, decided on the same day as *Atlanta Motel*, the Court held that Ollie's Barbecue was also within the reach of the statute because a substantial percentage of its supplies came from out of state.]

. . . The foregoing facts are more than enough, in my judgment, to show that Congress acting within its discretion and judgment has power under the Commerce Clause and the Necessary and Proper Clause to bar racial discrimination in the Heart of Atlanta Motel and Ollie's Barbecue. I recognize that every remote, possible, speculative effect on commerce should not be accepted as an adequate constitutional ground to uproot and throw into the discard all our traditional distinctions between what is purely local, and therefore controlled by state laws, and what affects the national interest and is therefore subject to control by federal laws. I recognize too that some isolated and remote lunchroom which sells only to local people and buys almost all its supplies in the locality may possibly be beyond the reach of the power of Congress to regulate commerce, just as such an establishment is not covered by the present Act. But in deciding the constitutional power of Congress in cases like the two before us we do not consider the effect on interstate commerce of only one isolated, individual, local event, without regard to the fact that this single local event when added to many others of as similar nature may impose a burden on interstate commerce by reducing its volume or distorting its flow.

Mr. Justice DOUGLAS, concurring.

Though I join the Court's opinions, I am somewhat reluctant here . . . to rest solely on the Commerce Clause. My reluctance is not due to any conviction that Congress lacks power to regulate commerce in the interests of human rights. It is rather my belief that the right of people to be free of state action that discriminates against them because of race, like the "right of persons to move freely from State to State occupies a more protected position in our constitutional system than does the movement of cattle, fruit, steel and coal across state lines." . . .

Hence I would prefer to rest on the assertion of legislative power contained in s 5 of the Fourteenth Amendment which states: "The Congress shall have power to enforce, by appropriate legislation, the provisions of this article"—a power which the Court concedes was exercised at least in part in this Act.

A decision based on the Fourteenth Amendment would

have a more settling effect, making unnecessary litigation over whether a particular restaurant or inn is within the commerce definitions of the Act or whether a particular customer is an interstate traveler. Under my construction, the Act would apply to all customers in all the enumerated places of public accommodation. And that construction would put an end to all obstructionist strategies and finally close one door on a bitter chapter in American history.

Notes/Queries/Readings

1. Justice Clark wrote that "voluminous testimony presents overwhelming evidence that discrimination by hotels and motels impedes interstate travel." Is there a difference between activity that "impedes interstate travel" and activity which has an effect on interstate commerce? Are they the same thing? Are they so closely intertwined that an effect on one necessarily has an effect on the other?

2. The Court conceded that Congress might have chosen other means to eliminate these kinds of racial discriminations. What other means did Congress have at its disposal? The Court had struck down earlier efforts by Congress to prohibit private acts of discrimination in *The Civil Rights Cases*, 109 U.S. 3 (1883). The Kennedy Administration feared that those cases might impede civil rights legislation predicated on the Reconstruction Amendments, and they successfully sought to have the legislation justified upon the congressional power to regulate matters that "affect" interstate commerce. For a history, see Gerald D. Gunther, *Constitutional Law*, 12th ed. (Westbury, N.Y.: Foundation Press, Inc., 1991), 148–49. Justice Douglas suggested in his concurrence that Congress might have relied upon the equal protection clause. Do you agree?

3. In what ways does this case resemble *Champion v. Ames*? Should the Court permit Congress to use its power to regulate interstate commerce to advance noncommercial ends, such as ending the moral vice of racial discrimination? To advance the ends of other constitutional provisions? Why or why not? Do these distinctions ultimately matter?

4. How would this statute have fared under the Canadian Constitution? See Comparative Note 6.6 (p. 255).

Maryland v. Wirtz
392 U.S. 183, 88 S. Ct. 2017, 20 L. Ed. 2d 1020 (1968)

Maryland v. Wirtz, National League of Cities v. Usery, and *Garcia v. San Antonio Metropolitan Transit Authority*, all of which are reprinted in the following pages, are another example of the rise and fall of a constitutional doctrine and the continued struggle among the justices over the integrity of that doctrine. In *Wirtz* Maryland, joined by twenty-seven other states, challenged the validity of amendments to the Fair Labor Standards Act extending its minimum wage and maximum hours coverage to schools and hospitals, including those operated by the states and their subdivisions. A federal district court concluded that these amendments were within the power of Congress. Opinion of the Court: *Harlan*, Black, Warren, Brennan, White, Fortas. Dissenting opinion: *Douglas*, Stewart. Not participating: Marshall.

Mr. Justice HARLAN delivered the opinion of the Court.

Appellants' . . . contention is that the commerce power does not afford a constitutional basis for extension of the Act to schools and hospitals operated by the States or their subdivisions. Since the argument is made in terms of interference with "sovereign state functions," it is important to note exactly what the Act does. Although it applies to "employees," the Act specifically exempts any "employee employed in a bona fide executive, administrative, or professional capacity (including any employee employed in the capacity of academic administrative personnel or teacher in elementary or secondary schools). . . ." We assume, as did the District Court, that medical personnel are likewise excluded from coverage under the general language. The Act establishes only a minimum wage and a maximum limit of hours unless overtime wages are paid, and does not otherwise affect the way in which school and hospital duties are performed. Thus appellants' characterization of the question in this case as whether Congress may, under the guise of the commerce power, tell the States how to perform medical and educational functions is not factually accurate. Congress has "interfered with" these state functions only to the extent of providing that when a State employs people in performing such functions it is subject to the same restrictions as a wide range of other employers whose activities affect commerce, including privately operated schools and hospitals.

It is clear that labor conditions in schools and hospitals can affect commerce. . . . Strikes and work stoppages involving employees of schools and hospitals, events which unfortunately are not infrequent, obviously interrupt and burden this flow of goods across state lines. It is therefore clear that a "rational basis" exists for congressional action prescribing minimum labor standards for schools and hospitals, as for other importing enterprises.

Indeed, appellants do not contend that labor conditions in all schools and hospitals are without the reach of the commerce power, but only that the Act may not be constitutionally applied to state-operated institutions because that power must yield to state sovereignty in the performance of governmental functions. This argument simply is not tenable. . . . [I]t is clear that the Federal Government, when acting within a delegated power, may override countervailing state interests whether these be described as "governmental" or "proprietary" in character. . . .

There remains, of course, the question whether any particular statute is an "otherwise valid regulation of commerce." This Court has always recognized that the power to regulate commerce, though broad indeed, has limits. . . . The Court has ample power to prevent what the appellants purport to fear, "the utter destruction of the State as a sovereign political entity."

But while the commerce power has limits, valid general regulations of commerce do not cease to be regulations of commerce because a State is involved. If a State is engaging in economic activities that are validly regulated by the Federal Government when engaged in by private persons, the State too may be forced to conform its activities to federal regulation. . . .

This Court has examined and will continue to examine federal statutes to determine whether there is a rational basis for regarding them as regulations of commerce among the States. But it will not carve up the commerce power to protect enterprises indistinguishable in their effect on commerce from private businesses, simply because those enterprises happen to be run by the States for the benefit of their citizens.

**Mr. Justice DOUGLAS, with whom
Mr. Justice STEWART concurs, dissenting.**

The Court's opinion skillfully brings employees of state-owned enterprises within the reach of the Commerce Clause; and as an exercise in semantics it is unexception-able if congressional federalism is the standard. But what is done here is nontheless such a serious invasion of state sovereignty protected by the Tenth Amendment that it is in my view not consistent with our constitutional federalism.

The case has some of the echoes of *New York v. United States* [1946], where a divided Court held that the Federal Government could tax the sale of mineral waters owned and marketed by New York. My dissent was in essence that the decision made the States pay the Federal Government "for the privilege of exercising the powers of sovereignty guaranteed them by the Constitution."

The present federal law takes a much more serious bite. . . . The impact is pervasive, striking at all levels of state government. As Judge Northrop said in his dissent below: "By this Act Congress is forcing, under the threat of civil liability and criminal penalties, the state legislature or the responsible political subdivision of the state (1) to increase taxes . . . ; (2) to curtail the extent and calibre of services in the public hospitals and [schools]; or (3) to reduce indispensable services in other governmental activities to meet the budgets of those activities favored by . . . Congress; or (4) to refrain from entering new fields of government activity necessitated by changing social conditions."

There can be no doubt but that the 1966 amendments to the Fair Labor Standards Act disrupt the fiscal policy of the States and threaten their autonomy in the regulation of health and education. . . .

Notes/Queries/Readings

(See notes and queries following the *Usery* and *Garcia* cases.)

National League of Cities v. Usery

426 U.S. 833, 96 S. Ct. 2465, 49 L. Ed. 2d 245 (1976)

In this case several cities and states sued in federal district court to test the validity of 1974 amendments to the Fair Labor Standards Act extending the statutory minimum wage and maximum hour provisions to employees of states and their political subdivisions. They argued that these provisions violated the principle of state sovereignty under the Tenth Amendment. A federal district court, following the decision in *Wirtz*, dismissed the suit, and the case was appealed to the Supreme Court. Opinion of the Court: *Rehnquist*, Burger, Powell, Stewart. Concurring opinion:

Blackmun. Dissenting opinions: *Brennan*, White, Marshall, *Stevens*.

Mr. Justice REHNQUIST delivered the opinion of the Court.

Nearly 40 years ago Congress enacted the Fair Labor Standards Act [which was upheld] as a valid exercise of congressional authority under the commerce power in *United States v. Darby*. . . . The original Fair Labor Standards Act passed in 1938 specifically excluded the States and their political subdivisions from its coverage. . . .

In a series of amendments beginning in 1961 Congress began to extend the provisions of the Fair Labor Standards Act to some types of public employees. The 1961 amendments to the Act extended its coverage to persons who were employed in "enterprises" engaged in commerce or in the production of goods for commerce. And in 1966, with the amendment of the definition of employers under the Act, the exemption heretofore extended to the States and their political subdivisions was removed with respect to employees of state hospitals, institutions, and schools. We nevertheless sustained the validity of the combined effect of these two amendments in *Maryland v. Wirtz* (1968). . . . [W]e have decided that the "far-reaching implications of *Wirtz* should be overruled, and that the judgment of the District Court must be reversed."

It is established beyond peradventure that the Commerce Clause of Art. I of the Constitution is a grant of plenary authority to Congress. That authority is, in the words of Mr. Chief Justice Marshall in *Gibbons v. Ogden* "the power to regulate; that is, to prescribe the rule by which commerce is to be governed." . . .

Congressional power over areas of private endeavor, even when its exercise may pre-empt express state-law determinations contrary to the result which has commended itself to the collective wisdom of Congress, has been held to be limited only by the requirement that "the means chosen by [Congress] must be reasonably adapted to the end permitted by the Constitution." *Heart of Atlanta Hotel v. United States* [1964].

Appellants in no way challenge these decisions establishing the breadth of authority granted Congress under the commerce power. Their contention, on the contrary, is that when Congress seeks to regulate directly the activities of States as public employers, it transgresses an affirmative limitation on the exercise of its power akin to other commerce power affirmative limitations contained in the Constitution. . . .

This Court has never doubted that there are limits upon the power of Congress to override state sovereignty even when exercising its otherwise plenary powers to tax or to regulate commerce which are conferred by Art. I of the Constitution. In *Wirtz*, for example, the Court took care to assure the appellants that it had "ample power to prevent . . . 'the utter destruction of the State as a sovereign political entity,'" which they feared. Appellee Secretary in this case, both in his brief and upon oral argument, has agreed that our federal system of government imposes definite limits upon the authority of Congress to regulate the activities of the States as States by means of the commerce power. In *Fry* [*v. United States* (1975)], the Court recognized that an express declaration of this limitation is found in the Tenth Amendment: "While the Tenth Amendment has been characterized as a 'truism,' stating merely that 'all is retained which has not been surrendered,' *United States v. Darby* (1941), it is not without sig-

nificance. The Amendment expressly declares the constitutional policy that Congress may not exercise power in a fashion that impairs the States' integrity or their ability to function effectively in a federal system." . . .

The expressions in these more recent cases trace back to earlier decisions of this Court recognizing the essential role of the States in our federal system of government. Mr. Chief Justice Chase, perhaps because of the particular time at which he occupied that office, had occasion more than once to speak for the Court on this point. In *Texas v. White* (1869), he declared that "[t]he Constitution, in all its provisions, looks to an indestructible Union, composed of indestructible States." . . .

It is one thing to recognize the authority of Congress to enact laws regulating individual businesses necessarily subject to the dual sovereignty of the government of the Nation and of the State in which they reside. It is quite another to uphold a similar exercise of congressional authority directed, not to private citizens, but to the States as States. We have repeatedly recognized that there are attributes of sovereignty attaching to every state government which may not be impaired by Congress, not because Congress may lack an affirmative grant of legislative authority to reach the matter, but because the Constitution prohibits it from exercising the authority in that manner. . . .

One undoubted attribute of state sovereignty is the States' power to determine the wages which shall be paid to those whom they employ in order to carry out their governmental functions, what hours those persons will work, and what compensation will be provided where these employees may be called upon to work overtime. The question we must resolve here, then, is whether these determinations are "'functions essential to separate and independent existence,'" so that Congress may not abrogate the States' otherwise plenary authority to make them.

Quite apart from the substantial costs imposed upon the States and their political subdivisions, the Act displaces state policies regarding the manner in which they will structure delivery of those governmental services which their citizens require. The Act, speaking directly to the States qua States, requires that they shall pay all but an extremely limited minority of their employees the minimum wage rates currently chosen by Congress. It may well be that as a matter of economic policy it would be desirable that States, just as private employers, comply with these minimum wage requirements. But it cannot be gainsaid that the federal requirement directly supplants the considered policy choices of the States' elected officials and administrators as to how they wish to structure pay scales in state employment. The State might wish to employ persons with little or no training, or those who wish to work on a casual basis, or those who for some other reason do not possess minimum employment requirements, and pay them less than the federally prescribed minimum wage. It may wish to offer part-time or summer employment to teenagers at a figure less than the minimum wage, and if unable to do so may decline to offer such employment at all. But the Act would forbid such choices by the States. The only "discretion" left to them under the Act is either to attempt to increase their revenue to meet the additional financial burden imposed upon them by paying congressionally prescribed wages to their existing complement of employees, or to reduce that complement to a number which can be paid the federal minimum wage without increasing revenue.

Our examination of the effect of the 1974 amendments, as sought to be extended to the States and their political subdivisions, satisfies us that both the minimum wage and the maximum hour provisions will impermissibly interfere with the integral governmental functions of these bodies. . . . If Congress may withdraw from the States the authority to make those fundamental employment decisions upon which their systems for performance of these functions must rest, we think there would be little left of the States' "separate and independent existence." . . . [T]he dispositive factor is that Congress has attempted to exercise its Commerce Clause authority to prescribe minimum wages and maximum hours to be paid by the States in their capacities as sovereign governments. In so doing, Congress has sought to wield its power in a fashion that would impair the States' "ability to function effectively in a federal system." This exercise of congressional authority does not comport with the federal system of government embodied in the Constitution. We hold that insofar as the challenged amendments operate to directly displace the States' freedom to structure integral operations in areas of traditional governmental functions, they are not within the authority granted Congress by Art. I, s 8, cl. 3.

With respect to the Court's decision in *Wirtz*, we reach a different conclusion. Both appellee and the District Court thought that decision required rejection of appellants' claims. Appellants, in turn, advance several arguments by which they seek to distinguish the facts before the Court in *Wirtz* from those presented by the 1974 amendments to the Act. There are undoubtedly factual distinctions between the two situations, but in view of the conclusions expressed earlier in this opinion we do not believe the reasoning in *Wirtz* may any longer be regarded as authoritative.

Mr. Justice BLACKMUN, concurring.

. . . Although I am not untroubled by certain possible implications of the Court's opinion—some of them suggested by the dissents—I do not read the opinion so despairingly

as does my Brother Brennan. In my view, the result with respect to the statute under challenge here is necessarily correct. I may misinterpret the Court's opinion, but it seems to me that it adopts a balancing approach, and does not outlaw federal power in areas such as environmental protection, where the federal interest is demonstrably greater and where state facility compliance with imposed federal standards would be essential. With this understanding on my part of the Court's opinion, I join it.

Mr. Justice BRENNAN, with whom Mr. Justice WHITE and Mr. Justice MARSHALL join, dissenting.

The Court concedes, as of course it must, that Congress enacted the 1974 amendments pursuant to its exclusive power under Art. I, s 8, cl. 3, of the Constitution "[t]o regulate Commerce . . . among the several States." It must therefore be surprising that my Brethren should choose this bicentennial year of our independence to repudiate principles governing judicial interpretation of our Constitution settled since the time of Mr. Chief Justice John Marshall, discarding his postulate that the Constitution contemplates that restraints upon exercise by Congress of its plenary commerce power lie in the political process and not in the judicial process. For 152 years ago Mr. Chief Justice Marshall enunciated that principle to which, until today, his successors on this Court have been faithful. . . .

My Brethren do not successfully obscure today's patent usurpation of the role reserved for the political process by their purported discovery in the Constitution of a restraint derived from sovereignty of the States on Congress' exercise of the commerce power. Mr. Chief Justice Marshall recognized that limitations "prescribed in the constitution," *Gibbons v. Ogden* [1824], restrain Congress' exercise of the power. Thus laws within the commerce power may not infringe individual liberties protected by the First Amendment. . . . But there is no restraint based on state sovereignty requiring or permitting judicial enforcement anywhere expressed in the Constitution; our decisions over the last century and a half have explicitly rejected the existence of any such restraint on the commerce power.

My Brethren thus have today manufactured an abstraction without substance, founded neither in the words of the Constitution nor on precedent. An abstraction having such profoundly pernicious consequences is not made less so by characterizing the 1974 amendments as legislation directed against the "States Qua States." . . . [M]y Brethren make no claim that the 1974 amendments are not regulations of "commerce"; rather they overrule *Wirtz* in disagreement with historic principles that *United States v. California* [1936] reaffirmed: "[W]hile the commerce power has limits, valid general regulations of commerce do not cease to be regulations of commerce because a State is involved. If a State is engaging in economic activities that are validly regulated by the Federal Government when engaged in by private persons, the State too may be forced to conform its activities to federal regulation." Clearly, therefore, my Brethren are also repudiating the long line of our precedents holding that a judicial finding that Congress has not unreasonably regulated a subject matter of "commerce" brings to an end the judicial role. . . .

The reliance of my Brethren upon the Tenth Amendment as "an express declaration of [a state sovereignty] limitation," not only suggests that they overrule governing decisions of this Court that address this question but must astound scholars of the Constitution. . . .

My Brethren purport to find support for their novel state-sovereignty doctrine in the concurring opinion of Mr. Chief Justice Stone in *New York v. United States* [1946]. That reliance is plainly misplaced. That case presented the question whether the Constitution either required immunity of New York State's mineral water business from federal taxation or denied to the Federal Government power to lay the tax. The Court sustained the federal tax. Mr. Chief Justice Stone observed in his concurring opinion that "a federal tax which is not discriminatory as to the subject matter may nevertheless so affect the State, merely because it is a State that is being taxed, as to interfere unduly with the State's performance of its sovereign functions of government." But the Chief Justice was addressing not the question of a state-sovereignty restraint upon the exercise of the commerce power, but rather the principle of implied immunity of the States and Federal Government from taxation by the other: "The counterpart of such undue interference has been recognized since Marshall's day as the implied immunity of each of the dual sovereignties of our constitutional system from taxation by the other."

. . . [M]ore significant for our purposes is . . . *United States v. California*, a case concerned with Congress' power to regulate commerce. . . . *California* directly presented the question whether any state-sovereignty restraint precluded application of the Federal Safety Appliance Act to a state owned and operated railroad. The State argued "that as the state is operating the railroad without profit, for the purpose of facilitating the commerce of the port, and is using the net proceeds of operation for harbor improvement, . . . it is engaged in performing a public function in its sovereign capacity and for that reason cannot constitutionally be subjected to the provisions of the federal act." Mr. Justice Stone rejected the contention in an opinion for a unanimous Court. His rationale is a complete refutation of today's holding:

That in operating its railroad [the State] is acting within a power reserved to the states cannot be doubted. . . .

The only question we need consider is whether the exercise of that power, in whatever capacity, must be in subordination to the power to regulate interstate commerce, which has been granted specifically to the national government.

The sovereign power of the states is necessarily diminished to the extent of the grants of power to the federal government in the Constitution. . . .

My Brethren do more than turn aside longstanding constitutional jurisprudence that emphatically rejects today's conclusion. More alarming is the startling restructuring of our federal system, and the role they create therein for the federal judiciary. This Court is simply not at liberty to erect a mirror of its own conception of a desirable governmental structure. . . .

It is unacceptable that the judicial process should be thought superior to the political process in this area. Under the Constitution the Judiciary has no role to play beyond finding that Congress has not made an unreasonable legislative judgment respecting what is "commerce." My Brother Blackmun suggests that controlling judicial supervision of the relationship between the States and our National Government by use of a balancing approach diminishes the ominous implications of today's decision. Such an approach, however, is a thinly veiled rationalization for judicial supervision of a policy judgment that our system of government reserves to Congress.

Judicial restraint in this area merely recognizes that the political branches of our Government are structured to protect the interests of the States, as well as the Nation as a whole, and that the States are fully able to protect their own interests in the premises. Congress is constituted of representatives in both the Senate and House elected from the States. *The Federalist* No. 45 (J. Madison). Decisions upon the extent of federal intervention under the Commerce Clause into the affairs of the States are in that sense decisions of the States themselves. Judicial redistribution of powers granted the National Government by the terms of the Constitution violates the fundamental tenet of our federalism that the extent of federal intervention into the States' affairs in the exercise of delegated powers shall be determined by the States' exercise of political power through their representatives in Congress. There is no reason whatever to suppose that in enacting the 1974 amendments Congress, even if it might extensively obliterate state sovereignty by fully exercising its plenary power respecting commerce, had any purpose to do so. Surely the presumption must be to the contrary. Any realistic assessment of our federal political system, dominated as it is by representatives of the people elected from the States, yields the conclusion that it is highly unlikely that those representatives will ever be motivated to disregard totally the concerns of these States. *The Federalist* No. 46. Certainly this was the premise upon which the Constitution, as authoritatively explicated in *Gibbons v. Ogden*, was founded. Indeed, though the States are represented in the National Government, national interests are not similarly represented in the States' political processes. . . .

We are left then with a catastrophic judicial body blow at Congress' power under the Commerce Clause. Even if Congress may nevertheless accomplish its objectives for example, by conditioning grants of federal funds upon compliance with federal minimum wage and overtime standards, there is an ominous portent of disruption of our constitutional structure implicit in today's mischievous decision. I dissent.

Notes/Queries/Readings

1. In *Maryland v. Wirtz*, Justice Harlan conceded that the "power to regulate commerce though broad indeed, has limits." What are those limits? Are there any limits short of "the utter destruction of the State as a sovereign political entity"? See also *Texas v. White*, 7 Wall. 700 (1869).

2. What understanding of judicial power does the majority in *National League of Cities* adopt? Is that understanding premised upon a view of the proper relationship between the states and the national government? How does it differ from the dissent's view of judicial power? Why, according to Brennan, "is it unacceptable that the judicial process should be thought superior to the political process in this area"?

3. What explains *National League*'s apparent retreat from the Court's post New Deal deference to congressional economic legislation?

4. How would you describe the differing approaches of Rehnquist, Blackmun, and Brennan in *National League*? Do these approaches really dictate the result of their reasoning? Or are their opinions driven by their larger visions of the Constitution? If so, what are these visions?

5. Suppose in the interest of promoting greater safety on the nation's highways, Congress were to pass a law requiring a federal driver's license of any person wishing to operate an automobile on any highway in the United States. The statute would have the effect of displacing the states in the issuance of drivers' licenses. Would *National League*

be of any help in deciding whether such a statute would survive constitutional analysis?

6. *National League of Cities* generated a great deal of commentary. Among the better works are Sotirios A. Barber, National League of Cities v. Usery: *New Meaning for the Tenth Amendment*, 1976 Supreme Court Review 161; Karen Flax, *In the Wake of* National League of Cities v. Usery: *A Derelict Makes Waves*, 34 Southern California Law Review 649 (1983); Charles A. Lofgren, National League of Cities v. Usery: *Dual Federalism Reborn*, 4 Claremont Journal of Public Affairs 19 (1977); Frank J. Michelman, *States' Rights and States' Roles: The Permutations of Sovereignty in* National League of Cities v. Usery, 86 Yale Law Journal 1165 (1977); Robert F. Nagel, *Federalism as a Fundamental Value:* National League of Cities *in Perspective*, 1981 Supreme Court Review 81; and Laurence H. Tribe, *Unraveling* National League of Cities, 90 Harvard Law Review 1065 (1977). See also Herbert Wechsler, *The Political Safeguards of Federalism: The Role of the States in the Composition and Selection of the National Government*, 54 Columbia Law Review 543 (1954).

7. *National League of Cities* provided the stimulus for other challenges to the federal regulation of state activities arguably within the ambit of a traditional governmental function. In each of these challenges the Court sustained the federal regulation, distinguishing *National League of Cities* and limiting it largely to its distinctive facts. See, for example, *Hodel v. Virginia Surface Mining & Reclamation Assn.*, 452 U.S. 264 (1981, upholding national surface mining standards throughout the states); *Transportation Union v. Long Island R. Co.*, 455 U.S. 678 (1982, upholding the application of the Railway Labor Act to a state-owned railroad); *Federal Energy Regulatory Commission v. Mississippi*, 456 U.S. 742 (1982, upholding the Public Utilities Regulatory Policies Act as applied to state public utility companies); and *Equal Employment Opportunity Commission v. Wyoming*, 460 U.S. 226 (1983, sustaining the application of the Federal Age Discrimination Act to state employees). At the same time, lower federal courts seemed hopelessly divided over what state activities were traditional governmental functions and thus within the protection of *National League of Cities*. The controversy on and off the Supreme Court over the reach of *National League of Cities* reached its climax in *Garcia v. San Antonio Metropolitan Transit Authority*, where the Court reconsidered its decision in the earlier case.

Garcia v. San Antonio Metropolitan Transit Authority

469 U.S. 528, 105 S. Ct. 1005, 83 L. Ed. 2d 1016 (1985)

The San Antonio Metropolitan Transit Authority (SAMTA) is a public mass transit authority that is a major provider of transportation in the San Antonio, Texas metropolitan area. In 1979, the Wage and Hour Administration of the Department of Labor issued an opinion that SAMTA's operations are not immune from the minimum wage and overtime requirements of the Fair Labor Standards Act (FLSA). SAMTA filed an action in federal district court, seeking declaratory relief. The district court held that a municipally owned mass transit is a traditional government function within the meaning of *National League of Cities* and thus exempt from the terms of the FLSA. Opinion of the Court: *Blackmun*, Brennan, Marshall, Stevens, White. Dissenting opinions: *Powell*, Burger, *O'Connor, Rehnquist*.

Justice BLACKMUN delivered the opinion of the Court.

We revisit in these cases an issue raised in *National League of Cities v. Usery* [1976]. In that litigation, this Court, by a sharply divided vote, ruled that the Commerce Clause does not empower Congress to enforce the minimum-wage and overtime provisions of the Fair Labor Standards Act (FLSA) against the States "in areas of traditional governmental functions." Although *National League of Cities* supplied some examples of "traditional governmental functions," it did not offer a general explanation of how a "traditional" function is to be distinguished from a "nontraditional" one. Since then, federal and state courts have struggled with the task, thus imposed, of identifying a traditional function for purposes of state immunity under the Commerce Clause.

In the present cases, a Federal District Court concluded that municipal ownership and operation of a mass-transit system is a traditional governmental function and thus, under *National League of Cities*, is exempt from the obligations imposed by the FLSA. Faced with the identical question, three Federal Courts of Appeals and one state appellate court have reached the opposite conclusion.

Our examination of this "function" standard applied in these and other cases over the last eight years now persuades us that the attempt to draw the boundaries of state regulatory immunity in terms of "traditional governmental functions" is not only unworkable but is also inconsistent with established principles of federalism and, indeed, with those very federalism principles on which *National League of Cities* purported to rest. That case, accordingly, is overruled.

The controversy in the present cases has focused on the . . . requirement . . . that the challenged federal statute trench on "traditional governmental functions." The District Court voiced a common concern: "Despite the abundance of adjectives, identifying which particular state functions are immune remains difficult." Just how troublesome the task has been is revealed by the results reached in other federal cases. Thus, courts have held that regulating ambulance services, licensing automobile drivers, operating a municipal airport, performing solid waste disposal, and operating a highway authority are functions protected under *National League of Cities*. At the same time, courts have held that issuance of industrial development bonds, regulation of intrastate natural gas sales, regulation of traffic on public roads, regulation of air transportation, operation of a telephone system, leasing and sale of natural gas, operation of a mental health facility and provision of in-house domestic services for the aged and handicapped are *not* entitled to immunity. We find it difficult, if not impossible, to identify an organizing principle that places each of the cases in the first group on one side of a line and each of the cases in the second group on the other side. The constitutional distinction between licensing drivers and regulating traffic, for example, or between operating a highway authority and operating a mental health facility, is elusive at best.

We believe, however, that there is a more fundamental problem at work here, a problem that explains why the Court was never able to provide a basis for the governmental/proprietary distinction in the intergovernmental tax-immunity cases and why an attempt to draw similar distinctions with respect to federal regulatory authority under *National League of Cities* is unlikely to succeed regardless of how the distinctions are phrased. The problem is that neither the governmental/proprietary distinction nor any other that purports to separate out important governmental functions can be faithful to the role of federalism in a democratic society. The essence of our federal system is that within the realm of authority left open to them under the Constitution, the States must be equally free to engage in any activity that their citizens choose for the common weal, no matter how unorthodox or unnecessary anyone else—including the judiciary—deems state involvement to be. Any rule of state immunity that looks to the "traditional," "integral," or "necessary" nature of governmental functions inevitably invites an unelected federal judiciary to make decisions about which state policies it favors and which ones it dislikes. . . .

We therefore now reject, as unsound in principle and unworkable in practice, a rule of state immunity from federal regulation that turns on a judicial appraisal of whether a particular governmental function is "integral" or "traditional." Any such rule leads to inconsistent results at the same time that it disserves principles of democratic self-governance, and it breeds inconsistency precisely because it is divorced from those principles. If there are to be limits on the Federal Government's power to interfere with state functions—as undoubtedly there are—we must look elsewhere to find them. . . .

The central theme of *National League of Cities* was that the States occupy a special position in our constitutional system and that the scope of Congress' authority under the Commerce Clause must reflect that position. . . .

What has proved problematic is not the perception that the Constitution's federal structure imposes limitations on the Commerce Clause, but rather the nature and content of those limitations. . . .

We doubt that courts ultimately can identify principled constitutional limitations on the scope of Congress' commerce clause powers over the States merely by relying on *a priori* definitions of state sovereignty. In part, this is because of the elusiveness of objective criteria for "fundamental" elements of state sovereignty, a problem we have witnessed in the search for "traditional governmental functions." There is, however, a more fundamental reason: the sovereignty of the States is limited by the Constitution itself. A variety of sovereign powers, for example, are withdrawn from the States by Article I, s 10. Section 8 of the same Article works an equally sharp contraction of state sovereignty by authorizing Congress to exercise a wide range of legislative powers and (in conjunction with the Supremacy Clause of Article VI) to displace contrary state legislation. By providing for final review of questions of federal law in this Court, Article III curtails the sovereign power of the States' judiciaries to make authoritative determinations of law. Finally, the developed application, through the Fourteenth Amendment, of the greater part of the Bill of Rights to the States limits the sovereign authority that States otherwise would possess to legislate with respect to their citizens and to conduct their own affairs.

The States unquestionably do "retai[n] a significant measure of sovereign authority." They do so, however, only to the extent that the Constitution has not divested them of their original powers and transferred those powers to the Federal Government. In the words of James Madison to the Members of the First Congress: "Interference with the power of the States was no constitutional criterion of the power of Congress. If the power was not given, Congress could not exercise it; if given, they might exercise it, although it should interfere with the laws, or even the Constitutions of the States." . . .

As a result, to say that the Constitution assumes the continued role of the States is to say little about the nature of that role. Only recently, this Court recognized that the purpose of the constitutional immunity recognized in *National League of Cities* is not to preserve "a sacred province of state autonomy." With rare exceptions, like the guarantee, in Article IV, s 3, of state territorial integrity, the Constitution does not carve out express elements of state sovereignty that Congress may not employ its delegated powers to displace. . . . The power of the Federal Government is a "power to be respected" as well, and the fact that the States remain sovereign as to all powers not vested in Congress or denied them by the Constitution offers no guidance about where the frontier between state and federal power lies. In short, we have no license to employ freestanding conceptions of state sovereignty when measuring congressional authority under the Commerce Clause.

When we look for the States' "residuary and inviolable sovereignty," in the shape of the constitutional scheme rather than in predetermined notions of sovereign power, a different measure of state sovereignty emerges. Apart from the limitation on federal authority inherent in the delegated nature of Congress' Article I powers, the principal means chosen by the Framers to ensure the role of the States in the federal system lies in the structure of the Federal Government itself. It is no novelty to observe that the composition of the Federal Government was designed in large part to protect the States from overreaching by Congress. The Framers thus gave the States a role in the selection both of the Executive and the Legislative Branches of the Federal Government. The States were vested with indirect influence over the House of Representatives and the Presidency by their control of electoral qualifications and their role in Presidential elections. U.S. Const., Art. I, s 2, and Art. II, s 1. They were given more direct influence in the Senate, where each State received equal representation and each Senator was to be selected by the legislature of his State. Art. I, s 3. The significance attached to the States' equal representation in the Senate is underscored by the prohibition of any constitutional amendment divesting a State of equal representation without the State's consent. Art. V.

The extent to which the structure of the Federal Government itself was relied on to insulate the interests of the States is evident in the views of the Framers. James Madison explained that the Federal Government "will partake sufficiently of the spirit [of the States], to be disinclined to invade the rights of the individual States, or the prerogatives of their governments." *The Federalist* No. 46. In short, the Framers chose to rely on a federal system in which special restraints on federal power over the States inhered principally in the workings of the National Government itself, rather than in discrete limitations on the objects of federal authority. State sovereign interests, then, are more properly protected by procedural safeguards inherent in the structure of the federal system than by judicially created limitations on federal power.

We realize that changes in the structure of the Federal Government have taken place since 1789, not the least of which has been the substitution of popular election of Senators by the adoption of the Seventeenth Amendment in 1913, and that these changes may work to alter the influence of the States in the federal political process. Nonetheless, against this background, we are convinced that the fundamental limitation that the constitutional scheme imposes on the Commerce Clause to protect the "States as States" is one of process rather than one of result. Any substantive restraint on the exercise of Commerce Clause powers must find its justification in the procedural nature of this basic limitation, and it must be tailored to compensate for possible failings in the national political process rather than to dictate a "sacred province of state autonomy." . . . Insofar as the present cases are concerned, then, we need go no further than to state that we perceive nothing in the overtime and minimum-wage requirements of the FLSA, as applied to SAMTA, that is destructive of state sovereignty or violative of any constitutional provision. . . .

In these cases, the status of public mass transit simply underscores the extent to which the structural protections of the Constitution insulate the States from federally imposed burdens. When Congress first subjected state mass-transit systems to FLSA obligations in 1966, and when it expanded those obligations in 1974, it simultaneously provided extensive funding for state and local mass transit. . . . In short, Congress has not simply placed a financial burden on the shoulders of States and localities that operate mass-transit systems, but has provided substantial countervailing financial assistance as well, assistance that may leave individual mass-transit systems better off than they would have been had Congress never intervened at all in the area. Congress' treatment of public mass transit reinforces our conviction that the national political process systematically protects States from the risk of having their functions in that area handicapped by Commerce Clause regulation.

This analysis makes clear that Congress' action in affording SAMTA employees the protections of the wage and hour provisions of the FLSA contravened no affirmative limit on Congress' power under the Commerce Clause. The judgment of the District Court therefore must be reversed.

Justice POWELL, with whom the Chief Justice, Justice REHNQUIST, and Justice O'CONNOR join, dissenting.

The Court today, in its 5–4 decision, overrules *National League of Cities v. Usery* [1976], a case in which we held that Congress lacked authority to impose the requirements

of the Fair Labor Standards Act on state and local governments. Because I believe this decision substantially alters the federal system embodied in the Constitution, I dissent.

Whatever effect the Court's decision may have in weakening the application of *stare decisis*, it is likely to be less important than what the Court has done to the Constitution itself. A unique feature of the United States is the *federal* system of government guaranteed by the Constitution and implicit in the very name of our country. Despite some genuflecting in the Court's opinion to the concept of federalism, today's decision effectively reduces the Tenth Amendment to meaningless rhetoric when Congress acts pursuant to the Commerce Clause. . . .

To leave no doubt about its intention, the Court renounces its decision in *National League of Cities* because it "inevitably invites an unelected federal judiciary to make decisions about which state policies it favors and which ones it dislikes." In other words, the extent to which the States may exercise their authority, when Congress purports to act under the Commerce Clause, henceforth is to be determined from time to time by political decisions made by members of the Federal Government, decisions the Court says will not be subject to judicial review. I note that it does not seem to have occurred to the Court that it—an unelected majority of five Justices—today rejects almost 200 years of the understanding of the constitutional status of federalism. In doing so, there is only a single passing reference to the Tenth Amendment. Nor is so much as a dictum of any court cited in support of the view that the role of the States in the federal system may depend upon the grace of elected federal officials, rather than on the Constitution as interpreted by this Court.

Today's opinion does not explain how the States' role in the electoral process guarantees that particular exercises of the Commerce Clause power will not infringe on residual state sovereignty. Members of Congress are elected from the various States, but once in office they are Members of the Federal Government. Although the States participate in the Electoral College, this is hardly a reason to view the President as a representative of the States' interest against federal encroachment. We noted recently "[t]he hydraulic pressure inherent within each of the outer limits of its power." The Court offers no reason to think that this pressure will not operate when Congress seeks to invoke its powers under the Commerce Clause, notwithstanding the electoral role of the States.

The Framers believed that the separate sphere of sovereignty reserved to the States would ensure that the States would serve as an effective "'counterpoise" to the power of the Federal Government. The States would serve this essential role because they would attract and retain the loyalty of their citizens. The roots of such loyalty, the

Founders thought, were found in the objects peculiar to state government. For example, Hamilton argued that the States "regulat[e] all those personal interests and familiar concerns to which the sensibility of individuals is more immediately awake." *The Federalist* No. 17. Thus, he maintained that the people would perceive the States as "the immediate and visible guardian of life and property," a fact which "contributes more than any other circumstance to impressing upon the minds of the people affection, esteem and reverence towards the government." . . .

Thus, the harm to the States that results from federal overreaching under the Commerce Clause is not simply a matter of dollars and cents. Nor is it a matter of the wisdom or folly of certain policy choices. Rather, by usurping functions traditionally performed by the States, federal overreaching under the Commerce Clause undermines the constitutionally mandated balance of power between the States and the Federal Government, a balance designed to protect our fundamental liberties.

In *National League of Cities*, we spoke of fire prevention, police protection, sanitation, and public health as "typical of [the services] performed by state and local governments in discharging their dual functions of administering the public law and furnishing public services." . . . Not only are these activities remote from any normal concept of interstate commerce, they are also activities that epitomize the concerns of local, democratic self-government. In emphasizing the need to protect traditional governmental functions, we identified the kinds of activities engaged in by state and local governments that affect the everyday lives of citizens. These are services that people are in a position to understand and evaluate, and in a democracy, have the right to oversee. We recognized that "it is functions such as these which governments are created to provide . . ." and that the States and local governments are better able than the National Government to perform them.

The Court maintains that the standard approved in *National League of Cities* "disserves principles of democratic self-governance." In reaching this conclusion, the Court looks myopically only to persons elected to positions in the Federal Government. It disregards entirely the far more effective role of democratic self-government at the state and local levels. . . . [Federal] legislation is drafted primarily by the staffs of the congressional committees. . . . Federal departments and agencies customarily are authorized to write regulations. . . . The administration and enforcement of federal laws and regulations necessarily are largely in the hands of staff and civil service employees. These employees may have little or no knowledge of the States and localities that will be affected by the statutes and regula-

tions for which they are responsible. In any case, they hardly are as accessible and responsive as those who occupy analogous positions in state and local governments.

In drawing this contrast, I imply no criticism of these federal employees or the officials who are ultimately in charge. The great majority are conscientious and faithful to their duties. My point is simply that members of the immense federal bureaucracy are not elected, know less about the services traditionally rendered by States and localities, and are inevitably less responsive to recipients of such services, than are state legislatures, city councils, boards of supervisors, and state and local commissions, boards, and agencies. It is at these state and local levels—not in Washington as the Court so mistakenly thinks—that "democratic self-government" is best exemplified.

The Court emphasizes that municipal operation of an intracity mass transit system is relatively new in the life of our country. It nevertheless is a classic example of the type of service traditionally provided by local government. It is local by definition. It is indistinguishable in principle from the traditional services of providing and maintaining streets, public lighting, traffic control, water, and sewerage systems. Services of this kind are precisely those with which citizens are more "familiarly and minutely conversant." *The Federalist* No. 46. State and local officials of course must be intimately familiar with these services and sensitive to their quality as well as cost. Such officials also know that their constituents and the press respond to the adequacy, fair distribution, and cost of these services. It is this kind of state and local control and accountability that the Framers understood would insure the vitality and preservation of the federal system that the Constitution explicitly requires.

Justice O'CONNOR, with whom Justice POWELL and Chief Justice REHNQUIST join, dissenting.

The Court today surveys the battle scene of federalism and sounds a retreat. Like Justice Powell, I would prefer to hold the field and, at the very least, render a little aid to the wounded. I join Justice Powell's opinion. I also write separately to note my fundamental disagreement with the majority's views of federalism and the duty of this Court.

In my view, federalism cannot be reduced to the weak "essence" distilled by the majority today. There is more to federalism than the nature of the constraints that can be imposed on the States in "the realm of authority left open to them by the Constitution." The central issue of federalism, of course, is whether any realm is left open to the States by the Constitution—whether any area remains in which a State may act free of federal interference. . . . The true "essence" of federalism is that the States *as States* have legitimate interests which the National Government is bound to respect even though its laws are supreme. If federalism so conceived and so carefully cultivated by the Framers of our Constitution is to remain meaningful, this Court cannot abdicate its constitutional responsibility to oversee the Federal Government's compliance with its duty to respect the legitimate interests of the States. . . .

In the decades since ratification of the Constitution, interstate economic activity has steadily expanded. Industrialization, coupled with advances in transportation and communications, has created a national economy in which virtually every activity occurring within the borders of a State plays a part. The expansion and integration of the national economy brought with it a coordinate expansion in the scope of national problems. This Court has been increasingly generous in its interpretation of the commerce power of Congress, primarily to assure that the National Government would be able to deal with national economic problems. . . .

It is worth recalling the cited passage in *McCulloch v. Maryland* [1819] that lies at the source of the recent expansion of the commerce power. "Let the end be legitimate, let it be within the scope of the constitution," Chief Justice Marshall said, "and all means which are appropriate, which are plainly adapted to that end, which are not prohibited, but consist with the letter *and spirit* of the constitution, are constitutional [emphasis added]." The spirit of the Tenth Amendment, of course, is that the States will retain their integrity in a system in which the laws of the United States are nevertheless supreme.

It is not enough that the "end be legitimate"; the means to that end chosen by Congress must not contravene the spirit of the Constitution. Thus many of this Court's decisions acknowledge that the means by which national power is exercised must take into account concerns for state autonomy. . . . The operative language of these cases varies, but the underlying principle is consistent: state autonomy is a relevant factor in assessing the means by which Congress exercises its powers.

The problems of federalism in an integrated national economy are capable of more responsible resolution than holding that the States as States retain no status apart from that which Congress chooses to let them retain. The proper resolution, I suggest, lies in weighing state autonomy as a factor in the balance when interpreting the means by which Congress can exercise its authority on the States as States. . . .

It has been difficult for this Court to craft bright lines defining the scope of the state autonomy protected by *National League of Cities*. Such difficulty is to be expected whenever constitutional concerns as important as federalism and the effectiveness of the commerce power come into conflict. Regardless of the difficulty, it is and will remain the duty of this Court to reconcile these concerns in the final instance. That the Court shuns the task today by appealing to the "essence of federalism" can provide scant comfort to those who believe our federal system requires something more than a unitary, centralized government. I would not shirk the duty acknowledged by *National League of Cities* and its progeny. . . .

Notes/Queries/Readings

1. What methods of constitutional interpretation did Justice Blackmun use in his majority opinion? Do they differ from the approaches used by Chief Justice Rehnquist?

2. Are the various opinions in this case premised, at bottom, on different understandings of federalism? Or are they premised on different understandings about the proper role of courts in giving life to those visions?

3. In her dissent, Justice O'Connor suggested that judicial withdrawal from the "battle scene" of federalism leaves the states without effective protection from the centralizing tendencies of the national government. Is "constitutional protection" for the states synonymous with "judicial" protection? How would the majority respond? Consider *Federalist* 39, where Madison wrote that the federal government will be "disinclined to invade" the rights of the states. Do you agree? For an extended argument that counsels judicial restraint, see Jesse Choper, *Judicial Review and the National Political Process: A Functional Reconsideration of the Role of the Supreme Court* (Chicago: University of Chicago Press, 1980).

4. For additional reading, see Martha A. Field, Garcia v. San Antonio Metropolitan Transit Authority: *The Demise of a Misguided Doctrine*, 99 Harvard Law Review 84 (1985); William W. Van Alstyne, *The Second Death of Federalism*, 83 Michigan Law Review (1985); Andrzej Rapaczynski, *From Sovereignty to Process: The Jurisprudence of Federalism after* Garcia, 1985 Supreme Court Review 341; Symposium, *Federalism, Separation of Powers, and the Legacy of* Garcia, 1996 Brigham Young University Law Review 329; Eduard A. Lopez, *The Constitutional Doctrines of State Immunity from Federal Regulation and Taxation after* Garcia v. San Antonio Metropolitan Transit Authority, 4 Journal of Law & Policy 89 (1978); and Thomas H. Odom, *The Tenth Amendment after* Garcia: *Process-Based Procedural Protections*, 135 University of Pennsylvania Law Review 1657 (1987).

United States v. Lopez

514 U.S. 547, 115 S. Ct. 1624, 131 L. Ed. 2d 626 (1995)

Alfonso Lopez, Jr., a twelfth-grade student, was indicted and convicted of knowingly possessing a firearm at a school zone in violation of the Gun-Free School Zones Act of 1990. The act makes it a federal offense "for any individual knowingly to possess a firearm at a place that the individual knows, or has reasonable cause to believe, is a school zone." It defines a school zone as in or on the grounds of a public, parochial, or private school or within a distance of one thousand feet from the school grounds. Lopez appealed, claiming that the act exceeded Congress's power under the commerce clause. The U.S. Court of Appeals agreed and reversed the district court. Opinion of the Court: *Rehnquist*, Kennedy, O'Connor, Scalia, Thomas. Concurring opinions: *Kennedy*, *Thomas*. Dissenting opinions: *Stevens*, *Souter*, *Breyer*, Ginsberg.

Chief Justice REHNQUIST delivered the opinion of the Court.

We start with first principles. The Constitution creates a Federal Government of enumerated powers. . . . The Court, through Chief Justice Marshall, first defined the nature of Congress's commerce power in *Gibbons v. Ogden* [1824]. . . . The commerce power "is the power to regulate; that is, to prescribe the rule by which commerce is to be governed. This power, like all others vested in Congress, is complete in itself, may be exercised to its utmost extent, and acknowledges no limitations, other than are prescribed in the constitution." The *Gibbons* Court, however, acknowledged that limitations on the commerce power are inherent in the very language of the Commerce Clause:

> It is not intended to say that these words comprehend that commerce, which is completely internal, which is carried on between man and man in a State, or between different parts of the same State, and which does not extend to or affect other States. Such a power would be inconvenient, and is certainly unnecessary.
>
> Comprehensive as the word "among" is, it may very properly be restricted to that commerce which concerns more States than one. . . . The enumeration presupposes something not enumerated; and that something, if we regard the language or the subject of the sentence, must be the exclusively internal commerce of a State.

[*NLRB v. Jones & Laughlin Steel Corp.* (1937), *United States v. Darby* (1941), and *Wickard v. Filburn* (1942)] ushered in an era of Commerce Clause jurisprudence that greatly expanded the previously defined authority of Congress under that Clause. In part, this was a recognition of the great changes that had occurred in the way business was carried on in this country. Enterprises that had once been local or at most regional in nature had become national in scope. . . .

But even these modern-era precedents which have expanded congressional power under the Commerce Clause confirm that this power is subject to outer limits. In *Jones & Laughlin Steel*, the Court warned that the scope of the interstate commerce power "must be considered in the light of our dual system of government and may not be extended so as to embrace effects upon interstate commerce so indirect and remote that to embrace them, in view of our complex society, would effectually obliterate the distinction between what is national and what is local and create a completely centralized government." Since that time, the Court has heeded that warning and undertaken to decide whether a rational basis existed for concluding that a regulated activity sufficiently affected interstate commerce.

Consistent with this structure, we have identified three broad categories of activity that Congress may regulate under its commerce power. First, Congress may regulate the use of the channels of interstate commerce. Second, Congress is empowered to regulate and protect the instrumentalities of interstate commerce, or persons or things in interstate commerce, even though the threat may come only from intrastate activities. Finally, Congress' commerce authority includes the power to regulate those activities having a substantial relation to interstate commerce. . . .

We now turn to consider the power of Congress, in the light of this framework, to enact [the Act before us]. The first two categories of authority may be quickly disposed of: [The Act] is not a regulation of the use of the channels of interstate commerce, nor is it an attempt to prohibit the interstate transportation of a commodity through the channels of commerce; nor can [the Act] be justified as a regulation of an activity that substantially affects interstate commerce.

First, we have upheld a wide variety of congressional Acts regulating intrastate economic activity where we have concluded that the activity substantially affected interstate commerce. . . . [These examples show that] where economic activity substantially affects interstate commerce, legislation regulating that activity will be sustained.

The Government's essential contention, in fine, is that we may determine here that [the Act] is valid because possession of a firearm in a local school zone does indeed substantially affect interstate commerce. The Government argues that possession of a firearm in a school zone may result in violent crime and that violent crime can be expected to affect the functioning of the national economy in two ways. First, the costs of violent crime are substantial, and, through the mechanism of insurance, those costs are spread throughout the population. Second, violent crime reduces the willingness of individuals to travel to areas within the country that are perceived to be unsafe. The Government also argues that the presence of guns in schools poses a substantial threat to the educational process by threatening the learning environment. A handicapped educational process, in turn, will result in a less productive citizenry. That, in turn, would have an adverse effect on the Nation's economic well being. As a result, the Government argues that Congress could rationally have concluded that [the Act] substantially affects interstate commerce.

We pause to consider the implications of the Government's arguments. The Government admits, under its "costs of crime" reasoning, that Congress could regulate not only all violent crime, but all activities that might lead to violent crime, regardless of how tenuously they relate to interstate commerce. Similarly, under the Government's "national productivity" reasoning, Congress could regulate any activity that it found was related to the economic productivity of individual citizens: family law (including marriage, divorce, and child custody), for example. Under the theories that the Government presents . . . it is difficult to perceive any limitation on federal power, even in areas such as criminal law enforcement or education where States historically have been sovereign. Thus, if we were to accept the Government's arguments, we are hard-pressed to posit any activity by an individual that Congress is without power to regulate.

Justice Breyer rejects our reading of precedent and argues that "Congress . . . could rationally conclude that schools fall on the commercial side of the line." Again, Justice Breyer's rationale lacks any real limits because, depending on the level of generality, any activity can be looked upon as commercial. Under the dissent's rationale, Congress could just as easily look at child rearing as "fall[ing] on the commercial side of the line" because it provides a "valuable service—namely, to equip [children] with the skills they need to survive in life and, more specifically, in the workplace." We do not doubt that Congress has authority under the Commerce Clause to regulate numerous commercial activities that substantially affect interstate commerce and also affect the educational process. That authority, though broad, does not include the authority to regulate each and every aspect of local schools.

To uphold the Government's contentions here, we would have to pile inference upon inference in a manner that would bid fair to convert congressional authority under the Commerce Clause to a general police power of the sort retained by the States. Admittedly, some of our prior cases have taken long steps down that road, giving great deference to congressional action. The broad language in [past] opinions has suggested the possibility of additional expansion, but we decline here to proceed any further. To do so would require us to conclude that the Constitution's enumeration of powers does not presuppose something not enumerated, and that there never will be a distinction between what is truly national and what is truly local. This we are unwilling to do. For the foregoing reasons the judgment of the Court of Appeals is Affirmed.

Justice THOMAS, concurring.

The Court today properly concludes that the Commerce Clause does not grant Congress the authority to prohibit gun possession within 1,000 feet of a school, as it attempted to do in the Gun-Free School Zones Act of 1990. Although I join the majority, I write separately to observe that our case law has drifted far from the original understanding of the Commerce Clause. In a future case, we ought to temper our Commerce Clause jurisprudence in a manner that both makes sense of our more recent case law and is more faithful to the original understanding of that Clause.

. . . [I]t seems to me that the power to regulate "commerce" can by no means encompass authority over mere gun possession, any more than it empowers the Federal Government to regulate marriage, littering, or cruelty to animals, throughout the 50 States. Our Constitution quite properly leaves such matters to the individual States, notwithstanding these activities' effects on interstate commerce. Any interpretation of the Commerce Clause that even suggests that Congress could regulate such matters is in need of reexamination.

[*E. C. Knight* (1895), *Schechter* (1935), *Carter Coal Co.* (1936), and related cases] all establish a simple point: from the time of the ratification of the Constitution to the mid-1930's, it was widely understood that the Constitution granted Congress only limited powers, notwithstanding the Commerce Clause. Moreover, there was no question that activities wholly separated from business, such as gun possession, were beyond the reach of the commerce power. If anything, the "wrong turn" was the Court's dramatic departure in the 1930's from a century and a half of precedent.

Justice BREYER, with whom Justice STEVENS, Justice SOUTER, and Justice GINSBURG join, dissenting.

The issue in this case is whether the Commerce Clause authorizes Congress to enact a statute that makes it a crime to possess a gun in, or near, a school. In my view, the statute falls well within the scope of the commerce power as this Court has understood that power over the last half-century.

I

In reaching this conclusion, I apply three basic principles of Commerce Clause interpretation. First, the power to "regulate Commerce . . . among the several States" encompasses the power to regulate local activities insofar as they significantly affect interstate commerce. See *Gibbons v. Ogden* (1824), *Wickard v. Filburn* (1942).

Second, in determining whether a local activity will likely have a significant effect upon interstate commerce, a court must consider, not the effect of an individual act (a single instance of gun possession), but rather the cumulative effect of all similar instances (i.e, the effect of all guns possessed in or near schools). . . .

Third, the Constitution requires us to judge the connection between a regulated activity and interstate commerce, not directly, but at one remove. Courts must give Congress a degree of leeway in determining the existence of a significant factual connection between the regulated activity and interstate commerce—both because the Constitution delegates the commerce power directly to Congress and because the determination requires an empirical judgment of a kind that a legislature is more likely than a court to make with accuracy. The traditional words "rational basis" capture this leeway. Thus, the specific question before us, as the Court recognizes, is not whether the "regulated activity sufficiently affected interstate commerce," but, rather, whether Congress could have had "*a rational basis*" for so concluding.

II

Applying these principles to the case at hand, we must ask whether Congress could have had a *rational basis* for finding a significant (or substantial) connection between gun-related school violence and interstate commerce. . . . As long as one views the commerce connection, not as a "technical legal conception," but as "a practical one," the answer to this question must be yes. Numerous reports and studies—generated both inside and outside government—make clear that Congress could reasonably have found the empirical connection that its law, implicitly or explicitly, asserts.

. . . Congress obviously could have thought that guns and learning are mutually exclusive. Congress could therefore have found a substantial educational problem—teachers unable to teach, students unable to learn—and concluded that guns near schools contribute substantially to the size and scope of that problem.

Having found that guns in schools significantly undermine the quality of education in our Nation's classrooms, Congress could also have found, given the effect of education upon interstate and foreign commerce, that gun-related violence in and around schools is a commercial, as well as a human, problem. . . .

In recent years the link between secondary education and business has strengthened, becoming both more direct and more important. . . . Increasing global competition also has made primary and secondary education economically more important. . . . Finally, there is evidence that, today more than ever, many firms base their location decisions upon the presence, or absence, of a work force with a basic education.

The economic links I have just sketched seem fairly obvious. Why then is it not equally obvious, in light of those links, that a widespread, serious, and substantial physical threat to teaching and learning *also* substantially threatens the commerce to which that teaching and learning is inextricably tied? . . . The only question, then, is whether the latter threat is (to use the majorities terminology) "substantial." And, the evidence of (1) the *extent* of the gun-related violence problem, (2) the *extent* of the resulting negative effect on classroom learning, and (3) the extent of the consequent negative commercial effects when taken together, indicate a threat to trade and commerce that is "substantial." At the very least, Congress could rationally have concluded that the links are "substantial."

To hold this statute constitutional is not to "obliterate" the "distinction of what is national and what is local," nor is it to hold that the Commerce Clause permits the Federal Government to "regulate any activity that it found was related to the economic productivity of individual citizens," to regulate "marriage, divorce, and child custody," or to regulate any and all aspects of education. . . .

In sum, a holding that the particular statute before us falls within the commerce power would not expand the scope of that Clause. Rather, it simply would apply preexisting law to changing economic circumstances. It would recognize that, in today's economic world, gun-related violence near the classroom makes a significant difference to our economic, as well as our social, well being. In accordance with well-accepted precedent, such a holding would permit Congress "to act in terms of economic . . . realities," would interpret the commerce power as "an affirmative power commensurate with national needs," and would acknowledge that the "commerce clause does not operate so as to render the nation powerless to defend itself against economic forces that Congress decrees inimical or destructive of the national economy."

Notes/Queries/Readings

1. What standards does Chief Justice Rehnquist propose for distinguishing between "what is truly national" and

"what is truly local"? Do those standards find their source in the constitutional text? In the original understanding of the commerce clause and the Tenth Amendment? In contemporary judicial understandings about the marketplace?

2. What is the original understanding of the commerce clause to which Justice Thomas refers? Is that understanding outdated in light of two centuries of economic development? If it is outdated, should the judiciary interpret it in ways that make it relevant for contemporary conditions? Is Justice Thomas suggesting that the Court's decisions striking down significant parts of the New Deal, as in *Schechter* and *Hammer*, were correctly decided after all?

3. What understanding of judicial power does the dissent by Justice Breyer adopt? Does the "rational basis" standard mean, in practice, that the Court will exercise no supervision over the commerce clause?

4. Justice Breyer insists that to uphold the statute in this case "is not to 'obliterate' the distinction" between what is national and what is local. Do you agree? What criteria does he offer to help us make the distinction?

5. Suppose we were to find that the Texas delegation in the Congress voted unanimously against the Gun-Free Zone law. Would this reality favor the majority opinion? Suppose, on the other hand, that Congress had vigorously debated the constitutionality of the law, concluding that it did not offend the values implicit in the Tenth Amendment. Would this reality argue for a passive judicial role?

6. For additional reading, see Chris Marks, "U.S. Term Limits, Inc. *v.* Thornton *and* United States *v.* Lopez: *The Supreme Court Resuscitates the Tenth Amendment*, 68 University of Colorado Law Review 541 (1997); Herbert Hovenkamp, *Judicial Restraint and Constitutional Federalism: The Supreme Court's* Lopez *and* Seminole Tribe *Decisions*, 96 Columbia Law Review 2213 (1996); and *Symposium: Major Issues in Federalism*, 38 Arizona Law Review 793 (1996).

United States v. Butler

297 U.S. 1, 56 S. Ct. 312, 80 L. Ed. 477 (1936)

The Agricultural Adjustment Act of 1933 was a New Deal measure designed to stabilize farm prices by maintaining a balance between the production and consumption of agricultural products. The act authorized the secretary of agriculture to reduce the acreage devoted to agricultural production. Farmers who took their acreage out of production through agreements with producers were to be compensated with funds raised by a processing tax levied on certain agricultural products. Following Butler's refusal to pay the processing tax, a federal district court found the taxes valid and ordered them paid. The court of appeals reversed, and the government appealed. Opinion of the Court: *Roberts*, Hughes, VanDevanter, McReynolds, Sutherland, Butler. Dissenting opinion: *Stone*, Brandeis, Cardozo.

Mr. Justice ROBERTS delivered the opinion of the Court.

. . . The government asserts that even if the respondents may question the propriety of the appropriation embodied in the statute, their attack must fail because Article 1, s 8 of the Constitution, authorizes the contemplated expenditure of the funds raised by the tax. This contention presents the great and the controlling question in the case. We approach its decision with a sense of our grave responsibility to render judgment in accordance with the principles established for the governance of all three branches of the government.

There should be no misunderstanding as to the function of this court in such a case. It is sometimes said that the court assumes a power to overrule or control the action of the people's representatives. This is a misconception. The Constitution is the supreme law of the land ordained and established by the people. All legislation must conform to the principles it lays down. When an act of Congress is appropriately challenged in the courts as not conforming to the constitutional mandate, the judicial branch of the Government has only one duty; to lay the article of the Constitution which is invoked beside the statute which is challenged and to decide whether the latter squares with the former. All the court does, or can do, is to announce its considered judgment upon the question. The only power it has, if such it may be called, is the power of judgment. This court neither approves nor condemns any legislative policy. Its delicate and difficult office is to ascertain and declare whether the legislation is in accordance with, or in contravention of, the provisions of the Constitution; and, having done that, its duty ends.

The question is not what power the Federal government ought to have, but what powers in fact have been given by the people. It hardly seems necessary to reiterate that ours is a dual form of government; that in every state there are two governments—the State and the United States. Each State has all governmental powers save such as the people, by their Constitution, have conferred upon the United States, denied to the states, or reserved to themselves. The federal union is a government of delegated powers. It has only such as are expressly conferred upon it and such as are reasonably to be implied from those granted. In this respect we differ radically from nations where all legislative power, without restriction or limitation, is vested in a parliament or other legislative body subject to no restrictions except the discretion of its members.

Article 1, s 8, of the Constitution, vests sundry powers in the Congress. But two of its clauses have any bearing upon the validity of the statute under review.

The clause thought to authorize the legislation, the first, confers upon the Congress power "to lay and collect Taxes, Duties, Imposts and Excises, to pay the Debts and provide for the common Defence and general Welfare of the United States." It is not contended that this provision grants power to regulate agricultural production upon the theory that such legislation would promote the general welfare. The Government concedes that the phrase "to provide for the general welfare" qualifies the power "to lay and collect taxes." The view that the clause grants power to provide for the general welfare, independently of the taxing power, has never been authoritatively accepted. Mr. Justice Story points out that, if it were adopted, "it is obvious that under color of the generality of the words, to 'provide for the common defence and general welfare', the government of the United States is, in reality, a government of general and unlimited powers, notwithstanding the subsequent enumeration of specific powers." The true construction undoubtedly is that the only thing granted is the power to tax for the purpose of providing funds for payment of the nation's debts and making provision for the general welfare.

Nevertheless, the Government asserts that warrant is found in this clause for the adoption of the Agricultural Adjustment Act. The argument is that Congress may appropriate and authorize the spending of moneys for the "general welfare"; that the phrase should be liberally construed to cover anything conducive to national welfare; that decision as to what will promote such welfare rests with Congress alone, and the courts may not review its determination; and, finally, that the appropriation under attack was in fact for the general welfare of the United States.

The Congress is expressly empowered to lay taxes to provide for the general welfare. Funds in the Treasury as a result of taxation may be expended only through appropriation. Article 1, s 9, cl. 7. They can never accomplish the objects for which they were collected, unless the power to appropriate is as broad as the power to tax. The necessary implication from the terms of the grant is that the public funds may be appropriated "to provide for the general welfare of the United States." These words cannot be meaningless, else they would not have been used. The conclusion must be that they were intended to limit and define the granted power to raise and to expend money.

How shall they be construed to effectuate the intent of the instrument?

Since the foundation of the Nation, sharp differences of opinion have persisted as to the true interpretation of the phrase. Madison asserted it amounted to no more than a reference to the other powers enumerated in the subsequent clauses of the same section; that, as the United States is a government of limited and enumerated powers, the grant of power to tax and spend for the general national welfare must be confined to the enumerated legislative fields committed to the Congress. In this view the phrase is mere tautology, for taxation and appropriation are or may be necessary incidents of the exercise of any of the enumerated legislative powers. Hamilton, on the other hand, maintained the clause confers a power separate and distinct from those later enumerated, is not restricted in meaning by the grant of them, and Congress consequently has a substantive power to tax and to appropriate, limited only by the requirement that it shall be exercised to provide for the general welfare of the United States. Each contention has had the support of those whose views are entitled to weight. This court has noticed the question, but has never found it necessary to decide which is the true construction. Mr. Justice Story, in his Commentaries, espouses the Hamiltonian position. We shall not review the writings of public men and commentators or discuss the legislative practice. Study of all these leads us to conclude that the reading advocated by Mr. Justice Story is the correct one. While, therefore, the power to tax is not unlimited, its confines are set in the clause which confers it, and not in those of section 8 which bestow and define the legislative powers of the Congress. It results that the power of Congress to authorize expenditure of public moneys for public purposes is not limited by the direct grants of legislative power found in the Constitution.

But the adoption of the broader construction leaves the power to spend subject to limitations. . . . Story says that if the tax be not proposed for the common defense or general welfare, but for other objects wholly extraneous, it would be wholly indefensible upon constitutional principles. And he makes it clear that the powers of taxation and appropriation extend only to matters of national, as distinguished from local, welfare.

We are not now required to ascertain the scope of the phrase "general welfare of the United States" or to determine whether an appropriation in aid of agriculture falls within it. Wholly apart from that question, another principle embedded in our Constitution prohibits the enforcement of the Agricultural Adjustment Act. The act invades the reserved rights of the states. It is a statutory plan to regulate and control agricultural production, a matter be-

Comparative Note 6.7

[In this case, the Privy Council struck down Canada's Employment and Social Security Act of 1935, the Dominion's equivalent of American "New Deal" legislation. Designed to alleviate the problem of unemployment, the Act established an unemployment insurance scheme to be paid for out of federal funds. The parliament passed the statute under its residual power to provide for the peace, order, and good government of Canada. In holding the act unconstitutional, the Privy Council affirmed the decision of the Canadian Supreme Court.]

Lord Atkin. . . . There can be no doubt that, *prima facie*, provisions as to insurance of this kind, especially where they affect the contract of employment, fall within the class of property and civil rights in the Province, and would be within the exclusive competence of the Provincial Legislature.

. . . A strong appeal [in support of the Act has been] made on the ground of the special importance of unemployment insurance in Canada at the time of, and for some time previous to, the passing of the Act. . . . It is sufficient to say that the present Act does not purport to deal with any special emergency. . . .

It only remains to deal with the argument . . . that the legislation can be supported under [the Dominion's power to raise] money by any mode or system of taxation. . . .

That the Dominion may impose taxation for the purpose of creating a fund for special purposes . . . could not as a general proposition be denied. . . . But assuming that the Dominion has collected by means of taxation [an unemployment insurance] fund, it by no means follows that any legislation which disposes of it is necessarily within Dominion competence. [The legislation may still] encroach upon the classes of subjects which are reserved to Provincial competence. It is not necessary that it should be a colourable device, or a pretense. If on the true view of the legislation it is found that in reality in pith and substance the legislation invades civil rights within the Province . . . the legislation will be invalid. . . . In the present case, their Lordships agreed with the majority of the Supreme Court in holding that in pith and substance this Act is an insurance Act affecting the civil rights of employers and employed in each Province.

Source: *Attorney General of Canada v. Attorney General of Ontario*, In the Privy Council. [1937] A.C. 355; III Olmstead 207.

---

yond the powers delegated to the federal government. The tax, the appropriation of the funds raised, and the direction for their disbursement, are but parts of the plan. They are but means to an unconstitutional end.

From the accepted doctrine that the United States is a government of delegated powers, it follows that those not expressly granted, or reasonably to be implied from such as are conferred, are reserved to the states or to the people. To forestall any suggestion to the contrary, the Tenth Amendment was adopted. The same proposition, otherwise stated, is that powers not granted are prohibited. None to regulate agricultural production is given, and therefore legislation by Congress for that purpose is forbidden.

It is an established principle that the attainment of a prohibited end may not be accomplished under the pretext of the exertion of powers which are granted. . . . The power of taxation, which is expressly granted, may, of course, be adopted as a means to carry into operation another power also expressly granted. But resort to the taxing power to effectuate an end which is not legitimate, not within the scope of the Constitution, is obviously inadmissible.

If the taxing power may not be used as the instrument to enforce a regulation of matters of state concern with respect to which the Congress has no authority to interfere, may it, as in the present case, be employed to raise the money necessary to purchase a compliance which the Congress is powerless to command? The government asserts that whatever might be said against the validity of the plan, if compulsory, it is constitutionally sound because the end is accomplished by voluntary co-operation. . . . The regulation is not in fact voluntary. The farmer, of course, may refuse to comply, but the price of such refusal is the loss of benefits. The amount offered is intended to be sufficient to exert pressure on him to agree to the proposed regulation. The power to confer or withhold unlimited benefits is the power to coerce or destroy. . . .

But if the plan were one for purely voluntary co-operation it would stand no better so far as federal power is concerned. At best, it is a scheme for purchasing with federal funds submission to federal regulation of a subject reserved to the states. . . .

Congress has no power to enforce its commands on the

farmer to the ends sought by the Agricultural Adjustment Act. It must follow that it may not indirectly accomplish those ends by taxing and spending to purchase compliance. The Constitution and the entire plan of our government negative any such use of the power to tax and to spend as the act undertakes to authorize. It does not help to declare that local conditions throughout the nation have created a situation of national concern; for this is but to say that whenever there is a widespread similarity of local conditions, Congress may ignore constitutional limitations upon its own powers and usurp those reserved to the states. If, in lieu of compulsory regulation of subjects within the states' reserved jurisdiction, which is prohibited, the Congress could invoke the taxing and spending power as a means to accomplish the same end, clause 1 of section 8 of Article 1 would become the instrument for total subversion of the governmental powers reserved to the individual states.

If the act before us is a proper exercise of the federal taxing power, evidently the regulation of all industry throughout the United States may be accomplished by similar exercises of the same power. It would be possible to exact money from one branch of an industry and pay it to another branch in every field of activity which lies within the province of the states. The mere threat of such a procedure might well induce the surrender of rights and the compliance with federal regulation as the price of continuance in business. . . .

The judgment is affirmed.

Mr. Justice STONE, dissenting.

The power of courts to declare a statute unconstitutional is subject to two guiding principles of decision which ought never to be absent from judicial consciousness. One is that courts are concerned only with the power to enact statutes, not with their wisdom. The other is that while unconstitutional exercise of power by the executive and legislative branches of the government is subject to judicial restraint, the only check upon our own exercise of power is our own sense of self-restraint. For the removal of unwise laws from the statute books appeal lies, not to the courts, but to the ballot and to the processes of democratic government.

The constitutional power of Congress to levy an excise tax upon the processing of agricultural products is not questioned. The present levy is held invalid, not for any want of power in Congress to lay such a tax to defray public expenditures, including those for the general welfare, but because the use to which its proceeds are put is disapproved.

As the present depressed state of agriculture is nation wide in its extent and effects, there is no basis for saying that the expenditure of public money in aid of farmers is not within the specifically granted power of Congress to levy taxes to "provide for the general welfare." The opinion of the Court does not declare otherwise. . . .

It is with these preliminary and hardly controverted matters in mind that we should direct our attention to the pivot on which the decision of the Court is made to turn. It is that a levy unquestionably within the taxing power of Congress may be treated as invalid because it is a step in a plan to regulate agricultural production and is thus a forbidden infringement of state power. The levy is not any the less an exercise of taxing power because it is intended to defray an expenditure for the general welfare rather than for some other support of government. Nor is the levy and collection of the tax pointed to as effecting the regulation. While all federal taxes inevitably have some influence on the internal economy of the states, it is not contended that the levy of a processing tax upon manufacturers using agricultural products as raw material has any perceptible regulatory effect upon either their production or manufacture. . . . Here regulation, if any there be, is accomplished not by the tax, but by the method by which its proceeds are expended, and would equally be accomplished by any like use of public funds, regardless of their source.

It is upon the contention that state power is infringed by purchased regulation of agricultural production that chief reliance is placed. It is insisted that, while the Constitution gives to Congress, in specific and unambiguous terms, the power to tax and spend, the power is subject to limitations which do not find their origin in any express provision of the Constitution and to which other expressly delegated powers are not subject.

Such a limitation is contradictory and destructive of the power to appropriate for the public welfare, and is incapable of practical application. The spending power of Congress is in addition to the legislative power and not subordinate to it. This independent grant of the power of the purse, and its very nature, involving in its exercise the duty to insure expenditure within the granted power, presuppose freedom of selection among diverse ends and aims, and the capacity to impose such conditions as will render the choice effective. It is a contradiction in terms to say that there is power to spend for the national welfare, while rejecting any power to impose conditions reasonably adapted to the attainment of the end which alone would justify the expenditure.

A tortured construction of the Constitution is not to be justified by recourse to extreme examples of reckless congressional spending which might occur if courts could not prevent—expenditures which, even if they could be thought to effect any national purpose, would be possible only by action of a legislature lost to all sense of public responsibility. Such suppositions are addressed to the mind accustomed to believe that it is the business of courts to sit in judgement on the wisdom of legislative action. Courts are not the only agency of government that must be assumed to have capacity to govern. Congress and the courts both unhappily may falter or be mistaken in the performance of their constitutional duty. But interpretation of our great charter of government which proceeds on any assumption that the responsibility for the preservation of our institutions is the exclusive concern of any one of the three branches of government, or that it alone can save them from destruction is far more likely, in the long run, "to obliterate the constituent members" of "an indestructible union of indestructible states" than the frank recognition that language, even of a constitution, may mean what it says: that the power to tax and spend includes the power to relieve a nationwide economic maladjustment by conditional gifts of money.

Notes/Queries/Readings

1. In his opinion for the Court, Justice Roberts describes the process of constitutional interpretation as a "power of judgment." The Court, he wrote, "has only one duty, to lay the article of the Constitution which is invoked beside the statute which is challenged and to decide whether the latter squares with the former." Do you agree? Recall our discussion in chapter 2. Is this a theory of interpretation, or is Roberts denying that interpretation is necessary?

2. In the introduction to this chapter, we argued that the Court's opinion validated the expansive, Hamiltonian reading of the spending power. Is that expansive reading consistent with the result in the case? Why or why not?

3. According to Justice Stone, what principles should guide constitutional interpretation and the application of the commerce clause? Does he allow for judicial review of Congress's determination of how it will regulate the economy?

4. In 1937, following the Supreme Court's change of attitude towards New Deal legislation, the Court sustained major provisions of the Social Security Act of 1935. In *Steward Machine Co. v. Davis*, 301 U.S. 548 (1937), the Court upheld an unemployment compensation scheme involving a tax on employers of eight or more persons and grants to the states to assist them in administering the compensation program. In *Helvering v. Davis*, 301 U.S. 619 (1937), the Court upheld the federal social security program. The law laid a special income tax on employees to be deducted from their wages and paid by their employers. The Court declared here, as in *Steward*, that the Social Security Act was a valid exercise of federal authority and did not invade the power of the states under the Tenth Amendment. Another question that arose in these cases was whether the federal taxes and expenditures served the "general welfare" within the meaning of Article 1, Section 8. In *Butler* the Court had made an independent assessment of the meaning of these terms. In *Helvering* the Court took—and has taken ever since—the position that "the discretion [to define the meaning of these terms] belongs to Congress, unless the choice is clearly wrong, a display of arbitrary power [and] not an exercise of judgment." "[T]he concept of the general welfare is not static," said the Court. "Needs that were narrow or parochial a century ago may be interwoven in our day with the well-being of the nation. What is critical or urgent changes with the times," and thus it is best to leave the decision to Congress as to whether the general welfare is involved. But if it is appropriate to leave the definition of the "general welfare" to Congress, why is it not equally appropriate to leave the definition of the term "commerce" to Congress?

United States v. Kahriger

345 U.S. 22, 73 S. Ct. 510, 97 L. Ed. 754 (1953)

This case involved a federal tax on illegal gambling operations. A 1951 tax statute required such gamblers to register with the Internal Revenue Service. Kahriger, who ran an illegal operation, was indicted in federal district court for willfully failing to register for and pay the occupational tax. The district court sustained his motion to dismiss the case and the government appealed. Opinion of the Court: *Reed*, Warren, Jackson, Burton, Clark, Minton. Concurring opinion: *Jackson*. Dissenting opinion: *Frankfurter*, Douglas (in part), *Black*.

Mr. Justice REED delivered the opinion of the Court.

The issue raised by this appeal is the constitutionality of the occupational tax provisions of the Revenue Act of 1951, which levy a tax on persons engaged in the business of accepting wagers, and require such persons to register with the Collector of Internal Revenue. The unconstitutionality of the tax is asserted on two grounds. First, it is said that Congress, under the pretense of exercising its power to tax has attempted to penalize illegal intrastate gambling through the regulatory features of the Act, and has thus infringed the police power which is reserved to the states. Secondly, it is urged that the registration provisions of the tax violate the privilege against self-incrimination and are arbitrary and vague, contrary to the guarantees of the Fifth Amendment.

It is conceded that a federal excise tax does not cease to be valid merely because it discourages or deters the activities taxed. Nor is the tax invalid because the revenue obtained is negligible. Appellee, however, argues that the sole purpose of the statute is to penalize only illegal gambling in the states through the guise of a tax measure. . . . [T]he instant tax has a regulatory effect. But regardless of its regulatory effect, the wagering tax produces revenue. As such it surpasses both the narcotics and firearms taxes which we have found valid.

Appellee's second assertion is that the wagering tax is unconstitutional because it is a denial of the privilege against self-incrimination as guaranteed by the Fifth Amendment.

Since appellee failed to register for the wagering tax, it is difficult to see how he can now claim the privilege even assuming that the disclosure of violations of law is called for. . . . If respondent wishes to take wagers subject to excise taxes under s 3285, he must pay an occupational tax and register. Under the registration provisions of the wagering tax, appellee is not compelled to confess to acts already committed, he is merely informed by the statute that in order to engage in the business of wagering in the future he must fulfill certain conditions.

Reversed.

Mr. Justice FRANKFURTER, dissenting.

. . . Constitutional issues are likely to arise whenever Congress draws on the taxing power not to raise revenue but to regulate conduct. This is so, of course, because of the distribution of legislative power as between the Congress and the State Legislatures in the regulation of conduct.

. . . [W]hen oblique use is made of the taxing power as to matters which substantively are not within the powers delegated to Congress, the Court cannot shut its eyes to what is obviously, because designedly, an attempt to control conduct which the Constitution left to the responsibility of the States, merely because Congress wrapped the legislation in the verbal cellophane of a revenue measure.

Congress, which cannot constitutionally grapple directly with gambling in the States, may compel self-incriminating disclosures for the enforcement of State gambling laws, merely because it does so under the guise of a revenue measure obviously passed not for revenue purposes. The motive of congressional legislation is not for our scrutiny, provided only that the ulterior purpose is not expressed in ways which negative what the revenue words on their face express and, which do not seek enforcement of the formal revenue purpose through means that offend those standards of decency in our civilization against which due process is a barrier.

I would affirm this judgment.

Mr. Justice BLACK, with whom Mr. Justice DOUGLAS concurs, dissenting.

The Act creates a squeezing device contrived to put a man in federal prison if he refuses to confess himself into a state prison as a violator of state gambling laws. The coercion of confessions is a common but justly criticized practice of many countries that do not have or live up to a Bill of Rights. But we have a Bill of Rights that condemns coerced confessions, however refined or legalistic may be the technique of extortion. I would hold that this Act violates the Fifth Amendment.

Notes/Queries/Readings

1. The district court's decision to dismiss Kahriger's case was based on *United States v. Constantine*, 296 U.S. 287 (1935). In this case, the Supreme Court struck down a "special excise tax" of $1000 on retail liquor dealers as a penalty under the guise of a tax and thus an invasion of the state's police power. In dismissing the case, the district court said that "while the subject matter of this legislation so far as revenue purposes is concerned is within the scope of Federal authorities," the tax is unconstitutional mainly because it is a vice control measure and thus an infringement on the police power reserved to the states by the Tenth Amendment.

2. Justice Frankfurter wrote in his dissent that "the motive of congressional legislation is not for our scrutiny." Why should congressional motive be out of bounds? Would an inquiry into motive be relevant to questions of comity? Would such an inquiry itself violate the doctrine of comity? Or is the doctrine grounded instead in separation of powers?

South Dakota v. Dole
483 U.S. 203, 107 S. Ct. 2793, 97 L. Ed. 2d 171 (1987)

Congress, in an effort to reduce highway accidents, enacted the National Minimum Drinking Age Amendment of 1984. In passing the statute, Congress tried to induce the states to establish a uniform drinking age of twenty-one years. The statute was designed to stop young people from commuting to border states where the drinking age was lower than twenty-one. It was also based on the finding that young people who drink and drive cause a disproportionate number of automobile accidents. The statute directs the secretary of transportation to withhold a percentage of otherwise allocable federal highway funds from those states in which persons less than twenty-one years of age are lawfully permitted to purchase or possess any alcoholic beverage. South Dakota, which permits persons nineteen years of age or older to purchase beer containing up to 3.2 percent alcohol, sued the secretary of transportation, claiming that the statute exceeded Congress's spending power and violated the Twenty-First Amendment. The district court ruled against the state, and the court of appeals affirmed. Opinion of the Court: *Rehnquist*, White, Marshall, Blackmun, Powell, Stevens, Scalia. Dissenting opinions: *Brennan, O'Connor.*

Chief Justice REHNQUIST delivered the opinion of the Court.

. . . [W]e need not decide in this case whether [the Twenty-First] Amendment would prohibit an attempt by Congress to legislate directly a national minimum drinking age. Here, Congress has acted indirectly under its spending power to encourage uniformity in the States' drinking ages. As we explain below, we find this legislative effort within constitutional bounds even if Congress may not regulate drinking ages directly.

The Constitution empowers Congress to "lay and collect Taxes, Duties, Imposts, and Excises, to pay the Debts and provide for the common Defence and general Welfare of the United States." Art. I, s 8, cl. 1. Incident to this power, Congress may attach conditions on the receipt of federal funds, and has repeatedly employed the power "to further broad policy objectives by conditioning receipt of federal moneys upon compliance by the recipient with federal statutory and administrative directives." . . . The breadth of this power was made clear in *United States v. Butler* [1936], where the Court, resolving a longstanding debate over the scope of the Spending Clause, determined that "the power of Congress to authorize expenditure of public moneys for public purposes is not limited by the direct grants of legislative power found in the Constitution." Thus, objectives not thought to be within Article I's "enumerated legislative fields," may nevertheless be attained through the use of the spending power and the conditional grant of federal funds.

We can readily conclude that the provision is designed to serve the general welfare, especially in light of the fact that "the concept of welfare or the opposite is shaped by Congress." Congress found that the differing drinking ages in the States created particular incentives for young persons to combine their desire to drink with their ability to drive, and that this interstate problem required a national solution. The means it chose to address this dangerous situation were reasonably calculated to advance the general welfare. The conditions upon which States receive the funds, moreover, could not be more clearly stated by Congress. And the State itself, rather than challenging the germaneness of the condition to federal purposes, admits that it "has never contended that the congressional action was . . . unrelated to a national concern in the absence of the Twenty-first Amendment." Indeed, the condition imposed by Congress is directly related to one of the main purposes for which highway funds are expended—safe interstate travel. . . .

Our decisions have recognized that in some circumstances the financial inducement offered by Congress might be so coercive as to pass the point at which "pressure turns into compulsion." Here, however, Congress has directed only that a State desiring to establish a minimum drinking age lower than 21 lose a relatively small percentage of certain federal highway funds. Petitioner contends that the coercive nature of this program is evident from the degree of success it has achieved. We cannot conclude, however, that a conditional grant of federal money of this sort is unconstitutional simply by reason of its success in achieving the congressional objective.

Here Congress has offered relatively mild encouragement to the States to enact higher minimum drinking ages than they would otherwise choose. But the enactment of such laws remains the prerogative of the States not merely in theory but in fact. Even if Congress might lack the power to impose a national minimum drinking age directly, we conclude that encouragement to state action found in s 158 is a valid use of the spending power. Accordingly, the judgment of the Court of Appeals is

Affirmed.

Justice O'CONNOR, dissenting.

My disagreement with the Court is relatively narrow on the spending power issue: it is a disagreement about the application of a principle rather than a disagreement on the principle itself. I agree with the Court that Congress may attach conditions on the receipt of federal funds to further "the federal interest in particular national projects or programs." I also subscribe to the established proposition that the reach of the spending power "is not limited by the direct grants of legislative power found in the Constitution."

United States v. Butler (1936). Finally, I agree that there are four separate types of limitations on the spending power: the expenditure must be for the general welfare, the conditions imposed must be unambiguous, they must be reasonably related to the purpose of the expenditure, and the legislation may not violate any independent constitutional provision. Insofar as two of those limitations are concerned, the Court is clearly correct that s. 158 is wholly unobjectionable. Establishment of a national minimum drinking age certainly fits within the broad concept of the general welfare and the statute is entirely unambiguous. I am also willing to assume, arguendo, that the Twenty-first Amendment does not constitute an "independent constitutional bar" to a spending condition. . . .

We have repeatedly said that Congress may condition grants under the spending power only in ways reasonably related to the purpose of the federal program. In my view, establishment of a minimum drinking age of 21 is not sufficiently related to interstate highway construction to justify so conditioning funds appropriated for that purpose.

The Court reasons that Congress wishes that the roads it builds may be used safely, that drunken drivers threaten highway safety, and that young people are more likely to drive while under the influence of alcohol under existing law than would be the case if there were a uniform national drinking age of 21. It hardly needs saying, however, that if the purpose of s 158 is to deter drunken driving, it is far too over and under-inclusive. It is over-inclusive because it stops teenagers from drinking even when they are not about to drive on interstate highways. It is under-inclusive because teenagers pose only a small part of the drunken driving problem in this Nation.

When Congress appropriates money to build a highway, it is entitled to insist that the highway be a safe one. But it is not entitled to insist as a condition of the use of highway funds that the State impose or change regulations in other areas of the State's social and economic life because of an attenuated or tangential relationship to highway use or safety. Indeed, if the rule were otherwise, the Congress could effectively regulate almost any area of a State's social, political, or economic life on the theory that use of the interstate transportation system is somehow enhanced. . . .

There is a clear place at which the Court can draw the line between permissible and impermissible conditions on federal grants. It is the line identified in the Brief for the National Conference of State Legislatures et al. As Amici Curiae:

Congress has the power to spend for the general welfare, it has the power to legislate only for delegated purposes. . . . The appropriate inquiry, then, is whether the spending requirement or prohibition is a condition on a grant or whether it is regulation. The difference turns on whether the requirement specifies in some way how the money should be spent, so that Congress' intent in making the grant will be effectuated. Congress has no

power under the Spending Clause to impose requirements on a grant that go beyond specifying how the money should be spent. A requirement that is not such a specification is not a condition, but a regulation, which is valid only if it falls within one of Congress' delegated regulatory powers.

While [*United States v.*] *Butler's* authority is questionable insofar as it assumes that Congress has no regulatory power over farm production, its discussion of the spending power and its description of both the power's breadth and its limitations remain sound. The Court's decision in *Butler* also properly recognizes the gravity of the task of appropriately limiting the spending power. If the spending power is to be limited only by Congress' notion of the general welfare, the reality, given the vast financial resources of the Federal Government, is that the Spending Clause gives "power to the Congress to tear down the barriers, to invade the states' jurisdiction, and to become a parliament of the whole people, subject to no restrictions save such as are self-imposed." This, of course, as *Butler* held, was not the Framers' plan and it is not the meaning of the Spending Clause. . . .

Notes/Queries/Readings

1. How does the Court distinguish between "relatively mild encouragement" and coercion? Does the spending power suggest such a distinction? If not, why is the distinction important?

2. Justice Rehnquist, as noted in earlier chapters, is an ardent defender of the independence and integrity of the states. His dissenting opinion in *City of Philadelphia v. New Jersey* (1978) and his majority opinion in *National League of Cities v. Usery* (1975) manifest his devotion to the rights of the states. What then explains his position in favor of the national government in *Dole*?

3. What is the difference between persuasion and an "unconstitutional condition"? For additional reading, see Richard Epstein, *Foreword: Unconstitutional Conditions, State Power, and the Limits of Consent*, 102 Harvard Law Review 4 (1988); Kathleen M. Sullivan, *Unconstitutional Conditions*, 102 Harvard Law Review (1989); and Albert J. Rosenthal, *Conditional Federal Spending and the Constitution*, 39 Stanford Law Review 1103 (1987).

Chapter 7

Foreign Affairs and Constitutional Crises

*I*n this chapter we consider two topics of undoubted significance for the life of any constitutional democracy: the power to conduct foreign relations and the power to respond to emergencies and constitutional crises. At first glance, these might seem unlikely partners, but the problems they raise for constitutional democracy are quite similar. Moreover, both issues have been the source of intense constitutional conflict at least since the Revolutionary War. One problem concerns the growth of presidential power and whether it can be squared with basic constitutional principles, such as the limitation and separation of power. A second problem concerns the terrible demands of war and crises and whether these demands can be met while maintaining our respect for constitutional principles.

First we consider the Constitution and foreign affairs. What falls under the rubric of "foreign affairs"? In the words of one scholar, foreign affairs and relations "constitute the relationship through which nations and their governments are bound together."[1] Thus defined, the topic covers a lot of ground. There are few issues of foreign affairs that do not also involve matters of commerce, or of federalism, or of the First Amendment and other civil liberties. Thus our study in this chapter will range across a wide variety of issues and topics.

Foreign affairs and constitutional crises are also inviting terrain for exploring the three perspectives—interpretive, normative, and comparative—we identified in the text introduction. The interpretive theme, especially concerning questions about what the Constitution is and what it includes, are especially prominent in this chapter. One consequence of the Founders' failure to deal with foreign affairs at any length in the Constitution is that interpreters must make use of a great variety of nontextual sources. History and practice together, scattered with occasional quotes from the *Federalist Papers* and Madison's *Notes*, and even more infrequently with Supreme Court opinions, provide us with the raw materials for interpretation. No student can fully understand the constitutional dimensions of foreign affairs without an appre-

---

[1] Carl J. Friedrich, *Constitutional Government and Democracy*, rev. ed. (Waltham, Mass.: Blaisdell Publishing Company, 1950), 76.

ciation of the ways in which past contests between presidents and Congresses supplement the written word.[2]

Questions about what to interpret typically overlap with questions about who should interpret. We have stressed that constitutional interpretation is not coextensive with judicial interpretation. In the field of foreign affairs, especially, constitutional interpretation is not the "peculiar province" of the Supreme Court. Indeed, the Court has tended to avoid these questions, claiming lack of authority and expertise. The Court has used a variety of devices, such as standing, ripeness, mootness, and especially the political questions doctrine (see chapter 3), to explain its unwillingness to oversee interbranch conflict.

The kinds of issues we have labeled "normative" also figure prominently here. We have seen in the past few chapters that the separation and distribution of power—concisely but misleadingly summed up in the phrase "checks and balances"—is a central feature of the constitutional order. The weedy growth of presidential power in the field of foreign affairs has put this principle to its strongest test. The rise of the "imperial presidency" forces us to reexamine assumptions we might otherwise take for granted. Why separate power, for example? What do we gain and at what expense? Additionally, and perhaps counterintuitively, foreign affairs issues also raise important questions about federalism or about the vertical distribution of power. Together, these two doctrines raise a single question: Is it possible to share power, or do the demands of foreign affairs require that the nation speak with a single, authoritative voice?

Another of our recurrent themes is the tension between constitutionalism's regard for individual liberty and the democratic impulse to majoritarian politics. War highlights this tension in disturbing ways. As we have suggested, the topic of foreign affairs and constitutional crises is especially useful for students of liberal arts because it forces us to confront issues of political theory and morality that we usually sidestep in other areas. To respect or to suspend the Constitution, to ignore it or to interpret it—these are ultimately questions of political morality, character, and identity. They ask us to define who we are as a people, what we believe, and why we believe it. War, observed Heraclitus, is the father of all things. If that is true, it is also true that the demands of war pose fundamental challenges to the maintenance of constitutional democracy.[3]

The Constitutional Basis and Structure of Foreign Affairs Powers

Separated and Shared Powers

Perhaps because they were intent on separating power, the Founders did not include in the constitutional document a general or comprehensive power to conduct foreign affairs. The Constitution does, however, include several provisions that relate directly to issues of foreign affairs. The most obvious of these is Article 1, Section 8, which gives Congress the power "To declare War," as well as the powers to provide for the common defense and general welfare, to raise and support armies, to provide and maintain a navy, and to define and punish offenses against the law of nations. In

---

[2] Louis Henkin, *Foreign Affairs and the Constitution* (New York: W. W. Norton & Company, 1975), vii, 3–4.

[3] See, e.g., John E. Finn, *Constitutions in Crisis: Political Violence and the Rule of Law* (New York: Oxford University Press, 1991); Carl J. Friedrich, *Constitutional Reason of State: The Survival of the Constitutional Order* (Providence, R.I.: Brown University Press, 1957); and Clinton Rossiter, *Constitutional Dictatorship* (Princeton, N.J.: Princeton University Press, 1948).

contrast, Article 2 makes the president the commander-in-chief, as well as giving him or her the power (with the advice and consent of the Senate) to make treaties. Thus the war power, broadly defined as the power to declare, to make, and to conclude war, is both separated and shared between the legislative and executive branches. There is nothing unique here. As we saw in earlier chapters, the American constitutional order is less a system of strictly separated power than one of shared powers and separate institutions.[4]

An Invitation to Struggle: Contests for Power Between Congress and the President

A few specific provisions aside, then, the Constitution is more notable for its silence than for its clarity concerning foreign affairs. In the words of one student, "The principal difficulty has been that, from the beginning, the compromises, irresolutions, oversights, and intentional silences of the Constitution left it unclear who had sail and who had rudder, and, most important, where is command."[5] The text tells us who may make treaties, for example, but it says nothing about who may break or cancel them. Similarly, the text tells us that the Congress has power to declare war, but it says nothing about when the president, as commander-in-chief, may utilize troops without prior legislative approval.

The consequence of silence is ongoing confusion and conflict between the branches, especially between Congress and the president. The Constitution is, in the words of the great scholar Edward Corwin, "an invitation to a struggle for the privilege of directing American foreign policy."[6] The history of that struggle begins as early as the administration of George Washington, when, in 1793, the president issued a Proclamation of Neutrality in the hostilities between France and Great Britain. In response, James Madison (along with Jefferson, Madison favored the French) complained publicly that the decision should be the joint responsibility of Congress and the president. In this case, Madison argued, joint responsibility was required because the constitutional text had committed to Congress the power to declare war, plainly a first cousin to the power to declare neutrality.

Writing as Pacificus, Hamilton defended Washington's decision, justifying "the right of the Executive . . . to determine the condition of the nation, though it may . . . affect the exercise of the power of the legislature to declare war. . . . The legislature is still free to perform its duties, according to its own sense of them. . . . The division of the executive power in the Constitution creates a *concurrent* authority in the cases to which it relates."[7] For his part, President Washington vowed in frustration that he "would be damned if he would be found in that place [the Senate] again. . . ."[8]

In our time the contest between presidential and congressional authority is no less intense. President Bush's decision to send troops to Kuwait in August 1990, for example, revived longstanding arguments about the power of the president to make war without congressional approval.[9] Fifty-four members of the House of Represen-

---

[4]Richard E. Neustadt, *Presidential Power*, rev. ed. (New York: John Wiley, 1976), 101.

[5]Henkin, *supra* note 2, at 271.

[6]Edward S. Corwin, *The President: Office and Powers*, 4th rev. ed. (New York: New York University Press, 1957), 171.

[7]Letters of Pacificus, #1 (*Works*, by A. C. Hamilton, ed., 1851), 7:76, 82–83.

[8]As quoted in Malcolm M. Feeley and Samuel Krislov, *Constitutional Law* (Glenview, Ill.: Scott, Foresman, 1990), 89.

[9]See, for example, J. Gregory Sidak, *To Declare War*, 41 Duke Law Journal 27 (1991), and Harold Hongju Koh, *The Coase Theorem and the War Power: A Response*, 41 Duke Law Journal 124 (1991).

tatives immediately filed suit in a United States District Court, asking it to enjoin the president's decision to send troops. Judge Harold Greene rejected the request, but he did note, in language reminiscent of Madison's complaints, that "If the executive had the sole power to determine that any particular offensive military operation, no matter how vast, does not constitute war-making but only an offensive military attack, the congressional power to declare war will be at the mercy of a semantic decision by the Executive." [10]

On 8 January 1991, four months after his decision to begin Operation Desert Storm, and a week before the deadline imposed on Iraq by the United Nations to remove all troops from Kuwait, President Bush asked Congress for a formal resolution supporting "the use of all necessary means" to give sanction to the deadline. President Bush was careful to note that he was *not* asking for—and did not believe he needed—congressional *approval* to use force. His independent authority as commander-in-chief, Bush argued, provided ample constitutional support for his actions. After much debate, Congress gave President Bush the resolution he had requested.

What are we to make of this continuing struggle? Two centuries of executive-legislative conflict in foreign affairs in general, and concerning the power to make war in particular, have yielded two certain truths. First, although the pendulum swings, the great trend has been toward the expansion of presidential power. Second, the constitutional text—and here text and history sing the same song—assigns no role to the judiciary in foreign affairs. With but a few exceptions, the Supreme Court has studiously avoided entering interbranch disputes over the allocation of foreign affairs powers. As this chapter's cases make clear, when the Court *has acted*, it has tended to support the growth of presidential power.

The Growth of the Imperial Presidency in Foreign Affairs

Whatever the Founders may have intended about shared authority and collective decision making, the president dominates foreign relations in the United States. Presidents make war, negotiate and abrogate treaties, enter into executive agreements, and generally represent American interests in the international community. The tremendous growth of presidential power was made possible in part by the division of authority contained in the constitutional text, but it was not an inevitable result of constitutional architecture. Instead, the swell has been a consequence of the Constitution's plasticity and, no less important, the demands of modern warfare and the dizzying pace of technological change.

The Constitution's ambiguity is best exemplified by the very language of Article 2, the source of executive authority. The first sentence of Article 2 states that "The executive power shall be vested in a President of the United States." Beyond this, however, the text has little to add. The remainder of Article 2 is a simple and short laundry list of specific powers that make up the "executive power" vested in the presidency. These powers include the position as commander-in-chief (itself a term whose meaning provokes argument), the power to execute the laws, the power to make treaties with the advice and consent of the Senate, the power to appoint ambassadors, and the responsibility to protect and defend the Constitution.

This skeletal structure stands in sharp contrast to Article 1 in two important ways. First, the catalogue of powers entrusted to Congress, in comparison to those listed in Article 2, is both long and comprehensive. Second, and of greater importance, one cannot find in Article 2 an explicit counterpart to Article 1's necessary and proper clause. You may recall that in the chapter 5 discussion of *McCulloch v. Maryland* (1819), we saw that the necessary and proper clause has been an important source of

---

[10] *Dellums v. Bush*, 752 F.Supp. 1141 (D.D.C. 1990).

"implied" legislative powers. The absence of a similar clause in Article 2, coupled with the relatively sparse explicit grants of power, has led some students to conclude that Article 2's miserly allocation of power to the president faithfully reflects the Founders' fears of expansive executive power. In the words of Daniel Webster, "I do not, therefore, regard the declaration that the executive power shall be vested in a President as being any grant at all; any more than the declaration that the legislative power shall be vested in Congress constitutes, by itself, a grant of such power." [11]

On the other hand, some folks argue that the first sentence of Article 2 literally vests in the president all of those powers that fall under the general rubric of "executive power." John Marshall, speaking not as chief justice but as a member of the House of Representatives, similarly argued, "The President is the sole organ of the nation in its external relations, and its sole representative with foreign nations." [12] On this understanding, Article 2 is an expansive, general grant of power to direct foreign affairs. Moreover, some proponents of presidential power have argued that the president may also act even in those areas the text assigns to Congress, presumably because such grants are not entrusted *only* to Congress. Unless Congress has chosen to use its power, and in ways that are plainly opposed to the president's use of the same power, the president is free to act. President Lincoln accordingly argued that his decision to suspend the writ of habeas corpus was constitutionally proper, even though, as Chief Justice Taney observed in *Ex Parte Merryman* (1861), the location of the power in Article 1 implies that it is entrusted to Congress. In addition, some presidents have argued that they possess an "inherent" power, sometimes called the power of prerogative, to take whatever action is necessary to protect the Union and the Constitution (though they are not necessarily one and the same or of equal weight, as Lincoln observed).

Scholarly debate has done little to resolve the conflict between these two very different understandings of Article 2 or the different visions of the relationship between Congress and the president that animate them. But the verdict of history is undeniable: With each decade the predominance of the executive in foreign affairs has become more complete. At least one scholar has thus concluded that the "history of the presidency is a history of aggrandizement. . . ." [13] The reasons for presidential dominance are not hard to find. As we saw in *Federalist* 70, the institutional structure of the presidency is highly conducive to leadership in a field, like foreign relations, that demands expediency, secrecy, diplomacy, political will, and "energy." In this sense, the Constitution enabled the growth of presidential power. The reasons that caused the expansion, however, lie in the growth of the United States as an international power and the persistence of international conflict. It is only a small exaggeration to claim that every war or armed squabble in which the United States has been engaged has resulted in the growth of presidential power.

The War Powers Resolution

Congress has alternately facilitated and challenged the rise of the imperial presidency. In 1964, President Lyndon B. Johnson sought and received from an all too willing Congress a blank check to escalate the undeclared war in Vietnam. The Tonkin Gulf Resolution authorized the president "to take all necessary measures to repel any armed attack against the forces of the United States and to prevent further aggression" by the Communist regime in Vietnam.

---

[11] *The Works of Daniel Webster*, 4 (17th ed., 1877), 186. Or, he might have added, of Article 3, which provides that "The judicial Power of the United States, shall be vested in one supreme Court. . . ."

[12] 10 Annals of Congress 613 (1800).

[13] Edward Corwin, *The President*, 5th ed. (New York: New York University Press, 1984), 29–30.

In 1973, Congress tried to reassert its constitutional authority by passing the War Powers Resolution (reprinted later in this chapter) over President Nixon's veto. The War Powers Resolution claims to be an effort to "fulfill the intent of the framers of the Constitution of the United States and ensure that the collective judgment of both the Congress and the President will apply to the introduction of United States Armed Forces into hostilities. . . ." The resolution seeks to buttress congressional power by requiring the president to consult with Congress before putting American troops into hostilities "or into situations where imminent involvement in hostilities" is likely. If the president cannot consult in advance of such action, then he or she must report to Congress within forty-eight hours and must terminate the action within sixty days of that report. Congress may extend the deadline by thirty days, or it may choose to authorize the continued use of American troops. The resolution also permits Congress to call back the troops by a joint resolution not subject to presidential veto.

The resolution raises important issues of constitutional theory. Many critics contend that it unconstitutionally infringes upon the president's power as commander-in-chief and that it may conflict with the Court's decision in *I.N.S. v. Chadha* (1983). Decisions about when to commit to troops, or when to withdraw them and why, these critics argue, are the very essence of the powers entrusted to a commander-in-chief.[14] On the other hand, the resolution's proponents see in the resolution, first, a renewed sense of congressional responsibility and second, a reiteration of the principle of separation of powers and collective decision making.

The Constitution in Crisis

The question of whether there are limits on presidential power to make war is just part of a larger problem: Is it possible to square constitutionalism's insistence upon limited government with the demands of crises and emergencies? Alexander Hamilton thought not, writing in *Federalist* 23 that "The circumstances that endanger the safety of nations are infinite, and for this reason no constitutional shackles can wisely be imposed on the power to which the care of it is committed." Implicit in Hamilton's counsel is a frank recognition of the inherent fragility of constitutional democracy. No government is immune from crisis. All states must weather threats to their existence and well being, be they threats of war, domestic instability, economic challenge, or crises of nature. Governments rarely prove able to resist the call for emergency powers that reach far beyond what would otherwise be permissible. The United States is no exception in this regard.

Crises are especially troublesome for a constitutional democracy because it is in them that the concept of limited power, so central to constitutional theory, seems of doubtful wisdom. Surely the first order of business when we are threatened must be survival and not, however glorious or principled it may appear in theory, respect for constitutional limits and parchment barriers. So, the first question we must face is perhaps the most basic and the most contentious: If it gets in the way, should we bother with the Constitution at all?

Crises and the Constitution

Almost every constitution makes some kind of provision for crises and emergencies. The most direct provision in the United States Constitution is Article 1, Section 9, which provides that in "Cases of Rebellion or Invasion" the writ of habeas corpus may

---

[14]Robert H. Turner, *The War Powers Resolution: Unconstitutional, Unnecessary, and Unhelpful*, 17 Loyola of Los Angeles Law Review 683 (1984); Stephen L. Carter, *The Constitutionality of the War Powers Resolution*, 70 Virginia Law Review 101 (1984).

be suspended if "the public safety may require it." But in contrast to most twentieth-century constitutions, the American Constitution is largely silent on the issue of emergency powers. It says nothing about what constitutes a crisis or who determines if there is one. It does tell us that someone (presumably Congress) may suspend the writ of habeas corpus, but it says nothing about martial law, emergency or military courts, or of the suspension of elections or civil liberties.

How should we respond to a crisis? In the abstract, we have only a few options and none of them are especially attractive. First, we might deny that there is any conflict between what necessity requires and what the Constitution permits. We can obviate the conflict between them in a number of ways. We might, for example, interpret the Constitution in ways that authorize whatever powers we think are required to resolve the crisis. Thus, we might read the Constitution to permit extensive restrictions on First Amendment freedoms if we think they are necessary to prosecute a war. Or, we might understand the Constitution to permit the president to suspend the writ of habeas corpus and to try civilians in military courts.

There are undoubtedly great advantages to using "interpretation" as a way to reconcile crises and the Constitution. By insisting that the Constitution governs all areas of our political life, we affirm our commitment to constitutional ideals, even though it may not always be possible to fully respect them. Furthermore, the continued applicability of constitutional rules and norms can provide a basis for citizens and other governmental officials to criticize and evaluate governmental policy. We thus retain a mechanism for ensuring accountability, among the most basic of constitutional ideals.

On the other hand, there are dangers with this approach as well. The first of these is one of practicality: If the Constitution may be interpreted to authorize whatever we need, whenever we need it, then what, if anything, will fall outside the pale? What are the limits to creative or expansive interpretation? The same objection has an important theoretical component as well. If we can interpret the Constitution in any way we like, what is its point? A Constitution that is infinitely plastic is arguably a Constitution that contains no limits on public power at all.[15]

A second alternative is to obviate conflict by simply ignoring the Constitution altogether. We might conclude, following Justice Jackson's dissent in *Korematsu v. United States* (1944) (the full decision is reprinted later in this chapter), that in some areas the Constitution does not and cannot apply. This, too, has the advantage of keeping the Constitution intact and in force (at least as regards some areas of public life), if at a subtle and dangerous cost. If the Constitution does not apply in a crisis, would it not be better, some critics ask, simply to acknowledge its limitations than to pretend that there is no conflict?

A third alternative suggests that we should squarely confront conflict and admit that there are times when the Constitution is incompatible with the expansive governmental powers that crises usually demand. This has the advantages of honesty and of maintaining respect for the integrity of constitutional ideals, instead of ignoring or warping them to fit our needs. This option of suspending part or all of the Constitution, however, also has a terrible price. First, it means, or has seemed to mean to some scholars, that governmental power in times of emergencies is effectively without constitutional limits.[16] Second, we might wonder, having suspended the Constitution, when and if we will ever restore it. This is not an idle concern. Crises have

---

[15] See Sotirios A. Barber, *On What the Constitution Means* (Baltimore: Johns Hopkins University Press, 1984).

[16] One of the authors of this book has argued that even when we suspend the Constitution, we must still respect a set of "basic constitutional principles" that transcend individual constitutional texts. See Finn, *supra* note 3.

long lives, and experience teaches that governments are likely to find unlimited powers addictive.

How Do Governments Respond to Crises?

At various times, all three of the approaches just described have been tried in the United States. Perhaps the most frequent course has been to ignore the Constitution. Consider, for example, the efforts of the Federal Bureau of Investigation to humiliate and discredit Martin Luther King and other leaders of the civil rights movements in the 1960s. Or earlier efforts to combat the "Red Menace." Whatever else may be said of the McCarthy hearings, a scrupulous regard for constitutional ideals was not one of their distinctive features.

As is true with the power of foreign affairs, the power to respond to crises has drifted to the executive branch. The growth of presidential power and the seeming inconsistency of limits on those powers raises a constitutional problem of the highest order. At least two theories have been advanced to reconcile the apparent conflict between our regard for constitutional limitations and the demands of crisis.

Inherent Powers and the Theory of Prerogative

The theory of prerogative power holds that the chief executive must have whatever authority is necessary to resolve a crisis that confronts the state. In the words of Arthur Schlesinger, Jr., "Crises threatening the life of the nation have happily been rare. But, if such a crisis comes, a President must act. . . ." Consequently, he or she "must be conceded reserve power to meet authentic emergencies," even if it means that he or she must go against the laws.[17] There are two questions we must address here. First, does the president possess these powers? Second, what, if any, are the limitations on these powers? The theory of prerogative dates at least from the time of the Roman Republic. Twice the Roman Senate dissolved itself and delegated the entire array of state power to Cincinnatus, an elderly farmer. On both occasions, Cincinnatus quashed the crisis and returned to his farm.[18] Thus the Republic was saved through the use of absolute and dictatorial power, the ends justifying the means. The most complete modern statement of the doctrine is by John Locke, who wrote that the executive must always retain the residual power "to act according to discretion for the public good, without the prescription of the law and sometimes even against it." Hamilton's argument in *Federalist* 41 that emergency powers "ought to exist without limitation, because it is impossible to foresee or to define the extent and variety of the means which may be necessary to satisfy them" recalls Locke's observation.

American constitutional history is replete with examples of presidents who have claimed some sort of prerogative. Although he was an articulate opponent of expansive presidential power before he assumed office, Thomas Jefferson relied on some version of the theory early in his tenure in office. In 1803, presented with an opportunity to purchase the Louisiana Territory at a cut-rate price of fifteen million dollars, Jefferson searched the Constitution in vain for the authority to act. In a letter to John Breckenridge, he concluded "The constitution has made no provision for our holding foreign territory, still less for incorporating foreign nations into our Union. The Executive in seizing the fugitive occurrence which so much advances the good of their country, have done an act beyond the Constitution."[19] Indeed, Jefferson was so convinced that the Constitution did *not* authorize him to act that he drafted a constitu-

---

[17] Arthur M. Schlesinger, Jr. *The Imperial Presidency* (New York: Popular Library, 1973), 17.

[18] See Clinton Rossiter, *Constitutional Dictatorship* (Princeton, N.J.: Princeton University Press, 1948), 15–19.

[19] *Writings*, VIII (Ford ed. 1892–1899), 244.

tional amendment that would have validated the purchase after the fact. Jefferson never acted on the amendment. He finally convinced himself that he possessed the power he needed because he was obligated to protect the Union. "A strict observance of the written laws is doubtless *one* of the highest duties of a good citizen, but it is not the *highest*," he wrote in a letter to J. B. Colvin. "The laws of necessity, of self-preservation, of saving our country when in danger, are of higher obligation."[20] Hence, "a strict and rigid observation of the laws [in some cases] may do harm."[21]

Jefferson's precedent found a receptive audience in later administrations. The principle of prerogative received its most expansive treatment in the hands of President Lincoln. Lincoln's prosecution of the Civil War led him to take a number of truly extraordinary measures, such as suspending the writ of habeas corpus, calling up state militias, blocking southern ports and harbors, and issuing the Emancipation Proclamation (which, following *Dred Scott v. Sandford* (1857), arguably took property without due process of law). None of these actions are authorized by the constitutional document. Nor were they authorized by statute, although Lincoln did later seek congressional approval for some of them. Explaining his actions to a Special Session of Congress, Lincoln argued that:

> I [understood] my oath to preserve the constitution to the best of my ability, imposed upon me the duty of preserving, by every indispensable means, *that government— that nation—of which that constitution was the organic law. Was it possible to lose the nation, and yet preserve the constitution? I felt that measures*, otherwise unconstitutional, *might become lawful by becoming indispensable to the preservation of the constitution, through the preservation of the nation.*[22]

More recently, President Theodore Roosevelt advanced a somewhat narrower version of the doctrine, stating that

> I declined to adopt the view that what was imperatively necessary for the Nation could not be done by the President unless he could find some specific authorization to do it. My belief was that it was not only his right but his duty to do anything that the needs of the Nation demanded unless such action was forbidden by the Constitution or the laws.[23]

Roosevelt's position seems to concede that there are some limits to the president's power, at least insofar as he may not act in ways that the Constitution explicitly forbids. The idea that there may be limits to the prerogative power, however, is one that Locke and Lincoln would have denied.[24]

The Constitutional Limitations Theory

In stark contrast to the theory of prerogative, the constitutional limitations theory holds that any exercise of presidential power must be fairly traced—directly or by implication—to one of the grants enumerated in Article 2. Best articulated by Chief

---

[20] Letter to J. B. Colvin, 20 September 1810.

[21] Finn, *supra* note 3, at 17.

[22] John Nicolay and John Hays, eds., *The Complete Works of Abraham Lincoln*, vol. 10 (New York: Francis D. Tandy, 1894), 65–68.

[23] Theodore Roosevelt, *Autobiography* (New York: MacMillan, 1931), 38.

[24] Consider another version of the stewardship theory, this time offered by Franklin Delano Roosevelt: "I cannot tell what powers may have to be exercised to win this war. The American people can be sure that I will use my powers with a full sense of my responsibility to the Constitution and to my country. The American people can also be sure that I shall not hesitate to use every power vested in me to accomplish the defeat of our enemies in any part of the world where our own safety demands such defeat. When the war is won, the powers under which I act automatically revert to the people—to whom they belong." 88 Cong. Rec. 7044 (7 September 1942).

Justice William Howard Taft (the only man to serve his country both as president and as Supreme Court justice), this position insists that any exercise of presidential power must ultimately find its source in the Constitution. "The true view of the Executive function is, as I conceive it, that the President can exercise no power which cannot be fairly and reasonably traced to some specific grant of power or justly implied and included within such express grant as proper and necessary to its exercise." [25] Hence, according to Taft, "There is no undefined residuum of power which [the president] can exercise because it seems to him to be in the public interest." [26]

Taft's position contends that there are no inherent powers, free of constitutional shackles, that belong to the presidency. As you read the cases in this chapter, consider the following questions. Are Locke and Hamilton correct in their insistence that there can be no limits on the president's power to conduct war or to respond to emergencies? If no such limits exist, then in what sense, if any, can we say that such powers are consistent with constitutional democracy? Alternatively, is Taft right in claiming that the president's powers must be traceable to Article 2? What limits might exist on those powers? What should a president do if he or she genuinely believes that some action—not sanctioned, or even prohibited by the Constitution—is necessary to save the nation? Finally, if there are limitations on the power of prerogative, who has the authority to enforce them?

Judicial Review and Foreign Affairs

So far our discussion has concentrated on the president and Congress. The constitutional text gives no hint that the judiciary has any role to play in the area of foreign affairs. No student this far along is likely to find this omission surprising. What *is* different is that the Constitution's failure to define powers and responsibilities in the area of foreign affairs, has mitigated strongly against *any* judicial involvement in the field. This is not to say that the Court has never acted. Still, this is an area of constitutional law and politics that has developed primarily without judicial supervision or involvement—in stark contrast, we shall see, to Germany, Canada, and several other constitutional democracies.

Extraconstitutional Sources of Power

Some justices have gone so far as to suggest that the field of foreign affairs has nothing to do at all with the Constitution, and hence nothing to do with judges. In the little known case of *Penhallow v. Dane* (1795), the Court addressed a conflict between two rival claimants to the legal title of a British ship seized by an American ship. Several of the justices suggested that the power to conduct war is entrusted to the national government as a principle of sovereignty. Consequently, the power to conduct war and foreign relations does not depend upon any specific provision in the Constitution.

The suggestion lingered about until 1936, when the Court heard a case that involved a challenge to a presidential proclamation that forbade the sale of arms to countries at war in South America. President Roosevelt's proclamation was based on a Joint Resolution of Congress, which had delegated to him the power to ban arm sales. The Curtiss-Wright Corporation was charged with selling arms to Bolivia and Paraguay, countries then involved in a border skirmish that eventually claimed over 100,000 lives.

---

[25] *Our Chief Magistrate and His Powers* (New York: Columbia University Press, 1916), 139, 156–57.
[26] *Ibid.*

Writing for the Court in *U.S. v. Curtiss-Wright Export Corporation* (1936, reprinted later in the chapter), Justice Sutherland sharply distinguished between the power to conduct domestic, or internal affairs, and the power to conduct foreign affairs. "The two classes of powers are different," he wrote, "both in respect of their origin and their nature. The broad statement that the federal government can exercise no powers except those specifically enumerated in the Constitution . . . is categorically true only in respect of our internal affairs." Elsewhere, reinforcing the point, Sutherland concluded that "the powers to declare and wage war, to conclude peace, to make treaties, to maintain diplomatic relations with other sovereignties, if they had never been mentioned in the Constitution, would have vested in the federal government as necessary concomitants of nationality." In other words, following *Penhallow*, the source of the powers to conduct foreign relations was not the Constitution, but rather the status of the United States as an independent and sovereign nation-state. Although the Court did not say so, this analysis is heavily grounded in history—Sutherland appealed repeatedly to the historical development of the nation—and in a particular political theory, that of nation-state nationalism. Consider if this understanding of the power to conduct foreign affairs can be reconciled with social contract theory, whether Lockean or Republican, or with the constitutional theory of the founding we explored in earlier chapters.

By and large, the Court has declined to adopt the "attribute of sovereignty" theory proposed by Sutherland in *Curtiss-Wright*. But in one other respect—its assertion that "the president alone has the power to speak in this vast external realm"—*Curtiss-Wright* is very much the norm: Only rarely has the Supreme Court challenged a presidential exercise of power. In *The Prize Cases* (1863), for example, a majority of the Court concluded that the powers to blockade southern ports and to announce that the Southern states were in a condition of "belligerency" were entrusted to President Lincoln. The cases began in April 1861, when President Lincoln blockaded two southern ports without seeking congressional approval. (Congress was not in session at the time.) In July, Lincoln called a special session of Congress to obtain approval for the blockade and for other actions he had taken on his own. In the meantime, Union forces had seized four southern ships as prizes of war. The ships' owners filed suit, claiming that the blockade proclamation, made without congressional authorization, was unconstitutional.

Writing for the majority, Justice Grier upheld the blockade and President Lincoln's decision to find the South in a state of belligerency, concluding that "The President was bound to meet it in the shape it presented itself, without waiting for Congress to baptize it with a name. . . ." Concerning judicial responsibility, Grier wrote that "Whether the President is fulfilling his duties, as Commander-in-Chief . . . is a question to be decided by him, and this court must be governed by the decisions and acts of the Political Department of the government to which this power was entrusted."

Justiciability and the Political Questions Doctrine

Justice Grier's reference to the "political departments" should remind us of the political question doctrine. Many if not most of the issues involved in foreign affairs arguably are entrusted by the Constitution to the "political" branches. As we saw in chapter 3, the political questions doctrine reaches as far back as Chief Justice Marshall's opinion in *Marbury v. Madison* (1803), where he observed that "Questions in their nature political, or which are, by the constitution and laws, submitted to the executive, can never be made in this court. . . ." In *Baker v. Carr* (1962), the Court advanced an elaborate set of criteria to determine when a case raises a political question. In addressing the area of foreign relations, Justice Brennan admitted that "resolution of such issues frequently turn on standards that defy judicial application, or involve the exercise of a discretion demonstrably committed to the executive or legislature. . . ." Nevertheless, Brennan continued, not every case that "touches foreign relations lies beyond judicial cognizance."

In the seminal case of *Youngstown Sheet & Tube Co. v. Sawyer* (1952, reprinted in chapter 4 and in this chapter), for example, the Court indicated that a president's claim of war is not always sufficient to ward off judicial scrutiny. *Youngstown* began with a threatened strike by the United Steel Workers. Fearing the strike would cripple the production of steel for the United States' war effort in Korea, President Truman issued an executive order directing his secretary of commerce to seize the mills and to ensure their continued operation. Under the seizure plan, the head of each plant became a "manager" under the direction of the United States government, although most of the technicalities of ownership, such as assets and liabilities, remained with the firms. Truman notified Congress of his action the next day, and Congress did nothing. The owners, however, obtained an injunction against the seizure. The president won a stay of the injunction and asked the Court to grant certiorari. Just one month later the Court decided the case for the steel companies.

In his majority opinion, Justice Black wrote that Truman's action "must stem either from an Act of Congress or from the Constitution itself." No act of Congress authorized the seizure, Black concluded, thus forcing the president to justify the seizure upon the basis of his constitutional authority. The majority concluded that the order could not be supported as an exercise of his power as commander-in-chief, for the "theater of war," no matter how broad, did not extend so far as to encompass the power to take possession of private property. The majority likewise concluded that the president's aggregate of executive powers could not support the seizure, which was an exercise not of executive power but of the lawmaking power, plainly entrusted to Congress.

The majority opinion said little about the role of the judiciary in overseeing such conflicts. In his concurring opinion, Justice Frankfurter was more direct. "The Framers . . . did not make the judiciary the overseer of our government . . . ," argued Frankfurter. "This eagerness to settle—preferably forever—a specific problem on the basis of the broadest possible constitutional pronouncements may not unfairly be called one of our minor national traits. . . . The path of duty for this Court, it bears repetition, lies in the opposite direction . . . So here our first inquiry must not be into the powers of the President, but into the powers of a District Judge to issue a temporary injunction in the circumstances of this case."

In his influential concurring opinion, Justice Jackson also addressed the separation of powers issues involved in the case more forthrightly. "A judge, like an executive adviser," he wrote, "may be surprised at the poverty of really useful and unambiguous authority applicable to concrete problems of executive power as they actually present themselves." Noting that "the art of governing under our Constitution does not and cannot conform to judicial definitions," Jackson constructed a tripartite framework (see chapter 4) for considering the relationship between executive and congressional power. In the end, though, like Justice Frankfurter, Jackson acknowledged the limits of judicial power, much as he had in *Korematsu*. "I have no illusion," he concluded, "that any decision by this Court can keep power in the hands of Congress if it is not wise and timely in meeting its problems. . . . We may say that power to legislate for emergencies belongs in the hands of Congress, but only Congress itself can prevent power from slipping through its fingers."

Youngstown indicates that the political question doctrine is not an absolute bar to judicial intervention. In *Dellums v. Bush* (1990), U.S. District Judge Harold H. Greene reiterated the point, writing that "While the Constitution grants to the political

branches . . . responsibility for conducting the nation's foreign affairs, it does not follow that the judicial power is excluded from the resolution of cases merely because
they may touch upon such affairs."

When issues touch foreign affairs directly, however, the normal course is for the
Court to keep to itself. On several occasions during the Vietnam War the Court
showed a reluctance to challenge the president, finding that the plaintiffs lacked
standing to sue or that the issues involved were political questions. In *Goldwater v.
Carter* (1979, reprinted later in this chapter) the Court refused to consider a challenge
to President Carter's decision to terminate our mutual defense treaty with Taiwan,
again finding a political question. The hands-off policy was reiterated in the case of
Dames and Moore v. Regan (1981). In this case, the Court upheld an order by President Carter, reaffirmed by President Reagan, that nullified the legal attachment of Iranian assets in U.S. banks that had been seized during the hostage crisis. Writing for
the majority, Chief Justice Rehnquist noted that in this case, there was no evidence of
congressional hostility to the president's actions, unlike in *Youngstown*. Thus the action was entitled to "the widest latitude of judicial interpretation."

War and Civil Liberties

No war or crisis is long underway before there is a claim that some civil liberty, be it
free speech, the right to property, or due process, is hampering the effort and must
therefore be suspended or curtailed. In the Civil War, for example, the federal courts
saw challenges to Lincoln's suspension of the writ of habeas corpus, which cleared
the way for the military to try approximately 17,000 civilians in military courts. In
1861, Chief Justice Taney, serving as a circuit court judge in Baltimore (at the time, all
of the Supreme Court justices also "rode circuit," or presided at circuit courts), received a petition of habeas corpus from John Merryman. Merryman, a civilian, had
been arrested at his home by the military and charged with helping the confederate
cause by blowing up several bridges. Taney issued the writ and ordered General
George Cadwalader, the commander of Fort McHenry where Merryman was being
held, to appear in court to explain the detention. Instead, Cadwalader sent a letter to
Taney in which he explained that Merryman was suspected of treason. He justified
the detention on the basis of President Lincoln's suspension of habeas corpus. In response, Taney ordered a federal marshal to arrest Cadwalader and to bring him to
court—a course of action destined to fail. Finally, in frustration, Taney wrote an
opinion excoriating Lincoln, concluding that the provision in Article 1 regarding the
suspension of habeas corpus entrusted the power to Congress

> *in language too clear to be misunderstood by anyone. . . . I can see no ground
> whatever for supposing that the president, in any emergency, or in any state of
> things, can authorize the suspension of the privileges of the writ of habeas cor-
> pus . . . except in the aid of judicial power. . . . Nor can any argument be drawn
> from the nature of sovereignty, or the necessity of government, for self-defence in
> times of tumult and danger. The government of the United States is one of dele-
> gated and limited powers; it derives its existence and authority altogether from the
> constitution. . . .*

Taney's stinging rebuke of Lincoln is a manifesto for judicially enforceable limitations on presidential power, but it is worth considering Lincoln's response. Although
he released Merryman, Lincoln staunchly ignored Taney. Later, in the special session
of Congress, Lincoln defended the presidency's power of constitutional interpretation: "Now it is insisted that Congress, and not the Executive, is vested with [the power
to suspend the writ.] But the Constitution itself, is silent as to which, or who, is to

exercise the power. . . ." Elsewhere in the same speech, Lincoln offered a more direct challenge to Taney: "Are all the laws, *but one*, to go unexecuted, and the government itself go to pieces, lest that one be violated?" Lincoln did not invoke Locke or Jefferson by name, but he clearly defended the theory of prerogative power they had promoted.

In another case, a majority of the Supreme Court aligned itself with Taney's opinion in *Merryman*. In *Ex Parte Milligan* (1866, reprinted later in this chapter), the Court was faced with a request for the writ by Lamdin P. Milligan, a civilian who was sentenced to be hanged by a military court. In an opinion by Justice David Davis (who had helped to manage Lincoln's presidential campaign in 1864), the Court insisted that

> *The Constitution of the United States is a law for rulers and people, equally in war and in peace, and covers with the shield of its protection all classes of men, at all times, and under all circumstances. No doctrine, involving more pernicious consequences, was ever invented by the wit of man than that any of its provisions can be suspended during any of the great exigencies of government. . . . [T]he theory of necessity on which it is based is false; for the government, within the Constitution, has all the powers granted to it which are necessary to preserve its existence. . . .*

Notwithstanding this assertion of judicial power, consider two additional points. First, the Court's strong posture occurred in 1866, safely after the war was concluded. Second, even then the decision led to a direct confrontation with the Reconstruction Congress and ultimately led to the decision in *Ex Parte McCardle* (1868, reprinted in chapter 3). In *McCardle*, the Court upheld the constitutionality of a congressional statute that trimmed the Court's jurisdiction over habeas corpus cases. It was no secret that the statute was a slap on the Court's wrist by an angry Congress. The Court backed away from the challenge, noting that "We are not at liberty to inquire into the motives of the legislature. We can only examine into its power under the Constitution. . . ."

In the twentieth century impositions on individual liberty have been no less frequent or extensive. Many of these episodes are covered in other chapters. In chapters 11 and 12, for example, we shall consider a series of cases involving impositions on the freedoms of speech and religion justified on the basis of war. In this chapter we focus on cases that directly implicate the role of courts in mediating such conflicts, such as *Korematsu v. United States* (1944).

Korematsu began when the Japanese military invaded Pearl Harbor in 1941. A few months after the attack, a wide coalition of military, government, and civilian leaders began a campaign to intern Japanese and Japanese-Americans living on the West Coast. Ostensibly motivated by fear of espionage, the military, led by Commander General John L. Dewitt, asked the government to impose a curfew and later to intern Japanese-Americans in camps scattered throughout the West Coast. DeWitt's fears were unfounded, as he knew all too well: The FBI and the Office of Naval Intelligence had already concluded that any threat was at best minimal. Nevertheless, on 27 March 1942, President Roosevelt authorized the policy of internment.

Two years later, in the fall of 1944, Fred Korematsu—a Japanese-American citizen who did not report to the camps—was arrested by the police in Oakland, California. Fred gave a false name and a false address, but was easily found out and put in jail. With help from the American Civil Liberties Union, Fred appealed his conviction—and thus the constitutionality of internment—to the Supreme Court.

Writing for the majority, Justice Black upheld the program. Black began by noting that legal restrictions based on race are "immediately suspect" and subject "to the most rigid scrutiny." In this case, however, the legal restriction was based not on racial hostility to Japanese-Americans. If that were so, the Court said, "Our task would be simple." Instead, the policy was based on "pressing public necessity," at least as judged by the competent military authorities. "Here . . . we cannot reject as unfounded the judgment of the military authorities and of Congress."

In an impassioned dissent, Justice Murphy argued that the exclusion "Goes over 'the very brink of constitutional power' and falls into the ugly abyss of racism." Murphy conceded that "In dealing with matters relating to the prosecution and progress of war, we must accord great respect . . . to the judgments of the military authorities." Even so, Murphy continued, "it is essential that there be limits to military discretion." In another dissent, Justice Robert Jackson, chief prosecutor at the Nuremburg war trials, added that "It would be impracticable and dangerous idealism to expect or insist that each specific military command . . . will conform to conventional tests of constitutionality. The armed services must protect a society, not merely its Constitution. . . . But if we cannot confine military expedients by the Constitution, neither would I distort the Constitution to approve all that the military may deem expedient." Jackson's comments recall our discussion on pages 284–288 about how constitutional states should respond to emergencies. Jackson's suggestion that it is better not to distort the Constitution's meaning by approving all that the military deems expedient reflects a profound concern about the dangers of making the Constitution mean whatever it has to mean in an emergency.

Like President Lincoln's suspension of the writ of habeas corpus during the Civil War, *Korematsu* raises profoundly important and distressing questions about our commitment to civil liberties and whether it can be squared with the demands of war. Our study of war and civil liberties, then, much as our earlier study of foreign affairs and the growth of presidential power, is at bottom an inquiry into the limits of constitutional government and the price of constitutional ideals.

Foreign Affairs and Constitutional Crises in Comparative Perspective

The experiences of other constitutional democracies in dealing with foreign affairs and war is especially rich, in part because many of them, such as Ireland, Germany, Italy, and Canada, have constitutions that literally are the products of war and crisis. Unlike their American counterpart, most twentieth-century constitutions treat these issues at length and in detail. The practice has been to follow the counsel of Machiavelli, who wrote that "[N]o republic will ever be perfect if she has not by law provided for everything, having a remedy for every emergency and fixed rules for applying it." [27]

The influence of American constitutional ideals regarding foreign affairs has also been considerable, in no small part because Americans have "participated" in the restructuring of several constitutional states, such as Germany and Japan. Sometimes this influence extended to the inclusion of specific institutions and articles. In Germany and Japan, for example, American policymakers insisted upon some kind of a supreme court with powers of constitutional review. And in both countries, Americans insisted upon the inclusion of "renunciation-of-war" clauses. Article 9 of the Japanese Constitution thus pledges that "Aspiring sincerely to an international peace based on justice and order, the Japanese people forever renounce war as a sovereign right of the nation and the threat or use of force as a means of settling international disputes."

---

[27] Niccolo Machiavelli, *Discourses*, trans. and ed. by Bernard Crick (Harmondsworth, Eng.: Penguin Books, 1970), ch. 34.

At a general level, the influence of American constitutionalism has more to do with general norms and principles than with specific statements of policy or with the design of institutions. In the field of foreign affairs, the Founders' insistence upon principles of deliberation and accountability has been especially influential. A comparative analysis of foreign affairs and crises shows considerable variation in how different countries have attempted to realize these common ideals.

The Founders were committed to the principle that the powers of foreign affairs must be subject to public accountability. Sharing powers and separating institutions were the means to accomplish that end. There is room for doubt about whether that vision has been achieved in the United States. The unchecked growth of executive power, coupled with a servile Congress and a judiciary unwilling to mediate conflict or to impose substantive limits on the president's powers, raises questions about whether there are any effective, constitutionally derived, limits on the executive's power to conduct foreign relations and to make war.

A comparative perspective, however, suggests that other constitutional democracies have succeeded, at least in part, on making good on the principle of democratic accountability. As one observer notes, "The techniques of accountability surely do vary—some techniques are embodied in written constitutions and other formal instruments, while others are unwritten or informal . . . ; some do and some do not include control through constitutional courts or other judicial bodies."[28] The experiences of Japan and Germany, for example, indicate that the principle of shared legislative and executive decision making can be made to work effectively. Moreover, and perhaps in starkest contrast to American constitutional history, the experiences of Canada and Germany indicate that there may be a prominent role for constitutional courts to play in the area of foreign relations. If one of the purposes of comparative analysis is to find out what works, then Americans should pay especial attention to how other countries have tried to realize the ideals of deliberative decision making and public accountability.

Foreign Affairs and the German Basic Law

Like Article 9 of the Japanese Constitution, the Basic Law establishes a policy against war as a constitutional norm. Designed to facilitate Germany's peaceful inclusion in a stable international order, Article 26 provides that "Acts tending to and undertaken with the intent to disturb the peaceful relations between nations, especially to prepare for aggressive war, shall be unconstitutional." Other provisions explicitly call for the German state to participate in international arbitration and systems of mutual collective security.

The Basic Law also seeks to hold the powers of foreign affairs to a principle of accountability by simultaneously sharing and separating power. Hence, Article 32 gives to the federation the power to conduct foreign relations, although it conditions it with requirements to protect the *Länder* that far exceed any of the protections that American states receive. Article 59 gives to the president of the Republic the power to represent the state in international relations, a power that includes the authority to conclude treaties, albeit in conjunction with various state authorities. In deliberate contrast to the Weimar Republic (where the president could dismiss the chancellor and authorize the use of expansive emergency powers), however, the great burden

---

[28] Lori Fisler Damrosch, *Constitutional Control Over War Powers: A Common Core of Accountability in Democratic Societies?* 50 U. Miami Law Review 181, 183 (1995). Our analysis here has been heavily influenced by Professor Damrosch's pioneering article.

of executive power falls to the prime minister, or chancellor, nominated by the president but chosen by the Bundestag. Thus the German system is best understood as a parliamentary, or chancellor, democracy, in contrast to the presidentialism of the United States.

Article 73(1) further separates power by providing that the Federation has exclusive power to legislate regarding foreign affairs. Article 73(4) gives the Federation authority over treaties on commerce and navigation, and 73(10) gives the Federation power over the protection of the democratic order and the existence and security of the Federation.

In general, then, the Basic Law embodies the fundamental constitutional principle of separation of powers and embraces the principle of democratic accountability. In contrast to the United States, however, these principles are given force by a judiciary that does not hesitate to apply them. As we saw, the United States Supreme Court uses a variety of procedural devices and doctrines to avoid disputes, the most prominent of which is the political questions doctrine. In Germany, the doctrine has considerably less force, in part because the creators of the Federal Constitutional Court gave it expansive and far-reaching authority to resolve constitutional conflicts. As one of the authors of this book has observed,

> *The Court's main task, especially with regard to direct conflicts between levels and branches of government and to separation of powers conflicts, is to clarify constitutional meaning . . . and to lay down clear rules. . . . Indeed, the Constitutional Court was established precisely to resolve disputes that the American Supreme Court would dismiss as 'political.'*[29]

With no political question doctrine to hem it in, the Constitutional Court has developed an extensive body of case law in the area of foreign affairs. In a series of cases involving the installation of American intermediate range nuclear missiles, the Court addressed issues of critical significance to German foreign relations. In the *Missile Decision I* case, the Court heard a claim that the decision to deploy nuclear missiles on German territory violated Article 2(2) of the Basic Law, which guarantees the right to life. Although the Court finally dismissed the complaint because "it has not been shown that there can be a possible injury to [the complainant's] lives and health," the decision was a function of the Court's finding that the threat was from the action of foreign governments and not, as might be expected in the United States, on grounds that the matter was "political" and therefore out of bounds.[30]

In recent years a prominent source of political conflict in Germany has concerned the issue of whether the Basic Law permits units of the armed forces to participate in United Nations' sanctioned peacekeeping efforts, such as those in Somalia, Kuwait, and Bosnia. Article 24(2) of the Basic Law provides that "For the maintenance of peace, the Federation may enter a system of mutual collective security." Article 87(a)(2), however, states that "Apart from defence, the Armed Forces may only be used to the extent explicitly permitted by this Basic Law." The German government's decision to participate in NATO units stationed in Bosnia and Herzegovina under United Nations' authority led some members of the opposition party to file a complaint in the Federal Constitutional Court. Prior administrations had resisted participation in similar cases, claiming that it would be illegal for the state to permit active

---

[29] Donald P. Kommers, *The Constitutional Jurisprudence of the Federal Republic of Germany*, 2d ed. (Durham, N.C.: Duke University Press, 1997), 163.

[30] For a contrast, see *Greenham Women Against Cruise Missiles v. Reagan*, 755 F.2d 34 (2d Cir. 1985), where the Court dismissed a similar challenge to President Reagan's policy on cruise missiles as a political question.

participation by military units outside of NATO, presumably because such efforts would not be primarily "defensive." In a unanimous decision, the Court found that German participation in United Nations' peacekeeping operations would not necessarily violate Article 24(2). The Court found that the Article authorizes all those tasks that normally accompany membership in such collective security arrangements.

The complainants also argued that German participation had established new international obligations, which under Article 59(2) require Parliament's consent. The Court ruled, over sharp dissents (the Court split four to four), that the Article was not violated because the action did not yet amount to a change in an old, or assumption of a new, international obligation; hence, the federal government did not need to secure parliamentary approval before committing German troops to a United Nations mandate. The Court did conclude, though, that unless the Parliament had already declared a "state of defence," Parliamentary approval would be required for every deployment of troops in support of security council resolutions.

The Court's interpretation of Article 59 had the effect of insisting upon a principle of legislative decision making and accountability, even as it upheld the executive decision in question. One commentator thus concludes that "By presenting a Solomonic judgment where both sides could claim a partial victory and did not have to lose face, the Court succeeded very well in fulfilling the integrational functions of constitutional adjudication."[31] Moreover, the Court's careful and measured opinion underscores the judgment in the *Rudolph Hess* case (1980) which stressed the wide degree of discretion entrusted to the government:

> *The breadth of this discretion in foreign affairs has its basis in the nature of foreign relations. . . . Such events are not governed solely by the will of the federation, but rather are dependent on many circumstances over which it has little control. . . . The Constitution confers considerable discretion on foreign affairs agencies in assessing the practicality and feasibility of certain policies or actions.*[32]

Another highly politicized area in foreign affairs has concerned Germany's participation in the European Union. After Germany signed the Maastricht Treaty on European Union in 1992, the Constitutional Court was asked to decide if the Treaty violated Article 20 of the Basic Law, which provides that the Republic is a democratic and social federal state, in which all public authority emanates from the people. Also at issue was Article 38(1), which provides that members of the German Bundestag must be elected in general, direct, free, and secret elections. The complainants argued that under Maastricht, Germany had in effect transferred part of its sovereignty to the Union, thus potentially limiting the rights of German citizens. The Court concluded that the treaty did not violate the Basic Law, but in a complicated judgment it also insisted that future delegations of sovereign power to the Union would require a "strengthening of the democratic basis of the EU itself."[33]

The German Court's willingness to undertake a substantive review of a treaty's conformity with the Basic Law stands in sharp contrast to the American Supreme Court's decision in *Missouri v. Holland* (1920, reprinted later in the chapter). The Japanese experience follows Holmes's lead. In the important *Sunakawa* case (1959), the Japa-

---

[31] Markus Zockler, *Germany in Collective Security Systems—Anything Goes?*, 6 European Journal of International Law 274, 286 (1995).

[32] Kommers, *supra* note 29, at 154.

[33] For an insightful analysis of the decision, see Manfred H. Wiegandt, *Germany's International Integration: The Rulings of the Federal Constitutional Court on the Maastricht Treaty and the Out-of-Area Deployment of German Troops*, 10 American University Journal of International Law and Policy, 889, 896 (1995).

nese Court, in addressing the possibility that it might review a security treaty, concluded that

> *the security treaty possesses a highly political nature of great importance to the very existence of our country; that a decision as to the unconstitutionality of such treaty, as a matter of principle, does not involve a decision of the judicial courts; and that, accordingly, the constitutional review of such a treaty, unless it is recognized as being "clearly and obviously unconstitutional or invalid," lies outside the scope of constitutional review.*[34]

The absence of judicial review in the United States and Japan does not, of course, mean that the treaty-making process is necessarily without constitutional limits. We have stressed repeatedly, and especially in this chapter, that constitutional review is not coextensive with judicial review. In Japan, for example, one commentator has argued that the absence of judicial review "is not to say that constitutional control mechanisms are absent . . . , but rather that they have taken a largely nonjudicial form. . . . The real constitutional debate occurs in the legislature, in newspapers, and in gathering places."[35] As you read the cases in this chapter, consider whether judicial review would contribute to or impede the development of public discussions of the constitutional dimensions of foreign affairs.

Accountability and the Political Questions Doctrine in Canada

The active involvement of the German Constitutional Court in foreign affairs reflects a somewhat different understanding of the doctrine of separation of powers, as well as a more expansive role for judicial review, than does American jurisprudence. The Canadian approach comes closer to the German experience. In one respect, however, Canada differs from both the German and American traditions. The Basic Law and the American Constitution both insist upon some form of shared legislative and executive decision making. The power to conduct foreign relations in Canada, in contrast, falls within the prerogative power assigned to the executive alone. For example, at least as a matter of constitutional necessity, the Parliament in Canada plays no formal role in the making or conclusion of treaties. Nevertheless, the principle of democratic accountability is alive and well, in part because in practice most Canadian governments have sought the approval of Parliament before concluding treaties.

Judicial Review and the Political Questions Doctrine in Canada

In the leading case of *Operation Dismantle v. The Queen* (1985), the Canadian Supreme Court explicitly refused to embrace the political questions doctrine. *Operation Dismantle* involved efforts by groups of Canadian citizens to challenge a decision by the government to permit testing of American cruise missiles in Canada. The complaint charged that the policy violated Section 7 of the Charter, which guarantees the right to life and security of the person. The Court dismissed the case, holding that the plaintiffs had failed to establish a link between the tests and an increased threat of nuclear war. Nevertheless, Chief Justice Dickson concluded that "I have no doubt that disputes of a political or foreign policy nature may be properly cognizable by the courts."

---

[34] For a general discussion, see John M. Maki, *Court and Constitution in Japan* (Seattle: University of Washington Press, 1964), 348.

[35] See Damrosch, *supra* note 28, at 195.

In a separate and elaborate opinion, Justice Wilson rejected a lower court's finding that the case was nonjusticiable because such issues "involve moral and political considerations." Justice Wilson responded that "I think we should focus our attention on whether the courts *should* or *must* rather than on whether they *can* deal with such matters."[36] Contrast Justice Wilson's insistence upon the normative and moral imperative of judicial review with the studied pragmatism of Justice Brennan's opinion in *Baker v. Carr* (1962).

In Germany and in Canada, then, constitutional courts have been much more willing than have American courts to participate in disputes over foreign affairs. In this sense, a comparative perspective suggests that there may be institutional and structural ways to give force to principles of deliberative and shared decision making, ways that Americans have been reluctant so far to consider. Among those benefits may be an improved public understanding of foreign policy and its constitutional dimensions, which has added a degree of legitimation upon the conduct of various policies.[37] These kinds of benefits help to give everyday force to basic but sometimes abstract issues of constitutional theory. They also demonstrate, once again, that issues of theory are interlaced with thorny questions about the nature and limits of judicial power.

Selected Bibliography

Adler, David Gray, ed. and Larry N. George. *The Constitution and the Conduct of American Foreign Policy*. Lawrence: University Press of Kansas, 1996.

Corwin, Edward S. *Total War and the Constitution*. New York: Alfred A. Knopf, 1947.

Damrosch, Lori Fisler. *Constitutional Control Over War Powers: A Common Core of Accountability in Democratic Societies?* 50 U. Miami. Law Review 181 (1995).

Ely, John Hart. *War and Responsibility: Constitutional Lessons of Vietnam and Its Aftermath*. Princeton, N.J.: Princeton University Press, 1993.

Fairman, Charles. *The Law of Martial Rule*, 2d ed. Chicago: University of Chicago Press, 1943.

Finn, John E. *Constitutions in Crisis: Political Violence and the Rule of Law*. New York: Oxford University Press, 1991.

Fisher, Louis. *Presidential War Power*. Lawrence: University Press of Kansas, 1995.

Franck, Thomas, M. *Political Questions/Judicial Answers: Does the Rule of Law Apply to Foreign Affairs?* Princeton, N.J.: Princeton University Press, 1992.

Franklin, Daniel P. *Extraordinary Measures: The Exercise of Prerogative Powers in the United States*. Pittsburgh: University of Pittsburgh Press, 1991.

Friedrich, Carl J. *Constitutional Government and Democracy*. Waltham, Mass.: Blaisdell, 1968.

———. *Constitutional Reason of State: The Survival of the Constitutional Order*. Providence, R.I.: Brown University Press, 1957.

Glennon, Michael J. *Constitutional Diplomacy*. Princeton, N.J.: Princeton University Press, 1990.

———. *Too Far Apart: Repeal the War Powers Resolution,* 50 U. Miami Law Review 17 (1995).

Henkin, Louis. *Constitutionalism, Democracy, and Foreign Affairs*. New York: Columbia University Press, 1990.

———. *Foreign Affairs and the Constitution*. New York: W. W. Norton & Company, 1975.

Irons, Peter. *Justice at War*. New York: Oxford University Press, 1983.

Koh, Harold Hongju. *The National Security Constitution: Sharing Power After the Iran-Contra Affair*. New Haven: Yale University Press, 1990.

Lofgren, Charles A. *Government From Reflection and Choice: Constitutional Essays on War, Foreign Relations, and Federalism*. New York: Oxford University Press, 1986.

Mann, Thomas, E. ed. *A Question of Balance: The President, Congress, and Foreign Policy*. Washington, D.C.: The Brookings Institution, 1990.

Mansfield, Harvey C. Jr. *Taming the Prince: The Ambivalence of Modern Executive Power*. Cambridge: Harvard University Press, 1989.

---

[36] Contrast this approach with *Greenham Women Against Cruise Missiles v. Reagan*, 591 F.Supp. 1332 (1984).

[37] Thomas M. Franck, *Political Questions/Judicial Answers* (Princeton: Princeton University Press, 1992), 107–25. See also Damrosch, *supra* note 28, at 196ff.

May, Christopher. *In the Name of War: Judicial Review and the War Powers Since 1918*. Cambridge: Harvard University Press, 1989.

Neustadt, Richard E. *Presidential Power: The Politics of Leadership*, rev. ed. New York: John Wiley, 1976.

Nishimoto, Richard S. *Inside an American Concentration Camp: Japanese American Resistance at Poston, Arizona* with an introduction by Lane Ryo Hirabayashi. Tucson: University of Arizona Press, 1995.

Pyle, Christopher H. and Richard M. Pious, eds. *The President, Congress, and the Constitution*. New York: The Free Press, 1984.

Rossiter, Clinton. *Constitutional Dictatorship*. Princeton, N.J.: Princeton University Press, 1948.

———. *The Supreme Court and the Commander in Chief*

with Richard P. Longaker. Ithaca, N.Y.: Cornell University Press, 1976.

Schlesinger, Arthur M. Jr. *The Imperial Presidency*. New York: Popular Library, 1973.

Silverstein, Gordon. *Imbalance of Power: Constitutional Interpretation and the Making of American Foreign Policy*. New York: Oxford University Press, 1997.

Smith, Page. *Democracy on Trial: The Japanese-American Evacuation and Relocation in World War II*. New York: Simon & Schuster, 1995.

Vile, M.J.C. *Constitutionalism and the Separation of Powers*. London: Oxford University Press, 1967.

Wormuth, Francis. *The Royal Prerogative 1603–1699*. Ithaca, N.Y.: Cornell University Press, 1939.

State of Missouri v. Holland

252 U.S. 416, 40 S. Ct. 382, 64 L. Ed. 641 (1920)

In 1913, Congress enacted a law that placed limits on the number of certain migratory birds that could be killed by hunters. A federal district court found the act unconstitutional later that year, and the government did not appeal the decision. However, before the district court opinion was announced, the Senate passed a resolution asking President Wilson to negotiate a treaty with Canada about these hunting limits to firm the constitutional ground of the proposal. In 1916, a treaty went into effect enforcing such limits. Congress then passed new legislation to enforce the new treaty. Many states, however, saw this as an infringement on state sovereignty, and refused to enforce the new act. In 1919, the attorney general of Missouri, one of the nonenforcing states, was caught poaching. He challenged the constitutionality of the new act in district court. The district court upheld the act, and the Supreme Court granted certiorari. Opinion of the Court: *Holmes*, McKenna, Day, White, McReynolds, Brandeis, Clarke. Dissenting opinion: *VanDevanter*, Pitney.

Mr. Justice HOLMES delivered the opinion of the Court.

. . . [T]he question raised is the general one whether the treaty and statute are void as an interference with the rights reserved to the States.

To answer this question it is not enough to refer to the Tenth Amendment, reserving the powers not delegated to the United States, because by Article 2, Section 2, the power to make treaties is delegated expressly, and by Article 6 treaties made under the authority of the United States, along with the Constitution and laws of the United States made in pursuance thereof, are declared the supreme law of the land. If the treaty is valid there can be no dispute about the validity of the statute under Article 1, Section 8, as a necessary and proper means to execute the powers of the Government. The language of the Constitution as to the supremacy of treaties being general, the question before us is narrowed to an inquiry into the ground upon which the present supposed exception is placed.

It is said that a treaty cannot be valid if it infringes the Constitution, that there are limits, therefore, to the treaty-making power, and that one such limit is that what an act of Congress could not do unaided, in derogation of the powers reserved to the States, a treaty cannot do. An earlier act of Congress that attempted by itself and not in pursuance of a treaty to regulate the killing of migratory birds within the States had been held bad in the District Court. Those decisions were supported by arguments that migratory birds were owned by the States in their sovereign capacity for the benefit of their people, and this control was one that Congress had no power to displace. The same argument is supposed to apply now with equal force.

Whether the two cases cited were decided rightly or not they cannot be accepted as a test of the treaty power. Acts of Congress are the supreme law of the land only when made in pursuance of the Constitution, while treaties are declared to be so when made under the authority of the United States. It is open to question whether the authority of the United States means more than the formal acts prescribed to make the convention. We do not mean to imply that there are no qualifications to the treaty-making power; but they must be ascertained in a different way. It is obvious that there may be matters of the sharpest exigency for the national well being that an act of Congress could not

Comparative Note 7.1

The Constitution of the United States is explicit in article 1, section 10, clauses 1 and 3, on the incapacity of a state thereof to enter into compacts with foreign states; the Canadian Constitution is silent on whether a province may reach to treat with a foreign government. No doubt, a province, as a juridical person, may deal across provincial or international boundaries with persons or private agencies, and as well with subordinate units of foreign states. . . . A province that purported to treat on its own in this way, albeit on matters within its domestic competence, could not claim international validity for any ensuing agreement, nor would implementing legislation be valid when enacted in pursuance of a non-existing power to accept international commitments.

SOURCE: Neil Finklestein, *Laskin's Canadian Constitutional Law*. 5th ed., vol. 1 (Toronto: Carswell Press, 1986), 413.

deal with but that a treaty followed by such an act could, and it is not lightly to be assumed that, in matters requiring national action, "a power which must belong to and somewhere reside in every civilized government" is not to be found. What was said in that case with regard to the powers of the States applies with equal force to the powers of the nation in cases where the States individually are incompetent to act.

We are not yet discussing the particular case before us but only are considering the validity of the test proposed. With regard to that we may add that when we are dealing with words that also are a constituent act, like the Constitution of the United States, we must realize that they have called into life a being the development of which could not have been foreseen completely by the most gifted of its begetters. It was enough for them to realize or to hope that they had created an organism; it has taken a century and has cost their successors much sweat and blood to prove that they created a nation. The case before us must be considered in the light of our whole experience and not merely in that of what was said a hundred years ago. The treaty in question does not contravene any prohibitory words to be found in the Constitution. The only question is whether it is forbidden by some invisible radiation from the general terms of the Tenth Amendment. We must consider what this country has become in deciding what that amendment has reserved.

The State as we have intimated founds its claim of exclusive authority upon an assertion of title to migratory birds, an assertion that is embodied in statute. . . . The whole foundation of the State's rights is the presence within their jurisdiction of birds that yesterday had not arrived, tomorrow may be in another State and in a week a thousand miles away. If we are to be accurate we cannot put the case of the State upon higher ground than that the treaty deals with creatures that for the moment are within the state borders, that it must be carried out by officers of the United States within the same territory, and that but for the treaty the State would be free to regulate this subject itself.

As most of the laws of the United States are carried out within the States, and as many of them deal with matters which in the silence of such laws the States might regulate, such general grounds are not enough to support Missouri's claim. Valid treaties of course "are as binding within the territorial limits of the States as they are elsewhere throughout the dominion of the United States." No doubt the great body of private relations usually fall within the control of the State, but a treaty may override its power.

Here a national interest of very nearly the first magnitude is involved. It can be protected only by national action in concert with that of another power. The subject matter is only transitorily within the State and has no permanent habitat therein. But for the treaty and the statute there soon might be no birds for any powers to deal with. We see nothing in the Constitution that compels the Government to sit by while a food supply is cut off and the protectors of our forests and our crops are destroyed. It is not sufficient to rely upon the States. The reliance is vain, and were it otherwise, the question is whether the United States is forbidden to act. We are of opinion that the treaty and statute must be upheld.

Decree affirmed.

Notes/Queries/Readings

1. Holmes wrote that there are limits on the treaty-making power of the national government, "but they must be ascertained in a different way." Does he say what that way is? What limits does he identify upon the treaty-making power? Are there other limits? Consider the Court's opinion in *Reid v. Covert*, 354 U.S. 1 (1957), in which the Court ruled that an exercise of the treaty-making power could

Comparative Note 7.2

[The German-Vatican Concordat of 1933 provided for the religious education of Catholic children in Germany. After the Second World War, however, the state (*Land*) of Lower Saxony enacted an education statute that violated the treaty. The issue before the Federal Constitutional Court, as in *Missouri v. Holland*, was whether the state law takes precedence over a national treaty.]

[The] continued validity of the Concordat means that its terms still bind the signatories. Under the Basic Law, the Federal Republic of Germany—the Federation and [states] considered as a whole—is bound as a partner to the treaty. But, under the constitutional law of the Federal Republic, only the [states] can fulfill obligations arising from the educational provisions of this agreement. The Federation has no legislative authority over educational affairs. . . . Article 123 (2) states . . . that only those provisions of the Concordat remain in force insofar as they were valid when the Basic Law became effective, although they originate in a treaty not concluded by the [states], now exclusively competent to regulate the matter in dispute.

• • •

The supposition that Art. 123 (2) was intended to constitutionally bind [state] legislatures to treaty law, in addition to directing the continued validity of the law itself, would contradict the general relationship that the Basic Law establishes between the Federation and [the states].

Constitutionally binding [the states] to the educational provisions of the Concordat would flatly contradict their authority freely to make educational law within the limits of the Constitution.

The Constitutional principle of *Bundestreue* (federal loyalty) belongs among the constitutional standards imminent in the Basic Law. . . . *Bundestreue* demands that each part take into consideration situations of interest and tension which arise in the Federation. Thus one must conclude that the [state's] obligation of loyalty toward the Federation is to be taken particularly seriously in foreign relations, where the Federation alone is competent.

Nonetheless, no obligation of [states] to the Federation to observe the Concordat's educational provisions can be derived from the principle of *Bundestreue*:

The Basic Law's choice constitutionally to limit [states] in the denominational orientation of education only by Article 7 excludes any further obligation of the [states] toward the Federation in this area.

Source: *Concordat Case* (1957) in Walter F. Murphy and Joseph Tanenhaus, *Comparative Constitutional Law*, 226–29.

---

not deprive a citizen of constitutional liberties guaranteed by the Bill of Rights.

2. Does *Missouri v. Holland* leave the states without any substantial protection against national treaties? Some commentators have feared that such an expansive view of the power permits the national government to use its power over foreign affairs to dramatically increase its influence over the states in domestic affairs. Such concerns, for example, lay behind Senator John Bricker's 1954 proposal for a constitutional amendment requiring Congress to pass legislation before any treaty could become a law in the United States. Bricker's amendment failed, but only by one vote, and hardly a session of Congress passes without the introduction of a similar amendment. But consider: Would Bricker's proposal have offered any comfort to the states?

3. What role—if any—should the states play in the making of foreign policy? As we saw in chapter 5, the Constitution also separates power vertically, or between the national and state governments. In the field of foreign affairs, however, federalism has been less an imperative. Madison set forth the reason in *Federalist* 42, writing that "If we are to be a nation in any respect, it clearly ought to be in respect to other nations." Article 1, Section 9, thus provides that "No State shall enter into any Treaty, Alliance, or Confederation. . . ." And "No State shall, without the Consent of Congress, . . . enter into any Agreement or Compact . . . with a foreign power, or engage in War, unless actually invaded, or in such imminent Danger as will not admit of delay." Finally, the supremacy clause of Article 6 provides strong support for the preeminence of national authority.

The Supreme Court recently reaffirmed the preeminence of national authority in *Perpich v. Department of Defense* (1990). In this case the Court rejected a challenge by a state governor to a congressional policy that authorized the training of national guard troops (ostensibly under state control) outside of the United States. In his opinion for the Court, Justice Stevens observed that "several constitutional provisions commit matters of foreign policy and military affairs to the exclusive control of the National Government."

Nevertheless, there remain important ways in which the conduct of foreign affairs is influenced by federalism. On a theoretical level, some justices have suggested that the Constitution (in particular the Tenth Amendment) must provide some rudimentary limitations on national power, so that the national government could not, through a treaty, for example, abolish a state militia or alter the republican character of a state. On a practical level, the states may influence the conduct of foreign relations in innumerable ways, from passing "resolutions" concerning various matters of interest to them, to enforcing (or not) federal immigration or customs policies. (Henkin, 245–46).

4. Justice Holmes's reference to the "living constitution" is among the most quoted of Supreme Court opinions. For a discussion of its meaning, see William H. Rehnquist, *The Notion of a Living Constitution*, 54 Texas Law Review 693 (1976).

5. Article 59(2) of the German Basic Law provides that "Treaties which regulate the political relations of the federation or are concerned with matters within the legislative competence of the federation require the consent . . . of the organs competent for the enactment of federal law in the form of federal statutes." In the *Petersberg Agreement Case* (1952) certain members of the West German parliament challenged an executive agreement between the chancellor and the Allied powers, claiming that the agreement was a treaty within the meaning of Article 59 and thus required parliamentary approval. In its decision, the Federal Constitutional Court defined a treaty as an agreement concluded with a foreign state or an equally important international agency—a status the Allied powers did not attain. The *Commercial Treaty Case* (1952) concerned the meaning of the term "political relations" in Article 59.

Overall, the German Parliament has an important role to play—as does the Federal Constitutional Court—in the construction of German foreign affairs. On the other hand, Article 32(3) qualifies the power of the federal government to conduct foreign affairs by permitting the individual *Länder* to conclude treaties with foreign states in those areas where they have exclusive legislative competence, albeit subject to the approval of the national government. In the *Concordat Case* (1957, Comparative Note 7.2), the Federal Constitutional Court intimated that the federal power to make treaties would be limited by the extent of those reserved powers.

6. For additional readings on this case, see Charles A. Lofrgen, "*Missouri v. Holland* in Historical Perspective," in Phillip B. Kurland. ed., *1975 Supreme Court Review* (Chicago: University of Chicago Press, 1975); Clement E. Vose, "State Against Nation: The Conservation Case of *Missouri v. Holland*," Prologue (Winter 1984), 233.

Goldwater v. Carter

444 U.S. 996, 100 S. Ct. 533, 62 L. Ed. 2d 428 (1979)

In 1979, President Carter terminated a defense treaty with Taiwan without notifying the Senate. Senator Barry Goldwater and several other Senators sued, challenging the constitutionality of the action. The Court granted certiorari, but remanded the case back to the district court with orders to dismiss the complaint without hearing oral arguments. Concurring opinion: *Rehnquist*, Burger, Stewart, Stevens. Concurring in the result: *Marshall*. Concurring in the judgment: *Powell*. Dissenting in part: *Blackmun*, White. Dissenting opinion: *Brennan*.

Mr. Justice POWELL, concurring.

Although I agree with the result reached by the Court, I would dismiss the complaint as not ripe for judicial review.

This Court has recognized that an issue should not be decided if it is not ripe for judicial review. Prudential considerations persuade me that a dispute between Congress and the President is not ready for judicial review unless and until each branch has taken action asserting its constitutional authority. Differences between the President and the Congress are commonplace under our system. The differences should, and almost invariably do, turn on political rather than legal considerations. The Judicial Branch should not decide issues affecting the allocation of power between the President and Congress until the political branches reach a constitutional impasse. Otherwise, we would encourage small groups or even individual Members of Congress to seek judicial resolution of issues before the normal political process has the opportunity to resolve the conflict.

In this case, a few Members of Congress claim that the President's action in terminating the treaty with Taiwan has deprived them of their constitutional role with respect to a change in the supreme law of the land. Congress has taken no official action. In the present posture of this case, we do not know whether there ever will be an actual confrontation between the Legislative and Executive Branches. Although the Senate has considered a resolution declaring that Senate approval is necessary for the termination of any mutual defense treaty, no final vote has been taken on the resolution. Moreover, it is unclear whether the resolution would have retroactive effect. It cannot be said that either the Senate or the House has rejected the President's claim. If the Congress chooses not to confront the President, it is not our task to do so. I therefore concur in the dismissal of this case.

Mr. Justice Rehnquist suggests, however, that the issue presented by this case is a nonjusticiable political question which can never be considered by this Court. I cannot agree. In my view, reliance upon the political-question doctrine is inconsistent with our precedents. As set forth in the seminal case of *Baker v. Carr* (1962), the doctrine incorporates three inquiries: (i) Does the issue involve resolution of questions committed by the text of the Constitution to a coordinate branch of Government? (ii) Would resolution of the question demand that a Court move beyond areas of judicial expertise? (iii) Do prudential considerations counsel against judicial intervention? In my opinion the answer to each of these inquiries would require us to decide this case if it were ready for review.

In my view, the suggestion that this case presents a political question is incompatible with this Court's willingness on previous occasions to decide whether one branch of our Government has impinged upon the power of another. Under the criteria enunciated in *Baker v. Carr*, we have the responsibility to decide whether both the Executive and Legislative Branches have constitutional roles to play in termination of a treaty. If the Congress, by appropriate formal action, had challenged the President's authority to terminate the treaty with Taiwan, the resulting uncertainty could have serious consequences for our country. In that situation, it would be the duty of this Court to resolve the issue.

Mr. Justice REHNQUIST, with whom The Chief Justice, Mr. Justice STEWART, and Mr. Justice STEVENS join, concurring in the judgment.

I am of the view that the basic question presented by the petitioners in this case is "political" and therefore nonjus-

---

Comparative Note   7.3

[Anti-nuclear groups challenged the decision of Canada's Federal Cabinet to permit the testing of cruise missiles by the United States on Canadian territory. They alleged that the government's decision violated rights to life and security of persons protected by s. 7 of the Charter of Rights and Freedoms. Chief Justice Dickson delivered the opinion of the Court.]

In my opinion, if the appellants are to be entitled to proceed to trial, their Statement of Claim must disclose facts, which, if taken as true, would show that the action of the Canadian Government could cause an infringement of their rights under s. 7 of the Charter. I have concluded that the causal link between the actions of the Canadian government, and the alleged violation of appellants' rights under the Charter is simply too uncertain, speculative and hypothetical to sustain a cause of action. Thus, although the decisions of the Federal Cabinet are reviewable by the courts under the Charter and the government bears a general duty to act in accordance with the Charter's dictates, no duty is imposed on the Canadian Government by s. 7 of the Charter to refrain from permitting the testing of the cruise missile.

• • •

The approach which I have taken is not based on the concept of justiciability. I agree in substance with Madame Justice Wilson's discussion of justiciability and her conclusion that the doctrine is founded upon a concern with the appropriate role of the Courts as the forum for the resolution of different types of disputes. I have no doubt that disputes of a political or foreign policy nature may be properly cognizable by the Courts. My concerns in the present case focus on the impossibility of the Court finding, on the basis of evidence, the connection, alleged by the appellants, between the duty of the government to act in accordance with the *Charter of Rights and Freedoms* and the violation of their rights under s. 7. As stated above, I do not believe the alleged violation—namely, the increased threat of nuclear war—could ever be sufficiently linked as a factual matter to the acknowledged duty of the government to respect s. 7 of the Charter.

Source: *Operation Dismantle v. The Queen.* In the Supreme Court of Canada (1985) 18 D.L.R. (4th) 481, 485, 494.

ticiable because it involves the authority of the President in the conduct of our country's foreign relations and the extent to which the Senate or the Congress is authorized to negate the action of the President.

Here, while the Constitution is express as to the manner in which the Senate shall participate in the ratification of a treaty, it is silent as to that body's participation in the abrogation of a treaty.

I think that the justifications for concluding that the question here is political in nature are even more compelling than in *Coleman* because it involves foreign relations—specifically a treaty commitment to use military force in the defense of a foreign government if attacked.

The present case differs in several important respects from *Youngstown Sheet & Tube Co. v. Sawyer* (1952), cited by petitioners as authority both for reaching the merits of this dispute and for reversing the Court of Appeals. In *Youngstown*, private litigants brought a suit contesting the President's authority under his war powers to seize the Nation's steel industry, an action of profound and demonstrable domestic impact. Here, by contrast, we are asked to settle a dispute between coequal branches of our Government, each of which has resources available to protect and assert its interests, resources not available to private litigants outside the judicial forum. Moreover, as in *Curtiss-Wright*, the effect of this action, as far as we can tell, is "entirely external to the United States, and [falls] within the category of foreign affairs." Finally, as already noted, the situation presented here is closely akin to that presented in *Coleman*, where the Constitution spoke only to the procedure for ratification of an amendment, not to its rejection.

Mr. Justice BRENNAN, dissenting.

I respectfully dissent from the order directing the District Court to dismiss this case, and would affirm the judgment of the Court of Appeals insofar as it rests upon the President's well-established authority to recognize, and withdraw recognition from, foreign governments. In stating that this case presents a nonjusticiable "political question," Mr. Justice Rehnquist, in my view, profoundly misapprehends the political-question principle as it applies to matters of foreign relations. Properly understood, the political-question doctrine restrains Courts from reviewing an exercise of foreign policy judgment by the coordinate political branch to which authority to make that judgment has been "constitutional[ly] commit[ted]." But the doctrine

does not pertain when a Court is faced with the antecedent question whether a particular branch has been constitutionally designated as the repository of political decisionmaking power. The issue of decisionmaking authority must be resolved as a matter of constitutional law, not political discretion; accordingly, it falls within the competence of the Courts.

The constitutional question raised here is prudently answered in narrow terms. Abrogation of the defense treaty with Taiwan was a necessary incident to Executive recognition of the Peking Government, because the defense treaty was predicated upon the now-abandoned view that the Taiwan Government was the only legitimate political authority in China. Our cases firmly establish that the Constitution commits to the President alone the power to recognize, and withdraw recognition from, foreign regimes. That mandate being clear, our judicial inquiry into the treaty rupture can go no further.

Notes/Queries/Readings

1. As Justice Brennan's opinion makes clear, discussions about the meaning and application of the political question doctrine necessarily raise questions about the proper extent of judicial power. How does Justice Brennan's understanding of that relationship differ from the other opinions?

2. Justice Powell denied that the issue in this case presented a political question. Was he correct in claiming that "Interpretation of the Constitution does not imply lack of respect for a coordinate branch"?

3. In Germany and some other civil law countries with constitutional courts, the political questions doctrine is not a barrier to judicial involvement—any case, properly initiated by the proper party, may come before the Constitutional Court. Consequently, the Court may not avoid a judgment on the merits, as did the United States Supreme Court in *Goldwater*. See the *Inter-German Basic Treaty Case* (1973). On the other hand, the duty to decide does not necessarily mean that the Court will not defer to the political branches on the merits, as the Court made clear in the *Rudolf Hess Case* (1980). Both cases are reprinted in D. C. Umbach, ed., *Decisions of the Bundesverfassungsgericht—Federal Constitutional Court—Federal Republic of Germany*, published by the members of the Court. 2 vols. (Baden-Baden, Germany: Nomos Verlagsgesellschaft, 1992).

The State of Mississippi v. Johnson

71 U.S. (4 Wall.) 475, 18 L. Ed. 437 (1867)

After the Civil War ended, Congress enacted a series of statutes known as the Reconstruction Acts. These acts were, for all intents and purposes, an imposition of martial law on the states that joined the Confederacy. The state of Mississippi sued to enjoin President Andrew Johnson from enforcing two of the statutes enacted. Opinion of the Court: *Chase*, Nelson, Grier, Clifford, Swayne, Miller, Davis, Field, Wayne.

The Chief Justice CHASE delivered the opinion of the Court.

We shall limit our inquiry to the question . . . whether, in any case, the President of the United States may be required, by the process of this Court, to perform a purely ministerial act under a positive law, or may be held amenable, in any case, otherwise than by impeachment for crime.

The single point which requires consideration is this: Can the President be restrained by injunction from carrying into effect an act of Congress alleged to be unconstitutional?

It is assumed by the counsel for the State of Mississippi, that the President, in the execution of the Reconstruction Acts, is required to perform a mere ministerial duty. In this assumption there is, we think, a confounding of the terms ministerial and executive, which are by no means equivalent in import.

A ministerial duty, the performance of which may, in proper cases, be required of the head of a department, by judicial process, is one in respect to which nothing is left to discretion. It is a simple, definite duty, arising under conditions admitted or proved to exist, and imposed by law.

The case of *Marbury v. Madison* (1803) furnishes an illustration. A citizen had been nominated, confirmed, and appointed a justice of the peace for the District of Columbia, and his commission had been made out, signed, and sealed. Nothing remained to be done except delivery, and the duty of delivery was imposed by law on the Secretary of State. It was held that the performance of this duty might be enforced by mandamus issuing from a court having jurisdiction.

. . . [N]othing was left to discretion. There was no room for the exercise of judgment. The law required the performance of a single specific act; and that performance, it was held, might be required by mandamus.

Very different is the duty of the President in the exercise of the power to see that the laws are faithfully executed, and among these laws the acts named in the bill. By the first of these acts he is required to assign generals to command in the several military districts, and to detail sufficient military force to enable such officers to discharge their duties under the law. By the supplementary act, other duties are imposed on the several commanding generals, and these duties must necessarily be performed under the supervision of the President as commander-in-chief. The duty thus imposed on the President is in no just sense ministerial. It is purely executive and political.

An attempt on the part of the judicial department of the government to enforce the performance of such duties by the President might be justly characterized, in the language of Chief Justice Marshall, as "an absurd and excessive extravagance."

It is true that in the case before us the interposition of the Court is not sought to enforce action by the Executive under constitutional legislation, but to restrain such action under legislation alleged to be unconstitutional. But we are unable to perceive that this circumstance takes the case out of the general principles which forbid judicial interference with the exercise of executive discretion.

Had it been supposed at the bar that this court would, in any case, interpose, by injunction, to prevent the execution of an unconstitutional act of Congress, it can hardly be doubted that applications with that object would have been heretofore addressed to it.

Occasions have not been wanting. . . .

It will hardly be contended that Congress can interpose, in any case, to restrain the enactment of an unconstitutional law; and yet how can the right to judicial interposition to prevent such an enactment, when the purpose is evident and the execution of that purpose certain, be distinguished, in principle, from the right to such interposition against the execution of such a law by the President?

The Congress is the legislative department of the government; the President is the executive department. Neither can be restrained in its action by the judicial department; though the acts of both, when performed, are, in proper cases, subject to its cognizance.

The impropriety of such interference will be clearly seen upon consideration of its possible consequences.

Suppose the bill filed and the injunction prayed for allowed. If the President refuse obedience, it is needless to observe that the Court is without power to enforce its process. If, on the other hand, the President complies with the order of the Court and refuses to execute the acts of Congress, is it not clear that a collision may occur between the executive and legislative departments of the government? May not the House of Representatives impeach the President for such refusal? And in that case could this Court interfere, in behalf of the President, thus endangered by compliance with its mandate, and restrain by injunction the Senate of the United States from sitting as a Court of impeachment? Would the strange spectacle be offered to the public world of an attempt by this Court to arrest proceedings in that court?

These questions answer themselves.

The motion for leave to file the bill is, therefore, DENIED.

Notes/Queries/Readings

1. One reason for the Court's decision was the fear that the President would refuse to obey it and that the Court would then be "without power to enforce its process." Is this a constitutionally defensible reason for refusing to issue the order? Why or why not? Contrast the Court's decision with its ruling in *United States v. Nixon*, 418 U.S. 683 (1974), in chapter 3.

2. After the Court ruled, Georgia tried to invoke the Court's original jurisdiction by asking it to enjoin the secretary of war from enforcing the Reconstruction Acts. The Court refused to hear the case.

Youngstown Sheet & Tube Co. v. Sawyer

343 U.S. 579, 72 S. Ct. 863, 96 L. Ed. 1153 (1952)

In June of 1950, North Korea invaded South Korea. President Truman authorized the use of American troops in the conflict in what he called a "policing action" rather than a war. In December, 1951, several of the contracts between the United Steelworkers Union and the Youngstown Steel Company expired. The union called a strike in April 1952, during the heart of the Korean War. The strike would have halted almost the entire steel industry in the United States. Because the troops in Korea were already facing ammunition shortages, President Truman issued an executive order to seize the steel mills and place them under government control, stating that the closing of the mills would "immediately jeopardize and imperil our national defense." The day after, Truman reported to Congress the action he had taken, and stated that he would abide by any action taken by Congress. Congress did not take any action, so the steel companies obtained an injunction. The opinion of the Court, by Justice Black, and the concurring opinions by Justice Frankfurter and Justice Jackson are reprinted in chapter 4 at pages 133–138. Here we include only the dissenting opinion by Chief Justice Vinson.

Mr. Chief Justice VINSON, with whom Mr. Justice REED and Mr. Justice MINTON join, dissenting.

Those who suggest that this is a case involving extraordinary powers should be mindful that these are extraordinary times. A world not yet recovered from the devastation of World War II has been forced to face the threat of another and more terrifying global conflict.

Plaintiffs do not remotely suggest any basis for rejecting the President's finding that any stoppage of steel production would immediately place the Nation in peril.

Accordingly, if the President has any power under the Constitution to meet a critical situation in the absence of express statutory authorization, there is no basis whatever for criticizing the exercise of such power in this case.

The steel mills were seized for a public use. The power of eminent domain, invoked in that case, is an essential attribute of sovereignty and has long been recognized as a power of the Federal Government. . . . Plaintiffs cannot complain that any provision in the Constitution prohibits the exercise of the power of eminent domain in this case. The Fifth Amendment provides: "nor shall private property be taken for public use, without just compensation." It is no bar to this seizure for, if the taking is not otherwise unlawful, plaintiffs are assured of receiving the required just compensation.

Admitting that the Government could seize the mills, plaintiffs claim that the implied power of eminent domain can be exercised only under an Act of Congress; under no circumstances, they say, can that power be exercised by the President unless he can point to an express provision in enabling legislation. This was the view adopted by the District Judge when he granted the preliminary injunction. Without an answer, without hearing evidence, he determined the issue on the basis of his "fixed conclusion . . . that defendant's acts are illegal" because the President's only course in the face of an emergency is to present the matter to Congress and await the final passage of legislation which will enable the Government to cope with threatened disaster.

Under this view, the President is left powerless at the very moment when the need for action may be most pressing and when no one, other than he, is immediately capable of action. Under this view, he is left powerless because a power not expressly given to Congress is nevertheless found to rest exclusively with Congress.

Focusing now on the situation confronting the President on the night of April 8, 1952, we cannot but conclude that the President was performing his duty under the Constitution to "take Care that the Laws be faithfully executed"—a duty described by President Benjamin Harrison as "the central idea of the office."

Much of the argument in this case has been directed at straw men. We do not now have before us the case of a President acting solely on the basis of his own notions of the public welfare. Nor is there any question of unlimited executive power in this case. The President himself closed the door to any such claim when he sent his Message to Congress stating his purpose to abide by any action of Congress, whether approving or disapproving his seizure action. Here, the President immediately made sure that Congress was fully informed of the temporary action he had taken only to preserve the legislative programs from destruction until Congress could act.

The absence of a specific statute authorizing seizure of the steel mills as a mode of executing the laws—both the military procurement program and the anti-inflation program—has not until today been thought to prevent the President from executing the laws. Unlike an administrative commission confined to the enforcement of the statute under which it was created, or the head to a department when administering a particular statute, the President is a constitutional officer charged with taking care that a "mass of legislation" be executed. Flexibility as to mode of execution to meet critical situations is a matter of practical necessity.

. . . Faced with the duty of executing the defense programs which Congress had enacted and the disastrous effects that any stoppage in steel production would have on those programs, the President acted to preserve those programs by seizing the steel mills. There is no question that the possession was other than temporary in character and subject to congressional direction—either approving, disapproving or regulating the manner in which the mills were to be administered and returned to the owners. The President immediately informed Congress of his action and clearly stated his intention to abide by the legislative will. No basis for claims of arbitrary action, unlimited powers or dictatorial usurpation of congressional power appears from the facts of this case. On the contrary, judicial, legislative and executive precedents throughout our history demonstrate that in this case the President acted in full conformity with his duties under the Constitution. Accordingly, we would reverse the order of the District Court.

Notes/Queries/Readings

1. Immediately following the Court's decision the steelworkers called a strike that lasted for fifty-three days. No shortages ensued, in part because there was an "enormous inventory of steel on hand at the beginning of the strike." Maeva Marcus, *Truman and the Steel Seizure Case: The Limits of Presidential Power* (New York: Columbia University Press, 1997), 252.

2. In the case of *In re Neagle*, 135 U.S. 546 (1890), the Supreme Court considered a claim of inherent presidential powers that involved the Court itself. David Neagle, a United States marshal assigned to protect Justice Stephen Field after threats were made against the justice's life, shot and killed the man who had made the threats. California authorities arrested Neagle and charged him with murder. The federal government asked for his release, claiming that Neagle had acted in the line of his authority. Nevertheless, no statute had authorized the president to appoint bodyguards for the justices. The Court held that the president's power to execute the laws was not "limited to the enforcement of acts of Congress." Does the majority opinion in *Youngstown* cast doubt on the opinion in *Neagle*, perhaps by suggesting that in the field of domestic affairs, the president has no inherent or emergency powers?

3. Of what relevance was the absence of a congressional declaration of war in this case? Of what relevance was the congressional history of legislation, reviewed by Justice Black in his majority opinion, that considered, but decided against, giving the president the authority to seize the steel plants?

4. The various opinions in *Youngstown* utilize a wide variety of methods of constitutional interpretation. Justice Black's majority opinion begins with the claim that the president's power must stem from the Constitution itself or from an act of Congress. How does Justice Frankfurter's concurrence differ in its understanding of the separation of powers from the majority opinion? Does it rest also upon a different understanding of judicial power? What is the source for Justice Jackson's tripartite framework for the analysis of presidential power? Does it apply to the president's power in foreign affairs, or only to domestic affairs? Does the dissent rely primarily upon statutes and precedents, or does it look to some other source for guidance?

5. For additional readings, see Grant McConnell, *The President Seizes the Steel Mills* (University of Alabama, 1960); Alan F. Westin, *The Anatomy of a Constitutional Law Case* (New York: Macmillan, 1958); Edward S. Corwin, *The Steel Seizure Case: A Judicial Brick Without Straw*, 53 Columbia Law Review 53 (1953); Paul Kauper, *The Steel Seizure Case*, 51 Michigan Law Review 141 (1952).

The Prize Cases
67 U.S. (2 Black) 635, 17 L. Ed. 459 (1862)

After the Civil War began in April 1861, but before a special session of Congress was allowed to begin, President Abraham Lincoln instituted a blockade of all ports belonging to the Confederate states. During the period between this initial commencement of the blockade and Congress's subsequent ratification of the blockade, several ships were seized and their cargoes confiscated as "prize" because they attempted to break through the blockade. The owners of these ships sued to regain their cargoes, arguing that the blockade was illegal. Questions arising from these suits were certified to the Supreme Court. Opinion of the Court: *Grier*, Wayne, Swayne, Miller, Davis. Dissenting opinion: *Nelson*, Taney, Catron, Clifford.

Mr. Justice GRIER delivered the opinion of the Court.

. . . Had the President a right to institute a blockade of ports in possession of persons in armed rebellion against the Government, on the principles of international law, as known and acknowledged among civilized States?

The right of prize and capture has its origin in the "jus belli," and is governed and adjudged under the law of nations. To legitimate the capture of a neutral vessel or property on the high seas, a war must exist *de facto*, and the neutral must have a knowledge or notice of the intention of one of the parties belligerent to use this mode of coercion against a port, city, or territory, in possession of the other.

Let us enquire whether, at the time this blockade was instituted, a state of war existed which would justify a resort to these means of subduing the hostile force.

By the Constitution, Congress alone has the power to declare a national or foreign war. It cannot declare war against a State, or any number of States, by virtue of any clause in the Constitution. The Constitution confers on the President the whole Executive power. He is bound to take care that the laws be faithfully executed. He is Commander-in-chief of the Army and Navy of the United States, and of the militia of the several States when called into the actual service of the United States. He has no power to initiate or declare a war either against a foreign nation or a domestic State. But by the Acts of Congress of February 28th, 1795, and 3d of March, 1807, he is authorized to call out the militia and use the military and naval forces of the United States in case of invasion by foreign nations, and to suppress insurrection against the government of a State or of the United States.

If a war be made by invasion of a foreign nation, the President is not only authorized but bound to resist force by force. He does not initiate the war, but is bound to accept the challenge without waiting for any special legislative authority. And whether the hostile party be a foreign invader, or States organized in rebellion, it is none the less a war, although the declaration of it be "*unilateral*." . . .

This greatest of civil wars . . . sprung forth suddenly from the parent brain, a Minerva in the full panoply of *war*. The President was bound to meet it in the shape it presented itself, without waiting for Congress to baptize it with a name; and no name given to it by him or them could change the fact.

Whether the President in fulfilling his duties, as Commander-in-chief, in suppressing an insurrection, has met with such armed hostile resistance, and a civil war of such alarming proportions as will compel him to accord to them the character of belligerents, is a question to be decided by him, and this Court must be governed by the decisions and acts of the political department of the Government to which this power was entrusted. . . . The proclamation of blockade is itself official and conclusive evidence to the Court that a state of war existed which demanded and authorized a recourse to such a measure, under the circumstances peculiar to the case.

If it were necessary to the technical existence of a war, that it should have a legislative sanction, we find it in almost every act passed at the extraordinary session of the Legislature of 1861, which was wholly employed in enacting laws to enable the Government to prosecute the war with vigor and efficiency. And finally, in 1861, we find Congress . . . passing an act "approving, legalizing, and making valid all the acts, proclamations, and orders of the President, &c., as if they had been issued and done under the previous express authority and direction of the Congress of the United States."

Without admitting that such an act was necessary under the circumstances, it is plain that if the President had in any manner assumed powers which it was necessary should have the authority or sanction of Congress . . . this ratification has operated to perfectly cure the defect.

. . . [W]e are of the opinion that the President had a right, *jure belli*, to institute a blockade of ports in possession of the States in rebellion, which neutrals are bound to regard.

Mr. Justice NELSON, dissenting.

. . . [T]he right of making war belongs exclusively to the supreme or sovereign power of the State.

This power in all civilized nations is regulated by the fundamental laws or municipal constitution of the country.

Comparative Note 7.4

[In 1983 several persons filed constitutional complaints against the Federal Republic of Germany's deployment on its territory of weapons equipped with nuclear warheads. The deployment was taken under an accord of the North Atlantic Treaty Organization (NATO). The complainants charged that the presence of these weapons endangered their physical integrity and right to life in violation of Article 2 (2) of the Basic Law.]

[I]t is questionable whether the asserted violation of [the right to] life and limb by German sovereign power rises to the level of a real danger under the Basic Law. . . . Under the prevailing circumstances [we cannot make] judicially verifiable findings concerning such decisions in advance. Moreover, the possible violation of basic rights asserted [here] does not fall within the protective purview of these rights, since [basic rights] are aimed at German state action; . . .

. . . Because [we] lack legally manageable criteria [for deciding this case], the Federal Constitutional Court cannot determine whether or not the German state action challenged by complainants has any influence on decisions of the Soviet Union which may or may not trigger measures (a preventive or responsive nuclear strike) complainants fear. The federal organs responsible for the foreign and defense policy of the Federal Republic must make such evaluations. . . . To the extent that unpredictable areas of risk remain, as will often be the case, the political body constitutionally responsible for the decision must include these [considerations] in their deliberations and assume political responsibility. It is not the function of the Federal Constitutional Court to substitute its opinions for the opinions and deliberations of the competent political branch of the federation over and above standard legal handicaps in this area. This applies equally for the question of how the state should fulfill its affirmative legal duty to protect basic rights in the sphere of foreign policy and defense matter vis-a-vis foreign states.

SOURCE: *Pershing 2 and Cruise Missile Case*, I (1983) in Kommers, *Constitutional Jurisprudence*, 156–57.

By our constitution this power is lodged in Congress.

Now, in one sense, no doubt this is war, and may be a war of the most extensive and threatening dimensions and effects, but it is a statement simply of its existence in a material sense, and has no relevancy or weight when the question is what constitutes war in a legal sense, in the sense of the law of nations, and of the Constitution of the United States? For it must be a war in this sense to attach to it all the consequences that belong to belligerent rights.

. . . [A]mple provision has been made under the Constitution and laws against any sudden and unexpected disturbance of the public peace from insurrection at home or invasion from abroad. The whole military and naval power of the country is put under the control of the President to meet the emergency. . . . It is the exercise of a power under the municipal laws of the country and not under the law of nations; and, as we see, furnishes the most ample means of repelling attacks from abroad or suppressing disturbances at home until the assembling of Congress, who can, if it be deemed necessary, bring into operation the war power, and thus change the nature and character of the contest.

. . . I am compelled to the conclusion that no civil war existed between this Government and the States in insurrection till recognized by the Act of Congress 13th of July, 1861; that the President does not possess the power under the Constitution to declare war or recognize its existence within the meaning of the law of nations, which carries with it belligerent rights, and thus change the country and all its citizens from a state of peace to a state of war; that this power belongs exclusively to the Congress of the United States and, consequently, that the President had no power to set on foot a blockade under the law of nations, and that the capture of the vessel and cargo in this case, and in all cases before us in which the capture occurred before the 13th of July, 1861, for breach of blockade, or as enemies' property, are illegal and void, and that the decrees of condemnation should be reversed and the vessel and cargo restored.

Mr. Chief Justice TANEY, Mr. Justice CATRON and Mr. Justice CLIFFORD, concurred in the dissenting opinion of Mr. Justice NELSON.

Notes/Queries/Readings

1. The Court appears to hold that when the country is under attack the president may "recognize" that we are in

a state of war and act on the basis of his commander-in-chief powers. In all other cases, the congressional power to declare war must precede the president's action. Why did the Founders separate the power to conduct war and peace in this way? Is the separation they envisioned a constitutional impossibility in an age when international agencies and organizations play an important role in responding to conflict between countries? Is a presidential power to react but not to declare consistent with the actual practice of presidential war making in the twentieth century?

2. Can the *Prize Cases* be reconciled with *Ex Parte Milligan* (1866), reprinted later in this chapter?

3. Justice Grier wrote that "Whether the President in fulfilling his duties, as Commander-in-Chief, in suppressing an insurrection, has met with such armed hostile resistance, and a civil war of such alarming proportions as will compel him to accord to them the character of belligerents, is a question to be decided by *him,* and this Court must be governed by the decisions . . . of the political department of the Government to which this power was entrusted." Does this mean that there can be no judicial review of such a presidential decision? What understanding of the separation of powers underlies this view? How does it differ from the dissent's understanding?

United States Code
Title 50. War and National Defense
Chapter 33—War Powers Resolution

s 1541. Purpose and policy

(a) Congressional declaration

It is the purpose of this chapter to fulfill the intent of the framers of the Constitution of the United States and insure that the collective judgment of both the Congress and the President will apply to the introduction of United States Armed Forces into hostilities, or into situations where imminent involvement in hostilities is clearly indicated by the circumstances, and to the continued use of such forces in hostilities or in such situations.

(b) Congressional legislative power under necessary and proper clause

Under article I, section 8, of the Constitution, it is specifically provided that the Congress shall have the power to make all laws necessary and proper for carrying into execution, not only its own powers but also all other powers vested by the Constitution in the Government of the United States, or in any department or officer thereof.

(c) Presidential executive power as Commander-in-Chief; limitation

The constitutional powers of the President as Commander-in-Chief to introduce United States Armed Forces into hostilities, or into situations where imminent involvement in hostilities is clearly indicated by the circumstances, are exercised only pursuant to (1) a declaration of war, (2) specific statutory authorization, or (3) a national emergency created by attack upon the United States, its territories or possessions, or its armed forces.

s 1542. Consultation; initial and regular consultations

The President in every possible instance shall consult with Congress before introducing United States Armed Forces into hostilities or into situations where imminent involvement in hostilities is clearly indicated by the circumstances, and after every such introduction shall consult regularly with the Congress until United States Armed Forces are no longer engaged in hostilities or have been removed from such situations.

s 1543. Reporting requirement

(a) Written report; time of submission and information reported

In the absence of a declaration of war, in any case in which United States Armed Forces are introduced—

(1) into hostilities or into situations where imminent involvement in hostilities is clearly indicated by the circumstances;

(2) into the territory, airspace or waters of a foreign nation, while equipped for combat, except for deployments which relate solely to supply, replacement, repair, or training of such forces; or

(3) in numbers which substantially enlarge United States Armed Forces equipped for combat already located in a foreign nation;

the President shall submit within 48 hours to the Speaker of the House of Representatives and to the President pro tempore of the Senate a report, in writing, setting forth—

(A) the circumstances necessitating the introduction of United States Armed Forces;

(B) the constitutional and legislative authority under which such introduction took place; and

(C) the estimated scope and duration of the hostilities or involvement.

(b) Other information reported

The President shall provide such other information as the Congress may request in the fulfillment of its constitu-

Comparative Note 7.5

Article 40(13)

(1) Except for military exercises based on valid international agreements or peace maintenance activities performed on request of the United Nations Organization, the armed forces [Hungarian National Army and Border Guard] may cross state borders only with the prior consent of parliament. (Constitution of Hungary, 1990)

Article 26

(1) Any activities apt or intended to disturb peaceful international relations, especially preparations for military aggression, shall be unconstitutional. They shall be a criminal offense. (Basic Law, Federal Republic of Germany, 1949)

Article 87a

(1) The [German] Federation shall establish Armed Forces for defense purposes. Their numerical strength and general organizational structure shall be shown in the budget. (2) Other than for defense purposes, the Armed Forces may only be employed to the extent explicitly permitted by this Basic Law. (Basic Law, Federal Republic of Germany, as amended 1956)

Article 9

(1) Aspiring sincerely to an international peace based on justice and order, the Japanese people forever renounce war as a sovereign right of the nation and the threat or use of force as a means of settling international disputes.

(2) In order to accomplish the aim of the preceding paragraph, land, sea, and air forces, as well as other war potential, will never be maintained. The right of the belligerency of the state will not be recognized. (Constitution of Japan, 1947)

Article 230

In case of threats to the constitutional order of the State . . . the President of the Republic may, on request of the Council of Ministers, introduce . . . for no longer than 90 days a state of emergency in a part of or upon the whole territory of the State.

Article 231

The President . . . shall submit the regulation on the introduction of . . . a state of emergency to the Sejm [parliament] within 48 hours of signing such regulation. The Sejm shall immediately consider the regulation of the President. The Sejm, by an absolute majority of votes taken in the presence of at least half the statutory number of representatives, may annul the regulation of the President. (Constitution of Poland, 1997)

---

tional responsibilities with respect to committing the Nation to war and to the use of United States Armed Forces abroad.

(c) Periodic reports; semiannual requirement

Whenever United States Armed Forces are introduced into hostilities or into any situation described in subsection (a) of this section, the President shall, so long as such armed forces continue to be engaged in such hostilities or situation, report to the Congress periodically on the status of such hostilities or situation as well as on the scope and duration of such hostilities or situation, but in no event shall he report to the Congress less often than once every six months.

s 1544. Congressional action

(a) Transmittal of report and referral to Congressional committees; joint request for convening Congress

Each report submitted pursuant to section 1543(a)(1) of this title shall be transmitted to the Speaker of the House of Representatives and to the President pro tempore of the Senate on the same calendar day. Each report so transmitted shall be referred to the Committee on Relations of the Senate for appropriate action. If, when the report is transmitted, the Congress has adjourned *sine die* or has adjourned for any period in excess of three calendar days, the Speaker of the House of Representatives and the President pro tempore of the Senate, if they deem it advisable (or if petitioned by at least 30 percent of the membership of their respective Houses) shall jointly request the President to convene Congress in order that it may consider the report and take appropriate action pursuant to this section.

(b) Termination of use of United States Armed Forces; exceptions; extension period

Within sixty calendar days after a report is submitted or is required to be submitted pursuant to section 1543(a)(1) of this title, whichever is earlier, the President shall terminate any use of United States Armed Forces with respect to which such report was submitted (or required to be submitted), unless the Congress (1) has declared war or has enacted a specific authorization for such use of United States Armed Forces, (2) has extended by law such sixty-day period, or (3) is physically unable to meet as a result of an armed attack upon the United States. Such sixty-day period shall be extended for not more than an additional thirty days if the President determines and certifies to the Congress in writing that unavoidable military necessity respecting the safety of United States Armed Forces requires the continued use of such armed forces in the course of bringing about a prompt removal of such forces.

(c) Concurrent resolution for removal by President of United States Armed Forces

Notwithstanding subsection (b) of this section, at any time that United States Armed Forces are engaged in hostilities outside the territory of the United States, its possessions and territories without a declaration of war or specific statutory authorization, such forces shall be removed by the President if the Congress so directs by concurrent resolution.

s 1547. Interpretations from any law or treaty

Authority to introduce United States Armed Forces into hostilities or into situations wherein involvement in hostilities is clearly indicated by the circumstances shall not be inferred—

(1) from any provision of law (whether or not in effect before November 7, 1973), including any provision contained in any appropriation Act, unless such provision specifically authorizes the introduction of United States Armed Forces into hostilities or into such situations and states that it is intended to constitute specific statutory authorization within the meaning of this chapter; or

(2) from any treaty heretofore or hereafter ratified unless such treaty is implemented by legislation specifically authorizing the introduction of United States Armed Forces into hostilities or into such situations and stating that it is intended to constitute specific statutory authorization within the meaning of this chapter.

(b) Joint headquarters operations of high-level military commands

Nothing in this chapter shall be construed to require any further specific statutory authorization to permit members of United States Armed Forces to participate jointly with members of the armed forces of one or more foreign countries in the headquarters operations of high-level military commands which were established prior to November 7, 1973, and pursuant to the United Nations Charter or any treaty ratified by the United States prior to such date.

(c) Introduction of United States Armed Forces

For purposes of this chapter, the term "introduction of United States Armed Forces" includes the assignment of members of such armed forces to command, coordinate, participate in the movement of, or accompany the regular or irregular military forces of any foreign country or government when such military forces are engaged, or there exists an imminent threat that such forces will become engaged, in hostilities.

(d) Constitutional authorities or existing treaties . . . respecting use of United States Armed Forces

Nothing in this chapter—

(1) is intended to alter the constitutional authority of the Congress or of the President, or the provisions of existing treaties; or

(2) shall be construed as granting any authority to the President with respect to the introduction of United States Armed Forces into hostilities or into situations wherein involvement in hostilities is clearly indicated by the circumstances which authority he would not have had in the absence of this chapter.

s 1548. Separability of provisions

If any provision of this chapter or the application thereof to any person or circumstance is held invalid, the remainder of the chapter and the application of such provision to any other person or circumstance shall not be affected thereby.

Notes/Queries/Readings

1. Whatever its wisdom at the time, (it passed the House unanimously and the Senate with only two dissents), the Tonkin Gulf Resolution (1964) now serves as a symbol of the dangers of congressional acquiescence to presidential power. By 1967, Vietnam was the third largest war in which Americans had ever participated, at least as measured by troops abroad and the number of casualties. In many ways, the War Powers Resolution (1973) is a response to Tonkin Gulf.

2. Presidents routinely ignore the War Powers Resolution, seemingly without peril. President Ford notified but did not consult with Congress about his decision to rescue the crew of the *Mayaguez* and to evacuate Americans from Lebanon with U.S. troops. President Carter sent a military rescue force into Iran without consulting Congress, and President Reagan sent the marines into Lebanon and troops into Grenada, without conceding that the act applied to his action. More recently, President Bush did notify Congress before he sent troops to Panama; he was

careful, however, to make it clear that he was not asking for congressional consultation or advice.

3. Its proponents believe the War Powers Resolution is an effort to give life to one of the defining features of the American constitutional order—the principle that power should be shared and accountable. But whatever the merits of its appeal to original intent, in practice the War Powers Resolution has done little to hem in presidential power or to raise Congress to the status of a coequal partner. Does the Resolution's failure suggest that it is impossible to reconcile the "imperial presidency" with constitutional government? If constitutionalism means respect for limits on power, then what are we to make of the Resolution's failure to constrain presidential war powers?

4. Claims about respect for Founders' intent aside, how can we reconcile the Resolution with Hamilton's claim in *Federalist* 70: "Energy in the executive is a leading character in the definition of good government. It is essential to the protection of the community against foreign attacks." In the same paper Hamilton praises a single, energetic executive as the only branch capable of acting with "decision, activity, secrecy, and dispatch."

5. The War Powers Resolution is plainly an exercise of constitutional interpretation. To what extent are branches of government bound to respect the interpretations of coordinate branches? Does Congress's interpretation go to the limits of *its* power—or is it an interpretation about the extent of presidential power? Does it matter?

6. Do the *Prize Cases* (1863) tell us anything about the constitutionality of the War Powers Resolution? Does the Resolution authorize the president to respond to threats of attack without seeking congressional approval?

7. Both Germany and Japan include a renunciation of war in their constitutions. In both cases, however, the renunciation has done little to end sometimes heated discussions about who has the responsibility to conduct foreign relations.

8. Consider the various constitutional provisions included in Comparative Note 7.5. Would a similar provision in the United States Constitution help to clarify or to resolve disputes in the United States about the proper constitutional distribution of the power to conduct foreign affairs? Why or why not?

9. The literature on the War Powers Resolution is considerable. Among the better treatments are John Hart Ely, *War and Responsibility* (Princeton: Princeton University Press, 1993); Louis Henkin, *Constitutionalism, Democracy, and Foreign Affairs* (New York: Columbia University Press, 1990); Stephen L. Carter, *The Constitutionality of the War Powers Resolution*, 70 Virginia Law Review 101 (1984); Eugene V. Rostow, *Great Cases Make Bad Law: The War Powers Act*, 50 Texas Law Review 833 (1972); Michael Glennon, *The War Powers Resolution: Sad Record, Dismal Promises*, 17 Loyola of Los Angeles Law Review 657 (1984).

Persian Gulf Resolution Authorization for Use of Military Forces Against Iraq

H.J. Res. 77 (1991), Pub.L. 102–1, Jan. 14, 1991, 105 Stat. 3

Sec. 2. Authorization for use of United States Armed Forces.

(a) Authorization.—the President is authorized, subject to subsection (b), to use United States Armed Forces pursuant to United Nations Security Council Resolution 678 (1990) in order to achieve implementation of Security Council Resolutions 660, 661, 662, 664, 665, 666, 667, 669, 670, 674, and 677.

(b) Requirement for determination that use of military force is necessary.—Before exercising the authority granted in subsection (a), the President shall make available to the Speaker of the House of Representatives and the President pro tempore of the Senate his determination that—

(1) the United States has used all appropriate diplomatic and other peaceful means to obtain compliance by Iraq with the United Nations Security Council resolutions cited in subsection (a); and

(2) that those efforts have not been and would not be successful in obtaining such compliance.

(c) War powers resolution requirements.—

(1) Specific statutory authorization.—Consistent with section 8(a)(1) of the War Powers Resolution [section 1547(a)(1) of this title], the Congress declares that this section is intended to constitute specific statutory authorization within the meaning of section 5(b) of the War Powers Resolution [section 1544(b) of this title].

(2) Applicability of other requirements.—Nothing in this resolution supersedes any requirement of the War Powers Resolution [this chapter].

Sec. 3. Reports to Congress.

At least once every 60 days, the President shall submit to the Congress a summary on the status of efforts to obtain compliance by Iraq with the resolutions adopted by the United Nations Security Council in response to Iraq's aggression.

Notes/Queries/Readings

1. President Bush's decision to send troops to Kuwait in August 1990 revived arguments about the power of the president to make war without congressional approval.[39] Fifty-four members of the House of Representatives filed suit in a United States District Court, asking it to enjoin the president's decision to send troops. Judge Harold Greene rejected the request, but he did note, in language reminiscent of Madison's complaints in the Washington administration, that "If the executive had the sole power to determine that any particular offensive military operation, no matter how vast, does not constitute war-making but only an offensive military attack, the congressional power to de-

clare war will be at the mercy of a semantic decision by the Executive." [40]

On 8 January 1991, four months after his decision to begin Operation Desert Storm, and a week before the deadline imposed on Iraq by the United Nations to remove all troops from Kuwait, President Bush asked Congress for a formal resolution supporting "the use of all necessary means" to give sanction to the deadline. President Bush noted that he was *not* asking for—and did not believe he needed—congressional *approval* to use force. His independent authority as commander-in-chief, Bush argued, provided ample constitutional support for his actions. Congress gave President Bush the resolution he had requested.

2. Is the requirement in Section b of the resolution that the President report to the speaker of the house and the president pro tempore of the Senate an unconstitutional invasion of his powers as commander-in-chief?

[38]See, for example, J. Gregory Sidak, *To Declare War*, 41 Duke Law Journal 27 (1991), and Harold Hongju Koh, *The Coase Theorem and the War Power: A Response*, 41 Duke Law Journal 124 (1991).

[39]*Dellums v. Bush*, 752 F.Supp. 1141 (D.D.C. 1990).

United States v. Curtiss-Wright Export Corp.
299 U.S. 304, 57 S. Ct. 216, 81 L. Ed. 255 (1936)

In the 1930s, Bolivia and Paraguay were involved in a violent border dispute. In 1934, Congress passed a Joint Resolution authorizing the president to enforce an arms embargo against those countries if he believed that it would promote peace in the region. President Roosevelt immediately issued a proclamation to that effect. The Curtiss-Wright Corporation was indicted by the Department of Justice for violating the embargo. Curtiss-Wright challenged the indictment, arguing that Congress had made an unconstitutional delegation of legislative power to the executive. Opinion of the Court: *Sutherland,* Hughes, Van Devanter, Brandeis, Butler, Roberts, Cardozo. Dissenting opinion: *McReynolds*. Not participating: Stone.

Mr. Justice SUTHERLAND delivered the opinion of the Court.

Whether, if the Joint Resolution had related solely to internal affairs, it would be open to the challenge that it constituted an unlawful delegation of legislative power to the Executive, we find it unnecessary to determine. The whole aim of the resolution is to affect a situation entirely external to the United States, and falling within the category of foreign affairs. The determination which we are called to make, therefore, is whether the Joint Resolution, as applied to that situation, is vulnerable to attack under the rule that forbids a delegation of the lawmaking power. In other words, assuming (but not deciding) that the challenged

delegation, if it were confined to internal affairs, would be invalid, may it nevertheless be sustained on the ground that its exclusive aim is to afford a remedy for a hurtful condition within foreign territory?

It will contribute to the elucidation of the question if we first consider the differences between the powers of the federal government in respect of foreign or external affairs and those in respect of domestic or internal affairs. That there are differences between them, and that these differences are fundamental, may not be doubted.

The two classes of powers are different, both in respect of their origin and their nature. The broad statement that the federal government can exercise no powers except those specifically enumerated in the Constitution, and such implied powers as are necessary and proper to carry into effect the enumerated powers, is categorically true only in respect of our internal affairs. In that field, the primary purpose of the Constitution was to carve from the general mass of legislative powers then possessed by the states such portions as it was thought desirable to vest in the federal government, leaving those not included in the enumeration still in the states. That this doctrine applies only to powers which the states had is self-evident. And since the states severally never possessed international powers, such powers could not have been carved from the mass of state powers but obviously were transmitted to the United States from some other source. During the Colonial period, those powers were possessed exclusively by and were entirely under the control of the Crown. By the Declaration of Independence, "the Representatives of the United States of America" declared the United (not the several) Colonies to be free and independent states, and as such to have "full Power to levy War, conclude Peace, contract Alliances, establish Commerce and to do all other Acts and Things which Independent States may of right do."

As a result of the separation from Great Britain by the colonies, acting as a unit, the powers of external sovereignty passed from the Crown not to the colonies severally, but to the colonies in their collective and corporate capacity as the United States of America. Even before the Declaration, the colonies were a unit in foreign affairs, acting through a common agency—namely, the Continental Congress, composed of delegates from the thirteen colonies. That agency exercised the powers of war and peace, raised an army, created a navy, and finally adopted the Declaration of Independence. Rulers come and go; governments end and forms of government change; but sovereignty survives. A political society cannot endure without a supreme will somewhere. Sovereignty is never held in suspense. When, therefore, the external sovereignty of Great Britain in respect of the colonies ceased, it immediately passed to the Union.

The Union existed before the Constitution, which was ordained and established among other things to form "a more perfect Union." Prior to that event, it is clear that the Union, declared by the Articles of Confederation to be "perpetual," was the sole possessor of external sovereignty, and in the Union it remained without change save in so far as the Constitution in express terms qualified its exercise. The Framers' Convention was called and exerted its powers upon the irrefutable postulate that though the states were several their people in respect of foreign affairs were one.

It results that the investment of the federal government with the powers of external sovereignty did not depend upon the affirmative grants of the Constitution. The powers to declare and wage war, to conclude peace, to make treaties, to maintain diplomatic relations with other sovereignties, if they had never been mentioned in the Constitution, would have vested in the federal government as necessary concomitants of nationality. Neither the Constitution nor the laws passed in pursuance of it have any force in foreign territory unless in respect of our own citizens and operations of the nation in such territory must be governed by treaties, international understandings and compacts, and the principles of international law. As a member of the family of nations, the right and power of the United States in that field are equal to the right and power of the other members of the international family. Otherwise, the United States is not completely sovereign. The power to acquire territory by discovery and occupation, the power to expel undesirable aliens, the power to make such international agreements as do not constitute treaties in the constitutional sense, none of which is expressly affirmed by the Constitution, nevertheless exist as inherently inseparable from the conception of nationality. This the Court recognized, and in each of the cases cited found the warrant for its conclusions not in the provisions of the Constitution, but in the law of nations.

Not only, as we have shown, is the federal power over external affairs in origin and essential character different from that over internal affairs, but participation in the exercise of the power is significantly limited. In this vast external realm, with its important, complicated, delicate and manifold problems, the President alone has the power to speak or listen as a representative of the nation. He *makes* treaties with the advice and consent of the Senate; but he alone negotiates. Into the field of negotiation the Senate cannot intrude; and Congress itself is powerless to invade it. As Marshall said in his great argument of March 7, 1800, in the House of Representatives, "The President is the sole organ of the nation in its external relations, and its sole representative with foreign nations."

It is important to bear in mind that we are here dealing not alone with an authority vested in the President by an exertion of legislative power, but with such an authority plus the very delicate, plenary and exclusive power of the President as the sole organ of the federal government in the field of international relations—power which does not require as a basis for its exercise an act of Congress, but which, of course, like every other governmental power, must be exercised in subordination to the applicable provisions of the Constitution. It is quite apparent that if, in the maintenance of our international relations, embarrassment—perhaps serious embarrassment—is to be avoided and success for our aims achieved, congressional legislation which is to be made effective through negotiation and inquiry within the international field must often accord to the President a degree of discretion and freedom from statutory restriction which would not be admissible were domestic affairs alone involved. Moreover, he, not Congress, has the better opportunity of knowing the conditions which prevail in foreign countries, and especially is this true in time of war. He has his confidential sources of information. He has his agents in the form of diplomatic, consular and other officials. Secrecy in respect of information gathered by them may be highly necessary, and the premature disclosure of it productive of harmful results.

The marked difference between foreign affairs and domestic affairs in this respect is recognized by both houses of Congress in the very form of their requisitions for information from the executive departments. In the case of every department except the Department of State, the resolution directs the official to furnish the information. In the case of the State Department, dealing with foreign affairs,

Comparative Note 7.6

[Article 9 of Japan's Constitution renounces the sovereign right of the nation to engage in war and prohibits the maintenance of "war potential." (See Comparative Note 7.5.) The present case challenged the construction of an "Air Self-Defense Force (SDF) missile base" in Hokkaido. The extracts are from the decision of Sapporo's District Court and the Japanese Supreme Court.]

. . . [We] must therefore decide the issue whether the installation of defense equipment in question is unconstitutional or not. [Arguments based on the political question doctrine] are very vague. . . . Whenever the constitutionality of a statute is questioned the matter inevitably involves a question of a more or less political nature. . . . The defendant's argument, we believe, is not compatible with the principle of government by law, nor with judicial supremacy as provided by . . . the Constitution.

The Constitution clearly sets up legal norms in its Preamble and Article 9 on the issue of [self-defense]. . . . On the basis of the organization [and] scale . . . of the Self-Defense Forces . . . , it is clear that [it] is "an organization of men and materials with the purpose of carrying out battle with force against a foreign enemy." It, therefore, falls within the meaning of

the term of "armed forces" . . . whose maintenance is prohibited by Article 9, Paragraph 2 of the Forest Act. [Sapporo's High Court reversed, holding that the issue was political and hence nonjusticiable. SOURCE: Kenneth L. Port, *Comparative Law: Law and Legal Process in Japan* (Durham: Carolina Academic Press, 1996), 174.]

Whether or not the SDF corresponds to the so-called "war potential" prohibited by Article 9 of the Constitution is not a matter to be examined by the judicial branch. The question of possessing a Self-Defense Force as a means of self-defense or, if one is maintained, questions regarding the scale and levels of equipment and capability . . . are matters relating to the fundamentals of state governance; they are highly political matters . . . not ordinarily dealt with in judicial review by the judiciary, which has a purely judicial function and does not bear political responsibility to the people. . . . Even if the power of judicial review does extend to the matter of the constitutionality of the SDF, that Force is self-defense power based on our country's right of self-defense, not the "war potential" of Article 9, and is consequently constitutional. [*Naganuma Nike Missile Site Case*, I (1973)]

SOURCE: Lawrence W. Beer and Hiroshi Itoh, *The Constitutional Case Law of Japan, 1970 through 1990* (Seattle: University of Washington Press, 1996), 91.

---

the President is requested to furnish the information "if not incompatible with the public interest." A statement that to furnish the information is not compatible with the public interest rarely, if ever, is questioned.

When the President is to be authorized by legislation to act in respect of a matter intended to affect a situation in foreign territory, the legislator properly bears in mind the important consideration that the form of the President's action—or, indeed, whether he shall act at all—may well depend, among other things, upon the nature of the confidential information which he has or may thereafter receive, or upon the effect which his action may have upon our foreign relations. This consideration, in connection with what we have already said on the subject discloses the unwisdom of requiring Congress in this field of governmental power to lay down narrowly definite standards by which the President is to be governed.

In the light of the foregoing observations, it is evident that this Court should not be in haste to apply a general rule which will have the effect of condemning legislation

like that under review as constituting an unlawful delegation of legislative power. The principles which justify such legislation find overwhelming support in the unbroken legislative practice which has prevailed almost from the inception of the national government to the present day.

The result of holding that the joint resolution [is an] unconstitutional delegation of legislative power would be to stamp this multitude of comparable acts and resolutions as likewise invalid. And while this Court may not, and should not, hesitate to declare acts of Congress, however many times repeated, to be unconstitutional if beyond all rational doubt it finds them to be so, an impressive array of legislation such as we have just set forth, enacted by nearly every Congress from the beginning of our national existence to the present day, must be given unusual weight in the process of reaching a correct determination of the problem. A legislative practice such as we have here, evidenced not by only occasional instances, but marked by the movement of a steady stream for a century and a half of time, goes a long way in the direction of proving the presence of unassailable ground for the constitutionality of the practice, to be found in the origin and history of the power involved, or in its nature, or in both combined.

Notes/Queries/Readings

1. Two specific conclusions followed from Sutherland's analysis. First, the Court concluded that Curtiss-Wright's argument, that the congressional resolution empowering the president violated the nondelegation doctrine, was irrelevant because that constitutional limitation applies only to domestic affairs. Second, the absence of constitutional limitations on the power required the Court to abstain, for without guidance from the Constitution, the Court could do nothing more than express its opinion about the wisdom of the policy involved—clearly out of the bounds of proper judicial authority. As Justice Jackson noted in *Chicago & Southern Airlines, Inc. v. Waterman Steamship Corp* (1948),

> The very nature of executive decisions as to foreign policy is political, not judicial. . . . They are delicate, complex, and involve large elements of prophecy. They are and should be undertaken only by those directly responsible to the people whose welfare they advance or imperil. They are decisions of a kind for which the Judiciary has neither the aptitude, facilities, nor responsibility which has long been held to be in the domain of political power not subject to judicial intrusion or inquiry.

2. What precisely does the Court hold about the source of executive power in the field of foreign affairs? The theory advanced by the Court is sometimes called the "sole organ theory": the theory that the president is the sole organ of the nation in foreign affairs. The phrase comes from a speech by John Marshall when he was in Congress. Marshall defended a decision by President John Adams to extradite a fugitive under the controversial Jay Treaty, saying "The President is the sole organ of the nation in its external relations, and its sole representative with foreign nations."

Is that power completely untethered from constitutional restraints? One commentator has suggested that the Court transformed the president's "exclusive authority to communicate with foreign nations into exclusive policy-making authority." David Gray Adler, "Foreign Policy and the Separation of Powers: The Influence of the Judiciary," in Michael W. McCann and Gerald L. Houseman, eds., *Judging the Constitution* (Glenview, Ill.: Scott, Foresman, 1989), 160.

3. Does the majority opinion offer any guidance for distinguishing between "internal" affairs and "external" affairs? Does the distinction have any merit?

4. What conception of judicial power does the majority embrace?

5. In Comparative Note 7.6, the Japanese District Court wrote that "The Constitution clearly sets up legal norms in its Preamble and Article 9 on the issue of [self-defense]." Does this suggest, in contrast to *Curtiss-Wright*, that the powers of foreign affairs are governed by constitutional norms and not simply or exclusively by political considerations?

6. For a review of the decision, see Charles Lofgren, United States v. Curtiss-Wright Corporation: *An Historical Reassessment*, 83 Yale Law Journal 1 (1973).

Korematsu v. United States
323 U.S. 214, 65 S. Ct. 193, 89 L. Ed. 194 (1944)

On 7 December 1941, Japanese forces attacked the American naval station at Pearl Harbor. Almost immediately the Japanese forces swept across much of the western Pacific, fueling fears that an attack on the West Coast of the United States was imminent. Because of war hysteria, simple racism, and economic competition, local and national politicians, including Earl Warren, then attorney general for the state of California, began to clamor for the internment of local Japanese-Americans, citing the threat of sabotage and espionage. Several military leaders joined in, notably General John L. DeWitt, commander-in-chief of the West Coast forces, even though the Office of Naval Intelligence and the Federal Bureau of Investigation had discounted the existence of any threat. On 27 March 1942, President Roosevelt issued an executive order that gave the military authority to "relocate" Japanese-Americans to several internment camps located in the west. No formal charges were required to relocate a citizen, and there was no requirement that there be any particular evidence of a citizen's disloyalty or of criminal behavior. Fred Korematsu resisted the order and was arrested and convicted. The Supreme Court granted certiorari. Opinion of the Court: *Black*, Stone, Reed, Frankfurter, Douglas, Rutledge. Concurring opinion: *Frankfurter*. Dissenting opinion: *Roberts, Murphy, Jackson*.

Mr. Justice BLACK delivered the opinion of the Court.

It should be noted, to begin with, that all legal restrictions which curtail the civil rights of a single racial group are immediately suspect. That is not to say that all such restrictions are unconstitutional. It is to say that Courts must subject them to the most rigid scrutiny. Pressing public necessity may sometimes justify the existence of such restrictions; racial antagonism never can.

In the light of the principles we announced in the *Hirabayashi* case, we are unable to conclude that it was beyond the war power of Congress and the Executive to exclude those of Japanese ancestry from the West Coast war area at the time they did. True, exclusion from the area in which one's home is located is a far greater deprivation than constant confinement to the home from 8 p.m. to 6 a.m. Nothing short of apprehension by the proper military authorities of the gravest imminent danger to the public safety can constitutionally justify either. But exclusion from a threatened area . . . has a definite and close relationship to the prevention of espionage and sabotage. The military authorities, charged with the primary responsibility of defending our shores, concluded that curfew provided inadequate protection and ordered exclusion. They did so . . . in accordance with congressional authority to the military to say who should, and who should not, remain in the threatened areas.

Here, as in *Hirabayashi*, "we cannot reject as unfounded the judgment of the military authorities and of Congress that there were disloyal members of that population. . . ." It was because we could not reject the finding of the military authorities that it was impossible to bring about an immediate segregation of the disloyal from the loyal that we sustained the validity of the curfew order as applying to the whole group. In the instant case, temporary exclusion of the entire group was rested by the military on the same ground. The judgment that exclusion of the whole group was for the same reason a military imperative answers the contention that the exclusion was in the nature of group punishment based on antagonism to those of Japanese origin. . . . That there were members of the group who retained loyalties to Japan has been confirmed by investigations made subsequent to the exclusion. Approximately five thousand American citizens of Japanese ancestry refused to swear unqualified allegiance to the United States and to renounce allegiance to the Japanese Emperor, and several thousand evacuees requested repatriation to Japan.

We uphold the exclusion order as of the time it was made and when the petitioner violated it. In doing so, we are not unmindful of the hardships imposed by it upon a large group of American citizens. But hardships are part of war, and war is an aggregation of hardships. Compulsory exclusion of large groups of citizens from their homes, except under circumstances of direst emergency and peril, is inconsistent with our basic governmental institutions. But when under conditions of modern warfare our shores are threatened by hostile forces, the power to protect must be commensurate with the threatened danger.

We are thus being asked to pass at this time upon the whole subsequent detention program in both assembly and relocation centers, although the only issues framed at the trial related to petitioner's remaining in the prohibited area in violation of the exclusion order. Had petitioner here left the prohibited area and gone to an assembly center we cannot say either as a matter of fact or law, that his presence in that center would have resulted in his detention in a relocation center. Some who did report . . . were not sent to relocation centers, but were released upon condition that they remain outside the prohibited zone.

Since the petitioner has not been convicted of failing to report or to remain in an assembly or relocation center, we cannot in this case determine the validity of those separate provisions of the order. . . . Some of the members of the Court are of the view that evacuation and detention . . . were inseparable. . . . The power to exclude includes the power to do it by force if necessary. And any forcible measure must necessarily entail some degree of detention and restraint whatever method of removal is selected. But whichever view is taken, it results in holding that the order under which the petitioner was convicted was valid.

It is said that we are dealing here with the case of imprisonment of a citizen in a concentration camp solely because of his ancestry, without evidence or inquiry concerning his loyalty and good disposition towards the United States. Our task would be simple, our duty clear, were this a case involving the imprisonment of a loyal citizen in a concentration camp because of racial prejudice. Regardless of the true nature of the assembly and relocation centers—and we deem it unjustifiable to call them concentration camps with all the ugly connotations that term implies—we are dealing specifically with nothing but an exclusion order. To cast this case into outlines of racial prejudice, without reference to the real military dangers which were presented, merely confuses the issue. Korematsu was not excluded from the Military Area because of hostility to him or his race. He was excluded because we are at war with the Japanese Empire, because the properly constituted military authorities feared an invasion of our West Coast and felt constrained to take proper security measures, because they decided that the military urgency of the situation demanded that all citizens of Japanese ancestry be segregated from the West Coast temporarily, and finally, because Congress, reposing its confidence in this time of war in our military leaders—as inevitably it must—determined that they should have the power to do just this. There was evidence of disloyalty on the part of some, the military authorities considered that the need for action was great, and

Comparative Note 7.7

[Rudolph Hess, a cabinet minister in the Nazi government, was arrested in Britain and brought forward as an accused before the International Military Tribunal following Germany's surrender in the second World War. He was convicted of "crimes against the peace" and sentenced to life in prison. In this case his son sought a declaration by the Federal Constitutional Court that the continuation of his imprisonment violated his rights under the Basic Law.]

The breadth of this discretion in foreign affairs has its basis in the nature of foreign relations. Such events are not governed solely by the will of the federation, but rather are dependent on many circumstances over which it has little control. In order to facilitate the realization of the federation's political goals within the framework of what is constitutionally permissible . . . the Constitution confers considerable discretion on foreign affairs agencies in assessing the practicality and feasibility of certain policies or actions.

SOURCE: *Rudolph Hess Case* (1980) in Kommers, *Constitutional Jurisprudence*, 154.

---

time was short. We cannot—by availing ourselves of the calm perspective of hindsight—now say that at that time these actions were unjustified.

Affirmed.

Mr. Justice FRANKFURTER, concurring.

The provisions of the Constitution which confer on the Congress and the President powers to enable this country to wage war are as much part of the Constitution as provisions looking to a nation at peace. And we have had recent occasion to quote approvingly the statement of former Chief Justice Hughes that the war power of the Government is "the power to wage war successfully." Therefore, the validity of action under the war power must be judged wholly in the context of war. That action is not to be stigmatized as lawless because like action in times of peace would be lawless. To talk about a military order that expresses an allowable judgment of war needs by those entrusted with the duty of conducting war as "an unconstitutional order" is to suffuse a part of the Constitution with an atmosphere of unconstitutionality. . . . To recognize that military orders are "reasonably expedient military precautions" in time of war and yet to deny them constitutional legitimacy makes of the Constitution an instrument for dialectic subtleties not reasonably to be attributed to the hardheaded Framers, of whom a majority had had actual participation in war. If a military order such as that under review does not transcend the means appropriate for conducting war, such action by the military is as constitutional as would be any authorized action by the Interstate Commerce Commission within the limits of the constitutional power to regulate commerce. And being an exercise of the war power explicitly granted by the Constitution for safeguarding the national life by prosecuting war effectively, I

find nothing in the Constitution which denies to Congress the power to enforce such a valid military order by making its violation an offense triable in the civil courts. To find that the Constitution does not forbid the military measures now complained of does not carry with it approval of that which Congress and the Executive did. That is their business, not ours.

Mr. Justice ROBERTS:

. . . [T]he indisputable facts exhibit a clear violation of Constitutional rights. . . . [E]xclusion was but part of an over-all plan for forcible detention. . . .

The two conflicting orders, one of which commanded him to stay and the other which commanded him to go, were nothing but a cleverly devised trap to accomplish the real purpose . . . which was to lock him up in a concentration camp. . . . Why should we set up a figmentary and artificial situation instead of addressing ourselves to the actualities of the case?

Mr. Justice MURPHY, dissenting.

This exclusion of "all persons of Japanese ancestry, both alien and non-alien," from the Pacific Coast area on a plea of military necessity in the absence of martial law ought not to be approved. Such exclusion goes over "the very brink of constitutional power" and falls into the ugly abyss of racism.

In dealing with matters relating to the prosecution and progress of a war, we must accord great respect and consideration to the judgments of the military authorities who are on the scene and who have full knowledge of the military facts. The scope of their discretion must, as a matter of necessity and common sense, be wide. And their judgments ought not to be overruled lightly by those whose training and duties ill-equip them to deal intelligently with matters so vital to the physical security of the nation.

At the same time, however, it is essential that there be definite limits to military discretion, especially where martial law has not been declared. Individuals must not be left impoverished of their constitutional rights on a plea of military necessity that has neither substance nor support. Thus, like other claims conflicting with the asserted constitutional rights of the individual, the military claim must subject itself to the judicial process of having its reasonableness determined and its conflicts with other interests reconciled.

The judicial test of whether the Government, on a plea of military necessity, can validly deprive an individual of any of his constitutional rights is whether the deprivation is reasonably related to a public danger that is so "immediate, imminent, and impending" as not to admit of delay and not to permit the intervention of ordinary constitutional processes to alleviate the danger. . . . Being an obvious racial discrimination, the order deprives all those within its scope of the equal protection of the laws as guaranteed by the Fifth Amendment. It further deprives these individuals of their constitutional rights to live and work where they will, to establish a home where they choose and to move about freely. In excommunicating them without benefit of hearings, this order also deprives them of all their constitutional rights to procedural due process. Yet no reasonable relation to an "immediate, imminent, and impending" public danger is evident to support this racial restriction. . . .

It must be conceded that the military and naval situation in the spring of 1942 was such as to generate a very real fear of invasion of the Pacific Coast, accompanied by fears of sabotage and espionage in that area. The military command was therefore justified in adopting all reasonable means necessary to combat these dangers. In adjudging the military action taken in light of the then apparent dangers, we must not erect too high or too meticulous standards; it is necessary only that the action have some reasonable relation to the removal of the dangers of invasion, sabotage and espionage. But the exclusion, either temporarily or permanently, of all persons with Japanese blood in their veins has no such reasonable relation. And that relation is lacking because the exclusion order necessarily must rely for its reasonableness upon the assumption that all persons of Japanese ancestry may have a dangerous tendency to commit sabotage and espionage and to aid our Japanese enemy in other ways. It is difficult to believe that reason, logic or experience could be marshalled in support of such an assumption.

That this forced exclusion was the result in good measure of this erroneous assumption of racial guilt rather than

bona fide military necessity is evidenced by the Commanding General's Final Report on the evacuation from the Pacific Coast area. In it he refers to all individuals of Japanese descent as "subversive," as belonging to "an enemy race" whose "racial strains are undiluted," and as constituting "over 112,000 potential enemies . . . at large today" along the Pacific Coast. In support of this blanket condemnation of all persons of Japanese descent, however, no reliable evidence is cited to show that such individuals were generally disloyal, or had generally so conducted themselves in this area as to constitute a special menace to defense installations or war industries, or had otherwise by their behavior furnished reasonable ground for their exclusion as a group.

Justification for the exclusion is sought, instead, mainly upon questionable racial and sociological grounds not ordinarily within the realm of expert military judgment, supplemented by certain semi-military conclusions drawn from an unwarranted use of circumstantial evidence. Individuals of Japanese ancestry are condemned because they are said to be "a large, unassimilated, tightly knit racial group, bound to an enemy nation by strong ties of race, culture, custom, and religion." They are claimed to be given to "emperor worshipping ceremonies" and to "dual citizenship." Japanese language schools and allegedly pro-Japanese organizations are cited as evidence of possible group disloyalty, together with facts as to certain persons being educated and residing at length in Japan. It is intimated that many of these individuals deliberately resided "adjacent to strategic points," thus enabling them "to carry into execution a tremendous program of sabotage on a mass scale should any considerable number of them have been inclined to do so."

The need for protective custody is also asserted. The report refers without identity to "numerous incidents of violence" as well as other admittedly unverified or cumulative incidents. From this, plus certain other events not shown to have been connected with the Japanese Americans, it is concluded that the "situation was fraught with danger to the Japanese population itself" and that the general public "was ready to take matters into its own hands."

The main reasons . . . appear . . . to be largely an accumulation of much of the misinformation, half-truths and insinuations that for years have been directed against Japanese Americans by people with racial and economic prejudices—the same people who have been among the foremost advocates of the evacuation. A military judgment based upon such racial and sociological considerations is not entitled to the great weight ordinarily given the judgments based upon strictly military considerations.

No adequate reason is given for the failure to treat these Japanese Americans on an individual basis by holding investigations and hearings to separate the loyal from the disloyal, as was done in the case of persons of German and Italian ancestry. . . . It is asserted merely that the loyalties of this group "were unknown and time was of the essence." Yet nearly four months elapsed after Pearl Harbor before the first exclusion order was issued; nearly eight months went by until the last order was issued; and the last of these "subversive" persons was not actually removed until almost eleven months had elapsed. Leisure and deliberation seem to have been more of the essence than speed. And the fact that conditions were not such as to warrant a declaration of martial law adds strength to the belief that the factors of time and military necessity were not as urgent as they have been represented to be.

I dissent, therefore, from this legalization of racism. Racial discrimination in any form and in any degree has no justifiable part whatever in our democratic way of life. It is unattractive in any setting but it is utterly revolting among a free people who have embraced the principles set forth in the Constitution of the United States. All residents of this nation are kin in some way by blood or culture to a foreign land. Yet they are primarily and necessarily a part of the new and distinct civilization of the United States. They must accordingly be treated at all times as the heirs of the American experiment and as entitled to all the rights and freedoms guaranteed by the Constitution.

Mr. Justice JACKSON, dissenting.

Now if any fundamental assumption underlies our system, it is that guilt is personal and not inheritable. . . . But here is an attempt to make an otherwise innocent act a crime merely because this prisoner is the son of parents as to whom he had no choice, and belongs to a race from which there is no way to resign.

. . . [I]t is said that if the military commander had reasonable military grounds for promulgating the orders, they are constitutional and become law, and the Court is required to enforce them. [There are] several reasons why I cannot subscribe to this doctrine.

It would be impracticable and dangerous idealism to expect or insist that each specific military command in an area of probable operations will conform to conventional tests of constitutionality. When an area is so beset that it must be put under military control at all, the paramount consideration is that its measures be successful, rather than legal. The armed services must protect a society, not merely its Constitution. The very essence of the military job is to marshal physical force, to remove every obstacle to its effectiveness, to give it every strategic advantage. Defense measures will not, and often should not, be held within the limits that bind civil authority in peace. No Court can require such a commander in such circumstances to act as a

reasonable man; he may be unreasonably cautious and exacting. Perhaps he should be. But a commander in temporarily focusing the life of a community on defense is carrying out a military program; he is not making law in the sense the Courts know the term. He issues orders, and they may have a certain authority as military commands, although they may be very bad as constitutional law.

But if we cannot confine military expedients by the Constitution, neither would I distort the Constitution to approve all that the military may deem expedient. This is what the Court appears to be doing, whether consciously or not. I cannot say, from any evidence before me, that the orders of General DeWitt were not reasonably expedient military precautions, nor could I say that they were. But even if they were permissible military procedures, I deny that it follows that they are constitutional. If, as the Court holds, it does follow, then we may as well say that any military order will be constitutional and have done with it.

In the very nature of things military decisions are not susceptible of intelligent judicial appraisal. They do not pretend to rest on evidence, but are made on information that often would not be admissible and on assumptions that could not be proved. Information in support of an order could not be disclosed to Courts without danger that it would reach the enemy. Neither can Courts act on communications made in confidence. Hence Courts can never have any real alternative to accepting the mere declaration of the authority that issued the order that it was reasonably necessary from a military viewpoint.

Much is said of the danger to liberty from the Army program for deporting and detaining these citizens of Japanese extraction. But a judicial construction of the due process clause that will sustain this order is a far more subtle blow to liberty than the promulgation of the order itself. A military order, however unconstitutional, is not apt to last longer than the military emergency. Even during that period a succeeding commander may revoke it all. But once a judicial opinion rationalizes such an order to show that it conforms to the Constitution, or rather rationalizes the Constitution to show that the Constitution sanctions such an order, the Court for all time has validated the principle of racial discrimination in criminal procedure and of transplanting American citizens. The principle then lies about like a loaded weapon ready for the hand of any authority that can bring forward a plausible claim of an urgent need. Every repetition imbeds that principle more deeply in our law and thinking and expands it to new purposes. All who observe the work of courts are familiar with what Judge Cardozo described as "the tendency of a principle to expand itself to the limit of its logic." A military commander may overstep the bounds of constitutionality, and it is an incident. But if we review and approve, that passing incident becomes the doctrine of the Constitution. There it has a generative power of its own, and all that it creates will be in its own image. Nothing better illustrates this danger than does the Court's opinion in this case. It argues that we are bound to uphold the conviction of Korematsu because we upheld one in *Hirabayashi*.

In that case we were urged to consider only the curfew. . . . We yielded, and the Chief Justice guarded the opinion as carefully as language will do. . . . Now the principle of racial discrimination is pushed from support of mild measures to very harsh ones, and from temporary deprivations to indeterminate ones. And the precedent which it is said requires us to do so is *Hirabayashi*. The Court is now saying that in *Hirabayashi* we did decide the very things we there said we were not deciding.

I should hold that a civil court cannot be made to enforce an order which violates constitutional limitations even if it is a reasonable exercise of military authority. The courts can exercise only the judicial power, can apply only law, and must abide by the Constitution, or they cease to be civil courts and become instruments of military policy.

. . . I would not lead people to rely on this Court for a review that seems to me wholly delusive. . . . If the people ever let command of the war power fall into irresponsible and unscrupulous hands, the courts wield no power equal to its restraint. The chief restraint upon those who command . . . must be their responsibility to the political judgments of their contemporaries and to the moral judgments of history.

My duties as a justice as I see them do not require me to make a military judgment as to whether General DeWitt's evacuation and detention program was a reasonable military necessity. I do not suggest that the Courts should have attempted to interfere with the Army in carrying out its task. But I do not think they may be asked to execute a military expedient that has no place in law under the Constitution. I would reverse the judgment and discharge the prisoner.

Notes/Queries/Readings

1. Executive Order 9066, calling for the "evacuation" of Japanese-Americans on the West Coast, resulted in the internment of over 100,000 residents. The last of the internees were released from the camps in 1946. In 1983, after years of hard work by lawyers for the American Civil Liberties Union and the Japanese-American Citizens League, among others, Fred Korematsu's conviction was "vacated" by Federal District Judge Marilyn Hall Patel. Korematsu's lawyers had used a petition of *coram nobis*—an extremely unusual procedure—to force the government to prove that there had not been a "manifest injustice" or prosecu-

torial misconduct in the case. Judge Patel ruled in favor of Korematsu, finding there was "substantial support in the record that the government deliberately omitted relevant information and provided misleading information" to the Supreme Court.

2. In 1980, Congress created a Commission on Wartime Relocation and Internment of Civilians to review the decision. After hearings in 1981, the Commission unanimously concluded that the internment policy was a consequence of "race prejudice, war hysteria and a failure of political leadership. . . ." It recommended that Congress reimburse each of the 60,000 or so survivors of the camps with $20,000. Congress enacted the legislation in 1988, and President Reagan signed it into law.

3. *Korematsu* involves important questions about how the Constitution is interpreted and who interprets it. Consider: In his majority opinion, Justice Black purports to use strict scrutiny but upholds the policy. Justice Murphy, in contrast, professes to use the lowly rationality standard, but he strikes the program. What does this tell us about the integrity of these various standards of judicial scrutiny? What does it tell us about the integrity of constitutional interpretation more generally?

Similarly, Justices Black, Murphy, and Jackson approach the question of who interprets the Constitution in such cases in very different ways. Black and Murphy insist upon the principle of judicial accountability, albeit in starkly different degrees. Jackson, in contrast, cautions about the limits of judicial supervision, thus entrusting constitutional interpretation primarily to the "political branches," much as Justice Grier did almost a century earlier.

4. What theory of judicial power animates Justice Black's opinion for the majority? How does it differ from Justice Jackson's dissent? Would Jackson—later chief prosecutor at the Nuremberg War Trials—have ruled that the executive order was unconstitutional? Or would he have refused to consider its constitutionality? Is there a difference?

5. Can the decision in *Korematsu* be reconciled with the Court's expansive language in *Ex Parte Milligan* (1866)?

6. The essential issue in *Korematsu*, of course, concerns the tension between the community and the individual. War highlights that tension better than anything else. Consider: If our collective survival is really at issue, is it not foolish to risk that survival by an overly scrupulous attention to constitutional principle? Is the Constitution a suicide pact?

7. There is a peculiar twist to *Korematsu*: It is among the very first cases to establish that "legal restrictions which curtail the civil rights of a single racial group are immediately suspect." As we shall see in chapter 13, this test has become a cornerstone of judicial efforts to guarantee equal protection to racial minorities.

8. Canada also detained many of its citizens of Japanese ancestry. In 1945, after Japan had surrendered, the Government ordered the Labour Minister to deport any member of the Japanese race who had requested repatriation during the war. The orders included a provision authorizing the minister to deport the wife and children of a male already scheduled for deportation. In *Co-Operative Committee on Japanese Canadians v. Attorney-General for Canada*, (1947) A.C. 87, 3 Olmstead 458, the Privy Council upheld the orders. For a history, see Forrest E. La Violette, *The Canadian Japanese and World War II* (Toronto: University of Toronto Press, 1948). For a fictionalized account of the Canadian experience, see Joy Kogawa, *Obasan* (Boston: David R. Godine, Publisher, 1981).

9. Comparative Note 7.7 reprints an excerpt from a decision by the Federal Constitutional Court of Germany. Does the Court's decision mirror Justice Black's insistence upon deference to the military authorities in *Korematsu*?

10. There are many fine studies of the Japanese-American internment. Among the most useful are Peter Irons, *Justice at War* (New York: Oxford University Press, 1983); *Justice Delayed: The Record of the Japanese Internment Cases* (Middletown: Wesleyan University Press, 1989); Morton Grodzins, *Americans Betrayed* (Chicago: University of Chicago Press, 1949); Bill Hosokawa, *JACL In Quest of Justice: The History of the Japanese American Citizens League* (New York: William Morrow & Co., 1982). For a recent treatment that paints a somewhat less dark picture of the episode, see Page Smith, *Democracy on Trial: The Japanese American Evacuation and Relocation in World War II* (New York: Simon & Schuster, 1995). For a description of life inside the camps, see Richard Nishimoto, *Inside an American Concentration Camp: Japanese American Resistance at Poston, Arizona* (Tucson: University of Arizona Press, 1995). For a description from the point of view of a young girl, see Yoshiko Uchida and Joanna Yardley, *The Bracelet* (New York: Philomel Books, 1993).

Ex Parte Milligan
71 U.S. (4 Wall.) 2, 18 L. Ed. 281 (1866)

Lambdin P. Milligan was arrested by federal troops in October 1864, for being part of the "Sons of Liberty," a group dedicated to freeing Confederate prisoners from Union prisons in Indiana, Ohio, and Illinois. Milligan, an Indiana resident, was tried by a military tribunal, convicted, and sentenced to death by hanging. Milligan's attorney petitioned the federal circuit court for a writ of habeas corpus despite President Lincoln's suspension of that privilege. The case was certified to the Supreme Court. Opinion of the Court: *Davis*, Nelson, Grier, Clifford, Field. Concurring opinion: *Chase*, Wayne, Swayne, Miller.

Mr. Justice DAVIS delivered the opinion of the Court.

The importance of the main question presented . . . cannot be overstated, for it involves the very framework of the government and the fundamental principles of American liberty.

During the late wicked Rebellion the temper of the times did not allow that calmness in deliberation and discussion so necessary to a correct conclusion of a purely judicial question. Now that the public safety is assured, this question, as well as all others, can be discussed and decided without passion.

The controlling question in the case is this: Upon the facts stated in Milligan's petition, and the exhibits filed, had the military commission mentioned in it jurisdiction, legally, to try and sentence him? Milligan, not a resident of one of the rebellious states, or a prisoner of war, but a citizen of Indiana for twenty years past, and never in the military or naval service, is, while at his home, arrested by the military power of the United States, imprisoned, and, on certain criminal charges preferred against him, tried, convicted, and sentenced to be hanged by a military commission, organized under the direction of the military commander of the military district of Indiana. Had this tribunal the legal power and authority to try and punish this man?

No graver question was ever considered by this Court, nor one which more nearly concerns the rights of the whole people; for it is the birthright of every American citizen when charged with crime, to be tried and punished according to law. The power of punishment is alone through the means which the laws have provided for that purpose, and if they are ineffectual, there is an immunity from punishment, no matter how great an offender the individual may be, or how much his crimes may have shocked the sense of justice of the country, or endangered its safety. By the protection of the law human rights are secured; withdraw that protection, and they are at the mercy of wicked rulers or the clamor of an excited people. If there was law to justify this military trial, it is not our province to interfere; if there was not, it is our duty to declare the nullity of the whole proceedings. The decision of this question does not depend on argument or judicial precedents, numerous and highly illustrative as they are. These precedents inform us of the extent of the struggle to preserve liberty and to relieve those in civil life from military trials. The founders of our government were familiar with the history of that struggle; and secured in a written constitution every right which the people had wrested from power during a contest of ages. By that Constitution and the laws authorized by it this question must be determined. The provisions of that instrument on the administration of criminal justice are too plain and direct, to leave room for misconstruction or doubt of their true meaning. Those applicable to this case are found in that clause of the original Constitution which says, "That the trial of all crimes, except in case of impeachment, shall be by jury;" and in the fourth, fifth, and sixth articles of the amendments.

Time has proven the discernment of our ancestors; for even these provisions, expressed in such plain English words, that it would seem the ingenuity of man could not evade them, are now, after the lapse of more than seventy years, sought to be avoided. . . . The Constitution of the United States is a law for rulers and people, equally in war and in peace, and covers with the shield of its protection all classes of men, at all times, and under all circumstances. No doctrine, involving more pernicious consequences, was ever invented by the wit of man than that any of its provisions can be suspended during any of the great exigencies of government. Such a doctrine leads directly to anarchy or despotism, but the theory of necessity on which it is based is false; for the government, within the Constitution, has all the powers granted to it, which are necessary to preserve its existence; as has been happily proved by the result of the great effort to throw off its just authority.

Have any of the rights guaranteed by the Constitution been violated in the case of Milligan? and if so, what are they?

Every trial involves the exercise of judicial power; and from what source did the military commission that tried him derive their authority? Certainly no part of judicial power of the country was conferred on them; because the Constitution expressly vests it "in one Supreme Court and such inferior Courts as the Congress may from time to time ordain and establish," and it is not pretended that the commission was a Court ordained and established by Congress. They cannot justify on the mandate of the President; because he is controlled by law, and has his appropriate sphere of duty, which is to execute, not to make, the laws; and there is "no unwritten criminal code to which resort can be had as a source of jurisdiction."

But it is said that the jurisdiction is complete under the "laws and usages of war."

It can serve no useful purpose to inquire what those laws and usages are, whence they originated, where found, and on whom they operate; they can never be applied to citizens in states which have upheld the authority of the government, and where the Courts are open and their process unobstructed. This Court has judicial knowledge that in Indiana the Federal authority was always unopposed, and its Courts always open to hear criminal accusations and redress grievances; and no usage of war could sanction a military trial there for any offence whatever of a citizen in civil life, in nowise connected with the military service. Congress could grant no such power; and to the honor of our national legislature be it said, it has never been provoked by the state of the country even to attempt its exercise. One of the plainest constitutional provisions was, therefore, infringed when Milligan was tried by a Court not ordained and established by Congress, and not composed of judges appointed during good behavior.

Why was he not delivered to the Circuit Court of Indiana to be proceeded against according to law? No reason of necessity could be urged against it; because Congress had declared penalties against the offences charged, provided for their punishment, and directed that Court to hear and determine them. And soon after this military tribunal was ended, the Circuit Court met, peacefully transacted its business, no military aid to execute its judgments. It was held in a state, eminently distinguished for patriotism, by judges commissioned during the Rebellion, who were provided with juries, upright, intelligent, and selected by a marshal appointed by the President. The government had no right to conclude that Milligan, if guilty, would not receive in that Court merited punishment; for its records disclose that it was constantly engaged in the trial of similar offences, and was never interrupted in its administration of criminal justice. If it was dangerous, in the distracted condition of affairs, to leave Milligan unrestrained of his liberty, because he "conspired against the government, afforded aid and comfort to rebels, and incited the people to insurrection," the law said arrest him, confine him closely, render him powerless to do further mischief; and then present his case to the grand jury of the district, with proofs of his guilt, and, if indicted, try him according to the course of the common law. If this had been done, the Constitution would have been vindicated, the law of 1863 enforced, and the securities for personal liberty preserved and defended.

Another guarantee of freedom was broken when Milligan was denied a trial by jury. The great minds of the country have differed on the correct interpretation to be given to various provisions of the Federal Constitution; and judicial decision has been often invoked to settle their true meaning; but until recently no one ever doubted that the right of trial by jury was fortified in the organic law against the power of attack. It is now assailed; but if ideas can be expressed in words, and language has any meaning, this right—one of the most valuable in a free country—is preserved to every one accused of crime who is not attached to the army, or navy, or militia in actual service.

This privilege is a vital principle, underlying the whole administration of criminal justice; it is not held by sufference, and cannot be frittered away on any plea of political necessity. When peace prevails, and the authority of the government is undisputed, there is no difficulty of preserving the safeguards of liberty; for the ordinary modes of trial are never neglected, and no one wishes it otherwise; but if society is disturbed by civil commotion—if the passions of men are aroused and the restraints of law weakened, if not disregarded—these safeguards need, and should receive, the watchful care of those intrusted with the guardianship of the Constitution and laws. . . .

It is claimed that martial law covers with its broad mantle the proceedings of this military commission. The proposition is this: that in a time of war the commander of an armed force (if in his opinion the exigencies of the country demand it, and of which he is to judge), has the power, within the lines of his military district, to suspend all civil rights and their remedies, and subject citizens as well as soldiers to the rule of his will; and in the exercise of his lawful authority cannot be restrained, except by his superior officer or the President of the United States.

If this position is sound to the extent claimed, then when war exists, foreign or domestic, and the country is subdivided into military departments for mere convenience, the commander of one of them can, if he chooses, within his limits, on the plea of necessity, with the approval of the Executive, substitute military force for and to the exclusion of the laws, and punish all persons, as he thinks right and proper, without fixed or certain rules.

The statement of this proposition shows its importance; for, if true, republican government is a failure, and there is an end of liberty regulated by law. Martial law, established on such a basis, destroys every guarantee of the Constitution, and effectually renders the "military independent of and superior to the civil power"—the attempt to do which by the King of Great Britain was deemed by our fathers such an offence, that they assigned it to the world as one of the causes which impelled them to declare their independence. Civil liberty and this kind of martial law cannot endure together; the antagonism is irreconcilable; and, in the conflict, one or the other must perish.

This nation, as experience has proved, cannot always remain at peace, and has no right to expect that it will always have wise and humane rulers, sincerely attached to the principles of the Constitution. Wicked men, ambitious of power, with hatred of liberty and contempt of law, may once fill the place occupied by Washington and Lincoln; and if this right is conceded, and the calamities of war again befall us, the dangers to human liberty are frightful to contemplate. If our fathers had failed to provide for just such a contingency, they would have been false to the trust reposed in them. They knew—the history of the world told them—the nation they were founding, be its existence short or long, would be involved in war; how often or how long continued, human foresight could not tell; and that unlimited power, wherever lodged at such a time, was especially hazardous to freemen. For this, and other equally weighty reasons, they secured the inheritance they had fought to maintain, by incorporating in a written constitution the safeguards which time had proved were essential to its preservation. Not one of these safeguards can the President, or Congress, or the Judiciary disturb, except the one concerning the writ of habeas corpus.

. . . [I]t is insisted that the safety of the country in time of war demands that this broad claim for martial law shall be sustained. If this were true, it could be well said that a country, preserved at the sacrifice of all the cardinal principles of liberty, is not worth the cost of preservation. Happily, it is not so.

It will be borne in mind that this is not a question of the power to proclaim martial law, when war exists in a community and the Courts and civil authorities are overthrown. Nor is it a question what rule a military commander, at the head of his army, can impose on states in rebellion to cripple their resources and quell the insurrection. The jurisdiction claimed is much more extensive. The necessities of the service, during the late Rebellion, required that the loyal states should be placed within the limits of certain military districts and commanders appointed in them; and, it is urged, that this, in a military sense, constituted them the theater of military operations; and, as in this case, Indiana had been and was again. . . . If armies were collected in Indiana, they were to be employed in another locality, where the laws were obstructed and the national authority disputed. On her soil there was no hostile foot; if once invaded, that invasion was at an end, and with it all pretext for martial law. Martial law cannot arise from a threatened invasion. The necessity must be actual and present; the invasion real, such as effectually closes the Courts and deposes the civil administration.

It follows, from what has been said on this subject, that there are occasions when martial rule can be properly applied. If, in foreign invasion or civil war, the Courts are actually closed, and it is impossible to administer criminal justice according to law, then, on the theatre of active military operations, where war really prevails, there is a necessity to furnish a substitute for the civil authority, thus overthrown, to preserve the safety of the army and society; and as no power is left but the military, it is allowed to govern by martial rule until the laws can have their free course. As necessity creates the rule, so it limits its duration; for, if this government is continued after the Courts are reinstated, it is a gross usurpation of power. Martial rule can never exist where the Courts are open, and in the proper and unobstructed exercise of their jurisdiction. It is also confined to the locality of actual war. Because, during the late Rebellion it could have been enforced in Virginia, where the national authority was overturned and the Courts driven out, it does not follow that it should obtain in Indiana, where that authority was never disputed, and justice was always administered.

The Chief Justice CHASE delivered the following opinion.

. . . [T]he opinion which has just been read . . . asserts not only that the military commission held in Indiana was not authorized by Congress; from which it may be thought to follow, that Congress has no power to indemnify the officers who composed the commission against liability in civil Courts for acting as members of it.

We cannot agree to this.

. . . Congress has power to raise and support armies; to provide and maintain a navy; to make rules for the government and regulation of the land and naval forces; and to provide for governing such part of the militia as may be in the service of the United States.

It is not denied that the power to make rules for the government of the army and navy is a power to provide for trial and punishment by military Courts without a jury. It has been so understood and exercised from the adoption of the Constitution to the present time.

Nor, in our judgment, does the fifth, or any other amendment, abridge that power.

We think, therefore, that the power of Congress, in the government of the land and naval forces and of the militia, is not at all affected by the fifth or any other amendment. It is not necessary to attempt any precise definition of the boundaries of this power. But may it not be said that government includes protection and defence as well as the regulation of internal administration? And is it impossible to imagine cases in which citizens conspiring or attempting the destruction or great injury of the national forces may be subjected by Congress to military trial and punishment in the just exercise of this undoubted constitutional power? Congress is but the agent of the nation, and does not the security of individuals against the abuse of this, as of every other power, depend on the intelligence and virtue of the people, on their zeal for public and private liberty, upon official responsibility secured by law, and upon the frequency of elections, rather than upon doubtful constructions of legislative powers?

Congress has the power not only to raise and support and govern armies but to declare war. It has, therefore, the power to provide by law for carrying on war. This power necessarily extends to all legislation essential to the prosecution of war with vigor and success, except such as interferes with the command of the forces and the conduct of campaigns. That power and duty belong to the President as commander-in-chief. Both these powers are derived from the Constitution, but neither is defined by that instrument. Their extent must be determined by their nature, and by the principles of our institutions.

We by no means assert that Congress can establish and apply the laws of war where no war has been declared or exists.

Where peace exists the laws of peace must prevail. What we do maintain is, that when the nation is involved in war, and some portions of the country are invaded, and all are exposed to invasion, it is within the power of Congress to determine in what states or districts such great and imminent public danger exists as justifies the authorization of military tribunals for the trial of crimes and offences against the discipline or security of the army or against the public safety.

In Indiana, for example, at the time of the arrest of Milligan and his co-conspirators, it is established by the papers in the record, that the state was a military district, was the theatre of military operations, had been actually invaded, and was constantly threatened with invasion. It appears, also, that a powerful secret association, composed of citizens and others, existed within the state, under military organization, conspiring against the draft, and plotting insurrection, the liberation of the prisoners of war at various depots, the seizure of the state and national arsenals, armed cooperation with the enemy, and war against the national government.

We cannot doubt that, in such a time of public danger, Congress had power, under the Constitution, to provide for the organization of a military commission, and for trial by that commission of persons engaged in this conspiracy. The fact that the Federal Courts were open was regarded by Congress as a sufficient reason for not exercising the power; but that fact could not deprive Congress of the right to exercise it. Those Courts might be open and undisturbed in the execution of their functions, and yet wholly incompetent to avert threatened danger, or to punish, with adequate promptitude and certainty, the guilty conspirators.

There are under the Constitution three kinds of military jurisdiction: one to be exercised both in peace and war; another to be exercised in time of foreign war without the boundaries of the United States, or in time of rebellion and civil war within states or districts occupied by rebels treated as belligerents; and a third to be exercised in time of invasion or insurrection within the limits of the United States, or during rebellion within the limits of states maintaining adhesion to the National Government, when the public danger requires its exercise. The first of these may be called jurisdiction under MILITARY LAW, and is found in acts of Congress prescribing rules and articles of war, or otherwise providing for the government of the national forces; the second may be distinguished as MILITARY GOVERNMENT, superseding, as far as may be deemed expedient, the local law, and exercised by the military commander under the direction of the President, with the express or implied sanction of Congress; while the third may be denominated MARTIAL LAW PROPER, and is called into action by Congress, or temporarily, when the action of Congress cannot be invited, and in the case of justifying or excusing peril, by the President, in times of insurrection or invasion, or of civil or foreign war, within districts or localities where ordinary law no longer adequately secures public safety and private rights.

We think that the power of Congress, in such times and in such localities . . . may be derived from its constitutional authority to raise and support armies and to declare war, if not from its constitutional authority to provide for governing the national forces.

We have no apprehension that this power, under our American system of government, in which all official authority is derived from the people, and exercised under direct responsibility to the people, is more likely to be abused than the power to regulate commerce, or the power to borrow money. And we are unwilling to give our assent by silence to expressions of opinion which seem to us calculated, though not intended, to cripple the constitutional powers of the government, and to augment the public dangers in times of invasion and rebellion.

Mr. Justice WAYNE, Mr. Justice SWAYNE, and Mr. Justice MILLER concur with me in these views.

Notes/Queries/Readings

1. Can the Court's decision, particularly its claim that the "Constitution of the United States is a law for rulers and people, equally in war and peace, and covers with the shield of its protection all classes of men, at all times, and under all circumstances," be reconciled with *Korematsu*?

2. Can the ruling against President Lincoln's orders for the trial of civilians by military courts be reconciled with the Court's earlier decision to uphold Lincoln's blockade of the southern ports in *The Prize Cases* (1863)?

3. John P. Frank concluded that "Ex parte Milligan is one of the truly great documents of the American Constitution, a bulwark for the protection of the civil liberties of every American citizen." (*Ex Parte Milligan*, 44 Columbia Law Review 639 [1944]). Is he correct?

4. *Milligan* was not well-received by Congress. Radical Republicans had enacted statutes that provided for military trials for some civilians. Many saw the Court's decision in *Milligan* as a direct threat to the constitutionality of their entire program for Reconstruction. Some of those Republicans, including Congressman John Bingham, announced that if the Court did not back down, Congress would propose a constitutional amendment that would call for "the abolition of the tribunal itself." The threat was real. In 1868, Congress had begun impeachment proceedings against President Johnson. Congress further reacted by depriving the Court of jurisdiction over certain classes of habeas corpus petitions. In *Ex parte McCardle* [1869], the Court took a more cautious approach, noting that Article 3, Section 2 gave Congress authority to regulate the Court's appellate jurisdiction (see chapter 3). Moreover, the Court went to great lengths to note that "We are not at liberty to inquire into the motives of the legislature."

5. For additional reading on the Court and the Civil War, see Harold Hyman, *A More Perfect Union* (New York: Knopf, 1973); Charles Fairman, *Reconstruction and Reunion, 1864–1888*. Part 1, vol. 6, of *History of the Supreme Court of the United States* (New York: Macmillan, 1971).

Declaration
of Independence

(Adopted in Congress 4 July 1776)

The Unanimous Declaration of the Thirteen United States of America

When, in the Course of human events, it becomes necessary for one people to dissolve the political bonds which have connected them with another, and to assume among the powers of the earth, the separate and equal station to which the Laws of Nature and of Nature's God entitle them, a decent respect to the opinions of mankind requires that they should declare the causes which impel them to the separation.

We hold these truths to be self-evident, that all men are created equal, that they are endowed by their Creator with certain unalienable Rights, that among these are life, liberty and the pursuit of happiness. That to secure these rights, Governments are instituted among Men, deriving their just powers from the consent of the governed. That whenever any Form of government becomes destructive to these ends, it is the Right of the People to alter or to abolish it, and to institute new Government, laying its foundation on such principles and organizing its powers in such form, as to them shall seem most likely to effect their Safety and Happiness. Prudence, indeed, will dictate that Governments long established should not be changed for light and transient causes; and accordingly all experience hath shown that mankind are more disposed to suffer, while evils are sufferable, than to right themselves by abolishing the forms to which they are accustomed. But when a long train of abuses and usurpations, pursuing invariably the same Object evinces a design to reduce them under absolute despotism, it is their right, it is their duty, to throw off such Government, and to provide new Guards for their future security.—Such has been the patient sufferance of these Colonies; and such is now the necessity which constrains them to alter their former Systems of Government. The history of the present King of Great Britain is a history of repeated injuries and usurpations, all having in direct object the establishment

of an absolute Tyranny over these States. To prove this, let Facts be submitted to a candid world.

He has refused his Assent to Laws, the most wholesome and necessary for the public good.

He has forbidden his Governors to pass laws of immediate and pressing importance, unless suspended in their operation till his Assent should be obtained; and when so suspended, he has utterly neglected to attend to them.

He has refused to pass other Laws for the accommodation of large districts of people, unless those people would relinquish the right of Representation in the Legislature, a right inestimable to them and formidable to tyrants only.

He has called together legislative bodies at places unusual, uncomfortable, and distant from the depository of their public Records, for the sole purpose of fatiguing them into compliance with his measures.

He has dissolved Representative Houses repeatedly, for opposing with manly firmness his invasions on the rights of the people.

He has refused for a long time, after such dissolutions, to cause others to be elected; whereby the Legislative powers, incapable of Annihilation, have returned to the People at large for their exercise; the state remaining in the meantime exposed to all the dangers of invasion from without, and convulsions within.

He has endeavored to prevent the population of these States; for that purpose obstructing the Laws for Naturalization of Foreigners; refusing to pass others to encourage their migration hither, and raising the conditions of new Appropriations of Lands.

He has obstructed the Administration of Justice, by refusing his Assent to Laws for establishing Judiciary powers.

He has made Judges dependent on his Will alone, for the tenure of their offices, and the amount and payment of their salaries.

He has erected a multitude of New Offices, and sent hither swarms of Officers to harass our people, and eat out their substance.

He has kept among us, in times of peace, Standing Armies without the Consent of our Legislatures.

He has affected to render the Military independent of and superior to the Civil Power.

He has combined with others to subject us to a jurisdiction foreign to our constitution, and unacknowledged by our laws; giving his Assent to their Acts of pretended Legislation:

For quartering large bodies of armed troops among us:

For protecting them, by mock Trial, from punishment for any Murders which they should commit on the Inhabitants of these States:

For cutting off our Trade with all parts of the world:

For imposing Taxes on us without our Consent:

For depriving us in many cases, of the benefits of Trial by Jury:

For transporting us beyond Seas to be tried for pretended offenses:

For abolishing the free System of English laws in a neighboring Province, establishing therein an Arbitrary government, and enlarging its Boundaries so as to render it at once an example and fit instrument for introducing the same absolute rule in these Colonies:

For taking away our Charters, abolishing our most valuable Laws, and altering fundamentally the Forms of our Governments:

For suspending our own Legislatures, and declaring themselves invested with power to legislate for us in all cases whatsoever.

He has abdicated Government here, by declaring us out of his Protection and waging War against us.

He has plundered our seas, ravaged our Coasts, burnt our towns, and destroyed the lives of our people.

He is at this time transporting large Armies of foreign Mercenaries to compleat the works of death, desolation and tyranny, already begun with circumstances of Cruelty & perfidy scarcely paralleled in the most barbarous ages, and totaly unworth the Head of a civilized nation.

He has constrained our fellow Citizens taken Captive on the high seas to bear Arms against their Country, to become the executioners of their friends and Brethren, or to fall themselves by their Hands.

He has excited domestic insurrections amongst us, and has endeavored to bring on the inhabitants of our frontiers, the merciless Indian Savages, whose known rule of warfare, is undistinguished destruction of all ages, sexes and conditions.

In every stage of these Oppressions We have Petitioned for Redress in the most humble terms: Our repeated Petitions have been answered only by repeated injury. A Prince, whose character is thus marked by every act which may define a Tyrant, is unfit to be the ruler of a free people.

Nor have We been wanting in attention to our British brethren. We have warned them from time to time of attempts by their legislature to extend an unwarrantable jurisdiction over us. We have reminded them of the circumstances of our emigration and settlement here. We have appealed to their native justice and magnanimity, and we have conjured them by the ties of our common kindred to disavow these usurpations, which, would inevitably interrupt our connections and correspondence. They too have been deaf to the voice of justice and of consanguinity. We must, therefore, acquiesce in the necessity, which denounces our Separation, and hold them, as we hold the rest of mankind, Enemies in War, in Peace Friends.

WE, THEREFORE, THE REPRESENTATIVES OF THE UNITED STATES OF AMERICA, in General Congress, Assembled, appealing to the Supreme Judge of the world for the rectitude of our intentions, do, in the Name, and by Authority of the good People of these Colonies, solemnly publish and declare, That these United Colonies are, and of Right ought to be FREE AND INDEPENDENT STATES; that they are Absolved from all allegiance to the British Crown, and that all political connection between them and the State of Great Britain, is and ought to be totally dissolved; and that as Free and Independent States, they have full Power to levy War, conclude Peace, contract Alliances, establish Commerce, and to do all other Acts and Things which Independent States may of right do. And for the support of this declaration, with a firm reliance on the protection of Divine Providence, we mutually pledge to each other our Lives, our Fortunes and our sacred Honor.

The United States Constitution

We the People of the United States, in Order to form a more perfect Union, establish Justice, insure domestic Tranquility, provide for the common defence, promote the general Welfare, and secure the Blessings of Liberty to ourselves and our Posterity, do ordain and establish this Constitution for the United States of America.

Article I

Section 1

All legislative Powers herein granted shall be vested in a Congress of the United States, which shall consist of a Senate and House of Representatives.

Section 2

Clause 1: The House of Representatives shall be composed of Members chosen every second Year by the People of the several States, and the Electors in each State shall have the Qualifications requisite for Electors of the most numerous Branch of the State Legislature.

Clause 2: No Person shall be a Representative who shall not have attained to the Age of twenty five Years, and been seven Years a Citizen of the United States, and who shall not, when elected, be an Inhabitant of that State in which he shall be chosen.

Clause 3: Representatives and direct Taxes shall be apportioned among the several States which may be included within this Union, according to their respective Numbers, which shall be determined by adding to the whole Number of free Persons, including those bound to Service for a Term of Years, and excluding Indians not taxed, three fifths of all other Persons. The actual Enumeration shall be made within three Years after the first Meeting of the Congress of the United States, and within every subsequent Term of ten Years, in such Manner as they shall by Law direct. The Number of Representatives shall not exceed one for every thirty Thousand, but each State shall have at Least one Representative; and until such enumeration shall be made, the State of New Hampshire shall be entitled to chuse three, Massachusetts eight, Rhode-Island and Providence Plantations one, Connecticut five, New-York six, New Jersey four, Pennsylvania eight, Delaware one, Maryland six, Virginia ten, North Carolina five, South Carolina five, and Georgia three.

Clause 4: When vacancies happen in the Representation from any State, the Executive Authority thereof shall issue Writs of Election to fill such Vacancies.

Clause 5: The House of Representatives shall chuse their Speaker and other Officers; and shall have the sole Power of Impeachment.

Section 3

Clause 1: The Senate of the United States shall be composed of two Senators from each State, chosen by the Legislature thereof, for six Years; and each Senator shall have one Vote.

Clause 2: Immediately after they shall be assembled in Consequence of the first Election, they shall be divided as equally as may be into three Classes. The Seats of the Senators of the first Class shall be vacated at the Expiration of the second Year, of the second Class at the Expiration of the fourth Year, and of the third Class at the Expiration of the sixth Year, so that one third may be chosen every second Year; and if Vacancies happen by Resignation, or otherwise, during the Recess of the Legislature of any State, the Executive thereof may make temporary Appointments until the next Meeting of the Legislature, which shall then fill such Vacancies.

Clause 3: No Person shall be a Senator who shall not have attained to the Age of thirty Years, and been nine Years a Citizen of the United States, and who shall not, when elected, be an Inhabitant of that State for which he shall be chosen.

Clause 4: The Vice President of the United States shall be President of the Senate, but shall have no Vote, unless they be equally divided.

Clause 5: The Senate shall chuse their other Officers, and also a President pro tempore, in the Absence of the Vice President, or when he shall exercise the Office of President of the United States.

Clause 6: The Senate shall have the sole Power to try all Impeachments. When sitting for that Purpose, they shall be on Oath or Affirmation. When the President of the United States is tried, the Chief Justice shall preside: And no Person shall be convicted without the Concurrence of two thirds of the Members present.

Clause 7: Judgment in Cases of Impeachment shall not extend further than to removal from Office, and disqualification to hold and enjoy any Office of honor, Trust or Profit under the United States: but the Party convicted shall nevertheless be liable and subject to Indictment, Trial, Judgment and Punishment, according to Law.

Section 4

Clause 1: The Times, Places and Manner of holding Elections for Senators and Representatives, shall be prescribed in each State by the Legislature thereof; but the Congress may at any time by Law make or alter such Regulations, except as to the Places of chusing Senators.

Clause 2: The Congress shall assemble at least once in every Year, and such Meeting shall be on the first Monday in December, unless they shall by Law appoint a different Day.

Section 5

Clause 1: Each House shall be the Judge of the Elections, Returns and Qualifications of its own Members, and a Majority of each shall constitute a Quorum to do Business; but a smaller Number may adjourn from day to day, and may be authorized to compel the Attendance of absent Members, in such Manner, and under such Penalties as each House may provide.

Clause 2: Each House may determine the Rules of its Proceedings, punish its Members for disorderly Behaviour, and, with the Concurrence of two thirds, expel a Member.

Clause 3: Each House shall keep a Journal of its Proceedings, and from time to time publish the same, excepting such Parts as may in their Judgment require Secrecy; and the Yeas and Nays of the Members of either House on any question shall, at the Desire of one fifth of those Present, be entered on the Journal.

Clause 4: Neither House, during the Session of Congress, shall, without the Consent of the other, adjourn for more than three days, nor to any other Place than that in which the two Houses shall be sitting.

Section 6

Clause 1: The Senators and Representatives shall receive a Compensation for their Services, to be ascertained by Law, and paid out of the Treasury of the United States. They shall in all Cases, except Treason, Felony and Breach of the Peace, be privileged from Arrest during their Attendance at the Session of their respective Houses, and in going to and returning from the same; and for any Speech or Debate in either House, they shall not be questioned in any other Place.

Clause 2: No Senator or Representative shall, during the Time for which he was elected, be appointed to any civil Office under the Authority of the United States, which shall have been created, or the Emoluments whereof shall have been encreased during such time; and no Person holding any Office under the United States, shall be a Member of either House during his Continuance in Office.

Section 7

Clause 1: All Bills for raising Revenue shall originate in the House of Representatives; but the Senate may propose or concur with Amendments as on other Bills.

Clause 2: Every Bill which shall have passed the House of Representatives and the Senate, shall, before it become a Law, be presented to the President of the United States; if he approve he shall sign it, but if not he shall return it, with his Objections to that House in which it shall have originated, who shall enter the Objections at large on their Journal, and proceed to reconsider it. If after such Reconsideration two thirds of that House shall agree to pass the Bill, it shall be sent, together with the Objections, to the other House, by which it shall likewise be reconsidered, and if approved by two thirds of that House, it shall become a Law. But in all such Cases the Votes of both Houses shall be determined by Yeas and Nays, and the Names of the Persons voting for and against the Bill shall be entered on the Journal of each House respectively. If any Bill shall not be returned by the President within ten Days (Sundays excepted) after it shall have been presented to him, the Same shall be a Law, in like Manner as if he had signed it, unless the Congress by their Adjournment prevent its Return, in which Case it shall not be a Law.

Clause 3: Every Order, Resolution, or Vote to which the Concurrence of the Senate and House of Representatives may be necessary (except on a question of Adjournment) shall be presented to the President of the United States; and before the

Same shall take Effect, shall be approved by him, or being disapproved by him, shall be repassed by two thirds of the Senate and House of Representatives, according to the Rules and Limitations prescribed in the Case of a Bill.

Section 8

Clause 1: The Congress shall have Power To lay and collect Taxes, Duties, Imposts and Excises, to pay the Debts and provide for the common Defence and general Welfare of the United States; but all Duties, Imposts and Excises shall be uniform throughout the United States;

Clause 2: To borrow Money on the credit of the United States;

Clause 3: To regulate Commerce with foreign Nations, and among the several States, and with the Indian Tribes;

Clause 4: To establish an uniform Rule of Naturalization, and uniform Laws on the subject of Bankruptcies throughout the United States;

Clause 5: To coin Money, regulate the Value thereof, and of foreign Coin, and fix the Standard of Weights and Measures;

Clause 6: To provide for the Punishment of counterfeiting the Securities and current Coin of the United States;

Clause 7: To establish Post Offices and post Roads;

Clause 8: To promote the Progress of Science and useful Arts, by securing for limited Times to Authors and Inventors the exclusive Right to their respective Writings and Discoveries;

Clause 9: To constitute Tribunals inferior to the supreme Court;

Clause 10: To define and punish Piracies and Felonies committed on the high Seas, and Offences against the Law of Nations;

Clause 11: To declare War, grant Letters of Marque and Reprisal, and make Rules concerning Captures on Land and Water;

Clause 12: To raise and support Armies, but no Appropriation of Money to that Use shall be for a longer Term than two Years;

Clause 13: To provide and maintain a Navy;

Clause 14: To make Rules for the Government and Regulation of the land and naval Forces;

Clause 15: To provide for calling forth the Militia to execute the Laws of the Union, suppress Insurrections and repel Invasions;

Clause 16: To provide for organizing, arming, and disciplining, the Militia, and for governing such Part of them as may be employed in the Service of the United States, reserving to the States respectively, the Appointment of the Officers, and the Authority of training the Militia according to the discipline prescribed by Congress;

Clause 17: To exercise exclusive Legislation in all Cases whatsoever, over such District (not exceeding ten Miles square) as may, by Cession of particular States, and the Acceptance of Congress, become the Seat of the Government of the United States, and to exercise like Authority over all Places purchased by the Consent of the Legislature of the State in which the Same shall be, for the Erection of Forts, Magazines, Arsenals, dock-Yards, and other needful Buildings;—And

Clause 18: To make all Laws which shall be necessary and proper for carrying into Execution the foregoing Powers, and all other Powers vested by this Constitution in the Government of the United States, or in any Department or Officer thereof.

Section 9

Clause 1: The Migration or Importation of such Persons as any of the States now existing shall think proper to admit, shall not be prohibited by the Congress prior to the Year one thousand eight hundred and eight, but a Tax or duty may be imposed on such Importation, not exceeding ten dollars for each Person.

Clause 2: The Privilege of the Writ of Habeas Corpus shall not be suspended, unless when in Cases of Rebellion or Invasion the public Safety may require it.

Clause 3: No Bill of Attainder or ex post facto Law shall be passed.

Clause 4: No Capitation, or other direct, Tax shall be laid, unless in Proportion to the Census or Enumeration herein before directed to be taken.

Clause 5: No Tax or Duty shall be laid on Articles exported from any State.

Clause 6: No Preference shall be given by any Regulation of Commerce or Revenue to the Ports of one State over those of another: nor shall Vessels bound to, or from, one State, be obliged to enter, clear, or pay Duties in another.

Clause 7: No Money shall be drawn from the Treasury, but in Consequence of Appropriations made by Law; and a regular Statement and Account of the Receipts and Expenditures of all public Money shall be published from time to time.

Clause 8: No Title of Nobility shall be granted by the United States: And no Person holding any Office of Profit or Trust under them, shall, without the Consent of the Congress, accept of any present, Emolument, Office, or Title, of any kind whatever, from any King, Prince, or foreign State.

Section 10

Clause 1: No State shall enter into any Treaty, Alliance, or Confederation; grant Letters of Marque and Reprisal; coin Money; emit Bills of Credit; make any Thing but gold and silver Coin a Tender in Payment of Debts; pass any Bill of Attainder, ex post facto Law, or Law impairing the Obligation of Contracts, or grant any Title of Nobility.

Clause 2: No State shall, without the Consent of the Congress, lay any Imposts or Duties on Imports or Exports, except what may be absolutely necessary for executing its inspection Laws: and the net Produce of all Duties and Imposts, laid by any State on Imports or Exports, shall be for the Use of the Treasury of the United States; and all such Laws shall be subject to the Revision and Controul of the Congress.

Clause 3: No State shall, without the Consent of Congress, lay any Duty of Tonnage, keep Troops, or Ships of War in time of Peace, enter into any Agreement or Compact with another State, or with a foreign Power, or engage in War, unless actually invaded, or in such imminent Danger as will not admit of delay.

Article II

Section 1

Clause 1: The executive Power shall be vested in a President of the United States of America. He shall hold his Office during the Term of four Years, and, together with the Vice President, chosen for the same Term, be elected, as follows

Clause 2: Each State shall appoint, in such Manner as the Legislature thereof may direct, a Number of Electors, equal to the whole Number of Senators and Representatives to which the State may be entitled in the Congress: but no Senator or Representative, or Person holding an Office of Trust or Profit under the United States, shall be appointed an Elector.

Clause 3: The Electors shall meet in their respective States, and vote by Ballot for two Persons, of whom one at least shall not be an Inhabitant of the same State with themselves. And they shall make a List of all the Persons voted for, and of the Number of Votes for each; which List they shall sign and certify, and transmit sealed to the Seat of the Government of the United States, directed to the President of the Senate. The President of the Senate shall, in the Presence of the Senate and House of Representatives, open all the Certificates, and the Votes shall then be counted. The Person having the greatest Number of Votes shall be the President, if such Number be a Majority of the whole Number of Electors appointed; and if

there be more than one who have such Majority, and have an equal Number of Votes, then the House of Representatives shall immediately chuse by Ballot one of them for President; and if no Person have a Majority, then from the five highest on the List the said House shall in like Manner chuse the President. But in chusing the President, the Votes shall be taken by States, the Representation from each State having one Vote; A quorum for this Purpose shall consist of a Member or Members from two thirds of the States, and a Majority of all the States shall be necessary to a Choice. In every Case, after the Choice of the President, the Person having the greatest Number of Votes of the Electors shall be the Vice President. But if there should remain two or more who have equal Votes, the Senate shall chuse from them by Ballot the Vice President.

Clause 4: The Congress may determine the Time of chusing the Electors, and the Day on which they shall give their Votes; which Day shall be the same throughout the United States.

Clause 5: No Person except a natural born Citizen, or a Citizen of the United States, at the time of the Adoption of this Constitution, shall be eligible to the Office of President; neither shall any Person be eligible to that Office who shall not have attained to the Age of thirty five Years, and been fourteen Years a Resident within the United States.

Clause 6: In Case of the Removal of the President from Office, or of his Death, Resignation, or Inability to discharge the Powers and Duties of the said Office, the Same shall devolve on the Vice President, and the Congress may by Law provide for the Case of Removal, Death, Resignation or Inability, both of the President and Vice President, declaring what Officer shall then act as President, and such Officer shall act accordingly, until the Disability be removed, or a President shall be elected.

Clause 7: The President shall, at stated Times, receive for his Services, a Compensation, which shall neither be encreased nor diminished during the Period for which he shall have been elected, and he shall not receive within that Period any other Emolument from the United States, or any of them.

Clause 8: Before he enter on the Execution of his Office, he shall take the following Oath or Affirmation:—"I do solemnly swear (or affirm) that I will faithfully execute the Office of President of the United States, and will to the best of my Ability, preserve, protect and defend the Constitution of the United States."

Section 2

Clause 1: The President shall be Commander in Chief of the Army and Navy of the United States, and of the Militia of the several States, when called into the actual Service of the United States; he may require the Opinion, in writing, of the principal Officer in each of the executive Departments, upon any Subject relating to the Duties of their respective Offices, and he shall have Power to grant Reprieves and Pardons for Offences against the United States, except in Cases of Impeachment.

Clause 2: He shall have Power, by and with the Advice and Consent of the Senate, to make Treaties, provided two thirds of the Senators present concur; and he shall nominate, and by and with the Advice and Consent of the Senate, shall appoint Ambassadors, other public Ministers and Consuls, Judges of the supreme Court, and all other Officers of the United States, whose Appointments are not herein otherwise provided for, and which shall be established by Law: but the Congress may by Law vest the Appointment of such inferior Officers, as they think proper, in the President alone, in the Courts of Law, or in the Heads of Departments.

Clause 3: The President shall have Power to fill up all Vacancies that may happen during the Recess of the Senate, by granting Commissions which shall expire at the End of their next Session.

Section 3

He shall from time to time give to the Congress Information of the State of the Union, and recommend to their Consideration such Measures as he shall judge necessary and expedient; he may, on extraordinary Occasions, convene both Houses, or either of them, and in Case of Disagreement between them, with Respect to the Time of Adjournment, he may adjourn them to such Time as he shall think proper; he shall receive Ambassadors and other public Ministers; he shall take Care that the Laws be faithfully executed, and shall Commission all the Officers of the United States.

Section 4

The President, Vice President and all civil Officers of the United States, shall be removed from Office on Impeachment for, and Conviction of, Treason, Bribery, or other high Crimes and Misdemeanors.

Article III

Section 1

The judicial Power of the United States, shall be vested in one supreme Court, and in such inferior Courts as the Congress may from time to time ordain and establish. The Judges, both of the supreme and inferior Courts, shall hold their Offices during good Behaviour, and shall, at stated Times, receive for their Services, a Compensation, which shall not be diminished during their Continuance in Office.

Section 2

Clause 1: The judicial Power shall extend to all Cases, in Law and Equity, arising under this Constitution, the Laws of the United States, and Treaties made, or which shall be made, under their Authority;—to all Cases affecting Ambassadors, other public Ministers and Consuls;—to all Cases of admiralty and maritime Jurisdiction;—to Controversies to which the United States shall be a Party;—to Controversies between two or more States;—between a State and Citizens of another State;—between Citizens of different States,—between Citizens of the same State claiming Lands under Grants of different States, and between a State, or the Citizens thereof, and foreign States, Citizens or Subjects.

Clause 2: In all Cases affecting Ambassadors, other public Ministers and Consuls, and those in which a State shall be Party, the supreme Court shall have original Jurisdiction. In all the other Cases before mentioned, the supreme Court shall have appellate Jurisdiction, both as to Law and Fact, with such Exceptions, and under such Regulations as the Congress shall make.

Clause 3: The Trial of all Crimes, except in Cases of Impeachment, shall be by Jury; and such Trial shall be held in the State where the said Crimes shall have been committed; but when not committed within any State, the Trial shall be at such Place or Places as the Congress may by Law have directed.

Section 3

Clause 1: Treason against the United States, shall consist only in levying War against them, or in adhering to their Enemies, giving them Aid and Comfort. No Person shall be convicted of Treason unless on the Testimony of two Witnesses to the same overt Act, or on Confession in open Court.

Clause 2: The Congress shall have Power to declare the Punishment of Treason, but no Attainder of Treason shall work Corruption of Blood, or Forfeiture except during the Life of the Person attainted.

Article IV

Section 1

Full Faith and Credit shall be given in each State to the public Acts, Records, and judicial Proceedings of every other State. And the Congress may by general Laws prescribe the Manner in which such Acts, Records and Proceedings shall be proved, and the Effect thereof.

Section 2

Clause 1: The Citizens of each State shall be entitled to all Privileges and Immunities of Citizens in the several States.

Clause 2: A Person charged in any State with Treason, Felony, or other Crime, who shall flee from Justice, and be found in another State, shall on Demand of the executive Authority of the State from which he fled, be delivered up, to be removed to the State having Jurisdiction of the Crime.

Clause 3: No Person held to Service or Labour in one State, under the Laws thereof, escaping into another, shall, in Consequence of any Law or Regulation therein, be discharged from such Service or Labour, but shall be delivered up on Claim of the Party to whom such Service or Labour may be due.

Section 3

Clause 1: New States may be admitted by the Congress into this Union; but no new State shall be formed or erected within the Jurisdiction of any other State; nor any State be formed by the Junction of two or more States, or Parts of States, without the Consent of the Legislatures of the States concerned as well as of the Congress.

Clause 2: The Congress shall have Power to dispose of and make all needful Rules and Regulations respecting the Territory or other Property belonging to the United States; and nothing in this Constitution shall be so construed as to Prejudice any Claims of the United States, or of any particular State.

Section 4

The United States shall guarantee to every State in this Union a Republican Form of Government, and shall protect each of them against Invasion; and on Application of the Legislature, or of the Executive (when the Legislature cannot be convened) against domestic Violence.

Article V

The Congress, whenever two thirds of both Houses shall deem it necessary, shall propose Amendments to this Constitution, or, on the Application of the Legislatures of two thirds of the several States, shall call a Convention for proposing Amendments, which, in either Case, shall be valid to all Intents and Purposes, as Part of this Constitution, when ratified by the Legislatures of three fourths of the several States, or by Conventions in three fourths thereof, as the one or the other Mode of Ratification may be proposed by the Congress; Provided that no Amendment which may be made prior to the Year One thousand eight hundred and eight shall in any Manner affect the first and fourth Clauses in the Ninth Section of the first Article; and that no State, without its Consent, shall be deprived of its equal Suffrage in the Senate.

Article VI

Clause 1: All Debts contracted and Engagements entered into, before the Adoption of this Constitution, shall be as valid against the United States under this Constitution, as under the Confederation.

Clause 2: This Constitution, and the Laws of the United States which shall be made in Pursuance thereof; and all Treaties made, or which shall be made, under the Authority of the United States, shall be the supreme Law of the Land; and the Judges in every State shall be bound thereby, any Thing in the Constitution or Laws of any State to the Contrary notwithstanding.

Clause 3: The Senators and Representatives before mentioned, and the Members of the several State Legislatures, and all executive and judicial Officers, both of the United States and of the several States, shall be bound by Oath or Affirmation, to support this Constitution; but no religious Test shall ever be required as a Qualification to any Office or public Trust under the United States.

Article VII

The Ratification of the Conventions of nine States, shall be sufficient for the Establishment of this Constitution between the States so ratifying the Same.

Amendment I (1791)

Congress shall make no law respecting an establishment of religion, or prohibiting the free exercise thereof; or abridging the freedom of speech, or of the press; or the right of the people peaceably to assemble, and to petition the government for a redress of grievances.

Amendment II (1791)

A well regulated militia, being necessary to the security of a free State, the right of the people to keep and bear Arms, shall not be infringed.

Amendment III (1791)

No soldier shall, in time of peace be quartered in any house, without the consent of the Owner, nor in time of war, but in a manner to be prescribed by law.

Amendment IV (1791)

The right of the people to be secure in their persons, houses, papers, and effects, against unreasonable searches and seizures, shall not be violated, and no Warrants shall issue, but upon probable cause, supported by Oath or affirmation, and particularly describing the place to be searched, and the persons or things to be seized.

Amendment V (1791)

No person shall be held to answer for a capital, or otherwise infamous crime, unless on a presentment or indictment of a Grand Jury, except in cases arising in the land or naval forces, or in the Militia, when in actual service in time of War or public danger; nor shall any person be subject for the same offense to be twice put in jeopardy of life or limb; nor shall be compelled in any criminal case to be a witness against himself, nor be deprived of life, liberty, or property, without due process of law; nor shall private property be taken for public use, without just compensation.

Amendment VI (1791)

In all criminal prosecutions, the accused shall enjoy the right to a speedy and public trial, by an impartial jury of the State and district wherein the crime shall have been committed, which district shall have been previously ascertained by law, and to be informed of the nature and cause of the accusation; to be confronted with the witnesses against him; to have compulsory process for obtaining witnesses in his favor, and to have the Assistance of Counsel for his defence.

Amendment VII (1791)

In Suits at common law, where the value in controversy shall exceed twenty dollars, the right of trial by jury shall be preserved, and no fact tried by a jury, shall be otherwise reexamined in any Court of the United States, than according to the rules of the common law.

Amendment VIII (1791)

Excessive bail shall not be required, nor excessive fines imposed, nor cruel and unusual punishments inflicted.

Amendment IX (1791)

The enumeration in the Constitution, of certain rights, shall not be construed to deny or disparage others retained by the people.

Amendment X (1791)

The powers not delegated to the United States by the Constitution, nor prohibited by it to the states, are reserved to the States respectively, or to the people.

Amendment XI (1798)

The Judicial power of the United States shall not be construed to extend to any suit in law or equity, commenced or prosecuted against one of the United States by Citizens of another State, or by Citizens or Subjects of any Foreign State.

Amendment XII (1804)

The Electors shall meet in their respective states and vote by ballot for President and Vice-President, one of whom, at least, shall not be an inhabitant of the same state with themselves; they shall name in their ballots the person voted for as President, and in distinct ballots the person voted for as Vice-President, and they shall make distinct lists of all persons voted for as President, and of all persons voted for as Vice-President, and of the number of votes for each, which lists they shall sign and certify, and transmit sealed to the seat of the government of the United States, directed to the President of the Senate;—The President of the Senate shall, in the presence of the Senate and House of Representatives, open all the certificates and the votes shall then be counted;—the person having the greatest number of votes for President, shall be the President, if such number be a majority of the whole number of Electors appointed; and if no person have such majority, then from the persons having the highest numbers not exceeding three on the list of those voted for as President, the House of Representatives shall choose immediately, by ballot, the President. But in choosing the President, the votes shall be taken by states, the representation from each state having one vote; a quorum for this purpose shall consist of a member or members from two-thirds of the states, and a majority of all the states shall be necessary to a choice. And if the House of Representatives shall not choose a President whenever the right of choice shall devolve upon them, before the fourth day of March next following, then the Vice-President shall act as President, as in the case of the death or other constitutional disability of the President. The person having the greatest number of votes as Vice-President, shall be the Vice-President, if such number be a majority of the whole number of Electors appointed, and if no person have a majority, then from the two highest numbers on the list, the Senate shall choose the Vice-President; a quorum for the purpose shall consist of two-thirds of the whole number of Senators, and a majority of the whole number shall be necessary to a choice. But no person constitutionally ineligible to the office of President shall be eligible to that of Vice-President of the United States.

Amendment XIII (1865)

Section 1. Neither slavery nor involuntary servitude, except as a punishment for crime whereof the party shall have been duly convicted, shall exist within the United States, or any place subject to their jurisdiction.

Section 2. Congress shall have power to enforce this article by appropriate legislation.

Amendment XIV (1868)

Section 1. All persons born or naturalized in the United States, and subject to the jurisdiction thereof, are citizens of the United States and of the state wherein they reside. No State shall make or enforce any law which shall abridge the privileges or immunities of citizens of the United States; nor shall any State deprive any person of life, liberty, or property, without due process of law; nor deny to any person within its jurisdiction the equal protection of the laws.

Section 2. Representatives shall be apportioned among the several States according to their respective numbers, counting the whole number of persons in each State, excluding Indians not taxed. But when the right to vote at any election for the choice of electors for President and Vice President of the United States, Representatives in Congress, the executive and judicial officers of a State, or the members of the Legislature thereof, is denied to any of the male inhabitants of such state, being twenty-one years of age, and citizens of the United States, or in any way abridged, except for participation in rebellion, or other crime, the basis of representation therein shall be reduced in the proportion which the number of such male citizens shall bear to the whole number of male citizens twenty-one years of age in such State.

Section 3. No person shall be a Senator or Representative in Congress, or elector of President and Vice President, or hold any office, civil or military, under the United States, or under any State, who, having previously taken an oath, as a member of Congress, or as an officer of the United States, or as a member of any State legislature, or as an executive or judicial officer of any State, to support the Constitution of the United States, shall have engaged in insurrection or rebellion against the same, or given aid or comfort to the enemies thereof. But Congress may by a vote of two-thirds of each House, remove such disability.

Section 4. The validity of the public debt of the United States, authorized by law, including debts incurred for payment of pensions and bounties for services in suppressing insurrection or rebellion, shall not be questioned. But neither the United States nor any State shall assume or pay any debt or obligation incurred in aid of insurrection or rebellion against the United States, or any claim for the loss or emancipation of any slave; but all such debts, obligations and claims shall be held illegal and void.

Section 5. The Congress shall have power to enforce, by appropriate legislation, the provisions of this article.

Amendment XV (1870)

Section 1. The right of citizens of the United States to vote shall not be denied or abridged by the United States or by any State on account of race, color, or previous condition of servitude.

Section 2. The Congress shall have power to enforce this article by appropriate legislation.

Amendment XVI (1913)

The Congress shall have power to lay and collect taxes on incomes, from whatever source derived, without apportionment among the several States, and without regard to any census of enumeration.

Amendment XVII (1913)

The Senate of the United States shall be composed of two Senators from each State, elected by the people thereof, for six years; and each Senator shall have one vote. The electors in each State shall have the qualifications requisite for electors of the most numerous branch of the State legislatures.

When vacancies happen in the representation of any State in the Senate, the executive authority of such state shall issue writs of election to fill such vacancies: *Provided*, that the legislature of any State may empower the executive thereof to make temporary appointments until the people fill the vacancies by election as the legislature may direct.

This amendment shall not be so construed as to affect the election or term of any Senator chosen before it becomes valid as part of the Constitution.

Amendment XVIII (1919)

Section 1. After one year from the ratification of this article the manufacture, sale, or transportation of intoxicating liquors within, the importation thereof into, or the exportation thereof from the United States and all territory subject to the jurisdiction thereof for beverage purposes is hereby prohibited.

Section 2. The Congress and the several states shall have concurrent power to enforce this article by appropriate legislation.

Section 3. This article shall be inoperative unless it shall have been ratified as an amendment to the Constitution by the legislatures of the several States, as provided in the Constitution, within seven years from the date of the submission hereof to the states by the Congress.

Amendment XIX (1920)

Section 1. The right of citizens of the United States to vote shall not be denied or abridged by the United States or by any State on account of sex.

Section 2. The Congress shall have power to enforce this article by appropriate legislation.

Amendment XX (1933)

Section 1. The terms of the President and Vice President shall end at noon on the 20th day of January, and the terms of Senators and Representatives at noon on the 3d day of January, of the years in which such terms would have ended if this article had not been ratified; and the terms of their successors shall then begin.

Section 2. The Congress shall assemble at least once in every year, and such meeting shall begin at noon on the 3d day of January, unless they shall by law appoint a different day.

Section 3. If, at the time fixed for the beginning of the term of the President, the President elect shall have died, the Vice President elect shall become President. If a President shall not have been chosen before the time fixed for the beginning of his term, or if the President elect shall have failed to qualify, then the Vice President elect shall act as President until a President shall have qualified; and the Congress may by law provide for the case wherein neither a President elect nor a Vice President elect shall have qualified, declaring who shall then act as President, or the manner in which one who is to act shall be selected, and such person shall act accordingly until a President or Vice President shall have qualified.

Section 4. The Congress may by law provide for the case of the death of any of the persons from whom the House of Representatives may choose a President whenever the right of choice shall have devolved upon them, and for the case of the death of any of the persons from whom the Senate may choose a Vice President whenever the right of choice shall have devolved upon them.

Section 5. Sections 1 and 2 shall take effect on the 15th day of October following the ratification of this article.

Section 6. This article shall be inoperative unless it shall have been ratified as an amendment to the Constitution by the legislatures of three-fourths of the several states within seven years from the date of its submission.

Amendment XXI (1933)

Section 1. The eighteenth article of amendment to the Constitution of the United States is hereby repealed.

Section 2. The transportation or importation into any State, territory, or possession of the United States for delivery or use therein of intoxicating liquors, in violation of the laws thereof, is hereby prohibited.

Section 3. This article shall be inoperative unless it shall have been ratified as an amendment to the Constitution by conventions in the several States, as provided in the Constitution, within seven years from the date of the submission hereof to the States by the Congress.

Amendment XXII (1951)

Section 1. No person shall be elected to the office of the President more than twice, and no person who has held the office of President, or acted as President, for more than two years of a term to which some other person was elected President shall be elected to the office of the President more than once. But this article shall not apply to any person holding the office of President when this article was proposed by the Congress, and shall not prevent any person who may be holding the office of President, or acting as President, during the term within which this article becomes operative from holding the office of President or acting as President during the remainder of such term.

Section 2. This article shall be inoperative unless it shall have been ratified as an amendment to the Constitution by the legislatures of three-fourths of the several States within seven years from the date of its submission to the States by the Congress.

Amendment XXIII (1961)

Section 1. The District constituting the seat of Government of the United States shall appoint in such manner as the Congress may direct:

A number of electors of President and Vice President equal to the whole number of Senators and Representatives in Congress to which the District would be entitled if it were a State, but in no event more than the least populous State; they shall be in addition to those appointed by the States, but they shall be considered, for the purposes of the election of President and Vice President, to be electors appointed by a State; and they shall meet in the District and perform such duties as provided by the twelfth article of amendment.

Section 2. The Congress shall have power to enforce this article by appropriate legislation.

Amendment XXIV (1964)

Section 1. The right of citizens of the United States to vote in any primary or other election for President or Vice President, for electors for President or Vice President, or for Senator or Representative in Congress, shall not be denied or abridged by the United States or any State by reason of failure to pay any poll tax or other tax.

Section 2. The Congress shall have power to enforce this article by appropriate legislation.

Amendment XXV (1967)

Section 1. In case of the removal of the President from office or of his death or resignation, the Vice President shall become President.

Section 2. Whenever there is a vacancy in the office of the Vice President, the President shall nominate a Vice President who shall take office upon confirmation by a majority vote of both Houses of Congress.

Section 3. Whenever the President transmits to the President pro tempore of the Senate and the Speaker of the House of Representatives his written declaration that he is unable to discharge the powers and duties of his office, and until he transmits to them a written declaration to the contrary, such powers and duties shall be discharged by the Vice President as Acting President.

Section 4. Whenever the Vice President and a majority of either the principal officers of the executive departments or of such other body as Congress may by law provide, transmit to the President pro tempore of the Senate and the Speaker of the House of Representatives their written declaration that the President is unable to discharge the powers and duties of his office, the Vice President shall immediately assume the powers and duties of the office as Acting President.

Thereafter, when the President transmits to the President pro tempore of the Senate and the Speaker of the House of Representatives his written declaration that no inability exists, he shall resume the powers and duties of his office unless the Vice President and a majority of either the principal officers of the executive department or of such other body as Congress may by law provide, transmit within four days to the President pro tempore of the Senate and the Speaker of the House of Representatives their written declaration that the President is unable to discharge the powers and duties of his office. Thereupon Congress shall decide the issue, assembling within forty-eight hours for that purpose if not in session. If the Congress, within twenty-one days after receipt of the latter written declaration, or, if Congress is not in session, within twenty-one days after Congress is required to assemble, determines by two-thirds vote of both Houses that the President is unable to discharge the powers and duties of his office, the Vice President shall continue to discharge the same as Acting President; otherwise, the President shall resume the powers and duties of his office.

Amendment XXVI (1971)

Section 1. The right of citizens of the United States, who are 18 years of age or older, to vote, shall not be denied or abridged by the United States or any State on account of age.

Section 2. The Congress shall have the power to enforce this article by appropriate legislation.

Amendment XXVII (1992)*

No law, varying the compensation for services of the Senators and Representatives, shall take effect, until an election of Representatives shall have intervened.

---

*This Amendment was proposed in 1789 as one of the original Bill of Rights. It was not until 1992 that the requisite number of states had ratified the proposal under Article V. In May, 1992 the archivist of the United States certified to Congress that the amendment had been ratified, notwithstanding serious doubts about the validity of the ratification process and the passage of two centuries between proposal and adoption.

First Inaugural Address

Abraham Lincoln

Fellow citizens of the United States: in compliance with a custom as old as the government itself, I appear before you to address you briefly and to take, in your presence, the oath prescribed by the Constitution of the United States, to be taken by the President "before he enters on the execution of his office."

I do not consider it necessary, at present, for me to discuss those matters of administration about which there is no special anxiety, or excitement.

Apprehension seems to exist among the people of the Southern States that by the accession of a Republican administration their property and their peace and personal security are to be endangered. There has never been any reasonable cause for such apprehension. Indeed, the most ample evidence to the contrary has all the while existed and been open to their inspection. It is found in nearly all the published speeches of him who now addresses you. I do but quote from one of those speeches when I declare that "I have no purpose, directly or indirectly, to interfere with the institution of slavery where it exists. I believe I have no lawful right to do so, and I have no inclination to do so." Those who nominated and elected me did so with full knowledge that I had made this and many similar declarations, and had never recanted them. And, more than this, they placed in the platform for my acceptance, and as a law to themselves and to me, the clear and emphatic resolution which I now read:

Resolved: that the maintenance inviolate of the rights of the States, and especially the right of each State to order and control its own domestic institutions according to its own judgment exclusively, is essential to that balance of power on which the perfection and endurance of our political fabric depend, and we denounce the lawless invasion by armed force of the soil of any State or Territory, no matter under what pretext, as among the gravest of crimes.

I now reiterate these sentiments; and, in doing so, I only press upon the public attention the most conclusive evidence of which the case is susceptible, that the property, peace, and security of no section are to be in any wise endangered by the now incoming administration. I add, too, that all the protection which, consistently with the Constitution and the laws, can be given, will be cheerfully given to all the States when lawfully demanded, for whatever cause—as cheerfully to one section as to another.

There is much controversy about the delivering up of fugitives from service or labor. The clause I now read is as plainly written in the Constitution as any other of its provisions:

No person held to service or labor in one State, under the laws thereof, escaping into another, shall in consequence of any law or regulation therein be discharged from such service or labor, but shall be delivered up on claim of the party to whom such service or labor may be due.

It is scarcely questioned that this provision was intended by those who made it for the reclaiming of what we call fugitive slaves; and the intention of the lawgiver is the law. All members of Congress swear their support to the whole Constitution—to this provision as much as to any other. To the proposition, then, that slaves whose cases come within the terms of this clause "shall be delivered up," their oaths are unanimous. Now, if they would make the effort in good temper, could they not with nearly equal unanimity frame and pass a law by means of which to keep good that unanimous oath?

There is some difference of opinion whether this clause should be enforced by national or by State authority; but surely that difference is not a very material one. If the slave is to be surrendered, it can be of but little consequence to him or to others by which authority it is done. And should any one in any case be content that his oath shall go unkept on a merely unsubstantial controversy as to HOW it shall be kept? Again, in any law upon this subject, ought not all the safeguards of liberty known in civilized and humane jurisprudence to be introduced, so that a free man be not, in any case, surrendered as a slave? And might it not be well at the same time to provide by law for the enforcement of that clause in the Constitution which guarantees that "the citizen of each State shall be entitled to all privileges and immunities of citizens in the several States?"

I take the official oath today with no mental reservations, and with no purpose to construe the Constitution or laws by any hypercritical rules. And while I do not choose now to specify particular acts of Congress as proper to be enforced, I do suggest that it will be much safer for all, both in official and private stations, to conform to and abide by all those acts which stand unrepealed, than to violate any of them, trusting to find impunity in having them held to be unConstitutional.

It is seventy-two years since the first inauguration of a President under our national Constitution. During that period fifteen different and greatly distinguished citizens have, in succession, administered the executive branch of the government. They have conducted it through many perils, and generally with great success. Yet, with all this scope of precedent, I now enter upon the same task for the brief Constitutional term of four years under great and peculiar difficulty. A disruption of the Federal Union, heretofore only menaced, is now formidably attempted.

I hold that, in contemplation of universal law and of the Constitution, the Union of these States is perpetual. Perpetuity is implied, if not expressed, in the fundamental law of all national governments. It is safe to assert that no government proper ever had a provision in its organic law for its own termination. Continue to execute all the express provisions of our National Constitution, and the Union will endure forever—it being impossible to destroy it except by some action not provided for in the instrument itself.

Again, if the United States be not a government proper, but an association of States in the nature of contract merely, can it, as a contract, be peaceably unmade by less than all the parties who made it? One party to a contract may violate it—break it, so to speak; but does it not require all to lawfully rescind it?

Descending from these general principles, we find the proposition that in legal contemplation the Union is perpetual confirmed by the history of the Union itself. The Union is much older than the Constitution. It was formed, in fact, by the Articles of Association in 1774. It was matured and continued by the Declaration of Independence in 1776. It was further matured, and the faith of all the then thirteen States expressly plighted and engaged that it should be perpetual, by the Articles of Confederation in 1778. And, finally, in 1787 one of the declared objects for ordaining and establishing the Constitution was "TO FORM A MORE PERFECT UNION."

But if the destruction of the Union by one or by a part only of the States be lawfully possible, the Union is LESS perfect than before the Constitution, having lost the vital element of perpetuity.

It follows from these views that no State upon its own mere motion can lawfully get out of the Union; that Resolves and Ordinances to that effect are legally void; and that acts of violence, within any State or States, against the authority of the United States, are insurrectionary or revolutionary, according to circumstances.

I therefore consider that, in view of the Constitution and the laws, the Union is unbroken; and to the extent of my ability I shall take care, as the Constitution itself expressly enjoins upon me, that the laws of the Union be faithfully executed in all the States. Doing this I deem to be only a simple duty on my part; and I shall perform it so far as practicable, unless my rightful masters, the American people, shall withhold the requisite means, or in some authoritative manner direct the contrary. I trust this will not be regarded as a menace, but only as the declared purpose of the Union that it WILL Constitutionally defend and maintain itself.

In doing this there needs to be no bloodshed or violence; and there shall be none, unless it be forced upon the national authority. The power confided to me will be used to hold, occupy, and possess the property and places belonging to the government, and to collect the duties and imposts; but beyond what may be necessary for these objects, there will be no invasion, no using of force against or among the people anywhere. Where hostility to the United States, in any interior locality, shall be so great and universal as to prevent competent resident citizens from holding the Federal offices, there will be no attempt to force obnoxious strangers among the people for that object. While the strict legal right may exist in the government to enforce the exercise of these offices, the attempt to do so would be so irritating, and so nearly impracticable withal, that I deem it better to forego for the time the uses of such offices.

The mails, unless repelled, will continue to be furnished in all parts of the Union. So far as possible, the people everywhere shall have that sense of perfect security which is most favorable to calm thought and reflection. The course here indicated will be followed unless current events and experience shall show a modification or change to be proper, and in every case and exigency my best discretion will be exercised according to circumstances actually existing, and with a view and a hope of a peaceful solution of the national troubles and the restoration of fraternal sympathies and affections.

That there are persons in one section or another who seek to destroy the Union at all events, and are glad of any pretext to do it, I will neither affirm nor deny; but if there be such, I need address no word to them. To those, however, who really love the Union may I not speak?

Before entering upon so grave a matter as the destruction of our national fabric, with all its benefits, its memories, and its hopes, would it not be wise to ascertain precisely why we do it? Will you hazard so desperate a step while there is any possibility that any portion of the ills you fly from have no real existence? Will you, while the certain ills you fly to are greater than all the real ones you fly from—will you risk the commission of so fearful a mistake?

All profess to be content in the Union if all Constitutional rights can be maintained. Is it true, then, that any right, plainly written in the Constitution, has been denied? I think not. Happily the human mind is so constituted that no party can reach to the audacity of doing this. Think, if you can, of a single instance in which a plainly written provision of the Constitution has ever been denied. If by the mere force of numbers a majority should deprive a minority of any clearly written Constitutional right, it might, in a moral point of view, justify revolution—certainly would if such a right were a vital one. But such is not our case. All the vital rights of minorities and of individuals are so plainly assured to them by affirmations and negations, guaranties and prohibitions, in the Constitution, that controversies never arise concerning them. But no organic law can ever be framed with a provision specifically applicable to every question which may occur in practical administration. No foresight can anticipate, nor any document of reasonable length contain, express provisions for all possible questions. Shall fugitives from labor be surrendered by national or State authority? The Constitution does not expressly say. May Congress prohibit slavery in the Territories? The Constitution does not expressly say. MUST Congress protect slavery in the Territories? The Constitution does not expressly say.

From questions of this class spring all our constitutional controversies, and we divide upon them into majorities and minorities. If the minority will not acquiesce, the majority must, or the government must cease. There is no other alternative; for continuing the government is acquiescence on one side or the other.

If a minority in such case will secede rather than acquiesce, they make a precedent which in turn will divide and ruin them; for a minority of their own will secede from them whenever a majority refuses to be controlled by such minority. For instance, why may not any portion of a new confederacy a year or two hence arbitrarily secede again, precisely as portions of the present Union now claim to secede from it? All who cherish disunion sentiments are now being educated to the exact temper of doing this.

Is there such perfect identity of interests among the States to compose a new Union, as to produce harmony only, and prevent renewed secession?

Plainly, the central idea of secession is the essence of anarchy. A majority held in restraint by constitutional checks and limitations, and always changing easily with deliberate changes of popular opinions and sentiments, is the only true sovereign of a free people. Whoever rejects it does, of necessity, fly to anarchy or to despotism. Unanimity is impossible; the rule of a minority, as a permanent arrangement, is wholly inadmissible; so that, rejecting the majority principle, anarchy or despotism in some form is all that is left.

I do not forget the position, assumed by some, that Constitutional questions are to be decided by the Supreme Court; nor do I deny that such decisions must be binding, in any case, upon the parties to a suit, as to the object of that suit, while they are also entitled to very high respect and consideration in all parallel cases by all other departments of the government. And while it is obviously possible that such decision may be erroneous in any given case, still the evil effect following it, being limited to that particular case, with the chance that it may be overruled and never become a precedent for other cases, can better be borne than could the evils of a different practice. At the same time, the candid citizen must confess that if the policy of the government, upon vital questions affecting the whole people, is to be irrevocably fixed by decisions of the Supreme Court, the instant they are made, in ordinary litigation between parties in personal actions, the people will have ceased to be their own rulers, having to that extent practically resigned their government into the hands of that eminent tribunal. Nor is there in this view any assault upon the court or the judges. It is a duty from which they may not shrink to decide cases properly brought before them, and it is no fault of theirs if others seek to turn their decisions to political purposes.

One section of our country believes slavery is RIGHT, and ought to be extended, while the other believes it is WRONG, and ought not to be extended. This is the only substantial dispute. The fugitive-slave clause of the Constitution, and the law for the suppression of the foreign slave-trade, are each as well enforced, perhaps, as any law can ever be in a community where the moral sense of the people imperfectly supports the law itself. The great body of the people abide by the dry legal obligation in both cases, and a few break over in each. This, I think, cannot be perfectly cured; and it would be worse in both cases AFTER the separation of the sections than BEFORE. The foreign slave-trade, now imperfectly suppressed, would be ultimately revived, without restriction, in one section, while fugitive slaves, now only partially surrendered, would not be surrendered at all by the other.

Physically speaking, we cannot separate. We cannot remove our respective sections from each other, nor build an impassable wall between them. A husband and wife may be divorced, and go out of the presence and beyond the reach of each other; but the different parts of our country cannot do this. They cannot but remain face to face, and intercourse, either amicable or hostile, must continue between them. Is it possible, then, to make that intercourse more advantageous or more satisfactory after separation than before? Can aliens make treaties easier than friends can make laws? Can treaties be more faithfully enforced between aliens than laws can among friends? Suppose you go to war, you cannot fight always; and when, after much loss on both sides, and no gain on either, you cease fighting, the identical old questions as to terms of intercourse are again upon you.

This country, with its institutions, belongs to the people who inhabit it. Whenever they shall grow weary of the existing government, they can exercise their CONSTITUTIONAL right of amending it, or their REVOLUTIONARY right to dismember or overthrow it. I cannot be ignorant of the fact that many worthy and patriotic citizens are desirous of having the national Constitution amended. While I make no recommendation of amendments, I fully recognize the rightful authority of the people over the whole subject, to be exercised in either of the modes prescribed in the instrument itself; and I should, under existing circumstances, favor rather than oppose a fair opportunity being afforded the people to act upon it. I will venture to add that to me the convention mode seems preferable, in that it allows amendments to originate with the people themselves, instead of only permitting them to take or reject propositions originated by others not especially chosen for the purpose, and which might not be precisely such as they would wish to either accept or refuse. I understand a proposed amendment to the Constitution—which amendment, however, I have not seen—has passed Congress, to the effect that the Federal Government shall never interfere with the domestic institutions of the States, including that of persons held to service. To avoid misconstruction of what I have said, I depart from my purpose not to speak of particular amendments so far as to say that, holding such a provision to now be implied Constitutional law, I have no objection to its being made express and irrevocable.

The chief magistrate derives all his authority from the people, and they have conferred none upon him to fix terms for the separation of the states. The people themselves can do this also if they choose; but the executive, as such, has nothing to do with it. His duty is to administer the present government, as it came to his hands, and to transmit it, unimpaired by him, to his successor.

Why should there not be a patient confidence in the ultimate justice of the people? Is there any better or equal hope in the world? In our present differences is either party without faith of being in the right? If the Almighty Ruler of Nations, with his eternal truth and justice, be on your side of the North, or on yours of the South, that truth and that justice will surely prevail, by the judgment of this great tribunal, the American people.

By the frame of the government under which we live, this same people have wisely given their public servants but little power for mischief; and have, with equal wisdom, provided for the return of that little to their own hands at very short intervals. While the people retain their virtue and vigilance, no administration, by any extreme of wickedness or folly, can very seriously injure the government in the short space of four years.

My countrymen, one and all, think calmly and WELL upon this whole subject. Nothing valuable can be lost by taking time. If there be an object to HURRY any of you in hot haste to a step which you would never take DELIBERATELY, that object will be frustrated by taking time; but no good object can be frustrated by it. Such of you as are now dissatisfied, still have the old Constitution unimpaired, and, on the sensitive point, the laws of your own framing under it; while the new administration will have no immediate power, if it would, to change either. If it were admitted that you who are dissatisfied hold the right side in the dispute, there still is no single good reason for precipitate action. Intelligence, patriotism, Christianity, and a firm reliance on him who has never yet forsaken this favored land, are still competent to adjust in the best way all our present difficulty.

In YOUR hands, my dissatisfied fellow-countrymen, and not in MINE, is the momentous issue of civil war. The government will not assail YOU. You can have no conflict without being yourselves the aggressors. YOU have no oath registered in heaven to destroy the government, while I shall have the most solemn one to "preserve, protect, and defend it."

I am loathe to close. We are not enemies, but friends. We must not be enemies. Though passion may have strained, it must not break our bonds of affection. The mystic chords of memory, stretching from every battlefield and patriot grave to every living heart and hearthstone all over this broad land, will yet swell the chorus of the Union when again touched, as surely they will be, by the better angels of our nature.

Understanding Supreme Court Opinions

Constitutional interpretation is not and should not be solely the province of judges. The task of ensuring fidelity to the values of the Constitution is one all governmental officials and citizens must share, a point underscored by Justice Frankfurter's dissent in *West Virginia v. Barnette* (1943). "Reliance for the most precious interests of civilization," he reminded us, "must be found outside of their vindication in courts of law. Only a persistent positive translation of the faith of a free society into the convictions and habits of actions of a community is the ultimate reliance against unabated temptations to fetter the human spirit."

Any citizen of the Constitution, therefore, must have some basic understanding of its rules, principles, and commitments. Judicial opinions construing the Constitution are an obvious and critically important source for learning about those commitments. Unfortunately, their odd form and peculiar cant[1] may make them seem inaccessible to many students. Our experience in teaching these materials has taught us that students may come to understand Supreme Court opinions more quickly and with somewhat less pain if they use some of the following tools.

How to Read an Opinion

A judicial opinion is both an act of explanation and one of persuasion. Most opinions purport to explain how the judge or judges arrived at the decision, usually by tracing a series of questions, answers, and arguments from a set beginning to a seemingly inevitable end. In this sense, a judicial opinion helps to assure the accountability of power—a fundamental constitutional imperative—by declaring publicly the reasons why a case has been decided in a particular way. An opinion is also an exercise in persuasion. Difficult cases, at least, often admit of more than one solution. Any judge who fails to say why his or her solution is preferable to another, no less obvious solution, is a judge who has failed to understand the difference between judicial *power*, or the capacity to reach a decision, and judicial *authority*, or when it is constitutionally appropriate to reach a decision. The latter requires an understanding of the proper nature and limits of judicial power in a constitutional democracy and why a judge has an obligation to tell us why—to persuade us—his or her solution is superior.

The twin purposes of explanation and persuasion suggest that when we read opinions we should remember that they often have more than one purpose—sometimes to settle a contested point of law, sometimes to teach, and sometimes to preach. The opinions are often directed to more than one audience, as well—sometimes the litigants alone, sometimes the legal academy, and sometimes the entire polity. As you read the opinions, you will also find it helpful to assess them in light of the three themes—interpretive, normative, and comparative—we identified in the introduction. Every opinion, for example, adopts one or more methods of constitutional interpretation. Similarly, in every opinion the justices wrestle—sometimes explicitly, sometimes not—with the political theory and ideals that inform the Constitution and give it meaning.

In every case, then, students should read for the following information:

1. Legal Doctrine. What question of law does the case raise? How do the judges or justices answer that question? What doctrines of law do they utilize or formulate? Does their an-

---

[1] See Lawrence M. Solan, *The Language of Judges* (Chicago: University of Chicago Press, 1993); Joseph Goldstein, *The Intelligible Constitution: The Supreme Court's Obligation to Maintain the Constitution as Something We the People Can Understand* (New York: Oxford University Press, 1992).

swer conform to existing legal doctrine or does it change it?

2. Institutional Role. Almost every constitutional case decided by the Supreme Court involves some question about the proper role of the Court in the political process. What understanding of judicial power does the majority embrace? Does the opinion envision a broad or a narrow role for the power of judges? Does that vision rest upon a particular understanding of democratic theory and of the authority of the community to govern itself through the means of majoritarian politics? Does it rest upon a particular view about when judges should protect individual liberty from regulation by a majority?

3. Method and Strategies of Constitutional Interpretation. Translating the "majestic generalities" of the Constitution into a practical instrument of governance requires interpretation. What methods and strategies of interpretation do the judges employ? Do they explicitly acknowledge their choices? Do they justify them? What sorts of justifications and evidence does the opinion marshal to support its argument?

4. Commentary on the American Polity. We wrote in the introduction that a course on constitutional law should be a "commentary on the meaning of America." Judicial opinions can be a rich source for such commentary. As you read them, consider what an opinion says about American history, about contemporary politics, about political theory, and about the success or failure of the American experiment.

How to Brief a Case

Seemingly endless generations of first-year law students have spent hours learning the law by "briefing cases." Some of us harbored doubts about the practice and gave it up as soon as we could, but case briefs *can* be an excellent tool for learning how to read judicial opinions. A good brief can help students focus on what is essential in a case and what is frill. Moreover, a brief can be a useful study tool at the end of the semester, when there may be a hundred or more cases to review for a final exam.

A case brief is essentially a short summary, no more than a page or two, of the main features of a case. A typical brief follows a format similar to this:

1. The Facts. In the United States the Supreme Court does not decide hypothetical cases or cases that are not ripe. Every case therefore rises in a particular factual context. The facts may or may not have a substantial influence on how the Court decides the case. The facts themselves are sometimes subject to interpretation and a source of disagreement among the justices. The facts should include the statute or policy challenged and the various constitutional provisions implicated in the case.

2. The Question Presented. What question of constitutional law does the case present? Frequently a case involves several constitutional provisions and consequently several con-

stitutional questions for resolution. We find it most useful to try to pose the questions in a format that yields a "yes–no" response.

3. The Holding. How does the Court answer the questions? Usually the response is contained in the majority opinion, but many times the decisive holding must be constructed through a reading of several different opinions in the case.

4. The Rationale. This is a summary and analysis of the reasoning and evidence the Court uses in its decision. What strategies and methods of interpretation does the opinion employ? What kinds of evidence does it muster on behalf of its argument? What are the implications of the opinion for future cases? How does the Court describe its role in the political process?

5. Concurring and Dissenting opinions. This should also contain a summary and analysis of the various opinions. In what precise ways do the concurring or dissenting opinions agree with or differ from the majority opinion?

6. Significance of the Case. Why is the case important? What general principles of constitutional law does this case create, reaffirm, or reject? Students may find it helpful here to consider again the questions we focused upon in the first section of this appendix. What does this case tell us about the Constitution? What does it tell us about the American polity?

Sample Brief: *Bowers v. Hardwick* (1986)

Bowers v. Hardwick
478 U.S. 186, 106 S. Ct. 2841, 92 L. Ed. 2d 140 (1986)

1. Facts of the Case. Hardwick committed consensual sodomy with another man in private. He was arrested for violating a Georgia law prohibiting sodomy. The law carried a prison term of no less than one year and no more than twenty years. Hardwick challenged the law, claiming it violated his constitutional rights to privacy, expression, and association. The federal district court rejected his claim, but the circuit court reversed, finding that Georgia's statute violated Hardwick's rights to private and intimate association. The state appealed to the United States Supreme Court.

2. The Question Presented.
   a. Does a statute criminalizing sodomy between consenting adults violate the right to privacy, as protected by the due process clause of the Fourteenth Amendment?
   b. Does the statute violate the freedom of intimate expression in one's home, as protected by the First Amendment?

3. The Holding.
   a. No. The right to privacy does not include a "fundamental right . . . to engage in sodomy. . . ."
   b. No. The right to intimate expression in one's home does not always make "otherwise illegal conduct" immune from regulation.

4. The Rationale. (White) Nothing in the constitutional text authorizes an individual to commit sodomy. In addition, the

Court's prior cases involving a right to privacy involve matters of family, marriage, and procreation. They do not extend to homosexual activity. Moreover, they make clear that private conduct is protected only when the interest or conduct "are implicit in the concept of ordered liberty" (*Palko*) or when "deeply rooted in this Nation's history and tradition." (*Moore*) Protection for homosexual sodomy does not satisfy these criteria; indeed, history and tradition show that sodomy has long been proscribed by the states. Consequently, the Court should be wary of creating a new fundamental right in their absence. Thus, there is no fundamental right to homosexual sodomy. The state must still advance a rational basis for the proscription of such conduct. Here, the state's rational basis is the protection of majoritarian moral preferences.

5. Concurring and Dissenting Opinions.
   a. Justice Burger, concurring: Proscriptions against sodomy have ancient roots and the state's ban against sodomy is supported by "a millennia of moral teaching. . . ."
   b. Justice Powell, concurring: If he had been convicted, Hardwick might have been imprisoned for twenty years. This might violate the cruel and unusual punishment clause of the Eighth Amendment.
   c. Justice Blackmun, dissenting: This case does not involve a right to homosexual sodomy, but instead whether individuals have a "right to decide for themselves whether to engage in particular forms of private, consensual sexual activity." Prior cases stand for the proposition that individuals have a right to privacy because it forms a central part of an individual's life. Hence the state may interfere with that right only when it has a compelling reason. The protection of a community's shared moral sense is not compelling because there "is no real interference with the rights of others. . . ."
   d. Justice Stevens, dissenting: The Georgia statute applies to heterosexual and homosexual activity alike. Prior cases make it clear that the state may not without a compelling reason interfere with the sexual conduct of unmarried heterosexual adults. (*Eisenstadt*) Moreover, Georgia has advanced no interest in selecting out homosexual activity except "habitual dislike for, or ignorance about, the disfavored group."

6. Significance of the Case. *Bowers* is important for several reasons. First, the majority opinion restates the criteria for determining what kinds of activity will be protected by the right to privacy. Second, its reassertion of those criteria is directly related to a specific understanding of the limits of judicial power in a democracy. The majority believes that the Court should not set aside majoritarian preferences absent a clear constitutional warrant for doing so. Similarly, the majority's use of precedent and appeals to history and tradition are informed by this understanding of judicial power. The dissenting opinions embrace a more expansive view of judicial power. Consequently, although they adopt similar methods of interpretation, they reach a different result from the majority. Finally, this case reflects the politics of sexuality and its prominence in the political and cultural life of the nation.

Selected Bibliography

Atiyah, P. S. and Robert S. Summers. *Form and Substance in Anglo-American Law: A Comparative Study of Legal Reasoning, Legal Theory, and Legal Institutions*. Oxford: Clarendon Press, 1987.

Carter, Lief. *An Introduction to Constitutional Interpretation: Cases in Law and Religion*. White Plains, N.Y.: Longman, 1991.

Goldstein, Joseph. *The Intelligible Constitution: The Supreme Court's Obligation to Maintain the Constitution as Something We the People Can Understand*. New York: Oxford University Press, 1992.

Levi, Edward H. *An Introduction to Legal Reasoning*. Chicago: University of Chicago Press, 1948.

Van Geel, T. R. *Understanding Supreme Court Opinions*. White Plains, N.Y.: Longman, 1991.

Glossary
of Terms

abstention   A doctrine holding that federal courts should not decide issues involving the interpretation of state law until the state's highest court has issued a decision on the question.

abstract judicial review   The authority of a court, such as the German Federal Constitutional Court, to decide cases in the absence of a real controversy and adverse parties, as would be required in the United States.

acquittal   A finding that a criminal defendant is not guilty.

admiralty   A law or court that pertains to the law of the sea and maritime concerns.

advisory opinion   An opinion by a court issued in a hypothetical or nonadversarial context, or in the absence of a concrete case or controversy.

affidavit   A written statement of facts made before a notary public or similar officer.

affirm   A decision by an appellate court to uphold or confirm a decision by a lower court.

amicus curiae   "Friend of the court"; a person or group, not a party to the case, invited by the court to submit a brief on an issue of concern to that group.

amparo   A procedure by which an individual or party may challenge the constitutionality of a law or policy by claiming a personal and direct harm; common in Latin American legal systems.

appeal   A request asking a higher court to decide whether the trial or lower court decision was correct.

appellant   A person who appeals a judicial decision.

appellate jurisdiction   When a court has the authority to review the judgment and proceedings of an inferior court.

appellee   The party who won the suit in a lower court and against whom an appeal is taken.

arguendo   "For the sake of argument"; assuming something to be true for purposes of argument.

arraignment   A formal proceeding in which the defendant is charged with a crime and must file a plea.

Basic Law   The Constitution of the Federal Republic of Germany.

bench memorandum   A memorandum about a case or an issue of law from a law clerk to a judge.

bench trial   A trial by a judge and without a jury.

Brandeis brief   A lawyer's brief that incorporates a wide variety of nonlegal materials, such as legislative findings, public policy, and social science.

brief   A written argument of law submitted by lawyers that explains to the judges why they should decide the case in their favor.

capital offense   A crime punishable by death.

case and controversy   A matter before a court in which the parties suffer real and direct harm and seek judicial resolution.

certification, writ of   A process where a lower court forwards a case to an appellate court because there are unresolved legal questions on which the lower court needs guidance.

certiorari, writ of   An order issued by the Supreme Court directing the lower court to transmit records for a case the Court has accepted on appeal. The primary means by which the Court sets its docket.

circuit court   An appellate court; in the federal judicial system each court covers several states; in most states their jurisdiction is by county.

civil law   A system of law based primarily on legislation and not on judicial decisions; common in Europe and Latin America. In common law systems, the civil law refers to laws and legal proceedings that are not criminal in nature and which concern relationships between private persons.

class action   A lawsuit filed by an individual or individuals on behalf of themselves and others "similarly situated."

comity   Courtesy; respect owed the various branches and levels of government.

common law   A legal system based primarily on judicial decisions rather than legislative action and statutory law.

complaint   A written statement by the plaintiff indicating how he or she has been harmed by the defendant.

concurrent powers   Powers held simultaneously between two or more levels of government.

concurring opinion   An opinion by a judge who agrees with the result reached by the majority but disagrees with all or part of the reasoning.

constitutional court   A court with the authority to review governmental action for its conformity with the Constitution; in the United States, these are courts created by or under the authority of Article 3.

conviction   A finding of guilt against a criminal defendant.

counsel   The lawyers in a case.

criminal law   The body of law that concerns offenses against the state and which may be penalized by fine or imprisonment.

declaratory relief   A request for or a decision by a court on a question of law or declaring the legal rights of the parties to a case, but without an order that any action be taken.

de facto   In fact or practice.

defendant   The person named in a civil complaint or, in a criminal case, the person accused of the crime.

de jure   In law or official policy.

deposition   An oral statement by a defendant or a witness, usually taken by an attorney, which may later be used at trial.

dicta (obiter dicta)   Statements by a court that are not strictly necessary to reach or that are not necessarily relevant to the result of the case. *Dicta* do not have the binding force of precedent.

discovery   The process before trial where attorneys investigate what happened, often by using interrogatories and by taking depositions.

dissenting opinion   An opinion filed by a judge who does not agree with the result reached by the majority of the court.

distinguish   To show why a case differs from another case and thus does not control the result.

diversity jurisdiction   The authority of federal courts to hear cases where the parties are citizens of different (or diverse) states.

docket   A record of court proceedings.

dual federalism   A doctrine of constitutional law providing that national powers should be construed in ways that do not needlessly invade the authority of the states.

due process   Fair and regular procedure; in the United States, there are two due process clauses, one in the Fifth Amendment and one in the Fourteenth Amendment.

en banc   "In the bench" or "full bench." Refers to cases where the entire membership of the court participates. In circuit courts, for example, cases are usually decided by a smaller panel of three judges.

equity   A branch of the common law where remedies for harm are governed by rules of justice and fairness, and less by strict legal rules and principles.

erga omnes   A decision by a court that binds everyone similarly situated, and not only the parties to the litigation.

error, writ of   A writ sent by a higher court to a lower court instructing it to send the case to the higher court to review for possible error.

ex parte   "From or on one side." A hearing where only one of the sides to a case is present.

ex post facto   "After the fact"; a law that makes something illegal that was not illegal when it was done or which increases the penalty for the act after it has occurred.

federal question jurisdiction   Jurisdiction based on the application of the United States Constitution, acts of Congress, and treaties of the United States.

felony   A crime that carries a penalty of more than a year in prison.

grand jury   A panel of citizens who determines whether prosecutors have enough evidence, or probable cause, to believe that an offense has been committed.

habeas corpus, writ of   "You have the body"; a writ sent to an officer or official asking him or her to explain why he or she has authority to detain or imprison a certain individual.

impeachment   The constitutional process where the House of Representatives may accuse high officers of the federal government of misconduct. The trial takes place in the Senate.

in camera   "In chambers"; when a hearing or trial is heard by a judge in private chambers.

incidenter   A decentralized method of constitutional review where such authority is shared among many courts and may be considered in any concrete case, without recourse to specialized constitutional procedures.

incorporation   In constitutional doctrine, the process by which various provisions of the Bill of Rights were made applicable to the states through the due process clause of the Fourteenth Amendment.

indictment   A formal charge by a grand jury against a defendant.

in forma pauperis   "In the manner of a pauper." The process where a person sues or appeals without paying the usual court fees by claiming poverty.

in haec verba   "In these words."

injunction   A judicial order that prohibits or compels the performance of a specific act to prevent irreparable damage or injury.

inter alia   "Among other things."

inter partes   A judicial decision that is binding only upon the parties to the case.

interrogatories   Written questions prepared by an attorney that must be completed, under oath, by the other party during the process of discovery.

ipse dixit   Asserted but not proved.

issue presented   The issue or controversy raised by the facts of the case.

judgment   A final decision by a court in a lawsuit. It usually determines the respective rights and claims of the parties.

judicial review   The authority of a court to review legislation and other governmental action for its conformity with superordinate constitutional provisions.

jurisdiction   The authority of a court to entertain a case.

jurisprudence   The study of law and legal philosophy.

justiciability   Whether a case may appropriately be heard by a court or is suitable for judicial decision.

legislative court   A court created by Congress under its Article 1 powers; judges on such courts generally do not receive lifetime tenure.

litigant   A party to a lawsuit.

majority opinion   An opinion by a majority of sitting judges or justices.

mandamus, writ of   "We command"; an order by a court to a governmental official directing that official to do something or take a particular course of action.

martial law   A condition where rule by military authorities replaces civilian authorities and courts martial replace civilian courts.

misdemeanor   A criminal offense punishable by less than one year of imprisonment.

moot   "Unsettled; undecided." Where the underlying dispute has been resolved or changed so that a judicial resolution of the controversy is not possible or must be hypothetical.

natural law/rights   A system of law or rights based upon "nature" or a deity or higher law that transcends human authority.

opinion   A written explanation by a judge that sets forth the reasons and legal basis for his or her decision.

opinion of the court   An opinion by a majority of the judges or justices hearing a case.

oral argument   Proceeding where lawyers explain their positions to the court and answer questions from the judges.

originalism   A method of constitutional interpretation that seeks the "original" meaning of the constitutional provision in doubt, or the intent of its drafters.

original jurisdiction   The authority of a court to hear a case in the first instance or as a trial court.

overrule   Where a decision by a court specifically repudiates or supersedes a statement of law made in an earlier case.

panel   A group of appellate judges, usually three, that decide cases. Also, a group of potential jurors.

parties   The litigants in a case, including the plaintiff and the defendant, or, on appeal, the appellants and appellees.

per curiam   "By the bench"; a collective decision issued by a court where no individual judge or justice claims authorship.

per se   "In or by itself"; in the nature of the thing.

petitioner   The party who seeks a writ or the assistance of the court.

plaintiff   A person who files the complaint in a civil lawsuit.

plea bargain   Where the prosecution and a defendant negotiate a guilty plea in exchange for a reduced charge or sentence.

plurality opinion   An opinion by a group of judges or justices that commands the most votes, but not an absolute majority.

police powers   The powers of a state or local government to protect the "health, safety, welfare, and morals of the community."

political question doctrine   A doctrine holding that questions primarily involving political instead of legal issues should not be decided by courts but instead left to the other branches of government.

positivism   A system of written law based upon rules and principles that claim their authority from a "sovereign"; positivism denies the existence of a "higher" law beyond the authority of human law.

precedent   A court decision in an earlier case that is similar to the case at hand.

preemption   A doctrine holding that issues and matters of concern to both the states and the national government become the prerogative of the national government, once it acts, and thus supersede any action by the states.

prima facie   "At first sight"; the evidence needed to establish a case until it is contested by opposing evidence.

principaliter   A method of constitutional review where such power is centralized and is divorced from the underlying factual or legal issue.

procedure   The rules that govern how a lawsuit proceeds. There are different rules for different areas of law and different courts.

prosecute   A decision by the state to charge someone with a crime.

quash   To vacate or annul.

record   A full written account of the proceedings in a lawsuit.

recuse   The process by which a judge decides not to participate in a case, usually because he or she has or appears to have a conflict of interest. In the normal course a judge will not set forth the reasons for his or her recusal.

remand   The process by which an appellate court sends a case back to a lower court for further proceedings.

reserved powers   Powers that remain with the states, as confirmed by the Tenth Amendment.

respondent   The party against whom action is sought or taken.

reverse   When an appellate court sets aside, or overrules, an erroneous decision by a lower court.

ripeness   A requirement that a case must be sufficiently developed factually before it may be heard by a court.

sentence   The punishment for a defendant convicted of a crime.

seriatim   To proceed one after the other or one by one. In the Supreme Court's early years, before John Marshall became chief justice, each member of the Court wrote a separate opinion in each case.

sovereign immunity   A doctrine holding that the state may not be sued without its consent.

special master   A person appointed by a court to hear evidence, to make findings, and to submit to the court recommendations about how to proceed in light of those findings; usually associated with original jurisdiction.

standing   A doctrine that requires a plaintiff to demonstrate that he or she has a real, direct, and personal interest in a case before the court will hear the case.

stare decisis   "Let the decision stand." The practice of adhering to settled law and prior decisions.

state action   Actions for which the state bears responsibility, either directly or indirectly; a requirement for a judicial remedy under the Fourteenth Amendment.

statute   A law passed by a legislature.

stay   To suspend or halt court proceedings.

subpoena   A command to a witness to appear and give testimony.

subpoena duces tecum   A command to a witness to produce documents.

summary judgment   A judicial decision made on the basis of statements and evidence presented for the record without a full trial, and where there is no dispute about the material facts or the law to be applied to the facts.

tort   A civil wrong or breach of a legal duty owed to another person.

vacate   To set aside.

venue   The location or jurisdiction where a case is tried.

verdict   The decision of a jury or a judge.

vested rights   A doctrine holding that long-standing property rights must be respected by the government absent an urgent claim of need.

writ   A written order by a court commanding an individual or a party to comply with its terms.

Chronological Chart of the Justices

Justice (Party)	Term	Appointed By	Replaced	State	Law School
John Jay (Fed)	1789–95	Washington (Fed)		N.Y.	
John Rutledge (Fed)	1789–91	Washington		S.C.	
William Cushing (Fed)	1789–1810	Washington		Mass.	
James Wilson (Fed)	1789–98	Washington		Penn.	
John Blair (Fed)	1789–95	Washington		Va.	
James Iredell (Fed)	1790–99	Washington		N.C.	
Thomas Johnson (Fed)	1791–93	Washington	Rutledge	Md.	
William Paterson (Fed)	1793–1806	Washington	Johnson	N.J.	
John Rutledge (Fed)	1795	Washington	Jay	S.C.	
Samuel Chase (Fed)	1796–1811	Washington	Blair	Md.	
Oliver Ellsworth (Fed)	1796–1800	Adams (Fed)	Rutledge	Conn.	
Bushrod Washington (Fed)	1798–1829	Adams	Wilson	Pa.	
Alfred Moore (Fed)	1799–1804	Adams	Iredell	N.C.	
John Marshall (Fed)	1801–35	Adams	Ellsworth	Va.	
William Johnson (DR)	1804–34	Jefferson (DR)	Moore	S.C.	
Henry Brockholst Livingston (DR)	1806–23	Jefferson	Paterson	N.Y.	
Thomas Todd (DR)	1807–26	Jefferson	new seat	Ky.	
Gabriel Duvall (DR)	1811–35	Madison (DR)	Chase	Md.	
Joseph Story (DR)	1811–45	Madison	Cushing	Mass.	
Smith Thompson (DR)	1823–43	Monroe (DR)	Livingston	N.Y.	
Robert Trimble (DR)	1826–28	J.Q. Adams (DR)	Todd	Ky.	
John McLean (Dem)	1829–61	Jackson (Dem)	Trimble	Ohio	
Henry Baldwin (Dem)	1830–44	Jackson	Washington	Pa.	
James M. Wayne (Dem)	1835–67	Jackson	Johnson	Ga.	
Roger B. Taney (Dem)	1836–64	Jackson	Marshall	Md.	
Philip B. Barbour (Dem)	1836–41	Jackson	Duval	Va.	
John Catron (Dem)	1837–65	Van Buren (Dem)	new seat	Tenn.	
John McKinley (Dem)	1837–52	Van Buren	new seat	Ky.	
Peter V. Daniel (Dem)	1841–60	Van Buren	Barbour	Va.	
Samuel Nelson (Dem)	1845–72	Tyler (Dem)	Thompson	N.Y.	
Levi Woodbury (Dem)	1845–51	Polk (Dem)	Story	N.H.	
Robert C. Grier (Dem)	1846–70	Polk	Baldwin	Pa.	
Benjamin R. Curtis (Whig)	1851–57	Fillmore (Whig)	Woodbury	Mass.	
John A. Campbell (Dem)	1853–61	Pierce (Dem)	McKinley	Ala.	

Justice (Party)	Term	Appointed By	Replaced	State	Law School
Nathan Clifford (Dem)	1858–81	Buchanan (Dem)	Curtis	Maine	
Noah H. Swayne (Rep)	1862–81	Lincoln (Rep)	McLean	Ohio	
Samuel F. Miller (Rep)	1862–90	Lincoln	Daniel	Iowa	
David Davis (Rep)	1862–77	Lincoln	Campbell	Ill.	
Stephen J. Field (Dem)	1863–97	Lincoln	new seat	Calif.	
Salmon P. Chase (Rep)	1864–73	Lincoln	Taney	Ohio	
William Strong (Rep)	1870–80	Grant (Rep)	Grier	Pa.	
Joseph Bradley (Rep)	1870–92	Grant	Wayne	N.J.	
Ward Hunt (Rep)	1872–82	Grant	Nelson	N.Y.	
Morrison Waite (Rep)	1874–88	Grant	Chase	Ohio	
John Marshall Harlan (Rep)	1877–1911	Hayes (Rep)	Davis	Ky.	
William B. Woods (Rep)	1880–87	Hayes	Strong	Ga.	
Stanley Matthews (Rep)	1881–89	Garfield (Rep)	Swayne	Ohio	
Horace Gray (Rep)	1881–1902	Arthur (Rep)	Clifford	Mass.	
Samuel Blatchford (Rep)	1882–93	Arthur	Hunt	N.Y.	
Lucius Q.C. Lamar (Dem)	1888–93	Cleveland (Dem)	Woods	Miss.	
Melville Fuller (Dem)	1888–1910	Cleveland	Waite	Ill.	
David J. Brewer (Rep)	1889–1910	Harrison (Rep)	Matthews	Kans.	
Henry B. Brown (Rep)	1890–1906	Harrison	Miller	Mich.	
George Shiras (Rep)	1892–1903	Harrison	Bradley	Pa.	
Howell E. Jackson (Dem)	1893–95	Harrison	Lamar	Tenn.	
Edward D. White (Dem)	1894–1910	Cleveland (Dem)	Blatchford	La.	
Rufus W. Peckham (Dem)	1895–1909	Cleveland	Jackson	N.Y.	
Joseph McKenna (Rep)	1898–1925	McKinley (Rep)	Field	Calif.	
Oliver Wendell Holmes, Jr. (Rep)	1902–32	T. Roosevelt (Rep)	Gray	Mass.	Harvard
William R. Day (Rep)	1903–22	T. Roosevelt	Shiras	Ohio	
William H. Moody (Rep)	1906–10	T. Roosevelt	Brown	Mass.	
Horace H. Lurton (Dem)	1910–16	Taft (Rep)	Peckham	Tenn.	Cumberland
Charles Evans Hughes (Rep)	1910–16	Taft	Brewer	N.Y.	Columbia
Edward D. White (Dem)	1910–21	Taft	Fuller	La.	
Willis Van Devanter (Rep)	1910–37	Taft	White	Wyo.	Cincinnati
Joseph R. Lamar (Dem)	1910–16	Taft	Moody	Ga.	
Mahlon Pitney (Rep)	1912–22	Taft	Harlan	N.J.	
James C. McReynolds (Dem)	1914–40	Wilson (Dem)	Lurton	Tenn.	Virginia
Louis D. Brandeis (Rep)	1916–39	Wilson	Lamar	Mass.	Harvard
John H. Clarke (Dem)	1916–22	Wilson	Hughes	Ohio	
William Howard Taft (Rep)	1921–30	Harding (Rep)	White	Ohio	Cincinnati
George Sutherland (Rep)	1922–38	Harding	Clarke	Utah	
Pierce Butler (Dem)	1922–39	Harding	Day	Minn.	
Edward T. Stanford (Rep)	1922–30	Harding	Pitney	Tenn.	Harvard
Harlan F. Stone (Rep)	1925–41	Coolidge (Rep)	McKenna	N.Y.	Columbia
Charles Evans Hughes (Rep)	1930–41	Hoover (Rep)	Taft	N.Y.	Columbia
Owen J. Roberts (Rep)	1930–45	Hoover	Stanford	Pa.	Pennsylvania
Benjamin Cardozo (Dem)	1932–38	Hoover	Holmes	N.Y.	
Hugo L. Black (Dem)	1937–71	F. Roosevelt (Dem)	Van Devanter	Ala.	Alabama
Stanley F. Reed (Dem)	1938–57	F. Roosevelt	Sutherland	Ky.	
Felix Frankfurter (Ind)	1939–62	F. Roosevelt	Cardozo	Mass.	Harvard
William O. Douglas (Dem)	1939–75	F. Roosevelt	Brandeis	N.Y.	Columbia
Frank Murphy (Dem)	1940–49	F. Roosevelt	Butler	Mich.	Michigan
James F. Byrnes (Dem)	1941–42	F. Roosevelt	McReynolds	S.C.	
Harlan F. Stone (Rep)	1941–46	F. Roosevelt	Hughes	N.Y.	Columbia
Robert H. Jackson (Dem)	1941–54	F. Roosevelt	Stone	N.Y.	
Wiley B. Rutledge (Dem)	1943–49	F. Roosevelt	Byrnes	Iowa	Colorado
Harold H. Burton (Rep)	1945–58	Truman (Dem)	Roberts	Ohio	Harvard
Fred M. Vinson (Dem)	1946–53	Truman	Stone	Ky.	Centre College

Justice (Party)	Term	Appointed By	Replaced	State	Law School
Tom C. Clark (Dem)	1949–67	Truman	Murphy	Tex.	Texas
Sherman Minton (Dem)	1949–56	Truman	Rutledge	Ind.	Indiana
Earl Warren (Rep)	1953–69	Eisenhower (Rep)	Vinson	Calif.	California
John Harlan Marshall (Rep)	1955–71	Eisenhower	Jackson	N.Y.	New York Law School
William J. Brennan (Dem)	1956–90	Eisenhower	Minton	N.J.	Harvard
Charles E. Whittaker (Rep)	1957–62	Eisenhower	Reed	Mo.	U. of Kansas City
Potter Stewart (Rep)	1958–1981	Eisenhower	Burton	Ohio	Yale
Byron R. White (Dem)	1962–93	Kennedy (Dem)	Whittaker	Colo.	Yale
Arthur J. Goldberg (Dem)	1962–65	Kennedy	Frankfurter	Ill.	Northwestern
Abe Fortas (Dem)	1965–69	Johnson (Dem)	Goldberg	Tenn.	Yale
Thurgood Marshall (Dem)	1967–91	Johnson	Clark	N.Y.	Howard
Warren E. Burger (Rep)	1969–86	Nixon (Rep)	Warren	Minn.	St. Paul College of Law
Harry A. Blackmun (Rep)	1970–94	Nixon	Fortas	Minn.	Harvard
Lewis Powell, Jr. (Dem)	1972–87	Nixon	Black	Va.	Washington & Lee
William H. Rehnquist (Rep)	1972–86	Nixon	Harlan	Ariz.	Stanford
John Paul Stevens (Rep)	1975—	Ford (Rep)	Douglas	Ill.	Northwestern
Sandra Day O'Connor (Rep)	1981—	Reagan (Rep)	Stewart	Ariz.	Stanford
William H. Rehnquist (Rep)	1986—	Reagan	Burger	Ariz.	Stanford
Antonin Scalia (Rep)	1986—	Reagan	Rehnquist	D.C.	Harvard
Anthony M. Kennedy (Rep)	1988—	Reagan	Powell	Calif.	Harvard
David H. Souter (Rep)	1990—	Bush (Rep)	Brennan	N.H.	Harvard
Clarence Thomas (Rep)	1991—	Bush	Marshall	Ga.	Yale
Ruth Bader Ginsburg (Dem)	1993—	Clinton (Dem)	White	D.C.	Columbia
Stephen G. Breyer (Dem)	1994—	Clinton	Blackmun	Mass.	Harvard

Key

Italics = Chief Justice   Dem = Democrat
Fed = Federalist   Rep = Republican
DR = Democratic Republican/Jeffersonian   Ind = Independent

Table of Cases

Index

Credits

Permission for reprinting published materials is gratefully acknowledged and we thank the following sources:

From Walter F. Murphy and Joseph Tanenhaus, *Comparative Constitutional Law: Cases and
Commentaries* (New York: St. Martin's Press, 1977). (Translations by Mrs. Renate Chestnut.)

From Lawrence W. Beer and Hiroshi Itoh, *The Constitution of Japan, 1970 Through 1990*
(Seattle: University of Washington Press, 1996).

From Sunita Parikh, *The Politics of Preference* (Ann Arbor: University of Michigan Press, 1997).

From *On Appeal: Courts, Lawyering, and Judging* by Frank M. Coffin, Copyright 1994 by W. W.
Norton & Company, Inc. Reprinted by permission of W. W. Norton & Company, Inc.

From *American Journal of Comparative Law*, Volume 42 (Spring 1994).